DUMBARTON OAKS STUDIES

ex IX so

EARLY CHRISTIAN
AND BYZANTINE
POLITICAL PHILOSOPHY

ORIGINS AND BACKGROUND

To
MILDRED BLISS
and
in revered memory of
ROBERT WOODS BLISS

Foreword

Habent sua fata libelli. The idea of writing a history of Early Christian and Byzantine political philosophy originated in England, in 1946, when I was elected by Trinity College to serve as the Birkbeck Lecturer at the University of Cambridge. It was suggested that I choose as the subject of my lectures the idea of kingship in the ancient Near East, its influence on Jewish political thought, on Greek thought, and especially on Hellenistic thought; and show to what extent Near Eastern and Greek political speculation had influenced both the Early Christians and the Byzantines. The interest which my audience manifested in the lectures encouraged me to continue my research and to publish a book devoted to these problems. The history of political ideas had attracted me from my early years—in 1923 I graduated from the Ecole des Sciences Politiques in Paris—and, as my research progressed, I became more and more convinced that it was necessary not only to examine the political ideas of the many cultures in the Near East, but also to show how the different civilizations of the pre-Christian era transmitted their ideas on kingship to each other, enriching them with new concepts which corresponded to their national, religious, or racial character, and to show to what extent the Jewish and Greek genius had absorbed, changed, or adapted them. Only when this process was clearly demonstrated in the different phases of its development could we understand the attitude of the Christians toward the political atmosphere of the Hellenistic period in which the Church was born, and see how the political system was formed by which the Byzantine Empire was governed for a thousand years.

While writing the chapters on ancient Eastern and on Jewish political and messianic ideas, I remembered with gratitude my teacher, J. Hejčl, Professor of Old Testament Studies on the Faculty of Theology in Olomouc. From 1912 to 1916 I learned the principles of the historical method in his seminar, comparing under his guidance Hammurabi's legislation with that of Moses, and the

Babylonian and Assyrian poetry with the Jewish Psalms on the Sun, on Kings, and on the Messiah. He wished me to become his successor on the faculty, but circumstances led me to a different field, that of Byzantine and Slavic studies. However, without the solid foundation which I owe to his instruction, I would not have had the courage to enter into such a dangerous and little-known field.

The first chapters of this book were written at the British Museum. I continued the research at Dumbarton Oaks, but it was interrupted when I was asked to give courses in Slavic history and civilization at Harvard University in 1951 and 1956. The publication of these courses in book form further delayed the continuation of my research, which I was able to conclude only at the beginning of 1964. The printing of the book presented certain difficulties, and I was unable to add to my research, and to the bibliography, publications which appeared after the beginning of 1964.

In quoting from the works of Greek and Latin classical writers, I have used the editions of the Loeb Library because they are easily accessible to English and American scholars. The reader will note that in some cases I have had to adapt the translations made by the editors to the Greek or Latin original. In quoting from Holy Writ, I have followed the King James Bible (English edition).

In order to avoid unnecessary repetition, and to help readers who may be interested only in certain parts of this book, it was decided to combine the bibliographical notices for chapters treating related problems.

I thank the Director of Dumbarton Oaks, Mr. John S. Thacher, and the Director of Studies, Professor Ernst Kitzinger, for undertaking the costly edition of my book in two volumes. My colleague, M. V. Anastos, now Professor at the University of California at Los Angeles, read the manuscript and gave me most useful advice on problems concerning the Greek, Hellenistic, Jewish, and Early Christian periods. I am most grateful to him for having shared with me his vast knowledge of these problems. Professor A. Alföldi, of the Princeton Institute for Advanced Study, read the chapter on the Hellenization of Roman political theory, and I am indebted to him for many corrections and additions to this chapter.

FOREWORD

I owe thanks to the superintendents and staff of the Reading Room at the British Museum, where I did my research in the difficult postwar years. The J. S. Guggenheim Memorial Foundation generously awarded me a scholarship in 1961, which enabled me to continue my research in European libraries.

Mrs. Fanny Bonajuto, Research Analyst to the Dumbarton Oaks Faculty, helped me greatly by revising the footnote quotations and in composing the Bibliography and the Index. Miss Julia Warner, of Dumbarton Oaks, was responsible for the editorial work, which was rather complicated owing to the special character of this book. I am most grateful for their devotion and faithful assistance.

I dedicate this book to Mrs. Bliss and to the pious memory of her husband, the Honorable Robert Woods Bliss. It is a humble homage to the generous founders of Dumbarton Oaks. Without their magnanimity, vision, and stimulating interest in Byzantine studies this book would not have been written.

June 1966   Francis Dvornik

CONTENTS

CONTENTS

VII The Kingdom of God 403

LIST OF ABBREVIATIONS

ACO *Acta Conciliorum Oecumenicorum*, ed. by E. Schwartz (Berlin-Leipzig, 1922–40)

AJP *American Journal of Philology*

Bonn Corpus Scriptorum Historiae Byzantinae (Bonn, 1828–97)

BZ *Byzantinische Zeitschrift*

CACSS Corpus Apologetarum Christianorum Saeculi Secundi, ed. by J. Th. Otto (Jena, 1847–81)

CAH The Cambridge Ancient History (Cambridge, 1923–39), 12 vols.

CIG *Corpus Inscriptionum Graecarum*, ed. by A. Böckh and others (Berlin, 1828–77)

CIL *Corpus Inscriptionum Latinarum*, ed. by Th. Mommsen and others (Berlin, 1862 seq.)

CJ *Corpus Iuris Civilis*, 2: *Codex Iustinianus*, ed. by P. Krueger (Berlin, 1929)

CSEL Corpus Scriptorum Ecclesiasticorum Latinorum, ed. by the Vienna Academy of Sciences (Vienna *et al.*, 1866 seq.)

CTh *Theodosiani Libri XVI cum Constitutionibus Sirmondianis*, ed. by Th. Mommsen (Berlin, 1905)

DJ *Corpus Iuris Civilis*, 1: *Digesta*, ed. by Th. Mommsen and P. Krueger (Berlin, 1928)

FHG *Fragmenta Historicorum Graecorum*, ed. by K. and Th. Müller (Paris, 1841–83), 5 vols.

GCS Die griechischen christlichen Schriftsteller der ersten drei Jahrhunderte, ed. by the Kirchenväter-Commission der Königlichen Preussischen Akademie der Wissenschaften (Leipzig,

1897–1941). Continued under the title: Die griechischen christlichen Schriftsteller der ersten Jahrhunderte, ed. by the Kommission für spätantike Religionsgeschichte der Deutschen Akademie der Wissenschaften zu Berlin (Berlin, 1953 seq.)

IGRR   Inscriptiones Graecae ad Res Romanas Pertinentes, ed. by R. Cagnat and others (Paris, 1901–1927), 4 vols.

IJ   Corpus Iuris Civilis, 1: Institutiones, ed. by P. Krueger (Berlin, 1928)

ILS   Inscriptiones Latinae Selectae, ed. by H. Dessau (Berlin, 1892–1916), 3 vols.

JBL   Journal of Biblical Studies

JHS   Journal of Hellenic Studies

Loeb   The Loeb Classical Library, Cambridge, Mass.

Mansi   G. D. Mansi, ed., Sacrorum Conciliorom Nova et Amplissima Collectio … (Florence-Venice, 1759–98)

MGH   Monumenta Germaniae Historica

NJ   Corpus Iuris Civilis, 3: Novellae, ed. by R. Schoell and W. Kroll (Berlin, 1928)

NTh   Leges Novellae ad Theodosianum Pertinentes, ed. by P. M. Meyer (Berlin, 1905)

OGIS   Orientis Graeci Inscriptiones Selectae. Supplementum Sylloges Inscriptionum Graecarum, ed. by W. Dittenberger (Leipzig, 1903–05), 2 vols.

Pauly-Wissowa   Paulys Real-encyclopädie der classischen Altertumswissenschaft, Neue Bearbeitung …, ed. by. G. Wissowa and others (Stuttgart, 1894 seq.)

PG   Patrologiae Cursus Completus, Series Graeca, ed. by J. P. Migne (Paris, 1857–66)

PL   Patrologiae Cursus Completus, Series Latina, ed. by J. P. Migne (Paris, 1844–80)

SB   Sitzungsberichte

TAPA   Transactions and Procedings of the American Philological Association

Teubner   Bibliotheca Teubneriana, Leipzig

Texte und Untersuchungen   Texte und Untersuchungen zur Geschichte der altchristlichen Literatur (Leipzig, 1883 seq.)

VT   Vetus Testamentum

ZAW   Zeitschrift für die alttestamentliche Wissenschaft und die Kunde des nachbiblischen Judentums

ZNW   Zeitschrift für die neutestamentliche Wissenschaft und die Kunde des Urchristentums

EARLY CHRISTIAN AND BYZANTINE
POLITICAL PHILOSOPHY

ORIGINS AND BACKGROUND

CHAPTER ONE

Oriental Ideas on Kingship: Egypt, Mesopotamia

Introduction — Origins of Egyptian divine kingship — Egyptian royal theology — The king, giver of life — Pharaoh the main factor in public worship — Egyptian idea of universality — Theocracy and hierocracy — Historical evolution of Mesopotamia — Sumerian ideas on the origin and character of kingship — Divine kingship in Mesopotamia? — Assyrian kingship — The idea of universality and of the King-Saviour — Kings impersonating gods — The king as intermediary between gods and subjects — Egyptian influence on royal symbolism in Assyria, among the Hurri and Mitanni.

What were the current trends of political thought in the East at the time when Christianity came into being? This question is supremely important and no inadequate answer permits a true appreciation of the words of the Founder of Christianity, words which were to serve as the basis upon which the early Christians erected the structure of their political philosophy.

It is natural to consider first the Jews of Palestine, for it was from their environment that Christianity spread both East and West. There is no need to examine in full detail the Jewish expectations of a Messiah and of the Kingdom He was to establish. These are matters for interpreters and historians of the Jewish creed; but it may be observed here that there are features of the Messianic role, including misinterpretations of it, which present aspects of special interest to our enquiry and will have to be studied more thoroughly. There is however one political notion for which the Jews cannot be held responsible: the deification of supreme rulers. Nevertheless, it affected both Jews and Christians to a considerable extent, since it formed the very atmosphere in which the states and nations of the ancient Middle East existed, and so it calls for examination.

POLITICAL PHILOSOPHY

The beginnings of this peculiar belief are lost in the mists which shroud the prehistory of the human race. As such, they lie outside our scope and are rather the concern of the anthropologist and the student of prehistory and of comparative history of religions. It is for them also to examine the various forms which the notion of kingship assumed among the primitive tribes, its early association by the human mind with ideas concerning deity and the convergence of the two lines of thought to survive together down to this modern age among some great Asiatic nations. The findings of J. G. Frazer revolutionized research in this matter.[1]

However, his contention that the kingly office and the supernatural character of kingship were introduced into primitive tribes by the medicine man or the public magician does not cover every aspect of the problem. It has proved untenable in the light of new evidence brought forward by other scholars. It is plain that the need for leaders, military commanders, and social organizers had a considerable bearing on the origin of kings; and something more than a belief in magic is required to account for their divinization. Rather was it a respect for authority, so innate in human beings, which instinctively focused in primitive minds on the chieftains, who thus came to represent divine power, the source of all authority. This would explain why the claim of kings and rulers to divine descent, or at least to a special character of sanctity is so general among primitive peoples the world over.

While these problems have a remote connection with the subject under consideration, they must be left to specialists.[2] It will, there-

---

[1] His theory is developed with particular emphasis in his book *The Magical Origin of Kings* (London, 1920). For a survey of these problems, see the article "King" in J. Hastings' *Encyclopaedia of Religion and Ethics* (Edinburgh, 1928), 7, p. 708 seq. Cf. also T. Hadfield, *Traits of Divine Kingship in Africa* (London, 1949) and Eva L. R. Meyerowitz, *The Divine Kingship in Ghana and Ancient Egypt* (London, 1960).

[2] See, for example, F. M. Cornford, *From Religion to Philosophy* (London, 1912), p. 102 seq. and A. M. Hocart, *Kingship* (Oxford, 1927). Cf., however, the critique of Hocart's book in H. Frankfort, *Kingship and the Gods* (see *infra*, note 12), p. 405. A critical review of works on sacral kingship published during the last century is given by C.-M. Edsman, "Zum sakralen Königtum in der Forschung der letzten Hundert Jahre," pp. 3–17, *The Sacral Kingship*, Suppl. to *Numen*, 4 (Leiden, 1959), which contains the communications of specialists given at the sixth International Congress for the History of Religions in Rome in 1955. Cf. also *ibid.*, pp. 63–70, the study by E. O. James, "The Sacred Kingship and the Priesthood."

fore, be more appropriate to make a general preliminary study of the evolution of political philosophy in the Middle East, the common cradle of Judaism and Christianity, limiting the survey to those problems which form an obstacle to the main field of our research.

During the millennia preceding the formation of the Jewish nation and its creed, great cultures and empires rose and fell in western Asia and northeastern Africa. They lived together on terms alternating between friendship and hostility, and represented in many ways the best that the human genius was able to produce with the means then at its disposal. Empires and cultures passed away and it fell to the modern scientist to discover the faint traces they left in the sands of Mesopotamia, Egypt, and the Sudan, and on the plains and rocks of Asia Minor, Media, and Persia; to decipher their literary documents and to discover from the inscriptions on the proud monuments of their kings the fascinating history of their political growth. But, forgotten though they lay for thousands of years, those cultures and empires left more abiding traces on the human mind than those to be gathered from the ingenious and noble monuments excavated from the ruins of their great cities; for other cultures and empires took their place and continued to build upon the human materials they had inherited. In the world of ideas there is a continuity which dovetails into the plans of a Providence, which uses every good deed of its creatures to further its designs.

The innovations brought about in the culture of the pre-Christian period were not so ephemeral as to preclude all possibility of survival in the ideological sphere, and one is amazed to observe, as modern discoveries bring them to light, how many Egyptian, Sumerian, Babylonian, Assyrian, and Persian features were incorporated in the books of the Old Testament and thus contributed to the rise and development of the Jewish nation. All those varied elements were thrown into the melting pot at the time of the conquests of Alexander the Great. They were remoulded by Greek genius and produced the Hellenistic culture against whose background Christianity drew its lifeblood in the first centuries of its existence. The great cultures which unconsciously shaped the right environment for Christ's words were the handiwork of the Egyptians, Sumerians, Babylonians, Assyrians, Hittites, and Persians. If these can be traced in the political, religious, and artistic growth of the Middle East, then it may well be asked to what extent those political formations left their mark upon the subsequent evolution of political ideology, and whether they influenced the Hellenistic world and early Christianity.

Attention must first be directed to the political thought of the Egyptians, since it was in Egypt that the idea of divinized kingship had developed into a firm political and religious system. In this and many other respects, Egyptian kingship differs in its origins and evolution from that of other cultured nations of the Middle East. One of the reasons why the concept of kingship was so highly and finely elaborated in Egypt, and why it remained the mainspring of all political and cultural life in the country, was that Egyptian culture as a whole was the product of one nation, which was able to preserve its individuality almost intact in its main features throughout the millennia of its history. In its divine kings, who had concentrated all political power in their own hands, the whole nation found leaders able to represent the might and growing influence of the Egyptian people at the greatest moments of their history. The conception of divine kingship gave the nation a firmly rooted political focus, which it could embellish with a spiritual power fitted to inspire its political development and expansion.[3] In this can be found the reason why the Egyptians retained the idea of divine kingship even after they had lost their native dynasties and were governed by foreign masters: Assyrians, Persians, Greeks, and Romans.

Uncertainty persists concerning the origins of Egyptian divine kingship.[4] There is a certain confusion in Egyptian accounts of the

---

[3] A clear picture of Egyptian civilization from the earliest times to the end of the New Kingdom is given in W. C. Hayes, *The Scepter of Egypt. A Background for the Study of the Egyptian Antiquities in the Metropolitan Museum of Art* (Cambridge, Mass., 1953, 1959), 2 vols. with a rich bibliography on ancient Egypt at the end of each volume. On Egyptian religious beliefs, cf. H. Kees, *Der Götterglaube im Alten Ägypten* (Leipzig, 1941), and H. Bonnet, *Reallexikon der ägyptischen Religionsgeschichte* (Berlin, 1952).

[4] Cf. H. W. Fairman, "The Kingship Rituals of Egypt" in *Myth, Ritual and Kingship*, ed. by S. H. Hooke (Oxford, 1958), p. 74. Cf. E. L. R. Meyerowitz, *op. cit.*, pp. 31–58, on the role of Hathor-Mother goddess, and other gods in prehistoric kingdoms.

creation of man and the organization of primitive human society. A text designated as "Memphite theology" and copied in the eighth century B.C. from a document probably dating from the first dynasty[5] calls Ptah "Father of all gods and creator of the universe." Even Atum (Aton), commonly worshipped in Lower Egypt as sun-god-creator, was created like other gods by Ptah.

The text mentions the nine main gods who reigned over Egypt and speaks of "the tragic death of the god Osiris who was drowned in his water." Osiris' son Horus contended for the dominion over Egypt with Seth. The earth-god Geb, acting as arbiter, divided the country between them, but then rescinded his decision and gave the whole land to Horus, because he was Osiris' only son. Osiris, who became the god of the Dead, was buried in Memphis, the new capital and center of the two parts of the country thus unified.

The main purpose of this cosmological speculation was to show that Egypt was primitively ruled by gods and that the unification of the two parts of Egypt was the realization of a divine plan.[6] Menes, the actual unifier of Egypt, and his successors were a kind of emanation of Horus on earth. In reality the name Horus— Falcon—is given to the kings beginning with the period of the unification of Egypt under the First Dynasty. The divine character of the king is expressed in many texts, where he is called simply "the god" or "the good god." There is no doubt that this mythical description of the origin of Egyptian divine kingship is based on certain historical events.[7]

[5] It was published with a commentary by H. Junker in two important studies, *Die Götterlehre von Memphis (Schabaka Inschrift)*, in the Abhandlungen der Preuss. Akademie der Wissenschaften, Phil.-hist. Kl., no. 23 (Berlin, 1940) and *Die politische Lehre von Memphis, ibid.*, no. 6 (Berlin 1941). Cf. E. Voegelin, *Order and History*, 1, *Israel and Revelation* (Louisiana Univ. Press, 1956), pp. 88–101.

[6] The idea of the existence of two kingdoms in Egypt before the unification, which was generally accepted by scholars in the nineteenth century, is being abandoned at the present time. According to available sources, there existed in the Nile delta only small, culturally homogeneous principalities with their own chiefs, who failed to offer a tenacious resistance to the conquerors coming from the south. There is little information on the rise of the Kingdom of Lower Egypt.

[7] These are interpreted by J. Pirenne in *Histoire des institutions et du droit privé de l'ancienne Egypte* (Brussels, 1932), 1, pp. 25–113.

The reunification of Egypt having been realized by a dynasty coming from Upper Egypt, it was quite natural that the religious system which the victors brought with them should become the official religion of the united country. Ptah, therefore, not Atum, who had previously been worshipped in the conquered land with its religious center at Heliopolis, became the supreme god. Horus, to whom Ptah had granted dominion over Egypt, not the sun-god Re of Heliopolis, became the ancestor of the kings. It was also logical that the document should stress the importance of Memphis, the new center of the kingdom founded allegedly by Menes, as opposed to the cities of Lower Egypt, especially Heliopolis. Memphis also appropriated Osiris, whose cult was popular in the conquered land, thus stressing that dominion over Upper and Lower Egypt belonged to Osiris' divine son Horus and to Horus' successors, who were his earthly incarnations.[8]

This divine origin of Egyptian kingship is also stressed by the worshipers of the sun-god Re. This can be learned from a papyrus now preserved in Turin[9] and originating in the royal archives of the Twentieth Dynasty of the Ramesides (1200–1090 B.C.), but reproducing with certainty a very old Egyptian tradition. According to this tradition, the sun-god Re was the first king of Egypt, thus inaugurating the period during which Egypt was ruled by divine dynasties. He was succeeded by his divine children and grandchildren—Sem, Geb, Osiris, Set, Horus, together with their divine wives. This period ended in tragedy, when Seth killed his brother Osiris.[10] Horus, the son of Osiris and Isis, avenged his father with the help of Anubis and Thoth, and inaugurated a new period in the legendary history of Egypt.[11]

[8] Cf. R. Anthes on the divine lineage of Horus in "Egyptian Theology in the Third Millennium B.C.," in *Journal of Near Eastern Studies*, 18 (1959), p. 169 seq.

[9] G. Farina, *Il Papiro dei Re restaurato* (Rome, 1938), p. 16 seq. Cf. for details A. Moret, *Du caractère religieux de la royauté pharaonique* (Paris, 1902), p. 6 seq. Cf. also C. J. Gadd, *Ideas of Divine Rule in the Ancient East* (Schweich Lectures, London, 1948), p. 33.

[10] The legend of Osiris, who was also believed to die and to rise again each year with the death and revival of Nature—cf. A. Erman, *Die Religion der Ägypter* (Berlin-Leipzig, 1934), p. 40—had a great influence on the evolution of Egyptian religion and also helped to create the erroneous impression that Osiris was the center and hub of Egyptian religion.

[11] During the Hellenistic period the divine rulership over Egypt was divided into three parts: the rule of gods, of demigods, and of men. The

The complicated notion of the divine character of the Pharaohs was further elaborated by Egyptian theologians. The divine incarnation of Horus in the king was achieved through the transmission of the lifegiving supreme principle, called Ka, by Horus to the king.[12] It was the peculiar Egyptian belief concerning man's personality which helped Egyptian theologians to frame this doctrine. According to the Egyptian view of the human personality, Man was composed not only of body, but also of Ba and Ka. The Ba—soul or, rather, ghost—was especially dependent on the body. The Ba is often pictured in the shape of a bird with a human head, returning to the mummy in the grave after having visited various places during the period between the owner's death and his burial.[13]

The Ka—spirit or vital force—was regarded as impersonal and as being present in different degrees of strength in various persons, or in the same person at various times. Unlike the Ba, the Ka of the common man was never pictured. The King's Ka was divine and endowed him with eternal life.

The origin and meaning of the Ka theology was long a subject of debate among specialists.[14] It was believed that the concept of the Ka originated in Lower Egypt, which was more advanced in religious speculation than the nomadic population of the more southerly Upper Egypt. On the other hand, however, the belief in the divine character of the king, regarded as an incarnation of Horus symbolized by a falcon, came from the South with the

---

Pharaonic period does not recognize such a division. Cf. Diodorus Siculus, *The Library of History*, I, 44, ed. by C. H. Oldfather (Loeb, 1933), I, p. 156.

[12] The theology of Egyptian kingship is analyzed by H. Frankfort, *Kingship and the Gods. A Study of Ancient Near Eastern Religion as the Integration of Society and Nature* (Chicago, 1948), especially pp. 24–47. See also the more recent publication and interpretation of early Egyptian inscriptions and representations of the rulers, by H. Brunner, *Die Geburt des Gottkönigs. Studien zur Überlieferung eines altägyptischen Mythos*, Ägyptologische Abhandlungen, 10 (Wiesbaden, 1964).

[13] On the Ba and Ka, see H. Frankfort, *Kingship*, p. 61 seq. Cf. also A. Erman, *Die Religion der Ägypter*, p. 209 seq. Cf. also E. L. R. Meyerowitz, *op. cit.*, pp. 109 seq., 130 seq.

[14] On the history of this controversy, see especially L. Greven, *Der Ka in Theologie und Königskult der Ägypter des Alten Reiches*, Ägyptologische Forschungen, Heft 17 (Munich-Glückstadt-New York, 1952), p. 35, and U. Schweitzer, *Das Wesen des Ka im Diesseits und Jenseits der alten Ägypter*, *ibid.*, Heft 19 (Glückstadt-New York, 1956), p. 13 seq.

conquerors and remained the most characteristic feature of Egyptian belief during the first dynasties. This seemed to indicate that the concept of the Ka must have been equally well known in Upper Egypt.

Only recently a possible solution to this problem has been postulated. The Ka appears to have developed from two different concepts of the divine. It is rooted in the magic-dominated, imaginative mind of the predominantly Hamitic and African population of Upper Egypt in prehistoric times. According to this view, the Ka was originally a kind of fetish numen of a tribe, which resided in the ruler, through whom it revealed its power. Because the Egyptian prehistoric rulers were kings of the falcon-god, the Ka most probably represented the essence which was ever present in Horus' falcon and which was incarnate in the living ruler. Through this magic-dominated outlook of the primitive Egyptians, the Ka brought about an essential unity of the King with the god Horus' falcon. In this religious system of Upper Egypt the Ka represented all manifestations of life that originated in Horus. Because the king was an incarnation of Horus through the Ka, the king became the only guarantee of existence and order for the state and for his subjects. The latter could only participate in the Ka of the Pharaoh but could not enjoy it independently.[15]

Such ideas did not correspond to the conceptions of the cosmic religion which had developed in the delta around Heliopolis, thanks to the contact of its population with the Semites.[16] The Heliopolitan theologians had to accept the creed of their new masters, but being more cultured they tried to soften this crude conception of the Ka and slowly introduced their own cosmic religious system into Memphis. They endeavored to bring the kings into relationship with their sun-god Re-Atum, not as his reincarnation, but as his sons. This attempt had already achieved some success during the rule of the Second Dynasty, because two kings of this dynasty at least manifested sympathy with the cult of Re.

---

[15] H. Stock, "Ägyptische Religionsgeschichte," *Saeculum*, 1 (1950), p. 624 seq., and U. Schweitzer, *op. cit.*, p. 16 seq. For general information, see also H. Bonnet, *Reallexikon der ägyptischen Religionsgeschichte*. On Ka, *ibid.*, pp. 357–362.

[16] See Stock's study, "Das Ostdelta Ägyptens," *Die Welt des Orients*, 1 (1947–52), p. 135 seq.

Thus it came about that Re-Atum was gradually admitted to equal standing with Horus in the college of royal deities.[17] King Chephren of the Fourth Dynasty was the first to call himself the son of Re (Sa-Re). The title deriving from Horus, however, still took precedence over that of Sa-Re. The introduction of the title of Sa-Re among the kings' nomenclature indicated that the protagonists of the worship of Horus, the theologians of Memphis, and the adherents of the religious system centering around Re-Atum, were waging a quiet but stubborn struggle for influence during the second half of the rule of the Fourth Dynasty.

This struggle probably weakened the authority of that dynasty. The priests of Heliopolis became so powerful that they overthrew the dynasty of Cheops and elevated one of their own high priests to the throne of Egypt. The legend preserved in the papyrus of Westcar depicts the coup d'état in very religious terms: Re rejected the dynasty of Cheops and replaced it by three kings whom he had begotten by the wife of the high priest. They were, therefore, his sons and the eldest of them became high priest in Heliopolis.[18]

This political upheaval inaugurated a new period in the history of the Egyptian ideology of kingship. The king ceased to be a god who was absolute master of the land and of the life of his subjects. This absolute power, rooted in the idea of the divine character of the ruler, found ruthless expression especially during the rule of the First Dynasty. The theory of divine kingship, softened by the more abstract conceptions of the Heliopolitan theologians, gained increasing influence at court and reached its highest peak during the rule of the Third and Fourth Dynasties. The magnificent pyramids and the Ka statues of the rulers of the Fourth Dynasty express most effectively the magnitude and the eternal character of the god-king.[19]

[17] Cf. J. Pirenne, *op. cit.*, p. 127 seq.
[18] Cf. H. Müller, *Die formale Entwicklung der Titulatur der ägyptischen Könige*, Ägyptologische Forschungen, Heft 7 (Glückstadt-New York, 1938), pp. 68-73, and J. Pirenne, *op. cit.*, 2, p. 1 seq.
[19] Cf. R. Anthes, *op. cit.*, p. 180: "The death of the king did not contradict his divine character. On the contrary it was the king's transition from Horus to Osiris which confirmed his existence as an eternal being." The author ventures a theory, for which there is no evidence, that the king's complete divinity and effective rulership became increasingly incompatible, and that this caused the final replacement of the concept of Horus by that of Re for the sole benefit of the royal power.

The king as son of Re is basically a man who had been chosen by the sun-god to reign over his subjects. It is in some way a kingship by the grace of God. The king is a man, but he is rendered divine by Re, who endows him with his Ka. It is now the conception of the king's Ka that is the only guarantee of the divine character of the ruler.

This transformation of the idea of kingship also implied a kind of democratization of the Ka concept. According to the mentality of the kingship deriving from Horus, the subjects could only participate in the king's Ka, which was exclusively his because of the incarnation of Horus in his person. When, however, the Ka was believed to be conferred by the God-Creator on a man, every Egyptian was believed from his birth to be in possession of a Ka, albeit much inferior to that of the king.

This belief exercised a considerable influence on the Egyptian cult of the dead. An image of the deceased, buried with him and hidden in the tomb, was regarded as a bearer of the Ka, the eternal vital force which had been given to the man who was now lying in the tomb. The image in which the Ka resided, guaranteed the further existence of the deceased in the world beyond. Only when, at the end of the Old Kingdom, the belief became current that every dead person was united with Osiris and obtained through him eternal life, was the practice of placing in the tombs images in which the Ka should reside discontinued. The Ka theology however continued to be preached.[20]

The concept of the divine character of the king as the son of a god remained almost unchanged in Egyptian history.[21] At every stage in the evolution of the Egyptian religious system, as well as when Re was replaced for a short period by Atum,[22] or later when

[20] See the documentation on this and further development in U. Schweitzer's convincing study *Das Wesen des Ka*, p. 18 seq.

[21] In his study, "Das Königtum im Mittleren Reich" in *The Sacral Kingship*, pp. 269–280, G. Lanczkowski shows how the conception of divine kingship was further weakened during the period of the Middle and New Kingdom. Cf. also *ibid.*, pp. 261–268, C. J. Bleeker's remarks on "The Position of the Queen in Ancient Egypt." For the Greco-Roman period of Egypt's history, see E. Otto, *Gott und Mensch, nach den ägyptischen Tempelinschriften der griechisch-römischen Zeit*, Abhandlungen der Heidelberger Akad. der Wissensch., Phil.-hist. Kl. (Heidelberg, 1964), pp. 63-83.

[22] Cf. *infra*, pp. 14, 42. A. Erman, *Die Religion der Ägypter*, p. 111 seq.

he was identified during the period of the New Kingdom (1570–950 B.C.) with Amon of Thebes, the king was invariably honored, not merely as God's representative, but as God's own son, rendered divine by the transmission of the god's Ka.

This is very clear from Egyptian documents transmitted to us. These also reveal that this belief was very firmly embedded in the minds of the Egyptians and that it cannot be regarded purely as theological speculation or political propaganda.

During the period of the New Kingdom the divine procreation of the king was imagined as happening in a more human way. When the supreme god had decided to give the Egyptians a royal successor to himself, he approached the queen as Ka-Mutef—the bull of his mother—and, taking over temporarily the body of the king, had intercourse with her. The queen became the mother of a god and the newly born Pharaoh became a fresh incarnation of the supreme god.[23]

It was therefore not illogical on the part of the Egyptians to imagine that all the gods collaborated in forming the body of the future king and that he virtually reigned from the very moment that he was conceived in his mother's womb. It was also a natural consequence that the future king should be depicted as being reared on the divine milk of the goddesses.[24]

The coronation of the king was neither more nor less than the realization of the promises given to him by the gods at the time of his conception and nativity. The gods played the main role in the

[23] See the study by H. Jacobsohn, *Die dogmatische Stellung des Königs in der Theologie der alten Ägypter*, Ägyptologische Forschungen, Heft 8 (Glückstadt-New York, 1939), p. 62 seq. L. Greven, *op. cit.*, p. 41 seq., has shown convincingly, in opposition to Jacobsohn, that this belief was a theological creation of the New Kingdom only. She also rightly rejected Jacobsohn's interpretation of the role of the Ka, according to which the supreme god and the ancestral ruling line were united with the reigning Pharaoh in the Ka. The Ka was, in the Old Kingdom, in no wise connected with the natural way of production. She considers the author's comparison of the God-father, son, and Ka-motif with the Christian Trinity erroneous.

[24] For details, see Moret, *Du caractère religieux*, p. 56 seq. An illustration of this belief can be taken from the account given by Sesostris (1965–1934 B.C.) of the founding of a temple. See A. Erman, *The Literature of the Ancient Egyptians*, trans. by A. M. Blackman (London, 1927), p. 50: "I conquered already as a babe and was great while yet in the egg.... He hath made me spacious to be lord of the Two Halves, as a child, ere the swaddling clothes were loosed for me...."

ceremony. It was they who performed the purification of the royal candidate. They acknowledged him as he was presented to them by the reigning king or by some of the gods. They assisted at the official publication and proclamation of the name of the new king, and it was they who afterwards handed to him the crowns of Upper and Lower Egypt. When all the mystic rites were completed, the king was finally kissed by the supreme god himself.[25]

According to Egyptian belief, the king was thus in some ways regarded as the earthly counterpart of all the national gods worshipped in the land. Because of the union of his Ka with the supreme god, the divinity could be worshipped in the person of the king; but the king could also be represented as worshipping his own Ka together with other divinities. As the king's Ka was directly associated with divinity, the king was as a matter of course the only mediator between the deity and his own subjects. His Ka was frequently represented as standing in front of him when the king intervened on behalf of his people. From the standpoint of the people, the Egyptian often addressed his prayers to the king's Ka or even an image of the king's Ka.[26]

The consequences of such beliefs for the Egyptians were far reaching. The concept of kingship was stretched to the highest degree. The king's Ka united not only the reigning king with the supreme god and with his ancestors, but also united the king's subjects with the divinity. As a result of this idea, the king participated in the creative power of the supreme god. It was to his Ka that the Kas of his subjects owed their existence. This concept illustrated in some pious expressions such as "my Ka comes from the king," "my Ka belongs to the king," "my Ka is the king." These expressions, with others of a similar kind, are the pious subject's acknowledgement that his Ka belonged to the god-creator.

[25] For the coronation ceremonies, see Moret, *op. cit.*, pp. 75–113. Cf. also H. Frankfort, *Kingship*, p. 105 seq. Great importance was attributed to the choice of Pharaoh's titles. See S. Schott, *Zur Krönungstitulatur der Pyramidenzeit*, Nachrichten der Akad. der Wiss. in Göttingen, Phil.-hist. Kl., no. 4 (1956), pp. 55–79. Cf. also H. Müller, *Die formale Entwicklung der Titulatur*. For a more detailed description of the coronation and other rituals of kingship, see H. W. Fairman, "The Kingship Rituals of Egypt," pp. 74–104.
[26] For documentation, see H. Jacobsohn, *op. cit.*, p. 60.

In the light of this doctrine, the king was unquestionably the one and only lord and owner of the earth, and, moreover, the only being who could validly distribute offices, fiefs, and imperial and social dignities. Expression was given to this belief when the king, in conferring a dignity upon someone, created the appointee's Ka, or united his own Ka with it. Phrases indicative of this thought seem to voice the conviction that the king actually conferred upon his subject that part of the divine power which went with the particular office.[27]

By virtue of his intimate union with the creator, the king was regarded as the actual author of the fertility of the fields and of cattle. He was also instrumental in causing the flooding of the Nile upon which not only the prosperity, but the very existence of Egypt depended.[28] As a matter of fact, the Pharaoh maintained the cosmic order (Maat) established by Re. Without the king chaos would prevail in nature and in human society.[29]

As a result of all this, the function of the Pharaoh assumed vital importance for Egypt. He became the sole fount of authority, the sole lawgiver and dispenser of justice.[30] These royal qualities are praised in numerous hymns composed in honor of the Pharaohs.[31] In these the king is hailed as the father of his subjects, the source of their joys and blessings, a stronghold of the country and of his soldiers, and also as a devouring lion attacking his enemies, consuming them with fire, filling the valleys with their corpses. This Egyptian court style is not only highly picturesque, but also important for a better understanding of ideas on Egyptian kingship. It will not be amiss to quote a few passages from the eulogies of the court to Rameses II, which are preserved in the great Abydos inscription.[32] They express more clearly than anything else Egyptian ideas on divine kingship.

[27] *Ibid.*, p. 61.
[28] For documentation, see H. Jacobsohn, *op. cit.*, p. 61 and H. Frankfort, *Kingship*, p. 59 seq.
[29] H. Frankfort, *Kingship*, pp. 9–12, 51 seq., 150, 231, 248, 309. I. Engnell, *Studies in Divine Kingship in the Ancient Near East* (Uppsala, 1943), p. 15. Cf. Ph. Derchain, "Le rôle du roi d'Egypte dans le maintien de l'ordre cosmique," *Le Pouvoir et le Sacré* (Brussels, 1962), pp. 61–73.
[30] Cf. H. Frankfort, *Kingship*, p. 51 seq.
[31] See especially A. Erman, *The Literature of the Ancient Egyptians*, p. 278 seq.: hymns on the accession of Merneptah and of Rameses IV. Cf. also the instruction of Sehetepibre, *ibid.*, p. 84 seq.
[32] J. H. Breasted, *Ancient Records of Egypt* (Chicago, 1906), 3, no. 265, p. 108.

We come to thee, O lord of heaven, lord of earth, Re, life of the whole earth, lord of duration, of fruitful revolution, Atum for the people, lord of destiny, creator of Renenet [goddess of birth, destiny, and good fortune], Khnum [creator god], who fashioned the people, giver of breath into the nostrils of all, making all the gods live, pillar of heaven, support of the earth ... adjusting the Two Lands, lord of food, plentiful in grain, in whose footsteps is the harvest goddess, maker of the great, fashioner of the lowly, whose word produces food, the lord vigilant when all men sleep, whose might defends Egypt, valiant in foreign lands ... our king, our lord, our sun ... breath of life, who makes all men live when he has shone on them.

In another address the court exalted the King's divine omnipotence.[33]

Thou art like Re in all that thou doest; that which thy heart wishes comes to pass ... If thou sayest to the water: 'Come upon the mountain,' the flood comes quickly after thy word, for thou art Re in limbs ... Thou art the living image on earth of the father, Atum of Heliopolis ... The seat of thy tongue is the shrine of truth, the god sits upon thy two lips ... thy heart is made into the likeness of (that of) Ptah, the creator of handicrafts. Thou art forever ....

When these eulogies are examined in the light of Egyptian theology, they cannot be regarded merely as long-winded adulations demanded by court etiquette. It must be remembered that the inscription was written under Rameses II during whose reign Egyptian royal theology seems to have received its final shape.

Another consequence of these beliefs was that the Pharaoh became the central figure and main factor in the public worship of the gods. This is illustrated by the fact that in all representations of public worship found in Egyptian temples, the king is depicted as performing sacrifices and religious rites. He may have performed the ceremonies in person on only very few occasions; but as the king was believed to be the sole representative of the people before the gods, so the priests who actually carried out the rites were

[33] *Ibid.*, no. 288, p. 120 seq.

considered to be acting as the king's representatives.[34] The king was also regarded as being the actual builder of all temples erected during his reign. The contributions of the faithful, although they might have been considerable, are never mentioned. The dedicatory addresses describe the king only as the builder and emphasize that the temples are to perpetuate the king's memory.[35]

But that was not all. Special feasts were given in honor of the king and the whole ceremonial, with prayers and sacrifices, served to reflect the unique position which the Pharaoh occupied in Egyptian life. The Egyptians not only accompanied the ceremony of the enthronement with a special liturgical ritual, but also inaugurated festivities to commemorate the anniversary of the king's coronation.[36] Particularly detailed information is extant concerning one special royal feast—the Sed festival. These details are not yet completely clarified by the specialists and it cannot be explained at present how and when the feast was inaugurated. The main significance of the festival is, however, clearly outlined in the ritual, of which the most important details are preserved in descriptions and illustrations in various Egyptian temples.[37]

This feast used to be celebrated on the thirtieth anniversary of the king's accession to the throne or on that of his designation as heir apparent. Some kings celebrated this "jubilee" before the thirtieth anniversary. It was also repeated at shorter intervals after having been celebrated once.

Great preparations were necessary for this occasion. Special buildings had to be erected near the king's favorite temple, with chapels for all the Egyptian gods, with a festival hall and a small palace for the king himself. All the Egyptian deities participated in this festival and received a visit from the king in their chapels. The ceremony was inaugurated by the old Egyptian war-god,

[34] Moret, *op. cit.*, pp. 115–208. See H. Kees, *Das Priestertum im ägyptischen Staat vom Neuen Reich bis zur Spätzeit* (Leiden-Cologne, 1953), pp. 1 seq., 30 seq.
[35] A. Erman, *Die Religion der Ägypter*, p. 186.
[36] Cf. A. Moret, *op. cit.*, p. 273 seq.
[37] See the bibliography concerning the festival in H. Frankfort, *Kingship*, p. 366 seq., and the description of the feast, *ibid.*, pp. 79–88. Cf. also the short resumé in L. Dürr's study "Reichsgründungen im antiken Orient," *Theologie und Glaube*, 20 (1928), p. 309 seq., and A. Moret, *op. cit.*, p. 235 seq.

whose statue was carried to the palace before that of the king and the king's standards. The climax to the celebrations was the reappointment of the king to his high office by all the gods. It was a kind of royal epiphany—a fresh revelation of the king in his divine character accompanied by solemn homage from the gods towards their earthly duplicate. The rites were concluded by the king offering many sacrifices to the gods and by a special ceremony known as a royal dance in the course of which a piece of land—probably symbolizing Upper and Lower Egypt—was dedicated to the gods.[38]

The concluding act of the ceremony appears to symbolize the universal character of Egyptian kingship. The king shot an arrow in the direction of each of the four points of the compass and was then solemnly enthroned four times, each time facing one of the four points. It must also be remembered that most of the ceremonies which the king had to perform were carried out twice, a repetition intended to symbolize the union of Upper and Lower Egypt as one realm under his sceptre. The title of Pharaoh as "Lord of the two Lands," seems, however, to have implied more than sovereignty over Egypt. It stressed the basic universality of the king's power. As the king was the incarnation of the sun-god, his realm naturally embraced "that which the sun encircled," namely, the whole earth. The Greeks seem to have interpreted the royal title in this sense, because they translated the "Two Lands" as ἡ οἰκουμένη —the whole world.[39] This particular belief could have provided the ideological foundation for the political expansion of Egypt which had been initiated by the Eighteenth Dynasty. Nubia, Ethiopia, and Libya were the first objects of this expansion. Thutmose I (ca. 1540 B.C.) conquered Syria and penetrated as far as the Euphrates. His conquests were defended and subsequently extended by Thutmose III. The tablets of Tell el-Amarna, which contain the archives of his successors Amenophis III and Amenophis IV, provide a

---

[38] Cf. S. Schott, *Zum Krönungstag der Königin Hatschepsût*, Nachrichten der Akad. der Wiss. in Göttingen, Phil-hist. Kl., no. 6 (1955), p. 204 seq.

[39] For details, see H. Frankfort, *Kingship*, p. 19. Cf. R. Anthes, *op. cit.*, p. 179. The idea of the universal rule of the king existed from the kingship of Horus on, but was clearly expressed only in later periods.

very clear picture of the spread of Egyptian culture and influence over neighboring lands.

The Egyptians were thus the first to build an empire which could claim a kind of universality—albeit within the limits of the narrow geographical horizons of the period. It stretched from Libya to Babylonia and Assyria and from Ethiopia to Cyprus and the islands of the Aegean. The Empire flourished from 1580 to 1350 B.C. and was replaced by the Second Empire founded by the Nineteenth Dynasty (1350–1205 B.C.) with Seti I and Rameses II as its greatest heroes.

The idea of a universal Egyptian Empire was most clearly expressed during the period of their expansion. In the hymn of victory in honor of Thutmose III, the god Amon-Re is presented addressing the Pharaoh thus:[40]

"I have given to thee might and victory against all countries. I have set thy fame [even] the fear of thee in all lands, thy terror as far as the four pillars of heaven.... I have come, causing thee to smite the uttermost ends of the lands, the circuit of the Great Circle (Okeanos) is enclosed in thy grasp."

Again the same Amon-Re addresses Seti I:[41] "I give to thee all might and all victory. I give to thee all lands, all countries beneath thy sandals". It is also significant that, as has been shown, the royal theology was fully elaborated during the reign of Rameses II, after the Egyptians had tasted the intoxicating flavor of political expansion over neighboring nations.

With these descriptions some light is thrown on the relationship of the kings to the priesthood. As the king was the only mediator between his subjects and the divine beings whom they venerated, he became the high priest of the Egyptian religious cult. But this circumstance did not eliminate the importance of the Egyptian priesthood. As the prosperity of the Egyptians depended upon the assiduous performance of a ritual, so a very intricate ceremonial developed around the theory of kingship. This came to regulate most of the Pharaoh's activities from his enthrone-

[40] J. H. Breasted, *Ancient Records of Egypt*, 2, pp. 263, 265.
[41] *Ibid.*, 3, p. 74.

ment through his daily life—his part in the ritual feasts, his contact with his subjects—until his own interment.[42] The rules for this ceremonial were drawn up by the priests who also maintained a careful check over their execution.[43] These circumstances and the generous gifts with which the Pharaohs endowed the principal temples naturally increased the influence of the priestly class to the detriment of that of the kings. So it happened that even Egypt experienced the rule of the priesthood when the power of the Pharaohs declined under the Twentieth Dynasty. The power of the high priests of the temple of Amon-Re in Thebes grew at the expense of the kings, and Hrihor, who was high priest during the reign of Rameses XII, gradually gathered all the real power in the land into his own hands and eventually succeeded the last king of the Rameside dynasty, about 1000 B.C.[44]

The kingship of the High Priest Hrihor, however, could not last. The new Tanite dynasty, which was perhaps of Libyan stock, obtained an ascendancy over the land and the high priests had to submit to the new Pharaohs, although Hrihor's descendants were able to maintain a marked influence over public affairs in Egypt during the rule of the Twenty-first or Tanite dynasty. Only during the period of the Twenty-second Dynasty did the high priesthood of Thebes become a kind of secundo-geniture of the reigning family.[45]

But this was not the definitive end of the hierocracy in Egypt. It seems that the descendants of Hrihor took refuge in Ethiopia, which was then under Egyptian sovereignty, and succeeded in gaining considerable influence in the native kingdom which was in process of formation there. According to the report of Diodorus,[46] the native Ethiopian kingdom was ruled by a theocracy, the real rulers being the priests who had obtained power over the kings,

---

[42] Cf. H. Kees, *Ägypten, Kulturgeschichte des alten Orients*, 1, Handbuch der Altertumswissenschaft, ed. by I. Müller and W. Otto, Abt. 3, Teil 1, Band 3 (Munich, 1933), pp. 172–185.

[43] Cf. Diodorus Siculus, *op. cit.*, I, 69 seq., *loc. cit.*, 1, p. 240 seq., on those customs and on the role of the priests in enforcing them.

[44] For details, see E. Meyer, "Gottesstaat, Militärherrschaft und Ständeswesen in Aegypten," *SB der Preuss. Akad. der Wiss.*, Phil.-hist. Kl. (Berlin, 1928), pp. 495–520. Cf. also J. H. Breasted, *A History of Egypt* (New York, 1912), pp. 464–536; esp. H. Kees, *Das Priestertum*, p. 160 seq.

[45] H. Kees, *Das Priestertum*, pp. 172 seq., 199 seq.

[46] Diodorus Siculus, *op. cit.*, III, 5 (Loeb, 1935), 2, p. 96 seq.

so that Amon and his priests became masters of Ethiopia. The god of Thebes once more secured his omnipotence and the influence of his priests regained its importance in Egypt when the Ethiopian dynasty succeeded in establishing its rule there (745–718 B.C.).[47]

Although this Egyptian hierocracy did not endure and proved to be only an incident in the political history of the land, it deserves to be recalled. It demonstrates that it was not impossible to transform a theocratic monarchy into a hierocratic dominion. Moreover the Egyptian priests never forgot the times when they reigned supreme in Egypt in the name of their god and represented the Ethiopian hierocratic theocracy as the ideal government. Many Greeks who came into contact with them during the period of Hellenic political adolescence were led into error by this circumstance, which was indeed the principal source for the misconception commonly held by the Greeks that Ethiopia had been the cradle of Egyptian civilization. It is an interesting incident which deserves mention in a history of Eastern political thought. Some of its features can be traced in the evolution of the political thought of other nations.

In spite of the great progress recently made in the interpretation of Egyptian ideas on kingship, there are still many problems relating to the subject which await a solution. Possibly a correct interpretation of the various symbols on royal standards [48]—some of them taken from the animal world—will illuminate the way to a better understanding of the ideas on kingship held by the primitive Egyptians. But such problems are rather the concern of the anthropologist.

Egypt is remarkable because it presents a divinized kingship in the last stage of its development. The prestige of the Pharaoh among neighboring populations must have been sufficiently ef-

---

[47] For details, see J. H. Breasted, *A History of Egypt*, p. 537 seq. Cf. H. Kees, *Die Hohenpriester des Amun von Karnak, von Herihor bis zum Ende der Äthiopenzeit*, Probleme der Ägyptologie, 4 (Leiden, 1964).

[48] So far the most exhaustive study of this subject is that of H. Frankfort, *Kingship*, pp. 91–95. Cf. also M. A. Canney, "Ancient Conceptions on Kingship," *Oriental Studies in Honour of Cursetji Erachji Pavry*, ed. by Jal Dastur Cursetji Pavry (London, 1933), p. 64. In this study the author compares, pp. 62–75, Egyptian conceptions with those of other Oriental nations.

fective to assure the influence of Egyptian culture over a wide area, and by implication also the influence of its political fabric. But in spite of the brilliance of Egyptian culture and its wide penetration, the Egyptian royal cult does not appear to have influenced the evolution of Eastern political thought as extensively as has often been assumed. The peoples of Mesopotamia, for example, the cradle of another advanced culture of the ancient world, reached their own conclusions on kingship, independently of Egypt.[49]

Mesopotamia, the valley between the rivers Tigris and Euphrates, depended for its existence upon irrigation from these waterways; but unlike Egypt, the valley was open to invasion from the western steppes and from the mountains to the north and east. Its political evolution was not as uniform as that of Egypt and its population consisted of a mixture of races. It was not national uniformity

[49] Great progress has recently been made in the study of Babylonian and Assyrian kingship. The works most pertinent to the subject include the following: Chr. Jeremias, *Die Vergöttlichung der babylonisch-assyrischen Könige*, Der Alte Orient, 19, Heft 3/4 (Leipzig, 1919) (his outline of evolution is, however, not clear). Cf. also A. Jeremias, *Handbuch der altorientalischen Geisteskultur*, 2nd ed. (Berlin-Leipzig, 1929), pp. 102 seq., 392 seq. B. Meissner gave a good summary in his fundamental work, *Babylonien und Assyrien* (Heidelberg, 1920, 1925), I, pp. 46–79, of what was known on the subject at that time. His observations were added to by Franz M. Th. Böhl in his important study, *Der babylonische Fürstenspiegel*, Mitteilungen der altorientalischen Gesellschaft, 11, Heft 3 (Leipzig, 1937), pp. 35–49. The remarks of C. W. McEwan on Mesopotamian kingship, *The Oriental Origin of Hellenistic Kingship*, The Oriental Institute of the Univ. of Chicago, Studies in Ancient Oriental Civilization, no. 13 (Chicago, 1934), pp. 7–17, do not give the correct interpretation of the matter. The best study so far is that written by R. Labat, *Le caractère religieux de la royauté assyro-babylonienne* (Paris, 1939). An exhaustive, although not complete bibliography on Oriental kingship is given by I. Engnell, *op. cit.* Most recently C. J. Gadd, *Ideas of Divine Rule in the Ancient East*, pp. 32–62 made a comparative study on kingship in the ancient Near East. There are numerous studies on the influence of Assyrian kingship on the evolution of Jewish Messianism. Particularly useful in this respect is that of L. Dürr, *Ursprung und Ausbau der israelitisch-jüdischen Heilandserwartung* (Berlin, 1925), pp. 16 seq., 74 seq. Interesting and new material on the history of Babylonia down to the reign of Hammurabi can be found in D. O. Edzard, *Die "Zweite Zwischenzeit" Babyloniens* (Wiesbaden, 1957). A select bibliography will be found in H. Schmökel, *Ur, Assur und Babylon* (Zurich, 1955). *Idem, Geschichte des alten Vorderasien*, Handbuch der Orientalistik, Band 2, Abschn. 3 (Leiden, 1957), is very useful. His dating of events and periods in Sumerian and Babylonian history is being followed in the present book. Cf. also *idem,* "Mesopotamien," in V. Schmökel and others, *Kulturgeschichte des Alten Orient* (Stuttgart, 1961), esp. pp. 85–108. W. von Soden published short monographs for general readers on prominent Babylonian and Assyrian rulers, *Herrscher im alten Orient* (Berlin, 1954).

which provided the cohesive formative power for a state, but cultural uniformity.

The cultural foundations of Mesopotamia were laid by its first primitive population, a people of unknown origin described by specialists as Asianic—the Sumerians.[50] Their political and cultural life evolved around cities, which were surrounded by cultivated lands made fertile through irrigation works carried out by the common effort of the inhabitants. The cities were often separated from each other by wide, desolate, and uninhabited tracts, which were crossed only by caravans because of the many dangers threatening the solitary traveller. A similar situation will be found in Greece, whose cultural life also evolved in cities separated from each other by mountainous regions. Difficulties of communication did not favor the formation of larger political entities; but here the similarity between ancient Mesopotamia and Greece ends. The political development of the city-states in the two countries was quite distinct.

The Sumerian city-states were organized on a religious basis. The supreme lord and master of each city was its national god. The city, all land, all cattle, and all the produce of the fields was his exclusive personal property. The temple of the god was the political and economic center of the city-states. The gods divided the produce of the fields among the people, and also regulated the citizen's obligations toward the community.[51] It was natural in such circumstances that the heads of the city-states should be representatives of the gods and that their first duty was to serve them. High priesthood was intimately connected with kingship.[52]

[50] On Sumerian culture, see the well-written, popular outline by A. Jeremias, *Die Weltanschauung der Sumerer*, Der Alte Orient, 27, Heft 4 (Leipzig, 1929), chap. 4. Cf. also the same author's *Der Kosmos von Sumer*, *ibid.*, 32, Heft 1 (Leipzig, 1932), chap. 1. It is acknowledged, however, that the author overemphasizes the importance of cosmic theories on Sumerian and Babylonian political ideas.

[51] Detailed documentation on this old Sumerian state socialism founded on a theocratic basis is to be found in P. A. Deirnel's important study "Sumerische Tempelwirtschaft," *Analecta Orientalia*, 2 (Rome, 1931), p. 71 seq.

[52] H. Frankfort, *Kingship*, p. 215 seq., tries to show that the basis of Mesopotamian political development was a kind of "primitive democracy." He elaborates Thorkil Jacobsen's ideas as expressed in his stimulating study

Such was the situation in the most important cities—Lagash, Nippur, Ur, Uruk, Kish, and others. The sovereigns of the cities were only the vicars (*ensi* or *patesi*) of the local gods and their high priests. When the prince of one city succeeded in extending his sovereignty over other cities, he claimed the title of *lugal*—great man.[53] There was, however, a period in the old Sumerian history when priesthood and kingship became separated and the priestly class gained considerable influence in the state. This happened in Lagash under the mighty King Entemena[54] who had extended his rule over many other city-states and was forced to devote more time to his royal duties (after 3089 B.C.).

The notion of an empire of more universal character was outlined in the old Sumerian period by Lugal-zaggisi, *Ensi* of Umma about 2375 B.C., who claimed to be master of all countries from the "Lower Sea" (the Persian Gulf), between the Euphrates and Tigris, as far as the "Higher Sea" (the Mediterranean).[55] It was however, not a Sumerian dynasty which succeeded in making good such a claim for a longer period. Semitic elements may have been settled on parts of Sumerian territory for a considerable time, for the dynasties of Kish seem to have been of Semitic origin from a

---

"Primitive Democracy in Ancient Mesopotamia," *Journal of Near Eastern Studies*, 2 (1943), pp. 159–172. Their arguments are, however, not convincing. Frankfort's distinction between the governor-high priest and the leader elected by city assemblies appears to be very artificial. Jacobsen's suggestion that the assemblies of gods described in Mesopotamian epics should be regarded as projections of the old assembly into the world of the gods is ingenious, but does not carry enough weight to upset evidence in the same literature that describes kingship as coming from heaven. The old Sumerian political system, as we know it in historical times, does not exclude the existence of a kind of council of elders—king's councillors—and of assemblies functioning in general as a court of law. The political organization of the Assyrian merchant colonies in Asia Minor is quite different. T. Fish, "Some Ancient Mesopotamian Traditions concerning Men and Society," *Bulletin of the John Rylands Library, Manchester*, 30 (1946), pp. 41–51, 53, is more precise, since he terms such assemblies "an oligarchy which on every state occasion took counsel together, in assembly, under the primacy of the king."

[53] Cf. B. Meissner, *Babylonien und Assyrien*, I, p. 46. See especially H. N. Halle, *Early Mesopotamian Royal Titles. A Philological and Historical Analysis* (New Haven, 1957).

[54] For details, see S. H. Langdon, "Early Babylonia and Its Cities," *CAH*, I, pp. 383–386.

[55] F. Thureau-Dangin, *Les inscriptions de Sumer et d'Akkad* (Paris, 1905), pp. 218–220.

very early period on.[56] These became so strong that Sargon, king of the Akkad in the northern part of Mesopotamia, not only denounced Lugal-zaggisi's overlordship, but imposed the rule of the Akkadians on all Sumerian territory. Sargon's dynasty ruled for almost two centuries (ca. 2350–2150 B.C.). After that the Sumerians of Ur became the masters of Mesopotamia (ca. 2150–1950 B.C.), but the new Semitic center which had arisen in Babylon rapidly outgrew not only the old city of Akkad, but also the Sumerian centers of Uruk, Ur, Lagash, Isin, and Larsa which had risen to prominence after Ur (ca. 1960–1700 B.C.).[57] Hammurabi, the king of Babylon (ca. 1728–1686 B.C.), assured permanent Semitic predominance over the whole of Mesopotamia. This Semitic element became so strong that the Kassites, who established their rule over the whole land (ca. 1600–1400 B.C.) lost their national individuality and became Semitized. These new invaders of Babylonia had come from the mountainous region which formed the confines of Persia and was called Elam by the Semites.

This mixture of races in Mesopotamia is, of course, of great importance for the evolution of the ideas on kingship of the Sumerians, Akkadians, Babylonians, and Assyrians. The latter were Semites from the mountainous region of the middle Tigris who finally—from 883 B.C. onward—became the political heirs of this millenary development. It is remarkable to observe how the Sumerian and Semitic elements influenced each other. The Semites accepted not only the Sumerian cuneiform mode of writing and literary tradition, but, in addition, effected some important exchanges with the Sumerians in religious belief. On the other hand, Semitic political ideas considerably enriched Sumerian political thought. The importance of the Sumerian element in the cultural evolution of their Semitic suzerains is illustrated by the fact that, even when the Sumerian language was completely replaced by the Akkadian tongue in public life, Sumerian remained a liturgical language down to recent times. This forms a curious parallel to

---

[56] S. H. Langdon, op. cit., p. 365 seq. On Semitic migration, see infra, p. 54 seq.
[57] On Larsa during the period of its independence, see the study by Ch. F. Jean, "Larsa d'après les textes cunéiformes (2187–1901)," Babyloniaca, 10 (1927–1928), pp. 161–239; 11 (1929–1930), pp. 1–64, 175–198.

the mediaeval evolution in the West where Latin maintains its position in Christian liturgy long after its disappearance as the language of a nation.

As can be seen from this account of the old Sumerian city-states, kingship was regarded there as being of divine origin: only gods were the real kings. This conception is further elaborated in Sumerian and Akkadian lists of gods and of royal dynasties, and in legends, such as that of Etana, which have been transmitted to us in fragments from the old Babylonian and Assyrian period, or in the myth concerning the creation of the world.[58] According to these descriptions, the primeval king is the supreme god, Anu. He is both king of gods and king of humans. Before his throne lay the insignia of kingship. The idea of kingship held by Enlil was, however, less abstract. Anu had little affection for human beings; but Enlil was the real master of the earth. He is called the supreme sovereign, master of the lands, king of kings, shepherd and prince.[59] Here it should be stressed that from the Sumerian period onward the title of shepherd was regarded as having an important kingly significance.[60] According to the myth of the Creation, the supreme god, Anu or Enlil, decided to establish on earth the kingship which

[58] For a general description, see B. Meissner, *Die babylonisch-assyrische Literatur*, Handbuch der Literaturwissenschaft (Potsdam, 1927–28), pp. 24 seq., 44 seq. R. Labat, *Le poème babylonien de la Création* (Paris, 1935), pp. 157–171 (Marduk's "supreme kingship"); S. H. Langdon, "The Legend of Etana and the Eagle, or the Epical Poem 'The city they hated'," *Babyloniaca*, 12 (1931), p. 10 seq. lines 6–14: "The pale-faced people, all of them had not yet set up a king. At that time no tiara had been worn, nor crown, and no sceptre had been studded with lapis lazuli. The chambers [probably throne rooms] had not been created together. The seven gates were locked against the host [of mankind]. Sceptre, crown, tiara and staff were [still] placed before Anu in heaven, there being no royal direction of her [Ishtar's] people. [Then] kingship descended from heaven...." On the list of kings, see the fundamental work by Th. Jacobsen, *The Sumerian King List*, The Oriental Institute of the University of Chicago, Assyriological Studies, 11 (Chicago, 1939), pp. 55–58, 166 seq. (antediluvian rulers), pp. 70–127, new critical edition of the text, which starts with the words: "When the kingship was lowered from heaven, the kingship was in Eridu(g)."

[59] For details, see K. L. Tallquist, *Akkadische Götterepitheta*, Studia Orientalia, 7 (Helsingfors, 1938), p. 300 seq.

[60] See the numerous examples gathered from Sumerian, Babylonian, Assyrian, and neo-Babylonian documents by A. Schott, *Die Vergleiche in den akkadischen Königsinschriften*, Mitteilungen der Vorderasiatisch-Ägyptischen Gesellschaft, 30 (Leipzig, 1926), p. 70 seq.

until then had existed only in heaven. He therefore created five cities and gave each one of them to a god. The gods then delegated their kingly powers in each city to a prince who administered them in the god's name. It was imagined that the human kings of this remote period lived and reigned for fabulously long periods. Then the deluge came and the kingship returned to heaven. It came back to earth only when the cities were rebuilt, after which it remained among men.

According to these legendary accounts, kingship was something abstract and had a separate existence. Its possession was disputed by the various cities[61] and when a city lost its independence, it was said that its kingship had departed, leaving it to lodge with its victorious rival. A defeated king would try to carry with him statues of the god of his city-state in order that he might safeguard the claim to sovereignty of the subjugated city, for the real kings of the cities were their gods. On the other hand, the first preoccupation of the victor was to render homage to the gods of the territory he had conquered so that he might receive from their hands the true sovereignty over the lands which he now occupied. Occasionally, however, the conqueror destroyed the gods of vanquished cities, or carried them home as the booty of his own gods.

A further consequence of these factors which affected the origins of kingship was the belief that the sublime office of king could be attained only by men who had been especially predestined and trained for it by the gods. In the Babylonian and Assyrian period this predestination was believed to be evidenced by the new king being a scion of a royal family chosen by the gods to govern in their name. Therefore, the kings were greatly occupied in maintaining an eternal union with their dynasties.[62] Here for the first time is encountered the idea of eternity in connection with kingship. This predestination was emphasized in the royal protocol by phrases stating that the god, after having chosen his representative, had fixed his regard upon him, had loudly and clearly pronounced the name of the chosen one, and, together with other gods, had

[61] For details, see R. Labat, *Le caractère religieux*, pp. 29–39.
[62] For documentation, see *ibid.*, p. 40 seq.

determined a favorable fate for him. It was a kind of divine and mystic investiture. This custom originated in the old Sumerian period and can be traced in the court style of all periods of Mesopotamian history, not excluding the Assyrian period.[63]

In accordance with these beliefs, the kings liked to call themselves sons of gods, who had chosen them as their special creatures. They claimed to possess special, divine qualities vouchsafed to them by the gods. Such expressions are also found in use from the old Sumerian period onward and are a prominent feature of the court style of the Babylonian and Assyrian era. They are, however, inclined to be vague and lack the dogmatic rigidity of similar expressions used in the Egyptian court style. They are not as explicit as their Egyptian counterparts in suggesting a real divine filiation of the Mesopotamian kings.[64] In this respect the kings of the old Sumerian period did not claim to be of divine nature, although they were well aware of the sublimity of their office, which set them high above the common man. The divinization of kings first appears during the reign of the Akkadian dynasty (2350–2150 B.C.). It seems that the Semitic conception of the power and might vested in divinity was the main reason for this deification. The Semites also modified the primitive Sumerian idea that the city-states were the exclusive property of the gods. In dividing conquered territory among their noble families, reserving the lion's share for themselves, they acted as supreme masters and used their own discretion in determining the portions to be allotted to the temples and the clergy. They claimed, therefore, to be divine, and wore the helmet with the double horn, the Semitic emblem of divinity.[65]

The Sumerian kings, who followed the Akkadian rulers (2150 to 1700 B.C.), retained their predecessors' claims to divine character.[66]

---

[63] For details, see *ibid.*, pp. 53–62. The phrase, "pronouncing the new king's name," might mean changing the present ruler's name. See H. Frankfort, *Kingship*, p. 23 seq. On p. 398, H. Frankfort calls the different phrases expressing the divine investiture "equivalent rather than complementary." Cf. also J. De Fraine, *L'aspect religieux de la royauté israélite* (Rome, 1954), pp. 169–186.

[64] Cf. J. De Fraine, *op. cit.*, p. 236 seq.

[65] For details, see Franz M. Th. Böhl, *op. cit.*, chap. 3, p. 40. Cf. also R. Labat, *op. cit.*, p. 7 seq.

[66] R. Labat, *op. cit.*, p. 9 seq.

They also tried hard to re-establish the principles of the old Sumerian theocracy. Gudea of Lagash, for example, revived the ideal of the king-high priest; but the Akkadians had so radically changed the old economic order that it was impossible to restore to their gods all the property of the city-states. The kings remained the sovereign possessors of the land and as, according to the old Sumerian conception, only a god could be in possession of the city-states, they claimed divine character in order to legitimize their own positions.

Evidence for this new practice is provided from the reigns of Kings Shulgi, Ishme-Dagan, Lipit-Ishtar and others. Statues of the kings were placed in temples erected in their honor and there, at ceremonies celebrating the inauguration of the building or coronation anniversaries, they were adored as gods. The hymns sung in the king's honor on those occasions give us a clear idea of this Sumerian ruler worship.[67]

It seems, however, that owing to their mortality, the divine kings were identified with gods of the underworld or gods of fertility, especially Abu and Tammuz.[68] There is evidence of a kind of restriction in Sumerian deification, while the superiority in rank of the heavenly gods over the divinized kings seems to have been strictly respected.[69]

The dynasty of Babylon (1750–1600 B.C.) did not completely repudiate its inheritance of Sumerian ideas on kingship, but it seems to have discarded the old conception of divine kingship. It is true that Hammurabi (*ca.* 1728–1686 B.C.) called himself not

[67] The liturgies for the worship of deified kings, together with the appropriate hymns, have mostly been published by S. Langdon, *Sumerian Liturgical Texts*, Univ. of Pennsylvania, Museum Publications of the Babylonian Section, 10, no. 2 (Philadelphia, 1917), p. 126 seq. Cf. also *idem*, *Babylonian Wisdom* (London, 1923), p. 22 seq. See also T. Fish, "The Cult of King Dungi during the Third Dynasty of Ur," *Bulletin of the John Rylands Library, Manchester*, 11 (1927), pp. 322–328; *idem*, "The Contemporary Cult of Kings of the Third Dynasty of Ur," *ibid.*, 12 (1928), pp. 75–82. Cf. the translation of Sumerian and Akkadian hymns by A. Falkenstein and W. von Soden, *Sumerische und akkadische Hymnen und Gebete* (Zurich-Stuttgart, 1953); royal hymns, *ibid.*, pp. 114–131.

[68] Cf. I. Engnell, *Studies in Divine Kingship*, p. 24 seq. The picture which the author gives of Sumerian kingship is, however, not clear. Cf. also the critical remarks by Frankfort, *Kingship*, p. 405, on Engnell's study. See also T. H. Gaster's review in *Review of Religion*, 9 (1945), pp. 267–291.

[69] This is rightly emphasized by F. M. Th. Böhl, *op. cit.*, p. 38.

only the sun(-god) of Babylon, but also "God of kings and brother of the God Zamama."[70] But he himself never claimed divinity—at least there is no extant proof thereof—and his successors all discarded the royal-divine title. It is probable that Hammurabi employed the expressions only metaphorically. The Assyrian kings of the later period also liked to call themselves "sun of the whole of mankind,"[71] an expression which can have only a metaphorical significance. The emphasis which Hammurabi placed upon his relationship to the gods had a figurative meaning; it expressed his intimacy with the gods and dependence on them and at the same time stressed the fact that his sovereignty over other princes was willed and sanctioned by the gods.

It seems that the deified Sumerian kings were not worshipped in those cities which provided the foundation of their power and where they regarded themselves as representatives of gods, but only in the cities which came under their sway.[72] It is true that during the reign of the Babylonian dynasty the practice of erecting statues of kings in temples was continued; but this was done not to make them objects of worship, but to give substance to the idea that the kings were always in the presence of gods and rendered them, therefore, continuous homage.[73]

The Babylonians also retained certain other practices inherited from the Sumerians, especially that of taking the oath in the name of the king; but contrary to Sumerian usage, the names of one or two gods were added.[74] Borrowings from Sumerian hymns on divinized kings are also to be found in the court style of the

[70] Code, cols. II, 13–14 (son of Sin), 55 (god of kings), 56 (son of Enlil); IV, 27–28 (son of Dagan, brother of the god Zamama); V, 4–9 (sun-[god?]— of Babylon). V. Scheil's edition of the Code is used here, *Textes élamites-sémitiques, Deuxième série*, Délégation en Perse, Mémoires, 4 (Paris, 1902): "Code des Lois de Hammurabi," pp. 11–162. H. Frankfort's suggestion (*Kingship*, p. 308) that in this instance the translation should be sun of Babylon, not *sun-god* of Babylon, is here accepted. Cf. also what he says on Hammurabi, pp. 300, 302, 306. A. Schott, *Die Vergleiche in den akkadischen Königsinschriften*, p. 92, also seems to favor the translation "sun" of Babylon.

[71] For documentation, see L. Dürr, *Ursprung*, p. 107. Cf. I. Engnell, *Studies in Divine Kingship*, p. 23.

[72] See H. Frankfort, *Kingship*, p. 301 seq., on this problem.

[73] Cf. the extremely interesting description of the significance of royal statues in Mesopotamia and their worship, in H. Frankfort, *Kingship*, p. 302 seq.

[74] R. Labat, *Le caractère religieux*, p. 226.

Babylonian period.[75] This indicates that the Amorite dynasty considered itself to be the heir of the Sumerians; but in ruler-worship its kings went their own way. Hammurabi himself initiated this new evolution when he made a clear distinction between kingship and priesthood. His legal reforms also terminated the old Sumerian social order. The divinization of kings reappeared only for a short period during the reign of the Kassite dynasty (1600–1400 B.C.).

The separation of kingship from priesthood introduced a danger. A strong king had no difficulty in keeping the priestly class in its appointed place. But both Egyptian and Sumerian history have shown that when the political power of a king declined, the priests were in a position to take the reins of government into their own hands. This danger threatened the Babylonian state at one time owing to the considerable power acquired by the clergy of the temple erected to Marduk, the principal divinity of the Babylonians.[76]

In the circumstances described, it is clear that the divine character of the Akkadian, Sumerian, and Babylonian kings could not be of the same nature as that of the Egyptian Pharaohs. According to the Egyptian royal theology, the king was a natural son of the sun-god and his reincarnation. In Mesopotamia one can refer only to a kind of adoption of the king by the gods as their child. The kings, when adopted by the gods, renounced their earthly parents. This explains why in invocations they affirmed that they had no father and no mother, an expression which became almost stereotyped and was also used by Assyrian kings who became the heirs of the Sumerians and Babylonians.[77]

The adoption was ratified not only by the king's solemn acceptance of divine parentage, but also by the presumption that the adopted one was reared on the divine milk of the goddesses. It may be that the procedure of adoption was founded upon juridical practice in Mesopotamia of which evidence is slight.

---

[75] See F. M. Th. Böhl, *op. cit.*, p. 40 seq. Cf. also the brief summarized statements on the Babylonian ruler cult made by R. Labat, *op. cit.*, at the end of his excellent study, p. 370 seq.

[76] Cf. B. Meissner, *Babylonien und Assyrien*, 2 p. 59 seq.

[77] For documentation, see R. Labat, *op. cit.*, pp. 63–69.

POLITICAL PHILOSOPHY

The evolution of the idea of kingship was completely different in Assyria than it was among the Akkadians, Sumerians, and Babylonians. It has been shown that the Akkadians and Babylonians had come under the magic spell of a Sumerian culture far superior to their own and that even in the political sphere Sumerian influence was marked. The Assyrians, although of Semitic origin like the Akkadians and Amorite Babylonians, were too remote from the centers of Sumerian culture to be greatly affected by it. Sumerian culture never became their traditional inheritance, although it affected them in their mountainous strongholds on the middle Tigris and helped them to form the fabric of their civilization. They had turned, especially during the second millennium B.C., not toward the south, but toward the north and northeast, whose wild and turbulent peoples made a considerable impact on their national life. In this way, the Assyrians forfeited to a great extent the purity of their Semitic race; they mixed with native Asianic elements and with peoples from Asia Minor, particularly the Hittites.[78] The cultural evolution of the Assyrians was partly shaped by this, and it also explains why their political ideas developed along lines that differed from those followed by the Sumerians, the Semitic Akkadians, and the Amorites. Unfortunately, it is not possible to analyze the Semitic and foreign elements in Assyrian ideas on kingship.

At the beginning of their history the Assyrians were ignorant of the title of king. Their overlord was both a religious chieftain and a military leader, whose political power was limited by an assembly usually called the *karum* and composed of members of a form of nobility and of certain wealthy citizens. Each important city had its assembly which decided all commercial and juridical matters brought before it. The *karum* of the capital—Ashur (Ashshur)—naturally had more competence than others, sharing political power with the sovereign. Its political importance is illustrated by the fact that it is mentioned, with the prince, in all important documents. The oath was taken in the names of the prince and the *karum*, and appeals were made not to the king as in Babylonia but to the *karum*.[79]

---

[78] On the Hittites, see *infra*, p. 45 seq.
[79] R. Labat, *op. cit.*, p. 15 seq. Cf. A. T. Olmstead, *History of Assyria* (New York-London, 1923), pp. 525–541, 598 seq.

The prince is also described as judge (*waklum*) as he presided over the tribunal, in which the *karum* participated; but the main basis of his political influence was religious. He gloried in the title of prince-vicar (*ishshak*) and priest of the god Ashur. Besides these titles, he is referred to in the inscriptions simply as prince, a word which means great (*rubu*). The title of king (*shar*) was introduced into Assyria by a usurper, Shamshi-Adad I (*ca.* 1748–1718 B.C.), but it did not come into common usage until five centuries later in the reign of Ashur-uballit I (*ca.* 1356–1320 B.C.). This can be learned from his correspondence with the Pharaoh, which is preserved on the tablets of el-Amarna.[80] The Assyrian prince simply took over the royal title previously used by the prince of the neighboring tribe of Mitanni, whom he had defeated. Ashur-uballit's reign marks the starting point of Assyria's rise to world domination. The defeat of the Mitanni, who had long exercized their hegemony over Assyria, was followed by the subjection of Baby-lonia. A new title, already used by Shamshi-Adad I (see *supra*), but discarded by his successors, was added to the name of the prince: "king of the totality" (of Babylonia). That of "lieutenant of Enlil" was also added, Enlil being the supreme deity of Babylonia. The identification of Ashur with Enlil soon enforced the unification of Assyria and Babylonia. Further expansion led to the assumption of the title "king of the four regions of the world," which clearly expresses the idea of universal empire.[81]

The Assyrian kings were able to make good their claim to universal empire insofar as was possible at this remote period.[82] Tiglath-pileser I (*ca.* 1116–1078 B.C.), one of the greatest of Assyrian conquerors, extended his sway as far north as Armenia and as far west as Cappadocia in Asia Minor, the seat of power of the Hittites.[83] Lebanon became his hunting ground and Egypt sent him a crocodile in acknowledgement of the importance of his political power. After a series of vicissitudes, Ashurnazirpal II (883–859 B.C.) opened a further chapter in Assyria's victorious conquests. These

[80] Letters 15,3; 16,3; *The Tell el-Amarna Tablets*, I, ed. by S. A. B. Mercer (Toronto, 1939), pp. 56, 58. Cf. A. T. Olmstead, *op. cit.*, p. 41 seq.
[81] For documentation, see R. Labat, *op. cit.*, pp. 17–20.
[82] For details, see A. T. Olmstead, *op. cit.*, pp. 55–97, 175–385.
[83] On the Hittites, see *infra*, pp. 45 seq., 56.

were continued by Shalmaneser III (858–824 B.C.), conqueror of
the Syrian confederacy and of Achab of Israel. They reached their
zenith under Tiglath-pileser III (745–727 B.C.), who broke the
power of the Hittites in Asia Minor and secured for Assyria the
great commercial highways to the Mediterranean and the Phoenician
seaports on the Syrian coast. The conquest of Egypt in 670 B.C.
under Asarhaddon was the crowning achievement. After Assyria's
days of glory had passed, Babylonia rose again for a short period.
Then, under Cyrus, from 539 B.C. Persia took over the inheritance
of both Assyria and Babylonia.

Assyria's great warrior kings provided their empire with a firm
organization on a military basis. But, in spite of their vast conquests, their domestic political power still had to be shared with
the principal *karum*, the assemblies of the lesser cities, and the
powerful nobility centered around the persons of the king's generals.
In this special respect the Assyrians may have been influenced by
the Indo-European Hittites. The Assyrian kings were not even
completely free to choose their successors. First, they were obliged
to secure favorable oracles from the gods, which meant that the
influence of the priestly class could not be neglected. After this
they had to acquire the approval of the assembly of the nobility
and of delegates of all the countries in the empire. It will be seen
how the Hittite kings had to wage a long and stubborn war
with their nobles[84] to save at least the principle of hereditary
succession.

From these premises it follows that the Assyrian kingship could
never pretend to absolute power. The mainspring of its power—and
this seems to be a Semitic feature—was religious. The Assyrian
kings constantly retained the functions of chief priest and participated actively in the worship of the gods. Never at any period
of Assyrian history was the king venerated as a god.[85]

[84] See *infra*, pp. 52, 53.
[85] Cf. R. Labat, *op. cit.*, pp. 21–25. This priestly character of the Assyrian king is also expressed in the coronation ceremonial. The king, not
the priests, offers the sacrifices to the gods before his coronation. This is
evident from the ritual of coronation dating from about 1220–1150 B.C.,
published by K. F. Müller, *Das assyrische Ritual, I: Texte zum assyrischen
Königsritual*, Mitteilungen der Vorderasiatisch-Ägypt. Gesellschaft, 41, Heft
3 (Leipzig, 1937), p. 8 seq.

KINGSHIP: EGYPT AND MESOPOTAMIA

As has already been indicated, both Egypt and Mesopotamia had provided prototypes for the Assyrian attempts to realize a universal empire. The title "king of the four regions of the world," which the Assyrian rulers had assumed and which expresses a tendency to thoughts of universality, is of Sumerian origin.[86] In the old Sumerian period, however, it was bestowed only on Anu and Enlil and on the sun-god. Sargon, conqueror of Sumeria and founder of the Akkadian Semitic dynasty, was the first to use this primarily divine title for himself in order to give expression to the extent of his political sway. Naram-Sin, the greatest warrior of the Akkadians also adopted this title for his personal glorification.[87] When the Sumerian dynasty of the city of Ur had assumed the heritage of the Akkadians, its kings continued to make use of this title, as did the Babylonian kings also.

The idea itself, therefore, was not invented by the Assyrians, although their kings succeeded in its realization more effectively than did their political competitors. It was the Babylonians, too, rather than the Assyrians, who were the first to impart to the idea of universality a profound moral significance. It must be emphasized that, even under Hammurabi, the idea was expressed in terms which revealed a much deeper understanding than was apparent in the Sumerian and Akkadian dynasties. Hammurabi declared in the introduction to his code that he was chosen to become a ruler of men in order to promote justice. He says this in his prologue and describes himself as "the king who holds in obedience the four quarters of the world."[88]

When the exalted Anu, the king of the Annunaki[89] [and] Enlil the lord of heaven and earth, who determines the destiny of the land, committed unto Marduk, first-born son of Ea, the dominion over all mankind, [and] made him great among the Igigi;[90] when

---

[86] Cf. A. Jeremias' account of the meaning of this title in his short study, "Die orientalischen Wurzeln der Idee von Weltherrschaft und Gottkönigstum," *Oriens; The Oriental Review*, 1 (Paris, 1926), p. 16.

[87] For documentation, see R. Labat, *op. cit.*, pp. 6–10.

[88] V. Scheil, *op. cit.*, p. 81 seq. Quotations are made here from the English translation by R. W. Rogers, *Cuneiform Parallels to the Old Testament* (New York, 1912), p. 398 seq. Cf. also H. Schmökel's monograph, *Hammurabi von Babylon* (Munich, 1958).

[89] Apparently the judge in the world hereafter.

[90] The gods and the spirits of the upper world.

they named the lofty name of Babylon, and made it great in the quarters of the earth, and erected for him [Marduk] therein an everlasting kingdom, whose foundations are established like heaven and earth; then did Anu and Bel call [me] Hammurabi by name, the exalted prince who honors the gods, to bring justice to prevail in the land, to destroy the wicked and the evil, that the strong may not injure the weak, that I may arise like Shamash over the black-headed men to enlighten the land and to further the welfare of men.... When Marduk sent me to rule men, and to promulgate justice, I put justice and righteousness into the language of the land and promoted the welfare of the people at that time. I ordered ....

Here follows the publication of the king's famous code.

In the prologue Hammurabi also stresses another quality which should adorn a universal ruler: to be a savior of his people by providing them with an abundance of all they need. Hammurabi declares that he was

the shepherd called Ulil ... who heaps up plenty and abundance, who made everything possible in completeness for Nippur and Durilu; the exalted supporter of Ekur, the powerful king who restored Eridu...; who brought together again the scattered inhabitants of Isin...; who increased the agriculture..., heaped up grain for the mighty Urash...; who gave pasture and watering places for Lagash and Girsu...; who gave life to the city of Adab...; who poured out prosperity over Mishlam...; who covered the people of Malgi in misfortune; who established their dwelling in riches....

Here the association of two ideas can be clearly seen: that of a universal king and that of a savior king. These were developed further in the Assyrian period. The Assyrian rulers liked to use the simpler title of "great king"; but the astrologers called them not only "kings of the universe," but also "images of Marduk, the divine master of the world."[91] The idea of world dominion is, moreover, clearly expressed in some Assyrian royal inscriptions,

---

[91] R. C. Thompson, *The Reports of the Magicians and Astrologers of Nineveh and Babylon in the British Museum* (London, 1900), p. 170 (quoted by A. Jeremias, *Handbuch d. altorientalischen Geisteskultur*, p. 108).

such as the Berlin inscription of Shalmaneser III (858–824 B.C.)[92]: "Shalmaneser, the great king, the mighty king, king of all the four quarters, the bold, the rival of the princes of the world, great kings, son of Ashurnazirpal, king of the world (*shar kishshati*), king of Assyria, son of Tukulti-Ninib, king of the world, king of Assyria...."

One of the mighty among the Assyrians, though inclined to oppose the coronation of the crown prince, nevertheless addressed Asarhaddon (680–669 B.C.):[93] "Now, O King, my lord, from the rising of the sun to its setting, Ashur has given you dominion." The idea of the savior-king is most forcefully expressed in a letter addressed by a courtier to King Ashurbanipal.[94]

Ashur, the king of the gods, proclaims the name of the king my lord for the dominion of the land of Assyria. Shamash and Adad, through their steadfast regard for the king my lord [and] his dominion of the lands, have established a gracious reign, orderly days, years of righteousness, abundant rains, copious inundations, and fair remuneration. The gods are graciously inclined. The fear of god is strong. The temples cause prosperity. The great gods of heaven and earth are favorably disposed to the king my lord. Old men dance, the youth sing, matrons and maidens are gay with laughter. The women are taken in marriage, they are embraced, they bring sons and daughters to birth. Reproduction is blest. To him whose sin condemned him to death, the king my lord has restored newness of life. Those who have been imprisoned for many years, you set free. Those who have been sick many days are recovered. The hungry are satisfied. The lean grow fat. The destitute are supplied with clothing.

---

[92] Translation by R. W. Rogers, *Cuneiform Parallels,* p. 298. See also *ibid.,* p. 305, the Calah inscription of Adad-Nirari III (809–782 B.C.). The Assyrian royal titles, "King of the World" (of totality) and "King of the Four Quarters" were inherited by the neo-Babylonian kings after the destruction of Assyria. This is clear from the inscriptions of Nabu-naid. S. H. Langdon, *Die neubabylonischen Königsinschriften* (Leipzig, 1912), pp. 218, 219. The title was inherited from Babylonia by Cyrus (see *infra* p. 122).

[93] L. Waterman, *Royal Correspondence of the Assyrian Empire* (Univ. of Michigan Press, 1930), Letter 870, vol. 2, p. 105.

[94] *Ibid.,* Letter 2, vol. 1, p. 3.

This intimate connection of the ideas of the universal king and the savior-king is significant for the further evolution of Oriental ideas on kingship. Combined with the idea of a new aeon—the opening of a new period in human history—an idea which had its roots in Iranian speculation—it exercized a marked influence on the the mind of man during the Hellenistic period, and through this channel reached Rome in the imperial era. As will be shown, it was further developed by another Semitic nation, the Jews, and became a basis for Jewish and Christian Messianism and political speculation.

The position of the Sumerian, Assyrian, and Babylonian kings is well defined by a saying which dates from the time of Asarhaddon (680–669 B.C.) and which has been newly interpreted in a translation by F. M. Th. Böhl:[95]

> The shadow of God is the prince
> and the shadow of the prince
> is the [other] men.

The writer who copied this proverb added the following explanatory note:

> The prince is here the king
> who is like an image of God.

These words express succinctly the two main roles of Mesopotamian kings, in relation to the gods and to their subjects. On the one hand they were images of gods—their representatives on earth; on the other they were intermediaries between men and the gods. This interpretation of the lines remains unchanged even if the "shadow" is understood in the sense of its legal application in the Akkadian language—that is, the protection afforded to a client by his patron in a lawsuit.[96] Even when it is given this meaning, the two roles of the king are aptly defined. The king, image of God on earth, is assured of God's special protection, while through the king, God's protection is extended to his subjects.

---

[95] *Op. cit.*, p. 48 seq. Cf. also R. Labat, *op. cit.*, p. 222. A good example of kingship is also reflected in the numerous similes and comparisons of kings in the royal inscriptions. For details, see A. Schott, *Die Vergleiche in den akkadischen Königsinschriften*, pp. 69–115.

[96] This has been rightly pointed out by H. Frankfort, *Kingship*, p. 406 seq.

KINGSHIP: EGYPT AND MESOPOTAMIA

The conception that kings were God's representatives upon earth naturally made them depositaries of divine law upon earth. They were the supreme judges of their subjects. This juridical and law-giving royal function, at first closely connected with the priestly side of kingship, was definitely regulated and given modern form by Hammurabi. From his time onward the kings sat in judgment over their subjects, not only with respect to religious laws, but also as supreme magistrates, enforcing laws which they had themselves promulgated in their capacity as lawgivers. Of course, the laws which they made had been revealed to them by the gods. Hammurabi himself, on the stele containing his code, is depicted in the act of receiving the laws from the sun-god Shamash, regarded as the god of justice, because the sun on its daily course through the firmament penetrated everywhere and nothing could escape its eyes.[97]

But there were certain moments in the lives of the Babylonians and Assyrians when the kings were believed to impersonate the gods in a particularly marked way. The Mesopotamians believed that there were certain solemn rites which could be performed only by gods; but if these same rites were to benefit humanity, they had to be repeated on earth by a man. In their eyes kings alone possessed the necessary qualifications to enact these rites; and when the kings were engaged in their performance, they actually personified the gods.[98]

The personal intervention of gods was deemed necessary in those rites that recalled the idea of the Creation. It was believed that the erection or restoration of a temple was an act associated with the idea of creation, and was at the same time the most important service which man could render to the gods. Therefore, when the gods suggested to a king that he should build a temple, he acted from that moment onward as the gods' special instrument and was guided and led by them in all the details relating to his task: the choice of site, the planning of the building, its dimensions, the

[97] For details, see R. Labat, *op. cit.*, p. 229. Cf. also *infra*, pp. 268, 288, 295, 309, 358. On the relief on Hammurabi's stele, see C. J. Gadd, *Ideas of Divine Rule*, p. 90 seq. Cf. also W. Eilers, *Die Gesetzesstele Chammurabis*, Der Alte Orient 31, Heft 3/4 (Leipzig, 1932).

[98] R. Labat, *op. cit.*, pp. 177 seq., 277 seq.

moulding of the bricks, and every aspect of its construction. As it was thought that the temple was a structure for all eternity, erected by the gods in heaven at the beginning of time, it became of the utmost importance that the king should reproduce on earth, as the earthly dwelling place of the gods, an exact replica of what they had built on high.[99] This belief explains why so many oracles were sought before the work was begun and throughout the period of its construction, so that there should be no possibility of misinterpreting the wishes of the gods. It explains, too, the numerous illustrations that depict the king engaged in the work of moulding or carrying bricks, or listening to instructions from the gods, or personally directing the work.[100] The dedication of the temple was performed on New Year's Day,[101] which marked the beginning of a new cycle in nature, recalling more than any other day the act of the creation of the earth and life, and thus being particularly fitted for the consecration of a temple which also evoked the same idea.

The other important occasion on which the king had to repeat on earth rites that were performed in heaven by the gods was the New Year festival. This was celebrated from the oldest Sumerian times probably twice a year, in the autumn and in the spring, that is to say, at the end of the summer and at the end of the winter, both seasons being destructive to nature—the summer with its oppressive heat perhaps more so than the winter. It was the festival celebrating nature's return to new life after the death brought about by winter's cold or summer's excessive heat. Here again the act of creation by the gods was recalled. The gods were the principal agents and the kings impersonated them on earth.[102] The main themes of the festival were the descent of the god

---

[99] Cf. A. Jeremias, *Handbuch*, pp. 114–116.

[100] For details, see R. Labat, *op. cit.*, p. 234 seq. Particular interest attaches in this respect to cylinder A of King Gudea. See the new translation of this document in *Revue biblique*, 55 (1948), pp. 403–437 (M. Lambert and R. Tournay, "Le Cylindre A de Gudéa").

[101] H. Frankfort, *Kingship*, p. 374.

[102] See the description of the festival in R. Labat, *op. cit.*, p. 161 seq. An exhaustive bibliography on the subject will be found in I. Engnell, *Studies in Divine Kingship*, p. 128 seq. The meaning of the New Year festival in primitive religions is well outlined by E. G. Kraeling, "The Real Religion of Ancient Israel," *Journal of Biblical Literature*, 47 (1928), p. 133 seq.

to the underworld, where he suffered and was slain—the death of nature—followed by his liberation and resurrection, symbolized by the victorious procession of the gods and the holy marriage of the resurrected god in his temple. The king had to represent the god and perform on earth the ceremony of the holy marriage; a priestess or a statue of the goddess represented the goddess-bride. It was believed that the reawakening of nature and the country's prosperity depended upon the performance of this ceremony. On that day the gods arranged the destinies of the king and of the land for the year to come.

It was the king who must perform in gestures the symbolic death, the god's fight with the powers of darkness, his triumph, and his reinstallation in power. Without the king the festival could not have been performed.

No less important was the king's function as the representative of his country and his people before the gods.[103] It was believed that by his service to the gods and by his own pious life he was responsible for maintaining the life of the country. It might also have been necessary for him to perform some ritual acts of manual labor in order to assure fertility to the land and prosperity to the people. As the salvation of his people depended upon the regularity and piety with which the king performed his services to the gods, he was obliged to carry out certain rites and ceremonies every day. Special calendars of feasts and monthly services were composed by the priests, showing the king's religious duties in the greatest detail. There were occasions upon which he was obliged to recite the penitential psalms to reconcile his people to the gods. These psalms, some of which belong to the best literary production of the ancient Near East, were primarily composed for the kings in their capacities as representatives of the people in the sight of the gods. They became the common property of the pious only much later, at the end of the process known as the democratization of religion.[104]

When misfortune had fallen upon the people or had threatened them, the king must intervene on their behalf before the gods; or he

---

[103] This is particularly well outlined by R. Labat, *op. cit.*, pp. 277–319.
[104] Cf. F. M. Th. Böhl, *op. cit.*, p. 46 seq.

must do penance for the sins of commission or omission which were believed to be responsible for whatever evil had befallen or was about to befall. The king's priestly advisers were constantly engaged in trying to anticipate what the gods had in store for the land and its people. The future could be read in the intestines of sacrificed animals and in the stars, and when priestly investigations revealed unfavorable signs, threatening the king or the prosperity of the people, detailed reports were made to the king, and at the same time a program of prayers, fasting, and solemn libations was drawn up to avert the impending catastrophe and to propitiate the gods.[105] Complicated rituals were devised for these purposes. When the ceremony to propitiate the gods had to be performed elsewhere than in the city where the king resided, the king's mantle was regarded as an essential before they could be carried out properly by the priest who impersonated the king by wearing it. When the omens were considered to be particularly menacing for the king or his land and it was thought that nothing short of the king's death would calm the anger of the gods, a substitute was found to stand in for the king and risk the possibility of death.[106]

These details and the whole literature on divination show the important role of the king in his capacity as the representative of his people before the gods. There is preserved in the library of Ashurbanipal (668–ca. 631 B.C.) an interesting document which illustrates as well the importance of divination as a political instrument, suggesting to the king his course of action and forewarning the people of their expectations. This is the so-called "Mirror of Princes" which is designed to keep the king mindful of his principal duties. The first half of this document reveals it to have been inspired by the copious literature which explains the significance of the omens observed in the entrails of animal sacrifices and

[105] On the importance of divination in the life of the Babylonian common people, see C. J. Gadd, *op. cit.*, p. 67 seq., and additional notes A, D, E–H. Interesting texts on liver divination were published by E. G. Klauber, *Politisch-religiöse Texte aus der Sargonidenzeit* (Leipzig, 1913).

[106] It is, however, erroneous to deduce from this habit that the Babylonians and Assyrians were familiar with human sacrifices. For details, see R. Labat, "Le sort des substituts royaux en Assyrie au temps des Sargonides," *Revue assyriologique*, 40 (1945–46), pp. 123–142. Cf. also G. Goossens, "Les substituts royaux en Babylone," *Analecta Lovaniensia biblica et orientalia*, 2nd Ser., fasc. 13 (Louvain, 1949), pp. 383–400.

in the stars, constellations, and heavenly bodies. It is possible that this literature originated in the later period of the Kassite dynasty and the document itself seems to have been written about 710 B.C.[107]

The text[108] is reminiscent of the exhortations thundered by the prophets of Israel before the thrones of their kings. It catalogues the evils which will befall the king, his high officers, and his generals if they fail to perform the duties which the gods demand of them. Apparently the first duty which a people expected from its king was that he should be just and strict in refusing favors or gifts while dispensing justice. He was also expected to insist that his subordinates behave in a similar manner. Particular emphasis was laid upon the preservation of certain privileges enjoyed by the cities of Nippur, Sippar, and Babylon. Dispensing justice and defending the special rights of the citizens were thus regarded as the principal duties of the king. Transgression in these respects by a king or his officers was punished severely by the gods.

The same idea is expressed by the confession which the king had to recite on the day of atonement preceding the celebration of the festival of the New Year. On that occasion he had to surrender his royal insignia—scepter, crown, tiara, and staff—to the high priest who deposited them before the statue of Marduk. Only after the king had made his confession and penance, had been humiliated by being slapped by the high priest, and had promised to observe all the gods' precepts, were the insignia restored to him, accompanied by the promise of divine protection and victory over his enemies.[109] This ceremony also illustrates the fact that the king's power, although absolute in theory, was limited by the precepts of the gods, who were especially insistent upon the proper administration of justice.

It has been shown that Assyrian ideas on kingship had developed under the marked influence of the Babylonian polity, which in its turn was a combination of old Sumerian and Semitic (Akkadian)

---

[107] For details, see F. M. Th. Böhl, *op. cit.*, pp. 23, 30.
[108] See F. M. Th. Böhl, *op. cit.*, pp. 3–11.
[109] For additional details, see bibliography and *infra*, p. 340 seq.

conceptions. Egyptian influence reached Assyria late and did no more than enrich Assyrian royal symbolism. The first example of this was the adoption of a winged sun-disk as the symbol of Shamash, the sun-god and god of justice. The Babylonians used a different symbol for the sun-god, a disk with a four-cornered star inside it.[110] The Assyrians must, therefore, have taken their symbol from the Egyptians, perhaps through the intermediary of their neighbors, the Mitanni or the Hittites, who, as will shortly be demonstrated, were affected by the cultural influence of Egypt during the second millennium B.C. Similar symbolism was also used by the Assyrians for their supreme god Ashur. In the middle of the sun-disk, however, Ashur was depicted with his bow. In order to illustrate the relationship of the sun-god and the king, the winged sun-disk was added to the different symbols which accompanied the portrait of the king.[111]

How closely the Assyrians followed the Egyptian example in this respect is shown by the relief found on an obelisk erected by Tiglath-pileser I (1116–1078 B.C.) now in the British Museum.[112] On this there may be observed a reproduction of the sun-disk with two hands outstretched toward the Assyrian king presenting him with a bow. This symbolism seems to have been inspired by Amenophis (Amenhotep) IV (1375–1358 B.C.). This religious reformer, also called Ikhnaton (Akhenaten), sought thus to symbolize[113] his supreme and only god Atum, who was to replace Amon-Re and all the other Egyptian gods.[114] Although Amenhophis' reforms did not endure in Egypt, he was regarded, because of his monotheistic tendencies, as a heretic by the "orthodox" clergy and his sun symbolism may have impressed those nations with whose rulers he was in frequent contact, as is shown by the correspondence preserved in Tell el-Amarna.

[110] Cf. B. Meissner, *Babylonien und Assyrien*, 2, p. 21.
[111] Cf., for example, B. Meissner, *op. cit.*, p. 6 (Asarhaddon); A. T. Olmstead, *History of Assyria*, p. 103 (Ashurnazirpal).
[112] G. Contenau, *La civilisation des Hittites et des Mitanniens* (Paris, 1934), p. 109.
[113] A. Moret, *Du caractère religieux*, p. 46. Cf. *infra*, pp. 255, 256.
[114] On this attempt at monotheism, see W. L. Wardle's study, "The Origins of Hebrew Monotheism," *ZAW*, N.S., 2 (1925), pp. 203–206. The most relevant bibliographical data will also be found there. On the famous hymns to Aton, see A. Erman, *The Literature of the Ancient Egyptians*, pp. 288–291.

During the second millennium B.C., Egyptian influence was more marked among the neighbors of the Assyrians—the Hurri, and the Mitanni, who belonged to the non-Semitic race of Mesopotamia called Asianic.[115] As they were settled on the upper Euphrates, between Assyria and Syria, they were more exposed to this Egyptian influence during the period of Egyptian expansion toward Syria. At that time the winged sun-disk appears in Mitannian art to represent the sun on its daily course across the heavens. Under the disk the royal throne is frequently pictured supported by mythical heroes.[116]

The kingdom of the Mitanni, intimately linked with that of the Hurri, experienced a short period of political expansion from the sixteenth century B.C. onward, but this disappeared from history at the end of the fourteenth century B.C. It is regrettable that little is known about this kingdom's political institutions, for in the case of both the Mitanni and the Hurri, an Aryan element comes to the surface for the first time in the history of political institutions.[117] The dynasty of the Mitanni was of Aryan origin, as was also their aristocracy. The regime was monarchic and hereditary, but constructed on a feudal basis. The king divided the land among the nobility which was obliged to provide him with military contingents in the event of war and which was also charged with the civil administration. It is an interesting example of the way in which a determined clan was able at that remote period to impose its sway upon an amorphous group of alien peoples and rule them successfully. As far as can be judged from existing documents, the civil code of the Mitanni also presented a curious mixture of Babylonian, Assyrian, and Aryan elements.

In one respect, however, this first appearance of the Indo-Europeans in Mesopotamia during the second millennium B.C. was of paramount importance for the evolution of Near Eastern civilization. It was they who acquainted the Babylonians and Egyptians with the horse—until then an animal virtually unknown in those countries. A curious document from the fourteenth century B.C.

---

[115] Cf. H. Schmökel, *Geschichte des alten Vorderasien*, p. 154 seq.

[116] G. Contenau, *op. cit.*, pp. 108, 109.

[117] See *infra*, pp. 46, 48, 50, for additional details on the appearance of the Aryans in Mesopotamia and Syria.

reveals this. This document is the famous first handbook on the training of horses, composed by Kikkulish from Mitannu.[118] The text, written in the Hittite language, contains some technical expressions which concern the racing of horse-drawn chariots and which are, without doubt, borrowed from the Indo-Europeans.

The use of horse-drawn chariots in battle assured a dominating position among the Kassites, the Hurri, and the Mitanni to the first Aryans who appeared amid these Asianic and Semitic peoples. From the second half of the second millennium B.C. the use of war chariots brought about radical changes in the battle technique of the Babylonians, Assyrians, and Egyptians. For several centuries to come, however, the horse was not used as a mount in those countries or in Asia Minor, Crete, and Greece, where the new tactics of war were also adopted.

The introduction of the horse was the first notable contribution by the Indo-European element to Near Eastern political history and civilization. More notable still was the contribution made by another Indo-European people—the Hittites—who introduced the Indo-European race to the history of political theories.

[118] Cf. B. Hrozný, *Die älteste Geschichte Vorderasiens und Indiens* (Prague, 1940), p. 132 seq.

CHAPTER TWO

Aryan Hittites and Near Eastern Semites

The first Aryan contribution to Near Eastern civilization — The Hittites in Asia Minor — Babylonian and Egyptian influences on Hittite ideas on kingship — Indo-European elements in the Hittite polity — Syro-Hittites; Syrian and Palestinian Semites — Egyptian court ceremonial according to the Tell el-Amarna Letters — Divine kingship in Syria and Palestine? — Ideas on kingship in Aramaic inscriptions — Documents from Mari and Ras Shamra-Ugarit betraying Babylonian and Hittite influences on the political ideas of Near Eastern Semites.

The Hittites must be credited with having introduced onto the stage of history that important part of the continent of Asia which is nearest to Europe: Asia Minor. This does not imply that that part of Asia had until then been completely cut off from the great centers of civilization on the Euphrates and Tigris rivers. The Mesopotamian culture which had originated with the Sumerians had penetrated far into the interior of Asia Minor long before the arrival of the Hittites. It is possible that the tribes which lived there at the time when the Sumerians flourished were akin to them and belonged to the same Asianic race. During the period of Semitic domination in Mesopotamia, cultural contact between the old Sumerian and the new Semitic centers in Mesopotamia and Asia Minor was maintained by Semitic colonists who had settled in Cappadocia. That was the situation in Asia Minor when the first waves of Indo-Europeans reached it.

At the end of the third millennium B.C. the great migration which brought the Indo-Europeans and the Indo-Iranians from the interior of Asia had commenced. They travelled from the Pamirs, over the Russian steppes, which they had already reached by then, toward Western Europe, the Balkans, and Greece, and also toward

45

the South—modern India and Iran. Some groups moved in the direction of Mesopotamia, lured by its riches. They seem to have attained first the mountainous marches known as Elam, and this would explain the presence of Aryan elements among the Kassites. They were followed by those other Aryans who established their supremacy over the Hurri and the Mitanni. Some Aryan tribes penetrated as far as Syria and established several dynasties there. Up to the present it has not been possible to reconstruct the history of this first Aryan incursion. It may, however, have contributed to the collapse of the power of the Hyksos and so have helped the Egyptians to recover their political independence and begin their conquest of Syria.[1]

Greater importance is attached to the Aryan penetration of Asia Minor, which the Indo-Europeans probably reached from the Bosphorus.[2] One of the first consequences of their arrival was the disappearance of the Semitic colonies in Cappadocia.[3] The Indo-Europeans did not drive away or exterminate the Asianic tribes established in Asia Minor, but by a systematic effort carried on through several centuries, they succeeded in regrouping most of these tribes and bringing them under their own strong influence. The leading Indo-European elements in Asia Minor became known by the name of the strongest of the Asianic tribes which they had dominated—the Hittites. Thus it was that the great Hittite Empire enjoyed two periods of power, the first from 1650 to 1500 B.C.—the

---

[1] For details, see E. Meyer, *Geschichte des Altertums*, I, pt. 2, 5th ed. (Stuttgart-Berlin, 1926), pp. 651 seq., 671 seq. The main bibliography concerning the different hypotheses by which specialists have tried to elucidate these problems is listed by A. Christensen in "Die Iranier," in *Kulturgeschichte des alten Orients*, Abschn. 3, Lief. 1, Handbuch der Altertumswissenschaft, Abt 3, Teil 1, Band 3, ed. by I. Müller and W. Otto (Munich, 1933), p. 209 seq.; F. Schachermeyr, *Indogermanen und Orient* (Stuttgart, 1944), p. 48 seq.

[2] B. Hrozný, *Die älteste Geschichte Vorderasiens und Indiens* (Prague, 1940), p. 121, favors the theory that they reached Asia Minor across the Caucasus.

[3] On these colonies, see A. Götze, *Kleinasien* (2nd ed.) = *Kulturgeschichte des alten Orients*, Abschn. 3, Unterabschn. 1, Handbuch der Altertumswissenschaft, Abt 3, Teil 1, Band 3, ed. by I. Müller, W. Otto, and H. Bengtson (Munich, 1957), pp. 64–81. Cf. the exhaustive study by R. S. Hardy, "The Old Hittite Kingdom," *The American Journal of Semitic Languages and Literatures*, 58 (1941), pp. 176–216, on the rise of the Hittites. *Ibid.*, pp. 178–185, interesting information concerning the political development of the colonies will be found.

KINGSHIP: HITTITES AND SEMITES

Old Empire—and the second from 1450 to 1200 B.C.—the New Empire. The first empire waged a victorious war against the Babylonians; the kings of the second empire disputed the possession of Syria with the Egyptians. The invasion of Asia Minor by tribes coming mostly from Thrace, on the one hand, and the pressure exerted by the Assyrians on the other hand, brought the Hittite power to an end. Their civilization survived, however, for over five centuries in Syria and during that time continued to exercize its influence on the evolution of the Middle East.

It is not easy to give a brief outline of the main features of Hittite ideas on kingship. Only since 1870 have Hittite monuments attracted the attention of archaeologists, while the numerous documents in cuneiform writing on the tablets found in the ruins of Hattushash, the former Hittite capital—modern Boghazköy—have been deciphered even more recently, thanks mainly to the efforts of Professor B. Hrozný of Prague University. They contain some important royal correspondence and, together with other documents, constitute the principal source for the study of Hittite political ideas.[4]

---

[4] A bibliography concerning the Hittite problem will be found in G. Contenau's *Éléments de bibliographie hittite* (Paris, 1922) and his "Supplément," *Babyloniaca*, 10 (Paris, 1927–28), pp. 1–68, 138–144. A more up to date bibliography is given in *Revue hittite et asianique*, 1 seq. (1930–). For general information, see G. Contenau, *La civilisation des Hittites et des Mitanniens* (Paris, 1934); R. Dussaud, "Les religions des Hittites et des Hourrites, des Phéniciens et des Syriens" in *Mana, Introduction à l'histoire des religions*, 1 (Paris, 1949), p. 333 seq.; J. Garstang, *The Hittite Empire* (London, 1929), pp. 8, 112; B. Hrozný, *op. cit.*, pp. 121–183. Particular value attaches to A. Götze's study *Kleinasien*, pp. 82–183. Cf. also the same author's *Hethiter, Churriter und Assyrer* (Oslo, 1936) and his more popular account, *Das Hethiter-Reich*, Der Alte Orient, 27, Heft 2 (Leipzig, 1928). See also E. Cavaignac, *Les Hittites* (Paris, 1950); O. R. Gurney, *The Hittites* (London, 1952) and Ch. L. Woolley, *A Forgotten Kingdom* (London, 1953). The main Hittite documents are published in *Boghazköi-Studien* (Leipzig) from 1917 to 1925 (under the direction of Otto Weber) and from 1925 onward in the *Hethitische Texte*, published in the *Mitteilungen der Vorderasiatisch-Ägyptischen Gesellschaft* (Leipzig) under the direction of F. Sommer. The Oriental Institute of Prague published the Hittite hieroglyphic inscriptions from 1933 onward. Cf. also B. Hrozný, "Inscriptions hittites hiéroglyphiques de Charchemish," *Archiv Orientální*, 6 (1934), pp. 207–266. Cf. also R. S. Hardy's study, *op. cit.*, p. 177. A select bibliography on the Hittites will be found in M. Riemschneider's general book *Die Welt der Hethiter* (Stuttgart, 1954). See the useful bibliography compiled by B. Schwartz, *The*

We learn from the texts of Boghazköy, first of all, that the Hittites had accepted the old Sumerian mythical descriptions of the gods succeeding each other in divine kingship. This is made particularly clear by the myth concerning the god Kumarbi, part of which is preserved on a tablet from Boghazköy.[5] In this particular case the Hittites took over a myth which had been further elaborated by the Hurri, who, for geographical reasons, must have transmitted to the Hittites other elements of Sumerian civilization.

This myth expresses not only the belief common to all the civilizations of the ancient Near East that kingship is of divine origin, but also another belief that every event on earth is a reflection of a similar event in heaven. The Hittite mentality subscribed to this belief with particular emphasis. From treaties concluded by certain Hittite kings with their neighbors, it is possible to discern how they associate their own political acts with the political acts of their gods, whom they invite to study and sanction the treaties,[6] as though these were being composed simultaneously on earth and in heaven. A particularly striking illustration of this attitude of mind is contained in a text translated by E. O. Forrer[7]:

> The gods of the country of the Hatti take nothing from you, the gods of the country of the Gasga, and they do not violate you in any way. But you gods of the country of the Gasga have started a conflict. You have thus chased away the gods of the country of the Hatti from their country and you have taken over their country. (In this way) have the men of Gasga

---

Hittites. A List of References in the New York Public Library (New York, 1939) and H. Schmökel, *Geschichte des alten Vorderasien*, Handbuch der Orientalistik, Band 2 (Leiden, 1957), p. 119 seq. Cf. also H. Otten, "Das Hethiterreich," in H. Schmökel and others, *Kulturgeschichte des Alten Orient* (Stuttgart, 1961), pp. 311–446.

[5] Published by E. O. Forrer, "Eine Geschichte des Götterkönigtums aus dem Hatti-Reiche," *Mélanges F. Cumont,* 2 = *Annuaire de l'Institut de Philol. et d'Hist. orient. et slaves,* 4 (Brussels, 1936), p. 690 seq.

[6] For example, the treaties concluded by Shuppiluliumash with the kings of the Mitanni and of the Nuhashshi. E. F. Weidner, *Politische Dokumente aus Kleinasien = Boghazköi-Studien,* 8 (Leipzig, 1923), pp. 29 seq., 45 : ". . . and the gods of the great king, of the king of the country of the Hatti, preceded us" in the campaign; also pp. 49 seq., 67 seq.

[7] "Eine Geschichte des Götterkönigtums," p. 689. The original text is published in *Keilschrifturkunden aus Boghazköi,* 4 (n.d.), 1, lines 7–20.

started a conflict. Thus have they [*you* in the text] taken away from the men of the Hatti their towns and have they [*you* in the text] chased them away from their land and field (and) from their vineyards. Therefore now the gods and the men of the country of the Hatti are clamoring for a bloody action.

With regard to kingship, it seems clear from the Boghazköy texts, that the Hittite king was first of all regarded as the supreme religious leader, rather than as military chieftain or paramount judge. There is still controversy among specialists concerning his relationship with divinity. One thing which seems to be agreed upon is that the king was regarded as divine after his death. When the king died, it was said simply that he became god.[8] In his protocol, the king boasted the titles of Labarna—founder of the first Hittite Empire—an equivalent of the Roman Augustus, of Great King, King of the Hatti, hero and beloved of a god.[9] The last of these titles indicates clearly that kingship was regarded as having been at least conferred by the god. But was the king regarded and worshipped as god during his life? None of the texts published so far indicates beyond doubt that he was.[10] It is true that in the royal texts are to be found such expressions as "son of the weather god." It is also true that the first wife of the king was called Tavananna—"mother of god"—the use of which can be explained by the fact that the king was regarded as divine after his death. The titles which express a close relationship with the supreme god—the weather god—can be explained by the fact that before the gods, the king personified his whole nation and was the only intermediary between his people and the divinities.[11] This

---

[8] Cf. F. M. Th. Böhl, *Der babylonische Fürstenspiegel*, Mitteilungen der altorientalischen Gesellschaft, 11, Heft 3 (Leipzig, 1937), p. 45. Murshilish II (1345–1315) says in his treaty with the kings of Amurru and Mira: "When my father became god, I, the Sun, occupied his throne." J. Friedrich, *Staatsverträge des Hatti-Reiches in hethitischer Sprache=Hethitische Texte*, 2 (Leipzig, 1926), pp. 7, 109.

[9] G. Contenau, *La civilisation des Hittites*, p. 159.

[10] I. Engnell, *Studies in Divine Kingship in the Ancient Near East* (Uppsala, 1943), p. 57 seq., seems inclined to believe that the Hittite kings assumed divine character from their nativity. The texts quoted by him in favor of this thesis are, however, not convincing. This is also the opinion of O. R. Gurney, "Hittite Kingship," in S. H. Hooke's symposium *Myth, Ritual and Kingship* (Oxford, 1958), p. 112 seq.

[11] Cf. R. Dussaud, *op. cit.*, p. 350.

circumstance gave him the right to claim a special relationship to the supreme god, a relationship which was best expressed in terms of a filial association with the divinity. Similar expressions have already been shown to have been used by the Babylonian kings at a period when they ceased to claim a divine nature.

Egyptian influence on Hittite ideas on kingship was particularly strong during the second Hittite Empire. The mightiest king of this period—Shuppiluliumash (*ca.* 1380–1346 B.C.)—was in the habit of referring to himself as *Shamshi*—"the Sun."[12] It would be going too far, however, to deduce from this that the king regarded himself as the equal of the sun-god.[13] Rather should this be envisaged as evidence of the influence of the Egyptian ruler cult on the evolution of Hittite ideas on kingship. The Hittite king adopted the titles of the Pharaoh, in order to demonstrate that they were on equal terms.

This Egyptian influence was responsible for the admission of the winged sun-disk to the royal symbolism of the Hittites—as was also the case with the Mitanni and the Assyrians. From the period of Shuppiluliumash onward the sun-god begins to occupy a most prominent place in the Hittite pantheon.[14] This imitation of Egyptian titles and court ceremonial induced the Hittites to refer to their king quite simply as "Our Sun." While there is a certain ambiguity about this title, it would not be justifiable to deduce from it that the Hittite kings wished to be regarded as incarnations of the sun-god.

As the representative of his people before the gods, the king was

[12] See the texts published by E. F. Weidner, *Politische Dokumente aus Kleinasien*, p. 4, line 14. His son Murshilish follows his father's example, *ibid.*, pp. 87, 91, 93, and *passim*. See also J. Friedrich, *Staatsverträge des Hatti-Reiches in hethitischer Sprache*, pp. 4, 5, 13, 15, 17, 19, 53, 55, 56, 59, 63, 65, 67, 107, 109, 111, 113, 115, 119, 121, 123, 125, 127, 131, 133, 135, 137, 139, 143, 145, 149. Another document from the end of the Hittite Empire shows that other Hittite kings of this period used constantly to be called "Sun;" see A. Götze, *Madduwattaš=Hethitische Texte*, 3 (Leipzig, 1928), *passim*. See also the newly discovered documents of the royal archives of Ras Shamra-Ugarit, correspondence between the King of Ugarit and Shuppiluliumash, in C. F.-A. Schaeffer's report, "Les fouilles de Ras Shamra-Ugarit," in *Syria*, 31 (1954), pp. 42–51.
[13] I. Engnell, *op. cit.*, p. 68.
[14] R. Dussaud, *op. cit.*, pp. 339, 352.

naturally the chief priest and leader of the religious cult.[15] In this respect, Hittite ideas on kingship were identical with those of the Sumerians, Babylonians, and Assyrians. The king appointed all priests, who deputized for him in the performance of ceremonies associated with the observance of the cult; but, as in Babylonia, there were certain rites requiring the king's active participation in person. These were associated with the great festivals, especially those of the sun-goddess, who was a particular object of veneration in the city of Arinna. The king presided over the liturgy, assisted in this case by the queen, who was considered to be a high priestess of the goddess. During the performance of these religious ceremonies, the king was obliged to wear a special dress, a voluminous and long mantle and a distinctive hat, at the same time carrying in his hand a rod with a curved end.

Following the example of the Babylonians and Assyrians, the king had to appease the wrath of the gods and avert from his people the dire misfortune threatened by various portents. In association with this, divination and magic flourished among the Hittites, their magicians following the procedures and incantations borrowed from the Babylonians. The sacred feast was also celebrated in person by the king, together with his nobles and his priests, in the temple after the manner of the rites handed down since the time of the Akkadian dynasty.

The expiation which the king had to perform on behalf of his people, was also based on Babylonian precept. There was provision for the use of a substitute for the king in these rites. Another man (*shar puhi*), or a bull or lamb, or the king's statue, or his robe could be used in place of the king to appease the wrath of the gods.[16] Penitential psalms were also recited by the king. Many devotional and penitential psalms and hymns are preserved, but they are only partly transliterated and translated. Nevertheless, Akkadian influence is clearly marked in this form of Hittite literature.

---

[15] Cf. O. R. Gurney, "Hittite Kingship," pp. 105 seq.

[16] *Ibid.*, p. 118. Unfortunately, information is scanty on the ceremony of coronation. There seems to have been an anointing with oil, a robing in royal vestments, a kind of coronation, a proclamation of the king's name—as in Egypt and Babylonia—and distribution of presents. There is almost no Hittite literature on kingship.

The participation of the queen in religious ceremonies, mentioned above, and the part which she played in state affairs, seems generally to be an Indo-European feature which is not found in the Egyptian and Mesopotamian polity. Another new element in ideas on kingship—the first Indo-European contribution to their evolution—is the elective nature of the king's appointment among the Hittites. Here the king had to be acknowledged as such by the members of his clan and by the nobles who formed the military class. The assembly of the nobles was called the *pankush*, which means the universality—probably a general council of all the nobility. The *pankush* also preserved other rights, which had the effect of limiting the power of the king; for example, the right of intervention in opposition to the king if he planned any misdeeds toward members of the royal family. It was also ordained that the nobles could be tried only by the *pankush* in which the king had no greater rights than any other individual member of the nobility.[17]

It can be imagined that this arrangement did not entirely suit the Hittite kings, who would have liked to enjoy the same royal prerogatives as their rivals of Babylonia and Egypt. After a prolonged struggle with the nobility they did succeed in establishing and maintaining a dynastic and hereditary principle. The rights of succession were fixed about the year 1500 B.C. by Telepinush, and according to this new constitution the succession was assured to the king's first son by his first wife. If the first wife had no son, the succession fell to the son by the second wife. If there was no son at all, the husband of the eldest daughter of the king's first wife became first in line. This arrangement remained in force throughout the existence of the second Hittite Empire. Despite this concession to the king, however, the nobility succeeded in preserving the other rights of the *pankush* mentioned above.

The *pankush* also appears to have continued to play an important role in the ceremony of the installation of the heir apparent. This again seems to be explained by the Indo-European idea that the king, who represented the nation before the gods, should be duly

[17] See the documentation concerning the election and succession of Hittite kings in A. Götze's study, *Kleinasien*, p. 85 seq.

52

acknowledged in this capacity through certain rites performed by the whole national and social group he was about to represent. This acknowledgment was made at the coronation of the heir apparent, when the ceremony consisted of anointing the crown prince, bestowing the royal insignia upon him, giving him a new name, vesting him with the royal robe, and placing a crown upon his head.[18] From then onward the heir took part in all royal functions, religious and political. By virtue of this he was assured of a thorough grounding in royal lore, thus providing the Hittites with continuity in political tradition and diplomatic practice.[19]

In other respects the Hittites were able to preserve their royal individuality. It is remarkable to observe, for example, that they did not follow the normal Oriental practice of embellishing monuments erected to their kings with boastful inscriptions. On the contrary, their inscriptions are conceived in an annalistic style and show a quite good historical sense. The Hittites were also the first to introduce a new kind of historical literature—the royal annals, which the Assyrians tried to imitate. The Hittites did **not** follow their Oriental neighbors in depicting their kings as displaying great proficiency and strength in hunting wild beasts. This kind of royal art, so popular among the Mesopotamian peoples and the Egyptians, failed to appeal to the Indo-European spirit of the Hittites.[20]

It can be seen that the contribution of the first Indo-Europeans to the civilization of the ancient Middle East in general and to the evolution of political ideas in particular was quite remarkable. It is amazing to observe how the Indo-European tribes, which penetrated into Asia Minor as carriers of a very primitive civilization, rose in a few centuries to become an important political power, able to dispute world domination—insofar as the Ancients were able to conceive of that—with the Babylonians, Egyptians, and Assyrians. They showed the same appreciation of the superior culture which they found as did the Semites when they conquered the land of the Sumerians. They were ingenious in the

---

[18] See *infra*, pp. 282, 283 on the origin of the rite of anointing.
[19] Cf. A. Garstang, *The Hittite Empire*, p. 8.
[20] A. Götze, *Kleinasien*, p. 92 seq.

adaptation of the different high cultural elements to their own racial conceptions. The most imposing feature of the achievements of the Hittites is their political unification of the different Asianic tribes under their domination. This ability on the part of a minority to create a solid state among heterogeneous races bears witness to the great qualities of the Indo-Europeans in fashioning important political edifices. Although their empire was eventually submerged by new waves coming from Europe to Asia Minor and from Assyria, their achievements presaged the role which the Indo-European and Indo-Aryan race would play in the future in world evolution and political ideology.

On the other hand, the Hittite civilization was able, from its center in Cappadocia, to maintain contact with the Aegean civilization which was about to inspire the Hellenes, who had moved toward Greece at the same time the Hittites crossed the Bosphorus into Asia Minor. In this way contact was maintained between the Asiatic and Aegean civilizations; and the waves of Thracians, sweeping over the great Asiatic peninsula, showed the way to the Hellenes, who, after having achieved a cultural level even higher than that of the Hittites, established their colonies on the Asiatic coast. From these they transmitted to Europe the best elements of the civilization of Asia.

But the influence of the Hittites did not end there. After the destruction of their empire in Asia Minor, they survived for five further centuries in Syria, where they continued to exercise a marked influence on the political and cultural evolution of that land and of Palestine, both of which were inhabited by Semitic populations. The Semites, coming from Arabia, entered this region in two main waves. The first, about 4000 B.C., swept principally towards Mesopotamia and the flood of this tide was marked by the subjugation of the Sumerians by the Akkadians.[21] The second between 2800 and 2600 B.C. was particularly violent and inundated not only Babylonia but also Syria and Palestine. As has been seen, the Amorites not only subdued the whole of Sumeria, but also founded a mighty Semitic empire under the first Babylonian

[21] Cf. *supra* p. 23.

dynasty. The Canaanites settled in Palestine and the mightiest of them all, the Philistines or Phoenicians, who occupied the coast of Palestine and infiltrated northward, at first called their land simply Canaan. Other Canaanite tribes, rendered familiar by the Bible, came either with the Philistines or in subsequent waves. These included the Edomites (Idumaeans), Moabites, Ammonites, and Hebrews. Then numerous Semitic tribes, probably mixed with the Hurri, penetrated as far south as Egypt (in about 1700 B.C.) and inaugurated the rule of the Hyksos—or Shepherd Kings as they were called by the Egyptians—over the land of the Nile.[22]

But this danger from the north has been shown to have awakened Egyptian interest in Palestine and Syria, with the result that when the Pharaohs had liberated themselves from the Hyksos, they began their expansion toward those lands. The local kings of Palestine and Syria became subject to the Pharaohs, who at the same time engaged their armies victoriously against the Hittites.

The Hittites started to advance towards Syria during the reign of Amenhotep III, and their penetration of northern Syria must have been on a greatly increased scale after the destruction of their empire in Asia Minor. From that period onward to the eighth century B.C. the Hittites of Syria are constantly mentioned in Assyrian annals. The Assyrians had good reason to be interested in them. The petty kings of the Hittites, although individually unable to create a solid political organization, were unanimous in their opposition to the Assyrians. They also succeeded in rallying to their cause the Semitic chiefs and the remnants of the Hurri who were still in those parts. The leadership in this anti-Assyrian confederation was assumed by the principal city-state of the Hittites, known as Karkemish.[23]

The Aramaeans, the most powerful of the Semitic nations, were also sworn enemies of the Assyrians. While they appear to have

---

[22] For more information on the early history of the Semites, cf. E. Meyer, *op. cit.*, 1, part 2, p. 377 seq., 2, part 2, p. 61 seq.

[23] Cf. the short but comprehensive description of Syro-Hittite evolution and cultural monuments in G. Contenau's work, *La civilisation des Hittites*, pp. 223–255. See also D. G. Hogarth, "The Hittites of Syria" in *CAH*, 3 (1925), pp. 132–147, and *ibid.*, "Hittite Civilization," pp. 148–168.

left Arabia with the Amorites and the Assyrians during the second Semitic migration, they seem also to have continued for a considerable time to lead a nomadic existence east of Mesopotamia. Thence they moved westward and settled in a large area of Mesopotamia, where Abraham, the forefather of the Israelites, lived among them for a time in Haran, their center on the upper Euphrates. From the second half of the twelfth century B.C. they were constantly at war with the Assyrians, under whose pressure they eventually moved into Syria.

The Aramaeans soon displaced the Hittites as the dominant power in Syria, and from their center in Damascus they endeavored constantly to extend their sway over the Israelites. When Achaz of Judah was menaced by them he called upon the Assyrians for help and Tiglath-pileser III decisively defeated the Aramaeans after taking Damascus in 732 B.C. Shortly after this, Sargon II of Assyria finally broke the last remnants of Hittite power and made the territory of Karkemish an Assyrian province.[24]

This brief account of the political development of Syria and Palestine[25] indicates the main points to be considered in a study of the political ideas of the Syrian and Palestinian Semites. First of all, the influence of Egyptian royal theology must have reached the Semites and undoubtedly left its mark upon them. But it is clear that whatever effect this might have had could have been offset by the influence of the Hittites, whose completely different ideas on kingship have already been explained. These influences were then succeeded by that of the Assyrians, whose political thought had features differing from those held by the Egyptians and the Hittites. Furthermore, account must be taken of the Amorites from Babylon, whose cultural influence was widespread. There was also the common racial ground upon which all the

---

[24] This was the end of the Hittites, but not of the Aramaeans. The growth of Aramaean influence is illustrated by the fact that from the eighth century B.C. onward Aramaic was not only the leading idiom in commercial and social intercourse in the Semitic East, but also the diplomatic language of the Jews and Assyrians. It finally replaced Hebrew as the vernacular in the second century B.C.

[25] See also the more comprehensive studies by O. Eissfeldt, *Philister und Phönizier*, Der Alte Orient, 34, Heft 3 (Leipzig, 1936), and by A. Alt, *Völker und Staaten Syriens im frühen Altertum, ibid.*, Heft 4 (Leipzig, 1936).

Semites met. Lastly the Aramaeans, who had been mingled with
the other Semites for a long period, can be credited with having
played a certain role in this respect, thanks to their predominance
in Syria and Palestine from the eighth century B.C. onward.

Valuable evidence concerning Egyptian influences is extant in
the form of the correspondence of the Semitic city-kings with the
Pharaohs, dating from the second half of the twelfth century B.C.,
which is preserved in the Tell el-Amarna tablets. These letters are
of some interest for the study of our subject, as they provide
additional information concerning Egyptian court style and ceremonial, as well as details concerning the ideas on kingship held
by the Semitic princes from northern Syria and the Phoenician
cities in central and southern Palestine.

Firstly, ample illustration may be found of the use of *proskynesis*
(adoration) in Egyptian court ceremonial. Almost every letter
starts with the words: "At the feet of my lord seven times and
seven times I fall down." Sometimes the number seven is omitted.[26]
In one instance we read: "eight times and seven times."[27] In
letters addressed to high Egyptian officials, the kinglets also use
the phrase, "at the feet of my lord I fall down"; but they never
add the number of times.[28] Later in this period, Zitrijara, probably
a Syrian city-king improved upon this practice when he assured
the Pharaoh,[29] "Seven (times) and sev(en) times, (with) back as
well as (with) belly, at the feet of the king, my lord, I fall down."
This formula was followed by Baiawa, another Syrian kinglet, in
one of his letters[30] and also by Zurata and Zatatna of Akko.[31] These
various gymnastics were especially favored by Shuwardata,[32] who
wished to ingratiate himself with the Pharaoh with whom he had

---

[26] E.g. Letters 49, 51, 58, 59, 207, 230, 252 in S. A. B. Mercer's edition of
The Tell el-Amarna Tablets, 2 vols. (Toronto, 1939); not the best but the
most convenient edition for non-specialists.

[27] Letter 84.

[28] E.g. Letters 62; 73 (Rib-Addi of Gubla to Amanappa, whom he calls
"my father"); 158 (Aziri of Amurru to Dudu—his "father").

[29] Letters 211, 4–6; 213, 7–9.

[30] Letter 215, 4, 5.

[31] Letters 232, 10, 11; 233, 14, 15; 234, 9.

[32] Letters 278 to 284.

been at enmity in the beginning of his reign. In this way a new
kind of *proskynesis*—an imaginary variety at least—was introduced
into the court style of Syrian and Palestinian kinglets and won
great favor with them.[33]

A letter composed by a north Syrian princeling, boasting an
Assyrian name, which complains about certain Hittite intrigues,
yields some valuable information concerning the ceremonial
procedure followed by the Pharaohs when they set their vassals
on their thrones:

> To the sun, the king, my lord, king of Egypt.
> Thus saith Addu-nirari, thy servant:
> At the feet of my lord I fall down.
> (Be)hold, when Manahbi(r)ia, king of Egypt, thy grandfather
> (T)a(ku), my (g)randfath(er), in Nuhashshe, established as king,
> and poured oil upon his head, then he spoke thus:
> "He whom the king of (Eg)ypt has made king (and poured oil
> upon his head)
> (shall no) one (overthrow)."[34]

This is the first mention of the use of anointing during the enthronement ceremonies, a ritual which was never employed at the enthronement of the Pharaohs.[35]

As there seems to be a process of evolution in the *proskynesis*,
so there is also a development in the titles given to the Pharaohs
by their vassal kings, who were quick to adopt the custom of
addressing the Pharaoh as "Sun."[36] The impression made on the
Hittites by this title, which they borrowed to apply to their own
kings, has been described. The Pharaohs themselves adopted the
same title in letters to their vassals.[37] Ammunira of Beirut, who
was particularly zealous in the cause of Egypt, even improved

---

[33] Letters 298, 13, 14; 299, 11; 301, 10, 11; 303, 11, 12; 304, 13, 14; 305,
13, 14; 306, 10, 11; 314, 9, 10; 315, 7; 316, 9; 319, 14; 320, 14; 322–328;
331.

[34] Letter 51, 2–9.

[35] H. A. Moret, *Du caractère religieux de la royauté pharaonique* (Paris,
1902), p. 75 seq.; H. W. Fairman, "The Kingship Rituals of Egypt," in
Myth, Ritual and Kingship, ed. by S. H. Hooke (Oxford, 1958), p. 78 seq.

[36] E.g. Letters 45, 49, 51, 53, 55, 60, 61, 67.

[37] Letter 99, 21 seq.: "And mayest thou know that the king is well, like
the sun in heaven." Letters 162, 78; 222a, 23: "The king is strong like the
sun, which is in heaven."

upon this. He repeatedly addressed the Pharaoh in one of his letters as: "My lord, my sun, my gods [in the plural!] the breath of my life,"[38] The final phrase sounds very Egyptian and shows that Ammunira had been diligent in his study of the Egyptian court style. His initiative was imitated by the kings of Sidon,[39] of Tyre, and of Amurru. The king of Tyre employed some particularly colorful expressions in his ten letters,[40] some of them worthy of an Oriental poet, for example:[41]

> To the king, my lord, (m)y gods, my sun .... I am the
> dust under the sandals of the king, my lord. My lord is the
> sun that rises over the lands day by day according to the
> determination of the sun, his gracious father, through whose
> friendly breath one lives, but mourns at his disappearance,
> who sets the whole land at rest by the power of (his) hand,
> who thunders in the heavens as Adad so that the whole land
> trembles at his thunder ..... He who hearkens to the king,
> his lord, and serves him in his place, over him the sun rises,
> and the good breath returns from the mouth of his lord....
> Verily, I have said to the sun, the father of the king, my lord:
> when shall I see the face of the king, my lord?

This kinglet says repeatedly how anxious he is to see the splendor of the king's countenance[42] and how he expects the king's "breath" (he means, word) to give him life, even life everlasting.[43] Aziri of Amurru follows the example of his royal colleague[44] and from then onward most of the princes of the vassal city-states address the Pharaoh as sun (*Shamash*) and god or gods.

The king of Tyre has been seen to compare the Pharaoh to the high god Adad, and two other instances of this particular practice can be quoted. Akizzi of Qatna addressed Amenophis III thus:[45] "Seven times at the feet of my lord, my Addu, I fall down."

---

[38] Letter 141, 1, 2, 6, 7, 10, 13, 14, 15, 37, 43.
[39] Letter 144, 2, 8.
[40] Letters 146–155.
[41] Letter 147, 1, 4–15, 41–44, 57–60. Cf. also 155, 47: "The king is the sun forever."
[42] Letters 151, 20; 152, 56.
[43] Letter 149, 25, 26.
[44] Letters 168, 1, 4, 9; 171, 13.
[45] Letter 52, 3, 4.

Abimilki of Tyre was even more expressive:[46] "I am the dust under the feet, the sandals of the king, my lord. O king, my lord, like the sun, like Adad in heaven thou art. May the king care for his servant." The last phrase and the whole content of the letter show why such flattering terms were employed.

Does the foregoing mean that the Semitic vassals of Egypt believed in the divine character of the Pharaoh and also that they had adopted in general the idea of divine kingship? To answer this question, it is necessary to examine in more detail some of the expressions employed by these writers of letters. In this connection the attitude of Rib-Addi requires special attention. He was a contemporary of Amenophis III (1411–1375 B.C.) and Amenophis IV (1375–1358 B.C.). His ideas on kingship can therefore be regarded as current not only at Gubla, that is Byblos,[47] where he represented the Pharaoh, but also among the other Syrian and Phoenician princes of this period.

Rib-Addi seems to have been aware that the Pharaohs were claiming a divine character. He appears to have referred to the Pharaoh as god on at least one occasion, in his letter to a high Egyptian official.[48] The passage is not well preserved; but this reading of it can be regarded as reasonably well founded. Nevertheless Rib-Addi gives the impression that he did not regard the Pharaoh as an authentic god. In almost all his letters[49] he expresses the wish that Baalat, the goddess of Gubla, will give power and strength to the Pharaoh. The phrase "May Baalat of Gubla give power to the king, my lord" is repeated so often and with such simplicity that one cannot avoid reading into it an expression of the writer's ideas on the Pharaoh's position in relation to

[46] Letter 149, 4–9. It would be presumptuous to draw any conclusion from Abimilki's Letter 155 to Amenophis IV in which he calls himself "servant of Shalmaiati." There is still controversy among specialists concerning the etymology of this name. It may stand for Amenophis IV or for a god venerated in Tyre. There is certainly no foundation for Engnell's suggestion (*op. cit.*, p. 83) that we have here "the local identification of the king with the vegetation deity."

[47] Cf. S. A. B. Mercer, *op. cit.*, 2, p. 836 seq.

[48] Letter 69, 5–7: "(May Ba'alat of Gubla, the goddess of the King, my lord, give to thee strength) be(fore the King, my lord, my god)."

[49] Letters 68, 70, 74, 75–81, 83, 85, 89, 92.

what he regards as true divinity. To Rib-Addi Baalat of Gubla was authentically divine and a being of a higher order than the Pharaoh. In his letter to Amanappa, a high ranking Egyptian official and general,[50] he delivers himself of this wish: "(May Baalat, the goddess of the king) thy lord, a(nd the goddess of Gubl)a, give (thee) strength in the presence of the king, (thy) lord." When he informs the general that he has no copper to send him, he invokes not the name of the king, but that of Baalat: "As true as Baalat of Gubla is exalted so there is no copper or axes of copper in my possession." On another occasion he writes:[51] "May Aman (the god of the king) thy lord, give thee strength (in the presence of)the king, thy lord." One passage is particularly striking. Rib-Addi, appealing for help, apostrophizes Amenophis IV[52]: "And behold the gods and the sun and Baalat of Gubla decre(ed) that thou sit upon the throne of thy father's house in thy land." This is reminiscent of the Babylonian belief that it was the gods who chose the kings, gave them their names, and decreed their sovereignty. Yet another trace of Babylonian court style can be detected in Rib-Addi's letters, when he indulges in the habit of calling the Pharaoh "the king of the lands, the great king," occasionally adding "the king of battle."[53]

The attitude of Rib-Addi toward the Egyptian ruler cult cannot be considered to support the assumption that the Semites of Syria and Palestine had accepted Egyptian ideas on divine kingship. The practice of calling the Pharaoh "god," adopted by numerous Semitic princelings, must be viewed in this light. Moreover, this conclusion is strongly supported by the fact that these princelings were by no means consistent in following this practice. There are a great many letters in which the divine title of the Pharaoh is omitted,[54] a condition which would hardly have been

---

[50] Letter 77, 4–11.
[51] Letter 86, 3. In letters 87, 5; 95, 3, 4, he adds his own divinity Baalat to the Egyptian sun god, Amon.
[52] Letter 116, 64–6.
[53] Letters 105, 2; 106, 2; 107, 2, 3; 108, 2, 3; 109, 2; 112, 2–4; 114, 2; 116, 2, 3; 117, 2; 119, 2, 3; 121, 2; 122, 2, 3; 123, 2, 3.
[54] For the sake of simplicity there are listed here only the Letters in which the divine title of the king is omitted. Letters 154, 155, (line 47: "The king is the sun forever"), 195, 199, 201, 202, 203, 204, 205, 206, 209,

admissible if the writers had been firm believers in the divine character of his kingly office. In addition, a few letters contain phrases which may be construed as affirming the estimation of the Semitic city-kings that their lord the Pharaoh could not be regarded as possessing the same degree of divinity as either his own or their gods. Aziri, for instance, who several times addresses the Pharaoh as "god" in his letters, attributes to the will of the Pharaoh's gods a misadventure which befell his messenger:[55] "The god(s of th)e king, m(y lor)d, have (not) permitted my messengers to e(sca)pe from the hand of (I)anhamu." Aziri, who also honors the Pharaoh with the title of "god," seems equally to be very conscious of the existence of varying degrees of divinity when he writes to the Pharaoh: "Thy gods and the Sun know indeed whether I lived not in Tunip."[56] Biridiya of Megiddo, while addressing the Pharaoh as "my gods" in one letter, acknowledges in another only the Pharaoh's gods: "If the gods of the king our lord, would ordain that we capture Labaiya, then we will bring him alive to the king, our lord."[57]

If all these circumstances are taken into account, it is probably justifiable to state that the Semitic kinglets of Syria and Palestine did not accept the Egyptian ideas on divine kingship. They adapted the Egyptian court style more or less perfectly to their own requirements.[58] But when they addressed the Pharaoh as "my god" or "my gods" they did not identify him with either his or their own national gods.

Unfortunately, the archives contain only a very few letters addressed to the city-kings by their subordinates. A chieftain who sent a letter to Rib-Addi calls him "Sun" and expresses the simple

---

211, 212, 216, 217, 218, 220, 221, 222, 223, 224, 225, 226, 228, 229, 230, 232, 234, 237, 239, 242, 244, 245, 246, 248a, 249, 250–265, 284, 285–290 (letters sent by Abdi-Hiba, king of Jerusalem), 317, 318, 334, 335.

[55] Letter 171, 9, 10.

[56] Letter 161, 32 seq. Cf. also Letter 209, 15 (Zishamimi, probably from Syria): "May the gods, who are with thee, smite my head," and Letter 250, 48 (Addu-Ur.Sag): "May the god of the king, my lord, preserve me."

[57] Letter 245, 3, 5.

[58] Here the life-giving function of the Pharaoh, which is often alluded to, might be especially stressed (e.g. Letters 74, 53 seq; 80, 31 seq.; 136, 41 seq.; 149, 24 seq.; 215, 16 seq.). Here again I. Engnell, op. cit., p. 92, goes too far in quoting them as an argument for his thesis of divine kingship.

wish:[59] "May the deity care for thy health (and) the health of thy house." When two of Aziri's officers sent him a warning when he was at the Pharaoh's court, they addressed him merely as their lord:[60] "At the feet of our lord we fall down. With our lord may it be well. And now with the lands of our lord may it be very well." This simple court style, which seems to have been generally observed in the chancelleries of the Semitic city-kings, does not support the assumption that their royal office conferred a real divine character on them.

This impression is strengthened by observations which can be made in a later period, when the Assyrians had driven the Egyptians out of Syria. A number of Aramaic inscriptions of this period from northern Syria are extant, and these give a very clear picture of the ideas on kingship which were then current in this region. Fortunately these inscriptions have been thoroughly studied from this point of view quite recently, so that there is no necessity here to go into detail.[61] An examination can, therefore, be confined to the results of these researches.

Under Assyrian rule, the city-kings definitely did not regard themselves as of divine origin or as sons of a god. It was believed, however, that kingship was conferred by a divinity, who was always the king's tutelary deity.[62] Once kingship had been conferred, then the divinity concerned became the tutelary deity of the whole dynasty. The right of succession now became hereditary, generally from father to son, but subject to confirmation by the Assyrian king, who reserved the right to make exceptions to this tacitly accepted rule. When the dynasty was changed, by

---

[59] Letter 96, 4, 5.
[60] Letter 170, 3, 4.
[61] K. F. Euler, "Königtum und Götterwelt in den aramäischen Inschriften Nordsyriens. Eine Untersuchung zur Formsprache der altaramäischen Inschriften und des Alten Testaments," *ZAW*, 56 (1938), pp. 272–316. I. Engnell's criticism (*op. cit.*, p. 205 seq.) of Euler's deductions sounds unconvincing.
[62] It should be added here that King Tabnith of Sidon calls himself priest of Ashtart (*ca.* 300 B.C.): "I, Tabnith, priest of Ashtart, king of the Sidonians, son of Eshmun-azar, priest of Ashtart, king of the Sidonians, lie in this coffin . . .," G. A. Cooke, *A Text Book of North Semitic Inscriptions* (Oxford, 1903), p. 26, inscr. 4, lines 1, 2.

extinction, usurpation or foreign intervention the tutelary deity changed also. It should be further noted that the divinity protecting the king could not be the leading national god and vice versa.

Some of the inscriptions reveal clear traces of the old Sumerian belief, which was adapted by the Amorites, that the gods of the land were its real masters. It is only by their will that the king maintains his status and it is they who sanction the treaties which the king concludes in their name. The king is no more nor less than the representative of the divine powers and his principal duty is to fulfill the wishes of the gods. While these considerations limited the king's importance, they nevertheless lifted him above the level of his subjects.

It is possible that in this respect, the influence of the Hittites may have made itself felt. It must be remembered that the Hittites had particularly developed the relationship between their gods and the land. It was their practice to associate their political actions and their national gods very intimately.[63] This was an inter-relationship of ideas which is an interesting feature of the political evolution of the ancient Middle East.

There is one point which merits special emphasis. The incriptions under discussion show a marked messianic character in relation to the names of some kings. For example, in an inscription found on the statue of the god Hadad at Zendjirli, King Panammu[64] exalts his tutelary deities, who set in his hand "the sceptre of blessing" (or abundance). Thanks to this aid, he had been able "to make disappear sword and complot from the house of his father." Everybody had plenty to eat; cities and villages had been built; abundance reigned in the land; the worship of the gods was well provided for.

Even more impressive is the Kalamu inscription from the same place, dating from the end of the ninth century B.C. The king describes himself and his reign in the following words:[65]

[63] Cf. also *infra* p. 69 on the Hittite influence of the deification of deceased rulers.

[64] Cf. for convenient details concerning the main inscriptions, G. Contenau, *La civilisation phénicienne* (Paris, 1928, 1939), pp. 336–337; French translations of the inscriptions, *ibid.*, p. 334 seq. For more numerous bibliographical details, consult I. Engnell, *op. cit.*, p. 94.

[65] The quotation is from the translation made by I. Engnell, *op. cit.*, p. 94 seq.

But I for the one was a father, and for the one I was a mother and for another I was a brother. And him who had not seen the face of a sheep I made owner of a flock, and (him) who had not seen the face of an ox I made the owner of cattle and owner of silver and owner of gold, and who had not seen linen from his youth in my days byssus covered him.

This is reminiscent of the description of Ashurbanipal's reign quoted above. It provides further evidence of the way in which the conception of an ideal savior king was establishing itself firmly in the Semitic mentality. In the case of the kings of northern Syria there can be no question of the connection of the two ideas: the universal king and the savior king. The messianic conception is expressed by this.

One further detail should be recalled in order to complete the picture. An inscription from the period when Syria and Palestine were under Persian domination shows that being just and righteous was regarded as the principal quality of kingship. Yehaw-milk, king of Byblos, after describing the altar and temple which he had built in honor of his protecting goddess, addresses himself to the goddess of Byblos asking her to let him live, to prolong his days and years, and to win for him the favor of both gods and people, because he is a righteous and just king.[66]

The archaeological material which has recently been discovered in Mari (modern Tel Hariri) is of considerable value in elucidating the degree to which Syria was associated with the culture of Mesopotamia. Ancient Mari, situated on the middle Euphrates, was an important focal point of communications. Here was the crossing of the highways leading on the one hand from southern Mesopotamia and the Persian Gulf to northern Mesopotamia and Assyria, and on the other hand from Mesopotamia to northern Syria and the Mediterranean. It was from this point that the old

---

[66] G. A. Cooke, *op. cit.*, p. 18 seq., inscr. 3, lines 9, 10: "May the mistress of Gebal bless Yehaw-milk and grant him life and prolong his days and years over Gebal for he is a righteous king. And may (the lady, m)istress of Gebal, give (him) favor in the eyes of the gods and in the eyes of the people of this land and the favor of the people of the lan(d). Cf. also *ibid.*, inscr. 62, line 19, p. 171 seq., an inscription of Panammu of Zendjirli from 745–727 B.C., and inscr. 63, lines 4, 5, p. 180, that of his son, Barrekub.

Sumerian and Akkadian cults penetrated Assur and Asia Minor, reaching not only the Assyrian colonies but also the Hittites. From here also they found their way to northern Syria to influence the Syro-Hittites and the Semites. As the recent discoveries referred to have shown, these cults existed first at Mari at the beginning of the second milennium B.C. and expanded from there along the lines just described.[67]

It is only logical to suppose that Sumerian and Akkadian ideas on kingship were conveyed to the Syrian Semites through the same channel. There is, indeed, a painting, discovered in the royal palace of Mari, which is particularly relevant to this subject. It represents Zimrilin, the last king of Mari and a contemporary of Hammurabi of Babylon, touching royal symbols—the circle and the sceptre—held by the goddess Ishtar, who is accompanied by other divinities. It was first thought that this scene represented the goddess presiding over the King's investiture; but it was later pointed out[68] that the circle and the sceptre appeared in Babylonia during the first Babylonian dynasty only and that they were

[67] Cf. G. Dossin, "Le panthéon de Mari," *Studia Mariana*, ed. by A. Parrot, Documenta et Monumenta Orientis Antiqui, 4 (Leiden, 1950), pp. 41–50. Cf. the rich bibliographical notice on the discoveries at Mari by A. Spycket, "Bibliographie de Mari," *ibid.*, pp. 127–138.

[68] See the well documented and convincing study by M.-Thérèse Barrelet, "Une peinture de la cour 106 du Palais de Mari," *ibid.*, pp. 9–35, especially p. 19. Cf. also *ibid.*, pp. 37–40, A. Parrot's commentary on Mme. Barrelet's study ("'Cérémonie de la main' et réinvestiture"). The letters from the royal archives of Mari, so far published, reveal little that is relevant to our subject. In the correspondence of Shamshi-Addu with his sons, mention is found of silver statues of the King and his son Iasmah-Addu; but it seems that only the accounts concerning the cost of the statues were to be placed in the temples of Ashshur and Dagan. It is not stated that the statues themselves were to be placed there. See G. Dossin, *Correspondance de Šhamši-Addu et de ses fils = Archives Royales de Mari*, 1 (Paris, 1950), p. 138 seq. (Letter 74). The Letters so far published, addressed to the king of Mari, are written in a very simple style. They start almost invariably with the words: "To my lord say this: thus speaks Kibri-Dagan your servant." There is no suggestion whatsoever of a cult of royalty. When the governor asks the king to visit his city he employs the phraseology: "Let my lord in the goodness of (his heart) come and kiss the foot of Dagan who loves him" (Letter 8, line 25). In another Letter he adds: "The ancients of the city continually come before Dagan and pray for my lord and the armies of my lord." See J. R. Kupper, *Correspondance de Kibri-Dagan, gouverneur de Terqa = ibid.*, 3 (Paris, 1950), pp. 31, 35. Nothing can be deduced from such phraseology in favor of a more intimate relationship between the king and the goddess Terga, such as divine filial relationship or any degree of divine status.

exclusive to gods—Shamash in particular—as symbols of sovereignty. Evidence that these two symbols can be assumed by kings is not found earlier than the neo-Babylonian period, which is many centuries later. The Mari painting can represent only a scene from a liturgical ritual in which the king played a prominent role as the intermediary between his people and the divinity.[69] Two interpretations are possible, first that the King is touching the statue of the goddess and inviting her to take her place in the liturgical procession, second that the king is saluting the goddess in his palace and receiving from her a renewal of his office. It is known from Babylonian ritual that statues of the gods, carried in solemn procession, were sometimes brought into the royal palace, the ceremony symbolizing the visit of the god to the king.

This calls for some study of the religious role of the Syrian and Palestinian kings, and material for the elucidation of this may be found in the texts which have been recently discovered at Ras Shamra, the ancient Ugarit, a Phoenician city in northern Syria.[70] There is already a considerable bibliography concerning the interpretation of these texts, most of it from the pen of C. Virolleaud.[71] Until the specialists have solved the many philological and religious problems involved, it is not possible for a historian to make any

[69] For details on the use of the circle and sceptre as symbols of sovereignty in kings, see R. Labat, *Le caractère religieux de la royauté assyro-babylonienne* (Paris, 1939), p. 87 seq. The author quotes a ritual from the period of the Seleucids, the Assyrian ritual and an inscription concerning the last king of Babylon, Nabu-naid.

[70] A useful introduction to the discoveries made at Ras Shamra will be found in J. Friedrich's short essay, *Ras Shamra. Ein Überblick über Funde und Forschungen*, Der Alte Orient, 33, Heft 1–2 (Leipzig, 1933).

[71] C. Virolleaud, *La légende phénicienne de Danel* (Paris, 1936); *idem, La déesse 'Anat, poème de Ras Shamra* (Paris, 1938); *Idem, La légende de Kéret, roi des Sidoniens* (Paris, 1936). Other texts were published by the same author in *Syria*, 13 (1932), pp. 113–163; 15 (1934), pp. 305–336 (Mort de Baal); 12 (1931), pp. 193–224, and 15 (1934), pp. 226–243 (La lutte de Mot et d'Aleïn); 16 (1935) pp. 247–266 (Chasses de Baal); 17 (1936), pp. 150–173 ('Anat et la Génisse); 16 (1935), pp. 29–45 (Révolte); 14 (1933), pp. 128–151 (Dieux gracieux); 17 (1936), pp. 209–228 (Nikal-Kosharot); 22 (1941), pp. 105 seq., 197 seq. (Le roi Kéret et son fils). Cf. also R. de Langhe, *Les textes de Ras Shamra-Ugarit et leurs rapports avec le milieu biblique de l'Ancien Testament* (Gembloux-Paris, 1945), 2 vols. Recently J. Gray, *The Legacy of Canaan*, Suppl. to *VT*, 5 (Leiden, 1957), esp. pp. 1–112; complete bibliography on pp. 217–228. Cf. also H. E. Del Medico, *La Bible cananéenne, découverte dans les textes de Ras Shamra* (Paris, 1950).

definite evaluation of these literary products.[72] There is, moreover, no point in discussing here the many intricate details which are still being hotly contested. So far, one thing seems to be established which is of importance for our subject. Some of the texts are of a liturgical character and dramatize the return of the rainy season after the deadly heat of summer which had arrested all life in nature. Baal, the god of rain, is defeated by Mot, the god of drought, and left impotent; but he is found and revived by his consort, Anat, who thwarts Mot and his aides and solemnly reinstalls Baal in his palace. It is indicated by the nature of the texts that the king was supposed to play a prominent role in the festivities accompanying these New Year celebrations by himself impersonating the god Baal.

Two legends, one relating to King Danel and the other to King Keret of Sidon, provide yet further details concerning the priestly role which the king was obliged to play, and concerning also his special relationship to the divinities. In both, the Kings are said to have brought many sacrifices for the gods. They practiced magic in order to learn the will of the gods. Their intimate relationship to gods is stressed and Keret is called son of the supreme god El. Danel is praised for having protected the rights of widows and orphans[73] and Keret's reign is said to have been blessed by widows.[74] This signifies that to render justice was the principal function of a king. Both Kings are promised progeny by the supreme god. The sacred marriage is commemorated in the hymn to the god Nikal and the goddess Kosharot.

All these texts betray a strong Babylonian, and sometimes also a Hittite influence. The Danel legend developed around the agrarian harvest cults, and—like some Babylonian epics—might have been recited as part of the liturgical ceremony in some parts of

---

[72] Cf. the review—detailed but not very clear—of the controversy in I. Engnell, *op. cit.*, pp. 97–110. *Ibid.*, pp. 110–173, provides the most detailed bibliography concerning all the texts in question. A complete bibliography dealing with Ras Shamra is to be found in C. F.-A. Schaeffer, *Ugaritica*, I and II, Mission de Ras Shamra 3 (Paris, 1939), 5 (1949), Bibliothèque archéol. et hist., 31, 47. Cf. also J. Nougayrol, "Textes accadiens et hourrites des archives est, ouest et centrales," *Le Palais royal d'Ugarit*, 3, Mission de Ras Shamra, 6 (Paris, 1955).

[73] C. Virolleaud, *La lég. phénic. de Danel*, p. 139.

[74] C. Virolleaud, *La lég. de Kéret*, p. 39.

Palestine. This relationship with Babylonian cults and traditions justifies the association of Syrian and Palestinian ideas on kingship with Babylonian ideas on the same subject. On this basis, it is quite legitimate to suppose that the Syrian and Palestinian Semites regarded their kings as beings especially chosen and protected by gods. Like the Babylonian kings, they were sons of gods, not by incarnation but by adoption.[75] It has been shown how the Assyrians whose kings were never regarded as gods, had nevertheless adopted Babylonian expressions to describe the relationship of their kings with gods.

Assyrian influences were also strong in Canaan and Palestine and it may be supposed that they made themselves felt in the sphere of political thought. The possibility of the infiltration of Hittite ideas must not be forgotten. Traces of such are apparent, it seems, in the sarcophagus of the Phoenician King Ahiram, dating from the beginning of the thirteenth century B.C. The King wears a beard and his hair is long like that of a god. He is represented seated on a throne with steps, adorned by winged sphinxes, as he accepts the homage of seven persons, the first of whom is holding the symbol of Oriental royalty—the flabellum or fan. If this scene can be interpreteted as representing homage being paid to a divinized king, it is admissible to discern in it an influence emanating from the Hittites, who regarded their kings as achieving divinity after death.[76]

---

[75] In this way the divine sonship of Keret can best be explained. On other titles of Keret, see C. Virolleaud, *ibid.*, p. 8. He is also called "soldier of the light of gods" (i.e. sun) and simply "servant and slave of El." El reveals himself to Keret as "father of humanity" (*ibid.*, pp. 37, 43, 51). All this seems to show that Keret's divine filiation should not be overemphasized. Cf. also R. de Langhe, *op. cit.*, 2, p. 416 seq., on the royal court of Ugarit and on the absence of evidence for divine kingship in the material so far discovered. Cf. J. Gray, *op. cit.*, p. 160 seq. On cultural Babylonian influence on Ugarit, see the paper by J. Nougayrol, "L'influence babylonienne à Ugarit, d'après les textes en cunéiformes classiques," *Syria*, 39 (1962), pp. 28–35.

[76] Cf. G. Contenau, *La civilisation phénicienne*, pp. 99 (figure 27), 231 seq. It is, however, not finally ascertained whether this represents homage being rendered to a divinized king. Four of the figures have been identified as women lamenting, a natural occurrence in Oriental funeral rites. Before the King there stands also a small table bearing food, which can be regarded as appropriate to a funeral scene. When King Kapara of Palu calls his father and grandfather *Ilim* (gods), he may have been influenced by the

There is a further feature which deserves mention, since it must undoubtedly have influenced Phoenician political evolution. It must not be forgotten that the chief Phoenician city-states —Sidon, Beirut, Byblos, Tyre—became important trading centers. It was quite natural that in cities whose wealth depended upon the commercial enterprise of their citizens, rich merchants should be given some voice in the administration and conduct of foreign relations. This practice has been shown to have been followed in Assyria and in the Semitic colonies in Asia Minor.[77] It was inevitable that a similar development should occur also in the Phoenician ports. Only the final stage in this process has been recorded; there is no direct information concerning its evolution. According to Arrian,[78] the historian of Alexander the Great, at Tyre the council of elders, comprising the most prominent citizens, was entitled to make decisions in the absence of the king, while at Sidon the council took action in opposition to the will of the king.

Hittite custom. B. Meissner, "Die Keilschrifttexte auf den steinernen Ortho-staten und Statuen aus dem Tell Ḥalâf," in *Aus fünf Jahrtausenden morgen-ländischer Kultur = Archiv für Orientforschung*, Beiband 1 (Berlin, 1933), pp. 71–79. I. Engnell, *Studies in Divine Kingship*, p. 81, sees this as "direct evidence of the king's divinity." This is in no way the case. Here is Meissner's translation of the inscription: "1. Palast des Kapara, des Sohnes des Hadianu. 2. Was mein Vater und mein Grossvater die Vergöttlichten (*sa abi-ia abi-abi-ia ilim lim*), 3. nicht getan haben habe ich getan. 4. Wer (meinen) Namen auslöscht und (seinen) Namen 5. hinsetzt, sieben seiner Söhne soll man vor der Wettergrotte 6. verbrennen, sieben seiner Töchter 7. soll man für die Ištar als Huren loslassen(?). 8. Abdi-ilu hat den Namen(?) des Königs geschrieben." A Phoenician inscription of King Azitawadd recently discovered in Cilicia and probably dating from about 740 B.C., reveals all the fine qualities that a good ruler should manifest, but there is no trace of a divine character being attrib-uted to the ruler. On this inscription, see the publication and studies by R. Marcus and I. J. Gelb, "A Preliminary Study to the New Phoenician Inscription from Cilicia," *Journal of Near Eastern Studies*, 7 (1948), pp. 194–198. *Idem*, "The Phoenician Stele Inscription from Cilicia," *ibid.*, 8 (1949), pp. 116–120. C. H. Gordon, "Azitawadd's Phoenician Inscription," *ibid.*, pp. 108–115. J. Obermann, *New Discoveries at Karatepe. A Complete Text of the Phoenician Royal Inscription from Cilicia*, Transactions of the Connecticut Academy, 38, 3 (New Haven, 1949).

[77] See *supra*, pp. 22, 41. Cf. G. Radet, *La Lydie et le monde grec au temps des Mermnades (687–546)* (Paris, 1893), pp. 90–94, on the influence exerted on policy in the later period by the Council of the elders in Asia Minor.

[78] Arrian, *Anabasis*, II, 15 seq., ed. by E. I. Robson (Loeb, 1929), 1, p. 182 seq. Cf. Quintus Curtius, *History of Alexander*, IV, 1, 15 seq., ed. by J. C. Rolfe (Loeb, 1946), 1, p. 164. The prophet Ezekiel (27 : 9) also speaks of the "elders" of Tyre.

It is clear from these instances that the power of local dynasts was considerably weakened, the scope of their activities curbed, and their prestige lowered by this development. The evolution of this practice was complete in Tyre after 570 B.C. when the monarchy was temporarily abolished in favor of a republic governed by judges.[79] In the colonies established by the Phoenicians the monarchic system had a stronger hold than it was able to retain in the mother country;[80] but it is not to be wondered at that in Carthage, the most important colony in North Africa, the government fell into the hands of the richest families, and a form of republic was established. The council of elders delegated executive power to two officials called suphetes, while the office of supreme magistrate frequently remained for too long in the same families, thus giving rise to a situation inimical to the state. This further evolution, however, is not relevant to the present subject.

It can thus be concluded that when the Semites addressed their kings as *Ilim* (gods) it was not their intention to bestow upon them the same degree of divinity which they reserved for their own gods. Indeed the very word had a much wider significance for them than it has for us now. *Ilu* (divine) was applicable not only to gods but also to spirits, demons, genii. The principal attributes of gods were power and might. Everything that manifested a power superior to that of the average man was considered to enjoy a degree of divine nature. Kings possessed supreme power upon earth and therefore they were *Ilim*. Their relationship to gods was naturally very intimate. They were chosen by gods, adopted by them as their sons, reared by them. They were the representatives of the gods upon earth. On certain occasions they even impersonated the gods before their subjects. They were in frequent communication with the gods in their dreams. They learned the will of the gods by magic and divination. They were the natural intermediaries between the gods and their subjects, the high priests impersonating the whole community before the

---

[79] Josephus Flavius, *Against Apion*, I, 157, ed. by H. St. J. Thackeray (Loeb, 1926), p. 224. Cf. the short notice on Phoenician political constitutions in G. Contenau, *La civilisation phénicienne*, pp. 96–98.

[80] On Phoenician colonization, see E. Meyer, *Geschichte des Altertums*, 2, pt. 2, p. 77 seq.

gods. All this explains why, for the primitive Semites, there was no sharp differentiation between god and king comparable to that which exists today. It is necessary to bear this in mind when studying Semitic ideas on kingship.[81]

[81] Cf. Th. H. Gaster, "Divine Kingship in the Ancient Near East," *The Review of Religion*, 9 (1944–45), p. 268. The author, when refuting the main thesis of I. Engnell, *Studies in Divine Kingship*, on Near Eastern divine kingship, proffers another explanation as to why the king was called *ilu* (p. 269): "The king is the type-man of the group, the focus and quintessence of its corporate life and existence. He symbolises only the living entity of his contemporaries, not the dead and the future.... That continuance likewise possesses its focus and quintessence and this is the local genius—the god. The king is but an avatar of a continuous, perpetual being; but as such he is its real incarnation, and his divine qualities are inherent, not conferred.... He is the god in his immediate, as distinct from his continuous aspect...." Cf. also his study, "'Ba'al is Risen....' An Ancient Hebrew Passion-Play from Ras Shamra-Ugarit," *Iraq*, 6 (1939), p. 123. This is an ingenious conception—to my mind too ingenious for the primitive Semite.

CHAPTER THREE

IRANIAN KINGSHIP

Eastern Iranian and Median monarchies — Formation of the Persian Empire — No traces of divine kingship in Iranian myths and oldest political organizations — *Hvarena* (kingly glory), the concrete apparition of light — The Aryan and Iranian character of this belief — *Hvarena* represented in the form of animals and elements. The god Verethragna, its bearer — Verethragna, personification of an abstract notion of might and power? — Priestly *Hvarena*, a Zoroastrian invention— Persian kings as successors of mythical heroes and representatives of Ahura Mazda — Zoroastrian influence on Achaemenid ideas of kingship? — Babylonian influences on Persian political ideas — Iranian and Oriental elements in Persian royal ceremonial — Evolution of royal symbols: tiara, throne — Persian idea of universality — The King-Savior and Zoroastrian eschatology — Conclusion.

While the Hittites were the first Indo-Europeans to contribute to the evolution of Oriental ideas on kingship, an influence both more important and of longer duration was that exercised by the other mighty Aryan nations which had occupied the Iranian plateau.

It is still impossible to determine at what period the Indo-Iranians took possession of their new homelands—Iran and India. They moved toward the South and Southeast most probably from the Russian steppes between the Black Sea, the Caspian Sea, and the Sea of Aral, whence the Indo-Europeans had commenced their migration toward Europe at the end of the third millennium B.C. The Indo-Iranians seem to have quitted their original homes at a later date and the details of their slow penetration are not known.

As has been seen, the advance guard had been the tribes which had infiltrated among the Kassites, the Hurri, and the Mitanni, and had penetrated as far as Syria. The general character of this penetration has been described, and it has also been shown to what extent these first Aryans had contributed to the military organization of the ancient Near East. Lack of reliable historical data prevents us from following the stages of the Aryan movement toward the Iranian plateau; but it seems to have been in the course of their penetration toward the South that they came into contact with the Assyrians, in the ninth century B.C. From this it can be inferred that their migration in the direction of the western Iranian plateau must have started much earlier than that date. Only one fact is known for certain— the Indians, the racial brothers of the Iranians, can be located in the Punjab as early as about 1600 B.C.[1]

There are certain indications which show that Eastern Iran was occupied by Aryan tribes at an earlier period than Western Iran. The most ancient part of the Persian sacred book, the Zend-Avesta —the oldest Yashts, which seem to have preserved a pre-Zoroastrian tradition[2]—contains the names of kings (kavi) who are not mythical personages, but might really have existed. The series, starting with Kavata and ending with Haosravah (Husravah), seems to have comprised five generations. This tradition is pre-Zoroastrian and provides an opportunity to reconstruct, at least on broad lines, the early history of Eastern Iran. It would thus appear that the first attempt to found a solid political structure in the form of a monarchy was made in Eastern Iran. This monarchy was in existence between 900 and 775 B.C.[3]

It is possible that Yasht[4] X, in honor of Mithra, contains an allusion to the existence of just such a higher political organization uniting the chieftains of the tribes under a supreme ruler —the *sastar* who is also mentioned in a hymn by Zoroaster—the

---

[1] E. Meyer, *Geschichte des Altertums*, I, pt. 2, 5th ed. (Stuttgart-Berlin, 1926), p. 899. On the early history of Iran, cf. F. W. König, *Älteste Geschichte der Meder und Perser*, Der Alte Orient, 33, Heft 3/4 (Leipzig, 1934), and R. Ghirshman, *L'Iran; dès origines à l'Islam* (Paris, 1951), pp. 58–108.

[2] For details, see *infra*, pp. 75, 86, 93, 98, Yashts XIII and XIX.

[3] This is the result of A. Christensen's research, *Les Kayanides*, Det Kgl. Danske Videnskabernes Selskab, Hist. fil. Meddelelser, 19, 2 (1932), pp. 17–35, which seems plausible. On the original and Zoroastrian parts of the Yashts V, VIII, X, XIII, XV, XIX, see *ibid.*, pp. 10–17.

[4] J. Darmesteter, *The Zend-Avesta*, pt.2: *The Sîrôzahs, Yasts and Nyâyis*, The Sacred Books of the East, ed. by F. M. Müller, 23 (Oxford, 1883), pp. 119–158.

Gatha XLVI, verse 1—as an enemy of the Prophet. In the Mithra Yasht the chiefs of the tribes are called *dahyupati*; but the title of *kavi* must have been known to its author because he also speaks of the *Hvarena* of the *kavi*—the mighty glory of the chieftains.[5]

After 775 B.C., there seems to have followed a period of disintegration of the East Iranian monarchy. The Kavi Vishtaspa, the main supporter of Zoroaster, who seems to have reigned about 650–600 B.C.,[6] is said in Yasht XIII to have fought other *kavi*. This indicates that in his time the East Iranian monarchy evidently no longer existed. In the sixth century B.C., the East Iranian tribes had to recognize the supremacy of Western Iran.

The first tribe from the west of the plateau to come into contact with the Assyrians was that of the Medes, who were divided into numerous clans. In 836 B.C. the Assyrian King Shalmaneser III[7] began to penetrate the Western Iranian plateau, and from that time onward reliable historical evidence is available from Assyrian inscriptions on the Medes and their neighbors the Persians, the two most important Iranian tribes. Peoples of non-Iranian origin who had settled in the country before the Aryan invasion continued to live in Iran.

Shalmaneser III subdued some Median chieftains and his conquests were continued and extended by his successors; but only a part of Media had to recognize Assyrian overlordship. The rest of the Medes and the Persians suffered from Assyrian invasions, but were able to maintain their independence.

From Assyrian annals describing these campaigns we learn that the political organization of the Medes must have been loose. All of the annals speak of numerous princes who had been forced to pay tribute to the Assyrians.[8] In spite of that, the first attempt at the formation of a Western Iranian monarchy was made by the

---

[5] Cf. H. S. Nyberg, *Die Religionen des alten Iran*, Mitteilungen der Vorderasiatisch-aegyptischen Gesellschaft, 43 (Leipzig, 1938), pp. 57, 292 seq., 438.

[6] A. Christensen, *Les Kayanides*, p. 33.

[7] For details, see G. G. Cameron, *History of Early Iran* (Chicago 1936), p. 143 seq. Cf. also the short outline of Iranian prehistory in A. T. Olmstead's book, *History of the Persian Empire* (Chicago, 1948), pp. 16–29. J. V. Prášek's *Geschichte der Meder und Perser* (Gotha, 1906, 1910) is still useful.

[8] Cf. E. Meyer, *op. cit.*, 3, 2nd ed. (Stuttgart, 1937), pp. 40, 140.

Medes and much more information is available about this Median venture than about attempts to establish a monarchy in Eastern Iran.

Herodotus[9] left a colorful account of the beginnings of the Median kingship and the emancipation of the Medes from Assyrian overlordship. According to him, the Medes, in order to end the anarchy and lawlessness which was rife among their different tribes, decided to establish a king. They offered this position to Deioces, son of Phraortes, who was known as a just and upright man among his neighbors.

One thing can be determined with certainty from this saga, which Herodotus might have learned from some authentic Persian source. The Assyrian King Sargon II reports that in 715 B.C., he defeated and captured a Median chieftain named Daiaukku, who seems to be identical with Herodotus' Deioces. It thus appears that it was the dynasty of this chieftain which had succeeded in uniting some Median tribes and in leading them in their struggle against the Assyrians.

According to Herodotus, the successor of Deioces was his son Phraortes, who extended his supremacy over the Persians also, but who is supposed to have perished in his attempt to subjugate the Assyrians. He was succeeded by Cyaxares and Astyages. In the narrative of Herodotus there now follows the legend of Cyrus, son of Astyages' daughter and the Persian Cambyses, whom Astyages wanted to have killed because it had been revealed to him in dreams that this son of a Persian would succeed him and become the master of the whole of Asia.

It was Kyaxares who, allied with Nabopolassar of Babylon, destroyed the once mighty Assyrian Empire, now weakened by the Scythian invasion, which had also slowed down the political evolution of Assyria. It was when Kyaxares had driven out the Scythians that he turned again on the Assyrians. After a prolonged and bloody struggle, he captured all the Assyrian strongholds—Ashur in 614, Nineveh in 612—and levelled them so completely that they remained forever in ruins. It was the end not only of a great empire, but of an entire nation as well. The Assyrian territory was divided

[9] *Historiae*, I, 96 seq., ed. by A. D. Godley (Loeb, 1931), I, p. 126 seq.

between the two victors and the way lay open for the Medes to make a new push toward the interior of Asia Minor where a new empire, that of Lydia, was rising. Cappadocia and Armenia fell under Median supremacy at the beginning of the sixth century B.C. The Persians seem to have started their conquest of the Elamite kingdom, badly disorganized and weakened by the struggle with Assyria, at the end of the seventh century B.C. The conquest of the whole territory, with Susa, which became the favorite residence of the Persian kings, may have been completed about the year 596 B.C. As the Persians recognized the supremacy of the Medes, the new Median Empire extended far toward the south, touching the eastern shore of the Persian Gulf. It is possible that at least a part of Eastern Iran, perhaps also Bactria, belonged to it.[10] Thus it seemed that the Medes were predestined to walk in the footsteps of the Assyrians, to conquer the rest of Mesopotamia with Syria and to penetrate through Lydia to the Aegean ports of Asia where flourishing Greek colonies were assuring a lively exchange of ideas and merchandise between the Asiatic mainland and Greece. A new empire, more universal than all that had preceded it in the

Middle East was in the process of formation.

Fate, however, did not permit the Medes to complete what their great King Cyaxares had begun. In 553 B.C. Cyrus II, the son of the Persian King Cambyses I, revolted against the Medes, thus realizing the dream which, according to the legendary tradition reported by Herodotus, had so greatly troubled Astyages, the last independent Median king. Herodotus' narrative describing how the Median army joined Cyrus is very probably based upon a reliable source.[11] In 550 B.C. Astyages was taken prisoner and his capital Ecbatana had to yield precedence to Susa, Pasargadae, and Persepolis, cities favored by the victorious Persian dynasty founded by Achaemenes. That Cyrus treated the defeated Astyages with

[10] Cf. E. Meyer, *op. cit.*, 3, pp. 143 seq., 163 seq. More details on Elam are given in G. G. Cameron, *op. cit.*, pp. 97–137, 185–211. See also F. W. König, *Geschichte Elams*, Der Alte Orient, 29, Heft 4, (Leipzig 1931); J. V. Prášek, *op. cit.*, 1, pp. 103–141.

[11] Cf. G. G. Cameron, *op. cit.*, p. 225 seq., with the indication of Greek and Babylonian sources. Cf. the short history of the Achaemenids in R. Ghirshman, *op. cit.*, pp. 108–181.

magnanimity may have helped the conqueror affirm his authority among the Medes. Further military and political successes followed each other with impressive rapidity. First came the defeat of the Lydian King Croesus and the occupation of his territory.[12] Croesus' new allies, the Babylonians and the Spartans, were too late with their help. The kings of Cilicia and Paphlagonia recognized Persian supremacy and the whole of Asia Minor was in Persian hands.

After these conquests Cyrus turned toward Eastern Iran, ruled now, after the collapse of the Eastern monarchy, by numerous local princelings, the *kavi*. He subdued Parthia, Aria, Bactria, and Sogdia. Even the Chorasmians in the Khiva Oasis along the Lower Oxus recognized the supremacy of Cyrus, who had now penetrated as far as the Indus valley.[13]

From Eastern Iran Cyrus was able to recruit enough warriors for his campaign against Babylonia, which was dissatisfied with the religious policy of its last King Nabu-naid. Babylon fell into his hands,[14] and again humane treatment of those whom he had defeated, in addition to shrewd political propaganda, helped Cyrus to win the sympathy of the vanquished. All the provinces of Babylonia, stretching as far as the boundary of Egypt, and all its vassals recognized the supremacy of Cyrus. The Jews, whose great prophet called Deutero-Isaiah had foretold the end of Babylon, and who had greeted Cyrus as one anointed by God,[15] were permitted to return from Babylonian captivity and to reconstruct their temple.

Cyrus' son, Cambyses, II, naturally struck against Egypt. After he had defeated the army of the last Pharaoh, Psammetich III, and had taken Memphis (525 B.C.) the fate of the once mighty Egyptian Empire was sealed. The Libyans and the Greek colonists of Cyrenaica recognized Persian supremacy, but the plan to subjugate the flourishing Phoenician city of Carthage had to be abandoned,

[12] On Lydia, see the study by R. Dussaud, "La Lydie et ses voisins," *Babyloniaca*, 11 (1929–1930), pp. 69–174; *ibid.*, p. 114, the explanation of the legend of Croesus dying on the pyre. Cf. also the older work by G. Radet, *La Lydie et le monde grec au temps des Mermnades (687–546)*, (Paris, 1893), which is still useful. On Croesus, see pp. 206–259.

[13] A. T. Olmstead, *op. cit.*, pp. 45–49, with references to sources. On Parthia, cf. N. C. Debevoise, *A Political History of Parthia* (Chicago, 1938), p. 3 seq., and J. V. Prášek, *op. cit.*, 1, p. 195 seq.

[14] E. Meyer, *op. cit.*, 3, pp. 181–187; A. T. Olmstead, *op. cit.*, pp. 49–58,

[15] Isaiah 13; 14; 21 : 9; 43 : 14 seq.; 44 : 28, 45.

because the Phoenicians of the Syrian coast, though subject to the Persians, refused to fight their own countrymen and without the help of their fleet a campaign against Carthage was unthinkable. The Ethiopians, however, became Persian vassals.[16]

Troubles which broke out after the sudden death of Cambyses brought the new empire to the brink of ruin; but the situation was saved by the energetic Darius, who, although a scion of the minor branch of the Achaemenids, came boldly forward to claim Cambyses' inheritance and to save the tottering empire. He dealt quickly with the usurpers in Media and Persia and defeated the rebellious Babylonians and Armenians. Thanks to his vigorous intervention, the Persian world empire was firmly re-established, from the end of 519 B.C., extending from the Nile to the Jaxartes and the Black Sea, and from the Hellespont to the river Indus. His energy was also responsible for a thorough reorganization[17] within the empire.

On the ruins of old national cultures a new political structure was thus erected by the vigorous Indo-European race. The dominant nation in the construction of this empire was faced with the colossal task of blending all the cultural elements, which were the fruits of its military victories, into a single unit. This would provide its empire with a more permanent basis and make it the channel whereby eastern civilization would be conveyed to the Mediterranean lands where a new culture—the Greek—was approaching maturity. The first phase of the unification of the two cultural worlds began under Darius (521–485 B.C.). The second, under Xerxes (485–465), was the more critical. Europe, on the verge of becoming Orientalized, was saved from this fate by the valiant Athenians, who led the first struggle waged by Europe against an Asiatic invader. However, though politically limited to Asia, the new world empire continued in many respects to exercize a marked influence on the cultural evolution of the human race.

[16] E. Meyer, *op. cit.*, 3, pp. 189–192. A. T. Olmstead, *op. cit.*, pp. 86–93.
[17] A. T. Olmstead, *op. cit.*, pp. 107–150. Cf. J. V. Prášek, *op. cit.*, 2, pp. 1–141. On the organization of the Persian Empire on the feudal basis, see G. Widengren's thorough study, "Recherches sur le féodalism iranien," *Orientalia Suecana*, 5 (1956), pp. 79–182. The author deals in more detail with the Parthian and Sassanian periods, but he does not omit the Achaemenid period.

The influence of the Persian Empire was particularly notable in the further evolution of political theory. Unfortunately a more detailed study of Persian political philosophy presents many problems, some of which cannot yet be adequately solved. First of all, the genuinely Iranian and Indo-European constituents in the Persian ideas on kingship must be discerned. Then, it would be important to discover to what extent these Iranian ideas were influenced by the political theories which the Persians had found in Assyria, Babylonia, and Egypt. A third important element—the religious element—must be considered. The rise of the Medes and Persians was accompanied by a fascinating religious movement inaugurated by Zoroaster. For the first time in human history there appeared an original religious thinker who preached belief in a god who was not a national deity but a universal being. His Ahura Mazda was to be worshipped, not merely by one nation or one city-state, but by all men. Zoroaster's religious system, although taking some Iranian beliefs as its point of departure, breaks with the religion of the forefathers of the Iranians in many respects. Zoroaster himself shows a very marked hostility toward some of these beliefs. Such a break with the past must have influenced profoundly the Old Iranian ideas on kingship, even though it was not complete. For after the prophet's death most of the Old Iranian ideas were reintroduced into his system. It must also—so it appears at first sight—have limited to a considerable extent Near Eastern influence on the further evolution of Persian political philosophy.

To ascertain the characteristic features of the Old Iranian ideas on kingship is a most difficult task. The problem is intimately connected with the prehistory of the whole Indo-European race and has hardly been touched by anthropologists and other specialists. Lack of historical evidence makes it almost impossible to arrive at a satisfactory and convincing conclusion. On the Iranians the only historical evidence extant derives from some Greek writers, especially Herodotus. Ctesias' work on Persia, written about 300 B.C., has been lost, with the exception of some fragments preserved by Nicolas of Damascus.[18] Of Dinon's work on Persia, dating from

[18] See the short but well outlined critical review of the main Greek sources for Persian history in E. Meyer, *op. cit.*, 3, pp. 128–131. Cf. also Carl

the fourth century B.C. only a few fragments survived, quoted by younger writers, especially Athenaeus. Some useful information is found in Xenophon's works, although in idealized form.

Of Zoroaster's original work very little is left: only some of his hymns, which are found among the Gathas. A few Yashts—not Zoroastrian, but of older date—reflect ancient Iranian beliefs and are of considerable interest for our investigation. The Persian sacred book, the Zend-Avesta, which contains the Gathas and the Yashts together with other sacred writings, is a work which was edited by many contributors from the Achaemenid period down to that of the Sassanian dynasty (third century A.D.). Some evidence is available from archaeological sources, especially statues and effigies of kings. There are inscriptions of the Achaemenid kings, but they are rare and some are too short to be of value for our purpose. It may easily be guessed from their style that the language was not yet fully developed and that the composition of the simplest literary works presented difficulties. It is impossible, therefore, to investigate closely all the details or to attempt to solve this problem. A few observations will, nevertheless, not be out of place.

There is no reliable evidence to show that the early Iranians had regarded their kings and chieftains as beings of a divine nature. So far as is known, there were no Old Iranian myths comparable to similar legends of the Sumerians and Akkadians concerning divine kingship in heaven. The Indo-European Hittites, have been seen to have preserved such a legend, which they had borrowed from the Hurri. The Zend-Avesta contains some passages, scattered throughout both the Gathas (the oldest part of this sacred book) and the earliest of the Yashts (composed after the Iranian tribes had settled on the Eastern Iranian plateau, which lead one

---

Clemen, *Die griechischen und lateinischen Nachrichten über die persische Religion*, Religionsgechichtliche Versuche und Vorarbeiten, 17, Heft 1 (Giessen, 1920/21). For a critical appreciation of Herodotus, Strabo, Theopompus, and Plutarch on Persian religion, consult E. Benveniste, *The Persian Religion According to the Chief Greek Texts* (Paris, 1929), pp. 22–117. On Iranian religious problems, see especially G. Widengren, *Hochgottglaube im Alten Iran* (Uppsala-Leipzig, 1938), and *idem, Stand und Aufgaben der iranischen Religionsgeschichte* (Leiden, 1955). The latter study appeared first in *Numen*, 1 (1954).

to the conclusion that they were governed by chiefs called *kavi*, who also performed certain sacred functions. Among the primitive Aryans, the word itself seems always to have denoted the performance of a religious rite.[19] It signifies a kind of priestly kingship, although priests (*karapan, usig*) are also mentioned by Zoroaster, and these latter names could designate different classes of priests, or perhaps priestly families. All these priestly classes, according to Zoroaster, were hostile to the preaching of his new gospel.

Such a political organization has been shown to have existed in Eastern Iran. But it can be presumed that the chieftains of the Western Iranian tribes exercised similar political and religious functions. The titles of these chieftains were, however, different in eastern and western Iran. It appears that the title *kavi* was of eastern Iranian origin. The western Iranians called their chiefs *chshayathiyas*. The title *dahyupati* (chief of the land) seems to be a Persian word. On the other hand, the official title of the Persian dynasty of the Achaemenids, "King of Kings"—*chshayathiya chshayathiya-nam*, whence the modern Persian royal title *shah* is derived—is of Median origin[20] and was first used by the kings of Media. Thus, the oldest known official royal titles show that to primitive Iranian tradition, insofar as it can be followed in historical documents, a divine character of kingship was unknown.

This seems to be further confirmed by the original Iranian mythical tradition. In the Zend-Avesta we find some legends that recall the Sumerian myths on the origin of kingship, while differing from them in one essential respect: the first kings on earth were not gods, but men regarded as heroes, gifted with immortality, but nevertheless men. According to the old Aryan myth preserved in the oldest part of the Zend-Avesta, the first king was Yima

---

[19] See H. S. Nyberg, *op. cit.*, pp. 48–51. Gathas XXXII, 12, 15; XLIV, 20; XLVI, 11, 14; LI, 14, 16; LIII, 2. A new translation of the Gathas is given by J. Duchesne-Guillemin, *Zoroastre; étude critique avec une traduction commentée des Gâthâ*, Les Dieux et les Hommes, 2 (Paris, 1948.) Cf. also the French translation by C. de Harlez, *Avesta, livre sacré du Zoroastrisme traduit du texte Zend*, Bibliothèque Orientale, 5 (Paris, 1881). An extensive bibliography on the Gathas will be found in the translation made by the Parsi High Priest Dastur Framoze Ardechir Bode, and Piloo Nanavutty, *Songs of Zarathushtra, The Gathas* (London, 1952).

[20] Cf. H. S. Nyberg, *op. cit.*, pp. 57, 344 seq.

In the first part of the sacred book, the Yasna IX, 3–5,[21] Yima is described as "brilliant...the most glorious of men who were sent into the world, one of the men whose sight was like that of the sun...." In this passage he is depicted as the king of the golden age when men did not die and everything prospered.

In another version of the myth,[22] Yima is connected in a rather confused way with the Flood and the end of the world. Acting upon instructions given by Ahura Mazda, Yima constructed a huge *var*, a subterranean fortress, where he gathered together specimens of all animals and plants and men. He governs this sheltered realm intending that when the world has been destroyed, the life which he has preserved will again repopulate the earth.[23]

The Yima-Gayomard myth—different from that of the *Urmensch*—must have been very popular with the Iranians. Zoroaster displayed a pronounced hostility toward it,[24] but did not succeed

---

[21] L. H. Mills, *The Zend-Avesta*, pt. 3, *The Yasna, Visparad, Âfrînagân, Gâhs, and Miscellaneous Fragments*, The Sacred Books of the East, ed. by F. M. Müller, 31 (Oxford, 1887), p. 232. Cf. also Yasht XIX, 31–38, J. Darmesteter, *Zend-Avesta*, pt. 2, p. 293 seq.

[22] Fargad II, J. Darmesteter, *The Zend-Avesta*, pt. 1, *The Vendîdâd*, The Sacred Books of the East, 4 (Oxford, 1880), p. 10 seq. Cf. also H. Lommel, *Die Yäšt's des Awesta*, Quellen der Religionsgeschichte, Gruppe 6, Bd. 15 (Göttingen-Leipzig, 1927), p. 196 seq., trans. on pp. 203–207. See also E. Herzfeld, *Zoroaster and His World*, 1 (Princeton, 1947), pp. 309–339.

[23] The myth evidently confuses the traditions of paradise and of the flood. Cf. E. Herzfeld, *ibid.*, p. 339: "With all its divergencies the myth of the *var* belongs to the motif of the ark of Noah. The Iranian legend, somehow, combined the flood with the expulsion from paradise. The fact that it mixes different motifs proves that it is not independent but had admitted elements from abroad, long before Zoroaster's time."

[24] Yasna XXXII, 8, J. Duchesne-Guillemin, *Zoroastre*, p. 255; L. H. Mills, *op. cit.*, p. 61. The Indians have a similar myth, but the Indian Yama became a god of death. Cf. J. Duchesne-Guillemin, *op. cit.*, p. 30 seq. The problem of the mythical *Urmensch* (first man) was thoroughly investigated by A. Christensen, *Le premier homme et le premier roi dans l'histoire légendaire des iraniens*, Archives Lundall, 14, pt. 1 (Stockholm, 1918). See especially pp. 9–101 on the giant Gayomard and the first human pair, Masyag and Masyanag, legends which he reconstructed from post-Zoroastrian Iranian tradition and which are not mentioned in the Yashts. Cf., however, R. Reitzenstein's and H. H. Schaeder's corrections and additions to Christensen's study, in *Studien zum antiken Synkretismus aus Iran und Griechenland* (Leipzig-Berlin, 1926), pp. 3–37, esp. 205–239: "Der Urmensch in der awestischen und mittelpersischen Überlieferung." H. H. Schaeder corrected and completed Christensen's researches and has shown that the myth of the *Urmensch* Gayomard was not unknown to Zoroaster. In his new edition and translation of some passages of the Iranian version of the Bundahishn, containing the myth of the *Urmensch*, he draws attention to a passage which

in deleting it from the memories of the Iranians. It appeared, as stated, in two versions in the sacred book of his followers after his death.

Yima is said to have been the son of Vivahvant, the sun-god. In spite of this, he is also said to have been the first man. This connection between the sun-god and the first man and king might lead us to a clearer understanding of another characteristic Iranian conception of kingship—"the awful royal glory" or *Hvarena* (*Hvarnah*), with which Iranian kings were believed to be endowed.[25]

What is this kingly glory of Iranian belief? The *Hvarena* is frequently mentioned in the Yashts. The greater part of Yasht

---

is of special interest (p. 230 seq.). According to the myth, when from the seed of the *Urmensch*, brought to death by the evil spirit, a plant had grown bearing the first pair of humans—Mahryag and Mahryanag—it is said that *farr* stood between them. The *farr* is the *Hvarena* (the glory) and it is identified in the text with the soul. See the study on the different traditions concerning Gayomard by Sven S. Hartman, *Gayōmart* (Uppsala, 1953). In numerous more recent Persian and Arab sources published by the author, Gayomard is said to be in possession of the royal *farr*. See the quotations on pp. 117, 161, 187, 196, 197, 211. One of these texts (p. 188) has Gayomard expel the bad spirits with the "divine farr which has been given to him." In some texts *farr* can be identified with the soul and mind.

[25] Cf. F. Dvornik, "Some Characteristic Features of the Old Iranian Political Philosophy," *Essays presented to Sir Jadunath Sarkar*, ed. by H. R. Gupta (Punjab Univ. Hoshiarpur, 1958), 2, pp. 76–85. S. K. Eddy, *The King is Dead* (Lincoln, Neb. 1961), p. 44, speaks of the *fravashi* (soul) of the king, which was venerated by his subjects. However, as even W.W. Tarn, whom he quotes in favor of his opinion, points out ("The Hellenistic Ruler-Cult and the Daemon," *Journal of Hellenic Studies*, 48 [1928], p. 206 seq.), we have no evidence for the belief that the Achaemenid king was supposed to have a *fravashi*, which the Greeks rendered as daemon. On the *fravashi* of the gods, see *infra*, p. 93. It is praised in Yasht XIII, 14–16 where it is said that all life in the world has its source in the *fravashi* of the gods. Eddy, in his chapter on Persian kingship, has nothing to say about the *Hvarena*, in spite of the abundant evidence that the Persians believed in its existence and attributed it to the Achaemenid kings. The author's main object is to show how the Near Eastern nations conquered by Alexander the Great had resisted Hellenization by his successors. It is clear that there were attempts at resistance in political, religious, and cultural matters, but the Hellenizing process was very profound in all fields, more profound than the author is ready to admit. As for the Bahman Yasht and the Oracle of Hystaspes, the documents which in Eddy's view best reveal the anti-Hellenic propaganda in Persia conducted mainly by the Magi, he overstresses their importance as basic documents for his thesis. The Magi cannot be presented as strict adherents to the political theory of the Achaemenid Empire. They had become more and more syncretistic, combining with the worship of Mithra and Anahita elements of Babylonian astrology, Asiatic cult practice, and some principles of Stoicism. See J. Bidez and F. Cumont, *Les Mages hellénisés* (Paris, 1938), 2 vols.

XIX is devoted to the praise of the *Hvarena*, or rather of those who possessed it. The "awful kingly glory" was created by Ahura Mazda.[26] It is depicted as "most conquering, highly working, possessing health, wisdom, and happiness, and is more powerful to destroy than all other creatures."[27] The *Hvarena* belongs first of all to Ahura Mazda as "[through it] Ahura Mazda made the creatures, many and good, many and fair, many and prosperous, many and bright." It belongs also to all the gods, especially to Mithra.[28] It was given by Ahura Mazda to all the heroes and *kavi* of the Iranian myths, all of them being enumerated in Yasht XIX. It was given by Ahura Mazda to all Aryan rulers. It made the ruler a lawful king and how it affected the lawful kings is described in the praise of Vishtaspa, the first *kavi* to give political support to Zoroaster and his new religion.[29] It "clave unto King Vishtaspa, so that he thought according to the Law, spake according to the Law, and did according to the Law; so that he professed that Law, destroying his foes and causing the Daêvas [evil spirits] to retire."

From all these descriptions of the *Hvarena* we can conclude with confidence that the Iranians conceived it as a concrete and shining apparition of light. This impression is conveyed with particular emphasis in the description of Mithra's splendid attire "driving forward from the shining Garonmâna [paradise] in a beautiful chariot...ever swift, adorned with all sorts of ornaments and made of gold." Four white heavenly stallions draw the chariot "on one golden wheel with a full shining axle." It was followed by the blazing spirit of fire and by the kingly glory. Such a description would fit a sun-god. In the same Yasht, Mithra seems to be identified in some way with the sun.[30] It is known that he was worshipped

---

[26] Sirôzah I, 9, 25; II, 9, 25, J. Darmesteter, *Zend-Avesta*, pt. 2, pp. 7, 8, 11, 15, 19. Yasht XII, 4, *ibid.*, p. 170.

[27] Yasht XIX, 9, 10, *ibid.*, p. 289 seq.

[28] Yasht X, *ibid.*, p. 119 seq., repeatedly praises Mithra's "brightness and glory." Behind Mithra's chariot drives Atar, the genius of fire, "all in a blaze, and the awful kingly glory." (Yasht X, 127, *ibid.*, p. 153).

[29] Yasht XIX, 84, *ibid.*, p. 306.

[30] Yasht X, 124, 125, 136, 142, 143, *ibid.*, pp. 152, 155, 157. Mithra was actually god of light and of the warm sunshine. His rays gave life to all living things. As god of light, which penetrates everywhere, he was said to have a thousand eyes and a thousand ears. Cf. G. Widengren, *Hochgottglaube*, p. 94 seq. On Mithra's *Hvarena*, *ibid.*, p. 108 seq.

locally in Iran as sun-god.[31] He was, indeed, a very popular god with the Iranians before Zoroaster. Some communities had regarded Mithra as superior to Varuna, who should be identified with Ahura Mazda.[32] Thus, the special connection of the *Hvarena* with Mithra can be easily understood. Mithra was accompanied by Verethragna who was the bearer of the *Hvarena*. Only after Zoroaster's teaching had been accepted by the communities of Eastern Iran, who worshipped Mithra as their supreme god, was the creation of the *Hvarena* attributed to Zoroaster's Ahura Mazda, and Mithra was then also made a creation of the supreme god.

The connection of the *Hvarena* with the sun-god and the description of its nature as having the appearance of a bright light,[33] are also strongly suggested by the might of Yima, who is represented as son of the sun-god. He was the first man on earth in possession of the *Hvarena*. Later tradition added two predecessors to Yima as king. In the original saga, however, Yima seems to have been regarded as the first and only king of the whole earth.[34] However, even in the new "edition" of the myth Yima was the last of three legendary kings—Haoshyangha, Takhma Urupa, Yima—who had possessed the *Hvarena* in visible form. The visible *Hvarena* entitled them to rule over the whole earth and over all *daēves* (evil spirits) and mortals. It made them free from illness and death.[35] "But when Yima began to find delight in words of falsehood and untruth, the glory was seen to flee away from him in the shape of a bird" (Yasht XIX, 34). From that time onward kings possessed the *Hvarena* only in invisible form and therefore they were not as

[31] H. S. Nyberg, *op. cit.*, pp. 60, 385.

[32] See *ibid.*, p. 99 seq. Cf. also what J. Duchesne-Guillemin, *Zoroastre*, p. 89 seq., says on Mithra. See also *infra*, p. 104 seq.

[33] In Yasht VI, 1, J. Darmesteter, *Zend-Avesta*, pt. 2, p. 86, the glory seems to be symbolized as the shining of the sun, and in Yasht VII, 3, *ibid.*, p. 90, as a radiance from the moon and stars and sometimes from the sun. However, it is not clear from the translation what kind of "glory" is meant in these passages.

[34] This was shown again more recently by E. Herzfeld, *op. cit.*, pp. 309–339, esp. p. 324.

[35] This is J. Hertel's interpretation, *Die awestischen Herrschafts- und Siegesfeuer* (Leipzig, 1931), Abhandl. d. Phil.-hist. Kl. d. Sächs. Akademie der Wiss., 41, no. 6, pp. 3 seq., 97, of the description of the *Hvarena* in Yasht XIX. On page 5, he interprets the punishment of Yima as being that he was degraded to the status of a nomad. Cf. also H. Lommel, *Die Yäšt's*, p. 173.

powerful against the *daëves* and mortals as the first legendary kings.

Sometimes the *Hvarena* was believed to become visible again. In this connection Xenophon's panegyric on Cyrus may be recalled.[36] In describing the war that Cyrus waged against the Assyrians, he writes: "As they [the Persians] proceeded night came on, and it is said that a light from heaven shone forth upon Cyrus and his army, so that they were all filled with awe at the miracle, but with courage to meet the enemy." The legendary report can be interpreted only in connection with the *Hvarena*.

Another similar report on Cyrus is preserved by Cicero[37] from Dinon's Persian annals of dreams: "Once upon a time Cyrus dreamed that the sun was at his feet. Three times, so Dinon writes, he vainly tried to grasp it and each time it turned away, escaped him and finally disappeared. He was told by the magi, who are classed as wise and learned men among the Persians, that his grasping for the sun three times portended that he would reign for thirty years." Interpreted in the above connection, it would mean that Cyrus would be in possession of the *Hvarena* for thirty years. The *Hvarena* is believed to have appeared in this case in visible form and is here again brought into closest connection with the sun.

The notion of the *Hvarena* is thus an old Aryan conception and seems to have been common to other Aryan nations. One kind of *Hvarena* was mentioned by Herodotus[38] when he recorded that all of the kings of the Scythians, of Aryan race, were successors of Targitaus, the founder of Scythian kingship, whose son Colaxaïs, although the youngest of three brothers, was the only one to capture the glowing gold which represented the kingship—again a concrete appearance of light—which came to him from heaven.

There is some evidence that a similar idea was not unfamiliar to the primitive Romans. Livy, at least, recounts a very curious story of the manner in which Servius Tullius, son of a slain enemy living in the house of King Tarquinius Priscus, was predestined to

[36] *Cyropaedia*, IV, 2, 15, ed. by W. Miller (Loeb, 1914), I, p. 330.
[37] *De divinatione*, I, 23, ed. by W. Armistead Falconer (Loeb, 1938), p. 274.
[38] *Historiae*, IV, 5–6, ed. by A. D. Godley (Loeb, 1938), 2, p. 202 seq.

become a king by the apparition of flames round his head when he was asleep.[39]

It is possible that this notion originated in the very remote past of the Indo-European race. The Iranians were, however, the only Indo-Europeans who had developed it into a definite system. They regarded the *Hvarena* as a strictly national distinction. Its Aryan character is often stressed in the Yashts. "The Turanian usurper Frangrasyan" prayed in vain for the *Hvarena*, "that glory...that belongs to the Aryan people."[40] Three times he "rushed down to the sea Vouru-Kasha [Aral Sea] ...wishing to seize the Glory that belongs to the Aryan nations, born and unborn, and to the holy Zarathustra. But the Glory escaped, the Glory fled away, the Glory changed its seat" and every time a new arm was produced in the sea.[41] The *Hvarena* was defended by Frangrasyan's principal opponent, the *Kavi* Haosravah (Husravah)—"he who united the Aryan nations into one kingdom." It was he who killed the Turanian who dared to attempt the usurpation of the *Hvarena*, which belongs only to the legitimate kings of the Aryan race.[42]

Another place where the *Hvarena* is said to have had a special seat is where the River Haetumant (Helmand) meets the Kansaoya Sea (Hamun), on the frontier between Iran and Afghanistan.[43] This region seems also to have been governed by a mighty

[39] Livy, *Roman History*, I, 39, ed. by B. O. Foster (Loeb, 1939), 1, p. 138: "At this time there happened in the house of the king a portent which was remarkable alike in its manifestation and in its outcome. The story is that while a child named Servius Tullius lay sleeping, his head burst into flames in the sight of many. The general outcry which so great a miracle called forth brought the king and queen to the place. One of the servants fetched water to quench the fire, but was checked by the queen, who stilled the uproar, and commanded that the boy should not be disturbed until he awoke of himself. Soon afterwards sleep left him, and with it disappeared the flames." The Queen and the King saw in the phenomenon a sure sign that the orphan child was predestined to kingship.

[40] Yasht V, 41, 42, J. Darmesteter, *Zend-Avesta*, pt. 2, pp. 64, 65.

[41] Yasht XIX, 56 seq., *ibid.*, pp. 300–302.

[42] Yasht IX, 17–22, *ibid.*, p. 114 seq. It is quite possible that, as H. S. Nyberg suggests (*op. cit.*, p. 258), the Iranians on the Aral Sea used to bury their dead kings (*kavi*) on an island in the sea. This would explain the location of the *Hvarena* in the sea. E. Herzfeld (*op. cit.*, p. 176) suggests that this connection of the *Hvarena* and water could be explained by a natural phenomenon—naphtha rising from the bottom of the sea being set ablaze. In any case, the whole story, in its legendary garb, reflects an episode from the early history of the Eastern Iranians.

[43] Yasht XIX, 66–8, Darmesteter, *Zend-Avesta*, pt. 2, p. 302.

Aryan dynasty in pre-Zoroastrian days. The *Hvarena* is said to be located there in a mountain "surrounded by waters, that run from the mountain." This probably means the residence or the burial place of the kavis.

It is not without interest to note that the two seas are connected in later Zoroastrian tradition with Zoroaster's eschatology. It is legitimate to interpret this, with H. S. Nyberg,[44] as an indication that, when Zoroastrianism had penetrated deep into the regions where the cult of Mithra and his *Hvarena* predominated, the tendency arose to bring the idea of *Hvarena*, so firmly rooted in Iranian minds, into the closest possible connection with Zoroastrianism.

Is it then possible to explain how the Iranians imagined *Hvarena* to be a concrete manifestation of light? This notion is a natural and logical deduction from the old Aryan doctrine on fire and light.[45] According to this doctrine, fire or light was the main element of the world and of life. Heavenly fire surrounds and penetrates the whole world. All goodness, beauty, truth, and might are nought but manifestations of fire. The incarnation of the heavenly fire or heavenly light is the god of heaven, who is, at the same time, the incarnation of supreme wisdom and might and, as storm god also, the giver of rain and of fire. All natural phenomena were thus regarded as a kind of incarnation of fire. In living beings it is again the interior fire or light residing in the heart which is the substance of strength, health, might, and wisdom. All abilities and capacities of the soul and body were thus, according to this doctrine, radiations of fire—thought, resolution, desire, wisdom, cleverness, strength, etc. The fire or light was the cause of seeing, of both spiritual and physical sight, the latter being the radiation of heart-fire through the eyes. *Hvarena* was, thus, in connection with this

[44] *Op. cit.*, p. 305. The objection raised against Nyberg's interpretation by E. Herzfeld (*op. cit.*, p. 178) seems unconvincing.

[45] For more detailed information, see J. Hertel, *Die arische Feuerlehre*, Indo-iranische Quellen und Forschungen, Heft 6 (Leipzig, 1925). A. Christensen in "Die Iranier," in *Kulturgeschichte des alten Orients*, Abt. 3, Lief. 2, Handbuch der Altertumswissenschaft, ed. by I. Müller and W. Otto (Munich, 1933), p. 221. On the further development of this doctrine, cf. A. Pagliaro, "Notes on the History of the Sacred Fires of Zoroastrianism," *Oriental Studies in Honour of Cursetji Erachji Pavry*, ed. by Jal Dastur Cursetji Pavry (London, 1933), pp. 373–385.

belief, another fire radiation, a source of might, victorious strength, and wisdom, which should adorn the king chosen by Ahura Mazda, the incarnation of heavenly fire.

Some elements in this doctrine may have been common to all Indo-Europeans in their remote prehistoric past.[46] It is at least remarkable that among most Indo-European nations, the supreme gods were, at one and the same time, a kind of incarnation of heavenly light, wisdom, and might, and also gods of storm and lightning. The opposite of this world of light, the world of darkness, whence came all evil spirits—incarnations of things inimical to Man—was also part of a common Indo-European belief. But the Indo-Iranians succeeded in developing this belief into a closely knit religious pattern. The Iranians played the leading role in this evolution. Zoroaster accepted the old doctrine concerning the heavenly fire and the inner fire in men's hearts, limiting himself in his reform to depriving it of all naturalistic attributes. So it happened that the *Hvarena*, or kingly glory, became such an important notion in Iranian ideas on kingship.

There is, however, another problem to be discussed. The *Hvarena* was often represented in other concrete forms, such as animals or elements. It has already been mentioned that the *Hvarena* was said to have resided in the Aral and Hamun Seas and in the River Helmand. Here it is brought into intimate contact with a mighty natural element—water. In another Yasht[47] the *Hvarena* cleaved "unto the Yima, the good shepherd, for a long time.... But when he began to find delight in words of falsehood and untruth, the Glory was seen to flee away from him in the shape of a bird."

In other passages of the Zend-Avesta, the *Hvarena* is referred to in connection with the god Verethragna, who was said to have appeared in different animal forms. In the Mithra Yasht[48] he is pictured as running before Mithra's chariot in the shape of a boar, "a sharp-toothed he-boar, a sharp-jawed boar, that kills at one stroke, pursuing wrathfully with a dripping face; strong, with iron

---

[46] Cf. J. Hertel, *Die arische Feuerlehre*, p. 8 seq.
[47] Yasht XIX, 31–8, J. Darmesteter, *Zend-Avesta*, pt. 2, pp. 293–295.
[48] Yasht X, 70–2, *ibid.*, p. 137.

feet, iron fore-paws, iron weapons, an iron tail, and iron jaws." A whole Yasht, the fourteenth, is devoted to this god. There he is described[49] as running first "in the shape of a strong, beautiful wind, made by Mazda; he bore the good Glory; the Glory made by Mazda." Afterward, he is pictured running in the shape of "a beautiful bull with yellow ears and golden horns"; then as "a beautiful, white horse, with yellow ears and a golden caparison." Then he is a "burden-bearing camel, sharp-toothed, swift." In his manhood he is pictured as a boar, a falcon (eagle?), a wild ram, a fighting buck, a youth at his full strength.[50] And always it is said that in all the shapes in which he appeared he was the bearer of the Glory, made by Mazda—the *Hvarena*.

In this connection two legendary stories transmitted by later Iranian tradition deserve to be recalled, for they seem to presume a connection between the *Hvarena* in the shape of an animal and the abstract idea of kingship. One story was told by Dinon (second half of fourth century B.C.) in his "Persia," now lost. The story was preserved by Athenaeus[51] and runs thus: Once, when Cyrus, who was at the time at the court of Astyages of Media, had gone with

---

[49] Yasht XIV, *ibid.*, p. 231 seq.

[50] For the translation and interpretation of Verethragna's animal incarnations, see E. Benveniste and L. Renou, *Vr̥tra et Vr̥θragna, étude de mythologie indo-iranienne*, Cahiers de la Société Asiatique, 3 (Paris, 1934), pp. 28–40. E. Benveniste's suggestion (*ibid.*, p. 34) that the bird incarnation should be interpreted as that of a falcon and not a raven (as translated by Darmesteter, *Zend-Avesta*, pt. 2, p. 236) is preferable. The description in the Yasht of the bird's characteristics fits the falcon better than the raven. Verses 19–21 read: "swiftest of all birds, the lightest of the flying creatures... overtaking the flight of an arrow.... He grazes the hidden paths of the mountains...the tops of the mountains...the summits of the trees, listening to the voices of the birds." J. Hertel, *Die awestischen Herrschafts- und Siegesfeuer*, p. 43, interprets the name of the bird *varegna*) as "killer of enemy"—*Feindetötung*. He therefore prefers to see this bird as an eagle ("Der Feindetötungsvogel ist der Adler"). Here he follows H. Lommel who translates "Adlervogel" (*Die Yäšt's*, p. 187). Let us add that Verethragna is called "bearer of the Glory made by Mazda" also in Fargard XIX, 37, Darmesteter, *Zend-Avesta*, pt. 1, p. 215. Cf. the remarks of E. Benveniste concerning the translation of this passage in the book quoted *supra*, p. 49 seq. According to him, the words have to be taken in their concrete sense. Verethragna is thus the flagbearer of the gods. The *Hvarena* is the flag. Verethragna "créé par les Ahuras [gods] pour incarner leur pouvoir offensif, les précède dans le combat en portant l'emblème du *ch'arnah* [*Hvarena*] qui lui sert d'étendard."

[51] *Deipnosophistae*, XIV, 633 d, e, ed. by Ch. B. Gulick (Loeb, 1937), 6, p. 416 seq.

his host's permission to visit his native Persia, the Median King prepared a great banquet for his nobles. During the feasting one of the singers who was entertaining the guests uttered a kind of prophecy, "how that a mighty beast had been let loose in the swamp, bolder than a wild boar; which beast if it got the mastery of the regions round it, would soon contend against a multitude without difficulty. And when Astyages asked, 'What beast?' he replied, 'Cyrus the Persian.'" The prophecy confirmed Astyages' suspicions concerning Cyrus and he tried vainly to summon him back from Persia. This story was probably invented after Cyrus had overthrown Astyages. The reference to Cyrus as a wild boar is very reminiscent of the boar incarnation of Verethragna.[52] Because this god was regarded as the bearer of the *Hvarena*, the likening of Cyrus, the future king of Persia, to a wild boar seems significant.

Another legendary story is told in a mediaeval Persian historical romance[53] describing the struggle waged by Ardashir and Ardavan. The story relates that a buck ran with Ardashir while he was riding his horse and attacking his adversary. When Ardashir had the buck lifted up to him, it became clear to all that he had won the fight and was the new king. Here again the connection between the *Hvarena* and the animal incarnation of Verethragna, the *Hvarena's* chief bearer, is clear. It is true that this legend is recalled in a late tradition; but this very circumstance shows that such conceptions of *Hvarena* must have been very deeply rooted in Persia.

The incarnation of the bearer of the *Hvarena* in so many animal forms seems at first sight to indicate a connection with prehistoric Iranian animism. The animal shapes of the divine bearer of the kingly glory also vaguely recall the Egyptian royal standards bearing emblems of animals. It is not impossible that anthropologists and prehistorians will have a word to say in explaining such phenomena. A historian can interpret only facts and occurrences for which there is some kind of historical evidence.

The evidence available on the Persian concept of *Hvarena* seems to indicate that the *Hvarena* was, at least in historical times,

---

[52] Cf. E. Benveniste and L. Renou, *op. cit.*, p. 68 seq.

[53] *Kārnāmak i Artaxšēr i Pāpakān*, chap. 3, quoted by H. S. Nyberg, *op. cit.*, p. 72. Cf. G. Widengren, *Hochgottglaube*, p. 152 seq.

regarded by the Persians as a manifestation of might and strength. This is indicated quite clearly in Yasht X, 16,[54] where *Hvarena* is used as a synonym for *kshathra* (might, sovereignty). Mithra is said to grant both *Hvarena* and *kshathra*. This idea is expressed in broader terms in Yasht XIII,[55] where the *Hvarena* is coupled with the word *raya* (power, might) and it is pointed out that all life and all activity in the world have their source in the "might and glory" of the *fravashi*—the inner power of the gods:

> Through their might and glory the waters run and flow forward from the never-failing springs...the plants grow up from the earth...the winds blow...the females conceive offspring... become blessed with children. Through their might and glory a man is born who is a chief in assemblies and meetings, who listens well to the [holy] words, whom Wisdom holds dear.... Through their might and glory the sun goes his way...the moon goes her way...the stars go their way.

Ahura Mazda created this might and glory and himself possesses it in full. The gods possess it because they are gods; but this might, glory, and strength are also given by Ahura Mazda to the heroes of Persian myths and to kings.

How could the extent of this might be described and measured? Were there not on all sides of man powerful animals boasting a measure of strength and qualities of might that had been denied to ordinary mortal man? The wild boar, the horse, the camel, the buck, the falcon or eagle, the bull, and the ram were admired, liked, and feared by primitive man because of these very qualities which he lacked in like measure. Could they not be used as illustrations and incarnations of the might and glory which were possessed by gods and which should also adorn the king chosen by

---

[54] Darmesteter, *Zend-Avesta*, pt. 2, p. 123. But see the interpretation given by H. S. Nyberg, *op. cit.*, p. 72. Darmesteter's translation is not clear on this point. On *kshathra*, see *infra*, p. 97.

[55] Yasht XIII, 14–16, Darmesteter, *op. cit.*, 2, p. 183 seq. See the interpretation of the passage given by H. Güntert, *Der arische Weltkönig und Heiland* (Halle, 1923), p. 215. Darmesteter's translation—"brightness and glory"—is changed by Güntert to "might and glory." The general context favors this alternative. All the deeds enumerated in the verses are notable exhibitions of might.

Ahura Mazda?[56] There were also some mighty elements, benevolent yet also terrible to man—wind and water.[57] To man both represent supernatural strength, and both illustrate for him the greatness of the might and glory of *Hvarena*.[58]

All the qualities admired in the animals mentioned and those that express a supernatural might and strength should be properties of gods in even greater measure. Verethragna, "the breaker of resistance"—for such is the meaning of his name—was created by Ahura Mazda to represent and embody this might and glory—

[56] In Yasht XIX, 68 (Darmesteter, *op. cit.*, 2, p. 302 seq.) is a passage which seems to confirm this interpretation. The effects of the *Hvarena* are described as follows: "And there comes with him a horse's strength, there comes with him a camel's strength, there comes with him a man's strength, there comes with him the kingly Glory." Cf. H. Lommel, *Die Yäšt's*, p. 183.

[57] The *Hvarena* residing in the Aral and Hamun seas and in the River Helmand. See *supra*, p. 88.

[58] It should be stressed that the primitive Slavs had many religious conceptions similar to those of the Iranians. The Slavic word to designate God—Bogŭ (wealth and giver of wealth)—corresponds to the Iranian Baga. They followed the Iranians in rejecting the common Indo-European symbolic name Diēus (worshipped sky) for the divinity, substituting the term "cloud" for "sky," and also used the equivalent form Deiwas (Daeva) to designate not God, but the demoniac being who was hostile to God. It is particularly interesting to note that the Slavic deity Svarogŭ has many features that connect him with the Iranian Verethragna. Like this Iranian deity, Svarogŭ "was also credited with being able to assume different animal and bird forms—as a falcon, a golden horned aurochs, a horse, a bear, or even as a whirlwind. The Slavs also connected Svarogŭ with fire, as the Iranians did with Verethragna. Svarogŭ like Verethragna was a warrior god, a giver of virility and strength. This virility—Slavic Jendrŭ, which is reminiscent of the Indian Indra—had various manifestations, a fact which the Polabian Slavs symbolized by providing their idols with several heads.... Like the Iranian Verethragna, the Slavic Svarogŭ is represented as generating the heat and light of the sun, called Chŭrsŭ Dažĭ-bogŭ by the Slavs...Chŭrsŭ (Chors) is obviously borrowed from the Iranian expression Churšid, designating the personified sun." Cf. F. Dvornik, *The Slavs, Their Early History and Civilization* (Boston, 1956), p. 49. The cult of Anahita seems also to have found imitation among the Slavs, and most of the Slavic words concerning worship and religious objects are borrowed from the Iranians. It is not yet possible to ascertain at what period the Slavs had been so profoundly influenced by Iranian religious beliefs. Some expressions are found too in the Baltic languages. This indicates that this borrowing must have occurred in prehistoric times when the Slavs and Balts formed one linguistic group. Other words and beliefs appear to have been borrowed from the Iranians at a much later period. If it were possible to determine more exactly the dates of this borrowing, it would be of great help to specialists in their study of Iranian religion. For more details and bibliography, see R. Jakobson, "Slavic Mythology," in Funk and Wagnalls' *Standard Dictionary of Folklore*, 2 (New York, 1950), p. 1025 seq.

the *Hvarena*, which was the standard of the gods. Verethragna was its bearer.

But all heroes should also be endowed with similar qualities. They could perform their deeds of valor and daring only because Ahura Mazda gave them the *Hvarena*. Therefore, they alone became "breakers of resistance" and Verethragna, the bearer of the *Hvarena* was embodied in them and his name became a racial name for the race of heroes.[59]

The kings were the successors of the heroes. They were also "breakers of resistance" in so far as they defended their people when they were attacked and continuously fought for their subjects' welfare. The bearer of the *Hvarena*, Verethragna, could thus be regarded as the personification of the reigning dynasty, of its dead and living kings. In fact, he was regarded as the one who assured the succession, because it was he who gave kings their sexual reproductive power to beget sons. It can be reasonably suggested, therefore, that primitively the chieftains and the tribal kings might have been called "Verethragnas."

In spite of this evolution, the traces of which can be followed in historic times in early Iran, no evidence is available that Verethragna was regarded by the Iranians as a primitive king—the *Urkönig*—who might have survived in mythical tradition as a god. This would have been a logical evolution among many other

[59] This is suggested by H. S. Nyberg, *op. cit.*, p. 79. The pages (69–81) which he devotes to Verethragna are most interesting, and his deductions, also partly supported by Benveniste's and Renou's researches, seem as firmly established as is possible in the present state of Iranian studies.

G. Widengren, too, accepted Nyberg's deductions in his *Hochgottglaube*, p. 371 seq. There is great merit in Widengren's promotion of Iranian studies. His work on Iranian kingship is not yet published, but he disclosed his main ideas on this subject in his *Hochgottglaube*, p. 352 seq., in his *Stand und Aufgaben der iranischen Religionsgeschichte*, p. 80 seq., and in his study "The Sacral Kingship of Iran," *The Sacral Kingship* (Leiden, 1959), pp. 242–257. He seems, however, to stress too strongly the divine character of the Iranian rulers. The position of the Iranian king appears "übermenschlich" rather than "göttlich"—superhuman rather than divine, and the attribution of this character to the king can be sufficiently explained by the gift of kingly glory and strength, the *Hvarena*, by the supreme god, first Ahura Mazda and later Mithra. The repeated confessions of the Achaemenid kings that they owed everything, the kingship, their righteous rule, and their victories, to Ahura Mazda seem to exclude the idea that they attributed to themselves a divine character. Perhaps further discoveries will help the specialists to give a more definite answer to this problem.

nations. Everything seems to point to the fact that Verethragna was a personification of the might and strength with which the gods, heroes, and rulers were supposed to have been endowed by Ahura Mazda. The *Hvarena*—might and strength—measured and illustrated by animal strength which was superhuman in man, and appearing as a concrete manifestation of light, should transform a king into a living hero, a new Verethragna, "breaker of resistance."

All this, however, does not mean that the king was a god, a visible incarnation of "god on earth." The *Hvarena*, given to him by Ahura Mazda, lifted the king above the average man, made him quite distinct from other mortals; but, although he was promoted to the race of heroes, the king did not become a god and was not regarded as such. Here lies the great difference between the Egyptian and old Akkadian conceptions and the Persian idea on the relation of kings to gods.

In the light of these considerations, it follows that the Persian conception of the god Verethragna is different from that concerning gods held by other Oriental nations. It approaches, in one way, a personification of an abstract notion. This appears strange at first; but such an interpretation corresponds to the Iranian conception of gods, which again differs from that of the Greeks. The gods of the Iranians were not anthropomorphic, as were those of the Greeks and the Sumerians. The Iranians were able to imagine gods in a more abstract form, as divinities, divine powers, divine centers of might and strength.[60] This is best illustrated by the fact that the primitive Iranians did not know any temples or altars. This considerably astonished the Greeks, as Herodotus remarks.[61]

Furthermore, in trying to discern the true meaning and concept of the *Hvarena*, it should not be forgotten that the Iranians had other notions, fundamentally abstract but expressed in an in-

[60] H. S. Nyberg, *op. cit.*, p. 369.
[61] *Historiae*, I, 131, ed. by A. G. Godley (Loeb, 1931), 1, p. 170: "It is not their custom to make and set up statues and temples and altars, but those who make such, they deem foolish, as I suppose, because they never believed the gods, as do the Greeks, to be in the likeness of men; but they call the whole circle of heaven Zeus, and to him they offer sacrifice on the highest peaks of the mountains; they sacrifice also to the sun and moon and earth and fire and water and winds."

dividualistic, concrete, and personified way. The main notion of this kind, common also to the Indians, was that of *Rta* or *Arta*.[62] This idea signified the right order—that is, cosmic order ruling the course of the stars and of nature, liturgical order—controlling the proper performance of prayer and sacrifice, and moral order governing the lives of men in the way of truth and rectitude. Although Arta was an abstract notion, it was also conceived in a concrete manner. As far as concerns the cosmic order, the *Arta* was located in the firmament. The Aurora at dawn was said to have awakened and to be leaving the seat of the *Arta*. It was imagined that *Arta* had its own charioteers, its own craft, its own cows, its own milk, as the other gods had. The place of sacrifice was also called the Seat of *Arta*.

The *Arta* was often associated with the sacrificial fire and, of course, with the principal gods—Mithra and, especially, Varuna, who was said to have created the *Arta*, because he had cleared the way for the sun and the moon and had made the nights to succeed the days. It was he who was said to be responsible for punishing evildoers. Zoroaster took over this ancient Indo-Iranian idea and called Ahura Mazda "Father of the *Arta*."

In spite of this personification of the *Arta*, of its being translated into a concrete form and of its intimate connection with gods, the *Arta* remained an abstract notion, expressed in the best way the primitive Iranians could conceive. A similar development can be observed concerning the Iranian notions of *sarvatah* (salvation, health, physical integrity), *amrta* (immortality), and *kshathra* (power, sovereignty, warlike valor).[63]

When this particular belief of the ancient Iranians is taken into consideration, the interpretation of Verethragna as an incarnation, concrete expression, or personification of the *Hvarena*, the might

[62] See the indication of sources and main bibliography concerning *Arta* in J. Duchesne-Guillemin's *Zoroastre*, pp. 58–68.

[63] J. Duchesne-Guillemin, *ibid.*, pp. 68–74. The author draws attention to some Assyro-Babylonian and Egyptian divinized and personified abstractions. The most striking is the Roman divinized abstraction of *Fides* and *Salus* (*ibid.*, pp. 67, 70) which seem to point to a common Indo-European root. Cf. also what H. S. Nyberg, *op. cit.*, pp. 330, 352, 368, has to say on the old Iranian notion of *Arta. Ibid.*, p. 352, interesting interpretation of the name of Artaphrenes, which should be Artaphernes (Arta-farnah), "whose *Hvarena* (*farnah*—a West Iranian version of *Hvarena*) comes from *Arta*."

and strength that resides in divine beings and that is reflected in the heroes and kings to whom Ahura Mazda gave it, becomes more comprehensible and more plausible.[64]

We have thus found that the conception of the kingly glory was an old Iranian notion and was not invented by Zoroaster or his followers. The prophet limited himself to adapting this ancient idea to his religious system, brushing aside Mithra and Verethragna, who were so intimately associated with the *Hvarena*, deeming it to be a creation of Ahura Mazda. But, as we have seen, after Zoroaster's death, his disciples thought it necessary to re-introduce Mithra and Verethragna into their master's religious teaching and to re-affirm the close relationship which they bore to the *Hvarena*.

Although Zoroastrianism is not responsible for the creation of the *Hvarena*, it seems that it made a contribution to the further evolution of the conception. Possession of the *Hvarena* is not only attributed to Zoroaster by his disciples, but—according to some passages in the Zend-Avesta—it is also given to priests. It cannot, however, be "forcibly seized." One can obtain it only by leading a virtuous and righteous life. This seems to be the meaning of the passage in Sirozah I, 25,[65] while the same idea is even more fully expressed in Yasht XIX, 53, 54:[66]

> "And whosoever of you, O men (thus said Ahura Mazda) O holy Zarathustra, shall seize that glory that cannot be forcibly seized, he has the gifts of an Athravan [priest]; whosoever shall long for the illumination of knowledge, he has the gifts of an Athravan; whosoever shall long for the fullness of knowledge, he has the gifts of an Athravan. And riches will cleave unto him giving him full welfare, holding a shield before him, powerful, rich of cattle and garments; and Victory will cleave unto

---

[64] It appears that Verethragna had, as his counterpart in West Iran, a god known as Zurvan. According to H. S. Nyberg's research (*loc. cit.*, p. 383) "Zurvān ist in gewisser Hinsicht die eigentliche Entsprechung des Westens zur Vĕrĕthragna-Vorstellung des Ostens; er ist der eigentliche Chwarĕnah-Träger des Westens." On the later history of Zoroastrianism and Zurvan, see the study by R. C. Zaehner, *Zurvan, a Zoroastrian Dilemma* (Oxford, 1955).

[65] J. Darmesteter, *op. cit.*, 2, 23, p. 11.

[66] *Ibid.*, p. 299.

him, day after day; and likewise Strength that smites more than a year. Attended by that Victory, he will conquer the havocking hordes; attended by that Victory, he will conquer all those who hate him.

This praise of the priestly *Hvarena* shows an interesting evolution toward a kind of democratization of the kingly glory akin to that seen in Egypt with the Ka, after the introduction of Sa-Re kingship. Zoroastrian priests started the same process which was, centuries afterward, to be observed in the Roman Christian Empire, when the halo—an imitation of the Persian *Hvarena*—distinguishing emperors was given to bishops and Saints who had deserved it by their virtuous and righteous lives.[67]

What were the consequences of the belief in the kingly glory and might as they affected the position of kings? First of all, as bearers of the *Hvarena*, the kings were expected to behave in all respects just as the more or less abstractly conceived Verethragna and his incarnations behaved. They were imagined to be, for example, killers of dragons, as were the great Persian heroes of mythical tradition—especially the great Keresaspa, who cooked his dinner on the dragon's skin.[68] This explains why the Persian kings were represented as killers of dragons and wild beasts.[69] If the heroes were regarded as giants, then the king could call himself Giant of Giants—*gigas gigantum*. This title is known from the Sassanid period, but may well have been already in use by the Achaemenids.[70] It corresponds to the conception of the king as the new Verethragna—"breaker of resistance." There are indications

[67] One can see from the above that the conception of the *Hvarena* remained rather vague and was never formulated in straightforward and unmistakable terms. Cf. in this respect H. Lommel, *Die Yäšt's*, pp. 168–175. Cf. also A. Christensen, *Les gestes des rois dans les traditions de l'Iran antique* (Paris, 1936), for his account of the royal glory in ancient Iranian literature.

[68] Yasht XIX, 40, Darmesteter, *op. cit.*, 2, p. 295.

[69] F. von Sarre, *Die Kunst des alten Persien* (Berlin, 1925), p. 13, figs. 16, 17: reliefs from Persepolis representing Darius as the killer of a monster and a lion. A. Gayet, *L'art persan* (Paris, 1895), p. 69, representations of kings fighting with griffins. *Ibid.*, p. 68, Darius' seal representing the King chasing lions, with the symbol of Ahura Mazda above his head. A. Alföldi, "Der iranische Weltriese auf archäologischen Denkmälern," *Jahrbuch der Schweitzerischen Gesellschaft für Urgeschichte*, 40 (1949–50), p. 24.

[70] A. Alföldi, *op. cit.*, p. 24.

that the old Persian rulers wore headdresses in the shape of a horse's head. Known representations of Achaemenid and Sassanian kings, however, do not bear out this supposition. So far only the heir apparent of the Sassanian King Varahran II is portrayed on his father's coins with such a headgear.[71] The King himself wears a crown. On the Sassanian relief of Nagsh-i-Rustam, a companion of King Narse also wears such a helmet,[72] and on the horse's head there is a pearl, or a fruit of the holy soma plant. The East Iranian King Napki is represented with a similar head-covering on his coins.[73]

Should this be explained as a reminiscence of the *Urmensch* and *Urkönig* of whom the Iranian kings were supposed to be an imitation or reincarnation?[74] And should it also be associated with Verethragna's equine incarnation? This is possible, although it must not be forgotten that the horse was an animal which had been domesticated by the Indo-Europeans and was in high esteem among all nomadic peoples, and we should, therefore, hesitate to attribute too much importance to this feature. The popularity of the horse among all Indo-Europeans in their prehistoric Asiatic seats would also explain why such headdresses were found also among other Indo-European peoples, above all, the Romans. The fact that the supernatural greatness of the kingly glory, the *Hvarena*, was measured by the energy and other qualities possessed by some animals should perhaps suffice to explain why the Iranians depicted their kings wearing headdresses representing such animals.

It is clear from the above that the possession of the *Hvarena*, a gift of the supreme god, made the Iranian kings superior beings in the eyes of their subjects. They were exalted above all other human beings and were the representatives on earth of the supreme god. The strength and might of Verethragna was in them and made them awe inspiring and terrible to behold, even for their own people. The Iranian kings were fully conscious of the high position they occupied among their subjects, as can be seen from the few

[71] F. Sarre and E. Herzfeld, *Iranische Felsreliefs* (Berlin, 1910), p. 72 (21). Cf. *ibid.*, p. 24 on Persian headwear.
[72] *Ibid.*, p. 85 (39).
[73] A. Alföldi, *op. cit.*, pp. 21 (no. 8), 34, note 106.
[74] *Ibid.*, p. 30.

inscriptions from the oldest Iranian period. No royal inscriptions from Media are extant, although the *Hvarena* (the *Farnah* in the Median form[75]) was also venerated by the Magi, the priestly class of old Media. When the Magi had accepted Zoroaster's teaching they became most zealous and fervent proselytizers. They adapted Zoroaster's teaching to the old Median faith, but the doctrine of the *Hvarena* (the *Farnah*) they left untouched.

From the short reign of Ariaramnes (*ca.* 640–615 B.C.), brother of Cyrus I (*ca.* 640–600), a gold tablet survives, on which the King boasted that he was a "Great King, King of kings, King of the land Parsa." The great god Ahura Mazda had given him the land Parsa, which possessed good horses and virile men. From this tablet it can be learned also that the king of Parsa before him was his father Teispes.[76]

From Cyrus II's reign only one longer inscription survives. It is written by Babylonian scribes in the royal court style of Babylon. Cyrus appears as a Babylonian ruler, to whom Marduk—whose hand he had held in his temple—had given the investiture of Babylonia. This inscription is important for an understanding of Cyrus' policy in general. The Persian King united the newly conquered land with his own Persia in a kind of personal union, a policy which was to be followed later in the Middle East by other rulers including Alexander the Great. This inscription will be discussed later in an attempt to determine to what extent Babylonian ideas on kingship had influenced the Persians.

We have to go as far as the reign of Darius to find inscriptions revealing old Persian ideas on kingship. The most informative is that upon the rock of the King's tomb in Naqsh-i-Rustam.[77] It starts with an eloquent eulogy of Ahura Mazda:

[75] H. S. Nyberg, *op. cit.*, p. 342. Cf. *supra*, p. 97.
[76] E. Herzfeld, "Āriyāramna, König der Könige," *Archäologische Mitteilungen aus Iran*, 2 (Berlin, 1930), pp. 113–127, Cf. also his other note concerning this inscription, "Xerxes' Charta von Persepolis," *ibid.*, 4 (1932), pp. 132–139. See *infra*, p. 122. Cf. what O. G. von Wesendonk, "The Title 'King of Kings'," *Oriental Studies in Honour of Cursetji Erachji Pavry*, pp. 488–490, says on the Assyrian origin of this title. See also R. N. Frye, "The Charisma of Kingship in Ancient Iran," *Iranica antiqua*, 4 (1964), pp. 36–54.
[77] A new edition and German translation in E. Herzfeld, *Altpersische Inschriften = Archäologische Mitteilungen aus Iran*, Ergänzungsband, 1 (Berlin, 1938), p. 4 seq.

A great god is Ahura Mazda who created this work superior over all, which became visible, who created peace for the man, who invested King Darius with (divine) wisdom and well being.

Says Darius the King: Through Ahura Mazda's will I am of such character: I love what is right, I hate what is not right. It is not my pleasure (to see) that the lower man should suffer injustice because of the higher man. What is right I love. The man who decides for the lie I hate. I am not vengeful and whoever is angry with me I restrain and I strictly dominate my own passion. Whoever tries to do well, I reward him according to his merit. Whoever has injured, I punish according to what he has injured. It is not my pleasure (to see) that injustice be done, neither is it my pleasure (to see) that when injustice is done, there be no punishment.

Darius goes further, to emphasize his sense of justice. After having praised his own military skill, as a good horseman, bowman, and spearman on foot and on horseback, he confesses that he owes this skill to Ahura Mazda. Readers of the inscription are exhorted to make known everywhere the greatness of the King's skill and valor.

Similar ideas are expressed by Darius in the monumental inscription of Behistun (Bisutun) which is, at the same time, the king's autobiography and one of the best sources for the study of his reign. It is composed in the three official languages, Persian, Elamite, and Akkadian, in cuneiform writing, and copies of it were sent to all parts of the empire. In introducing himself, Darius uses the following royal titles:[78] "I [am] Darius, the great King, the King of kings, the King of lands, son of Hystaspes, grandson of Arsames, the Achaemenid." After having stressed the royal character of the Achaemenid dynasty, Darius goes on (§ 5) "Says Darius the King: Through the will of Ahura Mazda I am King; Ahura Mazda gave me the kingship." He gave him also all the lands which the King enumerates. (§ 9) "Says Darius the King: Ahura Mazda gave me the kingship. Ahura Mazda gave [me] help

[78] F. H. Weissbach and W. Bang, *Die altpersischen Keilinschriften im Umschrift und Uebersetzung*, Assyriologische Bibliothek, 10 (Leipzig, 1908), p. 12 seq.

to attain the kingship. According to the will of Ahura Mazda I am in possession of the kingship."

All his political success Darius attributes to the help of Ahura Mazda.

> All this that I did, I did only according to the will of Ahura Mazda. Ahura Mazda helped me, and other gods who exist. [§ 62] Says Darius the King: Ahura Mazda and other gods who exist brought me help because I was not hostile, I was not a liar, I was not violent, neither I nor my dynasty. I ruled according to the law...and did no violence. The man who stood to my house, I protected him well, who treated my house badly, I punished severely. [§ 63] Says Darius the King: You who will later become king, the man who is a liar or a rebel, do not be his friend, punish such a man severely.

Both inscriptions are a kind of royal political creed of the Achaemenids. The protestation that all kingly power comes from Ahura Mazda is repeated in all other inscriptions of the reign of Darius. A majestic tone resounds in the following declaration:[79] "A great god is Ahura Mazda, who created this earth, who created yonder sky, who created man, who created fullness of blessing for man, who made Darius King, one King of many, one ruler of many."

This profession became a stereotyped phrase which is repeated at the beginning of other inscriptions of Darius and those of his successors Xerxes and Artaxerxes.[80]

Such outspoken declarations show clearly that the Achaemenids regarded kingship as a gift of Ahura Mazda. They indicate also that the Persians were expected to see in their kings representatives of Ahura Mazda on earth. The kings were far from claiming a divine character for themselves, but the logical deduction from these definitions of Persian kingship is that they occupied a lofty place in the life of the people, a place which put them above all other men, but below Ahura Mazda and other gods.

---

[79] The inscription NR a, of Naqsh-i-Rustam, in F. H. Weissbach and W. Bang, *op. cit.*, p. 35; F. H. Weissbach, *Die Keilinschriften der Achämeniden* (Leipzig, 1911), p. 87.

[80] F. H. Weissbach and W. Bang, *op. cit.*, pp. 37, 39, 41, 43, 47; F. H. Weissbach, *op. cit.*, pp. 99, 103, 107, 109, 111, 113, 117, 129; E. Herzfeld, *Altpers. Inschr.*, pp. 34, 38.

POLITICAL PHILOSOPHY

The almost monotheistic phraseology of these inscriptions poses another problem which cannot be neglected. This phraseology introduces a new notion into the evolution of ideas on kingship in the Near East. It differs profoundly from the polytheistic tenor of Babylonian and other Near Eastern inscriptions. Is this evolution in Persian religious thinking due to the direct influence of Zoroaster's religious reforms?

This problem is still under discussion among specialists, but everything suggests that, contrary to the opinions of E. Meyer[81] and E. Herzfeld,[82] most of the ideas expressed by Darius in his inscriptions must be regarded as pre-Zoroastrian. It is known that Zoroaster endeavored in his reform to replace the old Iranian divinities of nature by the worship of moral abstractions. But the supreme god (the Lord of Wisdom) Ahura Mazda of Zoroaster is not the Zoroastrian god par excellence, in spite of the close connection between Ahura Mazda and the prophet's religious reform.[83] There are very many reasons for believing that he was an ancient Iranian god who was not invented but only, as it were, promoted by Zoroaster.[84] It seems established that he must be identified with Varuna,[85] one of the two principal deities of the Indo-Iranians, the other being Mithra. Both were gods of the firmament—Varuna by day, Mithra by night. This divine pair was venerated in the four-

[81] E. Meyer, *Geschichte des Altertums*, 3, pp. 97–127. Cf. his article on Persia in *Encyclopaedia Britannica*, 21, 11th ed., p. 205. Cf. H. S. Nyberg, *op. cit.*, pp. 27–51, On p. 435 the author gives a short résumé of Meyer's ideas on Zoroaster.

[82] See especially E. Herzfeld's recent book *Zoroaster and His World*, in which he tries to defend his conviction that the Achaemenids were adherents of Zoroaster and that the *Kavi* Vishtaspa has to be identified with the ancestor of Darius.

[83] A general bibliography on Zoroaster up to 1928 will be found in A. V. W. Jackson's *Zoroastrian Studies* (New York, 1928), pp. xx–xxvi. More recent literature is mentioned in H. S. Nyberg's *Die Religionen des alten Iran*, in J. Duchesne-Guillemin's *Zoroastre*, and in R. C. Zaehner's *The Teachings of the Magi. A Compendium of Zoroastrian Beliefs* (London-New York, 1956), p. 151 seq.

[84] This problem is clearly outlined by E. Benveniste in his booklet, *The Persian Religion According to the Chief Greek Texts*, pp. 22–49, where the author states that the description by Herodotus of the Persian religious system reflects the pre-Zoroastrian religion, which was that of the first Achaemenids.

[85] See for details the discussion by H. S. Nyberg, *op. cit.*, p. 97 seq. Cf. also G. Dumézil, *Mitra-Varuna. Essai sur deux représentations indo-européennes de la souveraineté*, Bibl. de l'Ecole des Hautes Etudes, 56 (Paris, 1940), p. 66 seq.

teenth century B.C., by the first Aryans who had reached Asia Minor, as may be learned from the text of a treaty concluded between a Hittite and a Mitannian king.[86] Varuna succeeded in overshadowing Mithra among the Indians; but in Iran the evolution ran a different course. Some Iranian communities accepted Mithra as the supreme god, traces of how this evolved being observable in the Mithra Yasht referred to above. Other groups remained loyal to Varuna, now Ahura Mazda, the Lord of Wisdom, who became god of heaven and took over the functions of Mithra. Zoroaster belonged to such a community. It was he who brought these developments to a final stage, by trying to secure an undisputed supremacy for Ahura Mazda and to degrade other Iranian divinities to the level of moral abstractions brought into close association with Ahura Mazda. His reforms, however, were not welcomed with the enthusiasm which he had anticipated. The cult of the old Iranian deities was so deeply ingrained that, after Zoroaster's death, his disciples were forced to incorporate the old pagan creed into their master's teaching. So it came about that the Yashts, hymns of praise to ancient divinities, although collected at a later date, really represent an earlier stage of Iranian religious evolution than do the Gathas, which emanated from Zoroaster himself.

The Achaemenids evidently belonged to the group which had accepted Ahura Mazda-Varuna as the supreme god. It has been seen that they were not such strict monotheists as Zoroaster, because Darius also speaks of other divinities. Moreover, Darius employs the old Persian form of Ahuramazda as one word. All of this leads to an important conclusion; namely, that the purely Iranian element in the formation of the ideas on kingship of the Achaemenids was very strong.

It seems that Zoroastrian reforms, now incorporating the old Iranian creed, obtained a hold at the Achaemenid court only at the end of the reign of Darius and during that of his successor Xerxes. The main agents of this new evolution seem to have been

---

[86] The text of the treaty was published by H. Winkler in *Mitteilungen der deutschen Orient-Gesellschaft*, 35 (1907), pp. 1–59. See other bibliographical indications in A. Christensen, "Die Iranier," p. 209. Cf. H. S. Nyberg, *op. cit.*, p. 330 seq.

the Magi,[87] the priestly class of the Medes, whom Cyrus had allowed to settle in Persia. They were also mainly responsible for the adaptation of Zoroaster's ideas to the old Iranian belief, although one of them, Gaumatha, who led the revolt against Cambyses in Media, was a strict Zoroastrian and destroyed the places of worship of the old popular religion. Darius, after crushing the revolt, rebuilt these shrines, as he himself says in the Behistun inscription.[88] This detail might well be quoted as an example of religious tolerance as practiced by Cyrus and Darius. It also indicated, however, that Darius could not have been a zealous Zoroastrian, as many would like to picture him.

It was only under Xerxes that Zoroastrianism, in its revised form after the assimilation of the older creed, took a firm hold at court. In his inscriptions Xerxes followed the pattern drawn up by his father, but mentioned certain details which betray the fact that in this respect he went further than his father. Describing his crushing of a Babylonian revolt, Xerxes says that he destroyed the cult of the *daëves*,[89] employing here a term which Zoroaster used to designate those whose worship was proscribed. Artaxerxes II went even further. Besides Ahura Mazda, Artaxerxes II also mentions the gods Anahita and Mithra.[90] Thus, it was under Artaxerxes that Mithra, at one time ousted from the Persian heaven by Varuna-Ahura Mazda, began that glorious career which made him, in the Hellenistic period, the most popular of the gods and the only one who, for a time, became a serious rival and adversary of Christianity.

There is yet another detail in Darius' inscriptions which is important in our attempt to arrive at a definition of pure Iranian,

[87] On the complicated problem of the Magi, see the study by E. Benveniste, *Les mages dans l'ancien Iran*, Publications de la Société des Etudes Iraniennes, 15 (Paris, 1938). The whole question is discussed with skill by J. Duchesne-Guillemin, *Zoroastre*, pp. 113–120. Cf. also C. F. Lehmann-Haupt, "Wann lebte Zarathuštra?," *Oriental Studies in Honour of Cursetji Erachji Pavry*, pp. 251–280: Zoroaster lived about 550 B.C. On Zoroaster's teachings, see also G. Messina, *La religione mazdea* (Rome, 1951).

[88] F. H. Weissbach, *op. cit.*, p. 21 (§ 14); F. H. Weissbach and W. Bang, *op. cit.*, p. 15.

[89] E. Herzfeld, *Altpers. Inschr.*, p. 34. Cf. the analysis of the inscription in H. S. Nyberg, *op. cit.*, p. 364 seq.

[90] F. H. Weissbach, *op. cit.*, pp. 123 seq., 127 (Cyrus II), 129 (Artaxerxes III).

pre-Zoroastrian conceptions of kingship. The King emphasizes the necessity for the ruler to follow the way of truth, to avoid falsehood and to be just. His successors are exhorted to punish all liars. This recalls the contrast between *arta* (the right order) and *druj* (falsehood) which is preached by Zoroaster and which is the basis of his doctrine concerning retribution for men's deeds after their death. But even this important detail does not necessarily imply that Darius was a Zoroastrian during the whole length of his reign. There are indications which show that the generalizations of this contrast between the right order and falsehood, preached by Zoroaster, and its utilization for a belief in retribution, has its roots in the Indo-Iranian period and is therefore pre-Zoroastrian.[91]

It is, however, possible that at the end of his reign Darius was influenced in this matter by Zoroastrianism. A more attentive reading of the Behistun (Bisutun) inscription reveals that there is a marked difference between the last part (col. IV, from § 51 seq.) and the first part in the three preceding columns. It is in the last part of the inscription that particular stress is laid on the contrast between the right order and falsehood, and that expressions are used which certainly have the flavor of the oldest Zoroastrian compositions. The rebels are consistently called liars, because they had adhered to falsehood and had betrayed the right order of submission to the rightful King. Ahura Mazda and the other gods had helped the King because he did not follow the way of falsehood and his successors are exhorted to punish all "liars."

It is possible that this part was added to the rest of the inscription toward the end of Darius' reign.[92] If this is so, then it is legitimate to see here another argument in favor of the theory that Zoroastrianism in its new form, shaped by the Magi, established itself at the court of Darius at the end of his reign. But this

---

[91] For details, see J. Duchesne-Guillemin, *Zoroastre*, p. 129 seq.

[92] See the stimulating study by F. W. König, *Relief und Inschrift des Koenigs Dareios I. am Felsen von Bagistan* (Leiden, 1938), p. 79 seq. On pp. 34–59, the author gives a new translation of the inscription. König's opinion that from 519 to 486 B.C. the relief and the inscription were several times subjected to transformations and additions seems reasonably well founded and deserves careful attention on the part of specialists. A definite answer to this question will, however, be arrived at only when the original is more thoroughly studied on the spot, and when better reproductions of it are available.

does not mean that the notion itself was not pre-Zoroastrian. In the first part of the inscription (§§ 11 and 16) two of the rebels, Gaumatha and the Babylonians, are also called "liars" because they had refused to join Darius. The fact that Darius mentions too "the other gods," which, as we have said, makes it impossible for us to see him as a pure Zoroastrian, could likewise be invoked as an argument to show that Darius knew only the Magi-an form of Zoroastrianism, which was a compromise between Zoroaster's teaching and the old Iranian belief.

The influence of Zoroaster's religious reforms on Iranian political ideas under the Achaemenids has been seen to have been of no marked importance. It is now imperative to determine to what extent the old Oriental ideas on kingship, as they had developed for many centuries in the Middle East, had influenced the evolution of Persian political theory.

The main source in this respect is the inscription in which Cyrus' victory over the last Babylonian king, Nabu-naid is recalled. Cyrus presents himself as the king of Babylon, chosen by Marduk to replace the unworthy Nabu-naid.[93] All Babylonian formulas and phraseology used in connection with the divine choice of a king are employed in order to make Cyrus' seizure of the Babylonian throne appear normal and in accordance with the will of the gods. In the first part of the inscription it is recounted how the gods were infuriated by the treatment meted out to them by Nabu-naid, who removed their statues from their temples, carried them off to Babylon, and prohibited their worship in the cities which venerated them. Marduk thereupon took pity on his people and searched everywhere for a righteous prince. "He searched through all lands looking for him, nay he sought a just prince according to his heart's wishes, in order to take him by the hand. Cyrus, the king of Anshan, whose name he had pronounced, he called to rule over all." All these phrases are familiar from the Babylonian ritual of enthronement and the court style.

In the second part, Cyrus introduces himself with these following words:

[93] F. H. Weissbach, *op. cit.*, p. 3 seq.

IRANIAN KINGSHIP

I [am] Cyrus, the King of all, the great King, the mighty King, the King of Babylon, the King of Sumer and Akkad, King of the four quarters of the world, son of Cambyses, the great King... the eternal offspring of kingship, whose dynasty is beloved by Bal and Nabu, whose kingship they had designed to rejoice their own hearts.... Marduk, the great lord, rejoiced in my pious deeds, and he graciously blessed me, Cyrus, the King who worships him, and Cambyses, my own son, and all my warriors, and we praised in sincerity and with joy his exalted godhead.

This declaration was also a masterpiece of Persian political propaganda in the conquered country. It was, naturally, intended for the Babylonians and it would therefore be preposterous to see in it any proof that the Persians had accepted Babylonian ideas on kingship. However, a certain degree of influence cannot be denied. Cyrus, Cambyses, and Darius were not blind to the high cultural standards achieved by the Babylonians. As wise rulers, they not only respected the national customs and institutions in Babylonia; they also imitated some of them in Persia and in their entire empire. This is particularly the case with Persian legislation. Darius especially, after his experiences during the turbulent first years of his reign, had learned to appreciate the importance of a firm legal system, such as that of Hammurabi, binding together the motley gathering of nations of which his immense empire was composed. A comparison of his long inscriptions with Hammurabi's preface to his code shows that in the composition of the inscriptions, Darius followed the model given to him by this great Babylonian lawgiver.[94] This indicates that Babylonian influences did reach Persia and inspired the Persian version of the court style. Why, then, should this same influence be excluded from the formation of Persian political ideas?

As a matter of fact, this influence must have been first felt in Persia in the clearer formulation of the king's absolute power. In the old days of Iran, the royal power was most probably shared, in

---

[94] A thorough comparison of the inscriptions with the introduction to Hammurabi's code was made by A. T. Olmstead, *History of the Persian Empire*, pp. 120–128.

some respects, with the representatives of the tribes which had recognized the king's authority. While there is no direct evidence, it is known that in the "imperial" period, the chieftains of the six main Persian clans (the *vispati*) had a privileged position at the king's court. The king himself was the *vispati* of the tribe of Parsa, the principal Persian tribe. This tradition was still followed in the Sassanian period of Iranian history, and apparently was a survival from the early period when the chieftains were prominent persons with a certain political power. In the Sassanian period, however, the six dignitaries held only honorary office at the court and were without political influence.[95] This situation seems to have existed in Darius' time. On the tomb relief of Darius, six figures can be seen flanking the King. Two of them can still be identified as Darius' spear-bearer and baton-bearer, and these were evidently court functions of an honorary character.[96]

If it is true—and there are serious reasons for supposing so—that the figures of the two dignitaries were added to the Behistun relief at the end of Darius' reign,[97] then it is legitimate to find in this an echo of interior political complications, caused by a conflict between royal absolutism and the resentful *vispati*. In 490 B.C., Darius chose Xerxes, whose mother was Cyrus' daughter, from among his sons to be his heir and successor, rejecting his eldest son, whose mother was a daughter of Gobarva, his spear-bearer and a successful general. Such an act was naturally resented by Gobarva and his colleagues and Darius had to do something to placate them. He seems to have tried to do this by giving them a prominent place in the monumental reliefs commemorating his reign. Gobarva can also be identified as one of the dignitaries represented on Darius' tomb relief in Naqsh-i-Rustam. Gobarva, moreover, won

[95] A. Christensen, *L'Iran sous les Sassanides* (Copenhagen, 1936), p. 104; 2nd ed. (1944), p. 109.
[96] See the description, with bibliographical indications, in A. T. Olmstead, *op. cit.*, p. 229. Here once more the detailed study may be recalled by G. Widengren, "Recherches sur le féodalisme iranien," describing the feudal character of the Persian imperial regime.
[97] F. W. König, *op. cit.*, pp. 18–20. It seems that the addition of the figure of the third dignitary on the Behistun relief was planned. The wall behind the second figure looks polished, but the death of Darius in 486/5 B.C., interfered with the plan and the monument was left unfinished by Xerxes.

other distinctions, including, in the fifth column of the Behistun inscription, high praise for his generalship.

The above incident can therefore be regarded as tracing the steady progress of Persian royal absolutism, a progress which had gradually curtailed all the prerogatives which the Persian chieftains had enjoyed in the primitive period. Such a situation must have developed in Persia only as a result of influences from Oriental monarchies with which the Persians had come into close contact. Only one custom remained to recall the positions which the chieftains had once held: the royal princes were obliged to choose their principal wives from the families of the *vispati*.[98]

Jewish sources[99] recount moreover that the king had seven "councillors." They evidently occupied the posts of royal ministers entrusted with the administration of the empire. This information is confirmed by what Herodotus says about Cyrus, concerning whose youth he describes a charming scene—the future king of Persia was elected "king" by his playmates and the boy distributed the different offices among his comrades.[100] "Then he set them severally to their tasks; some to the building of houses, some to be his bodyguard, one (as I suppose) to be the King's Eye; to another he gave the right of bringing him messages; to each he gave his proper work."

It seems that Herodotus, when telling this tale, had in mind some of the most important offices at the Persian court. The commander of the bodyguard held at the same time the post corresponding to that of the modern vizier. The official called the "King's Eye" was the chief of the royal intelligence service, founded by Cyrus and well developed throughout the empire.[101] Another important function was that of the minister entrusted with the supervision of the construction of monuments, palaces, and cities. The bearer of

[98] Herodotus, *Historiae*, III, 84, ed. by A.D. Godley (Loeb, 1938), 2, p. 112. Herodotus confuses the chieftains of the Persian tribes with Darius' confederates in his conspiracy to seize the throne.

[99] Ezra 7 : 14; Esther 1 : 14.

[100] *Op. cit.*, I, 114, *loc. cit.* (1931), 1, p. 146 seq. Cf. also Xenophon, *Cyropaedia*, VIII, 1, 9, ed. by W. Miller (Loeb, 1914), 2, p. 308, on Cyrus appointing officers.

[101] Cf. H. H. Schaeder, "Das Auge des Königs," *Iranica = Abhandl. der Gesellsch. der Wiss. zu Göttingen*, Philol.-hist. Kl., Folge 3, no. 10, (Berlin, 1934), pp. 3–34.

messages could only be the director of the royal post, also founded by Cyrus. These seem to have been the most important of the seven ministers; but their functions were only consultative and administrative. The last word remained with the king, in whose hands all effective power was concentrated.

As in Babylonia, absolute royal power also extended over religious affairs. Cyrus introduced the Magi, the Median priests, into Persia.[102] The Zoroastrian calendar was introduced either by Darius at the end of his reign or by Xerxes, while Artaxerxes is said to have made important religious innovations. It will be recalled that he admitted to official worship of Mithra and Anahita, in addition to Ahura Mazda. It is also said that he permitted likenesses of Anahita to be made and installed in Babylon, Susa, and Ecbatana for public worship.[103]

This was an important innovation, for the Persians did not make simulacra of their gods. Ahura Mazda was represented, rather, in a symbolic way, as can be seen from the reliefs accompanying the inscriptions of Darius. But a study of this representation shows that in this respect also the Persians were influenced by other Oriental cultures. According to the Assyrian fashion, the supreme god is symbolized by a sun-disk, derived from the Egyptians and borrowed by the Assyrians from the Mitanni. Instead of Ashur, Ahura Mazda is represented in the center, with a cylindrical hat, flared at the top. The horns of divinity which adorn him are also borrowed from the Assyrians. He holds a ring, symbol of sovereignty, in his left hand, and the scrolls next to the disk should be identified either with the claw-like legs of the Egyptian goddess of truth, who used to be represented in the shape of a vulture, or, more probably, with those of the falcon of the god Horus, whose wings flank the sun-disk.

It appears that originally Ahura Mazda was symbolized by the sun-disk alone.[104] This would correspond to the customs of the

---

[102] Xenophon, *cyropaedia*, VIII, I., 23, *loc. cit.*, p. 316.
[103] Clement of Alexandria, *Cohortatio ad gentes* (*Protrepticus*), 5, PG, 8, col. 168.
[104] A sun-disk is found as a symbol of divinity in a Median tomb at Sakhna, described by E. Herzfeld, *Iran in the Ancient East. Archaeological Studies Presented in the Lowell Lectures at Boston* (London-New York, 1941), p. 201 seq.

primitive Iranians who, as has been shown,[105] never represented their gods in human form. The human figure was added to the sun-disk afterward, as a result of Assyrian influence, from the end of Darius' reign onward, when Zoroastrianism in its new form began to obtain a hold upon the Persian court. There are certain indications which show that the human figure now to be seen in the Behistun relief was added to the sun-disk with the claw-like feet during the last years of Darius' reign, when other additions were made to the relief and the inscription.[106]

It should be pointed out that in the relief of Naqsh-i-Rustam, mentioned above, Darius is presented in the same manner as the symbol of Ahura Mazda. This similarity is certainly intentional and is meant to emphasize the idea that the king is the representative on earth of the supreme god. The idea is further illustrated by the figures supporting Darius' throne who represent the thirty nations subject to his rule. The King towers high above them like an almost superhuman being. Only Ahura Mazda rises higher than he.

Another custom which developed at the court of the Achaemenids expressed the same idea once again. The description given by Xenophon[107] shows that when the Persian king appeared in a public procession his chariot was always preceded by the chariot of Ahura Mazda, "drawn by white horses with a yoke of gold and wreathed with garlands." Xenophon's description must date from a later period because, according to what he says, the chariot of Ahura Mazda was followed by two other chariots, one of them for the sun-god. This is the divine trinity—Ahura Mazda, Mithra, and Anahita. This change in official Persian theology was made by Artaxerxes II.

---

[105] See *supra*, p. 96. Cf. F. W. König, *Älteste Geschichte der Meder und Perser*, pp. 17 seq., 58 seq.

[106] For details, consult F. W. König, *Relief und Inschrift des Koenigs Dareios I.*, pp. 23–27. The artists who worked on the relief seem to have been inspired by a similar relief of Anubanini, king of a Semitic tribe in the Zagros mountains. See G. Hüsing, *Der Zagros und seine Völker*, Der Alte Orient, 9, Heft 3/4 (Leipzig, 1908), fig. 12, p. 16. Cf. also E. Herzfeld, *Iran in the Ancient East*, p. 254 seq. In his *Zoroaster and His World*, 2, p. 817, Herzfeld reasserts the Assyrian origin of this symbolism.

[107] *Cyropaedia*, VIII, 3, 11 seq., *loc. cit.* p. 354.

In the same passage Xenophon mentions another Persian custom illustrating the central position of the king in the life of the nation. Behind the chariots reserved for the divinities "followed men carrying fire on a great altar." This fire was not a symbol of the kingly glory—the *Hvarena*—but represented the royal hearth, the religious focus of the primitive state.[108] As will be shown, this custom survived the different phases of Iranian political history. It was taken over by the Roman emperors and, like the *Hvarena*, was adapted by the Christians for their liturgical use.

The whole description of the royal procession reveals that great pomp and solemnity were deployed in order to stress the prominent position of the king in and above the nation. According to Xenophon's description, Cyrus drove in a chariot—

> wearing his tiara upright, a purple tunic shot with white (no one but the king may wear such a one), trousers of scarlet dye about his legs, and a mantle all of purple. He had also a fillet about his tiara, and his kinsmen also had the same distinction, and they retain it even now. His hands he kept outside his sleeves.... And when they saw him they all prostrated themselves before him, either because some had been instructed to begin this act of homage or because they were overcome by the splendor of his presence, or because Cyrus appeared so great and goodly to look upon....

This description is completed by that given by Q. Curtius Rufus.[109] Although this author lived in the first century of our era, most probably under the Emperor Claudius, for his descriptions of Persian customs of the last years of the Achaemenid period he used older works, including probably that of Cetarchus (about 300 B.C., son of Dinon), which he may have known through the writings of Timagenes, who lived in the time of Augustus. Describing the march of the

---

[108] For Iranian ideas on fire, see J. Hertel, *Die arische Feuerlehre*. See also his study, *Die awestischen Herrschafts- und Siegesfeuer*. Diodorus Siculus, XVII, 114, 4, ed. by L. Dindorff and C. Müller (Paris, 1872), 2, p. 210, mentions the Persian custom observed on the death of a king: the holy fire that burned constantly in the palace was extinguished. Cf. C. Clemen, *Die griechischen und lateinischen Nachrichten über die persische Religion*, pp. 100, 139, on this custom.
[109] *History of Alexander*, III, 3, 10–26, ed. by J. C. Rolfe (Loeb, 1946), I, pp. 82–86. Cf. Herodotus, *op. cit.*, VII, 40, *loc. cit.* (1938), 3, p. 354.

Persian army led by the last king, Darius IV, he says that in front
of the King were carried silver altars with the sacred fire. Then came
the Magi, chanting their traditional hymns, and 365 young men—

> clad in purple robes, equal in number to the days of the
> whole year, for the Persians also divided the year into that
> number of days. After that, white horses drew the chariot
> consecrated to Jupiter [i.e., Ahura Mazda]; these were followed
> by a horse of extraordinary size, which they called the Steed
> of the Sun. Golden wands and white robes adorned the drivers
> of the horses. Not far off were ten chariots embossed with
> much gold and silver. These were followed by the horsemen
> of twelve nations of varying arms and customs.

The King's chariot was preceded by the "Immortals," the royal
bodyguard, always ten thousand in number. Then followed the
King's "relatives" (*cognati*), an honorary title conferred upon
members of the King's court and others who were admitted to
the King's banquets. The King was surrounded by two hundred of
the noblest "relatives" (*propinquiores*)—again probably an honorary title conferred upon courtiers admitted to a higher degree of
intimacy with the King. The King's chariot and his appearance
are described as follows:

> These preceded the King's chariot, in which he rode out-
> standing among the rest. Both sides of the chariot were
> adorned with images of the gods, embossed in gold and
> silver; the yoke was ornamented with sparkling gems, and on
> it rose two golden images, a cubit high, of the King's ancestors,
> one of Ninus, the other of Belus. Between these they had
> consecrated a golden eagle, represented with outstretched wings.
> The attire of the King was noteworthy beyond all else in
> luxury; a purple-edged tunic woven about a white center, a
> cloak of cloth and gold, ornamented with golden hawks which
> seemed to attack each other with their beaks; from a golden
> belt, with which he was girt woman-fashion, he had hung a
> scimitar, the scabbard of which was a single gem. The Persians
> called the King's headdress '*cidaris*'; this was bound with a
> blue fillet variegated with white.[110]

[110] Cf. C. Clemen, *op. cit.*, p. 149, on the historical reliability of this passage.

POLITICAL PHILOSOPHY

These descriptions of royal processions reveal certain customs of Persian court ceremonial which not only illustrate the outstanding position of the absolute monarch who was intimately associated with the gods, but also presage a further evolution of some royal symbols in the kingly ceremonial in general. First, the connection of the king with the sun: Quintus Curtius mentions also, at the beginning of the passage quoted above, that "above the tent [of the king] from which it might be seen by all, there gleamed an image of the sun enclosed in crystal."[111] This connection of the royal ceremonial with the sun, the worship of which must have increased among the Persians during the first Achaemenid period under Babylonian and Egyptian influences, explains why in the later period from the Parthian dynasty onward, the king was called the brother of the sun and of the moon. It inaugurates also the popularity of sun symbolism which will be constantly observed in the study of early political philosophy. The eagle appears here also, for the first time, as a symbol of royalty. It may be that in this connection the bird may be used for its association with magic. It is known, however, from another source that Artaxerxes II put the eagle on his military standard.[112] But in other passages[113] Xenophon attributes to Cyrus the choice of an eagle as a military ensign: "Now his ensign was a golden eagle with outspread wings mounted upon a long shaft. And this continues even unto this day as the ensign of the Persian king."

This correlation of the eagle with Persian symbols of royalty might be derived from the old Persian legendary tradition that the founder of the dynasty—Achaemenes—had been reared by an eagle.[114] It should be remembered, moreover, that the god Verethragna, the bearer of the *Hvarena*, sometimes appeared in the shape of a bird which might well have been an eagle.[115] In the

---

[111] In another passage (III, 3, 24, *loc. cit.* 1, p. 86) Quintus Curtius says that the King had 365 concubines—again the sacred number of the 365 days of the sun year.

[112] Xenophon, *Anabasis*, I, 10, 12, ed. by C. L. Brownson (Loeb, 1932), p. 338.

[113] *Cyropaedia*, VII, 1, 4, ed. by W. Miller, *loc. cit.*, p. 204.

[114] Aelian, *On Animals*, XII, 21, ed. by A. T. Scholfield (Loeb, 1959), 3, p. 40.

[115] See *supra*, p. 91.

light of this, the tradition concerning Verethragna's incarnation as a bird becomes more interesting. However, even in this respect, the Persians might have been influenced by Oriental traditions which they found in their new homeland. The eagle plays an important role in Egypt and in Syria, where it was associated with the sun-god.[116] The Sumerian myth of Etana and the eagle should also be recalled.[117]

There is evidence to show that in the early Persian period the "royal" bird was not the eagle, but the rooster, which the Greeks referred to as a Persian bird. Primitively, in Persia, the rooster was connected with the moon, but in a later period with the sun. On a Greek vase preserved at Naples, Darius I is represented with a tiara decorated with a rooster's comb. Some curious examples of the survival of this "rooster cult" have been pointed out recently.[118] Eventually, however, it was not the rooster but the eagle that carried the day in Persian royal symbolism, where it has retained its position to the present day. It seems that Oriental, especially Babylonian influences, helped this "thunderbolt" of birds to oust the rooster from this symbolic role.

The Persians inaugurated another royal tradition. It has been seen from the descriptions given by Xenophon and Quintus Curtius that they chose purple and red as the colors of royalty. For centuries since, these colors have been regarded as especially befitting kings.

Xenophon also describes the manner in which subjects rendered homage to their king by prostrating themselves on his approach. This is the famous *proskynesis*, the ceremony that so greatly displeased the Greeks. Isocrates in his Panegyric[119] severely condemned such "prostration to mortal man." Many Greeks saw in this habit a proof that the Persians paid homage to their kings as divinities; but this view is quite unjustified. It implies that the Greeks themselves reserved prostration exclusively for divine worship, but even this inference may not, apparently, be generalized.

[116] O. Keller, *Die antike Tierwelt*, 2 (Leipzig, 1913), p. 2 seq. Cf. also his *Thiere des classischen Alterthums in culturgeschichtlicher Beziehung* (Innsbruck, 1887), pp. 268, 447.

[117] See *supra*, p. 24.

[118] See A. Alföldi's study, "Der iranische Weltriese," pp. 24–26, for full documentation on the subject. Cf. also C. Clemen, *op. cit.*, p. 87 seq.

[119] *Panegyricus*, 151, ed. by G. Norlin (Loeb, 1928), 1, p. 216.

Herodotus,[120] in any case, is more lenient and sees in the *proskynesis* a form of greeting addressed by social inferiors to their betters. It would not seem, therefore, to have been exclusively a religious rite even for the Greeks. For the Persians it was the rite with which they honored their kings. At the same time, it demonstrates the elevated position which the king held in Persian eyes. It was the same kind of homage which was rendered unto gods.

Further, it is quite valid to see here a proof of Oriental influences upon Persian court ceremonial. Prostration was the form of homage which the subjects of the Egyptian Pharaohs paid to their rulers. The correspondence preserved in the Tell el-Amarna tablets[121] shows this. In letters addressed to Amenophis III and IV by their subjects, phrases such as this are constantly found: "To the Sun, the king, my lord, king of Egypt. At the feet of my lord, seven times and seven times I fall down." This makes clear the origin of the Persian *proskynesis*. Even this custom survived the Persian Empire and is still used in Christian liturgy.[122]

It is, perhaps, also correct to see Eastern influences in the evolution of the Persian royal tiara. On the royal reliefs mentioned above the kings wear an upright, cylindrical, head ornament, similar to that of the Assyrian kings. If A. Alföldi[123] is correct, primitively this was a headdress in the form of a horse's head, which was worn by the king. This might have some connection with primitive Iranian beliefs, by which the king was held to be some mythical creature who was half man and half beast, or at least a man whose superhuman strength and qualities were best illustrated by the strength and qualities of the horse. This had to give way to the more modern headdress of the Oriental kings of whom the Persians were the heirs.[124]

---

[120] *Op. cit.*, I, 134, *loc. cit.* (1931), 1, p. 174.

[121] See *supra*, p. 57 seq.

[122] See *infra*, pp. 655–657.

[123] Cf. his stimulating study, "Der iranische Weltriese," pp. 17–34, where a most comprehensive bibliography will be found.

[124] According to Athenaeus, who has it from Dinon, the tiara of the king was richly scented with two precious spices, *Deipnosophistae*, XII, 514 a, ed. by Ch. B. Gulick (Loeb, 1933), 5, p. 310.

Still another distinctive feature of Achaemenia royal head-dress was destined to inaugurate a new tradition in royal symbolism. On Darius' seal, for example, the King is shown wearing a lower *cidaris* surmounted by a serrated edge.[125] This kind of royal tiara can also be seen on coins issued by the Achaemenid kings from Darius I (521–485 B.C.) to Darius III (307–300 B.C.)[126] This peculiar form of tiara can be explained only in connection with the old Iranian belief in the *Hvarena*—the awful kingly glory. The points of the serrated rim symbolize fire and light, of which the *Hvarena* is an apparition. This was the origin of the crown with solar radiations which became so popular in the Hellenistic period, was adopted by the Romans, and ended its career only under the first Christian emperors.

The royal chariot, whose vivid colorings are described by Xenophon and Quintus Curtius, recalls another important item of royal symbolism—the throne. This subject was recently studied thoroughly by Professor Alföldi,[127] who showed how the primitive chariots in which the gods and chieftains of the nomad Iranians drove were slowly transformed into fixed seats, sometimes adorned with wheels as an echo of their origin in olden times. Frequently the wheel was used as a symbol of the sun and also of sovereignty. As a result of Babylonian influences, steps were added to the royal throne, to symbolize the seven spheres. A kind of tabernacle or canopy was then added—recalling the covered seat in a primitive wagon—and this was colored in reds and purples. A curtain, which might, too, have derived from the covers of the early form of conveyance, was accorded a symbolic role, intended to emphasize the unique character of the chieftain by secluding him from all other beings. It was from this particular thought that the practice developed for the king always to dine alone, hidden from his guests by curtains—a custom destined to outlive the Persian monarchy.

[125] See *supra*, p. 99. Cf. also E. Herzfeld, *Iran in the Ancient East*, pl. LV. A similar headdress is worn by Darius in the Behístun relief.

[126] J. J. M. de Morgan, *Manuel de numismatique orientale de l'antiquité et du moyen âge* (Paris, 1923–1936), I, pp. 35–41, Cf. also, p. 53, coin issued in 334 B.C. at Ephesus by Memnon, general under Darius III, and, p. 57, coins issued by the kings of Sidon.

[127] A. Alföldi, "Die Geschichte des Throntabernakels," *La Nouvelle Clio*, I–2 (1949–1950), pp. 537–566.

It has survived down to modern times in the ceremonial of the popes.

A vivid idea of the majestic and luxurious Persian royal throne can be obtained from the relief representing an audience given by the king found in Persepolis in the Hall of a Hundred Columns,[128] and from the description given by Athenaeus, based upon older reports.[129] We read here: "The throne on which he [the King] sat while transacting business was of gold, and round it stood four short posts of gold studded with jewels, and on them was stretched an embroidered cloth of purple." Attendants with a parasol and a fly-whisk—again, two Oriental symbols of kingship—stood behind the throne. In his right hand, the king held a sceptre resting upon the ground and in his left hand a lotus. Athenaeus also says:[130] "Whenever the king descended from his chariot, 'Dinon says,' he never leaped down, although the distance to the ground was small, nor did he lean on anyone's arms; rather, a golden stool was always set in place for him, and he descended by stepping on this; and the king's stool-bearer attended him for this purpose." Whenever the king left the palace, precious carpets from Sardis—on which "no-one but the king ever walked"—were spread upon the ground, between the ranks of his "Immortals" standing at attention. "He was never seen on foot outside the palace." Any man admitted to the presence of the king[131] first of all paid homage by prostration, refraining from rising until he had received permission to do so. Afterwards he stood, concealing his hands in his sleeves. This custom, originally probably only a security measure designed to preclude the possibility of an attempt upon the king's life, eventually became a ritual expressing the respect due to the king's august majesty. We learn from one of the reliefs that it was usual for frankincense to be burned before the throne—another custom destined to play an important role in ruler worship and in religious practice for centuries to come.

[128] F. Sarre and E. Herzfeld, *Iranische Felsreliefs*, pls. xxiii, xxiv, xxv.
[129] *Op. cit.*, XII, 514 c, *loc. cit.*, p. 312.
[130] *Ibid.*, 514 a, c, *loc. cit.*, p. 310 seq.
[131] Cf. the scene depicted in Esther 4 : 11; 5 : 1-3. Esther, presenting herself unannounced to the King, broke a strict rule of court etiquette. The King, extending his sceptre toward her, exempted her from the rule.

Two honorary titles conferred by the king upon his favorite courtiers have been remarked upon above. Herodotus[132] mentions an even older title *orosanges* (Benefactor of the King) which was bestowed upon men who had distinguished themselves on the field of battle or by performing some exceptional service for the king. They were also rewarded by lavish grants of land, and they made up a kind of Legion of Honor, the forerunner of all the modern noble orders. From the account left by Herodotus, it can be surmised that there was a special register of this "order," upon which the names of the members were recorded. Other distinctions could be won, some in the form of clothing in the royal colors—purple or a dark shade of red—some in the form of precious gifts—robes that the king himself had worn or, as a particularly noble prize, a horse that the king had ridden.[133] This custom survived not only in the Eastern monarchies, but also in Rome and Byzantium.

The lives of luxury led by the Persian kings, described vividly and not without accents of envy by the Greek writers, remind us of the ideas which the Assyrians had of the universal ruler whom they imagined to have achieved the ultimate ideal of happiness, enjoying all the blessings of this world. In the relief[134] showing Ashurbanipal banqueting with his queen in a vine-covered summerhouse in his garden, can be seen not only a representation of the universal king—rich, happy, and full of the joys of living, as the Assyrians imagined him to be—but many details of custom, dress, ornament, and attitude which were later to be incorporated in the reliefs of the Persian kings.[135] In this particular aspect of the royal way of life, the Persians brought to greater perfection a tradition which was already well developed among the Assyrians. Its roots, however, lay even deeper in Oriental ideas on kingship.

[132] *Op. cit.*, VIII, 85, *loc. cit.* (1930), 4, p. 82.

[133] Xenophon, *Cyropaedia*, VIII, 3, 3, *loc. cit.*, p. 348; Esther 6 : 7–8; 8 : 15. Cf. Plutarch, *Lives: Artaxerxes*, 5, ed. by B. Perrin (Loeb, 1926), 11, p. 134 seq. Plutarch speaks here also of curtains which covered the queen in her carriage and of the custom for the king to eat alone.

[134] See the reproduction in A. T. Olmstead, *History of Assyria*, p. 503.

[135] Frankincense, servants with fans, for example. The royal privilege—an umbrella held over the king's head—is also of Oriental origin. It appears first with Sargon, king of Akkad, and was favored particularly by the late Assyrian kings. This custom still survives in India. Cf. E. Herzfeld, *Zoroaster*, 2, p. 817.

This shows that, together with the customs and the setting, the Persians had also accepted the Assyrian idea of universality. Cyrus' account of his victory over Babylonia shows this very clearly. He employs all the Babylonian royal titles, including that of "King of the Four Quarters of the World." It is true that Darius and his successors used only Persian titles—king of kings, great king, king of the lands. The title "great king" does not, of itself, express the idea of a universal king. Shuppululiumash, king of the Hittites, had already called himself "Great King" in one of his letters to the Pharaoh.[136] On the gold tablet containing the only inscription by Cyrus I's brother, Ariaramnes, we find that he calls himself, "Great King, King of kings, King of Parsa."[137] This was before the Persians became vassals of the Medes.

Thus, we learn that these titles were ancient and did not express, by themselves, any idea of a universal empire. The title, "King of the Lands," however, was Babylonian and it had a connotation of universality. Darius was conservative in this respect, using the ancient Persian titles, and his successors followed his example. It can, however, be assumed that as a result of Assyrian and Babylonian influences, all these titles took on a fresh significance under Cyrus and his successors, and that they expressed Persian pretensions to universality. This appears to be confirmed by an inscription from Susa in which Darius calls himself: "King of [? on] this earth."[138] The Persians could not avoid the logical consequences of their conquests. The idea of a universal empire was already embedded in the minds of the Eastern peoples, and the vanquished princes were resigned to accepting it. According to Athenaeus,[139] who bases his report upon that of Chares, a writer who accompanied Alexander the Great, and upon that of Amyntas (of the same period), there was "in the bed-chamber [of the king] a golden vine, jewel studded, extended

---

[136] *The Tell el-Amarna Tablets*, Letter 41, ed. by S. A. B. Mercer (Toronto, 1939), I, p. 207.

[137] E. Herzfeld, *Altpers. Inschr.*, p. 2. Cf. A. T. Olmstead, *History of the Persian Empire*, p. 29. Cf. *supra*, p. 101.

[138] E. Herzfeld, *op. cit.*, p. 22: "(I Da)-rius the great king' the king of kings, the king of lands, the king on this earth." Even if we read "king *on* this earth," the phrase seems to stress the idea that Darius regarded himself as *the* king on this earth. This implies the idea of one universal king. Cf. also F. Sarre, *Die Kunst des alten Persien*, p. 8.

[139] *Deipnosophistae*, XII, 514 f, *loc. cit.*, p. 314.

over the bed. ... This vine had clusters composed of the costliest jewels." It is interesting to note that Ashurbanipal was also depicted banqueting in a summerhouse covered with a vine. Evidently the Persians took over this Assyrian symbol of the universal ruler who was blessed with all worldly goods. It may be that the legend reported by Herodotus[140] concerning the dream of Astyages was also created under the influence of those Oriental emblems symbolizing the idea of a universal ruler. The connection seems evident. The vine which sprang from the body of Astyages' daughter was said to have covered the whole of Asia.

Athenaeus speaks only of a vine in the king's bedroom. In the Sassanian period (third century A.D.) the vine is pictured as winding round a plantain tree on a vase representing the royal investiture.[141] This may be simply the evolution of a symbol, the tree having been added during the Sassanian period; but it is quite possible that both symbols had already been used by the Achaemenids. It is, in any case, significant that Darius was given a plantain tree by a Lydian prince,[142] as a sign of the prince's submission to his overlordship. It is possible that the origin of this symbol is to be found in the Tree of Life, which usually accompanied the portraits of Egyptian, Babylonian, and Assyrian kings. At least, here is the origin of the particular tree symbolism that appears in the throne rooms of Alexander's successors, in those of Arab rulers, and in Byzantium.[143]

From the Babylonian inscription of Cyrus, it can be deduced that the idea of the eternal duration of the king's rule had found acceptance in the Persian court style. It was not a Persian idea; but thanks again to the Persians, it survived in the Oriental court style and will be seen[144] continuing to play an important role in the evolution of political speculation. Another characteristic Sumerian and Babylonian kingly title—good shepherd—was also adopted by the Iranians, as can be seen from Yasht XIX, 31, where King Yima is called by that very term.

---

[140] *Historiae*, I, 108, *loc. cit.* (1931), 1, p. 138.
[141] Cf. A. Alföldi, "Die Geschichte des Throntabernakels," p. 553.
[142] Cf. A. Alföldi, *ibid.*, p. 552.
[143] See *infra*, p. 217.
[144] See, for example, pp. 510-512, *Roma aeterna*.

The idea of the king as the representative of God upon earth is intimately connected with that of him as savior—as also with the idea of the universal ruler. Thanks to Zoroaster's intervention, the Iranians had formed their own notions concerning the savior. It seems that Zoroaster had believed the establishment of the eternal kingdom to be at hand and expected that he would play a kind of savior-role as judge, appointed by Ahura Mazda, when the end of the world did come. But when the anticipated cataclysm failed to materialize, it became necessary to transfer its arrival to some remote future. So he preached the coming of a savior, Saoshyant, a man who would be given an even greater share of the *Hvarena*:[145] "That will cleave unto the victorious Saoshyant and his helpers, when he shall restore the world, which will [thenceforth] never grow old and never die, never decaying and never rotting, ever living and ever increasing, and master of its wish, when the dead will rise, when life and immortality will come, and the world will be restored at its wish."

The prophet's disciples worked further on this idea. According to their speculations, the savior would have two forerunners and all three would be the offspring of Zoroaster, his seed having been kept by Ahura Mazda in Lake Kasava. Every thousandth year a virgin would bathe in the lake and would conceive with Zoroaster's seed. The last of the three, Saoshyant, with the help of fifteen young men and fifteen virgins, would bring his work to a joyful conclusion—the purification and rejuvenation of the world. All men would have to go through the flames of nature's fire to be purified. Evil men would suffer torment by this ordeal, but they too would eventually be admitted to the purified world and would enjoy everlasting happiness. We know that in the later evolution of Persian religion, it was Mithra who took over the role of the Iranian savior.[146]

All this is a later evolution of the savior-idea, after the Iranians had accepted the modified doctrine of Zoroaster. But it has been shown that the first Achaemenids were not Zoroastrians. The

[145] Yasht XIX, 89, J. Darmesteter, *Zend-Avesta*, pt. 2, p. 306 seq.
[146] For details, see H. Güntert, *Der arische Weltkönig und Heiland*, pp. 395–417; H. S. Nyberg, *op. cit.*, pp. 30 seq., 188–232.

possibility cannot, therefore, be excluded that in the oldest Achaemenid period the Persian kings played, in the lives of their subjects, the same role of savior-king as did the Oriental kings. It is thus possible that during the New Year's festivities the Iranian kings enacted a role symbolizing the renewal of life in nature, as had the Sumerian, Babylonian, and Assyrian kings. No direct information on this subject is available. Athenaeus,[147] however, preserved an interesting detail which he copied from the lost work of Duris of Samos and which illustrates the position occupied by the king in relation to certain religious matters. This report states: "in only one of the festivals celebrated by the Persians, that to Mithra, the king gets drunk and dances 'the Persian' [national dance]; no one else throughout Asia does this, but everyone abstains on this day from the dance." The reliefs preserved in the royal residence of Persepolis[148] indicate what an important feast New Year's day was. The king, who held official receptions that day, accepted tributes and presents, distributed gifts himself, and invited his nobles to a great banquet. He was the central figure of the festivities.

The sacred character of the Iranian kingship is also manifested by other priestly functions performed by the king. The passage which most eloquently reveals that Achaemenid kings performed sacrifices is the exhortation given to Cyrus and the Persian elders by Cambyses (as related by Xenophon in his *Cyropaedia*). [149] "And as often as he [Cyrus] comes to Persia, it should be a sacred custom with you that he sacrifice on your behalf even as I do now. And when he is away, it might be well for you, I think, that that one of our family who seems to you the most worthy should perform that sacred office." This testifies as well to the seriousness with which the Achaemenid kings took their priestly functions.

It is apparent that the idea of the king-savior is mirrored to some extent in Iranian art, which was primarily employed in the service of the royal "cult." It has already been pointed out that

---

[147] *Deipnosophistae*, X, 434 e, *loc. cit.* (1930), 4, p. 468.
[148] See the detailed description given by A. T. Olmstead, *op. cit.*, pp. 272–88. Cf. S. K. Eddy, *The King is Dead*, p. 52 seq.
[149] *Cyropaedia*, VIII, 5, 26, *loc. cit.*, p. 406. Cf. G. Widengren, "The Sacral Kingship," p. 251 seq.

kings were often pictured in the act of slaying dragons or wild beasts. It seems evident that these motifs were taken from Oriental royal art; but a comparison with Egyptian, or especially Assyrian, representations of kings chasing wild beasts, brings an immediate awareness of a great difference in the whole composition. The Iranian scenes are idealized. Incredible monsters are often substituted for wild beasts. There is no life in the animals or in the figure of the king who is supposed to be slaying them. One has the impression that both king and beasts are symbols and that the whole picture is intended to represent the eternal struggle between good and evil, the king representing Ahura Mazda and the beast, Ahriman. The king plays the role of a savior who triumphs over all. A similar idea seems to have guided Darius and his artist in the Behistun relief, where the King is shown as victor over all false and lying kings.

It is therefore possible to imagine that kings were believed to carry on the role which the imaginary *Urmensch* was supposed to play—to fight the spirits of darkness. If the legend of the *Urmensch* Gayomard was known in Iran before Zoroaster's time, as seems probable, it would have been natural for the Iranians to see in their kings the chief protagonists continuing the struggle with Ahriman, a struggle in which the *Urmensch* succumbed. Some eschatological notions must have existed in primitive Iran before Zoroaster. Even here, Zoroaster and, later on, his disciples were only improving upon material which they had found on hand.

To this tradition may perhaps be attached the representation of the heroes fighting a bull, a lion, a griffin, and a griffin with a scorpion's tail found on the four side doors of the Hall of a Hundred Columns at Persepolis.[150] The heroes mentioned in Yasht XIX were also engaged in fighting Ahriman and his creatures. They were thus, in some ways, legitimate predecessors of the kings. The legend of the ancient Gilgamesh fights, related in the old Akkadian epic of Gilgamesh, probably influenced the growth of this ancient Iranian belief, and may have provided an additional inspiration to the artist.

[150] E. Herzfeld, *Iran in the Ancient East*, p. 257, pls. LXV, LXVI. Cf. also his *Zoroaster and His World*, 2, p. 822.

IRANIAN KINGSHIP

The savior symbolism in royal art must gradually have receded into the background as Zoroaster's eschatology was more widely accepted and developed by the priestly class—the Magi. It was not the kings but Zoroaster who was believed to be the one destined to carry on the work of the *Urmensch*, and it was from Zoroaster's seed that the true savior—the Saoshyant—and his two predecessors were expected to arise. In the later stages of this evolution, Mithra took over the role of savior. Therefore, in the Sassanian period of Iranian history, the savior idea was completely separated from theories concerning kingship.

When recapitulating Oriental political ideas in general, it must first of all be emphasized that they differed diametrically from our modern, Western notions on the state and political philosophy which have been shaped from the spiritual inheritance of Greece and Rome. For the Orientals, sovereignty did not reside in the people. It was of divine origin and, invested in kingship, it descended from heaven. Primitively, the insignia of kingship reposed before the thrones of the supreme gods, and it was the privilege of the gods to confer these insignia upon men specially chosen by them and specially protected by them. The first duty of the kings, therefore, was the service of the gods. They were images of gods on earth. They were the earthly representatives of the gods and the only mediators between mortals and the divinities. The kings were the main channel through which the gods communicated their blessings unto men.

This conception of kingship explains why the kings were regarded as central figures and pivots of the state and why the royal power was absolute and extended over all the riches of the land—nay, over all property and the very lives of their subjects. No limits could be imposed upon men who were chosen by gods as their representatives and who acted in the names of the gods. All authority on earth came from above.

The conception of the absolute power of kings was only occasionally tempered by exceptional circumstances in Assyria, in certain Semitic colonies in Asia Minor, among the Hittites, and probably also in ancient Iran, thanks mainly to Indo-European elements.

But not even these strong Indo-European influences were able to change the principal Oriental thesis on the power and position of kings. It was a thesis which continued to be professed by the whole Near and Far East through their millenary evolution down to modern times.

Does this evolution contain the answers to the questions of why it is still so difficult for the Oriental mind to understand democratic principles as developed in Western Europe and the New World, and why the people of the East submit so tamely to the appeal of men who have concentrated all effective power in their own hands?

The pronounced religious character of Oriental kingship and the intimate connection of kings with divinity find their explanation in the instincts which dominate the subconscious strata in human nature. It was instinctive for primitive man to approach as closely as possible the supernatural, whose existence was demonstrated so powerfully to him by the limitations of his own abilities in contrast to the superhuman forces in nature. He was impelled to make special efforts to secure nature's blessings for himself and to placate its anger toward him.

It was reasonable for primitive man to look for an intermediary between himself and the godhead, an intermediary who would be readily accessible to him and who, at the same time—thanks to his intimate relationship with divinity—had easy access to the godhead. The Egyptians went furthest in this respect when they imagined that their king was an incarnation of their supreme god and, consequently, that in the person of the Pharaoh, human and divine were blended. With the idea of the existence of an intermediary between god and man, the idea of the savior was intimately connected—the idea of saving man from divine anger and punishment and of securing the best possible conditions for human beings on earth.

In surveying Persian views on kingship, it must be agreed that the Iranians have merited a special place, regarding not only the development of Oriental political speculation, but also the history of political thinking in general. Marked progress can be seen in many respects. The notion of an absolute monarchy based on the hereditary principle and religious sanctions was more clearly defined. The relationship between king and divinity was put on a more natural basis. The king was deprived of a divine character, but his position as representative on earth of the supreme god, from whom he received all his authority, was stressed.

The king continued to be regarded as supreme lord in religious affairs too, but the priestly class gradually took over all the active functions in religious worship. Claims to universality were made good by the enormous expansion of Persian supremacy over all known cultural lands. Persian infiuence reached even Europe and, in spite of Greek victories, remained strong there.

Marked progress was also made by the Persians in royal symbolism and court ceremonial. In these respects, the Iranians, starting from what they found in the lands they had conquered, succeeded in elaborating a whole system of complicated ceremonial which fascinated and impressed human minds to such an extent that traces of it can still be discovered in modern court ceremony and in Christian liturgy.

Further, the Persians made great advances in the organization of their Empire and laid a foundation for the modern administration of a state. Improving on the system of the Assyrians, Darius divided the whole Empire into provinces with royal governors—the satraps—who concentrated all civil and military authority in their own hands. The royal garrisons in important centers were, however, commanded by generals who were directly responsible to the king. A special system of intelligence watched over the loyalty and integrity of the satraps and the people, and the royal post, established in all provinces, always despatched reports to the central government in record time.[151] The minting of a stable coin, the dareikos, which circulated throughout the Empire, helped to establish a firm monetary and economic basis, while at the same time it emphasized the centralization of authority in the hands of the king.

The tolerant religious policy of the Achaemenids showed a deep understanding of the spiritual needs of subjected peoples and also

[151] It is the author's intention to deal with the evolution of intelligence services in the ancient Near East in a special study.

demonstrated to a remarkable degree how different religious forces could be used to further the interests of the state.

Moreover, in the field of religion, the Persians, were able to find a new method of promoting unity among their subjects. Ahura Mazda was a supreme god, who could become the universal god of all peoples. The great law of this god was the promotion of the fight against falsehood, and it was this ethical principle which the king of kings, Ahura Mazda's representative, was obliged to carry into all the lands which god had given unto him. In this religion, there were many forces which, if used well, could appeal to the great majority of the people. All were called upon to fight the *druj* —falsehood and lies—and to promote the rule of truth and goodness. At the same time, the unchallenged rule of this king over all was given a supreme sanction, which the Oriental mind was accustomed to respect without hesitation.

Concerning the messianic character of Oriental kingship, it must be conceded that the idea of a coming savior owes a great deal to the Persians. It was certainly enriched and elaborated by them and developed to a point where it differed very considerably from the rather primitive conceptions of other Oriental religions. The idea was extended to the whole of mankind because Zoroastrianism presented the coming savior as one who would lead all men to eternal happiness in a new world kingdom, where there would be no sin, no death, no want. To separate the savior-idea from the king-idea and to put the savior-idea upon a more spiritual basis was also a remarkable achievement.

The Persians achieved all of this by blending old Asian, Egyptian, and Semitic political notions with other ideas, some of which were common to all Indo-European races, and by developing them in accordance with the Persian genius. However, in spite of the great progress made by the Iranians, political notions as formulated under the Achaemenids did not become the vital turning point in the evolution of political theory, or the basis of modern political thought. The Persians stopped half way. Laying too great an emphasis on the Persian and Iranian elements in their Empire, they failed to build a state in which all peoples would feel at home and equal. In regarding Ahura Mazda as a strictly Iranian god, they destroyed all chance of giving their Empire a common culture and religion. With the addition of old Iranian mythology and theology, the sublime ethical and religious values of Zoroastrian doctrine were considerably compromised and lost most of their appeal to other nations. The belief in one supreme being, who called upon all to fight for righteousness and truth, contained a basis upon which the ideas of the equality of all men and of their individual natural rights could have been developed. These ideas are the foundation of modern political thought, but the Persians missed the opportunity to further them. Fresh inspiration and new initiatives were needed to stimulate the progress of humanity along this path. They were found in another Indo-European race—the Greeks. The spiritual achievement brought to the Near East by the first great European conqueror, Alexander the Great, and blended there with Persian political and cultural accomplishments, became the basis of Hellenistic culture, the environment in which the first Jewish and Christian political thinkers were to work.

CHAPTER FOUR

FROM MYCENAE TO ISOCRATES

I. Greek migrations and Homeric kingship — Greek epic poetry — Crete, the Mycenaean Greeks, and Near Eastern civilizations — Egyptian influences on Minoan (Cretan) kingship? — Oriental political ideas in the Mycenaean monarchy? — Supreme kingship of Zeus.

II. The new migration and its consequences — Origin of city-states, decline of kingship — Regime of the aristocratic republics, new colonization — Codification, era of tyrants, the Spartan constitution — Origins of Athenian democracy — Pisistratus and Cleisthenes — Triumph of Athenian democracy — Athens' empire, Pericles' radical democracy — The Sophists and their influence on Greek political thought — Degeneration of radical democracy.

III. Longings for a better constitution, reminders of the past — Example of Persia — "Conversion" of Euripides — Plato's criticism of radical democracy — Plato's ideal state — Plato's second-best state — Aristotle on the state and the "best man" as ruler — Aristotle's homage to the tyrant Hermias — Xenophon on the monarchic regime — "Cult" of personalities — Isocrates' Panhellenic ideal — Isocrates and Philip — Isocrates and the monarchic idea.

I

In the third millennium B.C. the forefathers of the Greeks and of the other Indo-European nations left their common primitive home in the steppes of what is now southern Russia and central Asia and migrated into Europe. Followed by the Thracians and Illyrians, they first reached the Danube basin, and from about 2500 B.C. slowly penetrated the Balkan peninsula. Pressed by the Thracians, the forefathers of the Greeks journeyed farther and farther southward and by about 1600 B.C., if not earlier—the dates of their movements are very uncertain—they had settled most of modern Greece as far as the Peloponnesus.

The primitive population of this part of Europe, called Aegean by scholars, was of undetermined non-Indo-European descent. The natives had already developed a civilization superior to that of the newcomers, but the symbiosis of the two peoples was apparently rather peaceful. The newcomers accepted the higher culture of the natives, but imposed on them their leadership in political organization and development. The cultural and anthropological fusion of the native population with the new Indo-European invaders produced, in a long evolution during the second millennium B.C., the Hellenic man.

The history of Greece is very uncertain during this period of fusion which lasted until the twelfth century B.C., when the second Indo-European invasion of Greece, that of the Greek Dorians, took place. All this, however, at least bears out the belief that the earliest political organization of the Greeks must have shown some features which were common to all Indo-Europeans[1] and which have been observed also among the Hittites and the Iranians. Old Aryan institutions were monarchic, with a king at the head, but the king's power was not as absolute as it was among the Asianic and Semitic peoples. Here he was bound to consult the chief men of the community which he governed about all matters concerning his subjects. The decisions of the council and of the king were brought before the assembly of the people represented chiefly by the heads of families. All these prime features are to be found in primitive Greek society. The basis of Greek social and political organization was the family. It was customary for several families to group themselves into a brotherhood called a *phratria*, bound together by the ties of some common religious practices. Families descending from a common ancestor and living in common settlements formed a clan called *genos*. The villages of the clans were parts of a *phyle* or tribe, with a king at its head. When the king of a tribe became more powerful he could extend his sway over other tribes. In such a case a political community arose comprising several tribes, each retaning its separate identity, although its own political customs were merged into common institutions of the larger state.

---

[1] This is rightly stressed by F. Warncke, *Die demokratische Staatsidee in der Verfassung von Athen* (Bonn, 1951), p. 11 seq., with bibliographical indications concerning the primitive political and social structure of other Indo-European nations. Regarding the Slavs, cf. also F. Dvornik, *The Slavs, Their Early History and Civilization* (Boston, 1956), p. 57 seq.

In the formation of new political organisms in the adopted country, geography was the most important factor; the land which the Greek tribes occupied presented quite a different picture from Egypt, Mesopotamia, or Iran. No mighty rivers crossed the territories, the valleys formed by the smaller streams were often cut off by mountains, the sea isolated the many islands from the mainland and penetrated far into that mainland, forming deep bays and numerous peninsulas. Such a land, poor in natural resources and only partly suitable for extensive agriculture, was hardly able to inspire its inhabitants to found large-scale states. It could invite the formation of only small political units which tried to become self-sufficient and independent of other units, often separated from each other by natural impediments. Thanks to Homer, the supposed author of the *Iliad* and the *Odyssey*, the great Greek epics, information is available on the nature of Greek monarchies.[2] Kingship was a gift of Zeus who handed the sceptre to the king, and it was hereditary from father to son. The widowed queen could transfer the royal dignity to another family, should there be no other legitimate heir, by choosing a new husband. The king was supreme commander of the army, possessing the undisputed right of leading his people in war. The king also represented his people before the gods. He had to support and protect religious worship; he, was in fact, chief priest, himself performing the sacrifices when there was no special priesthood for a particular cult. It is important to note that the sacral functions were regarded as an essential part of kingship.[3]

The king is often said to have been also the chief justice. But it should be pointed out that the administration of justice was not regarded as an essential part of the king's prerogatives. Allusions to the judicial function of the king in the Greek epics are rather

[2] See the detailed notations of the relevant passages in the *Iliad* and the *Odyssey* concerning kingship in J. Busolt, *Griechische Staatskunde*, Handbuch der Altertumswissenschaft, Abt. 4, Teil 1, Band 1, Hälfte 1, 3rd ed. (Munich, 1920), pp. 317–341.

[3] There is absolutely no evidence of the existence of a divine kingship in Greece in the Mycenaean and Hellenic periods. Cf. H. J. Rose's study "The Evidence for Divine Kings in Greece," *The Sacral Kingship* (Leiden, 1959), pp. 371–378. This refutes A. B. Cook's argument for its existence in his book *Zeus, a Study in Ancient Religion* (Cambridge, 1914), 2, pp. 1121 seq., 1155 seq.; 3, p. 733.

scanty. Special judges, sometimes identified with the nobles, are mentioned more often. In addition, the assembly of the people is said sometimes to have administered justice in a rather primitive way.

This touches on the problem of the evolution of Greek justice, the most salient feature of which was that, among the primitive Greeks, the avenging of injustices and the punishment of transgressions were the responsibility of family chiefs. Primitively, the king was the highest judge only in the army, as supreme commander. Mention of special judges in the Greek epics reveals the changes introduced in this respect in later periods, characterized by the rise of the aristocracy. The nobles slowly established themselves as arbiters in judicial affairs, curtailing the rights of the family chiefs.[4]

The nobles and the people's assembly played a marked role in other respects too. The king was bound to consult the Council of Elders in all political decisions. The Council had only a deliberative right, but the king had no power to enforce his decision if it was opposed by the Council. Most probably the members of the Council were originally heads of clans that formed the tribes ruled by the king, but, with time, certain families obtained privileged positions and the composition of the Council thus became a kind of aristocracy.

There were also vassals, bound to obey the king's summons to go to war with their men and they, too, were among the new aristocratic members of the Council. These first traces of a primitive feudalism show the direction in which the evolution of Greek kingship was moving. The vassals were sometimes called kings, an indication that this title was becoming a designation for the aristocracy in general. This recalls the Persian titles "King of Kings"

---

[4] This was stressed especially by L. Bréhier in his study "La royauté homérique et les origines de l'état en Grèce," *Revue historique*, 84 (1904), pp. 1 seq., 15 seq., 19 seq.; 85 (1905), p. 11 seq. On primitive Greek justice, cf. G. Busolt, *op. cit.*, p. 330 seq. For fuller information, consult the following works: R. Hirzel, *Themis, Dike und Verwandtes. Ein Beitrag zur Geschichte der Rechtsidee bei den Griechen* (Leipzig, 1907); V. Ehrenberg, *Die Rechtsidee im frühen Griechentum. Untersuchungen zur Geschichte der werdenden Polis* (Leipzig, 1921); R. J. Bonner and G. J. Smith, *The Administration of Justice from Homer to Aristotle* (Chicago, 1930).

and "Great King." The king's vassals were, at the same time, representatives who spoke in behalf of their own troops in the army assembly, and the deliberations to which the king summoned them were connected with banquets held at the king's expense.

The assembly of the people, comprising all freemen of the tribes, was summoned by the king in order to hear and to approve the decisions made by the king and his Council. The assembly had no deliberative power. It was naturally composed of men doing field service and, therefore, in the early days, it was not distinguished from the army.

Besides the vassals and the Council, "king's friends" and "servants" are often mentioned.[5] The latter were the king's personal attendants, charged with the execution of different services. The former were the king's companions or retainers, who lived in his palace, ate at his table, and guarded him in battle.

It is clear from this short sketch of Homeric kingship[6] that the political ideas of the primitive Greeks differed considerably from those of Oriental peoples which have been discussed in the preceding chapters. The Homeric king was not the absolute master over his subjects that the Oriental king was. Early Greek political institutions provide elements which entitle us to speak about an evolution toward an aristocratic regime. Similar elements were found only among the Assyrians. It is possible that such a situation evolved in Assyria not only because of special internal conditions, but also because of influences from the Indo-European Hittites.

The question arises whether the political conditions described in the great Greek epic poems correspond to the earliest period of

---

[5] On the assembly and the "king's friends," see M. P. Nilsson, *Homer and Mycenae* (London, 1933), pp. 226–235.

[6] Inasmuch as this subject is dealt with in all handbooks of Greek history, more detailed study is omitted here. Greater detail and bibliographical notes will be found in J. Busolt's great work quoted above and in M. P. Nilsson's book, *Homer and Mycenae*, p. 212 seq. The latter develops ideas put forward in his lecture, "Das homerische Königtum," *SB d. Preuss. Akad. d. Wissensch.* (Berlin, 1927), p. 23 seq.; new edition in his *Opuscula selecta*, 2 (Lund, 1951–52), pp. 871–897. See also the short study by Joan Puhvel, "Helladic Kingship and the Gods," in *Minoica, Festschrift zum 80. Geburtstag von Johannes Sundwall*, ed. by E. Grumach, Deutsche Akademie der Wissenschaften zu Berlin, Sektion für Altertumswissenschaften, 12 (Berlin, 1958), pp. 327–333.

Greek history or whether they reflect the situation which existed at the time the poems obtained their present definitive shape. It would also be of interest to know whether there was any contact between the Greeks, settled in their new homes, and the important Oriental cultures, a contact which might also have influenced the evolution of Greek political institutions.

The answer to these questions can be given only when it is determined at what period the two great poems—the *Iliad* and the *Odyssey*—were composed. Specialists are not yet in accord on this problem. It seems, however, that the progress so far made by scholars in classical history and literature gives us a sufficiently solid basis for our own purposes. It has been pretty well established that both poems, but especially the *Iliad,* were intended to glorify deeds performed by some Greek heroes in the oldest, so-called heroic, period of Greek history.[7] They recall some historical events that occurred before 1200 B.C. The beginning of the eleventh century B.C. is marked by a cultural and political decline brought about by the Dorian invasion. The epic songs that had originated during the heroic period were preserved by minstrels through the subsequent centuries of cultural impoverishment and political chaos. To sing of the glory of bygone days had an especially stimulating significance in times of national downfall. The songs were carried from tribe to tribe and subjected to changes and additions, but they preserved their archaic features. The Greek colonists brought them to the Aegean Islands and Asia Minor, where they achieved their definitive form thanks to a great poet. His remarkable talent endowed them with new life, vigor, and cohesion, and made the *Iliad* one of the glorious products of human genius. There is not yet agreement among the specialists as to the exact time this poet, whom tradition calls Homer, arose. One can vacillate between the ninth and eighth centuries B.C., although the end of the eighth seems the most probable date.

Homer's achievement gave new impulse to Greek epic poetry. The school of minstrels which came into existence gave rise also to

---

[7] See for details the concise exposé of the controversy concerning Homer in M. P. Nilsson, *Homer and Mycenae*, pp. 1–55. The detailed study on the origin and transmission of epic poetry (*ibid.*, pp. 184–211) seems particularly convincing and gives a new approach to the whole problem.

the second poem, the *Odyssey*, which celebrates a hero of the Trojan war but also reflects the adventurous spirit that animated Greek colonists and merchants in the period of intensive colonizing activity.

It is thus established that the two immortal epics obtained their definitive form at a time much later than the events which they describe. This fact leads one to question the reliability of the information which they give about the oldest Greek political institutions. The prominent role given to the aristocracy in the poems —especially in the *Odyssey*—reflects, rather, the situation which arose in Greece after 1000 B.C., when kingship was definitely in decline. The important position of the aristocracy in cities founded by colonists was a natural consequence, and it seems that the two epics achieved their final form in this environment.

On the other hand, the monarchic idea is expressed in a very clear and almost uncompromising way in both poems. The famous dictum from the *Iliad* (book II, verse 204) may be recalled: "A multitude of masters is an evil thing, let there be one master." These words made a profound impression on the Greek mind, and will be found quoted again and again in support of the monarchic political system. Although the verse could be interpreted as the poet's criticism of the abuses of an aristocratic regime, it is more likely to be an echo of earlier times when the Greeks knew only one political system, the monarchy.

What happened in the heroic age of Greece? Cannot further documentation be found for this epoch that would help to define more clearly its political tendencies? Until recently little was known beyond what can be learned from the two great epics. But the rich archaeological discoveries made since 1886 on the initiative of H. Schliemann in Mycenae, in the Peloponnesus, and elsewhere has revolutionized our knowledge of ancient Greece. The extremely rich archaeological material testifies to a very high cultural level in Greece in the second millennium B.C. This civilization—called Mycenaean after the place where most of the discoveries were made, which seems also to have been the civilization's principal center—must have developed under influences emanating from Crete. Excavations, initiated there by A. J. Evans in 1900, revealed remains of a surprisingly well developed high culture, which was much older than the Mycenaean. It is called Minoan, for the palace of Minos at Cnossos on Crete, whose excavation has, more than anything else, revealed the riches of Cretan art.

Many problems concerning both civilizations are still subjects of controversy among specialists.[8] The nationality of the creators of Mycenaean art was hotly argued for a long time, but the Greek character of the people who were the bearers of Mycenaean culture is today sufficiently firmly established. Mycenaean civilization presents many characteristic features in housing, architecture, dress, and art which cannot be explained by a colonization or conquest of Greece by the Cretans. These features can be explained only by the adaptation of Minoan civilization in Greece by a new people, different from the Cretans, who were most probably of Asianic origin. The two great Greek epic poems describe artistic objects and some social conditions which could have existed only during the Mycenaean period. This circumstance completes the evidence for shifting the origins of Greek epic poetry to the Mycenaean period.

It must therefore be assumed that the Greeks, after having absorbed their new inhabitants, had sooner or later, at a date difficult to assess, started to build ships and to make expeditions to Crete, attracted there by the riches and culture about which they could have learned from the native population. The Cretans had colonies on the continent and some Greek tribes might have become tributary to them. It is possible that such expeditions were necessitated by the advent of new masses of Greeks looking for settlements in the peninsula, for the Greek immigration was ac-

[8] There is no room here for details. See, for example, the short and clear résumé of the controversy in M. P. Nilsson, *Homer and Mycenae*, pp. 56–86. Cf. also J. L. Myres, *Who Were the Greeks?* (Berkeley, 1930) and M. P. Nilsson's criticism (*op. cit.*, p. 57 seq.) of some of Myres's views. Cf. also M. Ventris and J. Chadwick, *Documents in Mycenaean Greek* (Cambridge, 1956). A. J. B. Wace gave a review of recent discoveries in ancient Greek history in his study "The History of Greece in the third and second Millenniums B.C.," *Historia*, 2 (1953–54), pp. 74–94, with recent bibliography. Cf. also L. R. Palmer, *Mycenaeans and Minoans* (London, 1961); F. Matz, "Minoan Civilisation," *CAH* (1962); V. R. d'A. Desborough and N. G. L. Hammond, "The End of Mycenaean Civilisation," *ibid.* More complete bibliography is given by B. E. Moon, *Mycenaean Civilization* (London, 1957–61), 2 vols.

complished in successive waves. Through the influence of Cretans brought back to Greece as prisoners, the open-minded Greeks, subjected to the appeal of a superior civilization, began the reorganization of their life according to the Cretan model, and commercial intercourse between the two lands completed the process.

If this is indeed what happened, then it is possible that, through their contact with Crete, the Greeks came under the influence of Near Eastern, especially Egyptian, civilizations. There is some evidence of intercourse between Crete and Egypt during the reign of the Twelfth and Thirteenth Dynasties. It was especially brisk from the sixteenth century B.C. on.[9] In the tomb of a governor of Upper Egypt under Thutmose III are shown offerings presented by the Keftiu, "the people from beyond," which show characteristics of Minoan art. The "tribute bearers" could only be Cretans. The same types of men are represented in other Egyptian tombs. The Egyptians certainly exaggerated when they called the Cretans their subjects. They could never have conquered the island as they had no fleet. In 1467 B.C. Thutmose III even had to employ Cretan sailors and boats to transport timber from the coast of Phoenicia to Egypt. Only later was this service performed by the Phoenicians.

On the other hand, Egyptian products reached Crete; not only objects of art but foodstuffs as well. Some religious forms must have been introduced from Egypt into Crete. The fragment of a steatite vase found in Crete and dating from the eighteenth century B.C. represents a festive procession in the middle of which a priest with an Egyptian *sistrum*—a musical instrument—leads young, singing, Cretan men.[10] Minoan writing also shows traces of the influence of Egyptian hieroglyphics.

[9] Cf. A. R. Burn, *Minoans, Philistines and Greeks* (London, 1930), p. 80 seq. See A. J. Evans, *The Palace of Minos at Knossos*, 1 (London, 1921), p. 17 seq., on cultural relationship between Egypt and Crete from the early dynasties on. For more details, see *ibid.*, p. 286 seq. ("Egyptian Monuments and Relations"). Cf. also *ibid.*, 2, pt. 1 (1928), pp. 192 seq., 209 seq. See also H. R. Hall, "Keftiu," *Essays in Aegean Archaeology presented to Sir Arthur Evans* (Oxford, 1927), pp. 31–41; S. Marinatos and M. Hirmer, *Kreta und das mykenische Hellas* (Munich, 1959).
[10] See the reproduction in A. J. Evans, *op. cit.*, 2, pt 1 (1928), p. 47, and in J. H. Breasted, *A History of Egypt* (New York, 1912), fig. 127. Cf. *ibid.*, p. 337 seq., on Egyptian cultural influences in Crete and in early Greece.

These influences also reached Greece proper, first indirectly through Crete and then directly through commercial intercourse. Thus, the finds of scarabs and bits of glazed ware with the name of Amenhotep III or Queen Tiy at Mycenae can be explained. Influences of Egyptian art are to be traced in the products of Mycenaean artists, especially in the drawing of landscapes and animal forms. The tombs of Mycenae have decorated ceilings similar to that found at Thebes in Egypt.

Attracted by the Syrian and Egyptian civilizations, the Greeks moved steadily toward those countries, as is shown by the history of their first attempts at colonization. Some Hittite texts have preserved evidence of Greek attempts to settle in southern Asia Minor. The letter of a vassal king asking for protection against this invasion seems to have been addressed to the Hittite King Murshilish II who ascended the throne in 1336 B.C. Although other Hittite evidence concerning the Greeks must be accepted with extreme caution, the authenticity of the letter seems reliably established. It attributes the attack to the brother of the king of Ahiyava. This name can refer only to the Achaean state in the Peloponnesus with its center at Mycenae.[11]

Later documents speak of Achaean attacks on Cyprus around the middle of the thirteenth century B.C. The island was colonized by the Greeks at the beginning of the twelfth century B.C. There is some probability that the Greek tribe of the Danaoi settled in Palestine at the beginning of the fourteenth century B.C., assuming that the tribe of the Danuna mentioned in one of the Tell el-Amarna Letters can be identified with it.[12] Even greater probability attaches to the supposition that the Achaeans participated in the attack on the Nile delta in 1221 B.C. The numerous tribes which attacked by sea and land were beaten off by Merneptah.[13] It seems that Greek attacks on Crete had forced a Minoan tribe—the

[11] Cf. the short résumé of discussions concerning the problem and the main bibliographical notices in M. P. Nilsson, *Homer and Mycenae*, p. 102 seq. Archaeological evidence favors the presence of Greeks in Syria and in Cyprus.

[12] Letter 151, 52 seq., S. A. B. Mercer, *The Tell el-Amarna Tablets* (Toronto, 1939), p. 497, of Abimilki, King of Tyre, announcing to the Pharaoh the death of the King of Danuna. For details, see A. R. Burn, *op. cit.*, p. 120 seq.

[13] See the Egyptian inscriptions in J. H. Breasted, *Ancient Records of Egypt*, (Chicago, 1906–7), 3, no. 1569 seq.

Philistines of the Bible—to seek their fortune elsewhere. Their attempt in company with other Asianic tribes to settle in the Nile Delta was repulsed by Rameses III (1190 B.C.) They settled on the southern coast of Palestine and were used by the Egyptians as mercenaries. The finding of Mycenaean pottery in their settlements shows, at least, that they were in some kind of relationship with the Greek Achaeans.[14]

The details of this steady penetration on the part of the Mycenaean Greeks toward the centers of the great Oriental civilizations are not yet clear. But sufficient evidence is available to establish the existence of cultural exchanges between the Greeks of the Mycenaean Age and Egypt and Syria, then under strong Babylonian cultural influence. Moreover, repeated attempts to establish colonies on the approaches to Egypt and Syria—on the southern coast of Asia Minor, on Rhodes, on Cyprus, and finally on the western coast of Syria and in the Nile delta—can be followed in general outline. These attempts were backed by the Achaean state, centered in Mycenae, and lasted from *ca.* 1400 to *ca.* 1200 B.C.

Thus, direct contact between the great Oriental civilizations and the Mycenaean Greeks is established beyond doubt. It may well be asked whether the influences emanating from these civilizations did not also make themselves felt in the political organization of the Mycenaean state and in other political centers of the period.

It seems natural to think first of all of the Cretans as possible transmitters of some Egyptian political ideas to the Mycenaean Greeks. When the frequent intercourse between the Egyptians and the Cretans is taken into consideration, one is inclined to think that the latter might have been influenced by the Egyptians in their political organization. But this expectation is doomed to disappointment. It is true that a monarchic regime had developed in Crete to supersede the primitive government by numerous chiefs of clans.[15] After a protracted evolution characterized by internal strife, two great centers were formed in Crete soon after 2000 B.C. —Cnossos on the northern coast and Phaistos in the south. The

---

[14] For details, see A. R. Burn, *op. cit.*, p. 141 seq.
[15] Cf. G. Glotz, *La civilisation égéenne* (Paris, 1923), p. 171 seq.

aspirations of the ruler of Cnossos to hegemony over the small city-states of the island were realized about 1500 when Phaistos with two other important centers—Haghia Triada and Mallia— were subjugated and the palaces of their kings destroyed. This, apparently, was carried out by Mycenaean Greeks who had established themselves at Cnossos. From then on the Minos of Cnossos—the name seems to have been a kind of dynastic title, like the Egyptian Pharaoh—was master of all vassal kings and, if there was any Egyptian influence on Cretan political organization, it must have begun at this time.

As later Greek sources show, the Minos of Cnossos was a representative on earth of the Minotaur—the bull-god. In later Greek tradition the Minotaur was brought into connection with Zeus. The supreme Greek god took the form of a bull and having approached Queen Pasiphae in the disguise of a cow, he begot Minos who was therefore regarded as his son. Minos obtained his divine vocation to govern men for only nine years. At the end of that period he was to present himself before his god in the sacred cave of the Labyrinth. God himself was then to decide whether he wished Minos to remain his representative for another nine years.[16] This mythical account seems at first to show traces of Egyptian influence. It should be recalled that, according to the Egyptians' belief in the period of the New Kingdom, the sun-god as Ka-Mutef, bull of his mother, approached the queen and, impersonating the king, had intercourse with her; so the future king of Egypt was another incarnation of the supreme god. The Cretans, who came from Near Eastern lands and were probably of Asianic origin, may have had some similar myths on superior beings in the form of animals.[17] This circumstance may have influenced them to accept the Egyptian mythical belief and to adapt it to their own national mythical tradition.

---

[16] Homer, *The Odyssey*, XIX, vs. 179, ed. by A. T. Murray (Loeb, 1931), 2, p. 240; Plato, *Minos*, 319 D, ed. by W. R. M. Lamb (Loeb, 1927), p. 414; Plato, *Laws*, 624 D, 630 D, ed. by R. G. Bury (Loeb, 1926), 1, pp. 2, 22; Strabo, *Geography*, X, 4, 8, 9, ed. by H. L. Jones (Loeb, 1928), 5, p, 128 seq.; Dionysius of Halicarnassus, *The Roman Antiquities*, II, 61, 1, ed. by E. Cary (Loeb, 1937), 1, p. 488. On the Labyrinth and Minotaur, cf. A. J. Evans, *op. cit.*, 1, p. 359.

[17] A. J. Evans, *op. cit.*, 1, p. 69, thinks of the myths of Gilgamesh and of Ea-bâni.

But when further study is devoted to the story a more critical attitude must be assumed toward the myth of the Minotaur and its supposed Egyptian origin. First of all, no archaeological evidence is available for its Cretan origin in Crete. The legend of the Minotaur is reported by a very late Greek tradition and seems to have been originally Greek.[18] It is possible that it originated in pre-Mycenaean Greece where some of the Greek tribes, especially the Athenians, were in a tributary relationship to Crete. There may have been in the origin and growth of this myth a certain connection with Cretan kingship, but its character cannot be determined. As to its connection with Egypt, nothing can be brought forward to substantiate this hypothesis.

There is, furthermore, no evidence from Cretan monuments to confirm the limitation of the rule of Cretan kings to nine years. The Greek tradition which reports it is again very late. It is quite possible even that this report on Cretan kingship is of late Greek origin, and developed only after the colonization of Crete by the Dorians. It is legitimate to detect here an echo of the Dorian custom which developed in Sparta, where every month the kings had to take an oath before the *ephoroi*—representatives of the people— that they would observe the laws in discharging their royal functions.[19] The ephors promised, on their part, to maintain the royal power undiminished as long as the king should be true to his oath. This critical review of the Greek tradition concerning Cretan kingship considerably reduces our knowledge of the political organization of the Minoan civilization. It eliminates almost completely the possibility of Egyptian influences.

A further comparison of Egyptian and Cretan kingship confirms this impression. The fact that the king was at the same time a priest[20] suggests no foreign influences. It was a common element of ideas on kingship among all Asianic and Semitic nations. There is certainly a difference between Egypt and Crete in the choice of regal emblems. The symbol of Minos' royal dignity was the sceptre

---

[18] Cf. M. P. Nilsson, *The Mycenaean Origin of Greek Mythology* (Berkeley, 1932), pp. 169 seq., 171, 176.

[19] See *infra*, p. 155.

[20] Cf. A. J. Evans, *op. cit.*, 2, pt. 2, p. 774 seq., on the priest-king relief.

and a double axe.[21] It seems too that the lily—the fleur-de-lis—
was the royal emblem. In one fresco—the priest-king relief—the
king is represented wearing a crown of lilies and a necklace of the
same kind, and marching through a field of lilies. There is nothing
of this sort in Egyptian royal symbolism. It is, however, quite
possible, although not at all sure, that in the choice of personal
names and titles and in the composition of a cartouche of their
royal seals the Minos were influenced by similar Egyptian customs.

Quite possibly the Cretans had imitated certain Egyptian
traditions in the administration of their state. The government of
Cnossos was, at least, strongly centralized and well developed; but
it is impossible to say more on this subject, since the numerous
tablets found in the ruins of the palace have not yet been deciphered. Nothing more precise is known on the divine character of
the king. However, it seems probable that in this respect the
influence of Egyptian royal theology could not have been very
profound. Crete was a small island and the king could hardly surround himself with an unapproachable majesty, as was possible in
the far flung Egyptian Empire. The Cretan regime apparently
also gave the aristocracy greater opportunity to participate in
court life and in matters of administration. The aristocratic families had their villas in the proximity of the royal palace,[22] in order
to be within easy reach of the king. Such intimacy with the royal
family does not suggest that the Minos was venerated, during his
life, as a god. According to the belief of his subjects, after his death
he was placed in Hades, as judge of the dead.[23]

This particular belief was connected with the main function
which the Minos exercised on earth—the administration of justice.

[21] *Ibid.*, 2, pt. 1, p. 273 seq. (sword of state and axe); 2, pt. 2, p. 776 seq.
(lily).

[22] G. Glotz, *op. cit.*, p. 174.

[23] *Ibid.*, p. 177. The problem of sacral kingship in Crete is not yet clarified. A. Furumark in a short study, "Was there a Sacral Kingship in Minoan
Crete?" *The Sacral Kingship*, pp. 369, 370, sees in the burial rites represented
on the Hagia Triada sarcophagus and in the griffins flanking the royal throne
in Cnossos indications of the divine character of the Minoan kingship. More
telling evidence for this thesis would be desirable. The explanation given
above should explain these symbols. In any case Egyptian influence can
hardly be proved after 1470, when the Mycenaean Greeks had settled at
Cnossos. The native Cretans could have developed their own beliefs before
coming to Crete.

The function of supreme legislator and judge was naturally intimately related with the king's character as representative and priest of the supreme god. It was his duty to transmit to his people the laws of the gods and to watch over their observance.[24]

Egyptian influence on the evolution of Cretan or Minoan kingship is thus very hypothetical, and this reduces to a minimum the possibility of Oriental influences on Mycenaean kingship, with Crete as the intermediary. Although the Mycenaean civilization is wholly built on the Minoan, direct evidence is lacking to indicate any marked influence of Cretan kingship on Mycenaean political institutions in the numerous states. One thing seems certain. As in Crete, so a strong monarchic regime started to develop in ancient, pre-Homeric Greece, especially in Argolis with its center at Mycenae. The archaeological finds at Mycenae and in its neighborhood indicate that the place was the seat of a monarch who ruled over several vassals. This is illustrated by the imposing palaces, fortified castles, well planned commercial roads, and the rich royal burial places. The might and renown of this monarch is echoed in the *Iliad* where Agamemnon is said to "rule mightily over all the Argives, and whom the Achaeans obey." He received the sceptre from Zeus "that he might be lord of many isles and of all Argos."[25]

This pre-Homeric, hereditary monarchy may, however, have developed in the Peloponnesus without any direct influence from abroad. Its basis was the old Greek social institutions, most of them characteristic of all Indo-European nations. The conquest of the land, the political subjugation of the natives, and expeditions against Crete necessitated strong leadership, a disciplined army, and a stable and continuous government. All this naturally prepared the way for a monarchic regime, more powerful than the political institutions which the Greeks had brought with them. Such a regime was established in Argolis in the Peloponnesus, with a center

---

[24] This function of the Cretan kings is particularly stressed in the later Greek tradition by all the authors quoted above. The law-giving function of the Minos must have particularly impressed Plato.

[25] Homer, *The Iliad*, I, vs. 79, II, vs. 108, ed. by A. T. Murray (Loeb, 1937), I, pp. 8, 58.

in Mycenae.[26] When the Mycenaean monarchy collapsed, overwhelmed by new invaders—the Dorians—the Greek political picture resumed the more aristocratic character which it had enjoyed previously, and which is described in other passages of the *Iliad* and the *Odyssey*.

Only one feature in the Mycenaean monarchy seems to suggest the possibility of a foreign, perhaps Egyptian, influence—the cupola graves of the kings. The nine tombs testify not only to the uninterrupted succession of mighty monarchs from about 1430 to 1230 B.C., but also to the growing progress of their might and of the general civilization of Mycenae. The technique of the construction of the tombs shows a gradual improvement. One tomb almost approached the proportions of the tombs of Egyptian Pharaohs. The rich decoration and lavish furnishing of these tombs testifies to a highly developed cult of dead kings in Mycenae. It is no wonder then that in Greek tradition these tombs were called treasuries. Buried with the king, in addition to the arms and utensils which he had used during his life, were, generally, numerous servants who were killed on his tomb in order to accompany their lord into the hereafter.[27]

These burial customs betray some similarity with the Egyptian royal cult, but it would be presumptuous to affirm that all were taken over from Egypt. It may be that the tombs were inspired by what the Greeks of Mycenae had heard about the burial places of the Pharoahs. If this is the case, the influence must have come to Greece directly without Crete as an intermediate stepping stone, because in Crete similar sepulchral constructions were made at a much later period under influences emanating from Mycenae.

Other burial customs could have developed in Mycenae from a common Indo-European tradition, free of any direct influence from Egypt. Nothing in the archaeological discoveries at Mycenae and elsewhere indicates that her kings were objects of a kind of divine

[26] A similar development could be observed in Boeotia where the kings residing in Gha (Gla) had established their supremacy over neighboring kings and princes.
[27] On the Greek burial customs of the Homeric period, cf. M. P. Nilsson, *Homer and Mycenae*, pp. 152 seq., 217 seq.

worship, although the cult of dead kings is certainly more marked in Mycenaean kingship than is indicated in the Homeric epics.

It is true that in the *Iliad* the dynasty of Achilles springs from Zeus; also those of Idomeneus and Priam.[28] The title *diogenes*, (born from Zeus) is given in the *Iliad* to Agamemnon, Achilles, Ajax, Eurypylus, and Patroclus. In another passage the same poet refers to the king, his sons, and some other aristocrats and warriors as "protected by Zeus."[29] In the *Odyssey* it is stated that the kings are descendants of Zeus;[30] there, however, the title *diogenes* is given only to Odysseus. The god Poseidon is said to have been the ancestor of the dynasty of Neleus.[31] This kind of divine filiation cannot, however, be taken as seriously as the Semitic ideas on relationship to gods. It is connected with the anthropomorphic trait of Greek ideas on gods and with hero worship, which we shall discuss later.[32]

There is one important conclusion which may be deduced from our investigation. Although direct influences of Oriental ideas of kingship on the political evolution of Mycenaean Greece cannot be found, these influences would inevitably have made themselves felt in Greece had the Mycenaean monarchy lasted longer. The Greeks of this period were instinctively gravitating more and more toward the Southeast where lay the centers of Near Eastern civilization. The colonization of the northern coast of Asia Minor, Crete, Cyprus, and of the Syrian coast were important attempts which would have brought the Greek mainland nearer and nearer to Babylonia and Egypt, and would have accelerated the penetration of Near Eastern civilization into Greece proper. It would have been natural for the Mycenaean monarchy to strengthen the absolutist tendency which has already been observed there. The new conquests in the Near East and the protection of established colonies could have been realized only if this penetration had been supported by the strong hand of an absolute monarch, the more so,

---

[28] *Iliad*, XXI, vs. 187 seq., XIII, vs. 449 seq., XX, vs. 213 seq., ed. by A. T. Murray (Loeb, 1939), 2, pp. 422, 36, 386.
[29] See for details and quotations, J. Busolt, *Griechische Staatskunde*, p. 320.
[30] *Odyssey*, XX, vs. 201 (Loeb, 1931), 2, p. 288.
[31] *Odyssey*, XI, vss. 254–257 (Loeb, 1938), 1, pp. 402, 404.
[32] See *infra*, pp. 218-220.

as the opposition to their penetration would have come from strong monarchic regimes. Thus it seemed at the end of the Mycenaean period that the Greek genius was about to attempt the fusion of Indo-European political institutions, adapting Oriental ideas of kingship to the Greek national character. This time the undertaking would certainly have been more interesting than that attempted by the Hittites and realized by the Iranians, for the Greek mainland was not completely surrounded by Oriental civilizations as were the Hittites and the Iranians.

But these possibilities failed to become realities. The Dorian invasion of the Peloponnesus terminated the Mycenaean monarchy and interrupted the promising evolution. The Greeks had to wait several centuries for a new opportunity to conquer the Near East. In the meantime their own political evolution underwent sweeping changes, and the blending of Near Eastern and Greek political ideas had to be realized under new circumstances and under the leadership not of the Mycenaean, but of the Macedonian, monarchy.

One important inheritance from the Mycenaean period, however, remained intact for centuries and was, unexpectedly, to play a marked role in the evolution of the blended Greco-Oriental political theories—the idea of the supreme kingship of Zeus.[33] We have seen that in the Middle East and in Egypt the heavenly order always reflected the actual political order on earth. This occurs most markedly in Mesopotamia where the supreme position in heaven goes from Enlil to Marduk or Ashur as political supremacy is won by the Sumerians, Babylonians, or Assyrians each of whom not only subjugates other peoples but brings their gods under the rule of its own national deity.

A similar situation developed in Greece in the Mycenaean period. Primitively, Greek deities had their dwelling in places or elements over which they were believed to rule. Zeus, the god of thunder and rain, was believed to dwell in the mountains, enveloped in clouds. Everything indicates that the pre-Hellenic term for "moun-

---

[33] See M. P. Nilsson, *The Mycenaean Origin of Greek Mythology*, p. 236. Cf. A. B. Cook, *Zeus, a Study in Ancient Religion*, 1, pp. 100–150. Cf. also M. P. Nilsson, *The Minoan-Mycenaean Religion and Its Survival in Greek Religion*, 2nd ed. (Lund, 1950).

tain" was "Olympus," a word for which a probable Greek etymology cannot be found. Many mountains in Greece and Asia Minor are designated by this name. As god of thunder and lightning, Zeus was particularly fitted to become the supreme god, although in the pre-Hellenic cult he did not occupy the most prominent place. This promotion of Zeus to king of gods was effected during the Greek heroic period—the Mycenaean age. A heavenly monarchy was imagined, formed on the pattern of the earthly monarchy of Mycenae. Just as the king was surrounded by his retinue and vassals, so Zeus was imagined to have placed all other gods in Olympus. He reigned over them as the king ruled over his vassals, invited them to assemblies, issued orders, and was respected as their supreme lord.

Many such descriptions can be read in the *Iliad* and *Odyssey*, descriptions which give quite a clear idea of the Greek state, of the gods, and of Zeus' undisputed supremacy. Homer located this divine state on the Olympus of Thessaly, the highest mountain of Greece, although primitively it was located in mountains surrounded with clouds or in heaven, symbolized by the clouds. From Homer's time on, the heavenly monarchy continued to be located on the Olympus of Thessaly. Through Homer, the divine monarchy of Zeus became one of the most popular beliefs of the Greeks. Thanks to Homer and to the fact that men are most faithful to old tradition in religion, this state of things was not changed when political ideas in Greece evolved from monarchy to democracy.[34]

These circumstances will be shown to have had a profound influence upon the evolution of political ideas in the coming ages.[35] Homer's divine monarchy of Zeus became the basis of theological speculations leading to a kind of pagan monotheism in a period when there was a mighty monarchy on earth which should naturally, according to both the old and contemporary opinion, reflect the heavenly monarchy. This idea will be seen to influence also

[34] For details, see M. P. Nilsson, *The Minoan and Mycenean Religion*, pp. 221–251, and *idem, Geschichte der griechischen Religion*, Handbuch der Altertumswissenschaft, Abt. 5, Teil 2, Band 1, 2nd. ed. (Munich, 1955), pp. 350–354.
[35] See, for example, *infra*, pp. 170, 185, 202.

the first Christian political thinkers[36] who certainly did not imagine that they were indebted to the Mycenaean Greeks.

II

The penetration of the Illyrians into northern Greece in the twelfth century B.C. led to the decay of the flourishing Mycenaean culture and to a complete upheaval in Greek political history.[37] First, Epirus and Aetolia were engulfed by the wave of the Illyrian invasion. Epirus which had been in greater part Hellenized and whose religious center was the sanctuary of Zeus in Dodona, became once more Illyrian. Aetolia, a flourishing land in Homeric times, lapsed into almost complete barbarism. A great many of the Aetolians crossed the Corinthian Gulf, subjected the native Greek population, and settled in the land which became known as Elis.

The Thessalians, a backward Greek tribe which had not been touched by the Mycenaean civilization, forced southward by the Illyrians, invaded the land called Thessaly, subjugated the inhabitants, and forced the rest of the Achaeans who had been driven into the mountains of Phthia, and other minor tribes, to become their tributaries. The superior culture of the subjugated natives, however, showed itself in the fact that the Achaean dialect prevailed over the Thessalian idiom in the new kingdoms.

A considerable portion of the Achaeans followed the Aetolians across the gulf and settled in the northern part of the Peloponnesus, in the land which came to be called Achaia. The Greek Boeotians were also forced out of Epirus and gradually settled in the land to which they gave their name. Here the remnants of the Aegean tradition survived for a long time in the city-state of Orchomenus.

---

[36] See *infra*, pp. 612–614.
[37] For a detailed history of Greece, see G. Busolt, *Griechische Geschichte bis zur Schlacht bei Chaeroneia* (Gotha, 1893–1904), 3 vols.; K. J. Beloch, *Griechische Geschichte*, 2nd ed. (Berlin-Leipzig, 1912–22), 3 vols., and the handbooks: J. B. Bury, *A History of Greece to the Death of Alexander the Great*, 2nd ed. (London, 1929); N. G. L. Hammond, *A History of Greece to 322 B.C.* (Oxford, 1959); H. Bengtson, *Griechische Geschichte von den Anfängen bis in die römische Kaiserzeit*, Handbuch der Altertumswissenschaft, Abt. 3, Teil 4, 2nd ed. (Munich, 1960).

Here the symbiosis of the conquerors with the natives was effected more peaceably than in Thessaly and the dialects of both coalesced in a new idiom, called Boeotian.

The most profound changes were, however, effected by the Dorians, one of the four major tribes of the Hellenes, along with the Achaeans, Aeolians, and Ionians. Moving from their old seats, probably in Macedonia and Thessaly, the Dorians penetrated the central lands of modern Greece, even occupying Delphi, the famous shrine of Apollo. Only a small part of the tribe, however, remained there, preserving its original name, Doris. The further wandering of the main Dorian group continued in several phases. It seems that a part journeyed from Naupactus by boat around the Peloponnesus, and settled in Crete, on the islands of Melos and Thera, and on the coast of southern Asia Minor. Their greatest achievement was, however, the gradual conquest of the Peloponnesus. Blocked by the Achaeans in the North and the Aetolians in the West, they sailed to the South and conquered Laconia where the majority of them settled after subjugating the natives. The conquest of Argolis was more difficult. Mycenae and Tiryns seem to have been destroyed at that time, but their native populations were only subdued and became amalgamated with the Dorians. More important was the third phase of the Dorian invasion, from the Saronic Gulf, which ended with the conquest of Corinth and Megara. The island of Aegina was also overcome after Argolis had been brought more firmly under their control.

Attica, which had been profoundly influenced by the Mycenaean civilization, was, thanks to its geographical situation, spared the horrors of the barbaric invasions which had affected the rest of Greece. However, even there the old population of Pelasgian or Greek stock had to accept the predominance of a new Greek tribe, akin to the Ionians and worshippers of their goddess Athena. The date of this event is uncertain, but the movement of the Athenians towards their new seats must have been connected in some way with the pressure exercised in the North by the Thracians and Illyrians, although it happened much earlier than the final migration of the Dorians, perhaps at the end of the second millennium B.C.

These upheavals also resulted in the foundation of Greek colonies on the coast of Asia Minor. The invaders forced many Achaeans and Aetolians to look for new homes in new lands. Together they founded several Hellenic colonies on the northwestern shore of Asia Minor and on the adjoining islands. This part of the sea coast became Aeolis, in Hellenic tradition. Ionian colonists settled in the middle of the western coast of Asia Minor where Ephesus, Magnesia, and Miletus became their most flourishing cities; Ionia was flanked in the south by Dorian settlements, which included Rhodes and other islands. So it happened that the Aegean Sea became a Greek lake.

All of this was accomplished under the leadership of tribal kings who led their people to new homes. Moreover, Athens also owed to its kings—legendary tradition attributed this deed to Theseus—the foundation of its commonwealth, which was probably realized in the ninth century B.C. through the union of Attica: all the smaller cities consented to surrender their own governments and to accept the central government in Athens.

Thus, Greece was again governed by kings, and they were many in number because the tribal division once more came to the forefront in Hellenic political life, and the geographical factor again played an important role in Greek history, making the formation of larger political units difficult. However, one new feature gradually appeared in Greek political life. In order to protect their tribes and to consolidate their own power, the kings encouraged their subjects to settle in walled cities. These were mostly constructed near or in the strongholds of the recently conquered Mycenaeans. So it happened that the Greek monarchy created the new form of political life, the *polis*, or city-state.[38]

Only the Dorians made an exception and broke completely with the Mycenaean tradition; they settled in unwalled, closely connected villages. But because these formed the center of power and

[38] For a detailed history of the *polis*, see G. Busolt, *Griechische Staatskunde*, p. 153 seq. Cf. also G. Glotz, *The Greek and its Institutions* (London, 1929). Both older and more recent bibliography on Greek state organization is given in V. Ehrenberg's *Der Staat der Griechen*, I (Leipzig, 1957–58), p. 101 seq. Cf. also W. W. Fowler, *The City-State of the Greeks and Romans* (London, 1952), pp. 1–183.

were fused into one locality called Sparta, they too can be assimilated to city-states, founded by the many tribal kings.

The concentration of the population in the cities, however, became fatal to Greek kingship. Living in close proximity to their subjects, the kings lost stature as all their human shortcomings —not so apparent when they resided in strongholds dominating the surrounding plains and villages—stood revealed.[39] Moreover, the desire to increase their power over the citizens, provoked opposition on the part of both the aristocracy and the common people. It was easy to organize plots among discontented subjects living in a secluded city; so it came about that in the new city-states the authority of the kings soon started to decline and that of the aristocracy to grow. This process lasted for many generations, but in the eighth century it was evident that the monarchic regime in Greece was disappearing.

This transformation in Greek political life was effected in different ways, which were seldom recorded by history. In some states only a part of the nobility obtained power, and such a regime was called an oligarchic constitution. The old monarchic regime persisted only in barbarous Macedonia, which was governed by a Greek dynasty, in Epirus, in remote Molossia, and in the African colony of Cyrene.

A special form of kingship survived in Sparta. The state was headed by two kings whose functions were hereditary in their families. This was probably the consequence of the fusion of two tribes which desired to retain their own kings even after the amalgamation. The dual kingship was regarded as less dangerous to the pretentions of the aristocracy. The powers of the kings were further limited by the Council of Elders (*gerontia*), whose twenty-eight members were chosen for life, from among the aristocracy, by the people's Assembly. The Council prepared matters which were to be laid before the Assembly, and functioned as a judge in criminal matters. A further curtailment of the royal powers was probably effected as early as the eighth century B.C. by the institution

---

[39] Cf. W. R. Halliday, *The Growth of the City-State* (Liverpool–London, 1923), pp. 69–110. On the decline of Greek kingship, cf. Ch. G. Starr, "On the Decline of the Early Greek Kings," *Historia*, 10 (1961), pp. 129–138.

of the ephors. Five ephors were selected by the Assembly for a year, and were originally entrusted with civil jurisdiction, but from the seventh century B.C. on, they became important political factors. The kings had to take an oath every month that they would observe the laws of the state. The ephors vowed to watch over the maintenance of royal powers as long as the kings were true to their oath.

In other city-states the functions of the kings were taken over by the nobles whose influence continued to grow, thanks to their predominance in the agrarian economy, the most important factor in the primitive society of the new states. When the lands were divided among the members of the tribes after the conquest, the nobles were given larger lots than were the ordinary citizens. They formed the Council which became the leading body in the state. The political and military functions of the one *basileus* were thus shared by many who, formerly subordinated to the *basileus*, now often claimed this title for themselves.

Even after the transformation of their constitution from a monarchy to an aristocratic republic, the new states continued to regard the divine cult as one of the main bases on which the state should be built. The priestly functions of the kings were to be executed by the highest magistrates, as one of their prerogatives. In some instances, a special officer was entrusted with the performance of all the religious functions of the state, and he inherited the royal title. Such was the case in Athens.[40] Its *archon basileus* became in this respect the heir of the Mycenaean priest-king.

Usually, the priests were entrusted only with the technicalities of the religious cult. The actual performance of the religious functions was a prerogative of the magistrates in the worship of the gods, the protectors of the state. The assembly of citizens decided all details concerning the official cult. The direction of the worship of gods whose cult was practiced by the different families, phratries, and tribes, was reserved to the heads of these social bodies. The

---

[40] Plato, *The Statesman*, 290 E, ed. by H. N. Fowler (Loeb, 1925), p. 122. See for details and references G. Busolt, *Griechische Staatskunde*, p. 348. Besides Athens, Chios, Miletus, Olbia, Siphnos, Ios, and Naxos also had a *basileus* for the performance of sacral functions.

priesthood enjoyed a privileged position only in special shrines, such as Delphi and Eleusis. There was a great difference in this respect between Near Eastern and Mycenaean kingship and the Greek city-states. Although the religious cult was regarded as the foundation of the city-states and played a great role in the life of the citizens, the priestly class could never rise to any importance in the political development of the states.

It should be noted, however, that in many new city-states there was a link with the Mycenaean tradition in that the temple of the city god was erected on the place where the palace of the Mycenaean kings had stood. The former residence of the king became thereby the residence of a god. This connection is also revealed by the architectural features of the temples in the new states. They were constructed in the style of the *megaron*, the principal room of the Mycenaean palaces.

Another connection with the Mycenaean tradition is provided by the fact that many cities chose goddesses as tutelary divinities (ἀρχηγέτις) of their states (Staatsgötter). In the Cretan and Mycenaean pantheons, goddesses were in the majority.

In general, the era of aristocratic republics in Greece was rather prosperous. It was the aristocracy which had to create a new political machinery, divide the administrative, judicial, and other functions among magistrates, and determine both the duration of their service and the way in which they should perform their respective duties.

During this era a new period of colonization was initiated. The causes of this new expansion of the Greeks were mostly political, apart from the growth of the population in the small states, and were brought about by trade or social conditions resulting from the family land system. It was natural that the aristocratic regime should create discontent by measures favoring only the ruling class of the states. Many free citizens disliked the rule of a few and demanded more rights for the mass of the people. It was in the interest of the ruling circles to encourage the discontented citizens to follow the example of their compatriots who had founded flourishing city-states in Asia Minor and to found new cities where they could play a leading role. The adventurous spirit was still alive among the Greeks and drove many of them to discover new lands. A new expansion in Asia Minor was barred by the resistance of the native Carians and Lycians, but one of the colonies there —Miletus—discovered new possibilities on the Black Sea coast where its merchants had penetrated. The city-state of Megara started the movement, and by founding Byzantium and Chalcedon, secured easy access to the Euxine Sea. Other cities followed and planted Greek colonies on Thracian shores, on the northern side of Asia Minor, and on the Chersonese.

The shores of Macedonia were also thickly colonized, but the greatest achievement was the colonization of Sicily and southern Italy. These areas were so thoroughly Hellenized that they were called at a later period Greater Greece—*Magna Graecia.*

Thus far, the Greek monarchies and the republican city-states were governed only by customary laws, whose interpretation and application by aristocratic magistrates did not always give satisfaction to the poorer citizens who were in the majority. Therefore, as the cities grew more prosperous and the citizens became more conscious of their rights, demands for a written law were heard on all sides, and, in order to preserve its authoritative position, the aristocracy was forced to give the people some satisfaction.

The seventh century is characterized as an era of codifiers and lawgivers, although the identity of only a few of them is known for certain. The first lawgiver of Athens was Dracon,[41] but his work was revised and completed by Solon the Wise. The laws of Sparta, attributed to the legendary Lycurgus, were codified at this period. The cities of Crete also were affected by this movement and the Code of one of them—Gortyn—has been preserved down to our own times.

The seventh century witnessed also a growing tension between the social classes in the cities. Trade and industry increased, and though it was chiefly the aristocracy who profited from the lively commercial intercourse, it led to the devaluation of their aristocratic privileges deriving from noble birth. Wealth became a more powerful factor

[41] On Dracon's laws concerning murder and on the importance of his legislation for the development of the Athenian *polis*, see the recent study by E. Ruschenbusch, "Φόνος. Zum Recht Drakons und seiner Bedeutung für das Werden des athenischen Staates," *Historia*, 9 (1960), pp. 129–154.

in politics. The poorer freemen, however, had little part in this economic transformation and suffered accordingly. Their number in the towns grew in proportion to the expansion of industry and the declining value of agriculture. Discontent with the reign of the privileged class became increasingly manifest and claims for more freedom and equality were heard everywhere. The economic distress resulting from the introduction of a money economy instead of the old system of exchange aggravated the situation.

All this had a profound effect on the political development of the Greek city-states. Members of the aristocratic class, envious of the ascendancy of their rivals, profited by this discontent among the masses and becoming their leaders, overthrew their rivals, took over the government, and introduced a new kind of monarchic system called tyranny.[42]

Now, for the first time it seems, Oriental influences helped to promote this development in the Greek polity. The name "tyrant," given to the self-appointed rulers, was the title of the rulers of the Asianic neighbors of Ionia—the Lydians. The first tyrants appeared in the Greek city-states that bordered on Lydia. The influence of the strongly organized Lydian monarchy made itself felt in Ephesus, Miletus, and in Mytilene on the island of Lesbos. It was under the government of the tyrant Thrasybulus that Miletus experienced its golden age and started its colonial expansion in the Euxine Sea.

Soon afterward, in the middle of the seventh century, central Greece had its first tyrants in Corinth, Sicyon, and Megara. Others arose in different parts of Greece. Though this political phenomenon became almost general at the same period, we cannot speak of an age of tyrannies preceding the establishment of democracies in Greece. Tyrants appeared in democracies also. Some of these tyrannies were prosperous and prepared the way for a more democratic government. Being, however, unconstitutional monarchs, the tyrants had often to maintain themselves by armed force and were inclined to oppress both aristocratic and popular groups.

Sparta was saved by its constitution from any upheaval caused

---

[42] Cf. G. Busolt, *Griechische Staatskunde*, p. 381 seq. See also P. N. Ure, *The Origin of Tyranny* (Cambridge, 1922).

by the rise of tyrannies; on the other hand, she was gradually transformed into a military and police state.[43] The only citizens who exercised full rights were the men from the five central settlements, the Spartiats. The Dorian population, settled on lands outside the center, and divided into about one hundred cities, formed a part of the Lacedaemonian state and supplied military contingents in case of war, but was excluded from participation in the military assembly called the *Apella*. These second-class citizens were called *perioikoi*. The subdued native populations of Laconia and of conquered Messenia were reduced to slavery and had to support the members of the *Apella* with the products of lands which they cultivated for the state.

The Spartiats renewed the state of war with these *helots* every year, and the danger of possible insurrection by the latter forced the Spartiats to introduce strict military discipline among the full citizens—state education of the youth from the age of seven years on and common meals for all men carrying arms—in order to be ready for battle at any time. The introduction of a new military tactic—the phalanx, a closed line of well trained infantry (hoplites) —enhanced the military prestige of Sparta.

The consequences of these economic developments were also felt among the three social classes in Athens. The rich landowners and the knights profited, but the independent peasants suffered serious losses. The class of poorer peasants and handicraftsmen, called *thetes*, had no political rights, but, with the development of the navy in which the *thetes* served as sailors, it began to gain some importance in public life.[44]

The attempt to establish a tyranny in Athens (632 B.C.) was, however, thwarted, and Solon's reforms saved the state from similar upheavals for at least two decades during which the democratic foundations laid down by him could be consolidated. Although refusing the claims of the impoverished peasants for a redistribution of the land, Solon alleviated their situation by

---

[43] On the Lacedaemonian state, see G. Busolt and H. Swoboda, *Griechische Staatskunde*, 2 (Munich, 1926), pp. 633–737.

[44] On the history of the Athenian state, see *ibid.*, pp. 758–1239.

annulling the mortgages and debts for which the debtors had pledged their own personal liberty, and by freeing all who had become slaves because of their indebtedness.

More important than Solon's social and monetary reform was his reform of the constitution. While retaining the old division into classes according to property, he admitted the *thetes* to the meeting of the Assembly (*ecclesia*), and thereby gave them a voice in the appointment of magistrates who were to be elected from the wealthier classes. Another, much bolder step toward a democratic constitution was the establishment of popular courts, to which all citizens were admitted. The judges were enrolled by lot. This court, called *heliaea*,[45] held jurisdiction over magistrates who could be judged by it on the performance of their duties when holding an office. The people thus obtained control over the administration.

Moreover, the Council, called the Areopagus and composed of aristocrats, was deprived of its deliberative functions, which implied the curtailment of its right to propose laws and administrative changes to the Assembly. It retained, however, its religious and judicial functions and was made the protector of the constitution and charged with the guardianship of the laws. The nine supreme magistrates—the archons—who were elected by the Assembly, became life members of the Areopagus after the end of their term of magisterial office.

Instead of the Areopagus, a newly created Council was charged with the preparation of proposals for the Assembly. It consisted of four hundred members, one hundred chosen from each of the four tribes. The *thetes* were, however, excluded from election to this Council.

Solon's reform of the Athenian constitution was rather cautious and conservative in many respects, especially since appointments to the highest offices were reserved for men of means, regarded as better fitted for the most responsible functions. Yet he should be regarded as the founder of Athenian democracy. Moreover, it is remarkable that he managed to bring about all of these vital changes

[45] See for its formation and history H. Hommel, *Heliaia* (Leipzig, 1927) = *Philologus*, Supplementband 19, Heft 2.

in a constitutional manner, since, as archon, he was, of course, provided with extraordinary powers.[46]

Solon's reforms, however, could not stop the strife among the parties or reconcile the differences among the social strata. Pisistratus, the energetic and ambitious friend of Solon, profiting by the prestige he acquired from his role in the victories of Salamis and Nisaea, sided with the extreme democrats composed of poor hill men and small farmers, and, seizing the Acropolis, became tyrant of Athens (560 B.C.). Driven out twice, he returned for a third time, and was even able to transmit the government of Attica to his sons. Nevertheless, because the Pisistratids left the constitution of Solon almost intact, their reign did not block Athens' way to a fuller democracy.

The extent to which the minds of the Athenians were imbued with the democratic ideas planted by Solon is illustrated by the events that followed the overthrow of the Pisistratids (510 B.C.). Although this was effected with the help of the Spartans, whose power had grown from their conquests in the peninsula and their domination of the Peloponnesian confederacy, the people revolted when the Spartans tried to impose on Athens an oligarchic regime. Cleisthenes, the promotor of the revolution against the tyranny, was once more victorious and, profiting by the experiences of the recent past, undertook the task of completing Solon's work and making democracy a reality. Abolishing the old division into Ionic tribes and *phratriai*, and disregarding the political parties formed after Solon's reforms, he divided the citizens into ten new tribes based on artificial geography. Each tribe had to choose fifty members, who formed the Council of Five Hundred, representing the whole of Attica, and became the supreme administrative authority. The Council obtained, too, the deliberative rights which Solon had given to his Council, and was also vested with some judicial

---

[46] Cf. F. Warncke, *Die demokratische Staatsidee in der Verfassung von Athen*, p. 41 seq. A detailed history of the Athenian democracy, with an extensive bibliography, is given by P. Cloché, *La démocratie athénienne* (Paris, 1951). Cf. B. Keil, *Die Solonische Verfassung in Aristoteles Verfassungsgeschichte Athens* (Berlin, 1892); A. H. M. Jones, *Athenian Democracy*, reprint, (London 1960). Cf. also C. Mosse, *La fin de la démocratie athénienne* (Paris, 1962).

functions. The business of the Council was carried out by the fifty
councillors of each tribe, who had to reside in Athens in turn, each
group during a tenth part of the year. Each tribe had also to elect a
general who commanded the hoplites, furnished by the tribes.

Although Cleisthenes also increased the number of citizens entitled
to take part in the Assembly, he did not alter Solon's conditions
for eligibility to the executive offices. The holders of the chief
financial posts and the nine archons were still chosen from the
members of the propertied classes, which thus controlled the
executive magistrates and the Areopagus. This was, however,
outweighed by the composition of the Council and the *ecclesia*
where the middle class prevailed.

It should be emphasized that the manner in which the Council of
Cleisthenes was elected led directly to a representative government as we know it in modern times. Every part of Attica was
represented according to the number of its citizens, and although
the Council could not legislate, it proposed the measures to be
taken, as is done by modern governments. This was, however, as
far as Greek statesmen dared to go. It never occurred to them
that a representative government could serve the needs of a state
better than an Assembly of all the citizens. They understood the principle of the sovereignty of the people in an absolutely literal sense. This
could be fully applied only in city-states of small size where
most of the citizens knew each other and could easily foregather
to legislate. Such was the Greek idea of a state.[47] Even Aristotle
could not imagine a larger Assembly than one over which the
voice of a herald could be heard.[48] This strict observance of the
principle of popular sovereignty prevented them from forming
larger political groups in which the citizens would not have been
able to exercise their rights personally.

The democratic regime implanted by Solon and reinforced by
Cleisthenes worked well in Athens. The enthusiasm of the citizens

[47] See, on the problem of representative government in general, J. A. O.
Larsen, *Representative Government in Greek and Roman History* (Berkeley-
Los Angeles, 1955). E. A. Freeman's *History of Federal Government in Greece
and Italy*, re-edited by J. B. Bury (London, 1893), is still very useful (pp.
1–556; attempts at federation in Greece).
[48] *Politics*, 1326 b, line 5, ed. by H. Rackham (Loeb, 1932), p. 556.

helped the state to repel a new attack by Sparta, to defeat the Boeotians and even to challenge the growing power of Persia, when the Ionian cities in Asia Minor revolted against Darius (498 B.C.), who had extended his supremacy not only over the whole of Asia Minor, but also over Thrace and Macedonia. The victorious repulse of the Persian invasion of Greece at the battle of Marathon (490 B.C.) revitalized the democratic tendencies. In order to strengthen the Council, a new method was introduced in the appointment of the nine archons. They were elected by lot from five hundred men chosen by the ten tribes for this purpose. The functions of the *archon polemarchos* were superseded by the ten generals who were henceforth elected by the Assembly and were given supreme command for a day each, in turn. Only in war time did the people assign the conduct of operations to one of the ten.

In this way the powers of the Assembly were strengthened, but the efficacy of the magistracy and of the military command weakened, to the detriment of the state. The introduction of ostracism (probably in 488 B.C.) assigned to the sovereign people the duty of preventing ambitious citizens from becoming dangerous to the community, a duty previously exercised by the Areopagus. This new measure, however, opened the way to the danger of misuse which could deprive the state of the services of able statesmen.

In spite of these perilous innovations, the Athenian democracy remained a very vital force. This was shown during the second invasion of Greece by Xerxes. Thanks to the foresight of their statesmen, especially of Themistocles, the Athenians built up a strong navy, manned by able oarsmen and sailors recruited from among the *thetes*. The victory of Salamis (September 480 B.C.) represented the triumph of Greek democracy over the absolute monarchy of Persia. The darker side of the constitutional reform, however, soon manifested itself in the ostracism of Themistocles (472 B.C.), the main architect of the great victory, and of his successor in command, Cimon, who had defeated the Persian army in Asia Minor in the battle of Eurymedon (466 B.C.).

Although the Spartans had the greatest share in the defeat of the Persian expeditionary force in Greece, especially in the battle of Plataea (479 B.C.), and although their leadership in the Hellenic resistance to Persia was readily recognized, they were unable to profit from their prestige and to form and dominate a closer federation of the Greek city-states. The main reason for this was not only their lack of a large fleet, but also the limitations which their constitution imposed on their state. It did not jibe with the democratic atmosphere of other Greek states, and the policy of the Spartan leaders was too conservative to take part in enterprises looking beyond their local interests in the Peloponnesus.

It was Athens which took the initiative in forming a large Greek political organization—the Delian League (478–477 B.C.)[49]—in order to continue the naval war with Persia and to liberate from its yoke all Greek cities on the Aegean coast and along the shores of the Euxine. Finally, about two hundred city-states adhered to the League. The Assembly met at Delos, where the treasury was also kept. But, although Athens could cast only one vote, it practically dominated the League, thanks to its prestige. After subduing recalcitrant members, Athens transformed the League into its empire. It was the only attempt made by a Greek city-state to form a political unit which could foreshadow a Panhellenic union.

But, the way in which Athens transformed the League into an empire provoked criticism in Corinth and Sparta which feared for their own safety. The fear and jealousy of Athens' enemies provoked the Peloponnesian war (431–404 B.C.). As a pretext they accused the Athenian empire of depriving many Greek states of their autonomy and endangering the political liberty of others. This shows how deeply political particularism was embedded in Greek minds.

The victories over the Persian army and navy, won under Athenian leadership, naturally exerted great influence on the political development of the state. The *thetes*, who supplied most of the mariners, also became an important factor in political life, and, because the sacrifices imposed by the wars were shared by all citizens, it seemed natural that the sovereignty of the people should be increasingly stressed, that the last vestiges of the aristo-

[49] On this and other Hellenic Leagues, or *symmachiai*, see J. A. O. Larsen, *op. cit.*, p. 46; recent bibliography, p. 207 seq.

cratic and oligarchic regime should disappear, and that every citizen should have equal rights in the state and access to all state offices.

The energetic statesman Ephialtes made the most daring move in this direction, a move which is described as the revolution of 462 B.C.[50] He proposed laws by which the Areopagus, the last bulwark of the aristocracy, was deprived of most of its privileges which were then transferred to the Council and the Assembly. The brilliant leader Pericles (ca. 495–429 B.C.) saw the opportunity to realize his own democratic dreams. The people must become really sovereign, and all important matters, all decisions concerning peace and war should be decided by the people alone. The people should be limited only by the laws which they themselves had instituted, and must enjoy full control over all executive offices. To realize this ideal, the members of the Council would be chosen exclusively by lot, in order to demonstrate that every citizen had an equal right to membership. It could not, however, become a governing body, because membership was limited to a year, and every member was responsible to the Assembly for the fulfillment of his duties.

The courts and all offices, except those of the general, financial officers and technicians were opened to all citizens. They were chosen by lot, could hold an office for only a year, and could not be reappointed. To make it possible for the poorest citizen to compete for the offices, all elected officers and councillors received a fixed salary. Any citizen who reached the age of twenty was admitted to the Assembly, and after he reached the age of thirty, he could sit in the court. On the other hand, however, citizenship was limited to legitimate children, both of whose parents were Athenian citizens.

a Thucydides, the historian of the Peloponnesian war and an edmirer of Pericles' political wisdom, has his hero pronounce an iloquent panegyric on Athenian democracy in the funeral oration in which Pericles honored the dead of the first year of the conflict.[51]

[50] For details, see C. Hignett, *A History of the Athenian Constitution* (Oxford, 1952), p. 193 seq., with bibliographical references.

[51] *History of the Peloponnesian War*, II, 35–46, ed. by Ch. F. Smith (Loeb, 1935), I, pp. 318–340. See the monograph by J. de Romilly, *Thucydide et l'impérialisme athénien* (Paris, 1951), pp. 99–136 (Pericles).

It clearly depicts the democratic ideal which Pericles wanted to realize in Athens, in opposition to the political system of Sparta.

In spite of the realization of the Athenian ideal of radical democracy, the new regime should rather be characterized as aristocratic when the number of its citizens is compared with the number of inhabitants in Attica. Almost three quarters of the population in Athens were slaves who had no political rights at all, and it was the work of the slaves in industry, agriculture, and domestic life that enabled the citizens to spend most of their time in the service of the state and in attendance at public festivals.

On the other hand, the radical democracy of Pericles presupposed the voluntary devotion, at all cost, of the individual citizen to the interests of the state, as well as the leadership of experienced statemanship. Pericles supplied this leadership during his lifetime, and the people manifested a high degree of loyalty to the state during the first years of the Peloponnesian war. But, because all offices could be held for only a short time, the constitution did not lead to a firm government.[52] Pericles dominated the Assembly, enjoying, thanks to his brilliant capacities, the confidence of the people, and he directed the votes of the citizens along sound and just lines. But after his death there was no-one who could win the confidence of the people, and the leaders of the different parties contended for the Assembly's favor, seeking approval for decisions they proposed in the interest of their parties.

Orators trained by the Sophists in rhetoric art, dominated the Assembly. The members of the Council, chosen at random by the drawing of lots and often of little wisdom and without experience in state affairs, could not exercise a commanding influence. Even the generals lacked sufficient influence to prevent the Assembly from reaching decisions at the behest of demogogic orators.

Moreover, in the fifth century, a widespread interest in philosophy had been awakened and was disseminated by the schools of the Sophists among the masses. The new tendency was characterized by Protagoras' thesis that man is the measure of all

[52] See the monograph by V. Ehrenberg, *Sophokles und Perikles* (Munich, 1956). Cf. the review by K. F. Stroheker in *Historia*, 6 (1957), pp. 506–508.

things.[53] It is, of course, debatable whether Protagoras actually uttered the words ascribed to him by Plato and what he meant by them.[54] He also seems to have attributed the origins of the social community to man's inborn social sense; solidarity among men, justice, and laws were, according to him, the basis of any social mind.[55] If this interpretation of Protagoras' teaching on the origin of the state is true, then his ideas anticipated, in some way, those of Plato and Aristotle.

There were, however, Sophists who propagated ideas the literal interpretation of which suggested that man's will and need should be the measure evaluating all things. This new philosophical trend led to emancipation from traditional opinions, beliefs, and prejudices. The tendency toward individualism, which was emphasized, also influenced political life unfavorably.[56] Until then, after the codification of customary laws and the overthrow of the aristocratic regime, the law—*nomos*—had been regarded as the supreme authority in the state, and this was recognized without hesitation by all citizens. It was almost generally believed that the laws were given to men by the gods and could, therefore, not be transgressed or changed. The emphasis on individualism, however, made disastrous inroads into this belief, and the conviction that positive law could be changed according to the interests of the citizens became general. In *Oedipus*[57]

---

[53] Plato, *Cratylus*, 385 E, ed. by H. N. Fowler (Loeb, 1926), p. 14. See E. Barker, *Greek Political Theory. Plato and his Predecessors* (London, 1918), p. 60 seq. *Idem, The Political Thought of Plato and Aristotle* (New York, 1959), p. 17 seq., on Pre-Socratics, Socrates, and minor Socratics. T. A. Sinclair, *A History of Greek Political Thought* (London, 1951), pp. 43–68. A succint and clear review of Greek political philosophy is given by M. Pohlenz, *Staatsgedanke und Staatslehre der Griechen* (Leipzig, 1923). On Protagoras, *ibid.*, 41 seq. See also, of course, J. Kaerst, *Geschichte des Hellenismus*, 1 (Leipzig-Berlin, 1917), pp. 53–88.

[54] See, on this problem, the study by A. Neumann, "Die Problematik des *Homo-Mensura* Satzes," *Classical Philology*, 33 (1938), pp. 368–379.

[55] See, on this new interpretation of Protagoras' teaching, D. Loenen, *Protagoras and the Greek Community* (Amsterdam, 1941), especially pp. 50–97.

[56] Cf. K. F. Stroheker, "Zu den Anfängen der monarchischen Theorie in der Sophistik," *Historia*, 2 (1953/54), pp. 381–412.

[57] *Oedipus the King*, vs. 868 seq., ed. by F. Storr (Loeb, 1939), 1, p. 78 seq. On the antithesis *nomos-physis* used by the Sophists, which often meant the proclamation of the right of the strong man over others, its different interpretations, and on the reaction against it, see the study by F. Heinimann, *Nomos und Physis. Herkunft und Bedeutung einer Antithese im griechischen Denken des 5. Jahrhunderts* (Basel, 1945), especially pp. 110–169.

the passionate defense of the divine origin of the unwritten law given by Sophocles reveals that the Sophists were attacking, in addition, the inviolability of natural law. The origin of law and of moral observances was discussed, and different theories on the genesis of a state were postulated. Was the state founded by the will of strong individuals, or by a convention of men through the conclusion of a social contract? Was the constitution of the state correctly conceived and constructed? Did it need to be reformed and to what extent?

Although the Sophists were not interested primarily in political theories, their teaching and activity opened the era of Greek political speculation. The different political systems—monarchy, oligarchy, democracy—were discussed according to their merits or defects, and there were those who even conceived an ideal political system that would satisfy the interests of both state and individual. In the second book of his *Politics*,[58] Aristotle recorded some of these ideas, paying special attention to the sketch of an ideal state made by Phaleas of Chalcedon and Hippodamus of Miletus. The latter divided the citizenry into three classes—peasants, artisans, and professional soldiers—giving only one third of the land to the private ownership of the peasants, while the rest of the land was to provide subsistence for the soldiers and revenue for the government, and should be in the hands of specialized administrators elected by the people. He rejected the choosing of officers by lot, and proposed rewards for citizens who came forward with new suggestions toward improving the state machinery.

Socrates (469–399 B.C.) also insisted that the state should be governed by men who know "the political art." To the wave of subjective individualism which questioned the foundation of morality, he opposed the belief in superior rules which govern the action of individuals. It is not the grasping of material wealth that makes man truly happy, but the knowledge of the rules that govern his actions and the virtue acquired in following them. In applying his teaching to politics, Socrates condemned the choosing of officers by lot, and objected to the system which granted sovereignty to an assembly of men who knew nothing of rulership.

[58] *Politics*, 1266 a–1269 a, *loc. cit.*, pp. 110–132.

Socrates' teaching could not arrest the development initiated by the Sophists. Individualism was deeply rooted even among professional politicians. The career of Alcibiades (*ca.* 450–404 B.C.), the successor of Pericles who had shown great promise,[59] illustrates this state of affairs more clearly than anything else. Respecting the interests of the state only when they coincided with his own, Alcibiades did not hesitate to betray his compatriots to the Spartans, and to enter into pacts with the Persians when his own interests demanded it. Many Athenians must have thought as Alcibiades did, for when he was recalled from exile, he was received with great enthusiasm.

A sharp criticism of some features of Athenian democracy can be read in an anonymous work, written by a contemporary of Alcibiades and erroneously ascribed to Xenophon. It was composed before the Peloponnesian war, between 431 and 424 B.C., by an emigrant from Attica.[60] It is a curious composition, for, although he was an enemy of democracy, the author argues in defense of the foreign and internal policy of Athens. Because he seems to have served formerly in the Athenian navy, he defends the imperialistic policy of Athens based on its sea-power. This inconsistency discloses that even this opponent of democracy was influenced by the doctrine of the Sophists, especially by Protagoras' theory of relativity.[61]

Radical democracy degenerated into the government of masses who decided in the Assemblies according to their whim, without regard to the interest of the state, favoring only the benefit of the lowest classes. Patriotic sentiment reached such a low ebb that the people demanded and were given compensation for the time spent in the Assemblies. The principle of absolute political freedom and equality, which was Pericles' ideal, put into practice by the irresponsible masses, prevented the rise of talented statesmen, because everybody who was above average was regarded as dangerous to democracy.

[59] See the monograph by J. Hatzfeld, *Alcibiade, étude sur l'histoire d'A-thènes à la fin du V*ᵉ *siècle* (Paris, 1940). Cf. also J. de Romilly, *op. cit.*, pp. 168–195.
[60] See the most recent edition, translation, and commentary by H. Frisch, *The Constitution of the Athenians*, Classica et Mediaevalia, Dissertationes, 2 (Copenhagen, 1942), p. 47 seq.
[61] H. Frisch, *ibid.*, pp. 106–129.

The propertied classes, being in a minority in the Assembly, formed secret groups where ways and means for the overthrow of democracy and the installation of an oligarchic regime were debated and plotted. By organizing a series of assassinations of prominent supporters of democracy, they terrorized the people and succeeded in 411 B.C. in changing the constitution. The number of members of the *ecclesia* with the right to speak and vote was limited to five thousand.[62] They were to be chosen from those men best qualified to serve the country as soldiers in war and from the wealthy who could contribute to the treasury. The payment of wages was limited to the army and navy, the nine archons, and the chairman of the Assembly and of the Council. A Council of Four Hundred was elected to choose the ten generals and a secretary, for the conduct of war and of state affairs.

However, the oligarchs did not remain in power for long. The changes made by them in the magistracy, accompanied by violent measures, were unpopular, and the hoplites, fearing an intervention by Sparta in favor of the new oligarchy, revolted. The Council of Four Hundred was abolished, but, instead of returning to radical democracy, the Assembly accepted a compromise. The government was to be in the hands of the Assembly of Five Thousand, and all pay for political functions was abolished. The people were thus, nominally the sovereign government, but with the poorer and most disturbing elements excluded from the Assembly and the magistracy, the limited democracy was greeted with relief by Socrates and all patriotic elements. Unfortunately, the compromise did not last, and shortly, perhaps as early as 410 B.C., radical democracy was re-established.

But the return to radical democracy could not save the decadent Athenian state. Old abuses were committed again, the conduct of the war against Sparta supported by Cyrus of Persia was in incompetent hands. The Athenian navy was destroyed by the skilful

---

[62] Cf. the recent study by G. E. M. de Ste. Croix, "The Constitution of the Five Thousand," *Historia*, 5 (1956), pp. 1–23. According to the author, this regime lasted from September 411 until about June 410. He regards it as more probable that even under this constitution all citizens had the basic political right to a seat in the Assembly and in the courts. Only the Council and the magistracies were reserved for citizen-hoplites.

Spartan admiral Lysander, and in the spring of 404 B.C. the Spartans occupied Athens. The city became a dependent of Sparta; her long walls were destroyed, her navy limited to twelve vessels, and the oligarchs, represented by thirty tyrants supported by Sparta, started their reign of terror. This triumph of the extreme oligarchs was short lived, and in 403, with the help of émigrés and moderate oligarchs, the government of the Three Thousand was instituted, with a Board of Ten, and democracy was finally again restored.

Military defeat had demonstrated the inefficiency of a radical democratic regime. But not even the Spartan oligarchic constitution proved satisfactory for the Hellenic cause, in spite of the victory over Athenian "democratic tyranny." The Spartans were no longer a well disciplined body. Equality in the agrarian economy in Sparta was a story of the past, and a class of property owners possessing large holdings existed. The victory undermined the moral basis of Sparta. Individualistic tendencies which disregarded the interest of the state also appeared. Even in foreign policy the Spartiat regime failed. The Spartans had acquired, by conquest or alliance, the hegemony of most of the Greek lands, and were replacing democratic regimes in Greek city-states with oligarchic constitutions unpopular to non-Spartans. The harshness with which they enforced their authority provoked a revolution in 395 by Athens, Argos, Corinth, and Thebes. The allies were supported by the Persian king whom the Spartans had alienated when they refused to let the Persians take control of the Asiatic Greeks. After winning King Artaxerxes over to their side by fulfilling their promises, the Spartans insured, with "The King's Peace" (386), their hold over the Greek mainland. They lost it, however, in 371, to the Thebans. The victors tried halfheartedly to supplant the Spartans, but had to revert in 361 to the principle of autonomy for all city-states, without a hegemony. Then the Athenians tried to build up a new, powerful, maritime confederacy (377), but they were not successful, and it soon disintegrated.

None of the city-states was able to bring about a union of all Hellenes in a mighty confederation, and the Greeks were forced to tolerate the humiliating intervention of Persia, their enemy, in their affairs. In the meantime, however, a strong monarchic regime in Macedonia, to the north of Greece, was being reinforced under Archelaus (413–399). Philip II (359–336 B.C.) laid the foundations for Macedonian greatness by creating a strongly centralized government. With his modernized army he extended his sovereignty over Thrace, Chalcidice, and Thessaly. He prided himself on his Greek ancestors whose line extended back to Heracles, and through adroit exploitation of the weakness of Greek city-states and their mutual dissensions he extended his influence deeper and deeper into Greece.

III

This short sketch of the development of political ideas in Greece from the twelfth to the fourth century B.C. has been necessary for a better understanding of the different currents of political speculation which stirred the minds of the finest Greek thinkers of the fourth century, and for emphasizing the profound change in political philosophy which was effected during this period of time. The failure of the Athenian radical democracy and of the Spartan aristocratic regime, and the appearance of a strong monarchy in the North of Greece induced the Hellenes to look for a better constitution and to view the monarchic regime with less distrust.

In order to understand this new development, it is necessary first to examine whether there survived through the era of the republican city-states any vestiges of the ancient Greek kingship which might have kept alive the idea that a monarchy might be the solution of the political problem.

In this respect it must be borne in mind that the great poems—the *Iliad* and the *Odyssey*—were the common possession of all Greeks and that the education of youth was based on the reading and memorizing of these epic compositions, wherein the supreme kingship of Zeus was stressed and primitive Greek kingship praised. It can readily be imagined that the peasants of Attica would often have preferred the mild rule of an Agamemnon or an Odysseus, as it was described in the recitation of these poems, to that of some tyrants, or of an aristocracy that cared only for its own interests, or of the radical democracy which brought a chaotic and irregular administration and dispensation of justice.

FROM MYCENAE TO ISOCRATES

Homer's ideas on the divine origin of kingship were revived by another poet: Hesiod says in his Theogony[63] that the Muses, especially Calliope, "attend on worshipful princes" from their birth on. Therefore, people look toward their prince "while he settles causes with true judgments.... And when he passes through a gathering, they greet him as a god with gentle reverence, and he is conspicuous amongst the assembled." Singers and harpers derive their talents from the Muses and Apollo, "but princes (*basilees*) are of Zeus."

Even Pindar may have evoked some memories of the ancient Greek past in his poems. In spite of the rationalism of the fifth century, his ideas on the deity and its intervention in human life still echo the sentiments of the age of Homer. Sisyphus, the mythical personage, is assimilated to the gods,[64] Tlepolemus of Tiryns the son of Heracles, venerated in Rhodes as the hero founder (*ktistes*), is also regarded as a god.[65] Pindar also follows Homer in acclaiming Heracles as a hero and a god.[66]

Pindar was also linked by friendship with Hieron, the tyrant of Syracuse, whose victory in the Olympic games he celebrated and who was, according to the poet, under the special protection of the gods.[67] These may have been no more than reminiscences, but they helped to keep the memory of the past and the traditions of old alive among Pindar's readers in a period of rationalism which was destroying mythical conceptions and leading the minds of the Greeks into more prosaic and realistic channels of thinking.

The belief that gods and men are of the same origin naturally helped, in people's minds, to bridge the gulf between humanity and divinity, and encouraged the veneration of men who, by their deeds, seemed nearer to the divine. Hesiod, when commencing his description of the five ages of the world, promises to relate "how the gods and mortal men sprang from one source."[68] Pindar starts his hymn to Alcimidas of Aegina with the following words:[69] "One

---

[63] *Theogony*, vss. 79–96, ed. by H. G. Evelyn-White (Loeb, 1936), p. 84.
[64] *Olympian Odes*, XIII, vs. 52, ed. by J. Sandys (Loeb, 1937), p. 136.
[65] *Ibid.*, VII, vs. 79, *loc. cit.*, p. 78.
[66] *Nemean Odes*, III, vs. 22, ed. by J. Sandys (Loeb, 1937), p. 336.
[67] *Olympian Odes*, I, esp. vs. 106 seq., *loc. cit.*, p. 14.
[68] *Works and Days*, vs. 108, ed. by H. G. Evelyn-White (Loeb, 1936), p. 11.
[69] *Nemean Odes*, VI, vs. 1, *loc. cit.*, p. 368.

is the race of men, one is the race of gods, and from one mother [*Gaia*, Earth] do we both derive our breath." Heraclitus shared a similar conviction.[70] Empedocles and the followers of Pythagoras thought that some men were gods or celestial demons, either fallen from heaven or charged with a supernatural mission.[71] According to this belief, Pythagoras was regarded by many of his disciples as either a god, a lunar demon, or the son of a god.

Even during the struggle for national existence the eyes of some political thinkers were turning to Persia, whose centralized government maintained peace in the immense Empire and assured to its citizens a material prosperity. It was an enemy to be hated and feared, but it also evoked awe by its achievements. It is only necessary to read Aeschylus' *Persians*, celebrating the victory of democratic Greece over the Persian monarchy, to see that, despite all its shortcomings, the Greeks were impressed by the magnitude of the Persian monarchy. Xerxes' mother is greeted in this work as the consort of a god,[72] and the chorus shrinks in awe from gazing upon the ghost of Darius.[73] The King then describes the building of the Empire by his ancestors and by himself.[74] The description of the Persian realm again reveals the poet's admiration. Darius is always treated with reverence and likened to god.[75]

It was, however, impossible for a long time to express any kind of sympathy for a monarchic regime, and any discussion of the advantages of such a constitution was quite out of order in Athens. Herodotus was the first who dared to do so, but he had to identify the discussion with the best regime in Persia before the accession of Darius. This work contains veiled criticism of the abuses of a

[70] Fragment 62, in H. Diels, *Die Fragmente der Vorsokratiker*, 6th ed., 1 (Berlin, 1951), p. 164.
[71] See, for details, A. Delatte, *Études sur la littérature pythagoricienne* (Paris, 1915), p. 270 seq.
[72] *The Persians*, vs. 155 seq., ed. by H. Weir Smyth (Loeb, 1938), 1, p. 120.
[73] *Ibid.*, vs. 694 seq., *loc. cit.*, p. 164.
[74] *Ibid.*, vs. 759 seq., *loc. cit.*, p. 174 seq.
[75] *Ibid.*, vs. 857, *loc. cit.*, p. 182: ἰσόθεος Δαρεῖος. Cf. the dissertation by V. N. Callahan, *Types of Rulers in the Plays of Aeschylus* (Chicago, 1944).

radical democracy,[76] and disguised praise of monarchy from the mouth of Darius himself.[77] "I hold that monarchy is by far the most excellent. Nothing can be found better than the rule of the one best man; his judgment being like to himself, he will govern the multitude with perfect wisdom, and best conceal plans made for the defeat of enemies." It is remarkable that Herodotus should have gone so far,[78] although in another passage he declared that the despotism which the Lacedaemonians were imposing on others was the most abominable and unjust regime on earth.[79]

Herodotus reproaches the Persian rulers for lack of the virtues of prudence and self-control, the Greek σωφροσύνη which should be practiced by a philosopher and a ruler. Xerxes is accused of hatred of the Greeks,[80] and Cambyses is called a madman because of his behavior in Egypt.[81] This is the way the Greeks generally depicted tyrants,

Of course, this censure of Persian monarchs was made under the pressure of circumstances—the war with Persia for Greek national survival. Herodotus' friend, the poet Sophocles, shared this sentiment.[82] Creon, although a legitimate king, is pictured—in *Oedipus the King*—as a tyrant devoid of self control, whose actions are dictated by offended pride. Oedipus, on the other hand, always acts only in the interests of the *polis*.

It is, however, interesting to find in Sophocles' dramas some passages which could have been interpreted by readers in the Hellenistic period as favorable to a monarchic regime, even as recommending it. Sophocles knew, for example, that a lawful king

[76] *Historiae*, III, 81, ed. by A. D. Godley (Loeb, 1938), 2, p. 106: "Nothing is more foolish and violent than a useless mob. And, indeed, to save ourselves from the insolence of a despot by changing it for the insolence of the unbridled common people—that were unbearable. Whatever the despot does, he does with knowledge; but the people have not even that; how can they have knowledge who have neither learnt nor for themselves seen what is best, but ever rush headlong and drive blindly onward, like a river in spate?"
[77] *Ibid.*, III, 82, *loc. cit.*, p. 108.
[78] K. F. Stroheker, *op. cit.*, p. 388 seq., sees in Herodotus' discussion the influence of the Sophist Protagoras.
[79] *Historiae*, V, 92, *loc. cit.* (1938) 3, p. 102.
[80] *Ibid.*, VII, 238, *loc. cit.*, p. 554.
[81] *Ibid.*, III, 30, 34, *loc. cit.*, I, pp. 38, 44.
[82] Cf. R. Camerer, *Zorn und Groll in der Sophokleischen Tragoedie* (Borna, 1936), not available to the author.

should be of royal blood;[83] Zeus is protector of kings, giving them his blessing and good fortune;[84] earthly reign is given to men by gods; the sceptre, called divine, is handed to the ruler by Zeus.[85]

The "conversion" of the famous tragic dramatist Euripides must have made the most profound impression in Athens and throughout Hellas. A zealous defender of Athenian democracy, Euripides based his main argument on the thesis that all men were naturally equal and that the Athenian political system was the best realization of the principle of equality. In his dramas he employs of course expressions on gods and rulers inherited from the past, but this does not hide his scepticism as to their true value.[86]

His enthusiasm for democracy was dampened, however, when he had to leave his state, which was torn by political strife, and find refuge at the court of Archelaus, King of Macedonia. The rule of this energetic and Hellenizing King impressed him, and, responding to the desire of his protector to have the origins of his family traced back to Heracles, he composed the play celebrating the deeds of one of the King's forefathers and bearing the same name, *Archelaus*. Of this, however, only fragments are preserved. There Euripides not only stresses the noble origin of the King (*eugeneia*), but also his nobility of soul, which can be acquired by suffering and virtue. This had been achieved by Heracles, the ancestor of the Macedonian dynasty, and by the forefathers of Euripides' protector. A "mirror" of a good ruler is sketched in the surviving fragments, in which the poet recommended for successful kingship not only the Greek *sophrosyne*, but also justice and piety.[87] This drama, probably

---

[83] *Ajax*, vs. 1291 seq., ed. by F. Storr (Loeb, 1939), 2, p. 106.; *Antigone*, vs. 174, *loc. cit.*, 1, p. 326; *Electra*, vs. 160 seq., *loc. cit.*, 2, p. 138.

[84] *Electra*, ibid.,; *Oedipus the King*, vs. 1235, *loc. cit.*, 1, p. 114.

[85] *Philoctetes*, vs. 137 seq., *loc. cit.*, 2, p. 378.

[86] There are, however, two passages in which the rule of a good king is praised. In the *Suppliants* (vs. 409 seq., ed. by A. S. Way. [Loeb, 1930], 3, p. 532) the herald exalts the rule of one man in Thebes, and in his *Erechtheus* (fragment 362, *Tragicorum graecorum fragmenta*, ed. by A. Nauck, [Teubner, 1889], p. 470) Euripides has the dying King give advice on good rulership to his son. In both cases Euripides probably had in mind Pericles' leadership in Athenian democracy. In the Hellenistic period this praise of the rule of one man could easily have been interpreted in a monarchic sense.

[87] *Archelaus*, fragments 237, 250, 254, 255, 256, 258, 259, ed. by A. Nauck, *loc. cit.*, pp. 430, 433–435.

never played in Athens, was regarded in Greece as a legitimization of Macedonian rule over the Greek cities, and in the minds of some political thinkers smoothed the path to a monarchic system.[88]

Even Euripides' last drama, *Iphigenia at Aulis*, shows that the poet was seriously preoccupied with the monarchic problem. In *Agamemnon* he tries to portray a good king anxious to devote himself to the good of his people. He again stresses the qualities which should distinguish a good ruler—sophrosyne—wisdom, and a sense of responsibility.[89] Fate did not permit Euripides to manifest his new conviction more clearly, but his last works should not be omitted in the history of the transformation of Greek democracy into Macedonian and then Hellenistic monarchy.[90]

Interest in political speculation had probably never been livelier in any area or time in history than in Athens in the first part of the fourth century. In order to secure a better insight into the problems this created, it is necessary to penetrate the political atmosphere which enveloped Greece and especially Athens, the cradle of democracy and the center of Greek culture. It is also advisable to study more thoroughly the writings of the political theorists of this period. Democracy was going through a serious crisis. Every intellectual who was also a true patriot saw that Pericles' radical democracy had proved to be a failure. It ended in the terrorist regime of the Thirty Tyrants. Then too, the unjust condemnation of Socrates by the resuscitated democracy in Athens (399 B.C.) was a profound shock, especially to his numerous pupils. It is from their ranks that the most serious and radical projects for constitutional reform originated.

Their general disappointment in the *polis* was expressed by Plato in books eight and nine of his *Republic* and summarized in his *Epistle VII*, written soon after 353 B.C. The philosopher, after reviewing the political situation, declares: "Looking at all the states

---

[88] For more details, see W. Nauhardt, *Das Bild des Herrschers in der griechischen Dichtung* (Berlin, 1940), pp. 67–83.

[89] Vss. 16, 46 seq., 78 seq. (admonitions of the old servant to Agamemnon), 337, 373 (Menelaus' admonition), ed. by A. S. Way (Loeb, 1930), I, pp. 8, 10, 12, 32, 36.

[90] Cf. K. F. Stroheker, *op. cit.*, p. 399 seq.

which now exist, I perceived that one and all they are badly governed; for the state of their laws is such as to be almost incurable
without some marvellous overhauling and good luck to boot." This
observation and the fate of Socrates induced the young philosopher
to abstain from active political life, and to devote his talent to
serious study of possible improvements and of the type of constitution that would be best for the Greek states.

According to Xenophon,[91] Socrates, stressing the necessity for
rulers of adequate knowledge, declared: "Kings and rulers are not
those who hold the sceptre, nor those who are chosen by the multitude, nor those on whom the lot falls, nor those who owe their
power to force or deception; but those who know how to rule."
Socrates' disciple improved on these words in a sentence which is
regarded as one of the most famous pronounced by Plato:[92] "Unless
either philosophers become kings in the city-states, or those whom
we now call our kings and rulers take to the pursuit of philosophy
seriously and adequately, and these two things, political power
and philosophic wisdom meet in one, and [unless] those of com-
moner nature, who at present pursue either to the exclusion of the
other, are compulsorily excluded, there can be no cessation of evil
for our city-states, nor, I fancy, for the human race either."

It was the standards set by Plato for the performance of a state
that led him to this conviction. The state had the same role as
the individuals of whom it was composed, namely, the realization
of social morality. It should not be a "pig state" whose role is
the satisfaction of material and animal instincts,[93] but a *Callipolis*[94]
whose aim is to lead all citizens to the realization of this moral ideal.
This can be achieved only when the citizens believe in the greatness
of this ideal. Without good training in philosophical knowledge, this
belief cannot be attained. Since the masses are not fit for such training,[95] is it not better for those men who have not "the divine and
intelligent principle indwelling in themselves" to be subject to the
government of the best man "who has within himself the divine

---

[91] *Memorabilia*, III, 9, 10, ed. by E. C. Marchant (Loeb, 1938), p. 228.
[92] *The Republic*, 473 D, ed. by P. Shorey (Loeb, 1937), 1, p. 508.
[93] *Ibid.*, 372 D, *loc. cit.*, p. 158.
[94] *Ibid.*, 527 C, *loc. cit.*, (1935), 2, p. 172.
[95] *Ibid.*, 494 A, *loc. cit.*, p. 42.

governing principle," to be almost slaves of such a man for their own good, "in order that we all so far as possible may be equals and friends under the government of the same character?"[96]

It follows from these premises that Plato rejected the principle of the absolute equality of all citizens that Pericles' democracy proclaimed. Only the most talented citizens are fit to rule and they must be given the highest education in philosophy and virtue. Their example and direction will lead the masses. Not the decision of the majority of the Assembly, but the judgment of men who are philosophers and who know how to govern should be law.[97] Others must fulfill the duties in the state for which they are best fitted.

In order to realize this specialization of the citizen's role in the service of society, Plato divided men into three classes.[98] The lowest class is to be composed of people whose main interests are in material things—lovers of wealth; the highest class is to be composed of intellectuals eager to acquire all philosophical knowledge—lovers of wisdom; and the middle class—lovers of honor—should be composed of professional soldiers, who defend both the classes and the interests of the state because they combine an ardent character with a virtuous zeal for justice and morality. Plato based these class distinctions on the three faculties which he attributed to the human soul—appetite, reason, and spirit.

The lowest, and largest class was assigned by him to minister to the daily needs of the community as agriculturists and artisans. They will need only an elementary education to enable them to fulfill their duties. They may marry and live as they please. The members of the two superior classes—the lovers of honor and the lovers of wisdom—who will have been endowed by the state with the best physical and intellectual training, will be forbidden any possessions, must live and eat together, like the Spartans, and should have no family life. Only the best of them will be selected as fit to

---

[96] *Ibid.*, 590 D, *loc. cit.*, pp. 406, 408.

[97] Cf. *Protagoras*, 319 C-D, 323 A, ed. by W. R. M. Lamb (Loeb, 1937), pp. 124, 126, 134.

[98] Although Plato shows a familiarity with the Egyptian custom of dividing society into castes, he does not seem to be influenced by it in this respect. It is improbable that he visited Egypt. See J. Kerschensteiner, *Platon und der Orient* (Stuttgart, 1945), pp. 44–55.

rule the state. They will not need any written laws because their abilities and education in philosophy will enable them to make just and appropriate decisions. In order to secure the reproduction of these classes, the state shall arrange, on the most opportune occasions, a kind of holy marriage between men and women of these classes. The children of these unions will be educated by the state from their birth. In order to guarantee the selection of professional soldiers and rulers from the most suitable specimens, the women shall be given the same education as men. Plato was thus the first to proclaim equality between men and women. Woman shall not, however, be allotted the same position in the state as man, because of the weakness of her nature.[99]

This was the ideal state proposed by Plato in his *Republic*,[100] and since he firmly believed it could be realized, he was disappointed when his ideas met with general disapproval. The communism and the abolition of family life prescribed for the two upper classes appeared to be the most shocking ideas to the people. But, in addition to ideas that were new, though hardly acceptable, Plato brought forward some proposals that were highly important in practical political life. For the first time, the necessity for a well trained professional magistracy to administer the state was stressed. The duty of the state to take care of the education of its citizens and to promote their spiritual and moral welfare was also outlined for the first time. Plato's request for a well trained army instead of a citizen militia was sound. So also was his desire to strengthen social feeling among the citizens in order to sustain their sentiments of obligation toward the state and the community, and to provide a bond of union for all citizens.

Although the ideal state, as outlined by Plato, was still based on the conception of the *polis* and appeared unrealizable to his

---

[99] *The Republic*, 457 A, *loc. cit.*, I, p. 450.

[100] For a detailed exposé, see E. Barker, *Greek Political Theory*, pp. 145–270; *idem*, *The Political Thought of Plato and Aristotle*, pp. 81–207; W. Jaeger, *Paideia: the Ideals of Greek Culture*, 2 (New York, 1943), pp. 198–370. An interesting interpretation of Plato's *Republic* is given by N. R. Murphy in *The Interpretation of Plato's Republic* (Oxford, 1951). For more complete bibliographical references on Plato's political ideas, see J. Luccioni, *La pensée politique de Platon* (Paris, 1958), pp. 323–331. Cf. also M. Vanhoutte, *La philosophie politique de Platon dans les Lois* (Louvain, 1954).

contemporaries, some of its principal characteristics encouraged them to familiarize themselves with the new theories which would one day lead to a complete transformation of Greek political philosophy. According to Plato, government was to be entrusted not to an Assembly or a Council, but to a few rulers, well trained in rulership and regarded as the best men available. He was even ready to accept the eventuality that among his "best men" one would attain to the greatest perfection and be able to rule alone with the help of the others.[101]

Moreover, Plato's belief that the initiative of a strong man could bring about his ideal state took him to Sicily three times—to the courts of Dionysius I, Dion, and Dionysius II.[102] But his expectations there were not realized, and this, together with the refusal of his contemporaries to accept his ideal state, induced him to outline the conditions in which the second-best state should be built.

His stay in Sicily did exercise some influence on him, however, as he seems to have been impressed by the Sicilian monarchy with its central government, able magistracy, and well trained and reliable army. This influence can be detected in his description of the second-best state in his *Statesman*. There, he still believes that the best constitution would establish government by one wise man who had attained a perfect knowledge of philosophy,[103] which would enable him to govern alone, through his own wisdom, without

---

[101] *The Republic*, 445 D, *loc. cit.*, 1, p. 422: "If one man of surpassing merit rose among the rulers, it would be denominated royalty (*baseleia*); if more than one, aristocracy." Cf. also 576 E, *loc. cit.* (1935), 2, p. 354: ' 'It is clear to everybody that there is no city more wretched than that in which a tyrant rules, and none more happy than that governed by a true king." Cf. also 587 B, *ibid.*, p. 396, on the contrast between tyranny and kingship. More pertinent is the passage in 580 B, C., *ibid.*, p. 368: "Shall I myself make proclamation that the son of Ariston pronounced the best man and the most righteous to be the happiest, and that he is the one who is the most kingly and a king over himself. Cf. C. Vering, *Platons Staat. Der Staat der königlichen Weisen*, 2nd ed. (Frankfurt a. M., 1932), pp. 79–93.

[102] He describes his bitter experiences in his *Epistle VII*, ed. by R. G. Bury (Loeb, 1942). On Dionysius I, see the recent publication by K. F. Stroheker, *Dionysios I. Gestalt und Geschichte des Tyrannen von Syrakus* (Wiesbaden, 1958), esp. p. 100.

[103] *The Statesman*, 291 E–303 E, *loc. cit.*, pp. 124–166. Plato often calls the wise ruler βασιλεύς.

recourse to the laws. This ideal, which he had described so boldly in his *Republic*, is—he declares after his experiences—hardly realizable on earth, because of the weakness of men. It should, however, always remain a goal before the eyes of rulers who should approach it as closely as possible in their rulership.

Therefore, in the second-best state, as Plato now saw it, wise men should establish a strict legislation and should rule according to law. Although maintaining the principle that government should be in the hands of wise men—philosophers, who know how to rule—he admits the possibility that even in the second-best state rulership could be exercized by only one wise man, and that, in any event, the number of wise men able to rule justly would never be great in a city-state. On the other hand, he adhered strictly to his principle of specialization among citizens in the service of the state. All must serve the interests of the state under the direction of a central government.[104]

The Statesman was written by Plato soon after 366 B.C. He completed the structure of his second-best state in his last dialogue, *The Laws*. He continued to defend his ideal state, with communism for the soldiers and rulers, but confessed that such an ideal could be realized only by gods or their sons. If, however, divine Providence were to allow the ascendancy of the best and wisest man to the head of a state, and if this man were given the strength to resist all temptations of luxury, ambition, and other vices that prevent men from ruling justly, then this man would not need any laws for his rule, because wisdom is higher than law.

Such a government was to be regarded as an ideal; in practice, however, rulers must govern according to laws. Imagining the foundation of a new state in Crete, he outlined a mixed constitution for it. There should be an Assembly and a Council. The many magistrates should be elected by competent citizens. In his proposed constitution, Plato minimizes the influence of the masses on government, adheres strictly to social morality as the norm of the state, and is most anxious to avoid any form of capitalism. Thirty-seven "Guardians of the Laws" should exercise control over all functionaries, and a Nocturnal Council should be given the power

[104] *Ibid.*, 305, *loc. cit.*, pp. 172 seq.

to revise the laws. Numerous details are given regulating all aspects of public and private life, and special stress is laid on the practice of religion.[105]

Plato's contemporaries might not have agreed with many of his ideas on the state, or on the constitution proposed for his best and second-best states. Much importance for the further development of political philosophy attached, however, to his repeated assertion that the state would be best administered if it were headed by one wise man who had attained the highest degree of philosophical and moral training. These views prepared the way for the advent of the monarchic idea, should a strong personality become ruler in a Greek state.

The founder of political science is, however, not Plato but Aristotle (384–322 B.C.) who had joined Plato's Academy in 367 B.C. at the age of seventeen, when his master was sixty years old and was aggrieved by the collapse of his plans in Sicily. Aristotle was of a much more practical nature than his master. He maintained the middle way between Plato's socialism and the individualism of the Sophists. In his political speculation, his practical mind followed an empirical method and he reached his recommendations and conclusions only after having studied 158 constitutions of the many Greek city-states.[106]

From this enormous mass of material collected by Aristotle and his students, only the 'Αθηναίων πολιτεία is preserved, discovered in 1890 on a papyrus in London.[107] Aristotle's authorship of this work has often been disputed,[108] but it seems certain that it at least originated in Aristotle's school under his supervision, though it was probably published only after his death. The first part is important for the history of the Constitution of Athens;

[105] For elaborate commentary on *The Statesman* and *The Laws*, see E. Barker, *Greek Political Theory*, pp. 271–382. On Plato's philosopher-king, see also J. Luccioni, *op. cit.*, pp. 147–187.

[106] See the main bibliography to Aristotle's political writing in M.-D. Philippe, *Aristoteles* (Bern, 1948), p. 43. Cf. W. Jaeger (*infra*, note 117), *Aristotle*, p. 259 seq.

[107] Ed. by H. Oppermann (Teubner, 1928), also by G. Mathieu and B. Haussoulier, *Aristote. Constitution d'Athènes*, Collection Budé (Paris, 1922).

[108] Recently by C. Hignett, *A History of the Athenian Constitution*. See the bibliography on the controversy, *ibid.*, pp. 1–32.

the second part gives a systematic review of contemporary political institutions. Even in this work some criticism of radical democracy can be discovered, probably as an influence of oligarchic writings.

Aristotle came from Stagiras in Chalcidice, on the border of Macedonia, and his father, a physician, enjoyed friendly relations with King Amyntas II of Macedonia. His stay in Assos with the tyrant Hermias and then at the Macedonian court from 343/2, probably until 338, as teacher of Philip's heir Alexander, all gave Aristotle the opportunity of becoming acquainted with both the light and shady sides of a rigid monarchic regime. These experiences induced him to devote more time to political speculation.

Aristotle's lectures on politics were later collected and edited by his disciples under the title *Politics*.[109] There he improves on Plato's teachings on the state. Man is a social being by nature, and in the state he finds not only his material autarchy but also the satisfaction of his moral needs. "Justice...is an element of the state; for judicial procedure, which means the decision of what is just, is the regulation of the political partnership."[110]

By showing that the state is a product of nature and is based on reason, Aristotle liquidates the theories of the Sophists on social contract, and of the Cynics, who taught that the wise man is self-sufficient and does not need a state. But he disagrees also with Plato's organic idea of the state, and disapproves of his excessive stress on the analogy of the state with the individual man when he declares: "A state is a composite thing, in the same sense as any other of the things that are wholes but consist of many parts ... a state is a collection of citizens."[111] He then gives the definition of a citizen: "A citizen pure and simple is defined by nothing else so much as by the right to participate in judicial functions and in office."[112]

---

[109] On the composition of Aristotle's *Politics*, see E. Barker, *The Political Thought of Plato and Aristotle*, pp. 255–263; discussion of Aristotle's policy, pp. 264–496. Cf. H. F. A. von Arnim, *Zur Entstehungsgeschichte der aristotelischen Politik*, Akad. der Wiss. in Wien, Phil.-hist. Kl., 200, Abhandl. 1 (Vienna-Leipzig, 1924).

[110] *Politics*, 1253 a, line 37 seq., ed. by H. Rackham (Loeb, 1932), p. 12.

[111] *Ibid.*, 1274 b, line 39 seq., *loc. cit.*, p. 172.

[112] *Ibid.*, 1275 a, line 22 seq., *loc. cit.*, p. 174.

Aristotle rejects Plato's communism, and having—in contrast to the celibate Plato—experienced a happy married life, he defends the family as the basis of human society and the state.[113] However, when expounding—in books seven and eight—his conception of the best constitution, he indicates that any dangerous accumulation of capital should be prevented by watchful measures on the part of the state. The best constitution recommended by Aristotle is akin to the second-best state of Plato. The latter's *Laws* are here followed by his pupil, often with approval. Although he did not complete his picture of the best state, he seemed to recommend for it a mixture of oligarchic, aristocratic, and democratic systems.

Discussing the qualities of the ruler in a well governed state, Aristotle agrees with Plato in his appreciation of the rule of the "best man":[114]

> If there is any one man so greatly distinguished in outstanding virtue, or more than one but not enough to be able to make up a complete state, so that the virtue of all the rest and their political ability is not comparable with that of the men mentioned, if they are several, or if one, with his alone, it is no longer proper to count these exceptional men a part of the state; for they will be treated unjustly if deemed worthy of equal status, being so widely unequal in virtue and in their political ability: since such a man will naturally be as a god among men.... There can be no law dealing with such men as those described, for they are themselves a law.

Further on Aristotle compares the superman–ruler to Zeus:[115]

> In the case of the best constitution there is much doubt as to what ought to be done, not as regards superiority in the other things of value, such as strength and wealth and popularity, but in the case of a person becoming exceptionally distinguished for virtue. It certainly would not be said that such a man must be banished and got out of the way; yet nevertheless no doubt men would not think that they ought to rule over such a man, for that would be the same as if they claimed to rule over

---

[113] *Ibid.*, 1263 b, line 15 seq., *loc. cit.*, p. 88 seq.
[114] *Ibid.*, 1284 a, *loc. cit.*, p. 240.
[115] *Ibid.*, 1284 b, line 26 seq., *loc. cit.*, p. 246.

Zeus, dividing up his spheres of government. It remains therefore, and this seems to be the natural course, for all to obey
such a man gladly, so that men of this sort may be kings in
the cities for all time.

These words are significant for the light they throw on the origin
of the monarchic idea in Greek political speculation. It is true that
Aristotle, like Plato, had his misgivings about the possibility that
any nation would produce such a man, and considered the realization
of a perfect ruler to be impossible; yet, he continued to discuss his
hypothetical paragon in all seriousness, which may suggest that the
same notion had haunted Greek minds before his and that a desire for
superior men had been common among philosophers and statesmen.

Not less revealing is the homage which Aristotle rendered to
the memory of his friend, the tyrant Hermias, when he learned, at
the court of Philip, of his tragic death at the hands of the treacherous
Persians. He apostrophies Virtue, "fairest prize in life," to die for
which is regarded in Hellas as the greatest good fortune, "better
than gold." Heracles, the Dioscuri, Achilles, and Ajax died for
Virtue, and Hermias is another such hero.[116]

It is significant that Aristotle casts the tyrant Hermias in heroic
guise. "The juxtaposition of Hermias with Heracles, and the Dioscuri, with Achilles and Ajax," says W. Jaeger,[117] "is not a trick of
the panegyric style; Aristotle does not intend to deck out his friend
in the pathetic paraphernalia of Homer's heroes. On the contrary,
all Hellenic heroism, from Homer's naive kind down to the moral
heroism of the philosopher, appeared to him as the expression of
one single attitude towards life, an attitude which scales the heights
of life only when it overcomes it."[118]

[116] Didymus, De Demosthene Commenta: Philippicon, 6, 22–36, ed. by H.
Diels and W. Schubart (Teubner, 1904), p. 11.
[117] W. Jaeger, Aristotle; Fundamentals of the History of his Development,
trans. by R. Robinson (Oxford, 1934), p. 118 seq. See also there the translation of the paean.
[118] Aristotles' homage to his martyred friend must have been interpreted
in the Hellenistic period as approval of the divinization of a ruler after death.
This is indicated by Lucian of Samosata who reports a rumor that
Aristotle brought sacrifices to Hermias as to a god; Lucian, Eunuchus, 9,
ed. by K. Jacobitz (Teubner, 1903), 2, p. 185. Of course, these rumors
were baseless.

This paean to a philosopher-tyrant is the more expressive if the situation in the Athens of 341, when Hermias was executed by the Persians, is borne in mind. Demosthenes' party was blackening the character of the dead tyrant, rejoicing that his agreements with Philip for common action against the Persians had been discredited, and hoping that after the revelation of this plot the Persians would be ready to conclude an alliance with Athens against Philip.

Aristotle's anti-Persian sentiments are also revealed by the epigram which he composed for Hermias' epitaph in Delphi.[119] There are indications here too that he sympathized with the Panhellenic ideas of Demosthenes' political adversaries. He knew, however, the narrowness of political life in the city-states, and, not being an Athenian by birth, he was more ready to accept a leader of superior qualities who would introduce some organic union into Greek political society and put an end to the humiliating interventions of the Persian kings in Greek political life.

The monarchic idea found an important protagonist in another disciple of Socrates, Xenophon (*ca.* 430–354 B.C.), the intrepid soldier who brought the Greek Army of the Ten Thousand safely back to Greece from the fateful expedition of Cyrus the Younger against Artaxerxes. Like Herodotus, Xenophon located his ideal ruler in Persia, in the person of Cyrus, the founder of Persian glory. His *Cyropaedia*, so important for our knowledge of Persian kingship, was also intended to expound to Xenophon's compatriots his own political convictions. It is not sure whether this political and philosophical romance Xenophon intended to oppose the ideas of Plato's *Republic*. His work, however, contributed not a little to the popularity of the monarchic regime among the Greeks, who read in it unstinting praise of the Persian administration.

It is possible that Xenophon's idea of depicting a Persian ruler as an ideal king was not original. Others may have preceded him, especially one of the most faithful disciples of Socrates, Antisthenes (*ca.* 455–*ca.* 360 B.C.).[120] The latter revered Heracles above all,

---

[119] Didymus, *op. cit.*, 6, 39–43, *loc. cit.*, p. 12.

[120] Photius in his *Bibliotheca*, codex 158 (PG, 103, col. 432), mentions that Antisthenes had written a treatise called *Cyrus*. In his *Banquet* and in his *Memorabilia* Xenophon has him participate in a discussion with Socrates.

because this hero had led a life of virtue which is—according to Antisthenes—the only basis of happiness. Cyrus was regarded by him as a model wise man, and the main principle of Antisthenes' political teaching was that dominion should be in the hands of wise men. He was, in this respect, even more outspoken than Plato and Aristotle.

Xenophon's political ideas are set out not only in his *Cyropaedia* but in his memoirs of Socrates, the *Memorabilia*, and in his *Agesilaus*, probably written after 360. This was intended to honor the memory of the Spartan King Agesilaus, who was greatly admired because of his Spartan virtue and his soldierly qualities. Although Xenophon himself, as a valiant soldier, was inclined to accept the principle of the right of the strong, he understood by this principle the man strong in virtue, and demanded that the ruler be virtuous, just, and a benefactor of his subjects. Rulership "is the noblest kind of excellence, the greatest of arts ... for [this art] belongs to kings and is dubbed kingly." It is impossible to excel in rulership without being a just man.[121]

With these principles in mind, Xenophon describes Agesilaus as follows:[122] "He never shirked toil, never shrank from danger, never spared money, never excused himself on the score of bodily weakness or old age: but believed that it is the duty of a good king to do as much good as possible to his subjects...though the most powerful man in the state, he was clearly a devoted servant of the laws."

Cyrus, on the other hand, is said to have regarded virtue as the strongest safeguard of the king's happiness.[123] He resolved to be a model to his subjects in religion, integrity, benevolence, temperance, and generosity. The ideal king must take care, first of all,

---

Only fragments are preserved of Antisthenes' works. Cf. what W. Weber says on Antisthenes in his address, *Zur Geschichte der Monarchie* (Tübingen, 1919), p. 16 seq.

[121] *Memorabilia*, IV, 2, 11, ed. by E. C. Marchant (Loeb, 1938), p. 276. Cf. III, 6, 2, *loc. cit.*, p. 204.

[122] *Agesilaus*, 7, 1 seq., in *Scripta Minora*, ed. by E. C. Marchant (Loeb, 1925), p. 112. Xenophon—as an aristocrat—admired Sparta, which he described in a special treatise. He came, however, to the conclusion that for uniting the Greeks and for spreading Hellenism throughout Asia Minor, the Spartan constitution was not suitable.

[123] *Cyropaedia*, VII, 5, 84, ed. by W. Miller (Loeb, 1914), 2, p. 300.

of the well-being of his people.[124] Cyrus is said to have defined this duty by comparing a king to a good shepherd:[125] "People quote a remark of his to the effect that the duties of a good shepherd and of a good king were very much alike; a good shepherd ought, while deriving benefit from his flocks, to make them happy...and in the same way a king ought to make his people and his cities happy, if he would derive benefits from them. Seeing that he held this theory, it is not at all surprising that he was ambitious to surpass all other men in attention to his friends." Thus, the king should be the best man[126] and a father of his people.[127]

Noble origin should also adorn the king. Xenophon has Artabazus proclaim[128] that he "would never leave the noblest and best of men [meaning Cyrus] and what was more than all, a man descended from the gods." And after his defeat, Croesus is said to have confessed to Cyrus:[129] "I was no match for you; for you are in the first place a scion of the gods and in the second place the descendant of an unbroken line of kings, and finally you have been practising virtue from your childhood on, while the first of my ancestors to wear a crown, I am told, was at the same time king and freedman. Therefore, as I was thus without knowledge, I have my just deserts."[130]

In the last phrase the necessity of a good education for a future ruler and the possession of natural talent is alluded to. Xenophon stresses those two qualities as essential for a good ruler in his minute account of Cyrus' education and talents. He reverts once more to this subject at the end of his *Oeconomicus*, when reviewing the qualities of a good master and repeating his conviction that the virtue of good rulership can be acquired only if the ruler is talented and has received a good education. This is a royal virtue and is part of the divine aspect of royalty.[131]

[124] *Ibid.*, VIII, 1, 21 seq., *loc. cit.*, p. 316 seq.
[125] *Ibid.*, VIII, 2, 14, *loc. cit.*, p. 338.
[126] *Ibid.*, VIII, 1, 37, *loc. cit.*, p. 322.
[127] *Ibid.*, VIII, 1, 1, 44, *loc. cit.*, pp. 304, 326; VIII, 2, 9, p. 336; VIII, 8, 1, pp. 438–440.
[128] *Ibid.*, IV, 1, 24, *loc. cit.*, 1, p. 322.
[129] *Ibid.*, VII, 2, 24, *loc. cit.*, 2, p. 240.
[130] Cyrus' descent from gods is mentioned also in the following passages: I, 6, 1 seq. *loc. cit.*, 1, p. 86; II, 1, 1, p. 132; IV, 1, 24, p. 322.
[131] *Oeconomicus*, 21, 11, ed. by E. C. Marchant (Loeb, 1938), p. 524: ἦθος βασιλικόν... καὶ τὸ μέγιστον δὴ θεῖον γενέσθαι. Marchant's translation of

POLITICAL PHILOSOPHY

In some passages of Xenophon's writing, a sharp, though disguised, criticism of Athenian radical democracy can be detected. He did not agree with the idea that all citizens should have equal shares in everything. His military experience taught him that everybody should be recompensed according to his merits and talents. He has Chrysantas address Cyrus in the following words:[132] "I do not believe that anything in the world is more unfair than for the bad and the good to be awarded equal shares." Cyrus' friends decided[133] "that each one should receive rewards according to his deserts, and that Cyrus should be the judge."

Xenophon also regards the military class from which Cyrus will choose his helpers as the privileged body in a state. However, in order to avoid the rise of too sharp a division between the upper and lower classes, he allows the talented young men of the lower class to participate in official education so that they may rejuvenate the upper class.

He believes that the distribution of offices and dignities in a state should not be left to the assembly of citizens, but would best be put in the hands of one ruler, the best man.

Xenophon is also convinced, like all disciples of Socrates, that the state should be based on the moral education of its rulers. He differs, however, from Plato's ethical ideal when he sees the goal of a state in its interior and exterior growth, which is manifested by the prosperity of its citizens and by its expansion beyond its frontiers. Obviously, such an ideal could be realized, not in the *polis*, strictly limited, as it was, within its frontier and by the number of its citizens, but only by a monarchy with an absolute ruler; further, according to Xenophon, this ruler should, of course, be the best man, well educated not so much in philosophy as in the practical administration, in the government of different peoples, in the dispensation of justice, and in the leadership of a large army.

---

this passage obscures the true meaning. For a more detailed analysis of Xenophon's political and social ideas, see E. Scharr's work *Xenophons Staats- und Gesellschaftsideal und seine Zeit* (Halle, 1919) and J. Luccioni, *Les idées politiques et sociales de Xénophon* (Paris, 1947), pp. 53 seq., 201 seq.

[132] *Cyropaedia*, II, 2, 18, *loc. cit.*, 1, p. 166.
[133] *Ibid.*, II, 3, 16, *loc. cit.*, p. 184.

FROM MYCENAE TO ISOCRATES

Xenophon was not a thinker of genius like Plato and Aristotle. However, he too belongs to the Socratic circle, and he developed some of his master's teachings on rulership in a much wider sense than other pupils of greater genius had done. He was of a soldierly and aristocratic nature, remote from Athenian political squabbles, and with wide experience gained through laborious expeditions in Persia. As he was a straight-forward man, he described his observations with a courageous open-mindedness. He did more for the progress of the monarchic idea in Greek political speculation than did more talented disciples of Socrates.

Xenophon was not alone in developing in Greece a kind of cult of strong personalities. Besides Cyrus and the Spartan King Agesilaus there were other strong rulers whose deeds had startled the Greeks of the mainland. In Syracuse Dionysius the Elder rose from the rank of an officer to become a tyrant.[134] Although the Athenian democrats had heaped the strongest condemnation on his head for the way in which he won dominion over Syracuse and other Sicilian cities, they soon had to confess that, thanks to his statesmanship and military capabilities, the Greek element in Sicily was saved from being engulfed by the Phoenicians of Carthage. But Dionysius was not entirely deaf to political philosophy. According to Plutarch, he gave to his three daughters names which recalled the main qualities of the "best man": Dikaiosyne, Sophrosyne, and Arete.[135] He even undertook some writing himself, and one short fragment attributed to him describes tyranny as the mother of injustice.[136] Dionysius invited writers and poets to his court, and through their writings the reputation of his rule as a profitable one for the Greeks became famous. Even Plato met him during his stay in Italy.

---

[134] Xenophon also chose a king of Syracuse—Hieron (478–467 B.C.)—in order to show, in an imaginary conversation between the King and the poet Simonides, that a tyrant who did not respect the interests of the people was less happy than a simple citizen, and to indicate the means by which a despot could win the affection of the citizens and happiness for himself.

[135] Plutarch, *Lives: Dion*, 6, 1, ed. by B. Perrin (Loeb, 1943), 6, p. 12; *idem, Moralia: Fortuna Alexandri*, 338 C, ed. by F. C. Babbitt (Loeb, 1936), 4, p. 448.

[136] Fragment 4, ed. by A. Nauck, *Tragicorum graecorum fragmenta*, p. 794: ἡ γὰρ τυραννὶς ἀδικίας μήτηρ ἔφυ.

Another such was Evagoras (*ca.* 435–374/3 B.C.), ruler of Salamis in Cyprus, who had not only shaken off the Phoenician domination, but had strengthened Hellenism in the whole island. For ten years he waged wars, not unsuccessfully, with Persia, while his court was filled with political émigrés from continental Greece.

In the north of continental Greece, Jason, tyrant of Pherae (*ca.* 380–370 B.C.), gained control over all Thessaly. He was an ally of the Thebans, a friend of Athens, and made a bold attempt to establish a Thessalian hegemony over Greece. For the first time there seemed to be some hope of the realization of a Panhellenic union, but these hopes were ended by an assassin.

The veneration and respect which these strong personalities enjoyed in the eyes of their Greek admirers is best illustrated by the words with which Isocrates describes the origins of Evagoras. He traces his dynasty back to Aeacus, son of Zeus, the ancestor of the family of the Teucridae.[137] Evagoras' successful reign must have fired the imagination of his grateful subjects, and legendary tales on his divine origin were rife. Isocrates, although hardly believing these, testifies at least to their existence when he says:[138] "I prefer to say nothing of the portents, the oracles, the visions appearing in dreams, from which the impression might be gained that he was of superhuman birth."

Summarizing his praise of Evagoras, Isocrates says:[139] "I believe that, if any men of the past have by their merit become immortal, Evagoras also has earned this preferment.... If any of the poets have used extravagant expressions in characterizing any man of the past, asserting that he was a god among men, or a mortal divinity, all praises of that kind would be especially in harmony with the noble qualities of Evagoras." Although Isocrates has no intention of deifying Evagoras, his words echo the respect that people, disillusioned by the excesses of radical democracy, had for strong rulers.

The Panhellenic idea was another element which helped to build a bridge between the old Greek political system of city-states

---

[137] *Evagoras*, 12 seq., ed. by Larue van Hook (Loeb, 1945), 3, p. 10 seq.
[138] *Ibid.*, 21, *loc. cit.*, p. 14.
[139] *Ibid.*, 70, 72, *loc. cit.*, pp. 42, 44.

and that of a more solid union. The idea of a Panhellenic union and of a war of retaliation against Persia gained ground rather slowly in the minds of the Greeks. The Sicilian rhetor Gorgias proclaimed in 408 B.C., in his Olympic speech[140] and in his *Epitaphios*,[141] that these two ideas should become the national program of the Hellenes, and a similar harangue was addressed to the assembled Greeks in Olympia in 388 by Lysias,[142] but these were rather academic and rhetorical productions which had no visible effect on Greek political life.

Xenophon and many others were sympathetic toward these ideas, but someone was needed who would devote to their realization all his rhetorical talent and all his strength. Such a man was Isocrates (436–338 B.C.), who had a firmly established conception of the national unity of all Hellenes. He included in his conception of Hellenes the Cypriots and the Macedonians, and believed in the superiority of the Hellenic race over the rest of humanity. Pointing proudly to the intellectual achievements of the Greeks, especially of the Athenians, he was not impressed by the Sophists Alcidamas and Antiphon, who proclaimed the equality of all men in the face of nature. For him all non-Greeks were barbarians and inferiors who should be forced to become servants of the Greeks.

The first condition for any success against Persia was, of course, the union of all Greeks.[143] Throughout his life Isocrates sought a leader who could achieve this union. As an Athenian citizen and patriot, he first hoped that Athens would realize such hegemony over other city-states and lead the Greeks against the Persians. He expressed this hope in his *Panegyricus* written for the Olympic festival in 380. There he praises the services rendered to all Hellenes

---

[140] Mentioned by Aristotle, *The "Art" of Rhetoric*, III, 14, 2, ed. by J. H. Freese (Loeb, 1939), p. 428. Cf. U. von Wilamowitz-Moellendorff, *Aristoteles und Athen*, 1 (Berlin, 1893), p. 172.

[141] Fragments 5 a, 5 b, in H. Diels, *Die Fragmente der Vorsokratiker.*, 2 (Berlin, 1952), p. 284 seq.

[142] *Olympic Oration*, fragment preserved by Dionysius of Halicarnassus, ed. by W. R. M. Lamb, (Loeb, 1930), pp. 684–689. On Lysias, cf. F. Blass, *Die attische Beredsamkeit*, 2nd ed., 1 (Leipzig, 1887), p. 339 seq.; on his *Olympiakos, ibid.*, p. 430 seq.

[143] Cf. the dissertation by J. Kessler, *Isokrates und die panhellenische Idee* (Paderborn, 1911). Cf. also F. Blass, *op. cit.*, 2 (Leipzig, 1892), pp. 8–331, and J. Luccioni, *Démosthène et le panhellénisme*, Publications de la Faculté des Lettres d'Algers, no. 40 (Paris, 1961).

by the Athenians during the Persian wars, and attacks the Spartans who had sided with the Persians and had forced the Athenians and their allies, through the ignoble "King's Peace" negotiated by their agent Antalcidas (386), to abandon to Persia the Greek cities of Asia Minor. The regime of Lysander imposed on the Greek cities after the Spartan victory in the Peloponnesian war came in for sharp criticism.[144] By its treatment of these cities and by its alliance with Persia, Sparta became unworthy of exercising hegemony over the Greeks. The movement for revenge against Persia was favorable in Isocrates' view because its might was declining. The Greeks should therefore accept the hegemony of Athens against the national enemy.

Isocrates' *Plataicus* seems to be a fictitious discourse written probably in 371 B.C. and propagating the idea of Athenian supremacy. This had been endangered by the ascendency of Thebes, which had conquered and destroyed the city-state of Plataea.[145] Thanks partly to Isocrates' *Panegyricus*, Athenian supremacy seemed likely to be realized. In 378 B.C. Athens had concluded the Second Confederacy with some of its previous allies, but the mistakes committed at the time of the Delian League were now repeated by Athens' leaders and the result was the Social War, inaugurated by the revolt of recalcitrant members of the Confederacy.

This was a great disillusionment for Isocrates. In his discourse *On the Peace* he made an impassioned effort to save the situation, exhorting his compatriots to conclude a just peace with their former allies and to respect, in the future, the freedom of other city-states. This discourse, probably written in 355 during the peace negotiations, shows that the author had almost lost the confidence in Athenian leadership that he had expressed so eagerly in his *Panegyricus*. The experiences of the last two decades had proved disconcerting. Isocrates had hoped that Timotheus, one of his pupils, who was elected *strategos* in 378 B.C., would be able to bring

---

[144] *Panegyricus*, 110–114, ed. by G. Norlin (Loeb, 1928), 1, p. 188 seq.

[145] Cf. G. Mathieu's and A. Brémond's edition of Isocrates' discourses (Paris, 1928–42, 2nd ed., 1950), 2, p. 72. See also Mathieu's detailed study *Les idées politiques d'Isocrate* (Paris, 1925), the best work on Isocrates. Cf. also H. Kehl, *Die Monarchie im politischen Denken des Isokrates* (Bonn, 1962).

about that unity. He accompanied him on his first expeditions and encouraged him by letters. Timotheus was a strong personality, but his imperialistic policy alienated the allies. He died in exile in 354 and in the *Antidosis*, written in 353,[146] Isocrates devoted an eloquent eulogy to him.

When he lost confidence in the Second Confederacy, Isocrates, looking for a strong man outside Athens who could realize his ideal, addressed a letter, probably in 368 B.C., to Dionysius the Elder, of Syracuse,[147] which praised the tyrant highly. The unfinished letter was evidently intended to appeal to Dionysius either to take the lead in or contribute toward the implementation of Isocrates' concept of union for all Greeks. This is interesting since in his *Panegyricus* Isocrates had attacked Dionysius for his alliance with Sparta.[148]

Isocrates also followed hopefully the exploits of Jason the Thessalian. It is possible that the latter was partly inspired by Isocrates' *Panegyricus* in extending his power over the whole of Thessaly, and in trying to establish Thessalian hegemony as a prelude to an attack on Persia. Apparently Isocrates met Jason in 373 B.C.,[149] and he speaks of their friendship in his letter *To the Children of Jason*: (Thebe and her half-brother Tisiphonus.)[150] Isocrates is said to have addressed a letter also to Alexander, son of Jason's brother Polydorus, who was slain at the instigation of his wife Thebe.[151]

Isocrates finally found his strong man in the Macedonian King Philip. His attitude toward the Macedonian dynasty had changed since 380 when he had judged Philip's father rather unfavorably in his *Panegyricus*.[152] His letter to Philip in 376 has not been preserved.[153] In his discourse *On the Peace*[154] Isocrates was more

---

[146] *Antidosis*, 101–141, ed. by G. Norlin (Loeb, 1929), 2, pp. 240–264.
[147] Letter 1, *To Dionysius*, ed. by L. van Hook (Loeb, 1945), 3, p. 372 seq.
[148] *Panegyricus*, 127, *loc. cit.*, p. 198.
[149] See Mathieu, *op. cit.*, p. 101.
[150] Letter 6, 1, ed. by L. van Hook, *loc. cit.*, 3, p. 434.
[151] L. Köhler, *Die Briefe des Sokrates und der Sokratiker* (Leipzig, 1928) = *Philologus*, Supplementband 20, Heft 11: Letter 28 of Speusippus, p. 45.
[152] *Panegyricus*, 126, *loc. cit.*, p. 198.
[153] Mentioned by Speusippus (L. Köhler, *op. cit.*, p. 45), but its authenticity is doubtful (*ibid.*, p. 117).
[154] *On the Peace*, 22, ed. by G. Norlin (Loeb, 1929), 2, p. 20.

hopeful and invited Philip to return to the Athenians the disputed city of Amphipolis, a former Athenian colony in Macedonia.

Isocrates expounded his heart's desire to Philip in a long address sent to him in 346. In the meantime Philip, cleverly exploiting the dissensions between Greek city-states and the troubles caused by the Social War, extended his authority over the whole north of Greece as far as Thermopylae. He ended the Sacred War for the possession of Delphi and, allying himself with Athens, also terminated the ten years of hostile relations with this city over the possession of Amphipolis.[155] The conclusion of the peace of 346 B.C. was a most appropriate occasion for inviting Philip to bring about the unity of Greece and to start the retaliatory war with Persia.

After pleading once more for the return of Amphipolis to Athens and stressing the importance to Philip of good relations with the most important Greek city-state, Isocrates confesses that harangues to the Athenians and citizens of other Greek states urging them to unite and to fight their common enemy were "as ineffectual as the legal codes and constitutions drawn up by the Sophists.... Those who desire not to chatter empty nonsense but to further some practical purpose, and those who think they have hit upon some plan for the common good must leave it to others to harangue at the public festivals, but must themselves win over someone to champion their cause from among men who are capable not only of speech but of action and who occupy a high position in the world."[156]

It was courageous of Isocrates to address such an invitation to an absolute ruler who was regarded by the party of Demosthenes as a barbarian and enemy of Greek culture, and it was no mere oratorical gesture for him to declare that, when he had disclosed his intention to write to Philip, many "were dismayed, fearing that because of my old age I had parted with my wits, ... insisting that I was applying myself to an absurd and exceedingly senseless undertaking."[157]

Isocrates was well aware that his enemies regarded the Macedonian as unworthy of the friendship of pure blooded Greeks. He acknowledged that not all Macedonians were Greeks, but regarded

---

[155] For details, see N. G. L. Hammond, *A History of Greece*, p. 533 seq.
[156] *Address to Philip*, 13, ed. by G. Norlin (Loeb, 1928), 1, p. 252 seq.
[157] *Ibid.*, 18, *loc. cit.*, p. 256.

them as intermediaries between the Greeks and barbarians. He praised their qualities and the friendly attitude of Philip's predecessors toward the Greek states, and plead with him to continue in this attitude.[158] He insisted especially on the descent of the Macedonian dynasty from Heracles.[159] This seemed to him to be the greatest recommendation of Philip to the Greeks and of the Greeks to Philip.

Of course, being a convinced democrat he repeatedly urged Philip not to touch the autonomy of the Greek states, but to be their unifier and leader in the war against Persia. He admitted having addressed himself first to Athens, which had liberated the Greeks twice from the Persian and once from the Lacedaemonian yoke. "But when I perceived that she cared less for what I said," confesses Isocrates,[160] "than for the ravings of the platform orators, I gave her up, although I did not abandon my effort.... Throughout my whole life I have constantly employed such powers as I possess in warring on the barbarians, in condemning those who opposed my plan, and in striving to arouse to action whoever I think will best be able to benefit the Hellenes in any way or to rob the barbarians of their present prosperity." It was not the "Great King" who should enjoy this prosperity, but the "descendants of Heracles, who because of his virtue was exalted by his father to the rank of a god."

In order correctly to present Isocrates' political ideas, it should be emphasized that in his Address he did not plead in any way for a federation of Greek states under Macedonian leadership. Rather, he exhorted Philip to desist from his plans for conquest in Greece and to make an alliance with Athens whose navy would be useful to him in the Macedonian conquest of Persia. He urged that other Greek states should accept the peace stipulations of 346 and cease their enmities.[161]

[158] *Ibid.*, 19, 107, 154, *loc. cit.*, pp. 256, 310, 336.
[159] *Ibid.*, 105, 132, *loc. cit.*, pp. 308, 324.
[160] *Ibid.*, 128 seq., *loc. cit.*, p. 322 seq.
[161] This is stressed by S. Perlman in his study "Isocrates' 'Philippus'—a Reinterpretation," *Historia*, 6 (1957) pp. 306–317. Unfavorable criticism of Isocrates' ideals was recently made by N. H. Baynes in his *Byzantine Studies and Other Essays* (London, 1955), chap. 8: "Isocrates," pp. 144–167, and by P. Cloché, *Un fondateur d'empire* (Saint-Etienne, 1955), pp. 159 seq., 189 seq. We cannot explore the details of these controversies. They are outlined by S. Perlman, who gives also a recent bibliography on Isocrates.

Upon learning in 342 B.C. that Philip had been wounded in a war with the Illyrians, Isocrates sent the King another letter.[162] He exhorted him to stop the war on the northern boundary of his realm and to concentrate all his power on the war with another barbarian, the king of Persia. Anxious to divert the Macedonian from any new attempt at conquest in Greece, he asked him once more to establish good relations with Athens whose help, or at least neutrality, would be welcome to Philip during his expedition into Asia. Once more Isocrates addressed the Athenians in his *Panathenaicus* in 339 B.C. There, when glorifying Agamemnon, he had Philip in mind.[163]

> He is the only man who was ever deemed worthy to be the leader of the armies of all Hellas. Whether he was elected by all or obtained this honor by himself, I am not able to say.... And when he obtained this power, he harmed no city of Hellas; nay, so far was he from injuring any one of them that, although he took command of the Hellenes when they were in a state of mutual warfare and confusion and great misfortune, he delivered them from this condition, and, having established concord among them... he collected the Hellenes into an army and led them forth against the barbarians.

In another passage he bitterly reproached the Spartans and Athenians for their negotiations with the Persians.[164] "In common we deliberate about nothing whatsoever, but independently we each send ambassadors to the King, expecting that the one of these two states to which he inclines in friendship will be invested with the place of advantage among the Hellenes, little realizing that those who court his favor he is wont to treat insolently."

However, Demosthenes and his party overcame Isocrates. But the defeat of the Athenian army at Chaeronea sealed Philip's triumph over the Greek city-states.

---

[162] Letter 2, *To Philip*, *I*, ed. by L. van Hook (Loeb, 1945), 3, p. 384 seq. Cf. S. Perlman, *op. cit.*, pp. 116, 117.

[163] *Panathenaicus*, 76 seq., ed. by G. Norlin (Loeb, 1929), 2, p. 418. Cf. the short study by F. Zucker, *Isokrates' Panathenaikos*, Berichte über die Verhandl. des Sächs. Akad. der Wiss. zu Leipzig, Phil-hist. Kl., 101, Heft 7. (Berlin, 1954).

[164] *Panathenaicus*, 160, *loc. cit.*, p. 472.

Now ninety-eight years old and in feeble health, Isocrates took up his pen again and wrote his last letter to Philip, urging him to bring to a happy fruition the union of all Greeks and to lead them against Persia. He ended his short missive with words which became famous and on which many Hellenistic political thinkers were in future to base their deductions:[165] "Be assured that a glory unsurpassable and worthy of the deeds you have done in the past will be yours, when you shall compel the barbarians...to be serfs of the Greeks, and when you shall force the King who is now called Great to do whatever you command. For then will naught be left for you, except to become a god."

To understand this statement, which seems extravagant, the content of Isocrates' Address to Philip must be recalled. There he exhorted him to follow the example of Heracles, whose deeds he had described:[166]

> For since you have no need to follow alien examples but have before you one from your own house, have we not then the right to expect that you will be spurred on by this and inspired by the ambition to make yourself like the ancestor of your race? I do not mean that you will be able to imitate Heracles in all his exploits; for even among the gods there are some who could not do that; but in the qualities of the spirit, in devotion to humanity, and in the good will which he cherished toward the Hellenes, you can come close to his purposes.

It should be borne in mind that, according to general Greek belief, Heracles, although a man, was raised by Zeus to the rank of a god. When these two statements by Isocrates are compared, it is legitimate to conclude that the rhetor really suggested that what happened to Heracles, because of his heroic achievements, could happen also to his descendant, Philip, if he should accomplish a deed similar to that for which Heracles is praised—the unification of all Greeks and leadership in their victory over the "barbarians."[167]

[165] Letter 3, *To Philip*, II, 5, ed. by L. van Hook, *loc. cit.*, p. 404.
[166] *Address to Philip*, 111–114, *loc. cit.*, p. 312 seq.
[167] In another passage of the same Address (151, *loc. cit.*, p. 336) Isocrates, praising Philip's achievements, says: "Indeed I believe that even your past achievements would never have reached such magnitude had not one of the gods helped you to succeed." Isocrates probably has in mind Heracles, Philip's ancestor.

Although basically a democrat, Isocrates had perhaps contributed more than any one of his contemporaries toward the dissemination of the monarchic idea in his own time and in the Hellenistic period. The principles set forth in his Letter to Evagoras' son and successor Nicocles, who was for some time his disciple in Athens, served as the first models for the guidance of a good prince and were by later generations understood only in this way. In many instances, when giving the prince his advice on how to rule and how to behave, Isocrates had in mind the misrule of the mass of citizens under radical democracy.

Isocrates confessed that the king is regarded by many as equal to the gods because of his exalted position and the power at his disposal, but that rulership is a very onerous responsibility involving many setbacks for the ruler.[168] The function of the king should be to relieve the state from any distress, to maintain its prosperity and to enlarge it.[169] He will achieve this by training his soul in virtue, in order to surpass everyone else in this respect. To reach this state, a good education is necessary.[170] The king should be a lover of men and a lover of his country, and should honor only those citizens who deserve it by their merits.[171] "It is monstrous that the worse should rule the better, and that the more foolish should give orders to men of greater wisdom." Here Isocrates probably had in mind the distribution of offices in the radical democracy without respect for the abilities of the office holders.

The good king should enact good laws and dispense justice without long delays—again, a possible criticism of popular lawsuits.[172] "In the worship of the gods, follow the example of your ancestors, but believe that the noblest sacrifice and the greatest devotion is to show yourself in the highest degree a good and just man; for such men have greater hope of enjoying a blessing from the gods."[173] This is the manner in which the king should practice his religion.

[168] *To Nicocles*, 5, ed. by G. Norlin (Loeb, 1928), 1, p. 42.
[169] *Ibid.*, 9, *loc. cit.*, p. 44.
[170] *Ibid.*, 11, *loc. cit.*, p. 46.
[171] *Ibid.*, 14, *loc. cit.*, p. 48.
[172] *Ibid.*, 17, *loc. cit.*, p. 50.
[173] *Ibid.*, 20, *loc. cit.*, pp. 50, 52.

Exhorting the Prince on his choice of friends, Isocrates again seems to have in mind the behavior of orators who flatter the assembly and the citizens, and refuse to follow the counsel of wise men:

> Do not give your friendship to everyone who desires it, but only to those who are worthy of you.... Subject your associates to the most searching tests.... Regard as your most faithful friends, not those who praise everything you say or do, but those who criticize your mistakes.... Distinguish between those who artfully flatter and those who loyally serve you, that the base may not fare better than the good.... Govern yourself no less than your subjects, and consider that you are in the highest sense a king when you are a slave to no pleasure but rule over your desires more firmly than over your people.[174]

The Letter to Nicocles deserves special emphasis because of its influence on other similar writings during the Hellenistic and Byzantine period. It served as a model to Agapetus, who wrote a guide for the conduct of a good ruler for Justinian the Great, and it inspired Photius when, for Boris-Michael, the converted Khagan of Bulgaria, he described the qualities of a good Christian ruler. Through the translations of these two writings into Western and Slavic languages, Isocrates' influence was extended to many countries in mediaeval Western and Slavic Europe.[175]

However, Isocrates' most outspoken defense of the monarchic system was in the short missive presented as a speech by Nicocles to his subjects, in which the Prince is said to explain his ideas on government. This missive was probably written between 372 and 365 B.C.

In his comparison of the oligarchic, democratic, and monarchic regimes, Isocrates has the Prince declare:[176]

> "Monarchies...make the highest award to the best man, the next highest to the next best, and in the same proportion to the third and the fourth and so on. Even if this practice does not obtain everywhere, such at least is the intention of

---

[174] *Ibid.*, 27–29, *loc. cit.*, pp. 54, 56.
[175] Cf. *infra*, pp. 712-714.
[176] *Nicocles or The Cyprians*, 15, 16, ed. by G. Norlin (Loeb, 1928), I, p. 84.

the polity.... Monarchies more than other governments keep
an appraising eye upon the characters and actions of men....
Who, then, that is of sound mind would not prefer to share
in a form of government under which his own worth shall not
pass unnoticed...?

Then follows a severe criticism of the system of annual appointments to offices in the Athenian democracy[177] which hampers good
administration, because the short tenure prevents the officials from
gaining any necessary "insight into public affairs or any experience in handling them...." The monarchies are better than any
other regimes also in mustering troops, handling them, and con-
ducting wars.[178] This is proved by facts.[179]

> For, in the first place, we all know that the Empire of the
> Persians attained its great magnitude, not because of the
> intelligence of the population, but because they more than
> other peoples respect the royal office; secondly, that Dionysius,
> the tyrant, taking charge of Sicily when the rest of it had been
> devastated by war and when his own country, Syracuse, was in
> a state of siege, not only delivered it from the dangers which
> then threatened, but also made it the greatest of Hellenic
> states; and again, we know that while the Carthaginians and
> the Lacedaemonians, who are the best governed peoples of the
> world, are ruled by oligarchies at home, yet, when they take
> the field, they are ruled by kings.... How could any one show
> more convincingly than through these instances that monarchy
> is the most excellent of governments?

Isocrates offers yet another reason for the superiority of a
monarchy over any other form of government:[180]

> And, if there is need to speak also of things old in story,
> it is said that even the gods are ruled by Zeus as king. If the
> saying is true, it is clear that the gods also prefer this regime;
> but if, on the other hand, no-one knows the truth about this

[177] *Ibid.*, 17, 18, *loc. cit.*, p. 86.
[178] *Ibid.*, 22, *loc. cit.*, p. 88.
[179] *Ibid.*, 23–25, *loc. cit.*, p. 90.
[180] *Ibid.*, 26, *loc. cit.*, pp. 90, 92. The problem of democracy and monarchy
in Isocrates' work is well illustrated in R. von Pöhlmann's study, *Isokrates
und das Problem der Demokratie*, SB der Königl. Bayer. Akad. der Wiss.,
Philos.-philol. u. hist. Kl., Abhandl. 1 (1913), esp. pp. 87–109.

matter, and we by our own conjecture have simply supposed it to be so, it is a proof that we all hold monarchy in the highest esteem; for we should never have said that the gods live under it if we did not believe it to be far superior to all other governments.

These were strong words for the Athenian radical democrats, and it is no wonder that Isocrates was accused of being a traitor to democracy. He defended himself in his *Antidosis*,[181] declaring that he had "expressed [himself] to Nicocles as a free man and an Athenian should, not paying court to his wealth nor to his power, but pleading the cause of his subjects, and striving with all [his] powers to secure for them the mildest government possible."

Isocrates' ideal government for Athens was that of Theseus, the legendary king, whose reign Isocrates idealized in his treatise *Helen*. But even in his description of Theseus' government, Isocrates stresses the main characteristic of a monarch, the quality of being a good and a wise man. According to him, Theseus was also of divine origin, of the progeny of Poseidon.[182] Like Heracles, he won immortal glory through his virtues.[183] His deeds were even more useful for men than those of Heracles. Although possessing absolute power, Theseus had only one goal—the good of all—and he reigned through benefactions to his subjects.[184] His government was so mild and respectful of the rights and good of the citizens that "he made the people masters of the government, and they on their part thought it best that he should rule alone, believing that this sole rule was more to be trusted and more equitable than their own democracy." Because of that, he was greatly beloved, and is still remembered gratefully by men.

His projection of his ideas into the history of the Athenian state, his idealization of the legendary founder of Attic unity, and his linking of the ideal past with the ideal future of his city-state saved Isocrates in the eyes of many of his compatriots. They also were anxious to improve the political system of their country, but were

---

[181] *Antidosis*, 70., *loc. cit.*, p. 224.
[182] *Helen*, 18, ed. by L. van Hook (Loeb, 1945), 3, p. 68.
[183] *Ibid.*, 21 seq., *loc. cit.*, pp. 70, 72.
[184] *Ibid.*, 36 seq., *loc. cit.*, p. 80. Cf. E. Mikkola, *Isokrates. Seine Anschauungen im Lichte seiner Schriften* (Helsinki, 1954), p. 213 seq.

not yet willing to go as far as Xenophon in his *Cyropaedia* and Isocrates in his Nicocles missive. Nevertheless, Isocrates' ideas were interpreted as monarchic by many, and helped considerably more than the writings of other contemporaries to prepare the way for Philip and his son Alexander.

Isocrates did not live to see the realization of his dreams. Philip, who was certainly influenced by Isocrates' exhortations and by his own experience, left the autonomy of the subjected Greek city-states generally untouched, contenting himself with hegemony over the new confederation. It was his son Alexander who realized, to a greater extent than could have been expected by Isocrates, his other ideal—the conquest of Persia and the founding of a world empire in which the Hellenes were to play the leading role, if not in its government, at least in its civilization. A new era, the Hellenistic, was about to begin.

CHAPTER FIVE

HELLENISTIC POLITICAL PHILOSOPHY

I. The ruler cult, the main feature of the Hellenistic age — The sacral character of the Macedonian kingship — Alexander's religious attitude, his deification as Pharaoh of Egypt — Alexander son of Ammon (Zeus) — Alexander's divinization by Greek cities — Greek origin and ceremonial of the cult — Hero worship and the ruler cult — The Athenian Assembly and the deification of Alexander, Antigonus, and Poliorcetes — Alexander's generals and his cult — The Ptolemaic ruler cult, its Greek and Egyptian character — Ruler-cult symbolism on Ptolemaic coins — Religious beliefs of the Seleucids, their ruler cult — Greek cities, symbolism on coinage — Parthia, Bactria, Armenia — The Attalids, Pontus, Comagene.

II. Theocritus and Callimachus on kingship — Historians and the masses — Archytas and the definition of the king as the law animate — Diotogenes on kingship — Hellenistic origin of his treatise (second century B.C.) — Sthenidas' fragment contemporary with Diotogenes' — Ecphantus on kingship — Oriental elements in Ecphantus' treatise — Ecphantus on the king's moral role; dating of his treatise — Ideas on kingship in Pseudo-Aristeas' Letter compared with those of Diotogenes and Ecphantus — Oriental influences on the development of some Hellenistic royal titles — Plutarch's ideas on kingship recalling those of Diotogenes' and Ecphantus — Hellenistic intellectuals' shyness on the divine character of kings.

I

The Hellenistic period, which opened with the conquests of Alexander the Great, brought about the fusion of the old Greek culture with that of the great Oriental traditions. There was apparently a similar exchange of Greek and Oriental ideas in the political sphere as well, but its nature and its limits are not easy to define. The fact is that the study of the Hellenistic period has long been neglected. Ever since the Renaissance scholars, carried away by their enthusiasm for classical Greek and Latin letters, have been fascinated by the majestic sweep of Demosthenes' eloquence.

They have been only too ready to share his conviction that the Macedonians Philip and Alexander were no better than barbarians, who put an end to the glorious days of classical Greece, destroyed the freedom of the Greek cities and their democratic institutions, and allowed the Greek genius to be polluted by unclean contact with the decadent East. This misconception placed the events of this period in a false light and paralyzed all efforts to explore them further until 1877, when J. Droysen[1] successfully disproved the old-fashioned opinion popularized by Demosthenes' *Philippics*. After long and lively controversies his view won the day. It is now commonly admitted that Philip's victory over the Greek cities marked the first step toward the Greek conquest of the East and that this was to lead to the creation of a great civilization, essentially Greek, yet so enriched with the cultural traditions of the East that its appeal transcended local frontiers and eventually benefited the whole human race. The foundations of Hellenistic culture were laid and the environment was created in which the first Christians lived and interpreted their faith.

Long neglect has unfortunately left many problems that must be solved before the Hellenistic period can be properly understood. This is equally true of its political evolution owing to its subsequent close association with Roman political thought and the growth of Christianity. Although great progress has been made during these last sixty years in the field of Hellenistic studies, unduly large areas remain to be explored.

Our study will, of course, be confined to the main problems. Of these, the most important concerns the growth of the notion of an absolute monarchy ruled by a divinized king, which was a feature of the political philosophy of the Hellenistic period.[2] Our discussion of the monarchic idea in the fourth century and of the survival of some traditions of the Homeric kingship shows that the Greeks of Philip's and Alexander's time were in general prepared to accept the rule of an absolute monarch. The way in which the Macedonians

---

[1] *Geschichte des Hellenismus* (Gotha, 1877).

[2] On other aspects of a Hellenistic state, see V. Ehrenberg, *Der Staat der Griechen*, Teil 2, *Der hellenistische Staat*, 2nd ed. (Leipzig, 1958), with a good selective bibliography. On kingship, see *ibid.*, pp. 19–34, 88.

imposed their supremacy, contenting themselves with a hegemony over sovereign city-states federated in the Corinthian League, facilitated this transition and silenced the opposition of the intransigent democrats. The problem remains, however, as to how the idea of a divinized monarch originated and what induced the Greeks to agree to the deification of Alexander the Great and, after the conqueror's death, to the practice of a special cult in honor of their rulers.

The various problems under discussion in connection with Alexander's deification must first be stated and their most likely solutions indicated; it will then be necessary to discuss the various stages which finally led the Greeks to accept a ruler cult. This will lead in turn to an examination of the ideological origin of this practice: Did it originate from purely Oriental premises, or practices imported from the East which Alexander conquered, or could it be traced to principles that were indigenous to Greek political philosophy and religion?[3]

It seems puzzling that the idea of the deification of a ruler should have originated at a period in Greek history which showed marked tendencies to rationalism. The old religion was no longer held in the same reverence as in former days and the intellectuals did not share their forefathers' awe of the gods. How, then, did it happen that the highly charismatic character of kingship should reappear at a period which seemed so alien to such ideas and in which the myths of old were losing their power of attraction?

Upon considering this question it should not be forgotten that the man who became the first object of such deification was a scion of an old dynasty which had long reigned over Macedonians, and that the latter had not been affected by the religious and political evolution of Greece proper. The old mythical traditions were still firmly believed in fourth-century Macedonia, and its dynasty venerated Heracles, son of Zeus, as its founder. The kingship had thus not yet been deprived of its charismatic character,

---

[3] C. W. McEwan, *The Oriental Origin of the Hellenistic Kingship*, Studies in Ancient Oriental Civilisation, 13 (Chicago, 1934).

and the dead kings seem to have been objects of a hero-cult similar to that given to the Mycenaean and Spartan kings after their deaths.

Alexander's mother seems to have been particularly inclined to mystic practices. She was also a descendant of an old Greek royal dynasty, that of the Molossi. Claiming descent from Chronos and Poseidon, she changed her name from Myrtale to the more divine Olympias. It should be stressed that Olympias had a profound influence on her son Alexander.

According to a scholium to the first Olynthiac discourse of Demosthenes (Ol. I,5), Philip's father, Amyntas, was honored by the citizens of Pydna with the dedication of a temple.[4] Philip himself is said to have been given cultic honors in Amphipolis. Although these two reports are regarded by some specialists as unreliable, there is no doubt about the reliability of Arrian's information disclosing that the citizens of Ephesus had erected a statue to Philip in the temple of Artemis.[5] Even if it is questionable to regard this gesture of the citizens, grateful for liberation from the Persians by the Macedonians, as an act of divinization of Philip,[6] the erection of the king's statue in a temple cannot be dismissed simply with the remark that such an honor had already lost all its charismatic character through frequent misuse. This can, perhaps, be accepted for the Greeks in Greece proper, but not for the Asiatic Greeks and the Macedonians. Moreover, the Asiatic city of Ephesus seems to have had a special veneration for Philip.[7]

Even if these instances are not regarded as cultic acts in their proper sense, they serve to explain how Philip could be so bold as to raise his own statue next to the statues of the twelve principal deities, becoming thus a *synthronos* of the gods,[8] during the nuptial cortège of his daughter Cleopatra in Aigai, and to build in Olympia

---

[4] Ch. Habicht, *Gottmenschentum und griechische Städte*, Zetemata, Heft 14 (Munich, 1956), p. 11.

[5] Arrian, *Anabasis of Alexander*, I, 17, 11, ed. by E. I. Robson (Loeb, 1929), 1, p. 74.

[6] Such is the meaning of Habicht, *op. cit.*, opposed by F. Taeger, *Charisma, Studien zur Geschichte des antiken Herrscherkultes*, 1 (Stuttgart, 1957), p. 174.

[7] See Habicht, *op. cit.*, p. 14.

[8] Diodorus Siculus, *The Library of History*, XVI, 92, ed. by I. N. Eyring (Cologne, 1793), 7, p. 217; ed. by L. Dindorf and C. Müller (Paris, 1855), 2, p. 128.

a temple where his own statue and the statues of his relatives had a place of honor.[9]

Such was the atmosphere in which Alexander had spent his early years. The belief in divine things continued to be manifested by him even when he had succeeded his father. He exercised his priestly functions conscientiously, and offered sacrifices to the gods before and after his military actions.[10] The frequent recourse to divination mentioned by his historians discloses his deeply mystical spirit.[11] Plutarch says explicitly that Alexander was imbued with the idea that he had a divine mission on earth.[12] He was proud of Heracles, the legendary founder of his dynasty, and was also devoted to Dionysus who was worshipped at the Macedonian court.

All this, together with the fact that he shared the Greek anthropomorphic conception of deities, puts the question of Alexander's deification in a different light. However, it is difficult to follow precisely how this idea had developed, and what was the role of Alexander in its realization. The main obstacle to our research is the lack of contemporary historical sources. The work of Callisthenes, whom he had chosen as his biographer, and that of Onesicritus are lost. Ptolemy's and Aristobulus' histories, both also lost, were used by Arrian about the middle of the second century A.D. The Life of Alexander by Plutarch and the treatise On Alexander's Fortune which is attributed to him are scarcely earlier. Quintus Curtius wrote a history of Alexander about a century earlier than Arrian, but his work is less reliable.[13] All of which

[9] Pausanias, *Description of Greece*, V, 20, 10, ed. by H. A. Ormerod (Loeb, 1926), 2, p. 500. The statement quoted by Joannes Stobaeus and attributed by him to Philip may be recalled here: "King Philip said that a king should remember that although he is a man, he yet wields quasi-divine power for the purpose of looking for what is beautiful and divine; but that he needs a human voice." Joannes Stobaeus, *Anthologium*, IV, 7, 21, ed. by C. Wachsmuth and O. Hense (Berlin, 1909), 4, p. 254.

[10] See the numerous quotations in L. Cerfaux and J. Tondriau's book, *Un concurrent du christianisme. Le culte des souverains dans la civilisation gréco-romaine* (Paris, etc., 1957), pp. 125, 126.

[11] See F. Taeger, *Charisma*, I, pp. 187, 188 with quotations of sources.

[12] *Moralia: Fortuna Alexandri*, 329 C, ed. by F. C. Babbitt (Loeb, 1936), 4, p. 398.

[13] For sources on Alexander's history see W. W. Tarn, *Alexander the Great* (Cambridge, 1948), 2, pp. 1–333 and C. A. Robinson, *The History of Alexander the Great*, I (Providence, 1953): An Index to the Extant Historians,

explains why so many problems concerning Alexander are still under discussion despite the considerable bibliography on his reign and his ideas.[14]

When Alexander embarked on his expedition against Persia, he did not seem to have any definite ideas on the character of his kingship except insofar as it was vouchsafed to him by the gods, in order to accomplish great things in imitation of his ancestor Heracles. The first stage of his divinization was accomplished in 332 B.C. when he invaded Egypt. He was greeted everywhere as liberator from the Persian yoke and was received with the honors which had been rendered to the Pharaohs. He was proclaimed to be the son of Re, and this was stated in the five royal titles given to the Pharaohs. The official enthronement took place at Memphis.[15] This deification, of course, was meant only for the Egyptians, and Alexander was wise enough to accept it in order to be regarded as the lawful ruler of conquered Egypt. This event, however, concerned neither the Macedonians nor the Greeks, nor even the Persians, whose lands he was about to conquer.

The Fragments. Cf. also L. Pearson, "The Diary and the Letters of Alexander the Great," *Historia*, 3 (1954), pp. 429–455; see also F. Pfister, "Das Alexander-Archiv und die hellenistisch-römische Wissenschaft," *Historia*, 10 (1961), pp. 30–67; *idem*, "Alexander der Grosse. Die Geschichte seines Ruhms im Lichte seiner Beinamen," *Historia*, 13 (1964), pp. 37–79. On Ptolemy's history of Alexander, see H. Strasburger, *Ptolemaios und Alexander* (Leipzig, 1934), and E. Kornemann, *Die Alexandergeschichte des Königs Ptolemaios I. von Aegypten* (Leipzig-Berlin, 1935).

[14] See the main bibliography in Cerfaux–Tondriau, *Le culte*, pp. 30–35. The most important monograph is still that by W. W. Tarn, *Alexander the Great*, in which he completes his previous studies on the King. Great progress in the study of Alexander was made by U. Wilcken, *Alexander der Grosse* (Leipzig, 1931), French trans. by R. Bouvier (Paris, 1952). Among other more recent works, the two following should be mentioned: C. A. Robinson, *The History of Alexander the Great*, Brown University Studies, 16, 26 (Providence, 1953, 1963) and F. Schachermeyr, *Alexander der Grosse. Ingenium und Macht* (Graz, 1949). R. Andreotti gives a succinct review of all recent publications on Alexander in *Historia*, 1 (1950), pp. 583–600: "Il problema di Alessandro Magno nella storiografia dell' ultimo decennio." Cf. also A. Gitti, "L'unitarietà della tradizione su Alessandro Magno nella ricerca moderna," *Athenaeum*, N.S., 34 (1956), pp. 39–57.

[15] This is mentioned only in the Alexander Romance, I, 34, ed. by W. Kroll, in *Historia Alexandri Magni* (Berlin, 1926), p. 37. There is no reason why we should not accept this information. No Greek author mentions it because the ceremony did not concern the Greeks. See U. Wilcken, "Zur Entstehung des hellenistischen Königskultes," *SB der Preuss. Akad. der Wiss.*, Philos.-hist. Kl. (Berlin, 1938), p. 299.

It should be pointed out in this connection that when Alexander had become master of Babylon, he again conformed to the customs of the land and made sacrifices to Marduk, re-establishing the old customs.[16]

The second phase in the process of Alexander's deification was his expedition or pilgrimage to the oasis of Siwah with its famous shrine and oracle of Ammon.[17] Specialists still disagree in their endeavors to explain what happened during this expedition. Some conclusions seem assured, however. It is generally agreed that this was not a military expedition, that it was Alexander's own idea, and that it met with the approval of both Macedonians and Greeks. The oracle was held in great esteem among the Macedonians, who had their own Ammoneion in Thrace, and the Greeks regarded its answers as almost infallible. The Egyptians, of course, rejoiced when they learned how their new Pharaoh respected their religious shrines.

It is most probable that the high priest saluted Alexander as the son of Ammon on his arrival before the oracle and in the presence of his military dignitaries. It is not known what oracle was given by the priests in the name of Ammon to Alexander, for the latter regarded it as his own personal concern and disclosed it only to his mother.

When deciding to make this pilgrimage, Alexander must have had in mind to imitate his model Perseus and his ancestor Heracles, both of whom were believed to have addressed themselves to the oracle.[18] The Spartan hero Lysander had also consulted Ammon of

---

[16] Arrian, *Anabasis*, III, 16, 5, *loc. cit.*, p. 274; VII, 17, 2, (Loeb, 1933), 2, p. 260 (called Belos).

[17] Cf. the recent publications by F. Schachermeyr, *Alexander der Grosse*, p. 204 seq., and, F. Taeger, *Charisma*, 1, pp. 191–208. The basic studies on this problem were published by U. Wilcken, "Alexanders Zug in die Oase Siwa," *SB. d. Preuss. Akad.* (Berlin, 1928), pp. 576–603, and "Alexanders Zug zum Ammon," *ibid.* (1930), pp. 159–176; cf. W. W. Tarn, *op. cit.*, 2, p. 346 seq. See also P. Jouguet, *Trois études sur l'hellénisme* (Cairo, 1944), p. 18 seq. and A. Gitti, "Alessandro Magno e il responso di Ammone," *Rivista storica italiana*, 64 (1952), pp. 531–547. Gitti follows the tradition of Aristobulus and Ptolemy preserved by Arrian. Cf., however, the critical review of A. Gitti's book *Alessandro Magno all'oasi di Siwah. Il problema delle fonti* (Bari, 1951), by H. Strasburger in *Gnomon*, 25 (1953), pp. 217–223.

[18] Arrian, *Anabasis*, III, 3, 1 seq., *loc. cit.*, 1, p. 230; for details, see W. W. Tarn, *op. cit.*, 2, pp. 350–359. Cf. also the discussion of sources and authors by Cerfaux-Tondriau, *Le culte*, p. 135 seq. and F. Taeger, *Charisma*, 1, p. 191 seq.

Siwah. The fact that Alexander was declared son of Ammon must have particularly impressed the Greeks, especially since the official historian Callisthenes substituted Zeus for Ammon. The Greeks of Asia were the first who accepted this proclamation and, according to the same author,[19] they brought to Memphis many oracles from their shrine at Miletus, one of them proclaiming Alexander son of Zeus. Alexander's divine birth was also confirmed by the Sibyl of Erythrae. When Alexander's religious attitude is taken into consideration, it will be agreed that these declarations made a great impression on him. This idea accompanied him to the hour of his death, although he did not make any attempt to establish a special cult in his own honor.

New achievements must have enhanced in Alexander the conviction that he was chosen by the gods to realize things which no man before him was able to accomplish. The flames of Persepolis, the magnificent residence of the Persian kings set on fire by the victor, emphasized to Macedonians and Greeks that a superhuman task—the final conquest of Persia—had been brilliantly terminated. New horizons were opening before Alexander. The idea of a universal empire, of supreme rule over the whole known *oikoumene*, is said to have led Alexander to India. Everywhere his Greeks found traces of Heracles and Dionysus who were believed to have penetrated to these remote regions. The refusal of the army to continue the march into unknown lands forced Alexander to return to Susa, but another plan is said to have haunted him, the conquest of Carthage and the building of a road from the city founded by him in Egypt and bearing his name, along the whole African coast to the Pillars of Heracles.[20]

[19] Callisthenes, Fragment 14, ed. by F. Jacoby, *Die Fragmente der griech. Historiker* (Berlin, 1927), Teil 2 B, Lief. 2, p. 645. See also Nearchos, Fragment 1, *ibid., loc. cit.*, p. 700.

[20] Cf., however, the study by R. Andreotti, "Die Weltmonarchie Alexanders des Grossen in Überlieferung und geschichtlicher Wirklichkeit," *Saeculum*, 8 (1957), pp. 120–166. The author warns, with good reason, against attributing to Alexander all the far reaching plans for world domination and human brotherhood mentioned by his biographers. See also his other study, "Per una critica dell' ideologia di Alessandro Magno," *Historia*, 5 (1956), pp. 257–302. Tarn's thesis on Alexander's supposed idea on "brotherhood and unity" of mankind (*op. cit.*, p. 339 seq.) is rejected by B. Badian in his study "Alexander the Great and the Unity of Mankind," *Historia*, 7 (1958), pp. 425–444. Such ideas were premature in Alexander's time.

To crown all these achievements Alexander requested the Greek cities of the Corinthian League to proclaim him divine.[21] This request, although reported only by Aelian, is accepted as genuine by most historians; it was recently challenged, however, by two scholars, J. P. V. D. Balsdon[22] and R. Andreotti.[23] The first, without denying Alexander's deification, attributed the initiative to the Greek cities themselves, acting upon a proposal by pro-Macedonian parties. The citizens agreed to this act because they expected that Alexander would return to Europe after the termination of his campaign in Asia. They believed that the granting of such an honor would ingratiate themselves to him and minimize the danger of his intervention in their autonomous status. Andreotti attributes the initiative to the Greek cities of Asia Minor; the gesture was subsequently imitated by the cities of the League.

For the purposes of the present investigation the most important point is that Alexander was divinized by the Greek cities. Even the authors who refuse to recognize Alexander as the initiator of the deification do not dispute its occurrence. The event is confirmed by contemporary writers, who speak of the opposition which such a proposal had provoked in Athens:[24] Demosthenes protested, but was silenced by Demades,[25] who reminded the opponents that a refusal would be a political blunder. In the end Demosthenes is said to have declared: "Let Alexander become son of Zeus and of Poseidon if he wishes."[26]

[21] Aelian, *Varia historia*, II, 19, ed. by R. Hercher (Teubner, 1887), p. 27.

[22] "The 'Divinity' of Alexander," *Historia*, 1 (1950), pp. 363–388, restated the view expressed by D. G. Hogarth, "The Deification of Alexander the Great," *English Historical Review*, 2 (1887), pp. 317–329.

[23] "Die Weltmonarchie," p. 155 seq.

[24] The main witness is Hyperides, *Epitaphios*, 21 seq., ed. by Chr. Jensen (Teubner, 1917), p. 102, and *In Demosthenem*, XXXI, 14 seq., XXXII, 2 seq., *loc. cit.*, p. 20; Dinarchus, *Against Demosthenes*, 94, in J. O. Burtt ed., *Minor Attic Orators* (Loeb, 1954), 2, p. 243: "At one time he [Demosthenes] made the proposal forbidding anyone to believe in any but the accepted gods and at another said that the people must not question the grant of divine honours to Alexander."

[25] According to Athenaeus, *Deipnosophistae*, VI, 251 b, ed. by C. B. Gulick (Loeb, 1929), 3, p. 130. After Alexander's death, Demades was fined ten talents for proposing the King's deification.

[26] Hyperides, *In Demosthenem*, XXXI, 14, *loc. cit.*; Fragment VII (VIII) in J. O. Burtt ed., *Minor Attic Orators* (Loeb, 1954), 2, p. 522. Timaeus also numbers Demosthenes among the opponents. His report is preserved by Polybius, *The Histories*, XII, 12 b, 3, ed. by W. R. Paton (Loeb, 1925),

Other cities followed. It seems that the cities were left free to choose the manner by which they issued the decree. Hyperides' report speaks of the erection of a picture of Alexander representing him as an invincible god, and of a temple with the necessary liturgical objects. It seems certain that Alexander was not called a new Dionysus.[27] This identification was effected only in the Ptolemaic period. Alexander himself had a great veneration for this divinized man, but there is no evidence that he regarded himself as his reincarnation. All cities sent their envoys to do homage to the divinized Alexander. Arrian[28] says expressly that they approached him as *theoroi*—ambassadors to a god—adorned with wreaths, and that they crowned him with golden crowns.

It is, however, far from certain that the initiative for Alexander's divinization came from Greek cities. First of all, Aelian's report can be discarded only with difficulty, especially as it is also echoed by later historians. The new thesis attributing the initiative to the cities has many weak points.[29] It seems safer, in the present state of research, to attribute the initiative to Alexander himself. This will appear the more probable if Alexander's religiosity is borne in mind. It has already been stressed that Alexander was profoundly religious and that he venerated the divinized Heracles as his ancestor and his model. After his military achievements Alexander could justifiably believe that he had surpassed his ancestor. Could he not thus claim the same honor which had been vouchsafed to Heracles?

4, p. 340. According to Plutarch (*Moralia: Apophthegmata Laconica*, 219, *loc. cit.* [1931], 3, p. 314), the Spartan Damis is said to have declared: "We concede to Alexander that, if he so wishes, he may be called a god." However, this saying may be only a Spartan variant of Demosthenes' dictum (Taeger, *Charisma*, I, p. 217). Cf., however, Aelian, *Varia hist.*, *loc. cit.*, whose report is similar to that of Damis.

[27] This has been shown already by A. D. Nock, "Notes on Ruler-Cult," *JHS*, 48 (1928), pp. 21–43. A profound study of this problem was made by Cerfaux-Tondriau, *Le culte*, pp. 148–161. See also W. W. Tarn, *op. cit.*, 2, p. 45 seq.

[28] *Anabasis*, VII, 23, 2, *loc. cit.*, 2, p. 282.

[29] Balsdon, although declaring that the initiative came from the Greeks, shows (p. 364 seq.) that there was not a single example of such divinization in Greece before Alexander. He discards all instances—Empedocles, Lysander, Clearchus—which were often regarded as precedents for such an act among the Greeks. How, then, did the Greeks come upon the idea of conferring such an unprecedented honor on Alexander?

Such an idea was suggested to his father Philip by Isocrates in the second long letter, the genuineness of which cannot be doubted. The orator presented Heracles to Philip as a model. It was not Philip but his son who surpassed Heracles and achieved something for which Isocrates, in his last letter, had promised Philip divine honors.[30] It is possible that Alexander never read Aristotle's *Politics*[31] since it was edited by the students who attended his lectures. Alexander was, however, accompanied by many Greek intellectuals who could easily have heard from Aristotle, or his disciples, his views concerning the conferment of the responsibility of government on the best man who, because of his superior life and achievements, would be like a god. Callisthenes, Alexander's biographer, was even a relative of Aristotle.

Aristotle was not the only one to have enunciated such ideas. Plato, as we have seen, had uttered similar thoughts and his writings may have reached Alexander; so may those of Antisthenes and other writers whose works are not preserved. In the middle of the fourth century the ideas discussed by Plato and his disciples, by Aristotle and others, must have been very frequent topics for speculation in Athens. Alexander could simply refer to these current ideas and ask the cities to draw the logical consequence from them.[32]

[30] The authenticity of this letter is rejected by Balsdon and Andreotti, but no new argument is brought forward. The repetitions of some passages or ideas contained in the long, genuine letter do not invalidate the authenticity of Isocrates' last writing. He was over ninety when he wrote it and old people like to repeat themselves especially when treating the same subject.

[31] It seems hardly probable that Alexander had learned of the possibility of deification from Aristotle when the latter was his preceptor. See, on this subject, P. Merlan's study, "Isocrates, Aristotle and Alexander the Great," *Historia*, 3 (1954), pp. 60–81. The author also gives a good explanation of the rivalry between Isocrates and Aristotle, revealed by Isocrates' writing to Alexander.

[32] It is now established that Alexander addressed himself only to the cities of the Corinthian League, and not to the Greek cities in Asia Minor. As has been shown, however, the latter had already proclaimed him son of Zeus; so it was unnecessary to appeal to them. The Greeks of Asia Minor were always more ready for such gestures than the Greeks in Europe. This is evidence of the influence of Oriental ideas on kingship among the Greeks of Asia. Cf. M. P. Nilsson, *Geschichte der griechischen Religion*, Handbuch der Altertumswissenschaft, Abteil. 5, Teil 2, 2nd ed. (Munich, 1961), vol. 2, p. 147 seq., on the worship of Alexander in the Greek cities of Asia.

It is thus evident that the idea of the divinization of a living ruler is of Greek and not of Oriental origin. The Oriental examples of divine kingship in Egypt and of the ruler's appointment by god as his representative in Babylon and Persia served only to accelerate the process in Alexander's mind and to confirm his own conviction. The initiative, probably in the form of a suggestion, emanated from him. The opposition in Athens may well have been provoked by the order sent to the *synhedrion* of the League to accept all political exiles. Although there was no connection between Alexander's order and his suggestion, some Athenians may have seen in it the possibility of other interventions by Alexander in their internal policy.

The cult rendered to the divinized monarch was also based on Greek and not Oriental traditions. This is shown by Hyperides' description of the honors given to Alexander in Athens—by picture, temple, and altar—and by Arrian's report of the coronation of Alexander by envoys from the League, who approached him decorated with wreaths as *theoroi*, as was the custom in religious ceremonies in Greece.

Alexander himself, while accepting the liturgical honors observed in Egypt, did not introduce any special liturgical ceremonial, although he took the Ammon-Zeus sonship seriously. The attempt to introduce the Persian *proskynesis* at his court for all his courtiers had nothing to do with the introduction of a royal cult, as has often been thought.[33] The incident at Bactra and the refusal of Callisthenes and others to render such homage to Alexander shows only that the King was introducing Persian ceremonial at his court, and was anxious to reconcile his new subjects to their new situation by accepting their customs. The *proskynesis* was particularly objectionable to the Macedonians and Greeks who interpreted it as a form of homage rendered to gods and concluded that the Persians venerated their kings as gods.[34] Even after the entourage of Alexan-

---

[33] See the controversy between P. Schnabel (*Klio*, 19 [1924], pp. 113–127), who saw in the *proskynesis* the introduction of a cult with an altar, and H. Berve, (*Klio*, 20 [1925], pp. 179–186), who opposed this thesis. L. R. Taylor's defense of Schnabel's thesis is not convincing (*The Divinity of the Roman Emperor*, Philological Monographs, no. 1 [Middletown, 1931], pp. 256–266).

[34] See *supra*, p. 117.

der had realized that this was not the case, the *proskynesis* continued to be regarded as a humiliating custom for free men.

It should be noted that Alexander's practice of adopting Persian garb and customs for political reasons, although it won him the sympathies of the subjugated Persians, initiated a long period of crisis (from 331 to 327) among the Macedonians which was marked by conspiracies against Alexander and by the execution of some of his formerly faithful followers—Parmenion, Alexander Lyncestus, Clitus, Callisthenes. Alexander's acceptance of Persian robes is attested by Aelian and Plutarch.[35] Athenaeus,[36] when quoting some ancient writers' descriptions of the luxury of Alexander's court, mentions several customs which are certainly Persian: the audience conducted from a luxurious throne, the awed religious silence in the ruler's presence, the purple robes, the accompaniment of musicians during solemn meals, the use of incense, the holy tree in the audience room. The author also reproaches Alexander with having worn vestments and emblems of different gods and of having partaken of sacred repasts in such attire. Athenaeus and his sources seem to see here a kind of divine epiphany, but this is incorrect. It is known that in the Greek cult the priests and celebrants often dressed as gods. The sacred repasts were also common.[37] Alexander continued, even as son of Ammon, to render sacrifices to Greek gods according to Greek ritual.[38] There is no evidence of the introduction of a ruler cult by him on the basis of Oriental religious traditions. It should be added that Athenaeus' sources are far from reliable.

The question now arises as to the considerations which induced the Greeks to decree divine honors for Alexander. E. Kornemann[39]

[35] Aelian, *Varia hist.*, VII, 8, *loc. cit.*, p. 84: Alexander threw the Persian garb worn by his friend Hephaistion on the pyre on which the body of his deceased friend reposed. Plutarch's *Moralia: Fortuna Alex.*, 329 C, D, *loc. cit.* (1936), 4, p. 396 seq.

[36] *Deipnosophistae*, XII, 537 d–539, *loc. cit.* (1933), 5, pp. 428–440.

[37] See P. Stengel, *Die griechischen Kultusaltertümer* (Munich, 1920), 3rd ed., p. 48. Cf., for details, S. Eitrem, "Zur Apotheose," *Symbolae Osloenses*, 10 (1932), p. 31 seq. Cf. also *ibid.*, 15–16 (1936), p. 132 seq.: "Der androgyne Herrscher."

[38] Cf., for example, Arrian, *Anabasis*, VI, 19, 4, 5, *loc. cit.*, 2, p. 160 seq. Alexander is said to have sacrificed, on Ammon's order, to different gods, according to different ceremonials.

[39] E. Kornemann, "Zur Geschichte der antiken Herrscherkulte," *Klio*, 1 (1902), pp. 51–146. A detailed bibliography, down to 1902, of the Greek

was the foremost champion of the theory that the ruler cult was a spontaneous growth which gradually evolved from the Greek practice of ancestor and hero worship. With all deference to the few who still maintain that Alexander's cult is wholly traceable to Greek ancestor and hero worship, it may be safely stated that this theory must be definitely abandoned. This does not mean that ancestor and hero worship had nothing to do with the process: on the contrary, it must have acted as an indispensable preliminary to prepare Greek minds for the later development. The worship of dead heroes was a familiar feature of old Greek religious practice: the ancestors of distinguished families, the founders of cities and prominent societies, well-known philosophers (e.g., Socrates and Plato, who was promoted to be a son of Apollo), athletes, and almost all the heroes of Greek mythology were honored, while the soldiers who gave their lives at the battles of Marathon and Thermopylae were remembered by annual festivities. The cult, which was also addressed to the heroes' graves and relics, degenerated in its last stages, when a profusion of beatifications of obscure personages by their cities or their families can be noted.[40]

A later feature of hero worship was the conferment by decree of heroic honors on the living. The first case of this kind to be traced in historical documents concerned Dion of Syracuse.[41] Nikias of the Island of Cos seems likewise to have been honored as a hero in his life time,[42] and the same distinction was conferred on Lysander, King of Sparta (*ca.* 405 B.C.). The islanders of Samos are reported to have gone even further and offered divine honors to Lysander;[43]

---

hero cult is to be found there. Cf. the criticism of this theory by W. S. Ferguson, "Legalized Absolutism en Route from Greece to Rome," *The Amer. Histor. Review*, 18 (1912–13), p. 33 seq. For particulars, see G. Herzog-Hauser, "Kaiserkult," Pauly-Wissowa, Supplementband, 4 (Stuttgart, 1924), col. 806 seq. Cf. also F. Pfister *Der Reliquienkult im Altertum* (Giessen, 1909, 1912), 2 vols., esp. vol. 2, pp. 401 seq., 466 seq., 545 seq., 581 seq.

[40] For a complete list with documentation of heroization before Alexander, see Cerfaux-Tondriau, *Le culte*, pp. 457–466: Annexe 1.

[41] Diodorus Siculus, *op. cit.*, XVI, 20, 6, ed. by C. H. Oldfather (Loeb, 1952), 7, p. 294.

[42] W. R. Paton and E. L. Hicks, *The Inscriptions of Cos* (Oxford, 1891), nos. 76–80, p. 125 seq., quoted by Cerfaux-Tondriau, *Le culte*, p. 108.

[43] Duris of Samos, fragment, *FHG*, ed. by K. Müller, 2, p. 484, no. 65; Plutarch, *Lives: Lysander*, 18, 3, ed. by B. Perrin (Loeb, 1916), 4, p. 280.

but his successor Agesilaus (*ca.* 394–358 B.C.) is said to have declined the offer made to him by the inhabitants of Thasos.[44]

These instances are interesting mainly because they suggest that Asiatic and Egyptian influence may have helped this later development of the hero cult. It seems only natural to suppose that the Greeks of the Aegean islands, living so near the Asiatic shores and within reach of their political and cultural influences, would be more liable than others to indulge in making gods of their living rulers. It may be that the Sicilians unconsciously imitated the Phoenicians who, having once been subject to the Egyptians, remained in some measure under their spell, but this is not certain.[45]

Although doubts have arisen concerning the reliability of the informants in the cases mentioned, this particular development in hero worship apparently did not spread rapidly to the Greek mainland. Macedonia and Thrace are, of course, an exception as has already been pointed out. In spite of his very critical examination of such cases, F. Taeger[46] had to confess: "Even the most careful critic cannot remove the fact that, in the fourth century, signs begin to become increasingly numerous that, at least in some Greek lands, the readiness was growing to elevate the man or, at least, to ask for his elevation." This statement is important, because it shows that the Greek mind was gradually being prepared for the idea of the divinization of a man.

In its initial stage, hero worship was distinguished from divine worship proper; heroes were honored, not as gods, but as demigods, divinized or quasi-divine beings. But at a later stage, instances can be quoted to show that the Greeks did not invariably draw the necessary distinction between the honors paid to their heroes and those paid to their gods.[47] This observation is important as it throws

---

[44] Plutarch, *Moralia*: *Apophthegmata Laconica*, Agesilaus, 25, *loc. cit.* (1931), 3, p. 256.

[45] See the critical remarks on the hero cult in Sicily and Greece in M. P. Nilsson's *Geschichte der griech. Relig.*, 2nd ed., 2, pp. 135–144. Lysander's honors seem to have been only ἰσόθεοι τιμαί. Cf. also M. P. Nilsson, *The Minoan-Mycenaean Religion and its Survival in Greek Religions*, p. 584 seq., on the Mycenaean origin of the hero cult.

[46] *Charisma*, 1, p. 164. See his documentation on many heroes of this period and his criticism on pp. 153–168.

[47] For instance Zeus Agamemnon, Zeus Asklepios, Diomedes, Menelaos, Helen. For particulars, see L. R. Farnell, *Greek Hero Cults and Ideas of Im-*

light on the gradual process of the Hellenic adoption of divinized royalty. It may also be recalled here that the period of Alexander showed marked tendencies toward rationalism; that the old religion was no longer held in the same reverence as in former days and that the intellectuals, not sharing their forefathers' awe for the gods, were inclined to reduce them to the level of mere heroes. Under these circumstances, the practice of offering not only hero worship but divine honors to a man after his death and after he had qualified as a hero becomes more intelligible.

But though the Greeks of the fourth century B.C., given their attitude toward hero worship, would have had no objection to Alexander's deification after his death, the serious difficuly arose that he was still alive. How was this rationalized?

There is something to be said for the ingenious explanation offered by E. R. Bevan.[48] Under certain circumstances the practice prevailed in ancient Greece of conferring on a personage the purely honorary insignia and distinctions of an office; though evidence of the practice dates only from the later periods of Ptolemaic Egypt, Julius Caesar, and Augustus, there can be no serious objection to assuming the practice to have existed in Alexander's time. This suggests that Athens and other Greek cities deified Alexander in anticipation of his posthumous dues.

This possibility is hinted at by Arrian in his *Anabasis*.[49] When speaking of the opposition of Callisthenes and the Macedonians to the practice of *proskynesis*, he has the Sophist Anaxarchus say that for the Macedonians "it would be far more just to reckon Alexander a god than Dionysus and Heracles," who had no connection with Macedonia. "For in any case there was no doubt that when Alexander had passed away from men they would honor him as a god; how much more just, then, that they should honor him in life rather than when dead, when the honor would profit him nothing."

mortality (Oxford, 1921), pp. 243, 278, 280, 290, 322, 323. Cf. also O. Gruppe, *Griechische Mythologie und Religionsgeschichte*, Handbuch der klassischen Altertumswissenschaft, Band 5, Abt. 2 (Munich, 1906), p. 1499 seq.
[48] "The Deification of Kings in the Greek Cities," *English Hist. Review*, 16 (1901), p. 632 seq.
[49] IV, 10, ed. by A. G. Roos (Teubner, 1907), p. 192 seq.; ed. by E. I. Robson (Loeb, 1929), 1, pp. 370, 372.

The words are probably imaginary. They seem, however, relevant enough to justify the conclusion that the promoters of Alexander's apotheosis resorted to the device of anticipatory honors to help the Athenians and other city-states overcome their reluctance to render divine honors to a living man.

The theory, introduced by Plato and Aristotle and discussed by their disciples, that the "best man" should become a ruler and should be honored as a god, also contributed to the acceptance of Alexander's deification. Alexander, by founding an immense empire which could in some way claim to be universal, achieved an even greater feat than that for which Isocrates would have liked to deify his father. This quite possibly was an additional contribution to the sweeping change in the Greek attitude. Alexander's empire was an innovation surpassing all previous political achievements of the Greek genius. Hitherto, Socrates and his followers had adumbrated a cosmopolitan citizenship in the abstract; but this time, the abstraction was transformed into palpable reality in Alexander's world-state. The feat undoubtedly impressed many Greek minds of the period, and Alexander, conqueror of Persia, the erstwhile foe of Greece's independence, must have struck the imagination as a hero for whom the usual honors were not sufficient. Further, it no doubt occurred to the thoughtful that the only way to reconcile the sovereignty of the Greek cities, so jealously guarded and so impatient of outside control, with the cosmopolitan monarchy founded by Alexander was to invest him with a supernatural character. To none other than a divine being could the proud city-states of Greece bend the knee without forfeiting their own sovereignty.[49a]

There is yet another consideration which may have persuaded the Athenian Assembly to ratify Alexander's apotheosis. This is suggested by a passage in Isocrates' Address to Philip. In his recommendation of the important city-states to Philip, Isocrates, speaking of Athens, emphasizes a fact which he felt should especially impress him, namely that Athens "aided Heracles to win his immor-

---

[49a] This opinion was put forward chiefly by the well-known specialist in Hellenistic thought, J. Kaerst, *Studien zur Entwicklung und theoretischen Begründung der Monarchie im Altertum* (Munich, 1898), p. 57 seq.

tality."[50] Isocrates probably had in mind the fact, reported by Diodorus Siculus,[51] that "the Athenians were the first of all other men to honor Heracles with sacrifices like as to a god, and by holding up, as an example for all other men to follow, their own reverence for the god they induced the Greeks first of all, and after them all men throughout the inhabited world, to honor Heracles as a god."

In other passages Isocrates stresses that Zeus had exalted his son Heracles that he might receive divine honors because of his virtues.[52] Yet, the above quotation suggests that the decision of the Athenian Assembly was an important factor in the divinization of Heracles. Why, then, could not another similar decision sanction the deification of Alexander?

The initiative taken by the Athenian Assembly in 307 in decreeing divine honors for Antigonus and Demetrius Poliorcetes seems to indicate that such a conclusion is plausible and that the Assembly vindicated the right of apotheosis in Athens. After Alexander's death (323) the Athenians had only one thing in mind, to regain their complete freedom and their democratic institutions. They initiated the uprising of Greek cities and the second regent, Antipater, who rushed from Asia to crush the uprising, was defeated. The Hellenic War thus initiated was, however, to be full of unpleasant surprises for the Athenians. It terminated with the destruction of the Athenian fleet—a bitter end for Athenian naval glory—with the subordination of Athens to Macedonia, and with the installation of an aristocratic government in Athens. This was re-established by Cassander, Antipater's successor in Macedonia, with the regency of Demetrius of Phalerum in the city.

In the meantime the general, Antigonus, was making a bold attempt in Asia to reunite all the lands of Alexander's kingdom. In order to win over the Greeks, he championed the principle of free dom for all Greek cities. The Athenians looked to him as their liberator. Finally, in 307 Antigonus made the decisive move and sent his son Demetrius Poliorcetes—"city—besieger"—to Athens with a strong navy. The citizens of Piraeus joined Poliorcetes

---

[50] *To Philip*, 33, ed. by G. Norlin (Loeb, 1928), 1, p. 264.
[51] *The Library of History* IV, 39, *loc. cit.* (1935), 2, p. 466 seq.
[52] *To Philip*, 132, *loc. cit.*, p. 324; *To Demonicus*, 50, *loc. cit.*, p. 34.

when they learned that he had come to liberate Athens. The Macedonian fortress in Piraeus was taken and Poliorcetes appeared in Athens.

The Athenians rejoiced at his promises to rebuild Piraeus and restore to the city its ancient freedom and democratic constitution. Their Assembly voted for the erection of gold statues to Demetrius and his father Antigonus, beside those of the Tyrannicides who were venerated as heroes, and for the coronation of the statues with crowns worth two hundred talents.[53] On the spot where Demetrius had first touched Athenian soil, an altar was erected to Demetrius "the Descender." The cult in the city was to be assured by a special priest. Two new tribes—the Antigonis and Demetrias—were added to the ten tribes of Cleisthenes and, accordingly, the number of senators was raised to six hundred. Two sacred vessels—Antigonia and Demetrias—were added to the other sacred triremes and the two rulers became eponymous heroes, as founders of the two new tribes. Both were officially termed god-savior *(theos-soter)*; also, unofficially, benefactor *(euergetes)*.

Their cult was combined with paeans, processions, sacrifices, and annual musical and theatrical performances. Another decree ordered their likeness to be woven with those of other gods into the *peplos* given to the goddess Athena in 306–305 and renewed every four years thereafter. The title "king" was decreed for Demetrius and Antigonus, although until then the latter had not yet used it. Moreover, the ambassadors, who were to transmit Athenian decrees to Antigonus, were authorized to call themselves *theoroi* (envoys to gods). It seems that Poliorcetes was even consulted as god-oracle in one instance, and that his decrees were declared as binding on gods and men.

Demetrius was also likened to Poseidon, who was greatly honored in Athens, and became a living *synnaos* of Athena when, in 304–303, he took up his abode in a part of the Parthenon.[54] He was also

---

[53] The main sources on the deification of Antigonus and Demetrius are *The Library of History* by Diodorus Siculus, XX, 46, ed. by R. M. Geer (Loeb, 1954), 10, p. 266 seq., and Plutarch's *Lives: Demetrius*, 10–13, *loc. cit.* (1920), 9, p. 24 seq.

[54] On Demetrius' coinage, see E. T. Newell, *The Coinage of Demetrius Poliorcetes* (London, 1927), esp. pp. 40, 41 (resemblance to Athena), and pp. 72, 87 (to Poseidon).

brought into intimate connection with Dionysus and a decree was voted by the Assembly that Demetrius should always be received in Athens with the honors due to Dionysus and Demeter.

The most extreme form of quasi-divine homage was rendered by the Athenians in 290 B.C., when, after recovering from his own and his father's misfortunes in Asia, Demetrius—now King of Macedonia—returned from Leucas and Corcyra to Athens. Athenaeus preserved a description of this reception written by Demochares, a contemporary of Demosthenes.[55] We read there: "Not only did the Athenians welcome him with offerings of incense and crowns and libations, but processional choruses also, and mummers with the elevated phallus met him with dancing and song; and as they took their places in the crowds they sang and danced, repeating the refrain that he was the only true god, while all the others were asleep, or making a journey, or non-existent; he, however, was sprung from Poseidon and Aphrodite, pre-eminent in beauty and embracing all in his benevolence." Athenaeus has also copied from the *Histories* of Duris of Samos the song flattering Demetrius and insulting other gods.[56] It is an interesting document illustrating the rationalistic tendency in religious matters in third-century Athens and the ease with which the Athenians accepted—but also rejected, as it later happened to Demetrius—a new man-god. Of course, political reasons dictated this behavior to the Athenians.[57] Nevertheless, all this illustrates that the Assembly vindicated the right of apotheosis.

The Athenians went too far in their enthusiasm and, according to Demochares whose report was preserved by Athenaeus, devoted

---

[55] *Deipnosophistae*, VI, 253 c, d, *loc. cit.* (1929), 3, p. 140. Cf. *FHG*, 2, p. 449.

[56] A good French translation with commentary is in Cerfaux-Tondriau, *Le culte*, p. 182 seq.; a German translation by F. Taeger in *Charisma*, 1, p. 271 seq. See also V. Ehrenberg, "Athenischer Hymnus auf Demetrios Poliorketes," *Die Antike*, 7 (1931), pp. 279–297.

[57] For details, see E. Cappellano, *Il fattore politico negli onori divini a Demetrio Poliorcete*, University of Turin, Publications of the Faculty of Letters, 6, fasc. 4 (Turin, 1954). Cf. also E. Manni, *Demetrio Poliorcete* (Rome, 1952). The different stages of Demetrius' divinization were described by K. Scott, "The Deification of Demetrius Poliorcetes," *AJP*, 49 (1928), pp. 137–166, 217–239. Cf. also W. S. Ferguson, *Hellenistic Athens* (London, 1911), p. 64, and J. Kaerst, "Demetrios," Pauly-Wissowa, 4 (Stuttgart, 1901), cols. 2769–2792. There is also an expression of sun symbolism in the song, Demetrius being compared to the sun surrounded by stars, his friends.

shrines and libations to Demetrius' entourage and to his courtesans. Even Demetrius is said to have been scandalized by such behavior.

Athens was not alone in its deification of Demetrius. Similar honors were decreed in Delos, at Sicyon, Samos, and in the cities of Euboea. These provide further illustrations of the rapid spread of the new practice in Greece. It would not have spread so rapidly if its basis had been of non-Greek, Oriental origin.

What makes the deification of Poliorcetes particularly interesting is the fact that this ruler cult is not connected with the cult of Alexander. The cult of the great conqueror, decreed by the Greek city-states in 324, did not endure in Greece. The political antagonism against Macedonia which erupted after Alexander's death explains why the continental Greeks did not join those of Asia Minor in the cult of the dead King. Of Alexander's generals, however, only Antipater refused to render divine honors to him after his death. Even after Antipater's death (319) Macedonia remained hostile to the ruler cult. With the exception of Antigonus I and Demetrius Poliorcetes, there are few cases in which it can be said with certainty that heroic honors had been rendered to a Macedonian ruler by Greek cities.[58]

The body of Alexander which should have been brought to Aigai in Macedonia, was seized by Ptolemy, son of Lagus, the governor of Egypt and founder of the Ptolemaic or Lagide dynasty, and was deposited in a magnificent sarcophagus—probably first in Memphis and then in Alexandria. His tomb became an important religious center. The Alexander cult also became the basis of the ruler cult in Ptolemaic Egypt.

During the bitter contests for Alexander's inheritance the other generals of the dead King also tried to profit from the prestige of their deified master. Peucestes, one of the generals most appreciated by Alexander, is said to have celebrated a great festival in Persepolis with sacrifices to gods to whose company he added Alex-

---

[58] See the quotations by Cerfaux-Tondriau, *Le culte*, pp. 171, 172. In this respect Lysimachus who established himself in Thrace seems to have been more fortunate.

ander and his father Philip, probably in order to win over the sympathies of Macedonians in his army.[59]

Another general, Eumenes, who wanted to avenge the murder of Perdiccas, elected first regent for Philip III, was the first to introduce into the ruler cult a new feature—the veneration of royal insignia. In order to strengthen his authority when reorganizing his army for an expedition (during which he was subsequently to meet his doom), Eumenes, claiming permission granted him by Alexander in a dream,[60] erected a royal throne in the tent of the high command, on which he placed a scepter, diadem, crown, and other emblems representing the insignia of the deceased supreme commander. An altar with a fire faced the throne and, before the deliberations, all the commanders offered sacrifice from a golden casket, presenting frankincense and the most costly of other kinds of incense, and making obeisance to Alexander as to a god.

This cultic display shows the influence of Persian court ceremonial, which included the bearing of fire before the Persian king every time he left his palace and the burning of incense in the audience hall. Without realizing it, Eumenes started a ceremonial which was to become an important feature in the later development of the ruler cult.

Ptolemy made the most of the fact that the body of the deified Alexander reposed in his capital. He outdid all his competitors and obtained a legitimate basis for his rule over a great part of Alexander's empire. He could even pretend to universal rule as the heir of Alexander. The dead King enjoyed, first of all, a municipal cult as founder (*ktistes*) of Alexandria. Because the heroic cult due the founders verged, at that time, on the divine, it is logical to conclude that Alexander-Ktistes was venerated as god in the magnificent mausoleum erected by Ptolemy II in Alexandria. This cult, of course, was purely Greek and concerned only the Greeks.[61]

---

[59] Diodorus, *op. cit.*, XIX, 22, *loc. cit.* (1947), 9, p. 288 seq. Cf. Plutarch *Lives: Eumenes*, 14, *loc. cit.* (1919), 8, p. 120.

[60] Diodorus, *op. cit.*, XVIII, 60,5–61,2, *loc. cit.*, p. 176 seq.; Plutarch, *op. cit.*, 13, 3 seq., *loc. cit.*, p. 116 seq.

[61] A short but clear outline of the development of the Hellenistic ruler cult was made by C. Lattey, "The Diadochi and the Rise of King-worship," *English Histor. Review*, 32 (1917), pp. 321–334. That the forms and technique imposed by the Lagides on Egyptian administration were also Greek was shown by C. Beaux, *Economie royale des Lagides* (Brussels, 1939).

Ptolemy I, however, also erected a state cult of Alexander which extended throughout the realm and was obligatory for all his subjects. If the body of Alexander did rest for some time in Memphis, as is reported by Pausanias,[62] Alexander was venerated in the temple where he reposed. Pausanias' report is doubted by many, but it is known for certain that Alexander's state cult had a center in Alexandria,[63] where a special temple was erected to him with an eponymous priest, chosen by the king from among the best families of the city. Not only Greek but also demotic documents were dated in his name. It seems that Ptolemy I started the Dionysiac tradition during Alexander's life, thus stressing his own ties with the god.[64]

It is important to note that in this cult Alexander was never called *theos* (god). He was regarded as being fully a god, and his name alone, like the names of other gods, indicated his divine character. The Dionysiac tradition concerning Alexander was further developed by Ptolemy II.[65] It was during his reign that the belief became general, thanks to the propaganda of court poets and writers, that Alexander had behaved during his life as a new Dionysus.

Ptolemy II also deified his father and his mother Berenice as god-saviors (*Theoi Soteres*),[66] and introduced a dynastic cult linking

---

[62] *Description of Greece*, I, 6, 3; 7, 1, ed. by W. H. S. Jones (Loeb, 1954), I, pp. 28, 34. Also Quintus Curtius Rufus, *History of Alexander*, X, 10, 20, ed. by J. C. Rolfe (Loeb, 1946), 2, p. 558.

[63] For details, see L. R. Taylor, "The Cult of Alexander at Alexandria," *Classical Philology*, 22 (1927), pp. 162–169.

[64] See Cerfaux-Tondriau, *Le culte*, p. 193, for details.

[65] This was shown definitively by A. D. Nock, "Notes on Ruler-Cult," *JHS*, 48 (1928), p. 21 seq. Cf. also J. Tondriau, "Notes Ptolémaiques," *Aegyptus*, 28 (1948), p. 176: Dionysos à Naukratis. *Idem*, "Le décret dionysiaque de Philopator," *Aegyptus*, 26 (1946), pp. 84–95.

[66] Ptolemy II celebrated their divinization by inaugurating a magnificent feast with Dionysiac features, called *penteteris*, with a quasi-Olympic *agon*. It is described by Callixeinus of Rhodes in Athenaeus' *Deipnosophistae*, V, 196–203 b, *loc. cit.* (1928), 2, pp. 386–418. See F. Bömer, "Pompa," Pauly-Wissowa, 21 (Stuttgart, 1952), col. 1954 seq. Ptolemy I also enjoyed a heroic cult in Ptolemais, founded by him. It is difficult to say whether he enjoyed there a divine or only a heroic cult. Cf. the criticisms of Ptolemy's legislation and reign by C. Préaux, "Quelques défauts de la politique intérieure de Ptolémée Philadelphe," *Aegyptus*, 13 (1933), pp. 547–554.

Alexander with the living rulers, himself, and his sister Arsinoe II (whom he had married, thus imitating a Pharaonic usage) called *Theoi Adelphoi*, the brotherly gods. After her death Arsinoe enjoyed another special, divine cult as the goddess Philadelphus.[67]

A further development of the dynastic cult was inaugurated by Ptolemy IV Philopator, who added to the official cult the names of the founders of the dynasty, Ptolemy I and his wife Berenice. A characteristic feature of the Ptolemaic ruler cult is the divinization of queens and princesses.[68] The most popular of these goddesses was Arsinoe II Philadelphus,[69] and most of the Ptolemaic queens imitated her divinized effigy on their coins.

All these cults were Greek, as were also the official titles given to the Ptolemaic rulers: Ptolemy I – Soter, Ptolemy II – Philadelphus, Ptolemy III – Euergetes, Ptolemy IV – Philopator, Ptolemy V – Epiphanes,[70] Ptolemy VI – Philometor. A reincarnation of deceased rulers in their successors is alluded to in the titles of Ptolemy VII – Neos Philopator, Ptolemy VIII – Euergetes II and Soter, Ptolemy IX – Philometor Soter II and Megistos Theos Soter, Ptolemy X – Alexander I and Theos Philometor, Ptolemy XI – Alexander II. Ptolemy XIII was regarded as an incarnation of Dionysus (Neos Dionysos).[71] These titles and their complication in

---

[67] P. Jouguet, *Trois études sur l'hellénisme*, p. 60, thinks that Ptolemy II established the cult of *Theoi Adelphoi* after the divinization of the dead Arsinoe, or at the same time. This is possible, but it seems more logical to suppose that the association of the brotherly gods with Alexander was already made during the life of Arsinoe (Cerfaux-Tondriau, *Le culte*, p. 204). The cult was richly endowed by the imposition of a special tax, and the priest of the *Theoi Adelphoi* and the priestess of Arsinoe were eponymous. Their names had to be mentioned in all official contracts.

[68] For details and bibliography, see Cerfaux-Tondriau, *ibid.*, pp. 193–201.

[69] Cf. E. Kiessling, "Zum Kult der Arsinoe im Fayum," *Aegyptus*, 13 (1933), pp. 542–546.

[70] On the origin and significance of this title which, although it seems to have been used by Ptolemy IV, appeared here for the first time as a ruler's epithet, see A. D. Nock, *op. cit.*, p. 38 seq. Cf. also J. Tondriau, "Notes Ptolémaïques," *loc. cit.*, pp. 171, 172. See also its use by the Seleucids, *infra*, pp. 234, 236. The title is not of Seleucid origin as suggested by F. Pfister, "Epiphanie," Pauly-Wissowa, Supplementband, 4 (Stuttgart, 1924), cols. 277–323. Cf. also the titles given to the kings in documents of the Ptolemaic period in U. Wilcken, *Urkunden der Ptolemäerzeit*, 2 (Berlin-Leipzig, 1935), p. 307 (Index).

[71] This is the only instance of the use of such a title. See A. D. Nock, *op. cit.*, p. 30 seq. See the analysis of Ptolemaic royal titles by W. Otto and H. Bengtson, *Zur Geschichte des Niederganges des Ptolemäerreiches*, Abhandl.

the later history of Ptolemaic Egypt indicate, furthermore, how the rulers tried to strengthen their tottering sovereignty by the introduction of new cult forms.[72]

Besides the Greek ruler cult there also existed in Ptolemaic Egypt the old Egyptian ruler cult. It is not certain whether the first Ptolemies were officially installed by the native priests, although it seems probable. In any event, after their succession to the throne the Ptolemies were regarded as divine sons of Horus. Their coronation was celebrated by the natives in the temple of Edfu. A sacred live falcon, "the living soul of Horus," played a prominent role in the ceremony.[73]

The famous Rosetta Stone, inscribed with a decree of a priestly synod at Memphis in 196 B.C.,[74] contains a very solemn formula of consecration of the young King Ptolemy V Epiphanes. This also shows that the Ptolemaic ruler cult had, at that time, been considerably assimilated to the old Pharaonic ruler cult.[75] The King is compared there to the Sun-Re, and called, in the old Pharaonic style, son of Zeus-Ammon, beloved of Ptah, illustrious in Upper and Lower Country. This is evidence that from the end of the second century B.C. the Ptolemaic ruler cult had been considerably Egyptianized. This process must already have started under the reign of

der Bayer. Akad. der Wiss., Philos.-hist. Abt., N. F., Heft 17 (Munich, 1938), pp. 238–240, with all bibliographical references. The Ptolemaic kings were often identified with different divinities, especially with Apollo-Helios, Eros, Heracles, Hermes, Poseidon, and Zeus. For details, see J. Tondriau, "Rois Lagides comparés ou identifiés à des divinités," *Chronique d'Egypte*, 45–46 (1948), pp. 127–146. Cf. also *infra*, pp. 234, 235.

[72] Cf., for details, Nilsson, *Geschichte der griech. Relig.*, 2nd ed., 2, p. 154 seq.

[73] See M. Alliot, "La fête égyptienne du couronnement du roi, au temple d'Edfou, sous les rois ptolémées," *Académie des Inscriptions et Belles-Lettres, Comptes Rendus, 1948* (Paris, 1949) pp. 208–219. The consecration ceremony at Memphis was perhaps called *protoklesia*. See P. Jouguet "Les débuts du règne de Ptolémée Philométor et la sixième guerre syrienne," *Revue de philol. de littér. et d'hist. anc.*, 10 (1936), pp. 208, 238. See also E. Otto, *Gott und Mensch nach den ägyptischen Tempelinschriften der griechisch-römischen Zeit*, Abhandlungen der Heidelberger Akademie der Wissensch., Phil.-hist. Kl., 1 (Heidelberg, 1964), pp. 63–83.

[74] See the translated text in E. R. Bevan, *A History of Egypt Under the Ptolemaic Dynasty* (London, 1927), p. 263 seq. Original text in *OGIS*, 1 (Leipzig, 1903), no. 90.

[75] The second title of Ptolemy V, besides Epiphanes, was Eucharistos which is certainly an older Egyptian epithet. Nock, *op. cit.*, p. 39, thinks that even Epiphanes is an Egyptian title. The hieroglyphic equivalents of these titles are "he who cometh forth" and "lord of beauties."

Ptolemy III, as seems indicated by another decree of a priestly synod held at Canopus in 237 B.C.[76] The decree conferred divine honors on Ptolemy III, his wife Berenice, and their daughter Berenice, who died in childhood. The King is given only his Greek titles, but the decree itself is written and the divinization made in the old Egyptian fashion.

The process of Egyptianization or assimilation to the old Pharaonic cult continued under Ptolemy IV. Another synod of Memphis, held in 217,[77] voted divine honors to Ptolemy IV after his victory over Antiochus III of Syria, and related the King to Ptah-Hephaistos, Re-Helios and Ammon-Zeus. Ptolemy IX Soter II is represented as priest of his own cult. This is again a further Egyptianization of the Ptolemaic ruler cult.[78] The Pharaohs were often represented as sacrificing to their own Ka.

Another Egyptian feature of the Ptolemaic ruler cult was the sharing of temple honors by the kings and queens with Egyptian gods.[79] The first who was given this honor was Arsinoe II. After her death she became a *synnaos*—sharing the temple—of all Egyptian gods in all temples. The *Theoi Adelphoi* were also made *synnaoi* of the principal Egyptian gods. The same honors were voted by the synods of Canopus and of Memphis to Ptolemy III, Ptolemy IV, and Ptolemy V.

Although faithful to the cult of the Greek gods,[80] the Ptolemies assumed the role of the Pharaohs in the Egyptian native religion.[81]

---

[76] *OGIS*, no. 56. Cf. E. R. Bevan, *op. cit.*, p. 208 seq. On the role which the priestly synods played in the worship of the Ptolemies, see W. Otto, "Aegyptische Priestersynoden in hellenistischer Zeit," *SB der Bayer. Akad. der Wiss.*, Abhandl. 2 (Munich, 1926), pp. 18–36. Cf. *idem*, *Priester und Tempel im hellenistischen Ägypten* (Leipzig-Berlin, 1905), 1, p. 72 seq.

[77] *Supplementum Epigraphicum Graecum*, ed. by J. J. E. Hondius (Leiden, 1923–60), 8, nos. 504 a and 467. Cf. E. R. Bevan, *op. cit.*, p. 232 seq.

[78] W. Otto, *Priester und Tempel*, 1, pp. 182, 183, 415.

[79] This has been shown conclusively by A. D. Nock in his thorough study "Σύνναος Θεός," *Harvard Studies in Class. Philol.*, 41 (1930), pp. 1–62, esp. p. 4 seq.

[80] On the introduction of the cult of Sarapis and a Greek adaptation of the cult of Isis, see Cerfaux-Tondriau, *Le culte*, p. 212 seq. Cf. also Nilsson, *op. cit.*, p. 155 seq. It seems that the Ptolemies' intention was to attach all Greeks to their kingdom through the propaganda of this Hellenized Egyptian cult. Cf. also A. Salač, *Isis, Sarapis, božstva sdružená* (Prague, 1915), on the spread of this cult.

[81] E. R. Bevan, *op. cit.*, p. 177 seq.

They appointed the most important priests, and conferred gifts and privileges on the temples.[82] Furthermore, the Egyptian priests of all major religious centers always remained loyal to the Ptolemies.

The epigraphic material from the Ptolemaic period is quite rich,[83] and is mostly in the form of addresses or dedications. It confirms the above deductions, but does not give many indications as to the development of the royal cult. The numismatic material is more expressive, and provides some new features which became important for the further evolution of the symbolism of divinized rulership in general.

At the beginning of his reign, Ptolemy I used for his coins, which were struck in the names of Philip Aridaeus and Alexander IV, the types of Alexander the Great.[84] About 316 B.C. he replaced the head of Heracles with a head of Alexander the Great wearing an elephant-skin. From 305 on he used the title *basileus* and struck coins not only with Alexander's head wearing either an elephant-skin or the horned symbol of Ammon, but also with his own head diademed and with the aegis around his neck. The eagle, often on fulmen, this combination being the Ptolemaic escutcheon, appears regularly on his and his successors' coins.

The idea of using coins for dynastic propaganda can be detected on the coins of Ptolemy II Philadelphus. The replete cornucopiae, which from his reign on frequently adorned Ptolemaic coins, clearly suggested the reign of prosperity and abundance secured by the rulers.

Ptolemy III initiated a bold innovation which found many imitators in later periods. A group of coins shows a bust of Ptolemy III, adorned with Helios' rays, wearing Zeus's aegis, and carrying Poseidon's trident combined with the sceptre.[85]

---

[82] W. Otto, *Priester und Tempel*, I, pp. 54–58.

[83] *OGIS*, p. 46 seq. Cf. Taeger, *Charisma*, I, pp. 251, 297 seq.

[84] B. V. Head, *Historia numorum*, 2nd ed. (Oxford, 1911), p. 847 seq. On the Alexander type on Hellenistic coins, see H. P. L'Orange, *Apotheosis in Ancient Portraiture* (Oslo, 1947), pp. 19–38: Heavenward-gazing Alexander, Transfigured Alexander. On pp. 39–48 he shows how this attitude was imitated by Hellenistic rulers.

[85] Head, *op. cit.*, p. 853. F. Taeger, *Charisma*, I, p. 300, sees in this innovation the influence of Egyptian royal ideology. The King appears here in the guise of three gods—Zeus, Helios, and Poseidon. The Egyptian influence, identifying the Pharaoh with Re-Helios, is possible. The Egyptianization of the Ptolemaic ruler cult has been shown to have started under this ruler.

Ptolemy IV Philopator struck gold coins with his own bust, wearing a diadem and a chlamys and with the bust of his wife Arsinoe III wearing a wreath and carrying a sceptre over her shoulder. A radiate bust appears again on Ptolemy V Epiphanes' coinage, with a sceptre over the shoulder of the King. The epithet *theos* appears for the first time on the coins of Ptolemy VI Philometor. Ptolemy VIII Euergetes II also liked to strike coins with his own radiate bust.

The Seleucid kings faced in their kingdom many problems which the Ptolemies were spared. The founder of the dynasty, Seleucus I Nicator (312–280 B.C.), who was appointed satrap of Babylon after Alexander's death, was defeated with the help of the first Ptolemy by Antigonus, but recovered his satrapy and ultimately became master of the whole Asiatic empire of Alexander, from the Aegean sea to the Indus.

There was no tradition of divinized kingship on the territory of the Seleucids. The Persians had great respect for their kings who, because of their *Hvarena*, were placed between gods and men but were regarded as being appointed by Ahura Mazda and ruling in his name. The Babylonian, Assyrian, and Hittite traditions did not know living, divine kings. Moreover, the religious beliefs of the Iranian and Semitic populations were very different from those of the Greeks.[86]

The Seleucids were well aware of this, and practiced a policy of benevolent tolerance in religious matters. Ahura Mazda continued to reign in Persia and Marduk in Babylon. The Seleucid rulers even constructed temples in honor of native divinities. In spite of all that, however, the Seleucids remained Macedonians and Greeks in their own religious beliefs. The Olympian divinities continued to be venerated in temples constructed by the rulers and by the citizens of numerous Greek municipalities newly founded by the Seleucids.

---

[86] For general information, see E. R. Bevan, *The House of Seleucus* (London, 1902), 2 vols. The best publication on the Seleucids is that by E. Bikerman, *Institutions des Séleucides* (Paris, 1938). See *ibid.*, pp. 236–257, on the monarchic cult. Cf. also M. Rostovtzeff, *The Social and Economic History of the Hellenistic World* (Oxford, 1951), I, pp. 429–542.

Apollo was regarded as the forefather of the dynasty[87] and Seleucus I consecrated to him the suburb of Antioch called Daphne, where he built a magnificent temple to Apollo and Artemis. Splendid games were organized in which the kings often participated personally.[88] The cult of Zeus Seleukios—the name may refer to the well-known Zeus of Seleucia Pieria, a Seleucid foundation[89]— was also propagated by the Seleucids.

All this indicates that the Seleucid ruler cult could hardly have Oriental origins. The founder of the dynasty abstained from proclaiming himself god, but he was anxious to express on his coins the sublime character of kingship. In 306 B.C. he substituted for the bust of Alexander-in-elephant-skin previously used, his own idealized portrait, in helmet adorned with the bull's horns and covered with panther's skin. The figure of Nike crowning a trophy on the obverse side symbolized the numerous victories of the King called Nicator—the Victorious.[90]

His son Antiochus I took the first step towards establishing a ruler cult by divinizing his dead father. A special temple with a priest was erected to the new god in Seleucia. Antiochus I was again deified after his death as Antiochus Apollo Soter. He earned the title Soter through his brilliant victory over the Galatian Gauls who had invaded Asia Minor.

It is believed that it was Antiochus III (223–187) who took the last step in the progress of the ruler cult by divinizing himself or, at least, by becoming a priest of his own cult. This recalls the Egyptian and Persian tradition regarding the king as the grand priest on earth. This may be learned from an edict issued by the King in 204, establishing a cult of his sister and Queen, Laodice.[91] She should have grand priestesses "who would wear gold crowns with the portrait of the Queen and whose names should be mentioned

---

[87] Cf. *OGIS*, nos. 212, line 14; 219, line 26; 227, line 5; 237, line 6.

[88] See the most important inscriptions concerning the temples, priests, and games of Daphne in *OGIS*, nos. 244, 245, 248.

[89] See Nock, "*Notes on Ruler-Cult*," p. 42: Zeus Seleukios.

[90] B. V. Head, *op. cit.*, p. 756 seq.

[91] *OGIS*, no. 224; new ed. by C. Bradford Welles, *Royal Correspondence in the Hellenistic Period* (New Haven, 1934), no. 36, p. 157 seq. Cf. U. Wilcken "Zur Entstehung des hellen. Königskultes," *SB der Preuss. Akad. der Wiss.*, p. 318 seq.

in the contracts after the names of the grand priests of our ancestors and of ourselves."[92]

This edict envisages the organization of the cult of the living queen throughout the empire. This implies that the cult of the royal ancestors and of the living king existed before 193 B.C. and that the office of grand priest was established for the supervision of the royal cult in his territory.

This official dynastic ruler cult, however, may already have been established by Antiochus I, a contemporary of Ptolemy II who created an official ruler cult in Egypt.[93] Although there is no direct proof that the Seleucids had followed the example of the Ptolemies in this respect, it seems logical to suppose that they could hardly have conceded this advantage to their Egyptian rivals.

A Ptolemaic influence on the Seleucid ruler cult is suggested also by the assimilation of certain Seleucid kings to their gods. An inscription from Seleucia Pieria speaks of priests of Seleucus I, called therein Zeus Nicator, and of his son Antiochus I, called Apollo Soter.[94] It is known that neither ruler had used such assimilation. It is therefore legitimate to see here an answer to Egyptian propaganda representing the founder of the dynasty with Zeus's features and comparing Ptolemy II with Apollo and Zeus.[95] It was Antiochus IV who seems to have identified himself with Zeus. This appears confirmed by the issue of coins depicting Zeus, on which he styles himself Theos Epiphanes—the god manifest.[96] He seems here

---

[92] Cf. also the copy of this edict found in Iran and published by L. Robert, "Inscriptions séleucides de Phrygie et d'Iran," *Hellenica*, 7 (1949), pp. 3–29. The text and a French translation, *ibid.*, pp. 7, 8. See there the bibliography on this edict and its publications.

[93] This has already been suggested by U. Wilcken, *op. cit.*, p. 321; also M. Rostovtzeff, "Πρόγονοι," *JHS*, 55 (1935), pp. 55–56, and Cerfaux-Tondriau, *Le culte*, p. 236. Cf. also E. R. Bevan, *op. cit.* 1, p. 177.

[94] *OGIS*, no. 245.

[95] Cf. J. Tondriau, "Rois Lagides," pp. 128–129, 130 (nos. 1, 4).

[96] See E. T. Newell, *The Seleucid Mint of Antioch* (New York, 1918), no. 63. Cf. *ibid.*, p. 23, on the religious policy of Antiochus IV. The same King seems to have followed the policy of syncretism in trying to identify the Greek Zeus Olympios with Zeus-Gad and Zeus-Baal Shamin. For details, see M. Rostovtzeff, "Le Gad de Doura et Séleucus Nicator," in *Mélanges syriens offerts à R. Dussaud*, 1 (Paris, 1939), p. 281 seq. See also *ibid.*, pp. 284–295, on the survival of the Seleucid ruler cult after the collapse of their empire. On the Se eucid religious policy, cf. E. R. Bevan, *op. cit.*, 2, p. 154 seq. and H. Seyrig, "Antiquités Syriennes," *Syria*, 20 (1939), pp. 296–302.

to have followed Ptolemy V in using the epithet Epiphanes. Similarly, it was apparently in imitation of Ptolemy IV Philopator, a
great propagator of the cult of Dionysus, that Antiochus VI and
Antiochus XII called themselves Dionysos.[97]

In one important matter the Seleucid ruler cult differed from the
Ptolemaic. The Seleucids do not seem to have insisted on becoming
synnaoi of native gods in their temples as did the Ptolemies.
Unfortunately, no direct proofs are extant concerning the existence
of a royal cult among the natives. One thing seems certain, namely
that, in spite of the sympathies they enjoyed among the native
priesthood, they did not receive divine epitaphs in cuneiform
documents.[98] However, even the natives in Babylonia and Elam
must have rendered some cultic homage to the Seleucid kings. A
tablet from Uruk, probably from the time of Antiochus III, mentions offerings of meat before the statues of the kings when the
regular sacrifices were performed.[99] Were these statues in native
temples or in the temples created for the royal cult? Lack of docu-
mentary evidence precludes a definite answer to these questions.
The fact that the rulers in the territory of the Seleucids were not
regarded as gods before the Macedonian conquest seems to have
exercised a restricting influence here.

Besides the official dynastic cult for the whole empire, which was
decentralized in the different satrapies, there naturally existed also
a municipal ruler cult.[100] The grand priest in the satrapies had no
right to intervene in the Greek cities in matters of the ruler cult.
It was up to the cities to decide what kind of honors they wanted
to decree to the rulers for their benefactions. In rendering divine
honors, some cities went further than was customary in the official

[97] See J. Tondriau, "Souverains et souveraines séleucides en divinités," *Le
muséon*, 61 (1948), pp. 171–182.
[98] A. D. Nock, "Σύνναος Θεός," p. 61.
[99] M. Rostovtzeff, *The Social and Econom. History of the Hellen. World*,
I, p. 437, 3, p. 1428. Cf. also Nilsson, *op. cit.*, p. 168 seq. According to *OGIS*,
no. 230, the high officer and grand priest Ptolemy Thraseas made a dedication to "Hermes, Heracles and the Great King Antiochus." F. Taeger,
Charisma, I, p. 317, rightly sees in it an exceptional case of Egyptian influence.
[100] See Cerfaux-Tondriau, *Le culte*, pp. 237–240 with bibliographical notes.
See in E. Bikerman, *Institutions des Seleucides*, pp. 243–246, a list of divine
and other honors decreed to the kings by Greek municipalities.

cult. The example of Antiochus II is especially significant. He was called simply *Theos* (god) by a decision of the city of Miletus, which thought itself particularly indebted to him. However, he was, *Theos* only for Miletus, not for the rest of the empire. In the official cult the ruler could be only *Theos Soter* or *Epiphanes*, but not simply *Theos* like the Olympian gods or Alexander. It was in the cities that the cult longest survived the extinction of the dynasty.[101]

Seleucid coinage does not reveal many new features in the symbolism of rulership.[102] A radiate head appears for the first time on the coins of the usurper Alexander-Bala (150–145). It is more pronounced on the coinage of Antiochus VI who called himself Dionysos. Stars and a radiate diadem indicate the deification of Antiochus IV Epiphanes. Cornucopiae are also used on the coins of Demetrius I Soter (162–150). Eagles adorned other coins. Oriental, Indian, and Iranian influences seem to have inspired frequent use of representations on the coins of elephants,[103] sometimes horned, and of horses, often horned.[104]

The epithet Epiphanes is very frequently used in the coinage. Antiochus X Philopator is the only ruler with the epithet Eusebes. This seems to show a certain slackening in the emphasis on divinized kingship and can be explained perhaps as a concession to the non-Greek population, or as due to influences coming from Cappadocia. The usurper Tryphon (142–139) is the first and only one

[101] Cf. M. Rostovtzeff, "Le Gad de Doura," *loc. cit.*, pp. 284–295.

[102] For details, see B. V. Head, *op. cit.*, pp. 756–773. Cf. also M.-Th. Allouche-Lepage, *L'art monétaire des royaumes bactriens* (Paris, 1956), pp. 27–42. At the beginning of his reign Seleucus I struck coins with Alexander's head with an elephant-skin, but without the horns, an attribute of Ammon. This indicates his opposition to the Ptolemies.

[103] Cf. the study by F. Matz, *Der Gott auf dem Elefantenwagen*, Akad. der Wiss. und der Lit., Abhandl. der Geistes- und Sozialwissenschaftlichen Kl., no. 10 (Mainz, 1953), esp. p. 730 seq. On pp. 742 and 750 he mentions the elephant holding a torch in his trunk on Antiochus VI's coins (P. Gardner and R. S. Poole, *The Seleucid Kings of Syria*, Catalogue of Greek Coins in the British Museum, 4 [London, 1878], p. 66, pl. 19, no. 12). He sees in it a symbol of light which later appeared again in the symbols of the ruler cult.

[104] The Seleucid kings also continued to wear Macedonian dress, military shoes, a purple mantle over their armour, and the felt hat (*causia*) with a diadem. Their dynastic symbol was the anchor. They sealed their documents with a ring bearing this symbol. Cf. M.-Th. Allouche-Lepage, *op. cit.*, p. 84.

in Syria to use the title Basileus Autocrator which was to become common in the Roman and Byzantine period.

Unlike the Ptolemies, the Seleucids do not seem to have profited from their ruler cult as much as their Egyptian rivals. Their last rulers seem to have laid less stress on the ruler cult. In this respect they differed from the last Ptolemies.

Tryphon may have been inspired in choosing his pretentious title by the example of the Parthian Arsacid dynasty whose kings used the title *Basileus Autocrator* from the period of Mithridates I (171–138? B.C.). Arsaces rebelled under Antiochus II Theos in 250 B.C. and founded an empire which extended over Seleucid Mesopotamia and in the East reached India. His dynasty ruled until A.D. 230. Although they regarded themselves as the heirs of the Achaemenids and had adopted Persian customs, organization, and religion, they were greatly influenced by the Hellenistic culture emanating from the lands of the Seleucids. This is particularly evident from their coinage which reveals titles used in the Seleucid and Ptolemaic ruler cult.[105]

The most frequent title is that of *Epiphanes*. At least seven kings are called *Euergetes*. The title *Eupator* is used only once, but seven rulers are called *Theopator* and six simply *Theos*. Queen Musa called Ourania Thea. These rulers seem, however, to have avoided any identification with a special god. It is difficult to say how serious the Parthian kings were in assuming their divine titles. In the Iranian religious atmosphere such a title probably lost most of its reality.

The epithets *Nicator* and *Nicephoros* too were adopted from Syria. The title *Dikaios*, emphasizing the love of justice of the kings, echoes the old Hellenic idea of a just ruler but seems also to betray Persian influence.[106] Many kings expressed their sympathy for Greek culture by the title *Philhellenos*. Old Iranian tradition appears

[105] For details, see B. V. Head, *op. cit.*, pp. 817–822. Cf. also A. Farkas, *Die Ikonographie der Partherkönige* (Aiud-Nagyenyed, 1933). See also R. Ghirshman, *Iran. Parthians and Sassanians*, trans. by S. Gilbert and J. Emmons, The Arts of Mankind ([London], 1962), pp. 15–117; coins, figs. 135–155 on pp. 114, 115. Cf. the short history of the Parthians in *idem*, *L'Iran. Dès origines à l'Islam* (Paris, 1951), pp. 216–258.

[106] See *infra*, p. 250.

in the title *Basileus Basileon*—King of Kings. Mithridates I (171–138 B.C.) was the first *Basileus Autocrator*. It is interesting to note that the title *Soter* is not to be seen on Parthian coinage. This seems to indicate that this title had been given to rulers for military and other deeds, which endowed them with the aspect of saviors of the state at critical periods. In spite of many reverses in the internal situation, Parthia did not suffer any catastrophic upheaval such as had often shattered other Hellenistic kingdoms.[107]

The title *Soter* was, on the other hand, popular in Bactria-Sogdiana, which became an independent kingdom in 250, being recognized so by the Seleucid Antiochus II. The country was exposed to many invasions threatening its very existence. At least thirteen kings were called Soter because of their military successes. Among other titles to be found on the coins are *Nicephoros*, *Euergetes*, *Epiphanes*, *Megas* (Great), *Nicator Aniketos* (Invincible), *Dikaios* (Just), *Philopator*. Only one ruler—Antimachus—called himself simply *Theos* and the only queen who had her own coinage[108]—Agathokleia—used the title *Theotropos*.

These are the only suggestions of a ruler cult in Bactria. The internal situation, with a racially mixed population which had a different religious attitude from that of the Greeks (who formed only a minority in the kingdom), was not favorable to the expansion of a ruler cult which was basically Greek.

The Hellenistic titles remained, however, on coins with Indian inscriptions. They were, of course, translated into the Indian idioms. Among them is found also the translation of the title King of Kings, which we miss on Greek coins of this Kingdom.[109]

A weak echo of the Hellenistic ruler cult reached even Armenia, but at a very late period. Tigranes III (12–6 B.C.) called himself *Theos Megas Neos*, and *Philhellenos* on his coins.[110] The title *Neos*

---

[107] Cf. F. Taeger, *Charisma*, I, p. 333.

[108] For details, see B. V. Head, *op. cit.*, pp. 832–845. Cf. also W. W. Tarn, *The Greeks in Bactria and India* (Cambridge, 1951, 2nd ed.) esp. pp. 90, 132, 138, 157, 180, 188, 261, 303, 437 seq., 446 seq. For more details, see M.-Th. Allouche-Lepage, *op. cit.*, esp. pp. 52 seq., 67 seq. Cf. also S. K. Eddy, *The King is Dead* (Lincoln, Nebraska, 1961), pp. 81–95 (Parthians and Bactrians).

[109] B. V. Head, *op. cit.*, p. 844.

[110] *Ibid.*, p. 754.

may be suggestive of the epithet *Epiphanes*. His predecessor had abandoned the title *Basileus Basileon* only when his kingdom became a Roman protectorate.

Hellenistic influences in political ideology in the small kingdoms and principalities on the borders of the Seleucid empire—Cappadocia, Pontus, Bithynia and others—are negligible. More important in this respect is the Attalid kingdom with its center in Pergamum, a Greek city. The first ruler, Philetaerus, still recognized Seleucus Nicator as his suzerain although he made himself independent in 284 B.C. It was Attalus I (269–197 B.C.) who, after assuming the royal title, raised his kingdom almost to the rank of a great power.

Philetaerus obtained divine honors after his death.[111] Because he and his successors generously favored Athens and other Greek cities, the latter offered them quasi-divine honors comparable to the cult decreed for Poliorcetes. Altars, sacrifices, and theatrical displays were voted by several cities for their benefactors.[112] However, they cannot be regarded as having been divinized during their life. Only after death were they believed to become gods and often called Soter and Euergetes. The cult became more intensive under the reign of Attalus I and was marked by a pronounced Dionysiac tendency. The queens also were given an apotheosis, with special priestesses charged to bring sacrifices in their honor.[113]

Another example of the Dionysiac character of the ruler cult is to be found in Pontus. Mithridates VI Eupator, who reigned over the kingdom from 120 to 63 B.C., called himself *Dionysos* and even *Neos Dionysos*.[114] It seems that this acceptance of such a title was intended to express the political aims of the king. Desiring to become a leader of the whole East against the Romans, Mithridates wanted to become a new Alexander. Dionysus appeared to him to

[111] *OGIS*, no. 764.

[112] For details and bibliographical notices, see Cerfaux-Tondriau, *Le culte*, p. 248 seq. On the penetration of Hellenic civilization into the small kingdom of Anatolia, cf. S. K. Eddy, *op. cit.*, pp. 163–182. On the conquest of these countries by the Romans, see D. Magie, *Roman Rule in Asia Minor to the End of the Third Century after Christ* (Princeton, 1950), I, p. 3 seq.

[113] Cf. the main inscriptions in *OGIS*, nos. 264 seq., especially 267, 280, 289, 297, 299, 301, 302, 309, 313. For the ceremonial of the cult, the inscription no. 764 from the gymnasium of Pergamum is especially instructive.

[114] B. V. Head, *op. cit.*, p. 501; *OGIS*, no. 370.

be the best bond to unite the Greeks and the East in opposition to Roman penetration.

An interesting development of the ruler cult is seen in the inscription on the monumental tomb which King Antiochus of Comagene had erected for himself on the summit of Nimrud-Dagh mountain. Comagene was a little kingdom which owed its existence to the disintegration of the Seleucid empire. Hellenization touched this territory, but Oriental and especially Persian traditions were still very strong. All this is reflected in the inscription.[115]

The King introduces himself in the main inscription as "Great King Antiochus, *Theos Dikaios Epiphanes Philoromaios Philhellenos.*" He regards himself as a scion of the Persian Achaemenids and, through the Seleucids, as a descendant of Alexander. Although accepting the divine titles, he does not affiliate himself with any of the gods, but declares that while his body would repose in this tomb, his soul would fly to Ahuramazda, whom he identifies with Zeus. He placed his statue with that of other gods, calling himself *synthronos*, but he distinguishes very clearly between the true gods and his divinized ancestors whom he regards only as heroes. He gave numerous prescriptions for the continuation of the ruler cult, instituting a priest with many privileges, ordering the erection of statues to his ancestors and to the living king and sacrifices and festivities on the royal anniversaries.

In this he imitated the example of the Seleucids, but the Persian tradition did not attribute to divine titles and honors the same significance as did the true Hellenistic ruler cult. Even the Persian *Hvarena* appears in his titles, interpreted in Greek as Tyche of the

---

[115] *OGIS*, no. 383. Cf. also short inscriptions with the same royal titles, *ibid.*, nos. 384–401, no. 402 in Gerger, and a longer inscription from Samosata (no. 404). Cf. P. H. Fraser, "Inscriptions from Commagene," *Annual Brit. School at Athens*, 47 (1952), pp. 96–101; F. K. Dörner and R. Naumann, *Forschungen in Kommagene*, İstambuler Forschungen, 10 (Berlin, 1939); J. Keil, "Basaltstele des Königs Antiochos I von Kommagene," *Serta Hoffilleriana* (Zagreb, 1940), p. 128 seq. See also Cerfaux-Tondriau, *Le culte*, pp. 254, 255 and F. Taeger, *Charisma*, I, pp. 427–433. A. J. Festugière, in a short study "Les inscriptions d'Asoka et l'idéal du roi hellénistique," *Recherches de Science religieuse*, 39 (1951) = *Mélanges J. Lebreton*, pp. 31–46, compared some principles of Indian political thinking with that of Hellenistic political philosophy. See also R. Ghirshman, *Iran, Parthians and Sassanians*, pp. 57–69, figs. 18, 71–80 (Nimrud Dagh); J. Neusner, "Parthian Political Ideology," *Iranica antiqua*, 3 (1963), pp. 40–59.

King. The apparent syncretizing is also interesting in the identification of Persian and other Oriental deities with Zeus, Apollo, Hermes, and Heracles. All this shows that the Hellenistic ruler cult, of Greek origin, could be only partially adopted in lands with strong Persian and Oriental traditions which had not known divinized kings before their conquests.

II

Upon establishing the origins and the main character of the Hellenistic ruler cult, it is fitting that we investigate the theoretical considerations which were destined to legitimize it, not only in the minds of the masses but also among intellectuals, who were not inclined to accept the divinization of a man. We must now determine what ideas made it popular, or at least acceptable, among the masses and whether there were any attempts on the part of the Hellenistic philosophers and thinkers to reconcile these radical new inroads in the religious sphere with the dignity of free-thinking men.

It is not easy to give an adequate answer to these questions because Hellenistic literature is only fragmentarily preserved. The new ideas on kingship must, however, have preoccupied many intellectuals and a considerable number of treatises on politics were written. Demetrius Phalereus, who died in Alexandria during the reign of Ptolemy Philadelphus, is said[116] to have "exhorted King Ptolemy to hold in great esteem and to read the books on kingship and on rulership. For what friends do not dare to say to kings, they write in books." Unfortunately the treatises known to Demetrius are all lost. This loss is the more regrettable as these writings were published at a period when the ruler cult was in its beginnings. It is therefore necessary to turn to other documents in order to follow this development.

From the early period of the ruler cult the works of two Hellenistic poets—Theocritus and Callimachus—may be quoted. They both wrote in Alexandria during the reign of Ptolemy Philadelphus.

[116] Joannes Stobaeus, *Anthologium*, IV, 7, 27, ed. by C. Wachsmuth and O. Hense (Berlin, 1909), 4, p. 255.

In one of his poems which has been preserved, Theocritus presents the king as the best man:[117] "A kind heart, loving the arts, a true gallant, and the top of good fellowship; knows well who is a friend, and still better who is not; like a true king, gives far and wide and says no man nay...."

This is a picture of a king such as most intellectuals would like to have: friendly, generous, loving the arts, wise, and knowing how to distinguish friends from foes. The new ideas on kingship are, however, expounded by Theocritus in his hymn on Philadelphus.[118]

He first invokes Zeus and the Muses in order to sing the deeds of the great man with dignity. Then he glorifies Philadelphus' divine origin. His divinized father and mother are enthroned in Olympus, with the god Alexander and with Heracles whose descendant the Soter (Philadelphus' father) was, through his mother Arsinoe, Lagus' wife, of the House of Macedonia. Philadelphus' birth was painless and marked by the appearance of an eagle, Zeus' bird, which was of good omen.

Then the wealth and power of Philadelphus' kingdom which Zeus bestowed on him are praised. The king's virtues and works for peace are extolled. He is a promotor of culture, generous to the gods and their temples, to foreign rulers, to his friends and to poets. He is the true *euergetes* (benefactor). His marriage with his sister is compared to the sacred union of Zeus with Hera.

Although praising the divine origin of his hero, Theocritus does not attribute a divine character to him. He places him among the demi-gods, praising him as a hero, and placing him between men and gods. The poem must have been written before the official introduction of the cult of *Theoi Adelphoi* in 271 B.C.

Callimachus expressed his ideas on kingship in his hymn on Zeus.[119] Kingship derives from Zeus. "And thou [Zeus] didst choose that which is most excellent among men...thou didst choose the

---

[117] Poem 14, vss. 61–63, in *The Greek Bucolic Poets*, ed. by J. M. Edmonds (Loeb, 1928), p. 172.

[118] Poem 17, *loc. cit.*, pp. 210–220.

[119] Hymn I, vss. 69–83, in *Callimachus and Lycophron, Aratus*, ed. by A. W. and G. R. Mair (Loeb, 1921), p. 44. Cf. W. Nauhardt, *Das Bild des Herrschers in der griechischen Dichtung* (Berlin, 1940), p. 87 seq.

rulers of Cities themselves, beneath whose hand...are all things that are: what is there that is not under the ruler's sway?... From Zeus come kings; for nothing is diviner than the kings of Zeus.... Thou hast bestowed upon them wealth and prosperity abundantly." Then he glorifies Philadelphus who outshone all kings.

Here again the king is regarded as a beloved creature of Zeus, almost divine, but not yet a god. Moreover, the absolute sovereignty of the king is accepted as a matter of fact. It is, however, a kingship only by god's grace; the most precious gift of Zeus, but not yet divine in itself.

This is, unfortunately, all that can be quoted from Hellenistic court poetry which has a direct relationship with the poet's ideas on kingship. The poems of Aratus and of Lycophron[120] yield nothing of interest and the lesser poets can be overlooked.

The Hellenistic historians were numerous, but their works are mostly known to us only in fragments. Only a few of these fragments are of interest for the present investigation. Theopompus, a pupil of Isocrates, protested against the exaggerations of the ruler cult.[121] His contemporary, Ephorus, also Isocrates' pupil, probably shared Theopompus' ideas in this respect. The historians of Alexander whose works were used by later historians—Arrian, Plutarch, Quintus Curtius—very often lacked enthusiasm for Alexander's divinization.[122] Duris is skeptical about it, Timaeus, Demochares and Phylarchus are more hostile. The greatest of them—Polybius —when referring to the different acts of the ruler cult, seldom suppresses a critical and rationalistic comment.

This reserved attitude on the part of so many Hellenistic writers towards the ruler cult can be explained also by the abuses which accompanied it—divinization of courtiers and mistresses, and the undignified behavior of some divinized rulers. The gods of Olympus, who were forced to accept the company of such new gods,

[120] Ed. by A. W. and G. R. Mair, *loc. cit.*, p. 380 seq.

[121] *FHG*, I, no. 277, p. 325: letter to Alexander protesting against Harpalus and the cult which the latter instituted in honor of his defunct courtesan Pythonike. Cf. *ibid.*, p. 283: Against Philip II.

[122] Details cannot be given here. For quotations and evidence, see F. Taeger, *Charisma*, I, pp. 381 seq., 397 seq. This book is not easy reading and often lacks clarity, but the references are reliable.

increasingly lost the respect of their worshipers. This also explains why the Oriental cults, which intrigued the Greeks by their mysteries and rites, started to attract them and penetrated ever more into western lands, overshadowing the cult of native deities.

How much the belief in the traditional gods had suffered is illustrated by the teaching of Euhemerus, a contemporary of the Diadochoi. He taught that the gods of popular worship were originally men whom people had divinized because of their deeds and the help given by them to mankind. In his doctrine the Greek and Egyptian anthropomorphism encountered growing rationalism among the intellectuals, and many could see in it a justification of the ruler cult.

The ruler cult was accepted by the masses, it appears, without reluctance and as a political necessity. How sincerely the people believed in the divinity of its rulers is not easy to determine. This belief could hardly have commanded deep religious feeling, however. Intellectuals possibly used the words *theos* and *theios* (god and divine) in a sense similar to that of Plato, or of Aristotle in his *Nicomachean Ethics*.[123] The latter speaks of "heroic and divine virtue" as the opposite of bestiality and quotes Homer's words on Hector who, on account of his surpassing valor seemed to be the son not of a mortal but of a god. "Hence if, as men say, surpassing virtue changes men into gods, the disposition opposed to bestiality will clearly be some quality more than human." This meaning suggested by Aristotle himself, may have helped the adherents of the Cynics, Epicurus, and the first Stoics to reconcile their teachings with realistic necessity in political life.

To the masses the divine kings appeared, above all, as their benefactors, saviors, and philanthropic patrons. These titles appear frequently on inscriptions and papyri.[124] In an absolute monarchy the king was the only central figure and the distribution of offices,

[123] On Plato, see the book by J. van Camp and P. Canart, *Le sens du mot* Ͽεῖος *chez Platon* (Louvain, 1956), Recueil de travaux d'histoire et de philol., Université de Louvain, 4th ser., fasc. 9, pp. 129 seq. (*Republic*), 213 seq. (*Politicus*), 305 seq. (*Laws*). Aristotle, *Nicomachean Ethics*, VII, 1, 1, ed. by H. Rackham (Loeb, 1939), p. 374.

[124] This was thoroughly investigated by W. Schubart, "Das hellenistische Königsideal nach Inschriften und Papyri," *Archiv für Papyrusforschung*, 12 (1936), pp. 1–26.

of justice and benefits, depended on his good will. It was thus natural that the suppliant letters addressed to the first Ptolemies so often ended with the phrase "savior and benefactor of all men" and that the kings' philanthropy and beneficence were invoked.[125] It should not be overlooked, however, that these titles, which can be traced far back in classical Greece,[126] did not in the early Hellenistic period have the kind of religious and mystical significance which they had had earlier and were later to acquire again.

In order to complete our knowledge of Hellenistic political philosophy, which can be only fragmentarily reconstructed from inscriptions and papyri, some writings on policy can be referred to. The fragments of these were fortunately preserved by Joannes Stobaeus in the sixth century A.D., chiefly in chapter seven of the fourth book of his Anthology.[127] So far, they have generally been assumed by specialists to be Pythagorean or Stoic treatises and for this reason have been neglected by the students of Hellenistic problems. It has been the great contribution of E. R. Goodenough[128] to have tried to make a satisfactory analysis of the different fragments for the first time. However, because his dating of these fragments from the Hellenistic period has been questioned,[129] it will be necessary to study them with more attention.

It is to be noted that many of the fragments insist on the identification of the king with the law-maker or with the law itself. One particular passage among the fragments is attributed to Archytas of Tarentum and quoted by Stobaeus from

---

[125] See O. Guéraud, Ἐντεύξεις, requêtes et plaintes adressées au roi d' Egypte au IIIᵉ s. avant J.C. (Cairo, 1931, 1932), 2 vols. Cf. the index of Greek words in vol. 2, pp. 274, 284, 286. Cf. the study by C. Spicq, "La Philanthropie hellénistique, vertu divine et royale," Studia Theologica, 12 (1958), pp. 169–191.

[126] For details, see E. Skard, Zwei religiös-politische Begriffe Euergetes-Concordia (Oslo, 1932), Acad. of Norway, Class Hist.-fil., no. 2., pp. 6–66. On the title Soter, see F. Dornseiff, Pauly-Wissowa, Reihe 2, Band 3 (Stuttgart, 1929), cols. 1211–1221, and G. Herzog-Hauser "Kaiserkult," ibid., Supplementband, 4, col. 810 seq.; F. Pfister, "Epiphanie," ibid., col. 306 seq.

[127] Joannes Stobaeus, Anthologium, IV, 7, 61 seq., loc. cit., 4, p. 263 seq.

[128] "The Political Philosophy of Hellenistic Kingship," Yale Classical Studies, 1 (1928), pp. 55–102.

[129] L. Delatte, Les Traités de la Royauté d'Ecphante, Diotogène et Sthénidas (Liège-Paris, 1942), Bibl. de la Faculté de Phil. et Lettres de l'Université de Liège, fasc. 97.

Archytas' treatise *On Law and Justice*.[130] This is his verdict about the law and the king: "Every community consists of the ruling element, the ruled, and a third element, the laws. Now, laws are of two kinds, the animate law (*empsychos nomos*), which is the king, and the inanimate, the written law. So, law is primary; for with reference to it, the king is lawful (*nomimos*), his rulership is fitting, the ruled are free, and the whole community is happy...."

The fragments attributed to Archytas are believed by A. Delatte[131] to be perhaps pre-Platonic or Pythagorean, but there are many reasons, especially those advanced by Theiler and Goodenough,[132] which incline us to take them, rather, as specimens of Hellenistic political thought, written anonymously, but attributed to the Pythagorean philosopher Archytas. The writer of the quoted fragment also uses the famous description by Plato and Aristotle of the perfect ruler, who in his opinion is more than an ideal legislator, for he himself is the law.

It would no doubt help the present inquiry and foster a better understanding of Hellenistic political philosophy if the fragment attributed to Archytas could be dated with greater accuracy; for if its pre-Platonic origin could be proved, it would indicate that the identification of the ruler with the law was already under discussion among Greek political thinkers at the Pythagorean period. In that case, the Pythagorean discussions and the descriptions by Plato and Aristotle of the superman who became law to his citizens would be but another instance of Persian influence on Greek political thought. One need only recall Xenophon's definition of the Persian king as the law personified;[133] a suggestive and sufficiently plausible similarity, since Persian influence was operative in other respects as well, especially in connection with the Greek notion of the monarchy.

[130] Joannes Stobaeus, *op. cit.*, IV, 1, 135, *loc. cit.*, p. 82 seq. The other fragment, *ibid*, IV, 5, 61, *loc. cit.*, p. 218 seq.

[131] A. Delatte, *Essai sur la politique pythagoricienne* (Paris, 1922), Bibl. de la Faculté de Phil. et Lettres de l'Université de Liège, fasc. 29, pp. 71–124, with French translation of the fragments.

[132] Cf. W. Theiler's review of Delatte's work in *Gnomon*, 2 (1926), pp. 147–156; E. R. Goodenough, *op. cit.*, p. 60 seq.

[133] *Cyropaedia*, VIII, 1, 22, ed. by W. Miller (Loeb, 1914), 2, p. 316, on Cyrus: τὸν δὲ ἀγαθὸν ἄρχοντα βλέποντα νόμον ἀνθρώποις ἐνόμισεν, ὅτι καὶ τάττειν ἱκανός ἐστι καὶ ὁρᾶν τὸν ἀτακτοῦντα καὶ κολάζειν.

HELLENISTIC POLITICAL PHILOSOPHY

This is a mere suggestion, as the Pythagorean origins of the fragments attributed to Archytas cannot be proved. It will be safer to look for the origin of this definition in the literature of classical Greece. Pindar[134] started the discussion in Greece of the function of the *nomos* (law), when he praised the law as *basileus* of all, living and dead. But already Euripides,[135] in describing the absolute power of a monarch, had said that in such a regime there "are no common laws, but one ruler, keeping the law in his private hands." One should also recall Plato's[136] observation on the ideal state: it would be governed by a wise man who was able to rule without laws.

Aristotle was more outspoken when he said that the ideal ruler would be like a god and that the best men ruling a state would not need written law because "they themselves are law."[137] In the *Nicomachean Ethics*[138] Aristotle came nearest the expression, though he employed the word *empsychos* in a different meaning.

In his treatise *On The Necessity for Kings to be Philosophers*, likewise only fragmentary, and preserved by Stobaeus,[139] the eclectic Stoic Musonius, who lived in the first century of our era, says explicitly, when using this definition of a king, that it was an ancient usage. After stating that the good king should as a ruler be sinless and perfect in word and deed, Musonius confirms his statement as follows: "Since he must be what the ancients called animate law, creating a law-abiding spirit and unanimity." This short clause incidentally proves that the concept of animate law as applied to kings must have been current in the first century of our

---

[134] Fragment 169, in J. E. Sandys ed., *The Odes* (Loeb, 1937), p. 604. See the short but thorough study on the meaning and history of Pindar's definition in Greek political thought by H. E. Stier, *Nomos Basileus* (Berlin, 1927).

[135] *Suppliants*, vs. 430 seq., ed. by A. S. Way (Loeb, 1930), 3, p. 534.

[136] *The Statesman*, 295, ed. by H. N. Fowler (Loeb, 1925), p. 136. Clement of Alexandria (*Stromata*, II, 4, 18, ed. by O. Stählin, GCS, 15 [1939], p. 122) says that Plato called the ideal statesman νόμος ἔμψυχος. Did he interpret the above passage, which does not contain these words, in this way?

[137] *Politics*, 1284 a, line 14, 1288 a, line 2, ed. by H. Rackham (Loeb, 1932), pp. 240, 270.

[138] V, 4, 7, *loc. cit.*, p. 276: ὁ γὰρ δικαστὴς βούλεται εἶναι οἶον δίκαιον ἔμψυχον. Cf. K. Oehler, "Thomas von Aquinas als Interpret der aristotelischen Ethik," *Philosophische Rundschau*, 5 (1957), pp. 135–152.

[139] *Op. cit.*, IV, 7, 67, *loc. cit.*, p. 279 seq. Cf. also O. Hense, *C. Musonii Rufi reliquiae* (Teubner, 1905), p. 37. On Musonius, cf. K. Praechter, *Die Philosophie des Altertums* (Berlin, 1926), p. 494 seq.

era and had been in use for a long time during the Hellenistic period. There does not appear to be any reason why Archytas' treatise should not be dated from the third, or from the end of the fourth, century B.C. The fragments reflect in many respects Pythagorean ideas and those of authors of the fourth century, namely Plato and Aristotle, and in all Archytas' fragments preserved by Stobaeus there is no trace of Stoic ideas or of Neopythagoreanism.[140]

Diotogenes is another author who may be quoted as using the words *empsychos nomos*, when characterizing the kingly office, in a way which suggests that it must have been familiar to his readers. Stobaeus[141] preserved a few fragments of Diotogenes' work *On Kingship* and there the following definition is given of a good king: "The most just man would be king, and the most lawful would be most just. For without justice no one would be king, and without law [there would be no] justice. For justice is in the law, and the law is the source of justice. But the king is animate law (*empsychos Nomos*) or is a legal ruler (*nomimos*). So for this reason he is most just and most lawful."

It is not difficult to trace in this statement the old Greek notion, familiar especially since Socrates, that the ruler must be a just man. Yet, it is also evident that Diotogenes has modified Aristotles' definition of the ideal ruler: "There can be no law to deal with such men...for they are a law unto themselves...." He goes further by saying that because the king, in virtue of his position, is himself the animate law and because justice is a product of law, therefore the king, who is law itself, must also, by the same token, be justice itself.

Diotogenes then describes the main functions of a king, following Aristotle in his description. The king is, at the same time, a general, a judge and a priest. The king must save the lives of his subjects; he is the *soter*. He must guide the state as a pilot steers his boat and the charioteer his chariot; he must care for his subjects as the physician cares for his patients. These titles are not Diotogenes'

[140] A. Delatte, *Essai sur la politique pythagoricienne*, p. 121 seq.
[141] *Op. cit.*, IV, 7, 61, *loc. cit.*, p. 263 seq. The translation quoted is by E. R. Goodenough, *op. cit.*, p. 65 seq.

invention,[142] but they became a commonplace in treatises on kingship. "The king is also the fashioner (*demiourgos*) of the organization of which he is the dictator."[143]

In giving judgement the king should act like god in his leadership and command of the universe. He must bring the whole kingdom into harmony with his leadership and benefit his subjects, thus becoming an *euergetes*. Because he is the best in the earthly realm, it is fitting that he should worship the best of all things—God. "The king bears the same relation to the state (*polis*) as God to the world; and the state is in the same ratio to the world as the king is to God. For the state, made as it is by the harmonizing of many different elements, is an imitation of the order and harmony of the world, while the king who has an absolute rulership, and is himself animate law, has been transformed into a deity among men."

This insistence on the imitation of God and the establishment of harmony among the subjects is an old Pythagorean idea, not unknown to Plato.[144] Diotogenes also used the comparison to a lyre and its harmonious sounds, another favorite Pythagorean simile. The author then describes how the king should behave. He should imitate the majesty of Zeus, be beneficent, inspire fear by his

[142] Aeschylus makes the comparison to a pilot, *The Seven against Thebes*, vss. 3, 62, 208, 652, ed. by H. N. Smyth (Loeb, 1938), 1, pp. 322, 326, 336, 374. Xenophon compares a king to a shepherd, surgeon, and pilot, *Memorabilia*, III, 3, 9, ed. by E. C. Marchant (Loeb, 1938), p. 180. Cf. also Plato, *The Statesman*, 298 C, 299 B, *loc. cit.*, pp. 148, 150; *Republic*, 551 C, ed. by P. Shorey (Loeb, 1935), 2, p. 264.

[143] Cf. Plato, *Gorgias*, 503 E, 504 A, ed. by W. R. M. Lamb (Loeb, 1939), pp. 454, 456. This is a clear allusion to the Pythagorean σύστημα, order, which is achieved by the collaboration of all δημιουργοί, craftsmen, who are building a house or a boat. A similar allusion to the world order, expressed in the succession of seasons and attributed to σοφία καὶ νοῦς, is to be found in *Philebus*, 30 C, ed. by H. N. Fowler (Loeb, 1925), p. 266.

[144] L. Delatte, *Les Traités*, p. 254, remarks rightly that Diotogenes here uses a comparison in a mathematical form which was used also by Archytas (Stobaeus, *op. cit.*, IV, 1 135, *loc. cit.*, p. 82, line 15), and by Plato, *Republic*, 508 C, 534 A, *loc. cit.*, pp. 102, 204. See *ibid.*, 591 C, D, *loc. cit.*, p. 410, as to how the wise man should "always be found attuning the harmonies of his body for the sake of the concord (ξυμφωνία) in his soul." In his *Laws*, 961 E, ed. by R. G. Bury (Loeb, 1926), 2, p. 542, Plato attributes the salvation of the city to the νοῦς of the ruler, using also the comparison with the νοῦς of the pilot, of the general, and of the surgeon. Diotogenes attributes this saving power to the king instead of to Plato's νοῦς. Cf. E. R. Goodenough, *op. cit.*, p. 67.

hatred of evil, be magnanimous, free from human passions,[145] and "draw himself up close to the gods, not in arrogance, but in high-mindedness and in the exceeding greatness of his virtue." If he acts in this way he will "affect the souls of those who see him no less than a flute or harmony." In general he should imitate Zeus the ruler of all things who is "awe-inspiring both by his pre-eminence and by the greatness of his virtues, gracious in his benefactions—father of gods and men."

Any attempt to date these writings more accurately is hampered by the fragmentary nature of their preservation. They do not seem, however, to contain anything which would force us to date them from the third century A.D., when Neopythagoreanism flourished.[146] Many points have been noted which link them with Plato and other political writers of the fourth century. It would perhaps be too daring, however, to suppose that they were written in the third century B.C., as W. W. Tarn suggested.[147] The cult of Poliorcetes could hardly have given such a stimulus to political thinkers as to inspire them to compose such a work. The fragments suggest, rather, a period in which the ruler cult was already well established in the Hellenistic kingdoms.

The emphasis on the imitation of god and on religious functions also supposes a more religious atmosphere than that of the fourth or third centuries. This atmosphere was being formed in the second century when the eastern mysteries started to penetrate among the Greeks. There are a few instances which suggest the era of the Hellenistic kings as the date of composition. The stressing of justice as the main function of the king recalls Antiochus I of Comagene who, most probably under Persian influence, called himself simply *Dikaios*. This title was also used by Parthian and Armenian kings in the Hellenistic period.

[145] This is a common feature in the recommendations given for a ruler by Plato, Aristotle, Xenophon, and Isocrates. Cf. L. Delatte, *op. cit.*, p. 256. If Diotogenes has in mind here the three parts of the soul, this does not mean that he is following the Neopythagoreans. He could have been inspired by Plato. Cf. *supra*, p. 182.

[146] Such is the opinion of L. Delatte, *op. cit.*, p. 282 seq.

[147] W. W. Tarn, *Alexander the Great and the Unity of Mankind*, Proceedings of the British Academy, (London, 1933) 19 p. 128.

HELLENISTIC POLITICAL PHILOSOPHY

In one instance there is even an echo of a phrase which seems to be of Pharaonic origin and appears in the Rosetta inscription of Ptolemy V.[148] The quality of εὐχάριστος, which, according to Diotogenes, should adorn the king,[149] must have been a commonplace in the Ptolemaic period; both Ptolemy V and Ptolemy VI are called Eucharistoi.[150]

There is yet another concept in Diotogenes' fragment which recalls the Hellenistic official court style, μισοπονηρία—hatred of evil.[151] This quality was ascribed to kings, and also sometimes to their officials, in so many inscriptions and papyri that it became a commonplace in official literature.[152]

Diotogenes' work is probably an attempt at a compromise between the official divinization of kings and the desire of the intellectuals to preserve a distance between kings, who are after all mortals, and gods. The author is evidently ready to go as far as possible to satisfy to the official creed in comparing the king with Zeus and in exalting his high position. "Just as God is the best of these things which are more honorable by nature, likewise the king is best in the earthly and human realm." But, in spite of all these eulogies the author does not break down the barrier between the divine and the human. Even when he says that the king as animate law has been transformed into a deity among men, he retains a certain reserve. When he says that the king is transformed into a divine being and that he transcends his subjects as god transcends his creatures, this still implies that god is above the king.[153] It is perhaps legitimate to see in this work

---

[148] Stobaeus, *op. cit.*, IV, 7, 61, *loc. cit.*, p. 264; καὶ μὰν τό τε δικασπολὲν καὶ διανέμεν τὸ δίκαιον. Cf. *OGIS*, no. 90, p. 154, line 3: ὁμοίως δὲ καὶ τὸ δίκαιον πᾶσιν ἀπένειμεν, καθάπερ Ἑρμῆς ὁ μέγας καὶ μέγας.

[149] Stobaeus, *op. cit.*, IV, 7, 62, *loc. cit.*, p. 269, line 12.

[150] *OGIS*, no. 90, pp. 147, 160, 161, 162, 165; no 92, p. 167; no. 94, p. 169; no. 97, p. 171 (Ptolemy V); no. 103, p. 180 no. 106, p. 184; no. 109, p. 188 (Ptolemy VI).

[151] Stobaeus, *op. cit.*, IV, 7, 62, *loc. cit.*, p. 267, line 9.

[152] See Schubart, *op. cit.*, p. 8: "Der Begriff, der in den Eingaben des Ptolemärstaates unendlich oft wiederkehrt"; a strange echo of the words in which Darius expressed his hatred of what is not right. Cf. *supra*, p. 102.

[153] L. Delatte, *Les Traités*, p. 255, rightly points this out, but his translation of this passage (p. 53), "le roi...figure Dieu parmi les hommes," is not exact. The words θεὸς ἐν ἀνθρώποις παρεσχημάτισται implies a stricter meaning than "figure Dieu."

the mild reaction of a Hellenistic thinker to the exaggerations of the ruler cult.

Taking all this into consideration, it seems reasonable to date this work in the second century B.C.[154] It originated most probably in Alexandria, the intellectual center of Ptolemaic Egypt.

Similar ideas appear in another fragment from a work on kingship attributed by Stobaeus to Sthenidas of Locri, a Pythagorean.[155] The fragment is, of course, not genuine. This is what the anonymous author says:

> The king must be a wise man, for so he will be a copy and imitator of the first God. For God is the first king and ruler by nature, while the other is so only by birth and imitation. The one rules in the entire universe, the other upon earth; and the one lives and rules all things forever and possesses wisdom (*sophia*) in himself, the other is temporal and has only understanding (*episteme*).[156] The king should imitate God by his generosity and mercy and by being like a father of his subjects. ... God is a supporter of all that is beautiful and a lawgiver to all. The king should also be such a leader. Without wisdom and understanding this cannot be achieved. Indeed, he who is both king and wise will be a lawful imitator and servant of God.

The distance between the divine and the kingly is kept intact in this fragment, even more clearly than in Diotogenes. The author did not call the king animate law, but when he says that the king should imitate God even as lawgiver, he is not far from the idea that the king is a law animate.

---

[154] L. Delatte, *ibid.*, in commenting on the fragments in question, is well aware that they echo Pythagorean, Platonic, and Aristotelian ideas. He often quotes them, but adds to these quotations passages taken from Neopythagorean writers and philosophers in order to prove that the fragments are of the second or third century A.D. The fragments in question reflect rather an intermediary period in the development of Hellenistic political philosophy, the works to which they belonged and prepared the terrain for the growth of ideas which blossomed during the third century A.D. in the works inspired by Neopythagorean philosophy.

[155] Stobaeus, *op. cit.*, IV, 7, 63, *loc. cit.*, p. 270 seq.

[156] Cf. Plato, *Laws*, 875 C, *loc. cit.*, p. 272: ἐπιστήμης γὰρ οὔτε νόμος οὔτε τάξις οὐδεμία κρείττων.

L. Delatte,[157] insisting on the fact that the author presents the king as a wise man, dates the fragment from the second Stoic period in the third century A.D. Goodenough,[158] however, rightly remarked that the "conception of imitating God is a bit of Pythagorean-Platonic mysticism which is essentially foreign to the nature of Stoicism" with its pantheistic ideas. That a wise man should be a ruler was a commonplace in the political literature of the fourth century. If there is any trace of Stoicism, it should be dated from the early Stoic period, before Poseidonius. This fragment, too, expresses ideas which were current in the second century B.C.

Another treatise on kingship, attributed by Stobaeus[159] to Ecphantus the Pythagorean, deserves study, though the fragments should be considered pseudonymous, since Ecphantus, a contemporary of Archytas, is supposed to have written in Attic Greek[159a] and the fragments are Doric.

This fragment first describes the harmony of the whirling universe, a doctrine which is characteristically Pythagorean and Platonic,[160] though Stoic ideas may possibly have inspired the author. He then proceeds to picture the universe as an agglomerate of worlds, each inhabited by citizens who are governed by the best of them, in representation of the deity. Here is what he says about the king:

> In our environment on the earth man has achieved the highest development, while it is the king who is most divine. He claims the lion's share of the better elements in our common nature. He is like the rest [of mankind], indeed in his earthly tabernacle, inasmuch as he is formed out of the same material; but he is fashioned by the supreme Artificer who, in making the king, used Himself as an archetype.[161] Accordingly, the king, as a

---

[157] *Les Traités*, p. 274 seq.

[158] *Op. cit.*, p. 74. He quotes also a paragraph from Stobaeus (*op. cit.*, II, 7, 3 f., *loc. cit.* 2, [1884], p. 49) stating: "Socrates and Plato agreed with Pythagoras that the end of life is to achieve a likeness to God."

[159] *Op. cit.*, IV, 7, 64–66, *loc. cit.*, 4, p. 271 seq.

[159a] Goodenough, *op. cit.*, p. 75.

[160] Cf. Plato, *The Statesman*, 269 C, *loc. cit.*, p. 50, where the whirling of the universe and its harmony is stressed.

[161] Cf. also another fragment attributed to Ecphantus, but differing from the fragment here quoted. It is found in Stobaeus, *op. cit.*, IV, 6, 22, *loc. cit.*,

copy of the higher king, is a single and unique creation, for he is on the one hand always intimate with the one who made him, while to his subjects he appears as though he were in a light, the light of royalty. For he is judged and approved by this light, as is the mightiest of winged creatures, the eagle, set face to face with the sun. Thus royalty is explained with the fact that by its divine character and excessive brilliance it is hard to behold, except for those who have a legitimate claim. For bastard usurpers are confuted by complete bedazzlement and by such vertigo as assails those who climb to a lofty height. But royalty is something with which people can live, if those who aspire to it are properly attuned to it and are able to use it. Royalty is, then, a sure and incorruptible thing, very hard for a human being to achieve by reason of its exceeding divinity.[162] ...And the one who lives in royalty ought to share in its immaculate nature and to understand how much more divine he is than the rest, and how much more divine than he are those other [the gods], to whom, by likening himself, he would do the best for himself and his subjects.

After declaring that the cosmic order should be taken as a pattern by both the king and his subjects, Ecphantus concludes this fragment: "So then I suppose that the earthly king can fall short in no particular of the virtue of the heavenly king; but just as the king is an alien and foreign thing which has come down from heaven to man, so anyone would suppose that his virtues were the work of God, and have become the king's through God.

Discussing further the king's relations with his subjects, Ecphantus declares the first and most necessary of all things for

4, p. 244 seq. L. Delatte, *op. cit.*, p. 177 seq., rightly points out that the idea of man's creation according to the image of God could have been suggested to Ecphantus by the Pythagorean Eurysus and by Timaeus or even by the narrative in Genesis. This is quite possible. But why should it be derived from Philo's interpretation? The Jewish doctrines were known in Alexandria in the second century B.C., as is testified by Aristeas' letter on the translation of the Hebrew Holy Books. Delatte himself admits that Ptolemy V is called "living image of God" (*OGIS*, vol. 1, no. 90, p. 142) and that, according to Plutarch (*Lives: Themistocles*, 27, 3, ed. by B. Perrin [Loeb, 1928], 2, p. 72), the Persian king was honored by his followers "as an image of God who saves everything."

[162] This recalls the Yashts praising the brilliance of the *Hvarena* which cannot be caught by a usurper. See *supra*, pp. 85–88.

"the human race to be the communion shared in by the king over men as well as by the master who rules all things in the universe...."
Only the perfect harmony existing between the king and his subjects can produce a common good, when the king has the same love for his subjects as God has for the universe and the things in it. And "there must exist complete good will, first, on the part of the king toward his subjects and, second, on the part of these toward the king, such as is felt by a father toward his son, by a shepherd toward his sheep, and by a law toward those who use it."

The value of the fragment lies in its demonstration of the debt of Hellenistic political philosophy to Oriental influence. Pseudo-Ecphantus' statements about the light of royalty, about the fashioning of the king by the supreme Artificer, and about the king being an alien and foreign entity that has come down from heaven are strongly reminiscent of Egyptian teaching which makes the king the image and son of the Sun, as well as of the Persian belief in the royal glory created by Ahura Mazda.[163] This latter surrounds the king like a halo of glory and justifies at the same time the king's legitimate claim, since that royal light was unobtainable by any upstart (Ecphantus uses the term bastard) in revolt.

At first, it would be difficult to say which influence, the Egyptian or the Persian, was uppermost in this Hellenistic representation of kingship; but the fact that Ecphantus describes the king as a copy of a higher being, as a unique and singular creation, an alien and foreign entity from Heaven on intimate terms with the One who made him, would recall the Egyptian concept of a ruler, particularly in the age of religious reform inaugurated by Amenhophis IV—Ikhnaton after 1375 B.C. This interesting experiment in Egypt's theological evolution was brought about by the imperial expansion of the Pharaohs who in the sixteenth century B.C. contrived to subjugate Asia and Africa and to found the first semblance of a universal empire. The inevitable consequence of this imperial

[163] Persian or Egyptian influence on this conception of Ecphantus is admitted also by L. Delatte, *op. cit.*, p. 202 seq. But why should the influence of Dion Chrysostom be preferable to Plutarch's conception of the luminous kingship (*ibid.*, p. 196 seq.) ?

universalism was a religious universalism which forced the local gods of Egypt to make room for the universal sun-god, not Amon-Re of the older dispensation, but Aton, an ancient Egptian name for the material sun, probably designating the solar disc.[164]

Beautiful hymns on the Sun-Aton were composed in Egypt at that period and discovered in the tombs of Tell el-Amarna. In one of these Ikhnaton and his wife, the beautiful Nefertiti, whose elegant bust is one of the treasures of the Berlin Museum, and whose picture is to be found in all books that treat of feminine beauty, are represented as having "come forth from his rays,"[165] emanating from the solar disc, and each is pictured as a hand.[166] This compares with Ecphantus' notion of a king as a "copy of a higher king," a "single and unique creation," "fashioned by the supreme Artificer," "an alien thing coming from Heaven." But even if this parallelism is accepted, it does not yet prove Egyptian influence on the Hellenistic concept of kingship, for it is not yet established whence Ikhnaton drew the inspiration for his religious reform. He may possibly have derived it from Asia which was then a part of the Egyptian Empire,[167] in which case Egypt's new political doctrine would have been borrowed from the Asiatic solar religion and therefore would have been rather Asiatic in its origin.

In any case, it should be remembered that the great religious and intellectual movement initiated by the young and sympathetic Pharaoh did not survive his reign. Many people in Egypt—the powerful priestly class, the artisans, and others—with their vested interests, were too much for him, so that his attempt at introducing a monotheistic creed into Egypt remained an isolated incident. Tutenkhamon, one of Ikhnaton's successors, restored Amon-Re and the old Egyptian cult.

[164] For further particulars, see the impressive chapter on the imperial age and monotheism in J. H. Breasted, *A History of Egypt* (New York, 1912), pp. 355–378.

[165] J. H. Breasted, *op. cit.*, p. 370.

[166] A. Moret, *Du caractère religieux de la royauté pharaonique* (Paris, 1902), p. 46. See the representations of Ikhnaton in A. Erman and H. Ranke, *Aegypten und ägyptisches Leben im Altertum* (Tübingen, 1923), pp. 135, 220.

[167] F. Cumont, *Astrology and Religion Among the Greeks and the Romans* (New York, 1912), p. 75 seq. It is possible that this theological Pharaoh was prompted by the Semites' star-worship to impose his reform on the Egyptian clergy.

Even if the Egyptian origin of Ikhnaton's reform is accepted, it is still possible that the new solar cult, despite its failure in Egypt, had come to stay in Asia, and reacted thence on Hellenistic and even Roman political philosophy.[168] There must have been some solar mysticism in Hellenistic ideas about kingship: it is well known that Hellenistic kings were often depicted on their coins with rays, evidently representing sunbeams, encircling their heads. It may also be that the solar mysticism implied in Pseudo-Ecphantus' description of the king was borrowed from the Asiatic solar and stellar worship.

Though some Pharaonic titles, especially those connected with the sun-god, came to the Ptolemies from ancient Egypt, all this sun symbolism was not therefore necessarily Egyptian. Rather is this some curious mixture of Asiatic, Egyptian, and Persian elements, the last of which must have been decisive, since the Pseudo-Ecphantus identifies the king with the law, i.e., the animate law, which was the basic notion of Hellenistic political thought. It is obvious that Pseudo-Ecphantus' solar radiation that shines upon the king is only a replica of the Persian *Hvarena* or kingly glory, the creation of Ahura-Mazda and the exclusive possession of kings.

Another instance of Oriental reaction on Hellenistic ideas of kingship as embodied in the Pseudo-Ecphantus fragments would be provided by the legend of the royal eagle compelling his young to stare at the sun. This was a favorite topic with Greek writers, chiefly Aristotle[169] and Lucian,[170] and it is recorded that only those eaglets which could gaze into the sun without their eyes watering were considered worth rearing by the parent eagles, the others being rejected as bastards. However familiar it was in Greece, the legend must have been of Oriental origin, for it was in Syria and in Egypt that the eagle was associated with the sun-god;[171] and the testing

[168] J. H. Breasted, *Development of Religion and Thought in Ancient Egypt* (New York, 1912), attributes the origin of the cult of the Roman emperor as *Sol Invictus* to Asiatic rather than to Egyptian influence.

[169] *Historia animalium*, IX, 34, 5, in *Aristotelis opera*, ed. by I. Bekker (Oxford, 1837), 4, p. 335.

[170] *Icaromenippus*, 14, ed. by A. M. Harmon (Loeb, 1929), 2, p. 290. On the eagle, cf. E. Oder, "Adler," Pauly-Wissowa, 1 (Stuttgart, 1894), col. 371 seq., esp. col. 374 on the Oriental origin of the eagle symbolism in royal art.

[171] O. Keller, *Thiere des classischen Alterthums* (Innsbruck, 1887), pp. 268, 447.

of the eaglets was associated with the royal dignity on the coins of Tigranes I, king of Armenia (*ca.* 140–55 B.C.).[172] This seems sufficient to establish the Asiatic character of this eagle symbolism.

One fragment in Pseudo-Ecphantus' treatise on kingship explains how the Hellenistic political philosophers visualized the king's moral role in relation to his subjects. Rulers should not base their rulership on force, reward, or punishment, but on the free will of their subjects, and these should be given every opportunity to see that the king is better and wiser than they are themselves. In illustration of this principle, which again is not only Platonic[173] and Aristotelian[174] but also, judging from Xenophon's account,[175] Persian, Pseudo-Ecphantus introduces the notion of Logos, a generative principle of Stoic philosophy, and applies it to the Logos of the king or to his relationship with God and his own kingly wisdom and virtue. Just as the divine Logos works on inert material and transforms it into animal and human life, so the king works on human minds through his Logos—an image of God reflecting his own kingly virtues—and awakens their better potentialities and transforms them into better beings. Men will thus imitate the king just as the king imitates God, and eventually they will live freely and spontaneously, without compulsion, in accordance with the divine law, and have no need for written codes of law to keep them on the right path of virtue.

The notion is not as new as it would seem. This insistence on the imitation of God by the king, recalls a passage in Plato's *Alcibiades*.[176] The first condition for becoming a good leader is to know oneself, says Plato. If the soul wants to know itself, it should consider another soul, like a mirror, and focus its eye on that part of the soul where its best faculty resides, that is the intelligence, and on any other part of a soul which resembles this. No other part

[172] Cf. E. R. Goodenough, *op. cit.*, p. 83; B. V. Head, *Historia numorum*, p. 772.
[173] *The Statesman*, 276 E, *loc. cit.*, p. 74.
[174] *Politics*, 1285 a, ed. by H. Rackham (Loeb, 1932), p. 250.
[175] *Cyropaedia*, I, 1, 5, ed. by W. Miller (Loeb, 1914), I, p. 8.
[176] *Alcibiades I*, 133 A–D, ed. by W. R. M. Lamb (Loeb, 1927), p. 210 seq. Cf. K. Oehler, *Die Lehre vom noetischen und dianoetischen Denken bei Plato und Aristoteles* (Munich, 1962).

of the soul can be called more divine than this, which is the seat of knowledge and thought. This part of the soul resembles God, and whoever looks at it and comes to know all that is divine will gain thereby the best knowledge of himself.

Eusebius[177] and Stobaeus[178] add to this passage the following: "Doubtlessly, because the true mirrors are clearer, purer, and more luminous than the mirror of the eye, so is God purer and more luminous than the best part of our soul...therefore we should regard God. He is the best mirror of human things for anybody who wants to know the quality of the soul and it is in Him that we can better see and know ourselves."

This additional passage is regarded by many editors of Plato's works as an interpolation, but its authenticity found a defender in P. Friedländer.[179] If it was added to the original, it was certainly done long before Eusebius, perhaps in the second century B.C. Many imitations of Plato's writings were composed in the second century, including probably the second treatise on Alcibiades which is certainly not genuine.

One fragment attributed to Diotogenes[180] gives a similar description of the kingly appearance, the virtues a king should display in order "to tune up the law-abiding city like a lyre, knowing well that the harmony of the multitude, whose leadership God has given him, ought to be attuned to himself." He concludes the description of the majesty and sublimity of the virtuous king: "So will he succeed in putting into order those who look upon him, amazed at his majesty, at his self-control and his fitness for distinction. For to look upon the good king ought to affect the souls of those who see him no less than a flute or harmony."

As a third instance of such a notion of kingship the pseudo-Aristotelian "Letter to Alexander," which is used as an introduction to the *De rhetorica ad Alexandrum*, may be quoted.[181] It is now acknowledged that in its present form this letter is the altered and

---

[177] *Praeparatio Evangelica*, XI, 27, 5, ed. by K. Mras, GCS, 43 (1956), p. 59.
[178] *Op. cit.*, III, 21, 24, *loc. cit.*, 3 (1894), p. 575.
[179] *Der grosse Alkibiades, ein Weg zu Plato*, 2 (Bonn, 1923), p. 14 seq.
[180] Stobaeus, *op. cit.*, IV, 7, 62, *loc. cit.*, 4, p. 266 seq.
[181] See the English translation by E. S. Forster, in W. D. Ross, *The Works of Aristotle Translated into English*, 11 (Oxford, 1924), and the edition and translation by H. Rackham (Loeb, 1937), pp. 266–274.

interpolated original prelude to the Rhetoric written not by Aristotle but by Anaximenes (*ca*. 380–320 B.C.),[182] with alterations on the subject of kingship introduced to adapt it to Hellenistic taste. One such alteration may be singled out as being particularly relevant. The anonymous interpolator addresses Alexander as follows:[183] "Again, you must realize that the model set before men is either the law, or else your life and your logos. In order, therefore, that you may excel all Greeks and barbarians, you must exert yourself to the utmost, so that those who spend their lives in these pursuits [which means, probably, those who make your life and logos their guide], using the elements of virtue in them to produce a beauteous copy of the model thus set before them, may not direct themselves towards ignoble ends, but make it their desire to partake in the same virtue."

When all this is taken into consideration, there seems to be nothing in Pseudo-Ecphantus' fragments which would exclude the possibility that the work was written during the second century B.C.,[184] perhaps about the same time as the Letter of Pseudo-Aristeas.

---

[182] Cf. E. R. Goodenough, *op. cit.*, p. 91 seq.; ed. by H. Rackham, *loc. cit.*, p. 260. E. S. Forster (*loc. cit.*, preface) attributes the work to "a Peripatetic writer contemporaneous with Theophrastus."

[183] Forster's translation, 1420 b, *loc. cit.*

[184] In order to show that the Pseudo-Diotogenes and Pseudo-Ecphantus' fragments were written in the third, or at the earliest in the second century A.D., L. Delatte made an extensive study of their dialect and vocabulary (*op. cit.*, pp. 59–119). He concludes from his research that the authors had used a variety of Dorian dialects mixing them with other Greek dialects. It is an artificial language used in order to give to their works an archaic and exotic character. This could have happened also in the second century B.C., especially if the authors were writing in Alexandria where the pure Dorian dialect was hardly used at that period. On pp. 94–104, L. Delatte studies Hellenistic linguistic elements in the treatises, coming to the conclusion that such words were common in writings from the second century A.D. on. When, however, the use of those words is compared with the vocabulary of Polybius, the linguistic material contained in *OGIS* and in F. Preisigke's *Wörterbuch der griechischen Papyrusurkunden* (Berlin, 1925–1931), 3 vols., it is found that only the word ἐπιπρεπής used by Diotogenes cannot be traced in documents previous to Lucian of Samosata. The word συνεκτικός appears in Plutarch and συνακτικός in Philodemus (110–40 or 35 B.C.) All other words can be traced in classical writers, in Polybius or the documents contained in *OGIS*, or in the papyrus material, if not in the same form, at least in a similar form and sense. Because Hellenistic literature is but fragmentarily preserved, the failure to find these three words in works before the Birth of Christ cannot be regarded as proof that these fragments could not have been written in the second century B.C.

The author built his conception of kingship on the basis laid down by Plato, Xenophon, and Aristotle, which he adapted to the new developments in political history. He is bolder than Diotogenes and enriched his conception with ideas of the first Stoic generation.[184a]

Some of the principles expounded by the authors of these fragments may be compared with another treatise on kingship which is hidden in the so-called Letter of Pseudo-Aristeas. This tells the legendary story of the translation of the Jewish Holy Scriptures into Greek by seventy-two Jewish Elders, on the invitation of Ptolemy II. This legendary account of the origin of the Septuagint is dated by its latest editor, M. Hadas,[185] shortly after 132 B.C. About one-third of the work, is however, an account of questions which King Ptolemy II asked the translators at seven banquets offered to them and of their answers. It is a common opinion among specialists that this part (sections 187 to 292) is a Hellenistic treatise on kingship which is of older date. This section contains nothing especially Jewish. It was written by a Hellenized Jew who wanted to demonstrate the great esteem which the great King Ptolemy II had for

[184a] Holger Thesleff has recently devoted a thorough study to the problems concerning the dating of the fragments on kingship in his work, *An Introduction to the Pythagorean Writings of the Hellenistic Period*, Acta Academiae Aboensis, Humaniora, 24, 3 (Abo, 1961). On pp. 65–75 he rightly rejects L. Delatte's late dating of the writings on kingship. Against Delatte's affirmation that the language used by the authors is a mixture of dialects which shows that the texts were written at a time when the Doric dialect was no longer spoken, Thesleff shows that the language is essentially Attic or *Koiné* with a strong Doric coloring. He rightly points out that Ecphantus could not have used Philo. "Some of the expositions of Philon and Ekphantos ultimately derive from the same source [p. 70]." He is inclined to date the texts in the middle of the third century B.C., that of Archytas in the middle or end of the fourth. He is of the opinion that, with the exception of Archytas, they were composed in Southern Italy. He thinks (p. 72 seq.) that "they were on the whole intended as philosophical propaganda for laymen, or as textbooks in philosophy."

[185] M. Hadas, *Aristeas to Philocrates (Letter of Aristeas)* (New York, 1951), p. 54. In his long introduction (pp. 1–90) the editor and translator reviews all that has so far been written on this document and gives a complete bibliography. W. W. Tarn, *The Greeks in Bactria and India* (Cambridge, 1938; 2nd. ed., 1951), p. 415, accepts the date *ca.* 100 B.C. Hadas' date is, however, to be preferred on the basis of the research by E. Bickermann, "Zur Datierung des Pseudo-Aristeas," *ZNW*, 29 (1930), pp. 280–298, who shows that the letter was most probably written between 145–127 B.C. Cf. D. W. Gooding, "Aristeas and Septuagint Origins: A Review of Recent Studies," *VT*, 13 (1963), pp. 357–379.

the Jews. The author of the Letter of Pseudo-Aristeas simply included this treatise in his account of the origin of the Septuagint, adding only two more questions and a few remarks on the presence of Greek philosophers (200–202, 235) at the discussions. He did this in order to show that the Jewish Elders were equal to the Greeks in philosophical lore because of their religion. For this purpose he made a stereotyped reference to God at the end of each answer. Every answer is, however, perfectly logical and understandable without this addition.

This treatise on kingship seems to have been written during the reign of Ptolemy III (247–222 B.C.).[186] Most of the principles expressed in Hellenistic documents and in the fragments preserved by Stobaeus are also at least alluded to in Pseudo-Aristeas. The imitation of God's gentleness is recommended by the first Elder to the King if he wants to preserve his kingdom unimpaired to the end (188, also 254). The essential quality of the kingship demands incorruptible justice (209, 212) to all men (189), impartiality to all in speech, humane action toward offenders (191, 208), and, above all "to rule oneself well, and not to be carried away by wealth and fame into unseemly and extravagant desires" (211). This latter kingly virtue is stressed in the answer of another elder (222, 223) to the question what is the highest rule: "To rule oneself and not to be carried away with passions. In the temper of all men there is some innate proclivity. In the majority it is likely that the cant is toward food and drink and pleasure, while for kings it is acquisition of territory and extent of fame. Yet in all things moderation is a good principle."

The king should be virtuous (272) and should not forget "that it is God who apportions fame and great wealth to all kings, and that no one is king by his own power" (224). Kings should take "the guidance of the laws, so that by just dealing they may repair the lives of men" (279). The king should also be a philosopher (256) who is "not carried away by impulses, but ponders the injuries which are the outcome of the passions, and performs the duties of

[186] W. W. Tarn, *The Greeks in Bactria and India*, pp. 426–427. Answer 252 recommends the king to judge petitions justly. It was only in the third century that petitions from his subjects could reach the Egyptian king. In the second century they were examined by special officials without reaching the king. This is Tarn's main argument for his dating of the treatise.

the moment properly, with emotions moderated." He has thus to "express his philosophy in his actions" (285). The king is exhorted to appoint righteous officers (280) and courageous commanders who, however, are "more concerned to save their men than to win a victory by reckless disregard for life." He should also keep an official record of his journeys and read the treatises on kingship (283). This is a new confirmation of the existence of a literature on kingship in the Hellenistic period.

How should the king treat his subjects? He should attract his subjects by benefactions, in order that they should be well disposed (*eunoia*) toward him (205). The king has to show his *eunoia* and benevolence toward all men (225). This *eunoia* of the subjects toward the king and of the king toward the subjects is stressed again and again (225, 230, 264, 265, 270).[187] Not only should the king be the *euergetes* of his subjects (249), but also *philanthropos epieikes* (gentle) (208, 265, 290). The king's role as savior (*soter*) is clearly alluded to (240, 292). He will fulfil it in applying justice and hating evil.

As a wise man, the king should "be conscious of no wrongdoing, and lead his life in sincerity" (260); he should act gently toward his good subjects and toward offenders (207), injure no man, help all men, and follow righteousness (232). He should show his *philotimia* (liberality) not only to those who are amicably disposed toward him, but also to those of an opposite disposition, in order to "win them to what is right and advantageous to themselves" (226, 227).

The author was also familiar with the comparison of the king's office to that of the pilot of a ship when he said: "Life is steered truly when the pilot knows to what haven he must set his course" (251). A faint allusion to this can also be read in 292 (δικαίως δὲ πάντα κυβερνῶν).

In the definitions of the king's role some influences are to be found of the early Stoa. When answering the questions, "how is fearlessness attained" and how is "right reason" (ὀρθὸς λόγος) acquired,

---

187 Cf. Pseudo-Ecphantus, in Stobaeus, *op. cit.*, IV, 7, 64, *loc. cit.*, 4, p. 276; ed. by L. Delatte, *op. cit.*, p. 32: ὅλαν δὲ τὰν εὔνοιαν χρὴ παρασκευάζεσθαι πρᾶτον μὲν παρὰ τῶ βασιλέως ἐς τὼς βασιλευομένως, δεύτερον δὲ παρὰ τῶνδε ἐς τὸν βασιλέα. Also, *ibid.*, IV, 7, 65, (Wachsmuth-Hense, 4, p. 278, Delatte, p. 34): χωρὶς εὐνοίας γὰρ ἀμάχανον ἐξομοιωθῆναι.

the Elders seem to have in mind the Stoic principle that when one is conscious of having done no evil, any external happenings and misfortunes are to be ignored as unimportant (293, 244). The following answer to the King's question as to how to avoid turning to ease or pleasure (245) echoes Stoic ideas on kingship (which the Macedonian King Antigonus Gonatas (277–239 B.C.) had tried to realize): "By being always aware that he is ruler of a large kingdom and leader of great multitudes, and that his mind must not be occupied with anything else, but think always of the care of these charges."

Stoic influence seems to appear also in the advice that the king should become "everybody's equal" (257, 283) and in the recommendation of humility (263). The request that the generals should respect human life (281) also echoes Stoic ideas. A Cynic-Stoic principle is expressed in the answer that the noblest by nature should be set over the people as king (288).[188]

Two expressions used by the author of the treatise reveal that he wrote during the Ptolemaic period. In speaking of the distribution of justice by the king (τὸ δίκαιον) he uses words similar to those of Diotogenes and to those found also on a Ptolemaic inscription.[189] When urging the king to hate evil, he uses, like Diotogenes, the word μισοπονηρία, which is a commonplace in Ptolemaic inscriptions.[190]

Upon reading the references to God added by Pseudo-Aristeas to the answers of the Elders it is impressive to see the way in which the author stresses God's care in governing the world and the king's obligation to imitate God. It is possible that the first exhortation to the imitation of God (188) was in the original treatise, but the others were added by the author in the second century B.C. Some of these may be quoted because they recall the prominent place which Pseudo-Diotogenes and Pseudo-Ecphantus attributed to God's action in the world which the king must imitate.

[188] This has been pointed out by M. Hadas in his commentary on the quoted sections.

[189] Cf. *supra*, p. 251, Pseudo-Aristeas, 212: εἰ τὸ δίκαιον ἐπὶ παντὸς προβάλλοι; 215: οὐδὲ ἐξουσίᾳ χρώμενος τὸ δίκαιον αἴρεις; 291: κομίζεσθαι τὸ δίκαιον ταχέως ἐν ταῖς διακρίσεσι; cf. also 280: τὰ δίκαια πράσσουσι (M. Hadas, *op. cit.*, pp. 182, 184, 214, 210).

[190] See *supra*, p. 251.

God is the *euergetes* of "the human race, providing them with health and food and all other things in due season" (190). God's methods in dealing with men, which the king must adopt, are gentle. He fulfills those of their petitions which are good for them and reveals to them in dreams the harmfulness of petitions which he does not fulfill. In spite of his majesty, he uses forbearance toward men (192). "God also by granting reprieves and displaying His sovereign power, implants awe into every mind" (194). "God rules all things, and in our fairest achievements it is not we ourselves who accomplish our intentions, but God in His sovereignty who consummates and guides the actions of us all" (195). The king should be beneficent because "God is the author of blessings to all men and His example must be followed" (205, 210). The king should be gentle and merciful because "God deals with all men with gentleness" (207) and is merciful (208). The king should honor justice because God is a lover of righteousness (209). "God governs the whole world with kindliness and without passion; His example Your Majesty must follow" (254). "For just as God benefits all men, so do you, in emulation of Him, benefit those subject to you" (281).

Some of these expressions recall vividly what Pseudo-Ecphantus says about God's government of the world and about the king's *mimesis* of God's government and virtues. Oriental influence is evident in Ecphantus' ideas on kingship, as has been shown. It is quite possible that even some Jewish notions had inspired him. In the second century B.C. this could easily have happened.

Oriental influences seem also to have deepened Ecphantus' conception of the *soter* idea. As has been shown, the Greeks seem to have had their own soteriological ideas, which had little in common with the messianic notions current in the East, since a number of Olympian gods, especially Zeus, Apollo, and Asclepius, were invoked as *Soteres*. Hermes, Poseidon, Pan, Serapis, and the Dioscuri were called saviors and some goddesses, such as Artemis, Athena, Nike, and Tyche enjoyed similar invocations.[191] Obviously, the sense of

[191] See, for details, F. Dornseiff, "Σωτήρ" in Pauly-Wissowa, Reihe 2, Band 3 (Stuttgart, 1929), cols. 1211–1221, and P. Wendland, "Σωτήρ," *ZNW*, 5 (1904), pp. 335–353.

those invocations was not messianic: the Greeks invoked their gods as *Soteres* because they expected to be delivered from evil and to secure their assistance in distress. Alexander was never regarded or venerated as *Soter*. The numberless *soter* titles that adorned the Hellenistic kings had a similar meaning to the *soter* title given to gods, without any Oriental messianic implication.

The influence of Oriental mysteries with messianic tones helped, however, to give a more profound meaning to the kingly *soter* title. Pseudo-Ecphantus seems to have been among the political thinkers who succumbed to the spell of the new Oriental ideas. In this new atmosphere even the titles *Euergetes* and *Epiphanes* started to acquire a more profound meaning.

It should be emphasized that other Greek and Hellenistic royal titles were also gaining deeper significance in the new Oriental atmosphere which was increasingly pervading the life of the Greek subjects of the Hellenistic kings. The title shepherd has been shown to have been given to the kings in Homeric times. It appears again and again in the Hellenistic period and it is legitimate to think that the use of this title by Babylonian, Assyrian, and Persian kings contributed to its dissemination and popularity. In the East it was often connected with the notion of a just king. A few examples will illustrate this fact.

This title is almost a commonplace, for example, in the inscriptions of the Sumerian king Gudea. Gudea is chosen by the god Ningirsu to be a good shepherd; he is "the shepherd chosen by the heart of Ningirsu."[192] He is addressed as shepherd, as good shepherd, and refers to himself: "I am the good shepherd." The same inscription bestows upon him the following praise: "The good shepherd Gudea was full of science and acted with great dignity."[193] Lugalzaggisi prays to remain forever "the shepherd who is the head."[194] Addahushu is called the shepherd of the people of Susa, shepherd of the god Shushinak.[195] Many other kings of the Sumerian period

[192] Cf. F. Thureau-Dangin, *Les inscriptions de Sumer et d'Akkad* (Paris, 1905), pp. 107, 119 (Statue B, col. II; Statue D, col. 1).
[193] *Ibid.*, pp. 141, 149, 157, 167, 169 (Cylinder A, cols. V [shepherd of the goddess Nina], XI, XVI, XXIV, XXV); pp. 177, 189 (Cylinder B, cols. II, XIII).
[194] *Ibid.*, p. 221 (vase fragment, col. III).
[195] *Ibid.*, p. 261 (brick and vase are used alternately).

pride themselves on being good shepherds of their people:[196] all of which proves the immense popularity of this royal title in the oldest epoch of Assyro-Babylonian history, the so-called Sumerian period. Judging from Hammurabi's inscriptions especially, as well as from other documents where he is called the shepherd of nations, the shepherd who brings salvation, and who received the shepherd's crook from Marduk,[197] the tradition must have been inherited by the Babylonian kings. It is the same tradition as can be traced during the period of the Assyrian and neo-Babylonian kings from Salmanassar[198] down to Sennacherib.[199] The use of the shepherd title can even be followed as far as Egypt,[200] where, however, its usage did not seem to be as widespread as in Babylonia, and where it seems to have been of foreign origin.[201] This should suffice to show how popular the title was throughout the East. The Persians apparently derived it from the Babylonians and in this again Greek political philosophy may have been influenced by the Persians from whom Plato,[202] who

[196] For instance, Gimilsin (*ibid.*, p. 287); Urninib, Pûrsin, Lipit-Ishtar (*ibid.*, p. 291); Sinmagir (*ibid.*, p. 293); Sinidinnam (*ibid.*, p. 297); Aradsin (*ibid.*, pp. 301, 305); Rimsin (*ibid.*, pp. 307, 311).

[197] For particulars, see T. W. King, *Letters and Inscriptions of Hammurabi* (London, 1898), vol. 2, p. 182 seq.; V. Scheil, *Textes élamites-sémitiques, deuxième série*, Ministère de l'Instruction Publique et des Beaux-Arts, Délégation en Perse, Mémoires, 4 (Paris, 1902), pp. 14, 118 (Code des Lois de Hammurabi, *recto*, col. I, line 51; *verso*, col. XXIV, line 43).

[198] L. Messerschmidt and O. Schroeder, *Keilschrifttexte aus Assur historischen Inhalts*, Wissenschaftliche Veröffentlichungen der Deutschen Orient-Gesellschaft, 16, 37 (Leipzig, 1911, 1922), vol. 1, nos. 13, 16, vol. 2, nos. 49, 59, 60.

[199] D. D. Luckenbill, *Annals of Sennacherib* (Chicago, 1924), pp. 23, 48, 55, 85, 117: Sennacherib is praised as "the wise shepherd," the "prayerful shepherd," "the pious shepherd," "the shepherd of nations." Cf. also A. Jeremias, *Handuch der altorientalischen Geisteskultur* (Leipzig, 1913), pp. 179 (Merodachbaladan), 221 (Leyden papyrus), 226. The whole problem was studied in detail and for the first time by L. Dürr, *Ursprung und Ausbau der israelitisch-jüdischen Heilandserwartung* (Berlin, 1925), pp. 116–124; and its importance in the evolution of Oriental political philosophy was best grasped by E. R. Goodenough, "Kingship in Early Israel," *Journal of Biblical Literature*, 48 (1929), p. 172 seq.

[200] For details, see L. Dürr, *op. cit.*, p. 120 seq.

[201] Cf. A. Erman and H. Ranke, *Aegypten und ägyptisches Leben im Altertum*, p. 73. Observe, however, what he says on p. 525, note 4: "The custom of calling the king the good shepherd who shepherds his people cannot be traced beyond the era of the New Empire (18th–20th dynasties, about 1580–1100 B.C.), and is probably of foreign origin. It corresponds to the ideal of nomadic tribes, not to that of a settled peasantry."

[202] *The Statesman*, 265 D, 268 A, *loc. cit.*, pp. 34, 44.

uses the metaphor, may have borrowed it. Xenophon, at any rate, was not the only one to know of it and of its popularity in the East, especially in Persia.

The conception of a just king seems to go back to the Sumerian period. Gudea's city was resplendent with justice and became similar to the sun-god.[203] The founder of the dynasty of Ur, Ur-Engur, takes pride in the institution of righteous laws which he promulgated under the guidance of the sun-god.[204] Dungi, his successor, is made to address the following prayer to the sun-god in a hymn composed in his honor after his divinization: "May the Sun-god place justice and righteousness in my mouth—the judge, maker of decisions, who rules the country; who makes justice exceedingly good."[205] Sinidinnam of Larsa is called "shepherd of justice who satisfied the heart of the Sun-god and of Tammuz."[206] Hammurabi, the author of the first known code of laws, declared in the prologue to the Code that he had received the law from the sun-god Shamash. On the bas-relief of the stele containing the Code, Hammurabi pictures himself in the attitude of adoration before Shamash, the source of the law which he had codified.[207] Shamash was regarded as the embodiment of the very concept of law and justice, as one gathers from some hymns composed in his honor.[208]

There exists one ancient hymn in particular which celebrates the stream of justice as brought forth by the gods and by them endowed with might, fire, wrath, splendor, and terror, and concludes with the apostrophe: "Thou judgest the cause of mankind. Mighty stream!

[203] Cylinder B, col. XVIII, 1–14, F. Thureau-Dangin, *op. cit.*, p. 113.

[204] See S. Langdon, *Sumerian Liturgical Texts* (Philadelphia, 1917), p. 126. The inscription, a clay peg from Lagash, was published by F. Thureau-Dangin, *Die sumerischen und akkadischen Königsinschriften*, Vorderasiatische Bibliothek, 1, Abt. 1 (Leipzig, 1907), p. 188, i, 1, line 15. See *idem, Les inscriptions de Sumer et d'Akkad*, p. 267.

[205] S. Langdon, *op. cit.*, p. 147.

[206] B. Meissner, *Babylonien und Assyrien*, 1 (Heidelberg, 1920), p. 149. The inscription was published by F. Thureau-Dangin, *Die sumerischen und akkadischen Königsinschriften*, p. 208, clay peg A, 2, lines 12–15.

[207] Code, *recto*, col. I, lines 28–49; cf. col. V, lines 1–25, in V. Scheil, Code des Lois de Hammurabi, *op. cit.*, pp. 14, 22.

[208] See A. Schmollmeyer, *Sumerisch-babylonische Hymnen und Gebete an Šamaš*, Studien zur Geschichte u. Kultur des Altertums, 1. Ergänzungsband (Paderborn, 1912), esp. nos. 5, 6, 9, 17, 25.

Exalted stream! Righteous stream!"[209] Evidently extolled by the poet as the stream of creation and justice, it reminds one forcibly of the Persian *Hvarena*, the royal glory, also depicted as created by God, reserved to kings who through the radiance of this stream become the law incarnate, the only source of justice in the realm.[210] The instances quoted are significant and indicative of a tradition in Babylonian religious and political life which goes back to the oldest period and can be traced through every age. It can therefore be concluded with some assurance that the Persian doctrine of *Hvarena* and of the kings as law incarnate took this evolution one stage further as the logical derivation from the doctrine that was part of the political philosophy of the ancient East and was mainly expanded by the Babylonians. This makes it all the more interesting to find in Plato's and Aristotle's writings political thought similar to that which was present in the earliest stages of Babylonian history and which culminated in the political philosophy of the Hellenistic period.

It is truly regrettable that the Hellenistic literature of political philosophy should survive in only a few fragments, although these do give us all the essentials of the notion of kingship as it developed in the Hellenistic period after Alexander the Great had promoted the divinization of kings into a principle. In addition to these fragments, this survey might be completed with an analysis of the ideas on kingship to be found in the works of Plutarch (*ca.* 46–120 A.D.), a late Platonist and author of the first century A.D. He read works on Alexander which were subsequently lost and he was acquainted with the political literature, not only of the fourth century B.C. but also of the whole Hellenistic period. He visited

---

[209] L. W. King, *The Seven Tablets of Creation*, Luzac's Semitic Text and Translation Series, 12, 1 (1902), pp. 128 seq. 200 seq.

[210] We may point out another parallel between this Babylonian Holy Stream and the Persian *Hvarena*. The hymn attributes the creation of all things to this Righteous Stream ("Oh Stream, Thou who createdst all things when the great gods dug thee out..."). The Zend-Avesta praises *Hvarena* not only as the source of law, but also as the creative energy by which Ahura Mazda created all things (Yast XIX, 10, in J. Darmesteter, *The Zend-Avesta*, pt. 2, The Sacred Books of the East, ed. by F. Müller, 23 [Oxford, 1883], p. 290). The Persians seem to have followed the Babylonians in this particular, too.

both Rome and Alexandria, but, being a continental Greek, he did not come as strongly under the influence of the Oriental trend in Hellenistic civilization as did his compatriots in Alexandria.

Plutarch's interest in political philosophy is manifested by the several treatises dealing with political problems to be found amongst his *Moralia*. The most relevant, as it best reveals what the author thought of kingship, is the short treatise—again only a fragment—entitled *To an Uneducated Ruler*.[211] As in others of his writings, Plutarch depends even here upon earlier writers for most of what he says on the ideal king; it will not be difficult to discover strong echoes of his reading of Hellenistic treatises on political ideas.

Plutarch starts with the notion of the king's Logos, which, according to him, consists in better knowledge or reason, implanted in the ruler by philosophy to act as his guardian and associate on the throne. Rulers are not usually very fond of their Logos, for by increasing their knowledge it might hamper their power to rule and cramp their action. They are in consequence not always open to advice. But this is not reasonable, since the Logos removes only what is dangerous in kingly power and leaves what is healthy and beneficial. The king of Sparta understood this so well that he limited his own power in the state by adding the ephors to his governmental system, convinced that by so doing he would minimize the danger of envy inherent in absolutism. But many rulers fail to understand this, and however much they try to impress people, can be likened to statues that are made to look impressive with all their heroic and divine trappings, but are stuffed inside with stones and sand.

The genuine ruler must first practice self-discipline and conform his life to high moral principles: nothing else will stimulate his subjects to righteousness. He should not follow other princes, least of all the Persian kings, who pretend that they are subject to no one; even the king is subject to law. Pindar had already said that

[211] It was again E. R. Goodenough who drew expert attention to this treatise, for parts of which he gives an excellent translation ("The Political Philosophy of Hellenistic Kingship," pp. 94–98)—which we have used occasionally—with a good commentary. See also a new edition and translation by H. N. Fowler, *Moralia: To an Uneducated Ruler*, 779–782 (Loeb, 1936), 10, pp. 52–70.

the law was king of all, whether living or dead; and even the Persian kings charged a servant to wake them every morning with the words: "Arise, O King, and take care of those things of which Ahura-Mazda has put you in charge." The law that rules over kings, however, is not the written, but the animate law, the Logos[212] "which dwells within him, protects him, and never for a moment leaves his soul without guidance."

Rulers are ministers of God, appointed for the purpose of fostering the well-being of men, and the distributors of the goods which the gods give them. The good things provided by nature and the sun cannot be enjoyed without law, justice, and the ruler, since justice is the purpose of the law and law is the handiwork of the ruler. The ruler is the image of God, who directs everything: hence, the ruler has no need of the art of Phidias, nor of Polycletus, nor of Myron. He makes himself alike to God by his virtue and thereby moulds himself into a being that is fair to behold and worthy of the Godhead. And just as God placed the sun, his resplendent image, and the moon in his heaven, so also stands the ruler in the city, God's likeness and effulgence, "when he dispenses God-like justice;"[213] and such also he is when he possesses intelligence, the Logos of God, not by virtue of his sceptre, or of thunderbolt, or trident, with which some of them have had themselves sculptured or painted thereby making their folly invidious to the Unattainable One. For God visits with nemesis those who copy his thunder and lightning and the radiation of sunbeams, whereas he takes his delight in enriching those who desire his virtue and wish to make themselves like unto him with beauty and love for mankind; and he shares with them the fine order, justice, truth, and mercy which surround him. Not fire, not light, nor the course of the sun, nor the rising and setting of the stars; no, not even eternity and immortality are more divine than these. For God is not made happy by reason of the duration of his life, but by the fact that he is a ruler of virtue. Such is true divinity, and to be ruled by virtue is a beautiful thing, too.

It is not true to say that whatever the king does is *ipso facto* right, and Anaxarchus who taught this was wrong. The king must

---

[212] Ἀλλ' ἔμψυχος ὢν ἐν αὐτῷ λόγος, *ibid*, 780 C.
[213] Homer, *Odyssey*, XIX, vss. 109, 111.

follow Zeus who himself is right and justice. Finally, after citing instances of rulers good and bad, Plutarch describes God presiding over nature whose changes cannot affect him and concludes: "And just as the sun in Heaven, surpassingly beautiful image of His, reveals His likeness in its reflection of Him to those who thus can see Him,[214] so He has created in the State the refulgence of high justice and of His attendant Logos, like a picture which those who have been blessed by philosophy with the gift of self-control can copy if they wish to shape themselves into the fairest of beings. But such a condition is realized by nothing else than the Logos, the fruit of philosophy."

Whoever follows the path traced by philosophy, receives a share in this royal spirit, but, as Plutarch shows by the example of Diogenes and Alexander the Great, none but the king can reach the highest step of royalty. Though Alexander almost envied Diogenes for his practice of philosophy, it must be remembered that, having more difficulties to face than the philosopher, Alexander could become greater even than Diogenes in that respect, whereas his failure would have been more serious than that of the average man. It is no easy task, and the greater the king, the more he needs the guidance of his Logos. His reasoning power must balance his power of authority and in this he must imitate the sun who reduces speed, insuring safety, as he ascends to greater heights. Unworthy kings are soon overthrown by the same Tyche who raised them to prominence. The dazzling light makes them dizzy. As leaky vases cannot hold water, unworthy kings cannot hold power but waste it through their sins.

It is easy to see that Plutarch's notions of kingship are in all essentials identical to the description we found in the most important Hellenistic fragments, those of Diotogenes, and even more of Ecphantus: an animate law which is identified with the prince; a law which is of his making; a prince who is the image of God and who by perfect imitation of Him must induce his subjects to be the same; and the better his knowledge or his Logos, the greater his likeness to God. There is notable progress in the concept

---

[214] Here Plutarch came under the spell of Oriental sun symbolism, but he is much more reticent than Pseudo-Ecphantus.

of the animate law which Plutarch identifies with the Logos, for he has the king become an incarnation of the universal law, which the Greeks considered divine, and, as such, he is an incarnate representation of the Logos.

Another characteristic of Plutarch's theory is that, in his opinion, whoever is guided by reason may to some extent be considered to represent animate law or the Logos, though the king, if guided by philosophy, incarnates it in the highest degree. This view recalls that of Ecphantus on the redeeming action of the king's good example. Plutarch lays greater stress on the principle that the king must be guided by his Logos which will attain mastery over the king's mind only by dint of philosophical training. This was also a Stoic ideal, which may have influenced him.

The frequent references to the sun as the most beautiful image of God, and the similes of divine radiation in the state as applied to the king also point to the popularity of sun symbolism in the Hellenistic period and its contribution to the theory of kingship.

It should be noted, too, that Plutarch twice specifically mentions the example of the Persian kings, which seems to point to the influence of Persian political thought on the Greek conception of animate law and its identification with the king. It would seem that even in Plutarch's time there was a certain consciousness of the dependence of these concepts upon Persian political thought.

An important conclusion remaining to be drawn from Plutarch's declarations is that, judging from the treatise quoted, this late Platonist placed kings very near to God: they had to possess the Logos or intelligence of God. They were to the state what God is to nature; they were the incarnation of law which in Greek opinion came from God. Yet nowhere is there one straightforward statement on the ruler's divinity. Instead, we find a spirited denunciation of those Hellenistic kings who cover their statues with trappings of heroic or divine significance and usurp symbols generally attributed to gods: sceptres, thunderbolts, tridents, or clusters of sunbeams.

This is not Plutarch's only reflection on the cult of divinized rulers, for similar remonstrations are to be found in his *Life of*

Alexander. For instance, after quoting some of Alexander's skeptical remarks about his own divine nature, the author concludes: "Consequently, judging from what has been said, Alexander himself was obviously in no wise convinced of, or blinded by, any belief in his divinity, but it helped him to enslave others."[215]

At times, when writing about the apotheosis of kings and their mimicry of the gods and their cult, Plutarch becomes almost sarcastic. For example, in his treatise *How to tell a Flatterer from a Friend*, he concludes in derision:[216] "Is not almost every king called Apollo, if he hums a tune? Dionysus, if he gets drunk? and Heracles, if he wrestles?" In his *On the Fortune or Virtue of Alexander* he has some hard things to say about the glamorous titles and claims of the Hellenistic kings:[217] "Some called themselves Benefactors (*Euergetes*), others Glorious Conquerors (*Callinicous*), others Saviors (*Soteres*) and others The Great (*Megalous*), but no-one could exhaust the list of the promiscuous marriages of those who, like horses, spent all their time among herds of women, their paederasty, their beating of timbrels among eunuchs, their perpetual dicing, their flute playing in theatres, their nights spent in banquets and their days in revels." In his *Isis and Osiris*, speaking of Antigonus the Elder, Plutarch says:[218] "When a certain Hermodotus in a poem proclaimed him to be the 'offspring of the Sun and a god,' [Antigonus] said: 'the slave who attends to my chamber-pot is not conscious of any such thing!'" In his essay on *How a Man may praise Himself without being Envied*, he singled out for praise those kings who showed no interest in their deification:[219] "Some who had no wish to be called gods or sons of gods, but Philadelphos, or Philometor, or Euergetes, or Theophilos, were not angered when people addressed them by those splendid but human titles." In *Romulus*, he is even more explicit on the subject:[220]

> We should therefore in no wise, in defiance of nature, send the bodies of good men to heaven, but firmly believe that in

[215] *Lives: Alexander*, 28, 3, ed. by B. Perrin (Loeb, 1919), 7, p. 308.
[216] *Moralia*, 56 F, ed. by F. C. Babbit (Loeb, 1927), 1, p. 302.
[217] *Moralia: Fortuna Alex.*, 338 C, *loc. cit.* (1936), 4, p. 448.
[218] *Moralia*, 360 D, *loc. cit.* (1936), 5, p. 58.
[219] *Moralia*, 543 D, E, ed. by P. H. de Lacy and B. Einarson, *loc. cit.* (1959), 7, p. 140.
[220] *Lives: Romulus*, 28, 8, *loc. cit.* (1928), 1, p. 182.

accordance with nature, their virtues and their souls raise them from the condition of men to that of heroes, from that of heroes to that of *daimones*, and that once they have been completely cleansed and purified as by the rite of initiation and have escaped from all that is mortal and subject to feeling, then, not by any law of the city, but with truth and right reason, they rise from the condition of *daimones* to that of gods and reach the fairest and most blessed consummation.

This passage is directly aimed at the many divine honors which cities used to decree to celebrate their rulers, and if read in context, it gives the impression that, according to Plutarch, no official declaration could turn a ruler into a god: only by a virtuous life and his imitation of God could a ruler deserve to be associated with divinity; then after a long process of purification his soul could reach its destiny. This is a very reasonable and sober compromise on divinized kingship, and it is interesting to note that the rites of initiation—the mysteries—which in Plutarch's days invaded the Roman Empire from the East, proved helpful to the philosophers of the first century A.D. in discovering this golden mean.

There are many other instances of this late Platonist's skepticism in matters of royal deification and cult,[221] and his attitude[222] is certainly of interest. Even if Plutarch's dislike of Nero and disgust for his vices, his flaunting of divine symbols, and his allowing himself to be placed in the pantheon may have warped his judgement, there is still more to that judgment than the mere private opinion of an intellectual of the later ruler-cult period. It

[221] Cf., for these and other quotations and particulars, Kenneth Scott, "Plutarch and the Ruler Cult," *Transactions and Proceedings of the American Philological Association*, 60 (1929), pp. 117–135.

[222] A similar attitude to the divine character of kings may be observed among the Scholiastes of Homer (Scholia II, A340, ed. by G. Dindorf, *Scholia Graeca in Homeri Iliadem* [Oxford, 1877], 3, p. 55). Homer, as can be read there, had already placed the king between gods and men, lower than the gods, but higher than men. Porphyry in his commentary on Homer (A.D. 243–*ca.* 304) is alleged to have written: "The Pythagoreans placed beside the godly and human kind a third venerable kind, the king or the wise man. Homer was the first to place kings between gods and men and to honor them by making them wise." At the end is a curious postscript which associates the notion of kingship described above with Indian political philosophy: "There is a saying that among the Hindus the Brahmans, who are their philosophers, on approaching kings, venerate them with the proskynesis."

should be emphasized that the descriptions of the kings' divine nature in the fragments of the early Hellenistic period are not invariably as clear as might be expected. Diotogenes and Ecphantus, for all they have to say about the divine character of the kings, the incarnate law, yet fight shy of raising them to the level of gods. This betrays the secret of the practice. The educated classes of the Hellenistic period apparently did not take the kings' divine claims very seriously and the kings themselves, though they made the claim, seldom really believed that they were gods. The general disbelief in the Olympian religion among intellectuals, the low esteem in which the gods of past ages were held, and the muddled notions that prevailed about the divinity of those Olympian gods (who were sometimes believed to have had mortal mothers, as was the case with Apollo and Dionysus, the most popular gods of the Hellenistic pantheon) were really responsible for the spread of the practice of apotheosis. It had little to do with genuine religious feelings; political reasons were paramount in the introduction of this new "religion," if such a term can be used. Divinization gave the kings a good hold in the Greek cities; it gave legal stability to the realm, since laws promulgated by divine kings could not be abrogated, and it proved a useful method for holding together the motley nations, whose racial character and political and cultural past often had nothing in common, under their rule. The myth gave the nation the necessary cohesion.

It should be noted once again that the idea of the king as animate law lay at the center of the whole system. Once the king was admitted to be law incarnate and therefore the only source of law in society, he became the essence of the state and in a way the state itself. The Hellenistic age must have been quite conscious of this, as nothing else can explain why the Hellenistic kings were so often called creators (Ktistes) of the state: No state could exist without law and justice and they were the only source of the law. The old Greek belief in the divine origin of the law lent the theory a certain mystical background which intellectuals, who had their own opinion on divinity in general, could respect. It was this concept which provided Hellenistic politico-philosophical speculation with a solid framework that stood up to the attacks of the most skeptical critics. It was also the most important contribution made by the Hellenistic age to political thought of all ages: a contribution which found favor with the Romans, was passed on to, and transformed by, the Jews and the Eastern Christians, and finally reappeared in a different shape in the West, where it left its mark on the political thought of the Middle Ages and occupied the political stage from the Renaissance to modern times.

CHAPTER SIX

Jewish Political Philosophy and the Messianic Idea

Moses and the Judges — Origin of the kingship; ceremonial of Saul's elevation — "Royal psalms," Egyptian and Babylonian parallels — The king a priest? — Foreign elements in Israelite kingship — The "kingly law" in Deuteronomy — The Messianic idea within the monarchic period — The Minor Prophets: kings and Messiah — Isaiah and Jeremiah on kingship and the Messiah — Ezekiel, forerunner of priestly rule — Deutero-Isaiah on the universal character of the messianic kingdom — Collapse of post-exilic national hopes; Zechariah on the growth of spiritual power over temporal — Jahweh's kingship — The Messiah's reign — The Suffering Servant of God — The last Prophets — Dangers of Hellenism — The Hasmonaean national state; Sadducees and Pharisees — Hellenistic political ideas in Jewish post-exilic Wisdom literature — Reaction in the apocalyptic literature, Enoch on the Messiah — Daniel — Sadducees and Pharisees on the Messiah — The Book of Jubilees written by a Sadducee or a member of the Qumran sect? — Belief in two Messiahs in Qumran Scrolls and the Testaments of the Twelve Patriarchs? — Herod and the Romans — Messianic kingdom in Solomon's Psalms — Final stage.

The concept of royalty as defined by Hellenistic political philosophers has been seen to convey a lofty picture of the ideal king as the incarnation and source of all law and justice: benefactor, savior, shepherd and father of his people, a manifestation of God's greatness to men, a faithful replica of God's virtue which by its example drew men nearer to God. This sublime conception of royalty was designed to offset the danger which always besets the concentration of absolute power in the hands of a single man, while the king's divinization made such concentration bearable and acceptable to his subjects.

Although this conception was based on Greek principles already defined by Plato, Aristotle, and other Greek thinkers, the older notions of the Babylonians, Persians, and Egyptians affected the growth of this politico-philosophical system. Since Judaism was the precursor of Christianity, the ideas of the Jews on kingship should next be studied in order to ascertain whether the Israelite concept of royalty borrowed notions from early Oriental peoples, to what extent Jewish political ideas were a genuine Jewish product, and, finally, how deeply they were influenced by other nations of the Middle East with which Israel was in daily contact. Once these questions have been answered, it can be established whether Hellenistic political philosophy had any influence on the growth of Jewish political and religious thought during the last three centuries before Christ. Since there were many Jews in countries where Hellenistic culture was predominant and since the influence of the Hellenistic world was far from negligible even in Palestine, it is valid to ask whether any attempts were made amongst the Jews to adapt Hellenistic political thought to their creed. The question is important, for if it can be answered in the affirmative, the task of the first Christian political thinkers must have been greatly facilitated. Not until it is answered shall we be able adequately to understand Christ's words—the basis for Christian political thought— and to fathom the early Christians' attitude toward the political problems of their day.

It is essential, therefore, to discover the component elements of Hebrew political philosophy and to trace their background in the history of Israel. Such an inquiry will be directly relevant to the problem under discussion. This should not lead us to neglect another aspect of Jewish royalty which was operative in Israel since the dawn of its history and became even more pronounced after the kings had vanished from the national stage—the royalty of the promised Saviour, whose expected arrival on earth fills the writings of the best Jewish thinkers. Though not directly affecting Jewish political philosophy, it had some bearing on the growth of political thought among the early Christians in the East. They daily fed their thoughts on the prophecies of the coming Saviour and tried to draw from these prophecies, as well as from Our Lord's words on the nature of His own kingship, a more graphic picture of the better kingdom which the Saviour had founded and which was to last for all eternity. Such speculations on the coming kingdom prompted Jews and Christians alike to frame a number of hypotheses that, rightly or wrongly, exercised a marked influence on the growth of Eastern political philosophy, which their study should clarify and complete.

The materials for this period are not abundant, but inquiries into kingship in early Israel have been facilitated once more by E. R. Goodenough.[1] In one short essay he has moved far ahead of previous interpreters of the Old Testament. First of all, the Israelites shared with other nations the conviction that God revealed His law to only one man, who thereby stood out as a sort of embodiment of the Lord's Law. So much results from the history of Moses. He was at first the only lawgiver and judge of his people. But when the task proved too much for him, he took the advice of his father-in-law, the practical-minded Jethro, and appointed judges familiar with his legislation to arbitrate all minor cases, reserving the more difficult ones for himself (Exod. 18: 13–27). This was the starting point of Hebrew political ideology and it is to be noted that lawgiving was the primary function of the first leader of Israel.

Philo, the famous Jewish philosophical and political writer of the Hellenistic period and a contemporary of the Founder of Christianity, saw evidence that Moses was a Jewish *nomos empsychos*.[2] Philo was clearly projecting into this early period notions that were current in his own time, and on such evidence it would be difficult to build a solid theory. Yet, it may be that Egyptian precedent had something to do with it. The writer of the history of Moses must

---

[1] "Kingship in Early Israel," *JBL*, 48 (1929), pp. 169–205. The same problem is treated from different angles by the following authors: W. Caspari, *Thronbesteigung und Thronfolge der israelitischen Könige*, Altorientalische Texte und Untersuchungen, 1, Heft 3 (Leiden, 1917); K. Galling, *Die israelitische Staatsverfassung in ihrer vorderorientalischen Umwelt*, Der Alte Orient, 28, Heft 3 (Leipzig, 1929). Useful remarks on the subject can be found in H. Gressmann *Der Messias* (Göttingen, 1929), pp. 2–63. See also J. Hempel, *Politische Absicht und politische Wirkung im biblischen Schrifttum*, Der Alte Orient, 38, Heft 1 (Leipzig, 1938), M. Buber, *Königtum Gottes*, 3rd ed. (Heidelberg, 1956), and especially J. De Fraine, *L'aspect religieux de la royauté israélite* (Rome, 1954), p. 74 seq.; A. R. Johnson, *Sacral Kingship in Ancient Israel* (Cardiff, 1955); idem, "Hebrew Conceptions of Kingship," *Myth, Ritual and Kingship*, ed. by S. H. Hooke (Oxford, 1958), pp. 204–235. Cf. also J. Pedersen, *Israel, Its Life and Culture*, 2 (London-Copenhagen, 1940) pp. 33–106. Recently K. H. Bernhardt, *Das Problem der altorientalischen Königsideologie im Alten Testament* (Leiden, 1961), Suppl. to *VT*, vol. 8, with complete bibliography.

[2] See *infra*, Chapter Eight.

have been familiar with Egyptian ideas of kingship; it is possible that in relating Moses' life story, he selected features that were likely to raise the great Jewish hero to the level of the Pharaohs. The story of Moses' upbringing at Pharaoh's court, his apprenticeship as a shepherd, perhaps also his rescue from a stream, often symbolized the wisdom that was to pervade the future king's body and soul.[3] Equally significant is the fact that Moses is called (in Exod. 7:1) "the God of Pharaoh" and Aaron, his brother, "thy prophet." We should of course beware of exaggeration: that Philo should explain Moses' story in his own sophisticated way is no argument that the original writer of Moses' life should have done the same. It is only too easy to read history backward and attribute to earlier periods political ideas which took subsequent centuries to come into being.

What is characteristic, none the less, is that the first Hebrew leader is exclusively portrayed as a lawgiver, so much so that when Jahweh gives His approval to the institution of the judges, He is made to say that He will take a portion of the legislative power (spirit) He gave to Moses and share it among the judges (Num. 11:11-25). A similar idea is found in the history of Moses' successor, Joshua (Josh. 3:7; 6:27).

Marked progress in Hebrew political thought was made during the period of the judges, the transitional stage between a nomadic life based on tribal organization and the beginnings of the national monarchy. The tribal framework still prevailed and the nomadic spirit, so averse to centralized power and so fond of unlimited political freedom, still possessed the hearts of the Hebrews. Their only ruler and king was Jahweh and whenever a national emergency called for a strong authority, emphasis was always laid on the judges' having been inspired by Jahweh to go forth and act in His name. But the personal qualities of the chosen leaders were be-

---

[3] Cf. Goodenough, *op. cit.*, p. 179. He is perhaps too emphatic on the point and more caution would seem advisable. The legend of the birth of Sargon may be noted as the model of a mythical tradition on the childhood of a famous ruler. See O. Weber, *Die Literatur der Babylonier und Assyrer*, Der Alte Orient, Ergänzungsband, 2 (Leipzig, 1907), p. 206. The similarity between the Sargon legend and the history of Moses is indeed interesting, but the motifs of the child's exposure in a basket lined with pitch and set adrift on the river are not identical in both cases.

coming ever more important; it is surprising how many Hebrew rulers—Othoniel, Ehud, Gideon, Tola, Samson (Judg. 3: 9–11, 15; 8:22 seq; 10:12; 13:5)—are called saviors of the nation on the grounds that, through their instrumentality, Jahweh saved His people from the enemy. There is *a priori* nothing eschatological or messianic about the designation of this *soter* title.

Though the judges did not by far enjoy the same social pre-eminence or wield the same political power as the kings and chief-tains of the Canaanites with whom the Jews came into contact, three similarities with their kingly functions are particularly evident: First, the office of the judge was a gift from Jahweh—close asso-ciation between kingship and divinity was at the root of all political philosophy in the East. Second, the main function of the judge was to dispense justice to his people and to be their military leader and "savior," as was the case with all Oriental kings. Finally, only harmonious association with Jahweh can guarantee a successful rule: The moment a judge breaks the covenant with Jahweh, he loses His support and his own functions. This latter characteristic has its parallel in some Oriental ideas which, as has been shown, were represented in their final stage of development by the Persian doctrine of *Hvarena*—a state which was liable to be forfeited by grievous sin.

At this period, foreign influences can already be discerned creep-ing into the ideological world of Israel to transform and complete its political institutions. Gideon's son Abimelech, who was looked upon as a usurper for having taken over his father's function not by the will of Jahweh but by violence, having slain his seventy brothers, allowed himself to be anointed (Judg. 9:8, "the trees went to anoint a king") near the sacred oak tree (Judg. 9:6).

Anointment can be regarded as an imitation of a Canaanite rite. The anointing of a Canaanite "king" by his Egyptian overlord Thutmose III (about 1447 B.C.)[4] is mentioned in the famous Amarna letters. The Israelites may have learned this practice from them, though the custom of anointing seems to have been familiar to

---

See *supra*, p. 58; cf. Hittiterite, p. 53. Cf. A. Bertholet, *A History of Hebrew Civilisation*, trans. by A. K. Dallas (London, 1926), pp. 113, 244.

their forefathers. Jacob is known to have consecrated the stone of Bethel by anointing it with oil. The origin of the custom is not clear. It may have been a common Semitic practice. It was also familiar to the Assyrians and to the Egyptians, although so far no text is known which includes anointing in the enthronement ritual of the Pharaohs.[5] It is, however, possible that anointment did form part of that complicated ceremonial, symbolizing the inviolability and sacrosanctity of the person concerned.[6]

The very performance of the rite near a stone pillar under an oak tree must be in imitation of a foreign practice,[7] though at a later stage of Israelite kingship both conditions became part of the ceremonial of royal enthronement. This can be inferred from the description of the enthronement of Joash, grandson of Ahaziah, who escaped the massacre of his family ordered by Athaliah. Acting on Jahweh's instruction, the priest Jehoiada, who had saved Joash, produced the boy in the temple where he had concealed him, "put the crown upon him and gave him the testimony, and they made him king and anointed him; and they clapped their hands and said, 'Long live the king'" (II Kings 11:5 seq.; cf. II Chron. 23:3 seq.). When she heard the noise, Athaliah came to the temple, and "she looked and behold the king stood by the pillar as the manner was, and the captains and trumpets by the king."[8] This is the

[5] Cf. W. Spiegelberg, "Die Symbolik des Salbens bei den Ägyptern," *Archiv für Religionswissenschaft*, 9 (1906), p. 144. There are apparently some indications in Egyptian documents suggesting anointment as part of the investiture of officials. See also J. Wellhausen, "Zwei Rechtsriten bei den Hebräern," *ibid.*, 7 (1904), p. 33 seq., and K. Vollers' reply, "Die Symbolik des Mash in den semitischen Sprachen, *ibid.*, 8 (1905), p. 97 seq. H. Gressmann, *Der Ursprung der israelitisch-jüdischen Eschatologie* (Göttingen, 1905), p. 258, points out that the anointing of the gods' statues was an important part of the daily dressing rite performed by the priests. See also *idem, Der Messias*, p. 5. W. Robertson Smith (*Lectures on the Religion of the Semites* [London, 1894], p. 383) may be nearest to the solution of the problem in deriving the anointing from the custom of the Semites and other nomads of rubbing the altars with the fat of the sacrificed animals.

[6] Cf. David's behavior when he learned about the killing of Samuel (I Sam. 24:7, 11; 26:9, 11, 23; II Sam. 1:14, 16. The cursing of a king was put on a par with the cursing of God (I Kings 21:10, 13; cf. Exod. 22:27; II Sam. 19:22; Prov. 24:21). The anointment was regarded as endowing the king with Jahweh's spirit. Cf. I Sam. 16:13; Judg. 14:6, 19.

[7] See J. G. Frazer, *Lectures on the Early History of the Kingship* (London-New York, 1905), p. 198 seq.

[8] In I Kings 7: 20–22 two pillars in the porch of the Temple are described. One is called Jachin which means "he will establish" and the other one Booz

only account extant of the enthronement of a Hebrew king in the later period, but it may be presumed that on other occasions, enthronements were performed in a similar manner. It is interesting that all the main features, such as the anointing and the adorning with crown and bracelet, which were introduced into the Hebrew ceremonial at that early period, probably under foreign influence, should have remained customary in later history.[9]

That Abimelech should have tried to set up a sort of monarchical regime in his mother's tribe in the hope of extending his own authority, proves that the idea of a monarchic system was making some progress among the Hebrews. The tendency may have arisen under his father Gideon, whose rule was firmer and more personal than that of other judges. But opposition to a monarchic regime was still very pronounced in Abimelech's days, as illustrated by the parable of Jotham (who escaped the fate of his murdered brothers) and of the trees that clamored for a king to rule over them but could find none to accept their offer—excepting only the bramble (Judg. 9 : 7-15).

There are also allusions in Saul's history to the existence of other Semitic influences that were absorbed by the Israelites in order to expand their own notions of kingship: the anointing of Saul by Samuel, the latter's prophecy that Saul would meet at the oak tree of Tabor three men who would give him two loaves of bread and that he would be filled with the spirit of Jahweh on joining a band of prophets (I Sam. 10:3-5). There is also the fact, strongly emphasized, that Saul overshadowed all the Israelites by his commanding appearance. Saul's eating of the loaves is said by Goodenough[10] to be a reflection of the Egyptian and Babylonian tradi-

which means "strength resides in him." The names symbolized the role of the king who may have stood between the two pillars during the coronation. Cf. J. Pedersen, *op. cit.*, p. 243.

[9] R. Patai in his study "Hebrew Installation Rites," *Hebrew Union College Annual*, 20 (1947), pp. 143-225, tried to reconstruct the Hebrew installation ritual on the pattern of African coronation rituals. The attempt, although interesting in its originality, cannot be accepted as successful. His interpretation of Saul's elevation on the pattern of African rites is especially strange, the author trying desperately to read into the simple scriptural account more than can be accepted in order to bring it closer to some African installation rites. His attempt was rightly rejected by J. De Fraine, *op. cit.*, pp. 198 seq., 210 seq., 278 seq., 332 seq.

[10] Goodenough, *op. cit.*, p. 186.

tion picturing the king as taking specific nourishment provided by the gods. This explanation cannot, however, be accepted. The loaves were rather a tribute to the king.[11] The necessity for kings to be filled with a godly spirit and to be conspicuous by their commanding stature, so much emphasized by the Babylonians, found its place in the account of Saul's ascent to the throne. He also was to be the savior of his nation from the pressure of its enemies (I Sam. 10:1).

In the account of Saul's election to royal dignity there seems to be a curious contradiction which obscures the history of monarchic rule in Israel.[12] It is first stated that the elders of Israel presented to Samuel their request for a king only because his sons did not walk in his footsteps, but turned aside after lucre, took bribes and perverted judgement (I Sam. 8 : 3, 4). The request displeased Samuel, so the account goes on, but surprisingly enough, the Lord is made to tell him (verse 7): "Hearken unto the voice of the people in all that they say unto thee: for they have not rejected thee, but they have rejected me that I should not be king over them" (cf. also I Sam. 10:19). Samuel is, however, ordered by the Lord "to protest solemnly unto them...and shew them the manner of the king that shall reign over them" (verse 9). He then enumerates all the evils that will befall Israel under monarchic rule. Such evils could hardly have been known to the Israelites at that time, unless Samuel were familiar with the Oriental monarchies of Egypt and Babylon with which the Israelites had only indirect contact in his days. The afflictions came upon the Jews at a much later period, when the Hebrew monarchy had been safely established by Solomon after the model of other Oriental monarchies.

Then there occurs the statement (I Sam. 9:16, 17) which makes the institution of the monarchy perfectly consonant with the Lord's designs for His people: "I will send thee a man out of the land of Benjamin, and thou shalt anoint him to be prince over my people Israel: for I have looked upon my people, because their cry is come unto me." Then after the account of the Ammonites' defeat

---

[11] See H. P. Smith, *A Critical and Exegetical Commentary on the Books of Samuel* (Edinburgh, 1951), p. 68.

[12] See, for details and bibliography, J. De Fraine, *op. cit.*, p. 89 seq.

by Saul, Samuel is made to deliver a long speech to his people and
again to rebuke the Israelites for having rejected the Lord in
preference to their own king (I Sam. 12:12 seq.). The Lord will
help them only as long as they and their king will observe His
commandments.

It is no wonder that so many specialists see in this confused account
the combination of two versions, the older one presenting the
institution of the Hebrew monarchy as an offshoot of natural
political growth which answered the needs of the Jews and tallied
with Jahweh's designs for the welfare of His people, and the later
addition made at a time when theocratic concepts permeated the
political mentality of Israel. The interpolator, according to this
hypothesis, looked upon the institution of the Hebrew monarchy as
something evil which amounted to no less than the dethronement
of Jahweh and a trespassing on the exclusive right of government
which the Lord had reserved to Himself. The insertion seemed all
the more plausible as there may have been in the original account
traces of the opposition which the introduction of a monarchic
regime must have provoked among tribes that had but recently
renounced their nomadic manner of living.

There occurs in the account of Saul's selection for the throne a
passage which seems to offer the best summary of what the Hebrews
thought of kingship. After the lengthy speech in which the prophet
tried to dissuade his people from their demand for a king, I Sam.
8:19, 20 continues: "But the people refused to hearken unto the
voice of Samuel; and they said, Nay, but we will have a king over
us; that we also may be like all the nations; and that our king may
judge us, and go out before us, and fight our battles."

It is true that the evils of a centralized monarchy as described
by the prophet in the above-quoted passage forcibly foreshadow
the unfortunate experience the Hebrews had later under their kings
as a result of the imitation of their neighbors' monarchic institutions. This is the very reason why many experts believe the passage
to be a post-Deuteronomic addition to the primitive and simple narrative. But even with this supposition, which remains hypothetical,
it is possible that the people's reaction was already present in the
first version, which at the very least is a straighforward account of

the people's desire for a king and tallies with verse 5 of the same chapter, where the crowd asks Samuel to "make us a king to judge us like other nations." The words, in this case, constitute a clear definition of early Hebrew kingship.

Two salient notions belong to the idea of the kingly office: law-giving, together with dispensation of justice, and the military protection of the nation. At the same time, the above passage makes it plain that the Hebrews adopted a monarchy under foreign influence: the words "that we also may be like all the nations..." shows this. In spite of that[13] the institution of the Israelite monarchy presents features which differ radically from the numerous small monarchies of its neighbors. It is not a usurpation by a strong personality. The wish of the people preceded its foundation, but the will of Jahweh was decisive.[14] It was Jahweh who chose the king and this choice was accepted and ratified by the people.

In the following period, Israelite political philosophy grew richer in ideas, and foreign, especially Babylonian, influences became more pronounced. And yet, even at that stage, stress was laid on the principle that the righteous king must first and foremost be a good law-giver and a just judge. Such was the case with David, for instance, as disclosed in particular by the words the woman of Tekoah addressed to the king: "As an angel of God, so is my lord the king to discern good and bad: and the Lord thy God be with thee...and my lord is wise, according to the wisdom of the angel of God, to know all things that are in the earth" (II Sam. 14:17, 20).

[13] Goodenough, *op. cit.*, p. 190, saw a foreign influence even in the acceptance of royal insignia—a crown and a bracelet (II Sam. 1:10). A bracelet was a distinctive ornament of Babylonian and Assyrian kings and used to be adorned with a solar rosette, which can be explained only in connection with the solar symbolism that surrounded the Oriental king. Even A. Bertholet, *op. cit.*, p. 245, accepts the historicity of the bracelet as a mark of Saul's royalty, though he entertains doubts about the diadem or crown as the first Hebrew King's royal distinctive mark. Cf. also H. P. Smith's commentary on the book of Samuel, *op. cit.*, p. 256. This is, however, not quite evident. The Hebrew word *ez adah*, used in this passage, seems to designate a metal plate protecting the forepart of the arm in battle. The Hebrew word for a bracelet is *zanid*.

[14] On the role of the people and religion in the creation of Israelite kingship, see L. Desnoyers' study "La politique et la religion dans l'établissement de la royauté en Israel," *Revue apologétique*, 45 (1927), pp. 1–19.

On another occasion Mephibosheth, when asking David for a fair decision against his accusers, said: "And he hath slandered thy servant unto my lord the king; but my lord the king is as an angel of God; do therefore what is good in thine eyes" (II Sam. 19:27). The appeal to the king as an angel or messenger of God is characteristic. Taken in their true sense, these words convey the fact that David was regarded as the legitimate messenger who brought to the ears of his people Jahweh's will and decisions in controversial and legal matters. In other words, the king is looked upon by his people as the only authentic interpreter of Jahweh's law: and the basic ideal of Jewish kingship, as of Babylonian kingship, was thus brought one stage further.

Equally interesting is Absalom's eagerness to offer himself to his country as a good and just judge, when he tries to oust his father from the throne (II Sam. 15:1–6)[15] and to mimic the pompous glamor of other kings, though Saul's court ceremonial had been of the simplest. This is yet another sign of progress in the Hebrew notions of kingship and of the growing influence of Egypt and Babylonia, where kings loved to surround themselves with all the pomp of royal pageantry.

The clearest expression of the same basic concept of kingship is found in the account of Solomon receiving from Jahweh the gift of wisdom. He saw the Lord in a dream, the usual method for Babylonian kings to learn the will of their gods and to hear of their selection for the royal office. Solomon, chosen by Jahweh to rule over Israel, humbly asks the Lord (I Kings, 3:9–13; II Chron. 1:7–13): "Give thy servant an understanding heart to judge my people, that I may discern between good and evil; for who is able to judge this thy great people?" The Lord was pleased with Solomon's request and gave him not only the wisdom he had asked for, but in addition, success, riches, and a long reign. It is difficult here to resist the temptation of comparing Solomon's prayer with that addressed by Dungi to Shamash for the gift of a spirit of justice and righteousness. Solomon's prayer illustrates as the essential functions of He-

---

[15] The passage seems to indicate that even the humblest subject had the right of appeal to the king. Cf. also II Sam. 14:1–20; II Kings 8:1–6; I Kings 3:16–28 (Solomon).

brew kingship the ability to receive Jahweh's will, to interpret it
rightly, and to judge the chosen people in accordance with that will.
And the whole history of Solomon's reign serves to show that such
was the foundation of his kingly power and greatness: "They feared
the king: for they saw that the wisdom of God was in him, to do
justice" (I Kings 3:28). Even the Queen of Sheba had to acknowledge
(I Kings 10:9) that "the Lord loved Israel for ever and therefore
made Solomon king, to do judgement and justice."

The same idea is set forth in another class of Hebrew literature,
the psalms, and some of those whose pre-exilic origin is beyond
doubt deserve examination. If it is surprising in the two instances
quoted to find David described as invested with divine gifts and
called an angel of God, the description of David's kingship as put
into the mouth of the dying King is even more so (II Sam. 23:1–7):[16]

> David, the son of Jesse, said,
> And the man who was
>   raised on high,
> The anointed of the God of Jacob,
> And the sweet psalmist of Israel, saith,
> The spirit of Jahweh spoke by me,
> And his word was upon my tongue.
> The God of Israel said,
> The Rock of Israel spoke to me:
> 'One that ruleth in the fear of God,
> He shall be as the light of the morning,
>   when the sun riseth,
> A morning without clouds.

The most startling words in this psalm are those that compare
David to the rising sun, and they will not be understandable until
they are placed side by side with the numerous passages in Egyptian and Babylonian documents where the king is identified with
the radiation of the sun.[17] The sun symbolism in this psalm is

[16] Cf. A. R. Johnson, *Sacral Kingship in Ancient Israel*, p. 14 seq.; *idem*,
"Hebrew Conceptions of Kingship," p. 209 seq.

[17] See S. Mowinckel, "'Die letzten Worte Davids,' II Sam. 23:1–7," in
ZAW, N.F., 4 (1927), pp. 30–58. The author proposes the following translation of Jahweh's words (verses 3–4, *loc. cit.*, p. 41): "Wenn ein Gerechter

certainly due to Babylonian inspiration, and with this in mind, it becomes easier to understand what is said about David in preceding passages: David, the exalted, "raised on high," "the anointed of the God of Jacob." These words recall the old Oriental court style in their emphasis on divine predestination to the kingly office. Owing to the exceptional relation in which he stands to the Spirit, David, with his primary mission to bring righteousness among men on earth, becomes a sort of incarnation of Jahweh's spirit. The Sumerian King Gudea, his successors, and Hammurabi could have used exactly the same terms as the psalmist. Once the fundamental principle of the *nomos empsychos* or incarnate law, to which Greek genius in the Hellenistic period so openly appealed, is recognized in the Babylonian documents, there is no reason why the same principle should not be acknowledged in a passage which is certainly pre-exilic, if not written by David himself.

A series of psalms called the "Royal psalms" has for many years attracted the attention of experts whose opinions have raised endless and heated controversies. But lately the general opinion seems to have veered round to the theory that these psalms were originally written by court poets for the celebration of the king's birthday or the anniversary of his enthronement. They have been carefully analyzed by H. Gunkel and R. Kittel,[18] and many of them

unter den Menschen herrscht, herrschend (in) Gottesfurcht, dann geht die Sonne auf am Morgen, an wolkenlosem Morgen (erstrahlt) (ihr Glanz)." But this reconstruction is unsatisfactory. Sun symbolism in this passage cannot be discounted and Mowinckel agrees to this on pages 34, 51, and 52. It is only by comparing this symbolism to the current hyperboles on kings being likened to the radiation of the sun that we shall be able to understand the curious association in this prophetic statement. Mowinckel dates the composition of this poem from the reign of Hezekiah or Josiah (*ibid.*, p. 58). Cf. also L. Dürr, *Ursprung und Ausbau der israelitisch-jüdischen Heilandserwartung* (Berlin, 1925), p. 110.

[18] H. Gunkel, "Die Königspsalmen," *Preussische Jahrbücher*, 158 (1914), pp. 42–68; R. Kittel, *Die Psalmen*, Kommentar zum Alten Testament, 13, 6th ed. (Leipzig, 1929). Cf. some readjustments and additions in L. Dürr, *op. cit.*, pp. 40 seq., 77, 80, 91 seq. See also the Register on p. 160 seq. The "Royal psalms" are the following: 2, 18, 20, 28, 45, 61, 72, 89, 101, 110, 132. See also H. Gunkel and J. Begrich, *Einleitung in die Psalmen*, pt. 2, Göttinger Handkommentar zum Alten Testament (Göttingen, 1933), pp. 140–171. Cf. Goodenough, *op. cit.*, pp. 198–201; also S. Mowinckel, *Psalmenstudien II. Das Thronbesteigungsfest Jahwäs und der Ursprung der Eschatologie*, Skrifter utgitt av det Norske Videnskaps-Akademi i Kristiania, II, Hist.-Filol. Kl., 1921, no. 6 (Christiania, 1922), pp. 178, 190, 303. Mowinckel's theory—

are certainly pre-exilic. In more ways than one, they recall the terms of the Egyptian, and especially the Babylonian court style, while in one instance they bear traces, as in the same class of Hebrew literature, of the divinization of royalty, once so popular in Egypt.

Those passages bearing on the Hebrew kings' primary function of dispensing justice and righteousness should be considered first. Psalm 45 must have been written in celebration of a Hebrew king's marriage and the following are the words of greeting to the royal bridegroom:

> Thou art fairer than the children of men;
> Grace is poured into thy lips:
> Therefore God hath blessed thee for ever.
> Gird thy sword upon thy thigh, O mighty one,
> With thy glory and thy majesty.
> And in thy majesty ride on prosperously,
> Because of truth and meekness and righteousness.[19]
> And thy right hand will teach thee terrible things.
>
> . . . .
>
> Thy throne, thou divine one, is for ever and ever;
> A sceptre of equity is the sceptre of thy kingdom.
> Thou hast loved righteousness and hated wickedness.
> Therefore God, thy God, hath anointed thee
> With the oil of gladness above thy fellows.

---

already suggested by P. Volz, *Das Neujahrfest Jahwes* (*Laubhüttenfest*) (Tübingen, 1912)—on the existence of a festival celebrating the yearly re-enthronement of Jahweh as King, although still defended by the so-called Scandinavian school, should be abandoned. There is no indication of its existence either in the Old Testament or in the Rabbinic literature. The psalms which are interpreted in this sense are not a convincing argument. The history of the controversy, with bibliographical indications, was clearly outlined by A. R. Johnson, "Living Issues in Biblical Scholarship. Divine Kingship and the Old Testament," *The Expository Times*, 62 (1950–1951), pp. 36–42. Cf. also in the same issue (pp. 4–9) N. W. Porteous, "Living Issues in Biblical Scholarship, Prophet and Priest in Israel." On the New Year Feast, see also N. I. Snaith, *The Jewish New Year Festival* (London, 1947) and L. J. Pap, *Das israelitische Neujahrsfest* (Kampen, 1933) and J. De Fraine, *L'aspect religieux*, p. 122 seq. with full bibliography. Cf. also *infra*, p. 304. on Johnson's theory.

[19] L. Dürr, *Ursprung*, p. 78, translates the verse as follows: "Glück auf, fahre hin für die Sache der Wahrheit und zeuge fürs Recht."

The first verses of Psalm 72 are perhaps even more significant:

> Give the king thy judgements, O God,
> And thy righteousness unto the king's son.
> He shall judge thy people with righteousness,
> And thy poor with judgement.
> The mountains shall bring peace to the people,
> And the hills, in righteousness.
> He shall save the children of the needy,
> And shall break in pieces the oppressor.
> They shall fear thee while the sun endureth,
> And so long as the moon, throughout all generations.

These two psalms best describe the Hebrew king's chief qualifications of justice, righteousness, and military valor which were so highly esteemed at the outset of Hebrew political organization in the days of the Judges. But justice and righteousness were valued far above military daring and it was precisely because of his instinctive love for justice and righteousness that a man was singled out and anointed by the Lord to rule over Israel.

The promise to love justice and integrity provides the main content of a declaration by a king of Judah on the day of his enthronement,[20] and Psalm 101 is in the nature of a royal proclamation (verses 2, 4, 5, 7, 8):

> I will behave myself wisely and in a perfect way.
> I will walk within my house with a perfect heart.
> A froward heart shall depart from me:
> I will know no evil thing.
> Who privily slandereth his neighbour, him will I destroy:
> Him that hath a high look and a proud heart will I not suffer.
> He that worketh deceit shall not dwell within my house:
> He that speaketh falsehood shall not be established before my
> Morning by morning will I destroy   [eyes.
> All the wicked of the land;
> To cut off all the workers of iniquity from the city of the Lord.

---

[20] R. Kittel, *Die Psalmen*, p. 325, calls the psalm "Regentenspiegel." Cf. H. Gunkel, *Die Psalmen*, 4th ed. (Göttingen, 1926), p. 433.

Such was also the kingly ideal of the ancient East. As for Egypt, there are two documents that have been assumed by many scholars to be prophecies of a coming savior and the prototypes of prophecies in the Old Testament, which clearly exemplify the Egyptian notion of kings as being the only source of justice, law, and right. The true character of both documents, the Papyrus of Leiden and the so-called prophecy of St. Petersburg, has already been revealed by A. H. Gardiner,[21] it now being admitted that both texts describe historical events in the form of a post-factum prophecy, and both attribute the scourges of civil war, devastation, and injustice that fell on Egypt to the want of a rightful king. "It is said: he is the herdsman of mankind. No evil is in his heart. When his herds are few, he spends the day in collecting them, while their hearts are on fire [?]. Would that he had perceived their true nature in the first generation [of men]; he would then have repressed evils, stretched forth [his] arm to stem them, destroyed their seed [?] and their inheritance.... There is no pilot [?] in their moment. Where is he [?] to-day? Is he sleeping? Behold, his might is not seen..." (Papyrus of Leiden, 12 1–3, 6).

The "prophecy of St. Petersburg," written about 2800 B.C., also announces the destruction of evil and the banning of injustice "when a king will come from the south.... Right will be restored to its place.... Injustice will be done away with. Rejoice, those who will see it and who will serve the king." Apparently, such "prophecies" were not uncommon in Egypt. In this class of literature, the advent of successful kings was announced by the gods in the manner of the Egyptian court style[22] for the country's deliverance from evil and the restoration of justice, right, and peace.

The same idea recurs in the instructions given to his son by Amenemhet I, (about 1980 B.C.), founder of the Twelfth Dynasty. Using himself as the example to emulate, the ruler writes: "I gave

---

[21] *The Admonitions of an Egyptian Sage, from a Hieratic Papyrus in Leiden* (Leipzig, 1909). *Idem,* "New Literary Works from Ancient Egypt: II. Pap. Petersburg 1116 B, *recto,*" *The Journal of Egyptian Archaeology,* I (1914), pp. 100–106. The latest translation of both documents is in A. Erman, *The Literature of the Ancient Egyptians,* transl. by A. M. Blackman (London, 1927), pp. 92–108, 110 seq. See discussion of problems and other bibliographical indications in L. Dürr, *Ursprung,* pp. 1–15.

[22] L. Dürr, *ibid.,* p. 14.

to the beggar; I fed the orphan; I admitted the lowborn as well as him who was of great account."[23] One of his main supporters, Khnumhotep, the king of Benihasan, wandered throughout the land seeking the eradication of sin, "resplendent like the sun-god Atum himself," and fixed the boundaries of the cities according to old records, because "he loved justice too much."[24] The same notion lies behind the praises lavished on the reigns of various Pharaohs, as, for instance, that of Rameses II[25] (1292–1225 B.C.) and of his successor Merneptah,[26] and runs through the hymn sung in honor of a new Pharaoh on the day of his ascent to the throne.[27] Typical of this is the hymn of greeting to Rameses IV on the day of his ascent, which is made to coincide with his subjects' deliverance from hunger, thirst, and want and presupposes the advent of a just and equitable regime. The wording of the hymn and its recital of sufferers who were relieved by the Pharaoh are strangely reminiscent of the recital of the "beatitudes" in Christ's Sermon on the Mount (Matt. 25:34 seq.).[28]

To the instances already quoted, with reference to Babylonia and Assyria and chiefly from the early period, may now be added some of later date, to show the persistent survival and revival of those ideas. In one of his inscriptions, King Neriglissar (559–556 B.C.) says among other things:[29]

> ...Marduk...singled me out from among many subjects...
> and because I gave heed to his power, to the prosperity of my life

---

[23] J. H. Breasted, *A History of Egypt*, 2nd. ed. (New York, 1912), p. 179.
[24] A. Erman and H. Ranke, *Aegypten und aegyptisches Leben im Altertum* (Tübingen, 1923), pp. 43, 101 seq. Two similar instances concerning high royal functionaries are quoted from the same period—a supreme judge and a monarch in the reign of Amenemhet's son. See *ibid.*, pp. 95, 105.
[25] J. H Breasted, *Ancient Records of Egypt* (Chicago, 1906–1907), 3, p. 120 seq., para. 288.
[26] *Ibid.*, para. 602 seq., p. 256 seq.
[27] On the ascent of Merneptah, see A. Erman, *The Literature of the Ancient Egyptians*, p. 278.
[28] A. Erman, *ibid.*, p. 279: "They that hungered are satisfied and happy and they that thirsted are drunken.
They that were naked were clad in fine linen and they that were dirty, have white garments.
They that were in prison are set free and he that was in bonds is full of joy. They that were at strife in this land are reconciled...."
[29] S. H. Langdon *Die neubabylonische Königsinschriften* (Leipzig, 1912), p. 214. Cf. Goodenough, *op. cit.*, p. 177.

and to my lowliness before the Godhead by daily striving to do well towards him, therefore he chose me and called me to the throne of this renowned land; for the eternal shepherding of his people, be my kingdom granted a just sceptre to make the land truly great; to my rulership he promised a just ruler's staff as a pledge for the salvation of the nation; he placed into my hand a scourge wherewith to curb the enemy; he put an imperishable crown on me for my kingship. Rivals and rebels, I put to nought; enemies, I crushed; opponents and traitors, I utterly consumed. I set up justice in the land. I ruled my widely scattered peoples in safety.

Three royal prayers to Shamash are still more significant. That addressed by King Dungi to Shamash has already been noted.[30] Another by King Nabu-naid (*ca.* 555–538 B.C.) invokes the sun-god in the following terms:[31] "May the gods Right, Justice, and Judgement, who are enthroned before thee, prepare, at thy exalted and unalterable command and by the inflexible orders of the great Godhead, the way of peace and justice for my feet.... Make the radiance of thy streaming light, the manifestation of rulership, the glory of royalty accompany me by my side as I plunder the lands of my enemies."

Another prayer to Shamash comes from Nebuchadnezzar (*ca.* 1146–1123 B.C.):

> Shamash, when Thou wilt take joyful possession of Thy splendid temple E-barra, behold the precious work I have accomplished. Thy lips announce me grace. May I, in accordance with thy just commands, be saturated with posterity. Grant me life into far distant days and a solid throne. Let my rule extend into eternity, my sceptre be just and my government be efficient. Adorn my kingdom for ever with that fair, kingly repute which brings salvation to mankind. Arm my troops with strong weapons in attack and battle. Thou, O Shamash, answer me rightly through equitable decision and dream. By thy sublime and unalterable command, may my

---

[30] See *supra*, pp. 268, 288.
[31] S. H. Langdon, *op. cit.*, p. 260; Goodenough, *op. cit.*, p. 177.

weapons launch forward and destroy the weapons of my foes.[32]

Of similar interest is the prayer uttered by the priest in the act of placing the diadem on the head of an Assyrian king at the ceremony of his enthronement: "The diadem on thy head means that Assur and Ninlil are masters of thy diadem. May they protect you for a hundred years. May thy foot in the temple and thy hands on the altar of Assur, thy God, prosper. May thy priestly reign and the priestly reign of thy sons be prosperous before Assur, thy god. May Assur give thy sceptre and thy land the right words, right hearing and compliance, right and justice."[33]

These and similar Babylonian documents share many ideas in common with the Hebrew royal psalms. Though these are naturally far superior in composition and trend, they will never be clearly comprehensible unless compared with corresponding productions and other documents of Egypt, Babylonia, and Assyria. The Hebrew king is portrayed as an ideal of beauty, exactly as the Egyptians and Babylonians portrayed their kings; his throne is forever and ever; his name is imperishable as the sun and the moon. Similar hyperboles are scattered in profusion over Egyptian and Babylonian documents.[34] One enthusiastic Hebrew poet even goes so far as to apostrophize him as "divine" (Ps. 45:7).[35] Such an encomium, so essentially Oriental, would never have been tolerated in Israel exept during the pre-exilic period. The passage survived only because its content, as well as that of other texts, was shifted to

[32] M. Jastrow, *Die Religion Babyloniens und Assyriens* (Giessen, 1905), I, p. 405. See also B. Meissner, *Babylonien und Assyrien*, I (Heidelberg, 1920), pp. 56 (Babylonia), 63 seq. (Assyria). For more instances of the kind, cf. L. Dürr, *Ursprung*, p. 77 seq.

[33] B. Meissner, *op. cit.*, p. 63.

[34] For Egypt, cf. Erman-Ranke, *Aegypten*, p. 324 seq.: Not thousands, but millions of years were promised by the gods to the Egyptian kings; they were to live for eternity, since the sun-god holds before his face the sign of life. In other documents, we read of God assuring the king: "I am giving thee years lasting into eternity.... As long as I am, wilt thou live on earth.... As long as the firmament holds will thy name endure, perpetually and for ever," etc. For Babylonia, see for instance Nebuchadnezzar's prayer quoted above, or that of Nabopalassar, the founder of the neo-Babylonian Empire, to Marlak (Jastrow, *op. cit.*, I, p. 400), where the king asks for the continuance of his reign into distant years. Also *ibid.*, pp. 394, 395, 396, 397, 403, 419.

[35] Cf. S. Mowinckel, *Psalmenstudien II*, p. 302 seq., and H. Gunkel, *Die Psalmen*, pp. 189–196.

the person of the divine Saviour. But such modes of address were in the best court style of Oriental, particularly Egyptian, chanceries.

Another variety of Oriental court terminology is found in such formulas as that calling the Israelite king a son of Jahweh (Ps. 2:7) trained by Him chiefly in warfare (Ps. 18:34). The divine adoption of kings, not their divine descent, is a Babylonian notion which must have found its way into Jewish ideology on kingship together with related ideas. There is no need, therefore, to see in Nathan's words calling David (II Sam. 7:13 seq.) Jahweh's son, or in Psalm 2:7, any traces of royal divinization. The words "Thou art my son; this day have I begotten Thee"[36] simply mean that the king was Jahweh's choice and became His adopted son on the day of his solemn proclamation. Such a manner of speaking sounded familiar to the Babylonians as it was part of their court style.[37]

Another royal song, Psalm 110, also reflects ancient notions on Hebrew kingship:

> The Lord saith unto my Lord, sit thou at my right hand
> Until I make thine enemies thy footstool.
> The Lord shall send forth the rod of thy strength out of Zion;
> Rule thou in the midst of thine enemies.
> Thy people offer themselves willingly in the day of thy power:
> In the beauty of holiness, from the womb of the morning,
> Thou hast the dew of thy youth.[38]
> The Lord hath sworn, and will not repent,
> Thou art a priest for ever
> After the order of Melchizedek.
> The Lord at thy right hand
> Shall strike through kings

---

[36] Cf. also Psalm 89, vs. 27: "I also will make him my first-born, the highest of the kings of the earth." See also S. Mowinckel, *Psalmenstudien II*, p. 302.

[37] For particulars, see E. Schrader, *Die Keilinschriften und das Alte Testament*, 3rd ed. (Berlin, 1903), p. 379; M. Jastrow, *op. cit.*, 1, pp. 152, 212. Cf. R. Kittel, *Die Psalmen*, p. 10 seq.; H. Gressmann, *Der Ursprung*, p. 256.

[38] The Hebrew manuscripts give several different versions of this line. It is impossible to find the true sense. C. A. Briggs in his *Critical and Exegetical Commentary on the Book of Psalms*, 2 (Edinburgh, 1907), p. 373, prefers the following reading: "Volunteers on the sacred [mountains] are thy people, in the day of thy host: From the womb of the morn come forth to thee the dew of thy youth."

In the day of his wrath.
He shall judge among the nations,
He shall fill the places with dead bodies;
He shall strike through the head in many countries.
He shall drink of the brook in the way;
Therefore shall he lift up thy head.

This poem again underlines the leading concepts of Hebrew kingship. Jahweh chooses his king, gives him the place of honor at his right hand. The king is the lawgiver and judge, he should be brave and the Lord will give him victory over all his enemies. Volunteers join his army like abundant drops of dew; they are his young men, full of enthusiasm. The king will go victoriously through many countries, in his haste not waiting for a cup but, like the men of Gideon (Judg. 7), drinking of the brook.[39]

This psalm is regarded as messianic by many scholars and possibly of Davidic origin.[40] But the coming Messiah was regarded as a king; thus even to him the leading principles of Hebrew kingship should be applied. Nor should one wonder at the use of phrases which are familiar to us from the Egyptian court style. It is known that the Pharaohs were often depicted as sitting on the right of the divinity or as holding their enemies under their footstool.

[39] Because of the uncertainty of the reading, it would be unwise to draw any conclusions from this passage. G. Widengren, in his study *Sakrales Königtum im Alten Testament und im Judentum* (Stuttgart, 1955), p. 49, sees in this drinking from the brook an old Israelite custom which was a part of the coronation ceremony. This is very hypothetical.

[40] C. A. Briggs, *op. cit.*, 2, p. 374, gives reasons for rejecting the Maccabean origin of the psalm. E. Sellin, *Introduction to the Old Testament*, trans. by W. Montgomery (London, 1923), p. 202, dates the psalm from the period of David. R. Kittel, *Die Psalmen*, p. 357, suggested that the psalm was written at a time when the Israelite priestly class grew conscious of its importance and began to question the royal privilege. This would place its composition in the eighth or seventh century B.C. See also H. Gunkel, *Die Psalmen*, p. 483 seq. R. H. Pfeiffer, *Introduction to the Old Testament* (New York, 1948), p. 630, dates it from the post-exilic period. This dating is rejected by W. O. E. Oesterley, *The Psalms* (London, 1955), p. 461. Cf. G. Widengren, *Psalm 110 och det sakrala kungadömet i Israel* (Uppsala Univ. Årsskrift, 1941). The most recent interpreter, R. Tournay, "Le Psaume CX," *RB*, 67 (1960), pp. 5–41, dates this psalm from the reign of Ptolemy III Euergetes (246–221 B.C.). He attributes to it a priestly origin and defines its messianic trend in the following words (p. 40): "Mais le messianisme du Ps. CX, s'il se relie foncièrement à David, type du Messie, comporte un élément original: c'est un messianisme sacral et sacerdotal."

The new element in Psalm 110 is that it attributes priestly characteristics to the king. It is the only passage in the books of the Old Testament where the priestly character of the king is stressed. Should it be interpreted in the same way as the priesthood of Egyptian and Assyrian kings?

The role which the Israelite kings played in religious organization is considerable.[41] David erected in Jerusalem the first altar to Jahweh (II Sam. 24:25), planned the construction of a temple, and laid down the details for religious practice (II Sam. 7:2–3; I Chron. 22–29). Solomon erected and dedicated the Temple (I Kings 5–13). King Jeroboam not only founded the sanctuary of Bethel, but also recruited the clergy and ordered the feasts to be celebrated yearly (I Kings 12:26–33). Joash published ordinances to be observed in the temple (II Kings 12:5–9), Josiah not only inforced their execution, but also reformed the cult (II Kings 22:3–7). The kings also enjoyed the right to appoint or to depose the chief members of the priestly class (II Sam. 8:17; 20:25; I Kings 2:26–27; 4:2).

Numerous texts also attribute to the kings the performing of sacrifices. Most of these passages can be explained in the sense that the kings ordered the sacrifices or made them possible by providing the sacrificial victims. There are, however, some texts which seem to imply more than this. Achaz, for example, is shown to have mounted the altar he had erected and to have initiated the sacrifice which was continued later by the priest (II Kings 16:12–16). A similar gesture is attributed to Jeroboam (I Kings 12:33; 13:1). David and Solomon are said to have blessed the people present in the sanctuary (II Sam. 6:18; I Kings 8:14). David seems to have worn a sacerdotal vestment (II Sam. 6:14).

From all this, it can be concluded that the "priestly" role gave the kings the rights to organize the cult, to watch over its execution with proper dignity, to provide the necessary sacrificial objects and to appoint the chiefs of the priestly class. But only very few cases seem to attribute to them the execution of priestly functions and

---

[41] Cf. G. Widengren, *Sakrales Königtum*, pp. 14–16. See, however, how K. H. Bernhardt rejects the theory defending the transfer of the sacral kingship from Melchizedek, priest-king of Jerusalem, to David, in his book, *Das Problem der altorient. Königsideologie*, p. 91 seq.

these do not prove that the king had a real priestly character.[42]
These interventions in religious practice can be explained by the
solemnity of the moment—the transfer of the ark, the first sacrifice
on a newly erected altar. But even in such cases the religious acts
were continued by the priests.[43] David's dance in front of the ark
especially can hardly be regarded as a sacerdotal function. It may
have been a ritual executed by the people, as seems indicated by
the exhortation in Psalm 150:4. Ritual dances are also mentioned
in Exod. 15:20, Judg. 21:21. An ephod similar to that worn by David,
was also worn by the boy Samuel (I Sam. 2:18). The blessing by
parents was regarded as an important ritual—the story of Jacob
and Esau need only be recalled (Gen. 27)—and the king was regarded as the father of his nation.

It should be emphasized that anointment was not intended to
endow the king with a priestly character. The anointment of the high
priest, and later of all priests, was introduced only after the disappearance of the kingship and it should be interpreted as giving to
the high priest a part of the sacred position and authority which
the anointed king had previously possessed.[44] He already possessed
the priestly character before anointment.

The theory concerning the role played by the Israelite king during the feast of the New Year, in imitation of the priestly functions of the Babylonian kings on the Day of Reconciliation, remains unproved. No evidence for the introduction of a New Year
feast by David can be found, and the quotations from psalms used
by the defenders of this theory are vague and can be explained
perfectly without the supposed royal performances during the
feasts. Not all the functions of Babylonian, Assyrian, or Egyptian
kings can be extended to the Israelite kings. The kingship in Israel
appeared late and was preceded by its own traditions of the patri-

[42] G. Widengren, *Sakrales Königtum*, p. 17 seq., puts too much stress on
the king's "high priestly" functions.

[43] Cf. A. R. Johnson, "Hebrew Conceptions," p. 213.

[44] See, for details, De Fraine, *op. cit.*, pp. 315–320. Cf. C. R. North, "The
Religious Aspects of Hebrew Kingship," *ZAW*, 50 (1932), p. 21: "In post-
exilic times the High Priest was, as far as might be, a king; for any evidence
that the high priests succeeded to the dignity of the kings is, with but little
qualification, evidence that their predecessors, the kings, were virtually
high priests."

archs Moses, Aaron, and the Judges. These traditions were within living memory and sometimes excluded a servile imitation of kingly functions customary in other nations. The Covenant with the Lord was concluded not with one representative of the people, but with the people as a whole, and this certainly influenced the evolution of the ideas on kingship in Israel.

This restriction on the priestly function of the ruler is also important for our investigation of the role of the first Christian emperors in the Church. It will be seen that in most ways the Byzantine emperors followed the example of their ideal "predecessors," David and Solomon, when organizing religious life and prescribing for cultic observances. But it must be remembered that though these biblical "predecessors" were often called priest-kings, they never actually acquired a priestly character.

The royal psalms give some further information on the king's enthronement. The Israelite texts make no mention of a royal sceptre, which was traditionally an essential part of Egyptian and Assyrian coronation. However, three royal psalms speak of a royal sceptre (Pss. 2:9; 110:2; 45:6). In the last instance the sceptre signifies the king's judicial function and in the others his executive power. Thus, the sceptre was not an exclusive royal emblem in Israel.

A diadem is mentioned in Psalm 89:39. It symbolizes an alliance of the king with Jahweh which seems to have been solemnly proclaimed at the coronation. It must have meant a solemn adoption of the king by Jahweh and a promise of victory. A decree of Jahweh is also mentioned in Psalms 2:7–9 and 132:11–12 recalling the alliance concluded by Jahweh with David and his descendants (II Sam. 7:8–16). This ceremony recalls the solemn proclamation of the five names of the new Egyptian king, declaring him to be the son of God and thus the legitimate king of both parts of Egypt.

The royal psalms contain several other descriptions and phrases for which the authors may have found inspiration in non-Hebrew literary production, e.g., Psalm 29. This poem is a prayer for victory before battle and the news of its successful issue is conveyed to the king through the oracle of the prophet by the choir that sings the prayer. Similar duologues must have been popular in the royal choruses of the Babylonians, as may be judged from the prayer of Ashurbanipal which was personally answered by the god Nabu.[45] The Egyptian prayer addressed by Rameses II to Amon-Re, when he was abandoned by all his troops at the battle with the Hittites, may also be quoted.[46]

There remains one feature which found its way from the Oriental court style into the general atmosphere of Hebrew kingship: the wish to see the national rule extended over the whole world. This idea is particularly noticeable in Psalms 2:8; 18:44; 45:6; 72:1–11; 89:26–28; 110. The feature, which was common to the Egyptian and Babylonian court styles, was taken over bodily by the Hebrew royal poets. Such national aspirations were, of course, natural in Egypt and Babylonia-Assyria, since both those countries succeded at various periods in imposing their rule on foreign nations and in making the first known bids for world dominion.[47] This pseudo-imperialism must have sounded somewhat strange coming from the lips of a Hebrew royal poet. But, taken in its true context, as part of a complete delivery, one item among many that were pla-giarized from the Oriental court style, it becomes simply part of a not unusual international exchange of ideas.

In Egypt and Babylonia the kings have been shown to have been regarded as saviors of their peoples, protecting them from disaster and guaranteeing to them prosperity and material well-being. The Israelites shared, at least in part, a similar conviction. This idea of a king-savior is best expressed in Psalm 72, which may have been composed for the coronation of Josiah, and is thus pre-Deuteronomic.[48] These are the most impressive verses:

[45] H. Zimmern, *Babylonische Hymnen und Gebete*, Der Alte Orient, 13, Heft 1 (Leipzig, 1911), p. 20; cf. also pp. 11–13 (Tammuz and his sister).

[46] Erman-Ranke, *Aegypten*, p. 467 seq.

[47] For particulars, see H. Gressmann, *Der Ursprung*, pp. 252 seq., 262 seq.; H. Gunkel, "Die Königspsalmen," p. 62 seq.; A. Jeremias, *Handbuch der altoriental. Geisteskultur*, 2nd ed. (Berlin-Leipzig, 1929), p. 178 seq.; L. Dürr, *Ursprung*, p. 92 seq. For Babylonia, see B. Meissner, *op. cit.*, p. 48 seq. Cf. also S. Mowinckel, *Psalmenstudien II*, p. 184. See K. H. Bernhardt, *op. cit.*, pp. 1–50, on the old and modern methods in the exegesis of psalms. See, on pp. 182–261, a thorough study of the royal psalms and their interpreta-tion, with more bibliography.

[48] E. G. Briggs, *op. cit.*, 2, p. 132. Cf. also A. H. van der Weijden, *Die Gerechtigkeit in den Psalmen* (Nijmegen, 1952). On this psalm, pp. 191–195, 199, 200.

Give the king thy judgments, O God, and thy
    righteousness unto the king's son.
He shall judge the people with righteousness,
    and thy poor with judgement.
. . . .

He shall judge the poor of the people, he shall
    save the children of the needy, and shall
    break in pieces the oppressor.
. . . .

He shall come down like rain upon the mown grass:
    as showers that water the earth.
In his days shall the righteous flourish;
    and abundance of peace so long as the moon endureth.
. . . .

He shall spare the poor and needy, and shall
    save the souls of the needy.
. . . .

There shall be an handful of corn in the earth upon
    the top of the mountains; the fruit thereof shall
    shake like Lebanon: and they of the city shall
    flourish like grass of the earth.

In these verses the psalm clearly expresses the basic principle: the material prosperity of the nation cannot be assured if the people are not righteous. Their righteousness depends, however, on the king's righteousness, which should be manifested by the conscientious execution of his judicial and legislative role. It is, however, only Jahweh who can inspire the king to maintain law and order in the interest of his people.[49]

There are a few passages in the books of the Old Testament indicating that material catastrophies—a prolonged drought or an outburst of the plague—could be attributed to the fact that the king had transgressed against Jahweh's laws. The whole dynasty and the whole nation could be involved in Jahweh's punishment for such transgressions.[50]

[49] See A. R. Johnson, *Sacral Kingship in Ancient Israel*, p. 7 seq.
[50] II Sam. 21:1–14; 24:10–25; compare also II Sam. 3:28 seq.; 14:9; Gen. 12:17; 20:3 seq. (Abraham's wife and the Pharaoh); I Kings 17:1; 18:1, 18 (Elijah and Achab); Jer. 15:4.

Only in one particular did Hebrew political philosophy differ from Egyptian and Babylonian: the Hebrews never consented to the divinization of their kings. The single instance of Psalm 45 where the king is addressed as the "divine one" is only a case of parallelism with the Egyptian court style and should not be taken literally. On the contrary, the royal psalms insist more than any other Hebrew document on there being but one God for the Israelites—Jahweh—to whom the king owes everything including his very elevation to the throne. He fights with Jahweh's assistance, is indebted to Jahweh for his victories and draws from him the inspiration to be fair in his judgments. The same dependence is found in Psalm 45 where, after addressing the king as a "divine one," the court poet proceeds to expose the king's human nature and to call attention to his indebtedness to God, his Lord, in the matter of his election: "Thou hast loved righteousness and hated wickedness: therefore God, thy God, hath anointed thee with the oil of gladness above thy fellows."[51]

The role which the king is supposed to have played during the ceremonies of the festivals is not as yet clear. The discussions concerning the New Year feast, started by S. Mowinckel, the founder of the so-called Scandinavian school, still continue. The idea that the festival was an imitation of a Babylonian festival and was concerned with the cyclic revival of the nation, celebrating the return of the national god to renew his kingship and that of his representative, the king,[52] should be rejected. If, in spite of the silence of the holy books and the Talmud, such a feast did exist, the solution offered by A. R. Johnson[53] would be more congenial to the spirit of Jewish religious conviction. He sees in the psalms which are supposed to show the existence of such a festival a description of the manifestation of Jahweh's sovereignty in the creation of the earth and his decision to choose Israel as his instrument in his "campaign against the forces of evil." In order to be capable

---

[51] See C. R. North, "The Religious Aspects," p. 21 seq. on this and other passages, which are quoted wrongly as proofs for the existence of divine kingship in Israel (especially Pss. 89:26 seq.; 2:7).

[52] Cf. G. Widengren, *Sacrales Königtum*, p. 62 seq., the ceremonial of the supposed festival. See *ibid.*, pp. 34–43: "Der König am Laubhüttenfest."

[53] *Sacral Kingship in Ancient Israel*, especially pp. 59, 133.

of this task the House of David has to fulfil "its own covenanted role of raising His chosen people to the required standard of social righteousness and thus forging a community which will be justified in serving as the moral and spiritual leaders of mankind. . . . Then the great 'Day' will dawn when He will be justified in intervening decisively in the affairs of men as the sovereign Ruler and Judge of mankind." It is a high conception which is supposed to have been brought each year before the eyes of the king and his people, but it still needs to be proved; one wishes that more evidence could be found for the existence of such a feast.[54]

The further development of Israelite kingship is marked by the emergence under Josiah of some new ideas which changed its initial character. This evolution was caused by the increased influence in Israel of the priestly class. After the erection by Solomon of the magnificent Temple of Jerusalem as the sole center of Hebrew worship, priestly influence was bound to benefit. It had not been insignificant politically as far back as the reign of Jehu (843–816 B.C.) of Samaria, who owed his accession partly to the priests' assistance. Again, the reign of Joash over Judah (837–798 B.C.) was made possible only by the revolt against the haughty Athaliah led by the high-priest Jehoiada (II Kings 11). These incidents were notable, as they foreshadowed a revolutionary change in the rela-

---

[54] See A. R. Johnson, "The Rôle of the King in the Jerusalem Cultus," *The Labyrinth*, ed. by S. H. Hooke (London, 1935), pp. 71–111, and his essays on "The Psalms" in *The Old Testament and Modern Study*, ed. by H. H. Rowley (Oxford, 1951), p. 194 seq. In his *Sacral Kingship in Ancient Israel* (p. 54) Johnson pointed out that the modification of his earlier views implied above all "the rejection of the view that the festival under discussion was concerned with the cyclic revival of the social unit, and the recognition that its orientation was not merely towards the following cycle of twelve months but towards a completely new era." Cf. also H. J. Kraus, *Die Königsherrschaft Gottes im Alten Testament* (Tübingen, 1951), p. 27 seq. and L. Černý's criticism in *The Day of Yahweh and Some Relevant Problems* (Prague, 1948), p. 27 seq. See also Johnson's short résumé of the theories of Mowinckel and the Scandinavian School and the restatement of his own ideas in his study "Hebrew Conceptions of Kingship," pp. 219–235. Cf. also J. Gray's review of Johnson's *Sacral Kingship*, in *VT*, 4 (1956), pp. 440–443. See the recent rejection of the "Ritual Pattern" by K. H. Bernhardt, *Das Problem der altorientalischen Königsideologie im A. T.*, pp. 51–66. This chapter was composed before I could profit from this work. Cf. also C. Hauzet, "L' interprétation des psaumes selon l'école 'Myth and Ritual,'" *Revue des sciences religieuses*, 33 (1959), pp. 321–342; 34 (1960), pp. 1–34.

tions between kingship and priesthood in Judah: whereas previously the kings had made priests, now they received their appointment from the high priest, who could count on the backing of the royal guards. The innovation was completed under Josiah, when (621 B.C.) the high priest discovered in the Temple the book dealing with moral and religious observances known today by the name of Deuteronomy. The pious King saw there the hand of Jahweh, and set about the reform of the central worship in Jerusalem in accordance with the prescriptions laid down in the book.[55]

The consequences of this reform are well known. First, the status of the clergy of Jerusalem was definitely stabilized, the worship centralized in the Temple there, and local worship on the high places forbidden. Another consequence was the introduction among the Jews of the Book-religion. Hitherto only the most general principles for the regulation of ethical, civil, and religious life had been outlined in the Book of the Covenant (Exod. 20:22–23:33). These were treated as custom, rather than as written law enforced by any authority, royal or otherwise, while forms of ceremonial observances were verbally regulated by the priests. Kings could only benefit by such conditions of legal uncertainty, since, as supreme judges, they were left free to act as the sole interpreters of Jahweh's will and the sole medium through which His decisions could be communicated. This was the very foundation on which the Hebrew notion of royalty and the Hebrew version of the—animate law—or *nomos empsychos* rested.

All this was changed by the adoption of Deuteronomy as the official law book. The possession of a sacred code which reflected the will of Jahweh, embodied the laws of the state, and provided all the necessary directions in matters of faith and life contributed

[55] For particulars, see R. Kittel, *Geschichte des Volkes Israel*, 1, 3rd ed. (Gotha, 1916), p. 290 seq.; 2 (1917), pp. 413 seq., 590 seq. *Idem, The Religion of the People of Israel*, trans. by R. C. Micklem (London, 1925), p. 153 seq. On the problem of the composition of the book, consult J. Hempel, *Die Schichten des Deuteronomium*, Beiträge zur Kultur- und Universalgeschichte, Heft 33 (Leipzig, 1914); H. Gressmann, "Josia und das Deuteronomium," *ZAW*, N.F., 1 (1924), p. 313 seq. The extensive bibliography in W. Baumgartner's study, "Der Kampf um das Deuteronomium," *Theologische Rundschau*, N.S., 1 (1929), p. 727 seq; G. v. Rad, *Deuteronomium-Studien* (Göttingen, 1947). Cf. also J. Pedersen, *Israel*, 2, p. 750 seq.: "Recent Discussions of the Deuteronomic Problem."

not a little to the stabilization of the legal and religious thought of the Hebrews. But at the same time it fettered royal freedom and prerogatives in legal matters and limited the personal initiative of the kings in the interpretation of Jahweh's will. They had to respect the codification of Jahweh's Law as a most sacred document and were soon to include in their venerations every prescription in its narrowest interpretation, to the possible detriment of Hebrew religious life and its spiritual depth, as well as of their own authority as lawgivers and Jahweh's mouthpieces.

The logical sequel is reflected in the notion of kingship enunciated in the book of Deuteronomy (17:14–20). It is one of the most debated passages in the book, which interpreters generally know by the name "Kingly Law." First of all, the king must be a Hebrew. The next injunction urges the king not to "multiply horses to himself" nor cause "the people to return to Egypt." This should be understood in the light of the context as a measure of protection against those Egyptian influences that were strong enough to reduce the Hebrew nation anew to political slavery.[56]

Then the writer enjoins the king to reduce his harem, not to have many wives, "neither silver nor gold."[57] There follows a passage which illustrates the profound innovation that overtook the old notion of Hebrew kingship (verses. 18–20):

And it shall be, when he [the king] sitteth upon the throne of his
    kingdom, that he shall write him a copy of this law in a book
    out of that which is before the priests, the Levites:

And it shall be with him, and he shall read therein all the days of
    his life: that he may learn to fear the Lord his God, to keep
    all the words of this law and these statutes, to do them:

---

[56] See H. Gressmann, "Josia und das Deuteronomium," *ZAW*, N.F., 1 (1924), p. 333 seq.

[57] J. Hempel, *op. cit.*, pp. 237–241, thinks that this passage was not written until after 608–607, under Jehoiakim or Zedekiah, as at that time the election of kings was not controlled by Judah, but by foreign powers. But this is not proof, as we have seen, that such a danger did not loom over Judah prior to that date. Yet, if Hempel's reading is correct, the passage would be more conclusive still with regard to the different stages of the new development and the effects of the Deuteronomic reform on the Jewish notion of kingship. As early as 1899, A. Bertholet, *Deuteronomium*, Kurzer Hand-Commentar zum Alten Testament, Abt. 5 (Freiburg i. B., 1899), p. 55, was inclined to date this passage from Zedekiah's time.

That his heart be not lifted up above his brethren, and that he
turn not aside from the commandment, to the right hand, or
to the left: to the end that he may prolong his days in his
kingdom, he, and his children, in the midst of Israel.

The words are clear enough as they stand, and they mark a
revolution in Hebrew thought: the king is no longer so much the
incarnation of Jahweh's spirit as the embodiment of a constitution
which he must be the first to observe before enjoining its strict
observance on his subjects. Though a curtailment of royal authority
is evident in the new conception, yet the fundamental notion of
the king's association with the law is preserved: Jahweh's will is
clearly laid down in the code, yet the king remains it chief ex-
ecutor.[58]

The change in Hebrew ideology on royalty is more perceptible
in Psalm 89, at least in part a post-Deuteronomic composition.[59]
There the poet exalts Jahweh as the source and origin of all righteousness, whereas the king's status is no longer pitched as high as
in other royal psalms, written in the preceding period (verses 13–18):
Jahweh's is transcendent. The king owes everything to Jahweh,
who exalted him as his first born over other kings (verse 27),
lavished on him His promises, and established a covenant with
him: "And my covenant shall stand fast with him" (verse 28). It
is the covenant which binds the king and his people to Jahweh, the
Lord's Law made known in the written code, on whose observance
will depend the extent of Jahweh's good will and protection (verses
30–34):

> If his children forsake my law,
> And walk not in my judgements;
> If they break my statutes,
> And keep not my commandments;
> Then will I visit their transgression with the rod,
> And their indignity with stripes.

[58] Cf. E. R. Goodenough, *op. cit.*, p. 201 seq.
[59] W. O. E. Oesterley, *The Psalms*, p. 397, divides the Psalm into three
parts. Verses 1–18 could have been composed in the northern kingdom about
788–747 B.C., verses 19–37 under Josiah, the rest under Jehoiakim.

But my mercy will I not utterly take from him,
Nor suffer my faithfulness to fail.
My covenant will I not break,
Nor alter the thing that is gone out of my lips.

This psalm also contains (verse 14) passages written in the spirit of the old Babylonian court style: "Justice and righteousness are the foundations of the Lord's throne; mercy and truth are seated before His face" (just as the Babylonians pictured their Shamash);[60] the king's throne is to last as long as the days of heaven (verse 29). There is even a trace of sun symbolism in the poet's words (verses 36–37): "His [David's] seed shall endure for ever, and his throne as the sun before me. It shall be established for ever as the moon...." The writer's insistence on the covenant definitely points to a post-Deuteronomic date of composition, at least of the middle section. But the whole trend of the psalm, especially in its description of the desolation that had fallen on the kingdom of David, points to a post-Deuteronomic period.[61]

The new manner of thought must have arisen among the Jews in the following period, chiefly under stress of the disasters that befell both Hebrew kingdoms, that of Israel and that of Jerusalem, when the prolonged disappearance of the royal institution from the national life of the defeated nation must have shorn royalty of much of its importance in Hebrew political thought. The covenant was left as the only relic of bygone days, the only witness to the intimate relationship that had existed between the humiliated nation and Jahweh. When the Jews recovered their independence, the renewed notion held its ground, as attested by a number of glosses, chiefly in the Books of Kings, which according to many critics of the Old Testament, are post-Deuteronomic. Such would be the case, for instance, with I Kings 3:14. After the account of Solomon's vision and Jahweh's promise to give him the wisdom he asked for, we read: "And if thou wilt walk in my ways, to keep my statutes and my commandments, as thy father David did walk, then I will lengthen thy days." These words sound quite out of place

---

[60] Cf. L. Dürr, *Ursprung*, p. 83.
[61] See R. Kittel, *Die Psalmen*, p. 293 seq; H. Gunkel, *Die Psalmen*, p. 396.

in their context, so that the possibility of their having been added as a gloss in the post-Deuteronomic spirit would be entirely acceptable.[62] But this problem may well be left to specialists.

So far, two notable results derive from our research into the development of Hebrew political thought. First, we have ascertained the vital and decisive character on this evolution of foreign influences, Babylonian and Egyptian, often through the medium of the Amorites. Indeed, the political growth of the Hebrews could scarcely be understood without those foreign infiltrations. Second, we have realized that the part played by the Hebrew king in the public life of his nation was more preponderant than was commonly believed: he was the bond between the chosen race and Jahweh, the interpreter of Jahweh's will, the giver of His laws, the channel by which Jahweh's salvation came to the people if he served, or Jahweh's punishment, if he sinned.

The royal psalms have further been shown best to embody Hebrew ideas on kingship. In their effort to conjure up the picture of the ideal king as Hebrew imagination conceived it, the poets have been found to borrow from the Babylonians and the Egyptians the picturesque and flattering imagery which those nations used to lavish on their rulers. The result is a highly impressive portraiture, true to the manner and style of the ancient East.

This portrayal delineates a king placed very near to Jahweh: His anointed, crowned by Him (Pss. 2: 2; 21:3); His adopted son (Ps. 2:7); chosen by Him (Pss. 45; 89:21) from among all the Israelites and sitting at His right hand (Ps. 110:1). Jahweh accompanies His chosen king on his military expeditions, destroys his enemies (Ps. 110:5) and makes him invincible (Pss. 72:9; 45:4–6). Jahweh even

---

[62] Two other passages of the same nature would suggest the same solution: I Kings 2:3, where David, shortly before his death, is reported as saying to Solomon: "And keep the charge of the Lord thy God, to walk in his ways, to keep his statutes, and his commandments, and his testimonies, according to that which is written in the law of Moses, that thou mayest prosper in all that thou doest, and whithersoever thou turnest thyself." In I Kings 6:11–13, the Lord is made to say to Solomon after the building of the Temple: "...Concerning this house which thou art in building, if thou wilt walk in my statutes, and execute my judgements, and keep all my commandments to walk in them, then will I establish my word with thee, which I spake unto David thy father. And I will dwell among the children of Israel, and will not forsake my people Israel." Neither passage seems to be an integral part of the narrative and their spirit is rather post-Deuteronomic.

gives him military directions (Pss. 18, 35). Because his Father is
Master of the universe, the king can aspire to world domination
(Pss. 2:8; 72:8–11; 89:26 seq.) and his father will give him "eternal"
life (Pss. 21:6; 72:17). He possesses superhuman knowledge, as
attested by the woman from Tekoah (II Sam. 14:17, 20). He is not
only a just regent (Pss. 72:1 seq.; 45:7; 101), but also an ideal of
piety (Pss. 20:3; 18:21–25). He is a priest, an authentic intermediary between Jahweh and His people, even in matters of worship
and ritual, and his priesthood will be with him for ever (Ps. 110:4).

The description of the Hebrew kingship, especially as conveyed
by the royal psalms, leaves the impression that the Jews, like the
Babylonians and the Egyptians, saw in their king some sort of a
superhuman being. As such, he embodied the soul of his people and
was at the same time the link between Jahweh and His people and
the channel for the conveyance of all His blessings.

What the person of the king meant to the Jews was best conveyed
in the Lamentations, a song composed immediately after the fall
of Jerusalem—in 586 B.C. (Lament. 4:20): "The breath of our
nostrils, the anointed of the Lord, was taken in their pits, of whom
we said, Under his shadow we shall live among the nations." The
portrayal of the king as the breath of life is again of Egyptian
origin, for it is found in Ikhnaton's hymns to the sun[63] and in a
hymn to the god of earth, Biris,[64] while it is frequently used in the
famous letters of Amarna. Though the designation is found to be
applied to the Jewish king only in this particular place, yet it
focuses the Jews' opinion of their king and defines his position in
the life of his people and in Judaic political thought in its pre-
exilic stage.[65]

Such then was the conception of Hebrew kingship in pre-exilic
days. It should be stressed once more that, in spite of some differ-

[63] A. Erman, *The Literature of the Ancient Egyptians*, p. 288.
[64] G. Roeder, *Urkunden zur Religion des alten Aegypten* (Jena, 1923), p.
50. Similar designations of Ikhnaton (Akhenaton), *ibid.*, pp. 74, 76; on
Amenophis III, *ibid.*, p. 157; on the problem, see H. Gressmann, *Der Ursprung*, pp. 27 seq., 49.
[65] Cf. also E. C. B. McLaurin, *The Hebrew Theocracy in the Tenth to the
Sixth Centuries B.C.* (Sydney, 1959), who analyzes ideas on God, man, and
society in the Books of Judges, Samuel, and Kings; cf. pp. 77–97, on the
"anointed."

ences, it was the common possession of the East, shared alike by Hebrews, Babylonians, Assyrians, and Egyptians as well as by other minor Asiatic nations. Its bearing on the subsequent evolution of the Jews and on the rise of Christian political thought lies in the hold it took on the minds of the prophets. They adapted it and transferred it to the ruler of the new everlasting and universal kingdom which the promised Saviour, a descendant of David, was expected to found. In his person the idealized picture of a king, as the imagination of poets and prophets had created it and which every human heart cherished, was to find its final consummation.

The idea of the coming of a Messiah has been the exclusive possession of the Hebrew nation ever since the dawn of its national existence. It sprang from the firm belief of the Israelites in Jahweh, the living and only God whose uniqueness implied domination over the world and all nations, and from the historical fact that this God had entered into special relationship with Israel.[66] Ever since the Covenant on Sinai, the Israelites were the chosen people and Moses was told by Jahweh: "Thou shalt say unto Pharaoh, Thus saith the Lord, Israel is my son, my first-born" (Exod. 4:22). "The Lord shall reign for ever and ever" (Exod. 15:18) over His people, sang Moses and the children of Israel. "The Lord is my strength and song, my salvation.... the Lord is a man of war.... Pharaoh's chariots and his host hath he cast into the sea" (Exod. 15:2–4). "Rehearse the righteous acts of Jahweh's rule in Israel," sang Deborah. "The Lord came down for me against the mighty.... Let all thine enemies perish, O Lord: But let them that love him be as the sun when he goeth forth in his might" (Judg. 5: 11, 13, 31). The two oldest religious and national songs, those of Moses, Miriam, and Deborah, will ever remain the freshest and richest expressions of this deep religious belief in Jahweh's might and in his intimate association with His chosen people. From this belief sprang the glowing expectation of the glorious day of Jahweh, when all His and His people's enemies would be crushed out of existence. But in this very belief in Jahweh's coming and his final victory

[66] Cf. H. Gross, *Weltherrschaft als religiöse Idee im Alten Testament,* Bonner Bibl. Beiträge, 6 (Bonn, 1953), p. 21 seq.

there lay also the notion of a mediator between Jahweh and His people. This notion is reflected in the words of Jacob's blessing of Judah (Gen. 49:10): "The sceptre shall not depart from Judah, nor the ruler's staff from between his feet, until be come whose he is: and unto him shall the obedience of the peoples be." There follows a colorful description of the new age which this intermediary will inaugurate after his advent; it will be an age overflowing with wine and milk. The intermediary will ride on an ass, the noblest mount in fashion at that time. More telling even are the words of Balaam's prophecy (Num. 24:17): "...There shall come forth a star out of Jacob, and a sceptre shall rise out of Israel...."[67]

This ancient Israelite notion of a future mediator found strong support in Hebrew ideas of kingship. It is essential to note that—as these two oldest prophecies confirm—the coming Messiah was visualized as a prince endowed with every royal quality. It naturally followed that, when a monarchy was established in Israel, the messianic expectations of the people should focus on the person of the king, since, from the days of David and Solomon, he occupied such a commanding position in the life of the nation. The influx of Egyptian and Babylonian notions on kingship then transformed the Jewish ruler into an active intermediary between Jahweh and His people and thereby made the amalgamation of the messianic idea with the kingly idea possible.

Once more, the royal psalms give voice to the messianic expectations thus enriched. They were written, it is true, in honor of a living king of either Judah or Israel, but the picture which the court poets conjured up before the king, his courtiers, and his people was that of an ideal king, endowed with all the excellence Jahweh expected from the man who was to convey His will to the

---

[67] Cf. L. Dürr, *Ursprung*, p. 62 seq., for the opinions of the foremost interpreters regarding the date and the composition of the two passages and their importance. See also the publication by E. Burrows, *The Oracles of Jacob and Balaam*, ed. by E. F. Sutcliffe (London, 1938). *Ibid.*, p. 80 seq. the two oracles in the Messianic prophecy. Cf. H. Schmidt, *Der Mythos vom wiederkehrenden König im Alten Testament*, Aus der Welt der Religion, Bibl. Reihe, 2d. ed. (Giessen, 1933). S. Mowinckel, *He that Cometh*, trans. by G. W. Anderson (Oxford, 1956), p. 12 seq., denies a messianic meaning to these prophecies.

people and destined to further all His designs and to realize the aspirations of the nation. It was on this ideal that the Hebrew poets fixed their eyes, with the additional advantage that by extolling this superhuman intermediary, they administered at the same time a useful lesson to the living ruler, the anniversary of whose enthronement or marriage they were singing. Such was the process by which the messianic idea grew to form the background of all court poetry. The more the reigning king fell short of the ideal king and of the perfection his subjects would have liked him to exhibit, the more they longed for the ideal king whose enchanting portrait the imagination of their poets was holding up before their eyes.

This desire must have grown as time went on, since even the most simple Jew and Israelite must have seen that the existing monarchy did not come up to any national or religious expectation; and to that desire, the first prophets must have contributed considerably when, in passionate terms, they exposed the hollowness of royal glory, denounced the corruption that was rife among courtiers and officials, or called down Jahweh's wrath on His people for the sins of its kings. The kingly ideal would never be realized by the present king—such was the burden of every prophetic warning—despite his privileged position and the hopes that centered in him; but that was no proof that such a king would never come. He will come, said the prophets, and his coming will put an end to every crime and injustice and accelerate the coming of Jahweh's day of triumph.

The decadence of the monarchy naturally evoked historical memories of happier days with a corresponding desire for their return. David was remembered as the ruler who came nearest to the ideal king and so became in the estimation of the prophets and of the people the prototype of the earthly king whose reign was so keenly looked forward to as a relief from present misery. By the same token, David became the prototype of the messianic king. The first stage in the growth of the Jewish messianic idea was thus completed within the period of the Jewish and Israelite monarchy; and here again the royal psalms are our witness (Pss. 89:3, 35, 49; 132:1, 11, 17).

314

When the new generation of prophets arose—the *Unheils-propheten* (Prophets of Doom)—all they had to do was to take over in toto a well established messianic tradition, and to improve on it. In fact, they depicted it so vividly and picturesquely that in the estimation of many, they received the credit for being the founders of Israelite Messianism.

It seems unlikely to expect from these prophets any new theories on kingship or any new definition of Israelite or Jewish political philosophy: their mission was to denounce the decadence of the old political and religious institutions and to preach the wrath of Jahweh to a people that had fallen away from Him and broken the covenant. Nothing but destruction, humiliation, and keen suffering could atone for such sin, cleanse Israel and Judah, and restore the covenant with Jahweh.

Their task was of course a thankless one. They had to make it clear that what had appeared to be the authentic instrument for Jahweh to hasten the day of His triumph[68]—the monarchy—had failed, that it would be discarded and that the end of political freedom was near. They knew, however, that they could rely on those faithful Jews and Israelites who, disillusioned by their own experience, were fast losing confidence in monarchic aspirations.

Yet, actual criticism of the monarchy in prophetic literature is, contrary to expectation, rather rare. That the first prophets, Amos, Hosea, Isaiah, Micah, Zephaniah and Nahum, should have referred to the kings so seldom, and contented themselves with general remonstrances addressed to the nation, the priests, and the administrative class, affords additional evidence of the kings' exceptional ascendancy over Israel and Judah. In spite of the bitterness they must have felt and the conviction that the kings' personal behavior and their policy of compromise with pagan infiltration was at the root of the trouble, the prophets never dared to attack the institution of the monarchy frontally. It still stood between Jahweh and His people. The few instances of a direct attack by a prophet on a king concerned mostly the kings of Israel, whose religious policy was more objectionable than that of the kings of Judah.

[68] Cf. what L. Černý says on the Day of Jahweh in his book, *The Day of Jahweh and Some Relevant Problems*, p. 53 seq.

Amos, for instance, is harsh on the king's officials (4:1) and warns Jeroboam, king of Israel, of his death (7:10 seq.) because of his violations of the Lord's laws, but he leaves the institution of the monarchy severely alone. Hosea also makes the political intrigues of the mighty responsible for the moral decadence of Israel, but he is more outspoken with respect to the king. According to him, kingship had degenerated since the days of Saul and the kings had made themselves vindicators of Israel's apostasy from Jahweh (9:15): "All their wickedness is in Gilgal [where the election of the first king took place]; for there I hated them: because of the wickedness of their doings I will drive them out of mine house: I will love them no more; all their princes are revolters."

It was not a long step from political to religious anarchy or revolt against the Lord: "Surely," the prophet had the rebels say, "now shall they say, 'we have no king: for we fear not the Lord: and the king what can he do for us?'" (10:3). But the kings were no better than the rebels (7:7): "They are all hot as an oven, and devour their judges: all their kings are fallen: there is none among them that calleth unto me."

These were strong words; but they could scarcely mean that Hosea branded the monarchy as such as an evil. His last words meant at most that Jahweh did not object to kings in general, but that he wanted only those who took their appointment from him and were faithful. Hosea is clearer in the next chapter (8:4): "They have set up kings, but not by me: they have made princes, and I knew it not." Jahweh wants God-fearing kings, subordinate to their Lord, as they had been in the first days under Saul and David. The present monarchy was a travesty of the original institution and Jahweh in his wrath prepared to eradicate it (13:10): "Where now is thy king, that he may save thee in all thy cities? and thy judges of whom thou saidst, Give me a king and princes? I have given thee a king in mine anger, and have taken him away in my wrath."[69]

Quite different was the association between prophet and king which obtained in Israel under Joash and the prophet Elisha, to

[69] For particulars, see E. Sellin, *Das Zwölfprophetenbuch*, 3rd ed. (Leipzig, 1929–30), p. 13 seq., and his interpretation of the passages quoted above. Cf. also B. Duhm, *Israels Propheten* (Tübingen, 1916), p. 120 seq.

whom Jehu's dynasty was indebted for its throne. When Elisha lay on his deathbed, "Joash, king of Israel, came down to him, and wept over him, and said, my father, my father, the chariot of Israel and the horsemen thereof" (II Kings 13:14). Jonah, who succeeded Elisha in the line of prophets, was a keen supporter of Joash's son Jeroboam II (II Kings 14:25). There was therefore in Amos' and Hosea's days a certain deterioration in the esteem for the kingship, but no explicit repudiation, as has often been asserted. But it is true that religious thinkers were fast losing the old conviction that the day of Jahweh would be brought nearer by the institution of the monarchy, as can be gathered from Amos' vehement outburst (5:18): "Woe unto you that desire the day of the Lord! Wherefore would ye have the day of the Lord! It is darkness and not light." These words, incidentally, show that eschatological expectations were commonly shared by the people of Israel, and that, therefore, they existed before the great prophets came on the scene. In Amos' time, the Israelites looked forward to the day of Jahweh as the only possible relief from their present miseries.[70]

Similar observations can be made on the writings of other prophets. Micah has some biting things to say about rulers and despots who exploit the poor (2:1 seq.; 3:1 seq.). But he proceeds optimistically to describe the final liberation of Israel by Jahweh, after His people have atoned for its iniquities, and the entry of the nation into the gathering place, with the king at its head (2:12 seq.): "I will surely assemble, O Jacob, all of thee; I will surely gather the remnant of Israel; I will put them together as the sheep of Bozrah; as a flock in the midst of their pasture, they shall make great noise by reason of the multitude of men. The breaker is gone up before them: they have broken forth and passed on to the gate, and are gone out thereat: and their king is passed on before them, and the Lord at the head of them."

Addressing himself to the mighty of his people, Micah carefully avoids mentioning the name of the king of Judah. This was not only because the House of David was held in higher esteem by the men of God than were the dynasties of Israel, which frequently owed their position to violence and revolution, but because the monarchy

[70] Cf. E. Sellin, *op. cit.*, p. 232, and L. Černý, *op. cit.*, p. 80 seq.

of Judah was instituted according to the will of Jahweh. Its kings were so securely entrenched in the popular mind that even when the prophets announced Jahweh's decision to punish His people by suppressing the monarchy, they treated the monarchs very leniently. The prophet Zephaniah adopted the same reverential attitude when he so forcefully announced the destruction of Jerusalem and of all its political and religious institutions (Zeph. 1:1 seq., 3:1 seq.).

Isaiah, who was the chief actor in the events of the concluding years of Judah's existence and in the political turmoil that preceded and accompanied the Assyrian invasion of Palestine, was equally considerate. In his reference to the final dissolution of Judah, he marshals the long train of dignitaries and notables who were driven into exile without even mentioning the king who headed them (Isa. 3:1 seq.). He is equally discreet when he fulminates against those "who grind the faces of the poor," though he must have been aware of the king's judicial supremacy and of his responsibility for the general breakdown of the judicature.[71]

The same primitive concept of royal dignity and the same respect for the king's privileged position in the life of the nation is apparent in other passages of Isaiah's prophecies. In describing the despair of the population, stricken by hunger and the scourge of war, he has them curse their king and their God (Isa. 8:21): "And they shall pass through it, hardly bestead and hungry: and it shall come to pass that, when they shall be hungry, they shall fret themselves, and curse by their king and by their God." This only means that Isaiah had lost none of the old deference to kingship as embodied in the law which prohibited cursing God or king and punished both sins by death (Exod. 22:28; I Kings 21:10). Isaiah shared the common belief that if the two sins came under the same punishment, the king must have come first after Jahweh.[72]

---

[71] Isa. 3:14, 15: "The Lord will enter into judgment with the elders of his people, and the princes thereof: it is ye that have eaten up the vineyard; the spoil of the poor is in your houses. What mean ye that you crush my people, and grind the face of the poor? saith the Lord, the Lord of hosts."

[72] The prophecy appended to Isaiah's writings announces the destruction of the Edomites who had benefited most by the collapse of Judah by set-

In the introductory account of the vision in which Isaiah received his mission from Jahweh, he felt so overwhelmed by the majesty of the Lord of Hosts whom he faced that he could find no better title for Jahweh than God the King: the power wielded by the king of Judah was in his estimation the only one that approximated the might of Jahweh.[73]

The principle which, judging from his writings, consistently inspired the attitude of the Prophet toward the King, was based on the assumption that kingship was a natural organism, essential to the political and religious life of the nation. Isaiah had implicit faith in Jahweh, and expected everybody to share it, especially the king. He claimed that the kingship of Judah should be based exclusively on religious motives and not until he had seen King Achaz, David's descendant, failing in this trust, did he throw up his mission in despair; this proved a bitter disappointment and the cause of the tragedy that arose between the King and his Prophet. Not until then did Isaiah realize the failure of the monarchy in Judah; thenceforth his visionary eye turned to the future and his prophetic spirit shifted all his hopes to the Messiah, whom he saw riding in the dimness of future generations. It was the turning point in the history of Judah. Isaiah thus ushered in the era in which none but Jahweh would be acknowledged as king of Israel. Henceforth, all eyes were to be focussed on the coming Saviour, as foretold by Isaiah, the moment David's successor lost his trust in God.

Jeremiah, the greatest of the prophets, modelled himself on Isaiah in this respect. After his election by Jahweh in 626 B.C., he

---

tling on a substantial portion of its lands. This gives evidence of the same kind, for the writer classes the loss of their monarchy among the worst disasters that befell the Edomites (Isa. 34:12): "They shall call the nobles thereof to the kingdom, but none shall be there; and all her princes shall be nothing."

[73] This seems to be the only plausible explanation for the Prophet's words. Cf. O. Procksch, *Jesaia*, I (Leipzig, 1930), p. 56. This, however, does not mean that Isaiah had initiated the custom of calling Jahweh "King," later popularized by Jeremiah. Jahweh's kingship is alluded to in Exod. 15:18; 19:6; Deut. 33:3 seq.; Judg. 8:23; I Sam. 2:8; Ps. 24. See the recent study by H. Gross, *op. cit.*, p. 22 seq., with indications of earlier studies on this problem. Cf. also A. R. Johnson, *Sacral Kingship in Ancient Israel*, p. 34 seq.: "The worship of Jahweh as Melek or 'King' was certainly no late development in the religious history of Israel but dates from at least the early years of the monarchy."

watched over the destinies of his people for forty eventful years. He saw five kings on David's throne. The best of them was Josiah (621–608), whose reign provided a peaceful sunset for the history of Judah. Josiah ended his life on the battlefield; three other kings, in exile. The Prophet himself vanished with the rest of the exiled nation.

For all his unfortunate experience with the rulers of Judah, Jeremiah never condemned the monarchic institution as such; he only tried to recall the kings and their officials to their duty towards Jahweh and finally announced their punishment for their disloyalty to God. His main theme was the king's duty to dispense justice and righteousness. He condemned in strong terms the corruption which prevailed in Judah and accounted so much for the people's suffering (Jer. 2:34 seq.) Only love of justice and right can save thy dynasty, he reminded the king in a striking passage (Jer. 22:3–5):

Execute ye judgement and righteousness, and deliver the spoiled out of the hand of the oppressor: and do no wrong, do no violence to the stranger, the fatherless, nor the widow, neither shed innocent blood in this place.

For if ye do this thing indeed, then shall there enter in by the gates of this house kings sitting upon the throne of David, riding in chariots and on horses, he, and his servants, and his people.

But if ye will not hear these words, I swear by myself, saith the Lord, that this house shall become a desolation.

King Jehoiakim is made to listen to the following words (Jer. 22:13–19):

Woe unto him that buildeth his house by unrighteousness, and his chambers by injustice: that useth his neighbor's service without wages, and giveth him not his hire:

That saith, I will build me a wide house and spacious chamber, and cutteth him out windows; and it is cieled with cedar, and painted with vermilion.

Shalt thou reign, because thou strivest to excel in cedar: Did not thy father eat and drink and do judgement and justice?

Then it was well with him.

He judged the cause of the poor and needy; then it was well. Was not this to know me? saith the Lord.

But thine eyes and thine heart are not but for thy covetousness, and for to shed innocent blood, and for oppression, and for violence, to do it.

Therefore thus saith the Lord concerning Jehoiakim the son of Josiah, king of Judah: They shall not lament for him, saying, ... Ah Lord! or, Ah his glory!

He shall be buried with the burial of an ass, drawn and cast forth beyond the gates of Jerusalem.

Jeremiah knew that the king was expected to be a good shepherd to his flock and had Jahweh remind him of his duty (Jer. 23:1–4): "Woe unto the shepherds that destroy and scatter the sheep of my pasture! saith the Lord. Therefore thus saith the Lord, the God of Israel, against the shepherds that feed my people: Ye have scattered my flock, and driven them away, and have not visited them; behold, I will visit upon you the evil of your doings, saith the Lord...." But when the Lord gathered again the remnants of his flock, then he will "set up shepherds over them which shall feed them: and they shall fear no more, nor be dismayed, neither shall any be lacking, saith the Lord." Hence the liberation of Israel is visualized as a renewal of the old monarchy with kings who will be good shepherds to their nation.

Elsewhere, Jeremiah so forcefully betrayed his conviction of a monarchy being essential to the welfare of his nation, that he visualized the redemption of his people as a restoration of a national government which would realize the religious and moral ideals of Israel (Jer. 30:21, 22): The prince of this state "shall be of themselves, and their ruler shall proceed out of the midst of them, and I will cause him to draw near, and he shall approach unto me.... And ye shall be my people, and I will be your God."[74]

The assurance that the new king will be of their own race, "out of the midst of them," recalls the Deuteronomic law (17:15 seq.)

[74] On this chapter, see P. Volz, *Der Prophet Jeremia* (Leipzig, 1922), pp. 189, 287, 296 seq. Cf. also Jer. 17:19–27, an interesting passage, which may not have been written by Jeremiah, but perhaps by a contemporary of Malachi.

that the king should always be a Jew. Similarly, the passage quoted above, in which Jeremiah condemns the display of pomp and luxury that so disgraced King Jehoiakim, also recalls the Deuteronomic law forbidding the king to surround himself with an extravagant court. Both of these passages show that Jeremiah, who had welcomed Josiah's reforms following the discovery of Deuteronomy, deliberately tried to carry the new Law into effect.

There exists among Jeremiah's writings a prophecy which shows that the author was fully alive to recent developments in Jewish political thought, as illustrated by the Deuteronomic law on kings, and to the growing influence of the priestly caste. This is how he views the liberation of the elected people and sees there the revival of the Davidic kingdom (Jer. 33:15–22):

> In those days, and at that time, will I cause the Branch of righteousness to grow up unto David; and he shall execute judgement and righteousness in the land.
> In those days shall Judah be saved, and Jerusalem shall dwell safely; and this is the name whereby she shall be called, The Lord our righteousness.
> For thus said the Lord: David shall never want a man to sit upon the throne of the house of Israel;
> Neither shall the priests the Levites want a man before me to offer burnt offerings, and to burn oblations, and to do sacrifice continually.
> . . . .
> As the host of heaven cannot be numbered, neither the sand of the sea measured; so will I multiply the seed of David my servant, and the Levites that minister unto me.

On close inspection, this prophecy is only a paraphrase of Jeremiah's famous messianic dictum (Jer. 23:5, 6): "Behold, the days come, saith the Lord, that I will raise unto David a righteous Branch, and he shall reign as king and deal wisely, and shall execute judgement and justice in the land. In his days Judah shall be saved, and Israel shall dwell safely: and this is his name whereby he shall be called, 'The Lord Our Righteousness.'" This dictum fails to describe the majestic dignity of the promised Saviour, the

Messiah being reduced to the state of a ruler over a liberated people after its return from captivity and resettlement in the promised land. This new kingdom is to last indefinitely and will be ruled by kings of the Davidic dynasty following each other in unbroken succession. The prophet's insistence on priestly privileges should not pass unnoticed.

If this prophecy was actually written by Jeremiah, under whose name it appears, it would provide additional evidence for the view that the great Prophet acquiesced in the king's new status as it emerged from Josiah's reform. But this attribution is questionable, for the prophecy seems to imply the abduction of the greater part of the nation into exile and the loss of its political independence. This makes it appear more likely that it was written by an anonymous prophet, perhaps a contemporary of Malachi.[75] Even so, the passage has its place in the history of Jewish political thought, for in either case, it shows that the Jews were so profoundly convinced of the indispensability of kings in their national and religious life that, even after the national disaster, they could see no salvation outside a resuscitated monarchy. However, in the years 500–450 B.C., when the prophecy may have been written, the priestly element was coming into its own, royalty was losing the monopoly of power and was left only with the alternative of sharing it with the clergy.

The prophet most active in this consummation was Ezekiel, who may rightly be called the forerunner of priestly rule in Israel. Like Jeremiah the son of a priest, Ezekiel, unlike his predecessor, could not conceive of any genuine worship of Jahweh without the existence of a Temple and a divine liturgy. During his captivity in 597 B.C., his faith in the reconstruction of the Temple and the restoration of its divine worship never wavered. This, not the restoration of the monarchy, lay at the center of Israel's redemption from captivity and its return to the homeland as he conceived it.

This does not mean that Ezekiel treated the monarchy as an evil or was ready to barter it for either a theocracy or a hierocracy, for the political reorganization he visualized included a king at its

---

[75] Cf. P. Volz, *loc. cit.*, p. 311.

head. He even went further than Jeremiah, whose redemption of the Jews from captivity was mainly meant to benefit Judah. Ezekiel prophesied the reunion of all Jews, whether of Israel or of Judah, and their gathering into one united kingdom which would be governed by one king, a second David (Ezek. 37:22 seq.): "I will make them one nation in the land, upon the mountains of Israel; and one king shall be king to them all: and they shall be no more two nations, neither shall they be divided into two kingdoms any more at all.... And my servant David shall be king over them; and they shall have all one shepherd.... And David my servant shall be their prince for ever. Moreover I will make a covenant: it shall be an everlasting covenant with them...."

These were Ezekiel's pre-exilic views, but they must have altered, for in another passage referring to the redemption of Israel, Ezekiel makes David only a prince, and Jahweh the overlord of Israel (Ezek. 34:22 seq.): "Therefore will I save my flock, and they shall no more be a prey; and I will judge between cattle and cattle. And I will set up one shepherd over them, and he shall feed them, and he shall be their shepherd. And I the Lord will be their God, and my servant David prince among them. I the Lord have spoken it." There is a theocratic ring to these words: Jahweh liberates His people and rules it without intermediary, while David, his servant, is kept for administrative purposes as the figurehead of the theocracy.[76]

Signs of profound alterations in the pre-exilic conception of kingship are also found elsewhere in Ezekiel. In referring to the corruption of Jerusalem before the exile, he first mentions the princes who devoured souls "like roaring lions" (Ezek. 22:25 seq.);[77] then the priests "who have done violence to my law"; the officials who were "ravening the prey like wolves"; and, lastly, the prophets and the people. The precedence given to priests over officials is significant and very unlike the manner of Jeremiah, who invariably mentioned the king first, then the princes or officials, followed by priests and prophets.[78] Evidently the priests had gained ground

---

[76] Cf. J. Hermann, *Ezechiel* (Leipzig, 1924), pp. 222 seq., 236 seq.
[77] See the translation in *ibid.*, pp. 137, 139.
[78] Jer. 1:18; 2:26; 4:9; 8:1; 13:13; 32:32; 44:17.

during the exile. The same impression may be inferred from Ezekiel's recommendations to priests and the prince in the renascent kingdom (Ezek. 44 seq.; 48:21 seq.).[79] During the exile, kings were only a memory of the past, and not a happy one at that, whereas the priests accompanied their people into exile and provided them with the sole consolation left to them. It was only to be expected that opinions on royalty should suffer in the process. Notable also is Ezekiel's emphatic command not to rebuild the royal palace in the vicinity of the Temple (Ezek. 43:7), where nothing should recall past sins and human weakness. Such words would have been impossible in pre-exilic days, when kings were enthroned next to Jahweh.

The change that raised Jahweh to an unprecedented position in Jewish national life and reduced the king to a subordinate rank marked to some extent a beginning of emancipation from the influence which Egypt, Babylon, and Assyria had wielded over Jewish political thought, and to that extent it signified progress. But the importance given to external worship, sacrifices, and ceremonies was a retrogression away from Isaiah and Jeremiah, who had laid stress on the relationship with Jahweh, personal, intimate, and sincere, even in the absence of outward display. The same was true of the growth of priestly influence, with its attendant danger of lust for power, always so liable to end in dereliction of sacerdotal duty.

In Ezekiel's insistence on a temple and organized worship,[80] one can detect the effects of the discovery of Deuteronomy and of Josiah's reform. The reform was encouraged by the prophetic and sacerdotal circles whose primary aim was to make organized worship the main center of religion and to enhance its magnificence by multiplying laws and prescriptions. In their anxiety to extend the new code to other fields of national life, they intensified their activities after the proclamation of Josiah's reform.

---

[79] See, for details, H. Gese, *Der Verfassungsentwurf des Ezechiel (Kap. 40–48) traditionsgeschichtlich untersucht*, Beiträge zur histor. Theologie, 25 (Tübingen, 1957). Cf. also O. Procksch, "Fürst und Priester bei Hesekiel," *ZAW*, N.F., 17 (1940–41), pp. 99–133, and L. H. Vincent, "L'autel des holocaustes et le caractère du Temple d'Ezéchiel," *Analecta Bollandiana*, 67 (1949), pp. 7–20.
[80] Cf. for the ideas of the prophets on cult, Th. Chary, *Les prophètes et le culte à partir de l'exil* (Tournai, 1955). On Ezekiel, *ibid.*, pp. 4–70.

Jeremiah immediately saw the danger of this tendency and, however much he believed in the reforms, warned his countrymen that, should this tendency prevail, their faith would lose its spiritual appeal and degenerate into book religion. But the Deuteronomic circle went on with its work and proceeded to introduce its legalism into the written books then known. They were inspired no doubt by religious and patriotic motives, for in their opinion the preservation of the state depended on the people's strict adherence to the covenant.

The exile, with its spasms of regret, penance, and contrition, only intensified the mood. As the nation realized that its present sufferings were but Jahweh's punishment for its many apostasies in the past, the Deuteronomic school—at least in the opinion of some experts—felt prompted to avert a similar fate for future generations. To that end they made a number of additions to the Books of Judges, Samuel, and Kings in order to enforce a strict observance of Jahweh's covenant. If this is true, these interpolations, made in a Deuteronomic spirit, reflected Deuteronomic opinions on the pre-Deuteronomic monarchy. This circumstance makes the study of Israelite ideas on kingship and on the part played by pre-exilic kings in national life difficult.

Isaiah, or, according to some specialists, an anonymous author known as Deutero-Isaiah who lived during the period of exile, appended to chap. 39 a document contained in chaps. 40–66. If this document was in fact written by an anonymous author, he probably spent some time with the exiles in Babylonia, though he must also have lived in Palestine. He may also have lived in Lebanon, since he speaks with such enthusiasm, though only incidentally, of the cedars of Lebanon and of the lands by the sea.[81] Like other prophets, he strikes a hopeful note and rouses in the stricken Jews an awareness of their role as the chosen people and of the glorious future which Jahweh has in store for them to lead all nations back to Jahweh's rule.

These poems give evidence of an exceptionally fertile imagination and of an idealism rich in pathos, but they are indifferent to

[81] B. Duhm, *op. cit.*, p. 29 seq.

the glories of Jewish kingship and sparing in their references to the monarchy. Jahweh is hailed as king of the liberated nation (Isa. 43:15; 44:6), and to display his majesty the writer delights in picturing kings and princes in adoration before him (Isa. 49:7, 23; 52:15). The poet looks upon the restoration of the Jewish community in Jerusalem as the revival of David's kingdom and the fulfilment of the promise made to this ideal king, though what he has in mind is rather David's spiritual mission to lead all nations to Jahweh by his deeds (Isa. 55:3 seq.). The promise, once made to David, is now transferred to the liberated nation which thereby becomes the trustee of all eschatological expectations. Israel's Davidic mission will be a spiritual and religious leadership over all nations. This is a new conception, entirely different from any previously encountered; it is a spiritualized version of the old concept of Israelite kingship and of its universal jurisdiction.

Isaiah's, or the so-called Deutero-Isaiah's, notable contribution to Jewish political thought was his portrayal of Cyrus, the conqueror who destroyed Babylonia and issued the edict for the liberation of the Jewish exiles. He is depicted as Jahweh's instrument for carrying out his will,[82] the first time that a Jewish writer referred to a foreign ruler in such terms, since none but a Jewish king could be called the Anointed of Jahweh and the shepherd of His choice (Isa. 44:28): "That saith of Cyrus, He is my shepherd, and shall perform all my pleasure...." "Thus saith the Lord to His anointed, to Cyrus, whose right hand I have holden, to subdue nations before him.... For Jacob my servant's sake, and Israel my chosen, I have even called thee by thy name: I have surnamed thee, though thou has not known me..." (Isa. 45:1 seq.).

The words bear a certain resemblance to the inscription on the famous Cyrus' cylinder made after the conquest of Babylon, and it is now generaly admitted that the Hebrew poet borrowed words current in the Babylonian court style,[83] another sign of Hebrew familiarity with the document.

[82] Cf. E. Jenni, *Die politischen Voraussagen der Propheten* (Zurich, 1956), p. 100 seq.
[83] Cf. especially R. Kittel's study, "Cyrus und Deuterojesaja," *ZAW*, 18 (1898), pp. 149–162, which settled the controversy about the affinity between Deutero-Isaiah and the Persian document. The inscription was published by

This daring declaration amounted to a revolution in Jewish political thought and religious belief. It was far reaching in its consequences, for it was to reconcile the Jews in later years to the unpalatable fact that their national state would never rise again and that Jahweh could use pagan princes to carry out his designs for the final redemption of his people. Yet the prophet, himself a patriot, knew how to play on national feeling, for he also saw the coming of Jahweh's day in the liberation of the exiles by Cyrus' intervention, in the rebuilding of Zion, in the setting up of Jahweh's kingdom. But he placed less stress on this than did Ezekiel, who minutely described the rebuilding of the Temple and the restoration of the nation.

Isaiah, or rather Deutero-Isaiah, saw the final goal of his eschatological dreams and visions rather in the manifestation of Jahweh, whose victory was that of his people's religion over all other religions. His prophecies represent the spiritual version of Israel's claim to be the chosen people, with no mention of universal political hegemony. This is remarkable, as the notion of a messianic kingdom in its political sense was still alive among the exiled Jews. For the prophet Isaiah, the new Zion was not the political, but the religious center of Jahweh's kingdom, in which all believers in Jahweh were as much his chosen people as the Israelites.

What is new and remarkable about these prophecies is that the seer puts all the stress on the universal character of the new kingdom and throws open its frontiers to all nations. His is the first message addressed to all pagans and the first invitation to them to join the faith of Jahweh.

The Jews were in sore need of such consolation as they could find in the prophet's words and in such of his visions as tallied with their own dreams. If they took some of them too literally and looked forward to the glories of an earthly kingdom, they were promptly disillusioned on their return to Jerusalem. For they discovered that the king of Persia was the only king available and

H. C. Rawlinson, *The Cuneiform Inscriptions of Western Asia*, 5 (London, 1884), p. 35, and by E. Schrader, *Keilinschriftliche Bibliothek*, Bd. 3, Hälfte 2 (Berlin, 1890), p. 120 seq. Cf. also W. F. Albright, *From the Stone Age to Christianity*, 2nd ed. (New York, 1946), p. 326 seq.

they had to rest satisfied with a mere satrap to represent him. The prophet Haggai, one of their spiritual leaders, surrendered to the inevitable, but the disappointment was bitter none the less when the home-coming produced none of the wonders foretold by the prophets and only an insignificant colony clustered around Jerusalem. The difficulties with the resident population were endless and assistance by the Persian government fell far short of the prophet's expectations. This was nothing like the great national kingdom so often foretold and so generally expected.

But there remained a glimmer of hope. The first satraps or Persian colonial governors, Sheshbazzar and Zerubbabel, were descendants of David, and they, especially the latter, as heirs of David and bearers of the royal tradition, became a rallying point for national aspirations. Haggai, true to the spirit of Ezekiel, still clung to the belief that delay in rebuilding the Temple was responsible for all the trouble; by dangling before their eyes the national kingdom as an approaching reality, he encouraged his countrymen's faith in the future promised by the prophets. Inspired by the words of Isaiah, he said (Hag. 2:21 seq.):

Speak to Zerubbabel, governor of Judah, saying, I will shake the heavens and the earth,
And I will overthrow the throne of kingdoms, and I will destroy the strength of the kingdoms of the heathen; and I will overthrow the chariots, and those that ride in them; and the horses and their riders shall come down, every one by the sword of his brother.
In that day, saith the Lord of Hosts, will I take thee, O Zerubbabel, my servant, the son of Shealtiel, saith the Lord, and I will make thee as a signet: for I have chosen thee, saith the Lord of hosts.[84]

The signet simile is a daring one, implying that, since a seal makes the king's orders official, Zerubabbel was to become the Lord's representative and the future king of Judah. Jeremiah once

---

[84] Cf. also Ecclesiasticus 49:11: "How shall we magnify Zerubbabel? And he was as a signet on the right hand...."

used the same figure of speech (Jer. 22:24): "As I live, saith the Lord, though Coniah the son of Jehoiakim king of Judah were the signet upon my right hand, yet would I pluck thee thence." The metaphor fitted Jewish kings and their main function as understood in pre-exilic days, i.e. law-giving and heralding the will of Jahweh. At the same time, Haggai, again under Isaiah's inspiration, predicted the world dominion of Israel and the world's subjection, but unable to follow his source of inspiration into the lofty heights where Isaiah felt so much at home, he materializes the notion and envisages it concretely as a political kingdom under a Davidic king. It is quite possible that indiscretions such as these, as uttered by Haggai and other nationally minded Jews, contributed to Zerubbabel's downfall, as it is easy to imagine their propaganda having been reported to the Persian king. Zerubbabel was replaced by a Persian satrap and the Jews had to resign themselves to further postponement of the Lord's day.

It is true that Haggai, influenced in his writings by the new thought initiated under Josiah and fostered during the exile, raised the high priest Joshua to a place next to the king, though at a respectable distance from the throne; but the distance is further reduced by Zechariah who invests the high priest with functions hitherto reserved to the king (Zech. 3:6 seq.): "And the angel of the Lord protested unto Joshua saying, Thus saith the Lord of hosts: If thou wilt walk in my ways, and if thou wilt keep my charge, then thou also shalt judge my house, and shalt also keep my courts, and I will give thee a place of access among these that stand by"; weighty words, such as no prophet would have dared to utter in pre-exilic days.

Zechariah goes even further. In another vision, he states how he was ordered by the Lord to take from the returning exiles the gold and silver they had brought and to make a crown with it for Zerubbabel, as he was to rebuild the Temple and rule over the messianic kingdom. Joshua the high priest would stand on his right and the council of peace would stand "between them both." The passage[85]

---

[85] Cf. E. Sellin, *Das Zwölfprophetenbuch*, p. 519 seq. The supposition that this passage was modified, probably after Zerubbabel's discomfiture, by an editor who left out the Prince's name and instead placed the crown on the High Priest's head is very hypothetical.

marks the turning point in the history of Jewish political thought. With the wrecking of their national monarchy, the Jews gradually lost the notion, shared with the Egyptians, the Babylonians, and the Assyrians, of the kings' indispensability in their national life. Royal power originally also included, besides secular authority, the right to represent the divinity and to approach it in the name of the nation in all official worship. In Zerubbabel's days, as interpreted by Zechariah, this royal power showed signs of losing its spiritual functions to the priests. This foreshadowed the dualism of the secular and the ecclesiastical powers, a distinction unknown to the East and to pre-exilic Judaism, but which was to enjoy a great future in the West. Western politicians and theologians who have elaborated on the distinction may have found in the vision of Zechariah promises of perpetual peace between king and high priest and adopted his words as a program, but they discovered in the course of time that it was easier for a prophet to weave dreams than for themselves to turn them into reality.

Zechariah's prophecies also foreshadowed the dominance of the spiritual power over the secular, the cherished ideal of the mediaeval Papacy. With the fall of Zerubbabel, only the priests were left to represent the once mighty kings, yet Zechariah and his contemporaries never despaired, as long as the high priest, the Temple and the religious cult remained to inspire them. After so many frustrations, the post-exilic Jews ceased to look upon their kings as the necessary link between the chosen people and Jahweh: the high priest, the Temple, and public worship would thenceforth replace the mediation of the prince. Thus ended the long process inaugurated by the Deuteronomies, accelerated by Ezekiel, and finally completed by the minor prophets of post-exilic days.

Though Zechariah's mission rather implied retrogression from the lofty stand of the so-called Deutero-Isaiah and Ezekiel, in one instance at least he did follow his predecessors: he too believed that all foreign nations would be crushed, that their riches would flow into the Temple, that the Temple was destined to be the center of Jahweh's kingdom from where the whole world would be governed, that many great nations would join Israel without detracting from its position as the chosen people, and that Jahweh would rule from

Zion. This rule Zechariah described in terms of the Persian notion of king of kings: Jahweh sits enthroned among His ministers and messengers who execute His orders and keep Him in touch with the world. More important, however, was that the rule was universal and that even pagan nations were admitted to the new kingdom. Thanks to Isaiah's poems, this idea of universalism was so deeply anchored in Jewish minds that not even a return to Ezekiel's exaltation of the Temple and its worship succeeded in obliterating it. The importance of the new transformation and the key to all further progress in Jewish political thought lay within this idea of universalism.

It is appropriate to note that, after Isaiah, the custom spread among the prophets of calling Jahweh King of Israel, or simply King, King of the hosts, King of nations.[86] To Jeremiah, Jahweh is "the Lord in Zion"; King of Jahweh's daughter Israel (Jer. 8:19 seq.); "King of nations," "everlasting King" (Jer. 10:7, 10); "King, whose name is the Lord of hosts" (Jer. 46:18; 48:15; 51:57). Jeremiah is followed by the so-called Deutero-Isaiah[87] and by the lesser prophets: Zephaniah (3:15), Zechariah (14:9, 16, 17), Malachi (1:14). The author of the prophetic poem (preserved amongst Isaiah's writings), who may have lived in the time of Alexander the Great,[88] expresses Jahweh's royal majesty in terms which the great prophets would never have dared to use (Isa. 33:22): "For the Lord is our judge, the Lord is our lawgiver, the Lord is our king; he will save us." He is then followed by the author of the Book of Daniel (Dan. 4:34), and, probably contemporary with him, the author of the apocalypse which is now embodied in Isaiah's book (chaps. 24–27).[89] He also yearned for the advent of the day when "the Lord of hosts would reign in Mount Zion, and in Jerusalem and before his ancients gloriously."[90]

[86] Cf. *supra*, p. 319.
[87] Isa. 41:21 ("King of Jacob"); 43:15 ("I am the lord, your Holy One, the Creator of Israel, your King"); 44:6 ("King of Israel"). Other designations are found in the following psalms: Ps. 5:2; 10:16; 24:7, 8, 9, 10; 29:10; 44:4; 47:2–7; 48:2; 68:24; 74:12; 84:3; 95:3; 98:6; 99:4; 145:1; 149:2. Cf. H. Gressmann, *Der Messias*, pp. 212–220.
[88] See O. Procksch, *Jesaia*, 1, p. 425.
[89] *Ibid.*, pp. 305–346.
[90] Isa. 24:23.

We have seen that Jahweh was invoked as King of Israel in the earliest days, since the practice of describing their gods as kings appears to have been common among all Semitic nations.[91] In any case, proper names derived from Melech, which indicate that Jahweh was commonly addressed as King, come into general use only after Jeremiah's time (Jer. 38:8: Ebed-melech);[92] if the title was conferred on Jahweh before Isaiah, it is significant that it grew more frequent after him. Various theories have been adopted in explanation,[93] but none are completely satisfactory. The solution can probably be found in the political and religious upheaval among the Jews during the periods immediately preceding and following the exile. The pre-exilic prophets' disappointing experience with their king must have prompted them to concentrate on Jahweh and on Him alone, and to dispense with the kings. By their unworthiness and their incapacity, the rulers had in the prophets' estimation forfeited their right to act as Jahweh's sons and representatives. Attention was then focussed on Jahweh as the only legitimate king of Israel, the earthly kings being discarded as useless tools.

This explanation fits in with the whole trend of the period, which was alive with eschatological expectations. The titles lavished on Jahweh were generally given an eschatological turn; thus an irresistible impression is created that the prophets turned their backs on earthly kings, conferred their titles on Jahweh, and looked to Him to provide the man who would bring about His and His people's great day.

If correct, this re-orientation of national policy marks a stage in Israel's progress and foreshadows a new era in its political thought. With the disappointing collapse of the old ideal of kingship and its promises, the prophets explored a new avenue that was to lead straight to pure theocracy, yet, at the same time, to call forth from the upheaval of a religious revolution a deeper and truer knowledge of God. Jahweh's new kingship also better conveyed his universality, since Jahweh was not only King of Israel, but of all nations. Thus,

---

[91] See *supra*, pp. 24, 33—35. Cf. O. Eissfeldt, "Jahwe als König," *ZAW*, N.F., 5 (1928), pp. 84–88, and especially W. Schmidt, *Königtum Gottes in Ugarit und Israel*, Beihefte zur *ZAW*, 80 (Berlin, 1961), pp. 1–59.

[92] Cf. O. Eissfeldt, *op. cit.*, p. 103 seq.

[93] *Ibid.*, pp. 81–84.

the narrow connotation of a national kingdom was widened and made to include the universal salvation that had been prepared by the Lord of hosts and would be carried out by the messenger of His choice. He would come to His people in the fullness of time, as the true consummation of a national monarchy that was meant only to be His shadow and forerunner.

It is in the context of these changing ideas that those psalms which hail Jahweh's enthronement as King of Israel should be explained.[94] These psalms which are numbered 47, 93, 96, 97, 98, and 99, supplement the royal psalms and continue their tradition. The eschatological meaning which many of the royal psalms convey, or which has been attributed to them, saved them from oblivion, in spite of a few features that must have been repugnant to contemporaries of the exilic or post-exilic period. They were followed by the psalms in praise of Jahweh's royal might and glory, so that the so-called "enthronement psalms" may be rightly regarded as the fitting adjunct to the prophets' tributes of praise addressed to the divine King of Israel.

It is now possible to appreciate how in the days of the greater and minor prophets the old notion of Israelite kingship underwent a period of alteration, receding gradually into the background of the national life to become increasingly spiritualized and focussed on Jahweh instead of on a political king. By the same token, it grew more universal in character, yet, however much transformed, it remained substantially the same. The greater Israel's punishment and persecution, the greater too its determination to look forward to Jahweh's Day when He would found His everlasting kingdom and hand over its leadership to the chosen people. But the question arose—would Jahweh act alone or through an intermediary? The kings of the old regime had been the authentic links between Jahweh and his people and the Israelites could not but expect a similar function from their ideal king. In that event, the new David would be superior to the feeble specimens the Jews knew. Consequently the notion of an intermediary was fated to

[94] Cf. J. Gray, "The Kingship of God in the Prophets and Psalms," *VT*, 11 (1961), pp. 1–29.

survive the Jewish national kingdom and to gather round the ideal monarch of their anticipations.

And this is exactly what is found in the writings of the prophets, expressed with increasing clarity, but always with the same conviction. The agent whom Jahweh would send to prepare his day and save his people was of course portrayed as the ideal king and on him were lavished all the epithets, suitably amplified, that were once reserved to the Hebrew kings. On going through the works of the prophets, the characteristic imagery of the Hebrew, Babylonian, Assyrian, and Egyptian court style is constantly seen.

First of all, the expected Messiah was glorified as a most righteous king, since in Eastern estimation righteousness and love of justice were held to be the leading attributes of ideal kings. Both Isaiah and Jeremiah made much of this messianic qualification so as to give heart to the many who were victimized by the royal officials. This is found at its best in the beautiful prophecy on the coming of the royal child (Isa. 9:6 seq.): "For unto us a child is born, unto us a son is given; and the government shall be upon his shoulders: and his name shall be called Wonderful, Counsellor, Mighty God, Everlasting Father, Prince of Peace. Of the increase of his government and of peace there shall be no end, upon the throne of David, and upon his kingdom, to establish it, and to uphold it with judgement and with righteousness from henceforth even for ever. The zeal of the Lord of hosts shall perform this." Elsewhere, Isaiah lingers on the righteousness of the "shoot out of the stock of Jesse" (Isa. 11:3–5): "And he shall not judge after the sight of his eyes, neither reprove after the hearing of his ears: but with righteousness shall he judge the poor and reprove with equity for the meek of the earth: and he shall smite the earth with the rod of his mouth, and with the breath of his lips shall he slay the wicked. And righteousness shall be the girdle of his loins, and faithfulness the girdle of his reins."[95]

---

[95] Cf. O. Procksch, *Jesaia*, I, p. 410. The same idea is believed to occur in more concise terms in another passage (Isa. 32:1) which, however, according to some specialists (cf. O. Procksch, *ibid.*, p. 410), may have been written by an anonymous prophet and survived under Isaiah's name: "Behold a King shall reign in righteousness, a prince shall rule in judgment." But according to E. J. Kissane, *The Book of Isaiah*, I, rev. ed. (Dublin, 1960),

Without enlarging on these messianic writings, it is sufficient to remember what has been said about the righteousness of Egyptian, Babylonian, and Hebrew kings. This would make it obvious that the Prophet, in portraying the righteous king, is mixing colors that had been used for centuries throughout the East. According to Isaiah, the messianic king he presages will be the personification of justice and therefore of law, since justice is the offshoot of law.

Jeremiah also falls back on Eastern materials in his portraiture of the Messiah: "Behold, the days come, saith the Lord, that I will raise unto David a righteous Branch, and he shall reign as king and deal wisely, and shall execute judgement and justice in the land: In his days Judah shall be saved, and Israel shall dwell safely: and this is his name whereby he shall be called, The Lord is our righteousness" (Jer. 23:5, 6). This passage, which is generally attributed to Jeremiah, is paraphrased by a prophet of a later period (Jer. 33:15, 16). Both Jeremiah and his commentator follow Isaiah and the many Babylonian inscriptions. The words "the Lord is our righteousness" imply that the future intermediary will personify justice and law.

The same spirit is apparent in the description of the coming mediator by the so-called Deutero-Isaiah (Isa. 42:1, 3, 6, 7): "Behold my servant, whom I uphold; my chosen, in whom my soul delighteth: I have put my spirit upon him; he shall bring forth judgement to the Gentiles. . . . A bruised reed shall he not break, and the smoking flax shall he not quench: he shall bring forth judgement in truth. . . . I the Lord have called thee in righteousness, and will hold thine hand, and will keep thee for a covenant of the people, for a light of the Gentiles. . . ." There is a ring of the court style about these words: the coming Saviour is God's chosen one; Jahweh's spirit is in Him just as the Babylonian gods were with their chosen kings; Jahweh will call His name just as Marduk called the name of his chosen king; Jahweh will hold his hand just as Marduk was pictured holding the hand of his earthly agent. It is interesting to

pp. 347, 350, this passage has no messianic meaning and has to be translated as follows: "If a king reigned with righteousness and if princes ruled with justice, and each were like a refuge from the wind and a shelter from the rain-storm. . . ." If this interpretation is correct, the passage must be attributed to Isaiah and all other combinations are pointless.

336

find that many epithets which this prophet used in hailing the coming Messiah and which so appealed to the hearts of the Christians, recalling to them the aura of Christmas, once came from the lips of Sumerian and Babylonian courtiers and poets.

We have seen that the Babylonians and Egyptians counted very generously and wished their kings thousands upon thousands of years of government and an eternal reign. The prophets did the same, allotting an eternal reign to the expected mediator between Jahweh and His people, as in Psalm 89, verses 29, 36, 37 (this was most probably written immediately after the collapse of Jerusalem and the kingdom),[96] in Isaiah 9:6 ("everlasting Father"), and in the words attributed to Jeremiah (Jer. 33:22). The prophet Joel (4:20) is equally generous, when he shifts the promise of eternal duration to Judah and Jerusalem, and so is Ezekiel after him (Ezek. 37:26; 43:7, 9).[97]

The pledge of eternity given to the Messiah's reign was, of course, implied in the oldest messianic promises and was therefore genuinely Israelite, but in trying to give expression to it, the prophets borrowed their terms from the Egyptian and Babylonian court style. They had recourse to the same device to extol the majesty of the mediator and his aristocratic origin. It was in this spirit that Micah rhapsodized over the Messiah's birthplace (Mic. 5:2): "But thou, Beth-lehem Ephratah, though thou be little among the thousands of Judah, yet out of thee shall he come forth unto me that is to be ruler in Israel; whose goings forth have been from of old, from everlasting." In like words did the Babylonian and Assyrian kings call attention to their origin, with special emphasis on the antiquity of their dynasties. Usurpers were called "sons of nobody."[98]

[96] Cf. G. W. Ahlström, *Psalm 89* (Lund, 1959), p. 20, on the different opinions concerning the date of this psalm. The author, of course, sees in this Psalm "eine Liturgie aus dem Ritual des leidenden Königs."

[97] Cf. L. Dürr, *Die Stellung des Propheten Ezechiel in der israel.-jud. Apokalyptik*, Alttest. Abhandl., 9, Heft 1 (Münster, 1923), p. 113 seq. Cf. *ibid.*, the treatment of Babylonian parallels to Ezekiel, with its description of the glory of renovated Jerusalem. Ezekiel used many Babylonian and Assyrian symbols in his description of Jahweh's manifestations, according to another study by L. Dürr, *Ezechiels Vision von der Erscheinung Gottes im Lichte der Vorderasiatischen Altertumskunde* (Münster i.W., 1917).

[98] Cf. Meissner, *Babylonien und Assyrien*, 1, p. 47 seq. Instances in connection with Hammurabi, Salmanassar and Asarhaddon will be found in L. Dürr, *Ursprung*, p. 252 seq.

It is in the same sense that Isaiah's insistence (Isa. 11:1, 10) on the Messiah coming up from the root of Jesse must be explained. Not content with tracing the origin of the ideal king to his forefather David, he goes further and traces him to David's father, the founder of the dynasty.[99] The prophets follow the same process of thought, when they call the Messiah the "Branch of David" or simply "the Branch" (Jer. 23:5; 33:15; Zech. 3:8; 6:12). Again, in affirming the universality of the Messiah's kingdom, prophets and poets may have been inspired by the court style, which makes all its kings rulers of the universe.[100] Yet, the idea was genuinely native to the Israelites, since it was implied in the Jew's conception of their Jahweh.

Likewise the names bestowed on the Messiah by Isaiah (9:6) recall the Babylonian liking for gracing their god or their king with the name "Counsellor." It was the epithet given to Marduk and Shamash; among the kings, the famous Hammurabi called himself the perfect counsellor.[101] Isaiah could therefore not claim to be original, when he called the coming Messiah "Wonderful, Counsellor." The title "Mighty God" is also an imitation, as valor and might were the common attributes of almost all the Babylonian gods. So was the title "father of his subjects," which Hammurabi claimed for himself; and many kings in pardonable self-praise commended the peacefulness of their rule on their inscriptions. Again, when Jahweh promised to rally his flock as a good shepherd and undertook, in the words of his prophets, to be a better shepherd than the present kings, we are reminded of the Babylonian and Assyrian kings who loved to call themselves good shepherds of their flocks. Even Balaam's prophecy (Num. 24:17) shows traces of the court style, where Babylonian rulers were often compared to the sun; and the Assyrian name for a king, *sharru*, meant resplendent, that which is striking. The title "Star of Jacob" also has its analogies in the court style, as do the comparisons of Jahweh with the shining sun or star found in the Hebrew poets (Deut. 33:2; Pss. 19:4;

---

[99] Cf. what H. Gressmann, *Der Messias*, p. 246 seq., has to say on the meaning of this passage.

[100] H. Gressmann, *Der Ursprung*, has already pointed out this parallelism, pp. 252 seq., 262 seq.

[101] For particulars, see L. Dürr, *Ursprung*, p. 113 seq., where the necessary bibliography will also be found.

50:2 seq.; 80:1; 112:4), and the identification of Jahweh with light found in the prophets (Mic. 7:8; the so-called Deutero-Isaiah, Isa. 60:19; cf. Ps. 27:1).

Of the same origins are the many references to conditions of life in the Messiah's new kingdom, whose blessings are mostly gifts of an earthly nature. Such visions were not borrowed from the old Oriental myths on the reopening of paradise by its mythical king, but rather from the old Oriental court style which described the reign of every good king as bringing forth gifts from nature, and from the ancient custom in the East of specifying every gift of God in terms of natural abundance, every affliction in terms of natural privation. One has only to look over the inscriptions of Sumerian and Accadian kings, chiefly the famous *patesi* of Lagash, Gudea,[102] to realize how anxious those rulers were to attribute to their reigns every gift of nature and to themselves the prosperity of their subjects. Little wonder, then, that the prophets, who lived in the same Oriental atmosphere and worked from the same Oriental materials, described the Messiah's future kingdom in analogous terms and gave free rein to their poetical enthusiasm to adorn it.[103]

The principle of Hebrew and Oriental kingship also seems to supply the solution to a problem which has worried modern interpreters of the Bible—the meaning of the presentation by Isaiah (or the so-called Deutero-Isaiah) of the Servant of God, suffering and led to death for the sins of others. It seems now to be generally admitted that the Servant in the "Servant Songs" (Isa. 42:1–7; 49:1–9; 50:4–9; 52:13, 14; 53:1–12) cannot be a personification of Israel,[104] but must refer to an individual being.[105] The Servant of

---

[102] Cylinder A, col. XI, 5–17, F. Thureau-Dangin, *Die sumerischen und akkadischen Königsinschriften*, Vorderasiatische Bibliothek, Bd. 1, Abt. 1 (Leipzig, 1907), p. 101; Cylinder B, col. XI, 15–25, *ibid.*, p. 133. For particulars and many other Babylonian parallels, see L. Dürr, *op. cit.*, pp. 94–105.

[103] Amos 9:13–15; Hosea 2:18 seq.; 14:6–9; Isa. 4:2; 11:6–9; Jer. 31:12, 21–24; Ezek. 34:25–31; 36:8–15; 47:1–12; Deutero-Isaiah 41:18–20; 48:21; 51:3; 55:12 seq.; 65:21 seq.; Anon. prophet in Isa. 25:6–8; 32:15–18; 35:1 seq.; Zech. 1:17; 8:12 seq.; 14:8; Joel 3:18.

[104] This thesis is still defended by O. Kaiser, *Der königliche Knecht* (Göttingen, 1959). H. Ringgren, *The Messiah in the Old Testament* (London, 1956), sees in the Servant a king.

[105] See the summary of this controversy and its bibliography in E. Sellin, *Introduction to the Old Testament*, pp. 127, 140 seq., and R. Pfeiffer, *Introduc-*

God is the eschatological intermediary who will be sent by the Lord to renew the covenant with liberated Israel and to be the light for all non-Israelitic nations.

The Servant of God is still represented by the Prophet as a king.[106] This would suggest that the role of sufferer atoning for his people, described in such moving terms in chapter 50: 4–9, in the last verses of chapter 52, and in chapter 53, is one of the traditional attributes of the king. This would be more certain if a parallel could be found in the Babylonian and Israelite traditions suggesting that such indeed was his obligation.

It is well known that the Babylonians had developed a very keen sense of atonement and expiation, as is indicated by the numerous penitential psalms so common in Babylon,[107] and by the New Year festivities, in the course of which one special day was appointed for the reconciliation of the temple and the people. Thanks to some recent discoveries,[108] the ritual of this atonement

---

tion to the Old Testament, pp. 454–480. For a more detailed account of the controversy on the meaning of the "Servant Songs," see P. Volz, *Jesaia*, 2 (Leipzig, 1932), pp. 149–196, and especially E. J. Kissane, *The Book of Isaiah*, 2 (Dublin, 1943), pp. lvi–lxviii, bibliography on p. lxix seq. On p. lxi Kissane summarizes his ideas on the composition of the Book of Isaiah in the following words: "The same individual who collected the prophecies of Isaiah now contained in chaps. 1 to 35, and added the historical section (chaps. 36 to 39), also appended this message to his fellow exiles in which he repeated for their benefit the teaching of the great prophet. In this hypothesis, the second part of the book would bear a certain analogy to the *Epistle to the Hebrews*, of which the ideas, according to many scholars (following Origen) are St. Paul's, the literary form the work of another. The ideas of chaps. 40 to 66 are those of Isaiah, their expression and the literary form in which they are presented to the exiles in Babylon are the work of the unknown prophet who compiled the whole book."

[106] This is abundantly clear in Isa. 49:1: "The Lord hath called me from the womb; from the bowels of my mother hath he made mention of my name"; words that recall the phrasing of the Babylonian court style which proudly declared the kings to be chosen by their gods, and to have received from them their name and their throne. Cf. Isa. 45:3, 4, where the prophet thus addresses Cyrus: "I have called thee by thy name... I have surnamed thee, though thou hast not known me...." Cf. the short introduction to the problem given by V. de Leeuw, "Le Serviteur de Jahvé. Figure royale ou prophétique," in L. Cerfaux and others, *L'attente du Messie* (Louvain, 1954), pp. 51–57. See also *ibid*, short studies on messianism given by B. Rigaux, pp. 15–30, by A. Decamps, pp. 57–84, and by J. Giblet, pp. 85–130.

[107] Mostly published by H. Zimmern *Babylonische Busspsalmen*, Assyriologische Bibliothek, 6 (1885). See also G. Widengren, *The Accadian and Hebrew Psalms of Lamentation as Religious Documents* (Uppsala, 1936).

[108] Last published by F. Thureau-Dangin, *Rituels accadiens* (Paris, 1921), part 3: "The Rites of the New Year Festivities in Babylon." See the English

can now be reconstructed with reasonable accuracy. It is notable that on that occasion the king had a special rite to perform and that he did so as the representative of his people. The ceremonies he performed were designed to abase him and to signify that, as a quasi-incarnation of his people, the king was doing penance and suffering, atoning for them all.

The king presented himself at the chief temple in Esagil bedecked in all his royal insignia, which the high priest took off him piece by piece and placed at the foot of Marduk's statue. The priest then returned to the king, slapped him on the face, took him to the statue, pulled his ears, and made him kneel down. There the king had to recite a prayer to assure the deity that he had done none of the wrongs enumerated in the prayer; he was then warned by the high priest to observe all the canons of the ritual and to shun all the wrongs just mentioned. He then received the high priest's assurance of the god's pardon and blessing and recovered his insignia. But that was not all: the high priest again slapped the king on the face, hard enough this time to draw tears, and these were taken as the pledge that the god would be propitious to him in the coming year. After another prayer addressed to the god of fire, the ceremony was concluded.

From this and other ritual texts it is made clear that the king acted not merely for himself, but in the name of his people. One prayer, which was recited for the king on the fourth of the month Nisan, twice calls him "Servant of God"[109] and the same designation repeatedly occurs in the penitential psalms which the king had to recite at frequent intervals. He thus played a leading part in the

---

translation of this part of the ritual in C. J. Gadd's study, "Babylonian Myth and Ritual," in *Myth and Ritual*, ed. by H. S. Hooke (Oxford, 1933), p. 53 seq. See also H. Zimmern, "Zum babylonischen Neujahrs-fest," *Berichte d. Kgl. Sächs. Ges. d. Wissensch. zu Leipzig*, Phil.-Hist. Kl., 58 (1906), Heft 3, pp. 126–156; 70 (1918), Heft 5, and his short account in *Das babylonische Neujahrsfest*, Der Alte Orient, 25, Heft, 3 (Leipzig, 1926).

[109] See F. Thureau-Dangin, *Rituels accadiens*, p. 99 seq. It is interesting to note that the Israelite king also used to be called on similar occasions "Servant of God," as is made evident from Ps. 89:39. Cf. also Hag. 2:23. Cf. also A. Bentzen, *King and Messiah* (London, 1955), pp. 29 seq., 48 seq., who however, explains this title in accordance with his theory of sacral kingship.

national penitential rites.[110] In Babylon, at the same ceremony, the custom of offering to the deity a figure clad in royal robes, which then was "immolated" instead of the penitent king, seems to have prevailed; or worse still, a living man, a slave, was killed as the king's substitute. On the other hand, the penitent king, in the course of the atonement ceremony, used to set slaves and prisoners free, or dress a man, chosen at random, in royal robes and permit him to parade as king for a few fleeting moments.[111]

It may thus be concluded that the Babylonian kings, as representatives of their people, had to perform some humiliating functions to conciliate the deity. Bearing in mind that the Israelites developed their notions of kingship under the direct influence of Babylonian political thought, many scholars believed it possible that this particular function of the Babylonian kings was introduced into Israelitic pre-exilic ritual. Unfortunately, we have very few references to the priestly functions of the Hebrew kings. The existence of a ritual of atonement is revealed in Leviticus 16. Nothing, however, is known about a role which the king might have played at such a ritual. Some further evidence can perhaps be found in the description of God's kingdom given by Ezekiel. He certainly insisted on the importance of priests and Levites in matters of worship and in the people's relations with God; yet (in chapters 44–46), he does reserve some liturgical functions to the king. On the fourteenth day of the first month (Ezek. 45:22–25)

---

[110] Cf. M. Jastrow, *Die Religion Bab. und Assyr.*, 2, p. 125 seq. Cf. also H. Zimmern, *Beiträge zur Kenntnis der babyl. Religion*, Assyriologische Bibliothek, 12 (Leipzig, 1899), p. 122 seq.

[111] Cf. B. Meissner, *op. cit.*, 1, pp. 48, 377. Other bibliographical indications and more particulars will be found in L. Dürr, *Ursprung*, pp. 134–143. It is possible that the origin must be sought in these Babylonian parallels for the Jewish custom of having a public criminal released by the governor on the eve of the Paschal feast, as Barabbas was released by Pilate at the Jews' request. The mock adoration of Christ by the Roman soldiers might be traceable to the same source. Cf. B. Landsberger, *Der kultische Kalender der Babyl. u. Assyr.*, Leipziger Semitistiche Studien, 6, 1–2 (1915), p. 117, note 1. This is what he writes about the scene described in Mark 15:6 seq.: "Ob auch als verstecktes Motiv der Erzählung von der Freilassung des Barabbas die Idee des symbolischen Tausches zugrunde liegt, so dass der büssende Heiland die Strafe des Verbrechers auf sich nimmt, während dieser freikommt, möchte ich nur anregen."

... shall the prince prepare for himself and for all the people of
the land a bullock for a sin offering.

And seven days of the feast he shall prepare a burnt offering to
the Lord, seven bullocks and seven rams without blemish
daily the seven days; and a he-goat daily for a sin offering.

And he shall prepare a meat offering, of an ephah for a bullock, and
an ephah for a ram, and an hin of oil for an ephah.

In the seventh month, in the fifteenth day of the month, shall he
do the like in the feast of the seven days; according to the sin
offering, according to the burnt offering, and according to the
meat offering, and according to the oil.

Other liturgical prescriptions for the prince to observe on the
Sabbath day are indicated by Ezekiel in chapter 46.

This seems significant. The Prophet was the forerunner of priestly
rule in Israel and, as already stated, was not in the least inclined
to give princes in the renovated kingdom any important say
in religious matters. That was the exclusive right of the priests. If,
notwithstanding this, he still allows the prince some liturgical
functions, it may well be concluded that this pre-exilic tradition
was so firmly rooted in Israel that even Ezekiel had to respect it
and make some allowance for it in the new Israelitic kingdom whose
organization and constitution he described so minutely.

Since Ezekiel refers to sacrifices to be offered by the prince for
the sins and the reconciliation of prince and people, it may be
presumed that in pre-exilic days Hebrew kings did have such a
right and such a duty. But there does not seem to be any evidence
to show that the Hebrews had ceremonies for the day of atonement after the Babylonian type, in which their kings performed the
same ministry as the Babylonian kings. Psalm 101 could be compared
to the "negative confession" which the latter were expected to recite
before the image of the deity on New Year's day, and can only be
understood as being a royal declaration on enthronement day. The
fact that the Israelites had no day of atonement on the Babylonian
model, does not mean that the celebration of such a day in Babylon
did not impress the captive Israelites.[112] In their distress they must

[112] It appears that the Israelites were impressed by the Babylonian New
Year Feast and Atonement Day, since similar feasts were introduced in

343

have felt and resented deeply the loss of their king, who as their legitimate mediator, would have been able to conciliate Jahweh and, by penance, mitigate His wrath. This loss occurred at a time when Israel needed her intercessor most, was most conscious of her sinful past and the need to atone for it.

It is thus not impossible that the author of the prophecies called Deutero-Isaiah, who was certainly familiar with the Babylonian court style and must have been equally well acquainted with the Babylonian kings' representative function on Atonement Day, should have witnessed the distress of his compatriots. It is easy to imagine how the great seer appraised the situation and, addressing his people, encouraged them by pointing out that Israel was second to no other nation. The Jewish king no longer reigned in Jerusalem and his people were scattered in exile, to be sure, but there still remained Jahweh's promise to send a mediator, a new king who would set Israel free and revive its old glory. This messianic king[113] would also act as expiator for his people before Jahweh. Being infinitely superior to any Babylonian or Hebrew king of the past, he would surpass all of them, taking upon himself responsibility for all the sins of his people, suffering instead of them and atoning to the last. There follows the pathetic picture, prophetically sighted in the distant future, of the messianic king, humiliated and led to slaughter (Isa. 53:3 seq.):

> He was despised, and rejected of men; a man of sorrows, and acquainted with grief; and as one from whom men hide their face he was despised, and we esteemed him not.
> Surely he hath borne our griefs, and carried our sorrows; yet we did esteem him stricken, smitten of God, and afflicted.

Israel after the return from exile. Cf. E. Auerbach, "Neujahrs- und Versöhnungs-Fest in den biblischen Quellen," *VT*, 8 (1958), pp. 337–343.

[113] See the illuminating study by C. R. North, *The Suffering Servant in Deutero-Isaiah. An Historical and Critical study* (Oxford, 1948). After discussing all the different theories on the identification of the Suffering Servant of God, the author comes to the conclusion that the Prophet could have been referring only to the promised and expected Messiah. More recent bibliography on the interpretation of Ebed Jahweh by authors of the "Pattern School" and its critical appreciation is found in K. H. Bernhardt, *Das Problem der altorientalischen Königsideologie im Alten Testament*, p. 184 seq.

But he was wounded for our transgressions, he was bruised for our
iniquities: the chastisement of our peace was upon him: and
with his stripes we are healed.

. . . .

He was oppressed, yet he humbled himself and opened not his
mouth; as a lamb that is led to slaughter, and as a sheep that
before her shearers is dumb; yea, he opened not his mouth.
By oppression and judgement he was taken away.

. . . .

And he made his grave with the wicked, and with the rich in his
death . . . .

This conjured up the vision of a king very unlike the Hebrew
and Babylonian rulers whose acts had been at most symbolic of
their own and their people's contrition. For the messianic king
there would be no death by proxy, no immolation of a counterfeit,
of a robed statuette, but free personal destruction, though he had
done no violence, "neither was any deceit in his mouth." A slap on
the face by the hand of a high priest would not suffice: the face of
this genuine king of Israel "was so marred more than any man,
and his form more than the sons of men" (Isa. 52:14). And he is
made to say of himself: "I gave my back to the smiters, and my
cheeks to them that plucked off the hair: I hid not my face from
shame and spitting" (Isa. 50 : 6). The picture of the Babylonian king,
Servant of God, humiliating himself before Baal for the benefit of
his people (a picture which impressed the Israelites as much as it
did the Babylonians) thus completely fades out before that of the
Israelite "Servant of God." The messianic king was to be the light
not only for the Israelites, but for the "Gentiles," to be Jahweh's
"salvation unto the end of the earth" (Isa. 49:6).[114] None had ever
thought of such an atonement before, yet such would be the real
"Servant of God." He would be more deserving of his title than
any Babylonian king.

The Babylonian parallel thus seems to place Deutero-Isaiah's
"Servant Songs" in their proper setting and in perfect consonance

[114] Cf. H. Gross, *Weltherrschaft als religiöse Idee im Alten Testament* (Bonn,
1953), p. 97 seq.

with the surroundings in which the exiled Jews found themselves.[115] It is easy to imagine the eagerness with which the faithful took in the prophetic words and the consolation which they found in them in their distress.

This explanation remains, of course, hypothetical,[116] but Jewish eschatology was thereby enriched with the idea of a suffering Messiah, doing penance for his people. However, the idea of a suffering Messiah was already implicit in the concept of an eschatological mediator sent by Jahweh to liberate his people and to bring about their common triumph over all nations. The same concept also included the

[115] The above solution was first suggested by E. Sellin, *Das Rätsel des deuterojesajanischen Buches* (Leipzig, 1908), pp. 98–111 (Babylonian Influences on the Author of the Songs), but was evolved by H. Schmidt, *Die Thronfahrt Jahves am Fest der Jahreswende im alten Israel* (Tübingen, 1927), and especially by L. Dürr, *Ursprung*, pp. 133–146. Also A. R. Johnson's study, "The Role of the King," which is an attempt to reconstruct the ritual of the Israelite feast of the Tabernacles, the possible Hebrew replica of the Babylonian New Year Festival (*loc. cit.*, p. 86 seq.). However interesting, this attempt, which also makes the psalms in celebration of Jahweh's kingship the mainstay of that liturgy, is at best arbitrary, since there is no evidence for dating their composition with any precision. Cf. also the study by W. O. E. Oesterley, "Early Hebrew Festival Rituals," *Myth and Ritual*, pp. 122–144. Dürr was followed in his interpretation by H. Riesenfeld, *Jesus Transfigured* (Copenhagen, 1947), p. 82 seq. I. Engnell in his study "The 'Ebed Yahweh Songs and the Suffering Messiah in 'Deutero-Isaiah'," *Bulletin of the John Rylands Library, Manchester*, 31 (1948), pp. 54–93 tried once more to find a connection between the suffering Messiah and the "Tammuz ideology." Cf. J. Klausner, *The Messianic Idea in Israel*, trans. by W. F. Stinespring (New York, 1955), pp. 143–184.

[116] S. Mowinckel, *He That Cometh*, pp. 187–257, after examining all other attempts at the solution of this difficult problem, comes to the conclusion that the Servant of God is not the Messiah, but a prophet who will accomplish the complete reconciliation of Israel with Jahweh through suffering according to Jahweh's will; a suffering king-Messiah could not be imagined by the Israelites. However, he concedes that the Servant is given by the poet certain royal titles and will be exalted by Jahweh like a king. "What no Messiah, as conceived by the Jewish national religion, could perform, the Servant performs... [p. 256]. They tacitly discard the Messiah, and quietly replace him with the Servant, as the overlord of kings and the plenipotentiary of God." The author has to confess that "it is nevertheless possible that the conception of the Servant was in many indirect ways influenced by the ancient Oriental idea [p. 257] of the sacred king and by the thought of the king's suffering and exaltation. It is, therefore, with justice that the Church has from the very beginning seen in Jesus Christ the true fulfillment of those prophecies. In this she has followed Jesus himself...." In any case, it cannot be denied that the poet here introduced into the conception of the Messiah new ideas on his true character, ideas which were not understood before Christ. See the synthesis of Mowinckel's messianic ideas given by J. Coppens, "Les origines du messianisme" in *L'attente du Messie*, pp. 31–38, and their criticism, written with due respect to this great scholar.

notion of intercession between Jahweh and his people and atonement for its sins. It can be imagined that the kings as temporary messiahs had previously symbolized such ideas, foreshadowing the ideal king who was expected. But once the national kings had vanished from the scene, these functions were transferred to the future Messiah, the final and supreme object of Israel's expectations.

It was this presentation of the Messiah that raised the hopes of the Israelites in the difficult days of their national regeneration under foreign domination. Diligent study of the old prophets prevented the new prophetic generation of Haggai, Zechariah, and Malachi from slipping from the high ideals they had upheld into a narrow national sentimentalism. This latter could only have led to a reconditioning of a politically independent state as the sole ideal of liberation. But the vividly colorful picture of the Messiah which they found in the writings of the old prophets, especially in Deutero-Isaiah, helped them to weather the crisis when the last hope of a national restoration vanished forever with the overthrow of Zerubbabel. Haggai (2:20 seq.) and Zechariah (3:8; 6:12 seq.) did go a long way in their predictions of a speedy revival of the national kingdom; yet they never forgot the lessons derived from the greater prophets, which had been well learned by the nation during its exile. Haggai appealed to the example of his predecessors and insisted on fostering inward purity, magnanimity, and faith (Hag. 2:13 seq.), while Zechariah was emphatic in his warnings against mere outward practices like fasting, when stripped of any ethical obligations (Zech. 7:4 seq.). Malachi (Mal. 1:10), much as he esteemed worship, sacrifice, and liturgical ceremonial, declared himself ready to close the Temple should the greatness of the Lord ever be marred and his name dishonored by unworthy offerings.

The conception of Jahweh held by the new prophets also followed the lines traced by their great predecessors. Zechariah did not even dare to report Jahweh's words as being addressed to himself, but was so permeated with the idea of Jahweh's transcendance that he contented himself with communicating with Jahweh through the medium of an angel (Zech. 1:13 seq.). As a result of a lengthy transformation of Hebrew theology, the Temple was no longer believed to be occupied by Jahweh in person, but only filled with his glory (Hag. 2:7 seq.). Similarly, the Deuteronomists allowed only the name of the Lord to dwell in the Temple (Deut. 12:5, 11, 21; 14: 24 ; 16:6, 11; 26:2) and in this sense are believed by many to have amended the accounts of how Jahweh took possession of the Tabernacle of Moses (Exod. 40:34) and of the Temple of Solomon (I Kings 8:10 seq.).[117]

A more profound comprehension of God and a closer association with Him can also be gathered from other literary compositions of the time, especially from Psalms 16 and 73, and from the graphic poem of Job—all witness to the profound transformation which the bitter years of exile and the trials of the post-exilic period had wrought in the souls of the Israelites. The transcendent character of Jahweh was further intensified by Ezra, the great law reformer

[117] Cf. R. Kittel, *The Religion of the People of Israel*, p. 184. This question cannot be answered with certainty as long as the problems connected with the composition of the Pentateuch, the Priestly Code, and Deuteronomy are not definitely solved. This must be left to specialists. It is interesting to note, however, that from this period onward, the notion of Jahweh becomes more and more transcendent. C. G. Montefiore remarks briefly in J. Abelson's book, *The Immanence of God in Rabbinical Literature* (London, 1912), p. 49 seq.: "As a matter of fact, Jahweh was very near in old days. . . . God became far off rather late, and then by immanence He had to be made 'near' again." Connected with this problem is the question of *cabod* (glory of Jahweh; *doxa* in the Septuagint) and of *shekinah*, which indicated the "presence" or "dwelling" of Jahweh in some special place. It is noteworthy that the word *shekinah* frequently occurs in apocryphal and rabbinical literature subsequent to this period. Cf. the book of J. Abelson quoted above and the recent penetrating study by G. H. Boobyer on *St. Mark and the Transfiguration Story* (Edinburgh, 1942), especially pp. 23 seq., 66 seq., 80–86. I should like to point out that this teaching of the shining glory of God offers many similarities to the radiation of the Egyptian and Babylonian sun-god. (see pp. 42, 255-258). The Persian concept of *Hvarena* or kingly glory, created by Ahura Mazda, can be traced to the same source. There should be nothing objectionable in the view that even the Jews were inspired in their theological thought by some Egyptian and Babylonian notions, since with them Jewish genius was able to outstrip the original ideas. For more complete information on *doxa* and its use in the Septuagint and in the New Testament, see G. Kittel and G. von Rad, *Theologisches Wörterbuch zum Neuen Testament*, 2 (Stuttgart, 1935), pp. 236–255 (δόξα). See also H. Kittel, *Die Herrlichkeit Gottes, Studien zur Geschichte und Wesen eines neutestamentlichen Begriffes*, Beihefte der *ZNW*, 16 (1934), especially pp. 135–182, the enumeration of all the places in the Old Testament, and in the Apocrypha with references to *cabod*. Brief observations can be found in the following publications: I. Abrahams, *The Glory of God* (Oxford, 1925); E. Burrows, S. J., *The Gospel of the Infancy and Other Biblical Essays*, The Bellarmine Series, 6 (London, 1940), pp. 101–110; L. Gillet, "Questions concernant la Chékinah," *Judaism and Christianity. Essays Presented to the Rev. Paul Levertoff* (London, 1939), pp. 32–38.

who came to Palestine,[118] probably during the reign of Artaxerxes
Longimanus, for the express purpose of recalling to the new community of Jerusalem the old prescriptions as codified in the important priestly document generally known among specialists as "P."
He had carefully purged all anthropomorphic elements from its
account of Jahweh's activities and shifted the emphasis to His
holiness.

Ezra's work made history and brought an important period of
Israel's national life to a definite close. The introduction of an
exhaustive code of laws regulated all liturgical and ethical questions of interest to the Jewish community. Coming as it did after
the disappearance of the monarchical regime, with its responsibility for all legislation and judgment, this code bridged the gap
left by the collapse of the monarchy and rendered all further
legislation, which had been the king's main function, unnecessary.

But shoals lay ahead. As the code abounded in ritual regulations,
so the emphasis on holiness in the approach to God was liable to
be misunderstood in terms of a rigid observation of ritual at the
expense of ethical obligations. Furthermore, as the ritual directions
were minute and complex and the ethical rules often too general
and vague, the necessity soon arose for amending or explaining the
law for practical application, a function which was actually performed first by the last prophets and their disciples, and later by
their spiritual successors and by the priests.

But after the Jews' return from exile, the importance of priests
rose proportionately with the gradual extinction of the prophetic
class. The priests were so numerous when the Temple had been
rebuilt and the liturgy reorganized that all influence and leadership had passed into their hands. It is in this environment that we
find Malachi (2:4) referring to a covenant which Jahweh had concluded with Levi. The priestly class thus usurped a position previously occupied by the kings, as, in fact, it was with them that the
Lord had entered upon a special covenant. This transfer of power
culminated under Joshua, the high priest, who rose to a position

---

[118] Cf. the study by H. Cazelles, "La mission d'Esdras," *VT*, 4 (1954),
pp. 113–140; R. H. Pfeiffer, *Introduction to the Old Testament*, p. 814 seq. On
the period of Nehemiah and Ezra, see W. O. E. Oesterley, *A History of Israel*,
2 (Oxford, 1932), p. 110 seq. (volume 1 was published by T. H. Robinson).

equal to that of Zerubbabel (Zech. 6:13), David's descendant and prospective king of the new Israel. After the King's removal, the High Priest was left as the sole repository of national authority and heir to the last relics of royalty. Priestly rule had come to stay.

This was not the only danger. The great prophets had raised the knowledge of Jahweh and of his relations with the created world to a very high level and bade fair to expand the Israelite creed into a world religion. But after the exile, when the nation became so absorbed in its law as almost to be identified with it, the creed, once so highly developed by the great prophets, slipped back into its old groove, to become again a national faith, characterized mainly by its peculiar law, the circumcision, and the Sabbath observance. Yet, the tidal wave which the prophets had stirred up and raised to so high a level that it seemed capable of overflowing national boundaries into the regions beyond, did not subside. Forced back into its national channel, it continued to move the hearts of the Israelites and to inspire occasional flashes of literary activity and religious fervor.

Two events prepared the ground for the final consummation. The first was the conquest of the Persian Empire by Alexander the Great, which led to the absorption of the small state of Judaea into the Greek world empire. As a consequence, the Jews came under the influence of Greek civilization, which was presently to coalesce with some elements of the Oriental already known to the Jews, and to blossom into Hellenistic culture. The Jews had hitherto been forced by circumstances to lean toward the East; now they enjoyed their first contact with the West.

The second event was the translation of the Old Testament into Greek. Initiated probably in the first half of the third century B.C.,[119] the Septuagint was to convey to the new world opened up by Alexander the Great the sublime religious notions which Israel had moulded out of elements that were native to the East.

It will be recalled that the old Greek world was not unfamiliar with many Oriental ideas and that, through the intermediary of Persia,

[119] See M. Hadas, *Aristeas to Philocrates* (*Letter of Aristeas*) (New York, 1951), p. 66 seq. See, for details, D. W. Gooding, "Aristeas and Septuagint Origins: A Review of Recent Studies," *VT*, 13 (1963), pp. 357–379.

there had also been ample opportunity for acquaintance with, assimilation and integration of Egyptian and Babylonian thought. Moreover, this work of cultural absorption and mutual influence went on in the four principal states that survived the disruption of Alexander's Empire and the conqueror's death in 323 B.C. Palestine then fell to the power of Ptolemy, the ruler of Egypt, and, in spite of bitter opposition from the Seleucids, whose empire centered in Syria, it remained under the Ptolemies until 198 B.C. This proved fortunate, as the Jews had much in common with the Egyptians, and the Ptolemies took a sympathetic view of the Jewish religion. Alexandria thus became an attractive center for the Jews, who settled there in great numbers and found there a unique opportunity to work out a synthesis of Hellenistic and Jewish civilizations.

However, before such a task could be attempted, the Jews had to go through an extended struggle with the new civilization. Greek culture had enjoyed a long sojourn in the Syriac cities of the Seleucid empire, where the Greek tongue and Greek literature were steadily supplanting the native Aramaic and Canaanite dialects; and the Semitic population took to Greek culture so readily that the old cities of the Phoenicians and the Philistines were soon able to contribute several distinguished names to the galaxy of Greek philosophers, thinkers, and writers. It is interesting to recall that it was a Syrian, Lucian of Samosata, who at a much later date (ca. A.D. 125–190) enriched Greek literature with a new literary composition, full of lively comments on topical subjects in journalistic style, which has caused him to be referred to as a forerunner of modern journalism. Old Punic and similar legends and tales, which circulated in the Syriac cities, gave way to Greek fables and stories; old manners and customs gave place to Greek modes of living. All this proves the attraction exercized on Semitic minds by Hellenistic civilization, with its gymnasia, stadia, hippodromes, and theatres, its stoas, its municipal institutions and senate, its cult of beauty and individuality, its religious displays.[120]

---

[120] This is well described by E. Bevan, *Jerusalem under the High Priests* (London, 1904), p. 33 seq.

No less obvious was the danger to the Jews when these modern ideas reached the walls of Jerusalem and its tiny Jewish world.

The menace was intensified by the fact that, as a result of an extraordinary succession of events, the Jewish priestly class happened to be most susceptible to the temptations of Hellenistic civilization. The community, which, during the Persian period, had clustered in and around Jerusalem, was small and poor, consisting mainly of peasants and artisans. The richer elements remained in Babylon, which gave the clergy in Jerusalem the chance to develop into an upper class. Enriched by the tithes which the faithful scrupulously paid to the Temple in obedience to the law, and invested, in the person of the high priest and his assistants, with extensive powers of political administration, the Jerusalem clergy had evolved into a rich and influential aristocracy, which at the same time represented, financially and intellectually, the élite of the city. Now it was this class which was laid open to the enticements of an easier life. The Jews of Alexandria and of the Syrian maritime cities only promoted the penetration of the new culture, which, to judge from the description of the life of members of the Tobiadae family by the Jewish historian Flavius Josephus,[121] gained ground not among the simple folk, but in the heart of Zion, chiefly among the young men of the ruling families.

It is quite possible that had the priestly aristocratic families been able to uphold the time-honored standards of Jewish morality and probity, the new way of life and thought might have scored greater success among all classes of Jews in Jerusalem and have ended in a compromise with the Jewish creed that would have made it more attractive to the Gentiles; but it was in this respect that they were the first to succumb to temptation which their new prosperity rendered so insidious. To make matters worse, it was a debased and corrupt form of Hellenism that had penetrated the Syrian cities when Palestine came under the rule of the Seleucids. The highly frivolous stories written in elegant Greek by the Hellenized Syrian, Lucian of Samosata, best illustrate that decadent form of Hellenism.

[121] *Jewish Antiquities*, XII, 154 seq., 239 seq., ed. by R. Marcus (Loeb, 1943), 7, pp. 80 seq,. 120 seq.

A reaction was bound to follow.[122] It came from the loyal believers, faithful to the letter of the law, called Hasidim, i.e., pious
men, mostly recruited from among the poorer classes, with a
sprinkling of priests. The High Priest Onias took the lead and
challenged the Hellenizing party organized and headed by the
priestly family of the Tobiadae. The conflict came to a head under
Antiochus Epiphanes (175–164 B.C.),[123] an eclectic monarch whose
character was full of contradictions. For all his partiality to Oriental despotism, he saw in the spread of Hellenism throughout
his realm the safest guarantee for the stability and unification of
the motley collection of races and cultures that made up his empire,
and decided not to cater to Jewish exclusiveness. He took the
Hellenizing Jewish party under his protection, and replaced the
High Priest Onias by his more amenable brother Jeshua-Jason,
who, however, presently had to vacate his place in favor of Menelaus,
a member of the Tobiadae. This pontiff, with excessive compliance,
allowed Antiochus (who had made a practice of meeting his financial difficulties by robbing the rich Syrian temples) to enter
the Temple of Jerusalem and help himself to its finest treasures
(I Macc. 1:21 seq.). But Hellenization penetrated even further. The
city was made into a strong garrison center, Jahweh was identified
with Zeus of Olympus, perhaps even with Antiochus, as another
manifestation of Epiphanes-Theos. The Temple was handed over to
the new creed as its religious center, while circumcision, sacrifices,
and observation of the Sabbath were forbidden under pain of
death.

After offering some passive resistance in the mountains for a short
period, the Hasidim at last gathered around their leader, the country
priest Mattathias, of the house of Hasmon, and his five sons, and

[122] See L. Cerfaux and J. Tondriau, *Un concurrent du christianisme. Le
culte des souverains* (Tournai, 1957), p. 242 seq., and especially V. Tcherikover,
Hellenistic Civilization and the Jews (Philadelphia, 1959), p. 160 seq. See also
W. O. E. Oesterley, *A History of Israel*, p. 217 seq.

[123] V. Tcherikover, *op. cit.*, p. 196 seq.; bibliography, p. 470. Ch. A. Kincaid,
"A Persian Prince, Antiochus Epiphanes," *Oriental Studies in Honour of
Cursetji Erachji Pavry*, ed. by Jal Dastur Cursetji Pavry (London, 1933),
pp. 209–219, tried to show Antiochus in a more sympathetic light. On
Jewish penetration by, and opposition against, Hellenism, cf. S. E. Eddy,
The King is Dead (Lincoln, Nebr., 1961), pp. 183–212 (The Jews to 166 B.C.),
213–256 (The Jews under the Hasmoneans).

entered upon their heroic struggle for religious freedom. One of them, Judas the Maccabee, distinguished himself in the field. Taking advantage of the political difficulties which hampered the regent Lysias in handling his superior forces, he scattered the troops of the Syrians, restored the worship of the Temple, rededicated its altar, and, notwithstanding several serious reverses, wrung from the Syrians in 162 B.C. the right of free exercise of the Jewish religion.[123a]

The pious and loyal Hasidim deserved their success, and their struggle would have lived forever in man's memory had the Maccabees been content with this achievement. But the conflict went on under Jonathan, Judas' brother, and by then its motive was not religious freedom, but lust for political and temporal power. The Hasmonaean brothers first procured the office of high priest as their family privilege, then they assumed command of the Jewish forces, and, finally, princely rank. A new dynasty was thus introduced into Jerusalem, under the suzerainty of the Seleucids (to 129 B.C.), but vying with other rulers in military exploits, luxurious court life, and political expansion. It looked like a return to the days of the last kings of Israel and Judah; and, indeed, Aristobulus, one of the Hasmonaeans, proudly took the title of king (103 B.C.)[124]

But the old Hebrew monarchy—with all its implications—failed to come to life again. The revolution in Jewish political thought during the last centuries had been too thorough and had gone too deep to allow for a return of dead and buried glories. Nor had political aggrandizement for the profit of a single dynasty been the object of the pious Hasidim's insurrection. Their zeal for the Hasmonaeans gradually cooled as the average pious Jewish peasant lost interest in the family ambitions of the new dynasty.

This opposition deserves to be noted, as the Hasmonaeans, though too often with outbursts of inhuman cruelty, did succeed to a great extent in restoring the national glory. They won political freedom for their nation: the old kingdom of Judah was

[123a] Cf. E. Bickerman, *The Maccabees*, trans. by M. Hadas (New York, 1947).

[124] For details on the Hasmonaean period, see W. O. E. Oesterley, *A History of Israel*, p. 272 seq. and V. Tcherikover, *op. cit.*, pp. 235–265.

independent again for sixty years, from the death of the Seleucid King, Antiochus Sidetes (in 129 B.C.), down to the Roman conquest. They extended the boundaries of their state considerably, by conquering the territory of the Samaritans, forcing the Edomites to embrace Judaism, resettling Jewish families in many Palestinian cities (after expelling the Hellenized and pagan native population), and reducing to subjection and Judaizing the Ituraeans (thereby becoming the creators of Galilee, the region from which the coming Messiah was to recruit most of his apostles). The Hasmonaeans were the ones who founded the Palestine which we know from the accounts in the Gospels, and their success must have filled many a patriotic heart with pride. The riddle is why they failed to rally the whole nation to their support.

The reason for this stems from the changes that took place in post-exilic Judaism. When the law became the sole authority in religious and social matters and when love and veneration for the law had found their way into the hearts of the majority, the principal excuse for a revival of a national monarchy had vanished. Pious Jews found sufficient guidance in the directives of the law, and when, as frequently happened, they were in doubt about its application to conduct (since the regulations were often couched in general terms), they had recourse to the many enlightened Jews who had made the study of the law their main business. These men commanded, in the eyes of the simpler folk, greater respect than royal officials could ever have laid claim to.

A new class thus came into existence in Jewish society, that of the scribes (*sopherim*), religious teachers and theologians who held the rank next to the clergy. This group flourished from the time of Ezra down to the conquest of Palestine by Alexander. Their influence asserted itself chiefly in the countryside where they presided over the gatherings of the faithful in their synagogues. These places of worship were first erected in foreign lands for the benefit of those Jews who were unable to visit Jerusalem and its Temple, and later, during the Maccabean period, became a feature of Palestinian cities and villages as well. The position of scribe in Israelitic life was taken over by the "rabbis" to whose elaborate casuistry pious people willingly conformed. Being in closer contact with the faithful than were the priests, who were confined to Jerusalem and specialized in liturgy, the rabbis eventually grew into a class which was more influential than the clergy.

It was only to be expected that these teachers would remain indifferent to politics, except in matters that concerned the law, and they jealously watched every trespass on their privileges and influence. Many of them belonged to the new party of the Pharisees, a name that first occurs under John Hyrcanus. It is also from this period that Flavius Josephus dates the final breach between the Hasmonaean dynasty and the Hasidim.[125] The Pharisees, or separatists, completely altered the political situation by refusing to endorse the nationalistic and dynastic aims of the Hasmonaeans. The latter naturally turned for support to the adherents of the priestly class, who, by instinct and self-interest, were hostile to the Pharisees. In the meantime, there arose among the clergy and the wealthier classes of Jerusalem a new party which went by the name of Sadducees, perhaps so called after Zadok, chief priest of the Temple in the time of David and Solomon; his descendants were entrusted by Ezekiel (44:10–15) with the service in the Temple. It soon became evident that its members and well wishers were faithful Jews and keen observers of the law, though naturally in opposition to the Pharisees, who questioned the monopoly of the priestly class in legal interpretation and who competed for ascendancy over the masses. The Hasmonaeans found their friends among the Sadducees, with the consequent and inevitable loss of the sympathies of the pious masses and their leaders, the Pharisees and the scribes. The result was that a movement which at the outset had gathered around the Hasmonaeans all that was sound and pious in Jewry, ended by splitting the nation into two com-

---

[125] *Jewish Antiquities*, XIII, 288 seq., *loc. cit.*, p. 372 seq. On the history of the Pharisees, see G. H. Box, "Pharisees," *Encyclopaedia of Religion and Ethics*, 9 (New York, 1928), pp. 831–836. Cf. also, *ibid.*, 11, pp. 43–46, his article "Sadducees." For details, see V. Tcherikover, *op. cit.*, pp. 253 seq., 493; and F. M. Abel, *Histoire de la Palestine* (Paris, 1952), 1, p. 219 seq. Cf. also R. T. Herford, *The Pharisees*, new ed. (Boston, 1962) and L. Finkelstein, *The Pharisees* (Philadelphia, 1938), 2 vols. See also A. Finkel, *The Pharisees and the Teacher of Nazareth* (Leiden, 1964), pp. 2–10 (bibliography on the Pharisees), pp. 18–22 (the role of the scribes), p. 58 seq. (the Pharisees and their controversial Halachic teaching).

peting camps, vying with each other for public favor and at variance on ideological issues.

Before examining the sequel to this new development, and its effect on the growth of political thought among the Jews, it is necessary to review the results of the clash between Hellenistic culture and Judaism in the ideological and literary field. These are best reflected in the literary products of the period, and a rapid survey of the most important works written during the pre-Maccabean and Maccabean periods makes it possible to see how the educated Jews formed opinions on kingship in Palestine in the light of Hellenistic principles, and to what extent they modified their own ideas as inherited from the previous period. First to be considered is a class of literature which certainly originated in pre-exilic days, but which was more fully cultivated in the later period we are dealing with—the so-called "Wisdom literature." It was written in a style which had already flourished in Egypt in the second millennium B.C.—the aphorisms of Ani, Amenemhet I, and Ptah-hotep being the most widely known examples[126]—and which was made popular at the Hebrew court by Solomon. The non-Jewish origin and the international character of this genre is acknowledged by the Jews themselves. The collection called Proverbs includes sayings by non-Israelite sages, the north Arabian kings Agur and Lemuel for instance. It belongs in its present form to this period, though it must be admitted that it includes also a nucleus of proverbs traceable to the time of Solomon and Hezekiah. It clearly marks the stages through which the Israelite notion of kingship passed, later to be developed in other literary products of the same genre—the Ecclesiastes, Jesus Ben-Sirach's Ecclesiasticus, the Wisdom of Solomon and the Book of Enoch.

The probably pre-exilic portion of Proverbs[127]—chapters 10–22—reveals what amounts to enthusiasm for the monarchy: "In the

---

[126] For particulars, see Erman-Ranke, *Aegypten*, p. 447 seq., and W. O. E. Oesterley, *The Wisdom of Egypt and the Old Testament* (London-New York, 1927). Cf. also H. Gressmann, *Israels Spruchweisheit im Zusammenhang der Weltliteratur*, Kunst und Altertum, 6 (Berlin, 1925).

[127] Cf. O. Eissfeldt, *Einleitung in das Alte Testament*, 2nd ed. (Tübingen, 1956), p. 581 seq.

multitude of people is the king's glory: But in the want of people is the destruction of princes.... The king's favor is toward a servant that dealeth wisely: but his wrath shall be against him that causeth shame" (Prov. 14:28, 35). These words serve as an introduction to the definition of the king's duties as envisaged in pre-exilic days (16:10–15):

A divine sentence is in the lips of the king:
His mouth shall not transgress in judgement.
A just balance and scales are the Lord's:
All the weights of the bag are his work.
It is an abomination to kings to commit wickedness;
For the throne is established by righteousness.
Righteous lips are the delight of kings;
And they love him that speaketh right.
The wrath of a king is as messengers of death;
. . . .
And his favor is as a cloud of the latter rain.

The words are eloquent and define kingship as the Orient conceived it and Israel adopted it. The stress laid on righteousness and right judgment shows that the wise author had before him the mental picture of a king as a framer of the law and its supreme interpreter. Similar ideas are expressed, though in different terms, in other passages (19:12; 20:2, 8, 26, 28; 22:11). Among these, there is one which recalls more than others the Hellenistic conception of kings as it is found in the description by Ecphantus[128] (Prov. 20:8): "The king that sitteth on the throne of judgement scattereth away all evil with his eyes."

This provides also an interesting reminiscence of the Persian concept of a shining kingly glory and of the Babylonian and Egyptian stream of sun rays emanating from the head of the king, son of the sun, or created by Shamash, the sun-god and the god of righteousness and justice. But in one instance the superiority of the Hebrew notion of kingship over the Egyptian and the Babylonian equivalent is evident. In chapter 21:1, the Hebrew sage declares: "The king's heart is in the hand of the Lord as the watercourses:

[128] See chapter V, pp. 253-255, 258.

He turneth it whithersoever he will." This declaration cuts right across other statements on the king's wrath and favor and reduces them to reasonable proportions by limiting the king's will to the Lord's and making it dependent on the Lord's decision.

This optimistically confident attitude toward the monarchy, so apparent in the oldest portion of Proverbs, disappears however in the second part (chaps. 22:17 to 29), which was collected later, probably under Hezekiah, after some unpleasant experiences with kings. A touch of skepticism already appears in Prov. 17:7; 19:10; 23:1-6; 25:15, and becomes evident in 28:15 seq.: "As a roaring lion, and a ranging bear; so is the wicked ruler over a poor people. The prince that lacketh understanding is also a great oppressor: but he that hateth covetousness shall prolong his days." Wise men still believed that the king's main function was to frame laws and dispense justice, but experience had taught them that theory and practice could be woefully at variance, judging from some proverbs gathered in chapter 29, verses 4, 12, 14, 26:

> The king by judgement establisheth the land:
> But he that exacteth gifts overthroweth it.

> If a ruler hearkeneth to falsehood,
> All his servants are wicked.

> The king that faithfully judgeth the poor,
> His throne shall be established for ever.

> Many seek the ruler's favor:
> But a man's judgement cometh from the Lord.

The following gives an idea of conditions in the kingdom of Israel, where princes followed each other in rapid succession through bloody revolution (Prov. 28:2): "For the transgression of a land many are the princes thereof; but by men of understanding and knowledge the state thereof shall be prolonged."

There are obvious differences between this portion of Proverbs and chapters 1-9 which were added to the collection at the time under review. Warnings against "strange women" (5:18 seq.; 7:5-27) are sufficient indication that the wise men who compiled

359

the collection in its present form and added the nine chapters as an introduction were well aware of the moral dangers that followed the new civilization into Jewish lands. Yet there is not one reference to the national monarchy, with the exception of one proverb which still harks back to the old Oriental doctrine on royalty as recast and perfected by Hellenistic philosophers. The wise men have Wisdom say (Prov. 8:14–16): "Counsel is mine, and sound knowledge: I am understanding; I have might. By me kings reign, and princes decree justice. By me princes rule, and nobles, even all the judges of the earth."

The words are unlimited in their application and could fit any ruler as the utterances of Hellenistic political thinkers. Now that the national kingdom had vanished, the Jewish wise men of the pre-Maccabean period were not particularly interested in it.

A similar attitude to kingship is adopted by the author of Ecclesiastes.[129] Hellenistic influences in this short work are, however, even more marked than in the introductory chapters of Proverbs. As the author himself observes, he is interested in every kind of wisdom and a glance through his work should make it plain that he must have been acquainted with the Epicurean, Stoic, and Heraclitean philosophers. This eclecticism precludes the possibility of the work having been written before 300 B.C. Greek philosophy influenced him in many ways and its contradictory teachings must have created some confusion in his mind. But for all his awkwardness in trying to suppress his scepticism, he remained at bottom faithful to his Jewish belief in a personal God and in God's future judgment of all nations.

Traces of Hellenistic political thought are equally visible in his few references to kingship. Though he introduces himself as a king of Jerusalem, he nowhere gives signs of any enthusiasm for a monarchy. Like all adherents of Hellenistic political ideas, he is convinced of the pre-eminence of royalty among men (Eccles. 2:12): "And I turned myself to behold wisdom, and madness and folly: for what can the man do that cometh after the king?" But he also has his doubts about the rightful use by kings and officials of royal powers (5:8,9): "If thou seest the oppression of the poor,

[129] On its composition and date, see O. Eissfeldt, *Einleitung*, pp. 605–617.

360

and the violent taking away of judgement and justice in a province, marvel not at the matter: for one higher than the high regardeth; and there be higher than they. Moreover, the profit of the earth is for all: the king himself is served by the field."

Again, Ecphantus' idea of the king being a wise man whose wisdom and goodness transfigure his appearance and make him radiant and attractive[130] runs through another description of kingship (8:1–5):

Who is as the wise man? and who knoweth the interpretation of a
    thing? A man's wisdom maketh his face to shine, and the
hardness of his face is changed.
I counsel thee, keep the king's command, and that in regard of the
    oath of God.
Be not hasty to go out of his presence; persist not in an evil thing:
    for he doeth whatsoever pleaseth him.
Because the king's word hath power; and who may say unto him,
    What doest thou?
Whoso keepeth the commandment shall know no evil thing; and
    a wise man's heart discerneth time and judgement.

A strain of scepticism concerning kingship can be observed in chapter 10, where the preacher says (10:4–7, 16, 17, 20):

If the spirit of the ruler rise up against thee, leave not thy place;
    for yielding allayeth great offences.
There is an evil which I have seen under the sun, as it were an
    error which proceedeth from the ruler:
Folly is set on great dignity and the rich sit in low place.
I have seen servants upon horses, and princes walking as servants
    upon the earth.
Woe to thee, O land, when thy king is a child and thy princes eat
    in the morning!
Happy art thou, O land, when thy king is the son of nobles, and thy
    princes eat in due season, for strenght, and not for drunkenness!
Curse not the king, no, not in thy thought; and curse not the rich
    in thy bedchamber: for a bird of the air shall carry the voice,
    and that which hath wings shall tell the matter.

[130] See *supra*, pp. 253-255.

There is nothing specifically Jewish about these short reflections on kings, and any non-Jew in Alexander the Great's Empire could have written exactly the same when that Empire was rent by quarrels between his successors. Yet, the Jews' attitude rises above change and injustice, knowing that there is somebody placed over the kings who will judge their doings.

Much the same view is found in the Wisdom of Jesus Ben-Sirach, generally called Ecclesiasticus because it was used in the early Church as a sort of catechism for the moral and social instruction of baptismal candidates. The collection was written about 200 B.C., and in Egypt, about 130 B.C., was translated from Hebrew into Greek by a descendant of the authors.[131] The book aims at contrasting Jewish with Hellenistic wisdom, which was finding its way into the Jewish world at that time. In Hellenistic wisdom are "evil imaginations which lead astray," but Jews should not be ashamed "of the law of the Most High, and the statute" (Ecclus. 42:1, 2) and of worship in the Temple (50). The law is supreme; worship should be held in great esteem, because the law has ordained it so (32:1 seq.). Good works must also be done because this is ordered by the law (29:9). These and other instances show the preponderant place which the law held in the life of a pious Jew. In such a world there was of course no room for a monarchy and Ben-Sirach leaves no one in doubt (17:17; 18:3; cf. also 50:15):

> For every nation He appointed a ruler,
>   But Israel is the Lord's portion,
> Whom He brought up as His first born with severity,
> Yet loving them (and) imparting to them the light of His love,
>   He forsook them not.
>   . . . .
>
> For He is the King of all things and they are in His power.

Aware, however, of the need for kings and rulers, he devotes a whole chapter to the art of ruling. The ruler must be wise in speech (9:17; 10:1-6):

---

[131] See the detailed discussion of this problem in R. H. Charles, *The Apocrypha and Pseudepigrapha of the Old Testament*, 1 (Oxford, 1913), pp. 291–294. Cf. O. Eissfeldt, *Einleitung*, p. 737 seq.

A wise ruler instructeth his people,
And the dominion of one that is discerning is well ordered.
As the ruler of a people so are his officers,
 And as the head of a city so are the inhabitants thereof.
A reckless king is the ruin of the city,
 And a city becometh populous through the insight of its
 princes.
In the hand of God is the dominion of every man,
 And in the sight of a ruler doth He set His majesty.
In the hand of God is the dominion of the world,
 And He placeth over it the right man.[132]

Many of these precepts to rulers could have come from the pen
of any Hellenistic philosopher, but as the Jewish creed subjected
everything to God, it possessed the advantage of authority and
forcefulness over other such writings. "A king to-day, to-morrow
he falleth" (10:10). "The throne of the proud hath God over-
turned, and He hath set the humble in place thereof" (10:14).
Ben-Sirach says (46:13) of the setting up a national monarchy in
Israel that:

. . . .
 Samuel, (who acted as) judge and priest.
 By the word of God he established the kingdom,
 And anointed princes over the people.

The divine origin of Israelite sovereignty is also maintained in the
passage in which the writer praises the Fathers of old (44:2 seq.):

Great glory did the Most High allot them,
 And they were great from the days of old.
(Men) who wielded dominion over the earth in their royalty,
 And men of renown in their might;

. . . .
Princes of nations in their statesmanship....

---

[132] Cf. R. H. Charles' translation (*Apocrypha*, I, p. 348):
 The rule over the world is in the hands of God,
 And at the right time He setteth over it one that is worthy,
 In the hand of God is the rule of every man,
 And He investeth the commander with his dignity.

363

Jesus Ben-Sirach, as previously noted, represents the old Jewish spirit in the Wisdom literature, and he was prompted to write for the purpose of stemming the infiltration of Hellenistic ideas into the Jewish world. But there exists in the same genre another book which also appears to oppose similar influences, the book called The Wisdom of Solomon. It was possibly written in the first century B.C. in Greek, presumably by two Hellenistic Jews, who in the first nine chapters seem intent on counteracting the teachings contained in Ecclesiastes, a work which shocked many Jews because of its avowed pessimism and numerous statements which they regarded as infected by Sadducean tendencies. The authors intended to confront this with the genuine wisdom which they attributed to Solomon.[133]

It is ironic to note that, in the first part of the book, the author, for all his anti-Hellenistic spirit, uses decidedly Hellenistic methods. He employs the chain-syllogism called *sorites*, commonly used by Stoic philosophers (Wisd. of Sol. 6 : 7–20), and adopts the classification of the cardinal virtues attributed to Plato and popular among Stoics when he states that Wisdom teaches self-control, prudence, righteousness, and manliness (8:7). His metaphor of the human body as a tent for the soul also has a Pythagorean and Platonic ring. For all that, he remains a Jew, and makes an honest attempt to apply the principles of the Jewish creed to the problems of daily life.

It is in this portion of the work that the most interesting passages on kingship are to be found. The second part, from chapter 10 onward, must have been written at an earlier period and probably

---

[133] See W. O. E. Oesterley, *The Wisdom of Solomon* (London, 1917), Introduction, pp. vii–xix. Extracts quoted are from this translation. See also the same author's *An Introduction to the Books of the Apocrypha* (London, 1935), pp. 196–227. Full information on the importance of the Wisdom literature in theology and the history of religion will be found in O. S. Rankin's book, *Israel's Wisdom Literature. Its Bearing on Theology and the History of Religion* (Edinburgh, 1936). Cf. also R. H. Charles' Introduction and translation (*Apocrypha*, 1, p. 518 seq.). Cf. G. Kuhn, *Beiträge zur Erklärung des salomonischen Spruchbuches* (Stuttgart, 1931), and O. Eissfeldt, *Einleitung*, p. 744. Cf. also the studies by different authors in *Wisdom in Israel and in the Ancient Near East. Presented to Professor Harold Henry Rowley*, ed. by M. Noth and D. W. Thomas (Leiden, 1960), and the remarks by S. Talmon, "'Wisdom' in the Book of Esther," *VT*, 13 (1963), pp. 419–455.

by another Jew who shared the same opinions. It has only one reference to the justice of God (12:13 seq.):

> For neither is there any God but Thee,
>   Who careth for all,
> That Thou shouldst show [to him] that
>   Thou didst not judge unjustly;
> Neither shall king or prince be able
>   To confront thee on behalf of those whom
>   Thou hast punished.
> For being righteous Thou rulest all things righteously,
> Deeming it alien from Thy power
> To condemn him that deserveth not to be punished.
> For Thy might is the origin of righteousness,
> And Thy being Lord of all maketh Thee to spare all.

These words offer a clear summary of the Jewish belief that all royal power issues from Jahweh, the only God and the sole source of righteousness.

Inspired by such a creed, the author could only profess contempt for the worship of kings and heroes, the leading feature of Hellenistic political philosophy as it revealed itself to the average pious Jew. Chapter 14, which treats of the folly and evil effects of idolatry (verses 17–22), is a standing condemnation of all such practices.

While the author of the second part addresses rulers and kings in general and ignores the national authorities, the author of the first part (who probably wrote about 50 B.C.) apostrophized the Jewish rulers (6:1 seq.):

> Hear, therefore, O kings, and understand,
> Learn, O ye judges of the uttermost parts of the earth;
> Give ear, O ye that rule over multitudes,
> And hold proud dominion over many nations.
> For your power was given you from the Lord,
> And your sovereignty from the Most High.
> Who shall search out your works, and scrutinize your counsels?
> For though you were officers of His Kingdom ye judged not
>   rightly,

Neither kept ye the Law,
Nor did ye walk according to the counsel of God.
Terribly and swiftly shall He come upon you,
For eternal judgement befalleth them that are in high place.
For the man that is of low estate may be forgiven in mercy,
But the mighty shall be mightily tested....
For you, therefore, O rulers, are my words,
That ye may learn wisdom and not fall away.

Notwithstanding high principles and their spirited defense, he seems to have imbibed at least some measure of Hellenistic political thought. His insistence on the necessity for rulers to be founts of wisdom is in line with the favorite Greek tenet that none but a philosopher is qualified to reign. This principle, elaborated by Socrates, Plato, and Aristotle, and adapted to the monarchical system by Hellenistic thinkers, exalts the king as some outstanding being, model of virtue and source of law and legal conduct. This is to be found in the words (6:20): "Thus, the desire for Wisdom leadeth unto a kingdom," kingdom here standing for ascendancy over the minds of men and conferred on him who sincerely desires true Wisdom. The following says the same thing in different words (6:24): "But the multitude of wise men is the salvation of the world, and a prudent king is the stay of his people."[134]

At another place, Wisdom is compared to the "reflection from the everlasting light" (7:26). Wisdom is "more beautiful than the sun, and above every constellation of the stars" (7:29). Such similes are suggestive of the solar symbolism so often met with in Egyptian, Babylonian, and Persian writings and borrowed by Hellenistic philosophers for the benefit of their deified kings, source and incarnation of all law.[135]

The Book of Enoch serves as a transition between the Wisdom literature and the apocalyptic writings, another class of letters much in vogue at this late period of Jewish history. The storm which

[134] Cf. especially Plato, *Republic*, 473 D, ed. by P. Shorey (Loeb, 1937), I, p. 508.
[135] Cf. also the study by T. Finan, "Hellenistic Humanism in the Book of Wisdom," *The Irish Theological Quarterly*, 27 (1960), pp. 30–48.

366

Antiochus Epiphanes raised against the Jews and their most sacred and cherished beliefs gave rise to this novel literary production. The apocalyptic literature was written by a new class of prophets, who set out to console and strengthen their compatriots in a grim struggle by conjuring up in their visions the final punishment that would overtake the enemies of the God of Israel and the splendid future which the promised Messiah would unfold to all the faithful. They drew largely on the great prophets for inspiration and interpreted their writings with consummate skill. They took the names of ancient patriarchs and prophets for disguise, as though it were not proper for any one to reveal new truths, once there was a law supplying all a Jew needed for regulating his life—one had only to explain what had been revealed to the patriarchs and prophets.

The Book of Enoch is a collection of six anonymous writings which circulated under the name of the Patriarch Enoch, but in fact date from various times between pre-Maccabean days and about the year 64 B.C.[136] In one Dream Vision, the so-called "Beast Apocalypse," a vivid account is given of the rising of the "pious" Jews under Judas Maccabeus. They are pictured as lambs who suddenly grow horns and start defending themselves against the aggressor (En.85–90). Then the master of the flock appears, mounts his throne and condemns the guilty to be burnt in the fiery abyss. In the end, the Gentiles are converted and the Messiah comes into his own as the ideal ruler over the New Jerusalem.

In another revelation, the so-called "Weeks Apocalypse," the defeat of the godless by the righteous will be followed by the rise of the messianic kingdom, outlined as a new heaven that will last (91:17) "many weeks without number for ever, and all shall be in goodness and righteousness, and sin shall no more be mentioned for ever." In this presentation of the messianic kingdom the old theme

---

[136] See W. O. E. Oesterley's Introduction to R. H. Charles, *The Book of Enoch (I Enoch)* (London, 1917), p. xiii seq. Quotations are from this translation. Cf. also F. C. Burkitt, *Jewish and Christian Apocalypses* (London, The British Academy, 1914), pp. 17–33; R. H. Charles' Introduction (*Apocrypha*, 2, p. 163 seq.); H. H. Rowley, *The Relevance of Apocalyptic. A Study of Jewish and Christian Apocalypses from Daniel to the Revelation*, 2nd. ed. (New York, 1947), and especially O. Eissfeldt, *Einleitung*, p. 763 seq. Cf. also D. O. Plöger, *Theokratie und Eschatologie* (Neukirchen, 1959), p. 37 seq., and D. Rössler, *Gesetz und Geschichte. Untersuchungen zur Theologie der jüdischen Apokalyptik und der pharisäischen Orthodoxie* (Neukirchen, 1960).

still lingers of the Messiah, as the ideal king, founding an earthly kingdom after triumphing over all the enemies of Israel and placing the chosen people in authority over the Gentiles. However, this vision spiritualizes the expectation, as the seer anticipates the dawn of a new age when sin shall be no more.

The idea is further developed in the Parables, the second part of the Book of Enoch (37–71, probably written before 63 B.C.) and the most appealing part of the collection. There most of the materials pertinent to our investigations are to be found and there, too, the link between the Wisdom literature and this new literary genre is most in evidence. The anonymous writer offers his parables to the reader as the words of wisdom revealed to Enoch (37:2, 3) and in the second parable he introduces the Messiah as the Son of Man and the supreme judge over kings, endowed with all righteousness (46:3 seq.):

> This is the Son of Man who hath righteousness,
> With whom dwelleth righteousness,
> And who revealeth all the treasures of that which is hidden,
> Because the Lord of Spirits hath chosen him....
> And this Son of Man whom thou has seen
> Shall raise up the kings and the mighty from their seats,
> And the strong from their thrones....
> And he shall put down the kings from their thrones and
>   kingdoms
> Because they do not extol and praise Him,
> Nor humbly acknowledge whence the kingdom was bestowed
>   upon them....

The same idea recurs in a beautiful passage which has the familiar ring of the Oriental court style (48:1–6):

> And in that place I saw the fountain of righteousness,
> Which was inexhaustible:
> And around it were many fountains of wisdom;
> And all the thirsty drank of them,
> And were filled with wisdom,
> And their dwellings were with the righteous and holy and elect.

And at that hour that the Son of Man was named
In the presence of the Lord of Spirits,
And his name before the Head of Days.
Yea, before the sun and the signs were created,
Before the stars of the heaven were made,
His name was named before the Lord of Spirits.
He shall be a staff to the righteous whereon to stay themselves
    and not fall,
And he shall be the light of the Gentiles,
And the hope of those who are troubled of heart.
All who dwell on earth shall fall down and worship before him,
And will praise and bless and celebrate with the song the Lord
    of Spirits.
And for this reason hath he been chosen and hidden before Him,
Before the creation of the world and for evermore....

The Son of Man, the Anointed of God, will be made to judge
the kings and the mighty. There follows a tribute to the wisdom
of the Son of Man, the Elect One (49:1–4):

For wisdom is poured out like water,
And glory faileth not before him for evermore.
For he is mighty in all the secrets of righteousness
And unrighteousness shall disappear as a shadow,
And have no continuance,
Because the Elect One standeth before the Lord of Spirits,
And his glory is for ever and ever,
And his might unto all generations.
And in him dwells the spirit of wisdom,
And the spirit which gives insight,
And the spirit of understanding and of might,
And the spirit of those who have fallen asleep in righteousness.
And he shall judge the secret things,
And none shall be able to utter a lying word before him,
For he is the Elect One before the Lord of Spirits according
    to His good pleasure.

Equally impressive is the description of the judgment of the
kings and the mighty by the Son of Man (62, 63): They will at last

see their mistake and in a belated repentance confess (63:4): "We have now learnt that we should glorify, and bless the Lord of kings and Him who is King over all kings."

It is difficult not to see in this enthusiastic description of the righteousness and wisdom of the Son of Man a reiteration of Hellenistic political thought, always so prone to attribute to the divinized kings the fullness of wisdom. Not they, however, are wise and righteous: there is but one king really wise and righteous, the Son of Man, the Elected One, the Messiah, and it is He whom the seer tries to evoke before the eyes of the righteous and troubled Jews. Those who arrogate His claims to themselves will one day be judged by that Son of Man, the only fountain of righteousness, and they will be condemned.

We may conclude with one more quotation from the Dream Visions (83–90), written probably between the years 135 and 76 B.C., and included in the collection. The passage is a straightforward formulation of the Israelite concept of God, creator of all things and supreme ruler (84:2, 3):

> Blessed be Thou, O Lord, King,
> Great and mighty in Thy greatness,
> Lord of the whole creation of the heaven,
> King of kings and God of the whole world.
> And Thy power and kingship and greatness abide for ever and
>   ever,
> And throughout all generations Thy dominion;
> And all the heavens are Thy throne for ever,
> And the whole earth Thy footstool for ever and ever.
> For Thou hast made and Thou rulest all things,
> And nothing is too hard for Thee,
> Wisdom departs not from the place of Thy throne,
> Nor turns away from Thy presence.

It should be noted that the author of the "Parables" in the Book of Enoch introduces a new notion into Jewish Messianic speculation. The Son of Man, as can be seen from the quotations, is different from the Messiah, the national king, descendant of David, as envisaged by official circles and the general public. He is created by Jahweh, but from the very beginning so that he pre-existed, hidden among the departed spirits, as a king of paradise (39:4-7), "standing before" the Lord of Spirits (49:2), waiting for the moment, predetermined by Jahweh, when he should appear on earth to judge the wicked and to glorify the just. His appearance will be a kind of epiphany. His name will be named "in the presence of the Lord of Spirits (48:2)— an echo of the Babylonian court style—and he will seat himself "on the throne of his glory" (69:29).

The author of the Parables is, however, neither the first nor the only one to speak about the Son of Man and describe his arrival. Daniel (7:13) saw in his vision the Son of Man coming "with the clouds of heaven....[137] And there was given him dominion, and glory, and a kingdom... his dominion is an everlasting dominion...." Other apocalyptic writings express similar ideas. The author of the Apocalypse of Ezra (after A.D. 70) saw the Son of Man coming with a violent wind from the sea and flowing with the clouds of heaven (IV Ezra 13:1 seq.) The Apocalypse of Baruch (written between A.D. 100 and 130) combines the coming of the Son of Man with a cloud rising from the sea (II Bar. 53) and with lightning (II Bar. 72).[138]

On the other hand, the kingdom of the Son of Man, in Enoch's conception, will, after the judgment, last forever in a new, transformed world. In this respect the other two late Jewish Apocalypses follow Enoch only in part. Their Son of Man remains a national Messiah. Ezra's Messiah will assure to the liberated faithful a blissful life for four hundred years; after that, they will die (IV Ezra 7:29). Only then will the eschatological Jahweh's Day of Judgment come. Moreover, his Messiah will spring from the seed of David (IV Ezra 12:32). Baruch seems more influenced by Enoch, as he thinks that the Messiah's "principate shall stand for ever, until the world of

[137] S. Mowinckel, *He That Cometh*, p. 351 seq., thinks that Daniel's Son of Man "is a pictorial symbol of the people of Israel." However, he acknowledges that the conception of such a "Man," who would come one day with the clouds of heaven, was familiar to the seer and his readers and must already have existed in Judaism about 200 B.C. or earlier.

[138] Cf. A. von Gall, Βασιλεία τοῦ Θεοῦ (Heidelberg, 1926), p. 423. The author compares the rise of the title "Son of Man" in the apocalyptic literature with that in the Gospels.

corruption is at an end, and until the Times aforesaid are fulfilled" (II Bar. 40:3).

It appears, thus, that, besides the official conception of a Messiah as being David's scion and the restorer of the national kingdom, there existed in late Judaism the conception of the Son of Man with characteristics taken from the idea of a national Messiah, but emphasizing his heavenly, universal character. He would inaugurate a new era after the judgment of the world. The kingdom, established by him, is spiritualized; the salvation of the simple and the return to paradise are stressed. The Son of Man becomes an eschatological figure, and the eschatological teaching expressed especially in Enoch's Book on the new aeon, the resurrection of men, the new kingdom of God, the paradise to which all the just may be admitted, certainly influenced the mentality of later Judaism. Nevertheless the new conception of the superterrestrial Son of Man could hardly overshadow the traditional messianic ideas.

The question arises as to how the new conception of a pre-existing Son of Man originated. E. Sjöberg, who devoted a thorough study to the problems connected with the origin and character of the Son of Man,[139] accepted the opinion of some other specialists[140] who sought a parallel in the world of Eastern religions. According to them, the Jewish conception of the Son of Man had its origin in the widespread Oriental ideas on Primordial Man—*Urmensch*— with a divine character, and in the Hellenistic "god Anthropos." The origin of this concept is connected with attempts to explain the genesis of the world. It was suggested that the cosmos had arisen in various ways from the body of Primordial Man. It will be appropriate to recall here the Persian eschatological savior Saoshyant. He was regarded as an incarnation not only of Zoroaster, but also of the Persian Primordial Man—Gayomard.[141] The Hellenistic "god

---

[139] *Der Menschensohn im äthiopischen Henochbuch* (Lund, 1946), p. 190 seq.

[140] See the bibliography in S. Mowinckel, *He That Cometh*, p. 422, note 2. On pp. 420–437 the author added interesting observations to Sjöberg's and other specialists' deductions. See especially O. Cullmann, *The Christology of the New Testament*, trans. by S. C. Guthrie and C. A. M. Hall (Philadelphia, 1959), pp. 137–192—a very competent discussion of this problem including both the Old and the New Testaments.

[141] Cf. *supra*, Chapter Three, pp. 124—127. See R. Reitzenstein, *Die hellenistischen Mysterienreligionen nach ihren Grundgedanken und Wirkungen*, 3rd ed. (Berlin, 1927), pp. 168 seq., 177 seq.

Anthropos"[142] is further a result of a mixture of Iranian and Chaldean ideas. These ideas also influenced the Jewish conception of the first man—Adam—in late Judaism.

It is thus possible that the pre-existing almost divine Jewish Son of Man is a variant of the Oriental myth of a Primordial Man. He cannot, however, be identified either with the first man—Adam —or with the Primordial Man himself. But if the connection between the two myths is valid, it is interesting to see how, once more, Oriental and Hellenistic ideas[143] influenced the conception of the Messiah in late Judaism, at least in certain circles. It must be remembered that this conception was not at all widespread.

The dependence of the seers on the myth of Primordial Man should not be exaggerated. It is clear that they had different ideas on the person and the task of the expected Messiah from those held by official circles and by the general public. They did not see in him merely an earthly king who had to renew the glory of Israel. They spiritualized his person and his kingdom and sought words and imagery which would better express their ideas than the royal titles and functions attributed a king.

The importance of the Book of Enoch lies, among other things, in its showing how strenuously the true Jewish spirit reacted against the encroachment of Hellenism. Itself the most un-Hellenic writing of this period in Jewish literature, its bearing on Christian origins is remarkable, because many of its ideas supply the background for a number of parables in the Gospels of Matthew, Mark, and Luke.[144] The book must have been read by the pious Jews of Jesus' day and its political bias apparently impressed the first Christians. Jesus Christ Himself appropriated the designation of Son of Man which the author of the Parables in the Book of Enoch had used with such relish for the Messiah, and had popularized among the Jews.[145]

[142] See C. H. Kraeling, *Anthropos and Son of Man*, Columbia Univ. Orient. Studies, 25 (New York, 1927), especially p. 128 seq. Cf. W. F. Albright, *From Stone Age to Christianity*, p. 290 seq.

[143] Especially Enoch, chaps. 17–36, or 41–44, 72–82, which treat of cosmogonic, cosmological, and astronomical problems and reflect many Egyptian, Iranian, and Greek ideas.

[144] See the interesting remarks on this subject in F. C. Burkitt, *op. cit.*, pp. 21–25.

[145] On this detail, cf. S. R. Driver, *The Book of Daniel*, The Cambridge Bible (Cambridge, 1901), p. 109 seq. Some passages in the Gospels (Matt.

The designation "Son of Man" has been shown to have come from another apocalyptic writer, whose work, the Book of Daniel, had the distinction of being classed among the canonical books of the Old Testament. Its publication in its present form was contemporaneous with the disastrous days of the persecution during the reign of Antiochus IV. It was intended to give courage to the faithful by recording the example of young men such as Daniel and his friends who had kept faith with the law and, for their loyalty, had been miraculously rescued by God. However, the narrative in the first part of the book probably contains some material of Babylonian origin. Even the story of Nebuchadnezzar's folly (Dan. 4) was probably included in the book for the particular benefit of Antiochus Epiphanes, whose pride outdistanced that of the Babylonian king, with the further hint that the proud Seleucid King would be called to account for his unwarranted attack on Israel.

The raising of Jewish morale was also the purpose of Daniel's visions (chaps. 7–12), which were doubtless written down in the first years of the Maccabean uprising, (167–165 B.C.),[146] although they contain some older narratives. The visions are recounted in forceful and dramatic style and throb with religious and patriotic fervor. This portion of the book is purely apocalyptic and its influence reached beyond contemporary Jewry, for it is also found in early Christian writings. It must certainly have heartened the long-suffering Jews to read that all those who had previously oppressed Israel had invariably incurred defeat and that even Antiochus IV Epiphanes, though he may have been "speaking great things" (chap. 7:8), would be repudiated by the Lord, as other proud rulers had been, for abuse of power.

24:30; 26:64; Mark 13:26; 14:62; Luke 21:27) seem to have been inspired by Daniel 7:13, and, in Driver's opinion, by Psalm 8:4.

[146] For particulars, see J. A. Montgomery, *A Critical and Exegetical Commentary on the Book of Daniel*, The International Critical Commentary (Edinburgh, 1927), pp. 88–99, which discusses the problems related to the composition of the book and gives a full bibliography. Cf. also R. H. Charles, *A Critical and Exegetical Commentary on the Book of Daniel* (Oxford, 1929), p. lxx seq. The most complete discussion of the history of the Book of Daniel, with detailed bibliography including also the fragments preserved in the Qumran Texts, will be found in O. Eissfeldt, *Einleitung*, pp. 633–654. Cf. also D. O. Plöger, *op. cit.*, pp. 19–36 (Das Danielbuch).

More comforting still to Jews, and later to Christians, was Daniel's spirited profession of faith in the resurrection of mankind, the divine judgment, and the everlasting life that was to be the lot of the righteous (chap. 12). The eloquent conclusion of this interesting book reveals to the chosen people, harassed and tortured to death as they were for their loyalty to the law, the terrifying vision of the Last Judgment: the consummation of the world, simultaneously with the resurrection of the righteous from their tortured bodies, now shining "as the brightness of the firmament," "as the stars for ever and ever," to enter everlasting life in raptures of joy, while their wicked persecutors are doomed to everlasting contempt.[147]

Besides its profession of faith in the resurrection, the Book of Daniel makes two other important contributions to the history of religion and the record of religious thought in the last stage of Jewish national life and the first of Christianity: it defined the Kingdom of God and it revealed a new aspect of the Son of Man— the Messiah and founder of the new Kingdom. Both contributions have a direct bearing on the problem with which we are dealing.

The triumph of the Kingdom of God over the kingdom of the world provides one of the leading ideas of the Book of Daniel. It pervades every chapter of its second part and is anticipated in chapter 2 by the dream of Nebuchadnezzar, pictured in the act of watching a stone falling upon a colossal statue, crushing it, and covering the earth. In enlarging on this vision, the seer borrows the words and the imagery of the prophets who preceded him to evoke Jahweh's final triumph and the dawning of Jahweh's Day.

The prophets Amos, Hosea, Isaiah, Jeremiah, Ezekiel, and Deutero-Isaiah in particular, never doubted the coming of Judgment Day, and they understood the final triumph over the Gentiles

---

[147] The observation made by H. L. Ginsberg in his short note "The Oldest Interpretations of the Suffering Servant," *VT*, 3 (1953), pp. 400–404, is of interest. He says that the author of the Book of Daniel, when speaking of the *Maskilim* (Enlightened or Enlighteners) who became, through their knowledge and also through their suffering and death, "justifiers of many" and would be resuscitated (Dan. 11–12), had in mind the Servant in Isa. 52:13–53:12, whom he identified with his *Maskilim*. This is the oldest interpretation of the suffering Messiah who through his suffering and death had to "justify many."

as implying either their conversion and incorporation into the new Kingdom, their subjection to the chosen people, or their destruction. But they painted the dawn of the Day and of the new era in colors too national and earthly: it would follow immediately on Israel's liberation from its oppressors, or its return to Jerusalem. In this respect, the seer in Daniel follows in their footsteps, since he also puts the coming of the Kingdom of God subsequent to the fall of Antiochus. Like other prophets, he telescopes events and places the final and ideal consummation of history in the near future, after the particular event which at the moment of writing was uppermost in his mind.

Yet, his presentation shows decided progress: it is certainly more eschatological than that of his predecessors, and ushers in the Kingdom of God after His final judgment of all men, whether just or unjust. There still lingers in his words the old ideal, so prevalent in the Old Testament, of Israel's universal domination and the anticipation of an earthly life of glory and triumph for its righteous sons; yet, there runs between the lines a faint and growing expectancy of an everlasting life that is spiritual and heavenly. The author of the Book of Daniel is also ahead of his predecessors in his extension of heavenly life to all the just, even outside Israel. In this respect, his presentation may be considered the final stage in the evolution of this particular theme in the Old Testament and it modifies the old concept of Jahweh's Day. In fact, it adumbrates the new Kingdom of God as it was revealed and defined by the promised Mediator, who by Jewish reckoning was to bring about the Day of Jahweh.[148]

This is how the seer introduces God's intermediary (7:13 seq.):

I saw in the night visions, and, behold, there came with the clouds
   of heaven one like unto a Son of man, and he came even to the
   Ancient of days, and they brought him near before him.
And there was given him dominion, and glory, and a kingdom, that
   all the peoples, nations, and languages should serve him: his
   dominion is an everlasting dominion, which shall not pass
   away, and his kingdom that which shall not be destroyed.

[148] Cf. S. R. Driver, *op. cit.*, pp. lxxxv–xc.

This designation of the Messiah, besides being vague, is very unusual. Though many have thought that Daniel's Son of Man symbolizes the glorified people of Israel (who are thereby promised world sovereignty)[149] the words actually can be applicable only to the Messiah,[150] who is depicted as similar to a man, something in the nature of an angelic prince. There was at the back of Daniel's portraiture of the Messiah the same notion of an ideal king that had so often served the prophets whenever they referred to Him.

Should any doubt remain as to the true significance of Daniel's Son of Man, it must be remembered that contemporary Jewish tradition would have understood the phrase as referring to the Messiah. We have seen how the Son of Man is found in the Parables, or Similitudes, of the apocryphal Book of Enoch (chaps. 37–71). The imagery which the writer uses in his description is evidently traceable, in many instances, to the vision recorded in Daniel, chapter 7. The seer of the Book of Enoch evidently refers to the Messiah and explains Daniel's conception as he saw it; but Enoch's Messiah, instead of being merely an angel-like being, one "like a son of man," *is* the Son of Man.

The author of the Parables considerably developed the idea and brought the Son of Man into far closer association with God than did Daniel. He also took up the ideas found in the Book of Daniel and further developed the notions of righteousness and gentleness with which the prophets Isaiah and Deutero-Isaiah (Isa. 9:7; 11:4 seq.; 42:3) had enhanced their portrayal of the Messiah. It may therefore be concluded that this passage of Daniel as interpreted by the Book of Enoch constitutes another important contribution to the development of the Messianic idea in the Old Testament. According to those two texts, the Messiah is a king, an ideal king, a fountain of righteousness; he resembles earthly kings only partially, for he is far above them, an angelic prince, very near to God—the Head of the days; his Kingdom, which will last forever,

---

[149] Cf. S. R. Driver, *op. cit.*, p. 103 seq., and S. Mowinckel, *He That Cometh*, p. 351 seq.

[150] J. Linder, *Commentarium in librum Daniel* (Paris, 1939), p. 309 seq. Cf. E. G. H. Kraeling, "Some Babylonian and Iranian Mythology in the Seventh Chapter of Daniel," *Oriental Studies in Honour of Cursetji Erachji Pavry*, pp. 228—231.

is not the same as an earthly kingdom. In this particular, the Books of Daniel and of Enoch point in the direction of the messianic concept as defined by Jesus Christ.[151]

The Book of Daniel also contains some striking passages, chiefly in the first part, which mark recent changes in Jewish political thought. Since this part seems to have been written in its original form in Babylonia by a loyal Jew who lived in an atmosphere of Babylonian and Persian ideas, some attempt might be expected at a compromise between the Oriental notions current there and Jewish notions as inspired by a belief in one God.

The whole of the first part exudes a Babylonian aura, with its oracular dreams and its magicians, though not every detail is correct. The author shows familiarity with the Oriental court style and when his heroes address Babylonian or Persian kings, they are always made to greet them with the typical "O king, live for ever" (Dan. 2:4; 3:9; 5:10; 6:6, 21). He also assumes the Eastern concept of absolutism, which allows kings to dispose of all their subjects and their belongings at will. In this, he certainly confuses Babylonian and Persian political thought. On one point only is he adamant: he takes his stand on the creed of his nation that all power on earth comes from God who gives it and takes it away from whomever he pleases. The subsequent extracts show this clearly.

In chapter 2:20 seq. Daniel is made to declare: "Blessed be the name of God for ever and ever: for wisdom and might are his: and he changeth the times and the seasons: he removeth kings, and setteth up kings: he giveth wisdom unto the wise, and knowledge to them that know understanding: he revealeth the deep and secret things: he knoweth what is in the darkness, and the light dwelleth with him. . . ."

In the same chapter (verse 37 seq.) Daniel addresses Nebuchadnezzar as follows: "Thou, O king, art king of kings, unto whom the

---

[151] It should be noted that in Daniel 7:13 the pre-existence of the Son of Man is not mentioned as it is in Enoch and that his Davidic origin is also not specified. It may be that the seer in Daniel seems not to be as much influenced by the myth of the Primordial Man as is Enoch. He uses this imagery, however, in order to express his idea of the Messiah, more sublime than that of the official circles.

God of heavens hath given the kingdom, the power, and the strength, and the glory; and wheresoever the children of men dwell, the beasts of the field and the fowls of the heaven hath he given into thine hand and hath made thee to rule over them all...." But the same King is told that he will be deprived of his position and live like a madman with the beasts for seven years (4:25) "till thou know that the Most High ruleth in the kingdom of men and giveth it to whomsoever he will." The King, after recovering his mental faculties and his kingdom, is made to declare (4:34 seq.): "...I blessed the Most High, and I praised and honored him that liveth for ever; for his dominion is an everlasting dominion, and his kingdom from generation to generation." With no less directness is the King's son Belshazzar told (5:18 seq.):

The Most High God gave thy father the kingdom, and greatness, and glory, and majesty,

And because of the greatness that He gave him, all peoples, nations, and languages trembled and feared before him: whom he would he slew, and whom he would he kept alive; and whom he would he raised up, and whom he would he put down.

But when his heart was lifted up, and his spirit was hardened that he dealt proudly, he was deposed from his kingly throne, and they took his glory from him:

....

... until he knew that the Most High God ruleth in the kingdom of men, and that he setteth up over it whomsoever he will.

The language of Oriental depotism has an unpleasant sound for anyone accustomed to a different political environment; yet, it must be admitted that the Jews discovered the only possible corrective to the plentitude of kingly power by establishing a more absolute power in the Most High, to whom all kings must render account for their deeds. He reserves to Himself the right to delegate His power to whomever He wishes, or take it from whoever fails to render due honor, praise, and obedience to Himself, the Most High, the true King of kings.[152]

[152] The messianic idea is also expressed in the prophecies of seventy "weeks"—the space of time which separates his contemporaries from the

379

The first clash between Hellenistic culture and Jewish religious and cultural traditions has been shown to have ended in a signal victory for the Jews. Those social circles which succumbed to the attractions of Hellenistic civilization were exterminated by Judas Maccabee, while the attack upon the Jewish spiritual inheritance met with determined resistance from pious Jewish writers, in whose opinion even the wisdom of Ecclesiastes was tinged with paganism. Yet, despite their resistance, the Jews were not altogether blind to what the new civilization had to offer and they adopted some innovations in the political field, though not without previous purification, to bring it into line with their own beliefs.

Again, their spirited fight on behalf of religious freedom and the Law inspired apocalyptic works. These contributed substantially to the history of the Jewish religion—and of religion in general—by their clear definition of the resurrection of the dead, the final judgment, the characteristics of the Kingdom of God and the personality of the Messiah, all favorite topics of Jewish theological speculation. But this was only one aspect of the evolution. Another arose from the very issue of the religious war and it will be of interest to consider for a moment this phase of Jewish national and religious history.

The writings which we have just studied, especially the Book of Daniel and the Parables of the Book of Enoch, came from the pens of pious Jews who belonged to a group characterized by devotion to the law, a group which supplied the Pharisees, the Essenes and other sects with most of their recruits. This party has already been seen fighting strenuously against the selfish dynastic policy of the Hasmonaeans, opposing especially the concentration of political and ecclesiastical power in the hands of that dynasty, whose members were attempting to combine the functions of chiefs and high priests. At this point a numerous and powerful party called the Sadducees came on the scene in support of the new Jewish national dynasty.

The Sadducees are reputed to have been worldly, wealthy, epicurean Jews, emancipated from the prescriptions of the law,

arrival of the Messiah. See the interpretation of Dan. 9:24–27 in J. Linder's *Commentarium*, pp. 364–414. One can see how deeply the author of the Book and his contemporaries believed in the Messianic idea.

denying the existence of an after-life, and placing their selfish, principles at the service of the existing political regime in Palestine. But lately serious doubts have been raised concerning this opinion.[153] It now appears that they were not as bad as they have been painted. Their leading principle was absolute fidelity to the law—held to be the only authority binding a Jew—and as a logical inference, they denied the existence of any other traditional law; this included such regulations as were advocated by the Pharisees to fill in the gaps left by the written law and to explain its obscurities. They did believe in a spiritual after-life, but not in the resurrection of the body, as this tenet was not included in the written law. Their dislike of the Pharisees was intensified by the fact that the Sadducees belonged to the priestly class who had been entrusted with the interpretation of the law since time immemorial. Naturally they resented any lay interference in a sphere of activity which they considered to be their professional privilege. But the party of the Pharisees was, both in its origin and in its acitivities, essentially a lay movement, recruited from among pious artisans and peasants. It might be considered as successor to the Hasidim, who had joined Mattathias of the priestly family of the Hasmonaeans in his fight against Hellenism. As the clergy formed a Jewish aristocracy to some degree, the Sadducees naturally recruited their adherents from among the priestly families and those wealthier Jews who were connected with them by matrimonial and other ties.

There was thus present in the rivalry between the two parties something of the never-failing antagonism between clergy and laity, mixed with the kindred jealousy between rich and poor. On top of this was the struggle for legislative powers. The Sadducees, representing the priestly class, claimed the right to frame new laws and regulations whenever the old ones proved inadequate; their claim had its justification in the post-exilic changes. Since the high priests

---

[153] Especially by R. Leszynsky, *Die Sadduzäer* (Berlin, 1912), the work that has contributed most to the clarification of this problem. However, Josephus in his *Jewish Antiquities* (XVIII, 1, 4, ed. by B. Niese, 3 [Berlin, 1892], p. 142 seq.) reproached them for their love of money and their implication in political affairs. See G. H. Box, "Sadducees" in Hasting's *Encyclopedia of Relig. and Ethics*, XI, pp. 43–46. On the origin and history of the Pharisees and Sadducees, see also E. Meyer, *Ursprung und Anfänge des Christentums*, 2 (Stuttgart, 1921), pp. 282–329. On the Essenes, see *ibid*, pp. 393–402.

had gradually stepped into the role of the national kings, they took it for granted that they had also inherited the royal privilege of framing laws, at least in liturgical and moral matters. But the Pharisees, in opposing this claim, considered the period of legislation to have definitely closed. They appealed to the body of unwritten tradition, which existed side by side with the written law, to compensate for the shortcomings of the code.

These differences necessarily affected the attitude of each party vis-à-vis the Hasmonaeans. When the Pharisees had turned away from the intruding dynasty and forced the rulers to look for support elsewhere, the change of alignment was bound to have its political repercussions. As it would have been poor strategy for the new dynasty to stress too much the Davidic origin of Israel's rulers, its supporters had to justify the regime in some other way. When the Hasmonaeans added the high priesthood to their political armory, they had, out of sheer decency, to look to the past for some plausible excuse, if only to placate the Pharisees. All this was bound to affect Jewish political thought as well as the current teaching about the Messiah and His kingdom.

Now that evidence concerning the history of the Sadducees has begun to come to light, these changes can be followed with at least reasonable confidence in their accuracy. Traces have been found in writings which may be attributed in Sadducees, or in works written by authors who were closely associated with the Pharisees, if not actually of their ranks. The ideas that were later to serve the Sadducees as their leading principles appeared for the first time in Ecclesiasticus, written by Jesus Ben-Elasa, or Ben-Sirach.[154] Not only is the whole tenor of this work alien to the dogma of the resurrection—one of the Sadducees' special aversions—but it betrays a strange indifference to David and to the promises made to his house by Jahweh. It admits to the covenant made by the Lord with David, but promptly proceeds to use the covenant made with Aaron to offset it. Whereas David's royal legacy passed down only from son to son, Aaron's went to all his seed—the obvious implication being that every priest was heir to Aaron's mission (Ecclus. 50:14-18) but not every descendant of David was his heir (Ecclus. 45:25).

[154] On his political ideas, see *supra*, pp. 362—364.

The next reference to David's legacy (chap. 47) is a feeble comment on the messianic promises made to David, as though their only purport was to give David a son, i.e., Solomon. The only unmistakable messianic reference to the House of David, which occurs in the thanksgiving at the end of Ecclesiasticus, 51:14, is suspected of being a later interpolation by a Pharisaic reader, and it is preserved only in the Hebrew text of the book.[155]

A similar attitude is adopted in the First Book of the Maccabees;[156] for example, I Macc. 2:57 says: "David, for being merciful, inherited the throne of a kingdom for ever and ever," but this is not meant to imply either the eternal duration of the Davidic kingdom or the Messiah's Davidic descent. That this meaning was not intended becomes evident in I Macc. 14:41, where the writer states that Simon and his successors will rule Israel as long as no authentic prophet is available: "King Demetrius had heard say... that the Jews and the priests were well pleased that Simon should be their leader and high priest for ever, until there should arise a faithful prophet and that he should be captain over them and should take charge of the sanctuary, to set them over their works, and over the country and over the arms, and over the strongholds...."

These words suggest that the Hasmonaeans and their followers were ready to compromise with the Pharisees, who objected to any ruler other than a descendant of David and believed that the Messiah would be of David's stock. The Pharisees were being asked to put up with the Hasmonaeans as merely temporary rulers over Judah, only so long as no faithful prophet was forthcoming to decide upon the next step. Another passage in the First Book (4:46) may bear out this interpretation; at least it shows that the Jews at the time were expecting a prophet who would decide on the disposal of the Temple altar that had been polluted by pagan sacrifices. The

---

[155] For particulars, see R. Leszynsky, *op. cit.*, p. 172 seq. The praises (Ecclus. 50) of the High Priest Simeon II (*ca.* 218–192) also indicate that the prestige of the priesthood in the nation was growing. The high priest had taken the place of the king. The Hebrew original was composed in Jerusalem about 190 B.C. and translated into Greek by the author's grandson in Egypt after 117 (O. Eissfeldt, *Einleitung*, pp. 737–741).

[156] Cf. on the author of the first book, F. M. Abel, *Les livres des Maccabées* (Paris, 1949), p. xxi seq.

Pharisees were at liberty to interpret this compromise to mean that the Hasmonaeans would vacate their place in favor of the Messiah, as foretold by the prophets (Deut. 18:18), whenever he should make his appearance. It is significant that the writer of the First Book of Maccabees was not more explicit, confining himself to no more than the announcement of an authentic prophet. His reticence makes one suspect that the Hasmonaeans and the Sadducees were not overly keen in their anticipation of a Messiah who, according to all Pharisaic glosses on the prophecies, was to be a descendant of David and was to inherit all his royal rights and prerogatives. As the Messiah's future kingdom was so often mistaken for an earthly state, it is quite understandable that a non-Davidic dynasty which intended to remain in power, would say little about the Messiah and His kingdom.

The Second Book of Maccabees seems to be of Pharisaic authorship.[157] The writer starts with the solemn declaration that God is the only king of Judah. To lend more weight to his words, he puts them into the mouth of Nehemiah, the same one who carried through Ezra's reforms (II Macc. 1:24): "O Lord, Lord God, the Creator of all things, who art terrible and strong and righteous and merciful, who alone art King and gracious, who alone suppliest every need, who alone art righteous and almighty and eternal, thou that savest Israel out of all evil, who madest the fathers thine chosen and didst sanctify them...." This serial enlargement on God's kingship and His righteousness reads like a veiled challenge offered to the Hasmonaean rulers and a reminder that they are not kings, since only God is Israel's king and source of all righteousness.

The whole trend of the Second Book of Maccabees is a tribute to Judas, the first to rally all the Hasidim and lead them in the fight for religious freedom. He, not Simon and his men, is the real hero, for he sowed where others reaped. Incidentally, the book weakens the reading of Exodus 19:6: "and ye shall be unto me a kingdom of priests, and an holy nation," quoted by the Sadducees in support of the priests' claim to royalty, and substitutes the following interpretation (II Macc. 2:17): "Now God, who saved all his people and restored the heritage to all, *and* the kingdom *and* the priest-

---

[157] On its author, see F. M. Abel, *op. cit.*, p. xxxiii seq.

hood, and the following. . . ." Here the priesthood is studiously dissociated from the kingdom, both being allotted as a legacy to the whole nation. Since the first book of the Maccabees (*ca.* 110–90 B.C.) seems to have been written before the second book (written *ca.* 40 B.C., though compiled from a larger work by an Alexandrian Jew about 120 B.C.), it is not impossible that the Pharisaic compiler of the second book was prompted to sing the praises of Judas Maccabee at the expense of Judas' successors, Jonathan, Simon, and John Hyrcanus. He was not deliberately hostile to the clergy, aiming his criticism only at the Sadducean priests. Moreover, it is well known that the book owed its popularity, especially in the Church of Rome, to its teachings on the resurrection, the prayers for the dead, and the intercession of the saints (II Macc. 7:9 seq.; 12:43 seq.; 15:11–16).[158]

If the Book of Sirach and the Books of Maccabees only skimmed the surface of some of the problems that divided Jewish society into two camps after the second half of the second century B.C., there remains an apocryphal work which seems better to reflect the Sadducean mind on our topic, the Book of Jubilees.[159] Here the writer apparently aimed at a reform of the Jewish calendar by advocating a stricter observance of the sabbatical years (periods of seven years) and of jubilees (periods of seven times seven years) and by urging the adoption of a solar calendar. He urgently recommends a number of usages that were certainly distasteful to the Pharisees;[160] he has very vague notions about the immortality of the soul (23:31; 7:29; 22:22; 24:31) and does not express faith

[158] For further particulars, see R. Leszynsky, *op. cit.*, p. 176 seq.; and the introduction to both books by R. H. Charles in his *Apocrypha*, 1, pp. 59–66, 125–131.

[159] R. H. Charles, "The Book of Jubilees," *Apocrypha*, 2, pp. 1–82, a reprint of his edition of the Ethiopic version published in 1895. It is also reprinted (*The Book of Jubilees*, Translations of Early Documents, 1st Ser. [London, 1917]) with an excellent introduction by G. H. Box. See also M. Testuz, *Les idées religieuses du livre des Jubilés* (Geneva-Paris, 1960) and the long review of this book in *VT*, 11 (1961), pp. 101–108. K. J. Klausner, *op. cit.*, at p. 302 seq., dates the composition of this book between 100 to 90 B.C., and, at p. 276 seq., the Book of Enoch from 110 to 68 B.C.

[160] These are listed in the commentary on the book in R. Leszynsky, *op. cit.*, p. 179 seq., and summarized by G. H. Box in his introduction, *op. cit.*, p. xv seq.

in the resurrection of the body; all indications that he was probably a Sadducee rather than a Pharisee.

The writer's views approach most closely the Sadducean attitude when discussing the coming of the Messiah and His kingdom, but there is nothing in the entire book to suggest that He might come from the House of David. The author rather dilutes the old Messianic promises once made to Judah by explaining the blessing as follows (Jub. 31:18): "A prince shalt thou be, thou and one of thy sons, over the sons of Jacob," the words "one of thy sons" being applicable to David, not to the Messiah. The whole book is significantly silent about the Davidic Messiah. It is even arguable that the writer eulogized Judah only because he associated him with Judas Maccabee, the hero of the new Hasmonaean dynasty, which at that moment combined supreme political and sacerdotal powers. Another reference (31:20) to the fullness of peace that shall fall to the lot of "all the seed of the sons of the beloved," when Judah shall be sitting on the throne of righteousness, may also be read as a veiled compliment to Judas Maccabee.

Some other passages (1:29; 23:29, 30) seem to bear out this explanation by suggesting that in the author's opinion the Messianic kingdom was already an accomplished fact at the time the book was written. According to him, this period coincided with an era of great prosperity under the blessed rule of the Hasmonaeans, particularly under Simon and John Hyrcanus; he found the rise of the kingdom apparently attributable to "the progressive spiritual growth of man and a corresponding transformation of nature. Its members were promised a span of a thousand years in perfect happiness and peace, with powers of evil under strict control and the Last Judgment to bring it to a close."[161]

In the light of this interpretation the book should help one to understand the extent to which Judaic ideas were modified in the Hasmonaean period and how the political experience of a new national dynasty was able to transform the old Messianic belief of Jews otherwise loyal to the prescriptions of the law. Actually, it is difficult to understand why the author tries to make so much of the

---

[161] R. H. Charles, *Apocrypha*, 2, p. 9, suitably summarizes in these concise words the author's ideas on the Messianic kingdom.

promise made to Levi, to whom and to whose descendants he attributes powers both priestly and political (31:51): "And they will be princes and judges, and chiefs of all the seed of the sons of Jacob; They will speak the word of the Lord in righteousness.... And they will declare My ways to Jacob and My paths to Israel. The blessing of the Lord will be given in their mouths to bless all the seed of the beloved." This reads like a plea for the Hasmonaeans' claim to combined priesthood and rulership. The same intention may be read into chapter 32:1, where it is claimed for Levi "that they had ordained and made him the priest of the Most High God, him and his sons for ever," words which in a way usurp the title given to the priest-king Melchizedek (Gen. 14:18) and imply that the new high priests could lay claim to political sovereignty.

In spite of all these appearances, the Sadducean origin of the book is not at all certain, although it may be said that the book was not written by a Pharisee,[162] but by a champion of priestly traditions and perhaps also of the Hasmonaean dynasty. There is, however, another possibility offering a better explanation for the origins and tendencies of the Book of Jubilees. It has been established that the calendar of the Jubilees corresponds to the calendar which has been used by the sect, probably Essenian, which had its headquarters "in the desert" at Qumran near the Dead Sea. Among the so-called Dead Sea scrolls, recently discovered, a calendar was found almost identical to that propounded by the author of the Jubilees and recorded also in the First Book of Enoch (72–80).[163]

---

[162] R. H. Charles declared the book to be a Pharisean production, but his opinion was rightly discarded by G. H. Box. The only sentence that has the Pharisaic touch is in chapter 16:18, where Israel is described as a future combination of kingdom, priests, and a holy nation—a Pharisaic comment on Exodus 19:6—and this may be taken for a later correction added in the Ethiopian text; in the Hebrew and Latin texts (Box, *loc. cit.*, p. xxxiii), as in Exodus, only "a kingdom of priests" is explicitly mentioned. It is well known that this passage used to be very popular among the Sadducees, who quoted it in justification of the usurpation of political power by the Hasmonaean high priests.

[163] For details, see A. Jaubert, "Le calendrier des Jubilés et de la secte de Qumrân," *VT*, 3 (1953), pp. 250–264; *idem*, "Le calendrier des Jubilés et les jours liturgiques de la semaine," *VT*, 7 (1957), pp. 35–61. E. Kutsch, "Der Kalender des Jubiläenbuches und das Alte und das Neue Testament," *ibid.*, 11 (1961), pp. 39–47, does not favor Jaubert's interpretation. Cf. also A. Finkel, *The Pharisees*, pp. 70–74.

J. Morgenstern[164] has shown that this calendar is a direct out-growth of the ancient pentecontad calendar which had been in vogue among the Semitic peoples of early Assyria, Babylonia, Syria, and Palestine. It divided the year into seven periods of fifty days each, and was essentially an agricultural calendar. In spite of different reforms, conservative elements, especially the peasants of Galilee, retained the old pentecontad calendar. When, at the end of the last quarter of the fifth century B.C., the priestly reformers introduced the lunar calendar (which became the official calendar of Judaism not only in Palestine, but also in the diaspora), the conservative, usually rural, elements of the Jewish community continued to follow the ancient pentecontad calendar.

The pentecontad calendar was maintained with particular tenacity by special Judaic sects, although with certain changes. The author of the Jubilees was therefore most probably a member of one of these sects, similar to, or identical with, that of Qumran. His passionate defense of the solar pentecontad calendar illustrates the deeply rooted opposition of the sectaries to the official priesthood, which had degenerated in their eyes and from whose leadership they had withdrawn. If this is so, then even the ideas on the Messiah which appear alien to the Pharisaic and official interpretation, and seem to echo Sadducean ideas, should perhaps be attributed to the beliefs of the Qumran sect concerning the coming Messiah.

The sect of Qumran seems to have been founded by a priest who in the discovered document is called Teacher of Enlightenment. He, or his successors, seems to have given to his followers a well-defined statute, called the Manual of Discipline,[165] regulating the

---

[164] "The Calendar of the Book of Jubilees, Its Origin and Its Character," *VT*, 5 (1955), pp. 34–76.

[165] See, on the discovery and editions of the Manual, A. Dupont-Sommer *Les écrits esséniens découverts près de la Mer Morte* (Paris, 1959), p. 83 seq. French translation. *ibid.*, p. 88 seq. A handy English translation by T. H. Gaster, *The Dead Sea Scriptures* (New York, 1956), p. 38 seq. On the founder of the Qumran community, see the detailed study by G. Jeremias, *Der Lehrer der Gerechtigkeit* (Göttingen, 1963). The author reviews all theories concerning his origin and character, and, on pp. 319–354, points out the differences between this Teacher's character and actions and those of Jesus Christ.

entire inner life of the members, their conduct and their relations with outsiders. It is related to the Zadokite Document,[166] which was discovered almost half a century ago in an old synagogue at Cairo and which can only now, since the discovery of the Qumran scrolls, be fully appreciated.

It appears from these documents that the sectaries had great veneration for the priesthood—priests being the recognized leaders of the congregation. Furthermore, they regarded themselves as the remnants of the faithful of Israel, separating themselves from the corrupt remainder of the nation and awaiting the renewal of the covenant and the liberation of the nation through the Messiah whose coming they regarded as imminent. This belief was so firmly embedded in their minds that one of them elaborated a detailed battle order for the war against the sons of Belial,[167] when the Messiah should come to lead them to the final triumph of God. A special ritual was planned for the communal banquet at which the Messiah—a layman, a kingly leader—should be present.[168]

The protocol regulating the session of dignitaries "in the event that the anointed [king] should be present among them" gives the first places to the high priest and the head of the Aaronite priestly families. Only when they are seated should the "anointed" come, followed by the chiefs of the armed forces. Not even the "anointed" can touch the food and wine before the high priest has blessed it and has served himself.

This reverence for the priesthood, so characteristic of the Qumran sect, seems to be reflected also in the Book of Jubilees when the author speaks so highly of Levi, attributing to his sons supreme priestly and judicial power. Priests wielded these powers in the

---

[166] See the last edition by C. Rabin, *The Zadokite Documents* (Oxford, 1954), English translation. The priests who directed the sect regarded themselves as true successors of Sadok (Zadok), mentionedb y Ezekiel (40:46), as did the Sadducees.

[167] J. van Der Ploeg, "La Règle de la guerre. Traduction et notes," *VT*, 5 (1955), pp. 373–420; T. H. Gaster, *op. cit.*, pp. 281–306. The first English translation of the new discoveries was made by M. Burrows in *The Dead Sea Scrolls* (New York, 1955) and *More Light on the Dead Sea Scrolls* (New York, 1958).

[168] "Manual of Discipline for the Future Congregation of Israel," trans. by T. H. Gaster, *op. cit.*, pp. 307–310. The author may have been inspired by the sacred meal described in Ezekiel 44:3.

congregation of Qumran (Manual, ix, 7) and were also assured of a privileged position after the final triumph of the army led by the Messiah. It is thus very likely that the author of the Jubilees was, if not a member of the same congregation, at least a sympathizer.

This exaltation of the Levitic priesthood in the Jubilees would be even more comprehensible if it were true that the community of Qumran was actually expecting two Messiahs—a high priest and a king. There is in the Manual of Discipline a passage which is interpreted by some specialists to mean this. Alluding to the prophecy in Deuteronomy 18:18, the author of the Manual orders that "until the coming of the prophet and of the Messiah(s) of Aaron and Israel, these men [the presbyters] are not to depart from the clear intent of the Law..."(ix, 11).

It is not certain, however, that such an interpretation is correct. Other specialists contest it. "Aaron and Israel" is understood, for example, as one unit by H. H. Rowley:[169] "the sect itself represents Israel and Aaron, and the title of the Messiah has reference to the character of the sect, and not his personal descent. The Messiah who shall arise from Aaron and Israel is thus the Messiah who shall arise from the sect." The Zadokite Document seems to confirm such an interpretation, because it repeats three times "the Messiah of Aaron and Israel" (xix, 10; xx, 1; xii, 23–39). Two other specialists[170] also suggest readings which eliminate the admission of two Messiahs.

On the other hand, the author of the Book of Jubilees, although favoring Levi and his descendants, the priests, is not denying the Davidic origin of the expected Messiah. From what he says about the Messiah it cannot be argued that he believed in the coming of

---

[169] *Op. cit.*, p. 41.

[170] L. H. Silbermann, "The 'Two Messiahs' of the Manual of Discipline," *VT*, 5 (1955), pp. 77–82, and W. S. LaSor, "'The Messiahs of Aaron and Israel'," *VT*, 6 (1956), pp. 425–429. M. Black, in his illuminating study "Messianic Doctrine in the Qumran Scrolls," *Studia Patristica*, pt. 1, ed. by K. Aland and F. L. Cross, 1, pp. 441–459 (= Texte und Untersuchungen, 63, [1957]), also speaks about one Messiah, regarding the other interpretation as a highly "debatable point." W. H. Brownlee, "John the Baptist in the New Light of Ancient Scrolls," *Interpretation*, 9 (1955), p. 81 seq., also accepts the one Messiah thesis.

two Messiahs, one from the tribe of Levi, the other of Davidic origin.

A similar tendency is to be found in another work, the Testaments of the Twelve Patriarchs. The editor and translator of this work, R. H. Charles,[171] dates its composition between 137 and 107 B.C. It was thought[172] that the author's primary aim was to induce the Pharisees to relent in their unfriendly attitude toward the Hasmonaeans and to convince them that the dynasty had a perfect right to combine the functions of high priests and rulers. As an illustration, he put on the stage twelve sons of Jacob and made them address their posterity from their death beds. Their general theme is magnanimity and concord, and an admonition to submit to lawful authority, which in their and the author's opinion, was vested in Levi and his descendants alone. The words of Reuben (2:10–12): "And bow before his [Levi's] seed, for on our behalf it will die in wars visible and invisible and will be among you an eternal king" were applied to the war which the Hasmonaean priestly family, especially John Hyrcanus had waged for the liberation and the glory of Israel. In a similar sense the exaltations of Levi, the founder of Israelite priesthood, were explained in chapters 5, 6, 8, and 9.

The discovery of the Qumran scrolls, however, induced the specialists to reach different conclusions concerning this apocryphal book. There are many affinities in the Testaments with the Qumran scrolls, which suggest that the author of the Testaments was familiar with the main documents of the sect.[173] Like the Qumran documents the author exalts Levi and the priesthood. He has little to say about sacrifices and uses the quotations from the same prophets —especially Isaiah—and from the Jubilees and Enoch's Apocalypse which are found in the Qumran Texts. He has the same theological principles and gives the same moral precepts as

---

[171] *Apocrypha*, 2, pp. 282–367. Cf. also W. O. E. Oesterley's introduction to the reprint of Charles' translation in Translations of Early Documents, 1st Ser. (1917), p. xvi seq. See O. Eissfeldt, *Einleitung*, p. 780 seq., with recent bibliography.

[172] For particulars, see R. Leszynsky, *op. cit.*, p. 248 seq.

[173] See especially the detailed comparison of quotations from the Testaments and the Qumran Texts, in M.-A. Chevallier's work, *L'Esprit et le Messie dans le bas-judaïsme et le Nouveau Testament* (Paris, 1958), pp. 117–119.

the sectarian writings. Everything indicates that he belonged to the Jewish sect which had its center at Qumran.

As the sect flourished from 200 B.C. to 70 A.D. the Testaments could have been written at any time during this period. E. J. Bickerman[174] places the composition of the Testaments in the first quarter of the second century B.C. He bases his conclusion on some historical allusions in the Testaments, on numismatic evidence, and on the fact that the work contains no allusion to the persecution under Antiochus IV or to the Maccabean struggles. This dating seems to be quite reliable and, of course, excludes every connection between this work and the political propaganda inspired by the Hasmonaean dynasty.

There is still one problem, concerning the coming of the Messiah as it is described in the Testaments, which needs clarification. The exaltation of Levi and the passage in Joseph's Testament[175] induced scholars to believe that the author expected two Messiahs, one from the tribe of Levi and the other from the tribe of Judah. The interpretation of a similar passage on the Messiah in the Qumran Manual of Discipline seemed to confirm the thesis that the author of the Testament, also expected two Messiahs, and gave precedence to the Levitic Messiah.

A more thorough investigation of the passages shows, however, that this is not the case. The most troublesome passage is contained in the so-called Messianic hymn in Levi's Testament (18:1, 2): "And after their punishment shall have come from the Lord, the priesthood shall fail. Then shall the Lord raise a new priest. And to him all the words of the Lord shall be revealed...." This is evidently an allusion to the coming of the Messiah. But because the author says that the old priesthood shall fail, the new priest-Messiah will not be a Levite priest. The author attributes to the Messiah a priestly character, but this does not exclude his descent from David. This illustrates, of course, the author's respect for the priesthood, as also stressed in the Testament of Simeon (7:1, 2):

---

[174] "The Date of the Testaments of the Twelve Patriarchs," *JBL*, 69 (1950), pp. 245–260.

[175] Test. of Joseph, 19:11: "And do ye, my children, honor Levi and Judah, for from them shall arise the salvation of Israel." (R. H. Charles, *Apocrypha*, 1, p. 353 seq.).

"Obey Levi and Judah...for from them shall arise unto you the salvation of God. For the Lord shall raise up from Levi as it were a High-priest, and from Judah as it were a King.... He shall save all...."[176]

When the author repeats that the salvation of Israel will come from Levi and Judah, his words do not mean that he expected two Saviours. From the tribe of Levi will arise a high priest, but the real Messiah-king will come from Judah. In this respect the author of the Testaments is in accord with the believers of Qumran.

The Testaments have many later Jewish and Christian interpolations. Basically, however, it is not a Judaic-Christian document as has recently once more been argued,[177] but a genuine Jewish work, representing the attitude of the sect, probably of Essenian character, which had its center at Qumran.

Insofar as the Messianic beliefs of this sect are concerned, it now seems generally agreed that its founder, the anonymous Teacher of Righteousness (who was persecuted by the official priestly authorities and exiled, perhaps to Damascus) cannot be regarded as their Messiah. For the Messiah, it was believed, would be resuscitated and would appear to his disciples.[178] The sectaries continued to expect a Messiah as their ancestors had—a king and founder of a new kingdom, who would lead the faithful Israelites to victory in the war against the sons of Belial.[179] Their expectation also had an eschatological character.

[176] Cf. also Test. of Judah, 21: "To me the Lord gave the kingdom, and to him [Levi] the priesthood, and He set the kingdom beneath the priesthood" (ibid., p. 322).

[177] M. De Jonge, The Testaments of the Twelve Patriarchs. A Study of their Text, Composition and Origin (Assen, 1953). His arguments are rightly discarded by F.-M. Braun, in his study "Les Testaments des XII Patriarches et le problème de leur origine," Revue biblique, 67 (1960), pp. 516–549.

[178] There is no space to enter into details of this complicated and prolonged discussion. The general reader will find a short, clear exposé with the main bibliography in J. Daniélou's publication, Les manuscrits de la Mer Morte et les origines du Christianisme (Paris, 1957), pp. 59–83. See, for details, B. Otzen, "Die neugefundenen hebräischen Sektenschriften und die Testemente der zwölf Patriarchen," Studia Theologica, 7 (Lund, 1954), pp. 125–157, especially p. 145 seq.

[179] The words with which the author introduces the protocol of the holy banquet are: "The following is a Session when God begets the Messiah [to be] with them"—if this reading is correct; specialists prefer sends instead of begets. Cf. also Gaster, op. cit., p. 279; it may contain a Messianic interpretation of

The criticisms which the Pharisees levelled at the Hasmonaeans were never so justifiable as under Alexander Jannaeus (102–76 B.C.), whose reign was the decisive period of Hasmonaean rule. Constantly in the field at the head of his army, he grossly neglected his high-priestly duties, the target of the Pharisees' concentrated attacks. He must have seen the danger of his policy, for on his death bed he advised his wife Alexandra Salome to give more freedom to the Pharisees. Alexandra (76–67 B.C.) maintained her husband's territorial gains, and, with the backing of her son Hyrcanus, who was formally invested with the high-priestly office, the Pharisees rose in influence. But the Sadducees, determined not to surrender their political gains without a struggle, rallied in revolt around Hyrcanus' brother, Aristobulus. When the crisis came to a head after the Queen's death, Aristobulus defeated his brother and forced him to abdicate. The counter action was soon to follow. Hyrcanus was induced by the governor of Idumaea, Antipater, father of Herod the Great, to re-open the fight and he forced his brother on the defensive.

At this stage an unexpected factor appeared on the scene in the form of the victorious Roman armies of Pompey, who were just then completing their campaign in Asia Minor and approaching the frontiers of Syria. In 63 B.C., Pompey entered the country and was invited by the contending parties to intervene. He first favored Aristobulus, but, suspecting treachery, then forced him to surrender. Jerusalem became a Roman possession, Hyrcanus was confirmed in his high priesthood, albeit with powers curtailed and confined purely to religious matters, and was permitted to govern Judaea. His position improved in 47 B.C., when he despatched Antipater at the head of a small army to the assistance of Caesar in his Alexandrine war. For his reward he was made hereditary

Psalm 2:7: "Thou art my son; this day have I begotten thee." The text "for blessing the president of the community" in the Supplementary Code of Qumran (ed. by Gaster, p. 91) also recalls some traditional Messianic features: Gen. 49:9 (Lion of Judah), Numbers 24:17 (Messiah as the Sceptre of rulers), and Isaiah 11:1–2, 5 (righteousness shall be his girdle, spirit of counsel). See, for details, M. Black, *op. cit.*, pp. 450, 451. Cf. also J. M. Allegro, "Further Messianic References in Qumran Literature," *JBL*, 75 (1956), pp. 174–187. Cf. also the interesting attempt at the solution of this problem given by L. Mowray, *The Dead Sea Scrolls and the Early Church* (Chicago, 1962), pp. 155–163.

ethnarch of Judaea, with the addition of a few cities. Antipater was appointed procurator of Judaea and made directly responsible to Rome. He, of course, took advantage of his position to favor his sons and place them in high positions.

The end result was that in 41 B.C. Hyrcanus lost his powers as a temporal ruler and Herod became king of Judaea. Thus the Hasmonaean dynasty and its hold on Judaea came to an end. The kingdom came under Roman rule and after some insurrections in Jerusalem its administration was distributed among the sons of Herod the Great: Archelaus, who had succeeded his father as king, was made no more than ethnarch of Judaea, Idumaea, and Samaria; Herod Antipas, tetrarch of Galilee and Peraea; Philip, tetrarch of Northern Palestine. Such was the new political setting in which the expected Messiah, Jesus Christ, was to found His new Kingdom. The last act of the political drama was enacted in the year A.D. 6, when the Romans deposed Archelaus for misgovernment and transferred the administration of Judaea to their own procurators with official headquarters in Caesarea, the new city built by Herod the Great.[180]

The loss of national independence, along with the end of the Hasmonaean dynasty—Israel's last claims to political glory—was by a strange irony of fate the work of an Idumaean aristocratic family. The conquest of Idumaea sealed the doom of its conquerors. Herod the Great, the founder of the Idumaean dynasty, knew no mercy and in order to preclude every possibility of a return of the Hasmonaeans, exterminated the whole family, without even sparing his own wife Mariamne, the last Hasmonaean princess. Outwardly faithful to the Jewish creed, which the Idumaeans had been forced to adopt, the Idumaean dynasty had no roots in the Jewish tradition. Herod the Great, in the true manner of a Hellenistic king, bent all his energies to the task of extending his kingdom and the powers of his dynasty.

The new political setting naturally affected the world of ideas. The collapse of the Hasmonaeans, who, with the exception of Queen Alexandra Salome, had always leaned on the aristocratic and

---

[180] A detailed summary of these events will be found in E. Bevan, *Jerusalem under the High Priests*, pp. 132–162.

priestly party, dealt the Sadducees a stunning blow from which they never recovered. The Pharisees were thus left in sole possession of the field and their influence over the people grew apace. This also meant the end of the Sadducean version of messianism. But, however much the Pharisees criticized the Hasmonaeans for usurping royal powers without being descendants of David, they could hardly welcome their successors, who were not even Jewish. Still, as their particular grievance had been the combination of priestly and royal powers by the Hasmonaean dynasty, they found consolation and a possibility of compromise in their attitude to the newcomers, since they were at any rate rid of one abomination. Under Herod, it is true, high priests were powerless, but that was better than being ruled by priest-kings. Besides, the Pharisees could always attribute the change to the nation's transgressions against the Lord's Law and to God's just punishment, and they could always cling to their belief that the House of David would rise again and assume power whenever the Messiah should make His awaited appearance.

A vivid account of what went on in the hearts of the faithful during this eventful period is found in the Psalms of Solomon,[181] eighteen beautiful songs composed after the Roman entry into Jerusalem. It is one of the finest products of the Pharisaic spirit, testifying to the deep sincerity and piety of the majority of the party and to the people's eager anticipation of the Davidic Messiah. These songs also provide a pointed definition of the Jews' political thought at that time.

The Pharisaic authors were certainly good patriots and the writer of Psalm 8 is alarmed by the threat of war from Syria:

> Distress and the sound of war hath my ear heard,
>   The sound of a trumpet announcing slaughter and calamity,
>   The sound of much people as of an exceeding high wind—,
> . . . .

---

[181] G. B. Gray, "The Psalms of Solomon" in R. H. Charles' *Apocrypha*, 2, pp. 624–652. Cf. also J. Viteau and I. Martin, *Les Psaumes de Salomon, Documents pour l'étude de la Bible* (Paris, 1911). Cf. O. Eissfeldt, *Einleitung*, pp. 754–758. Cf. also H. Braun, "Vom Erbarmen Gottes über den Gerechten. Zur Theologie der Psalmen Salomos," *ZNW*, 43 (1950–51), pp. 1–54.

And I said in my heart, Surely God judgeth us;
  A sound I hear [moving] towards Jerusalem, the holy city.
My loins were broken at what I heard, my knees tottered;
  My heart was afraid, my bones were dismayed like flax.

Later in the same psalm come words of dismay at Pompey's entry into Jerusalem, the surrender of the city by the princes, the capture of the fortress and of the ramparts, where blood flowed like water. Yet, nothing shakes the writer's confidence in the Lord. He knows that all has happened in consequence of the sins of the mighty who failed in their duty of righteousness (verses 8–14); "Behold, now, O God, Thou hast shown us Thy judgement in Thy righteousness; our eyes have seen Thy judgements, O God" (verses 30, 31).

He acknowledged the justice of the punishment and never condoned the Hasmonaeans' responsibility for so many sins, yet when he beheld princes and nobles carried away by the victorious Romans to the far West (Ps. Sol. 17:14), his heart was heavy and his patriotic spirit cried out to the Lord (Ps. Sol. 7:1, 3, 8): "Make not thy dwelling afar from us, O God.... Chasten us Thyself in Thy good pleasure; But give (us) not up to the nations.... For Thou wilt pity the seed of Israel for ever and Thou wilt not reject (them)...."

Political changes notwithstanding, the pious men who composed and sang these songs never lost the legacy of political thought they had inherited from their fathers; on hearing of the death of Pompey the pious Pharisee made these reflections (Ps. Sol. 2:30 seq.):

And I had not long to wait before God showed me the insolent
    one
  Slain in the mountains of Egypt,
  Esteemed of less account than the least, on land and sea;
  . . . .
He reflected not that he was man,
  And reflected not on the latter end;
He said: I will be lord of land and sea;
  And he recognised not that it is God who is great,

397

Mighty in His great strength.
He is king over the heavens,
　And judgeth kings and kingdoms...
　............
And now behold, ye princes of the earth, the judgement of the
　Lord,
　For a great king and righteous (is He), judging (all) that
　is under heaven.

Such was the principle of the author's political thought: the Lord is
over all kings and rulers, and all depend on Him even for their food
(Ps. Sol. 5:13); Israel is His own kingdom and His goodness will
be upon it (Ps. Sol. 5:21). "Blessed is the glory of the Lord, for He
is our King."

Utter confidence in the God of Israel is the theme of Psalm 17,
with its deep longing for a Messiah. The abject state of a once
mighty realm fallen prey to Gentiles and Idumaeans urges the
poet to look forward to a better future promised by the Lord, when
the Davidic Messiah will come. Promises forgotten by the Sadducees now recur to the mind with new meaning. The poet
apostrophizes the Lord (Ps. Sol. 17:1, 4): "Thou art our king for
ever and ever.... And the kingdom of our God is for ever over the
nations in judgement...." He then reminds Him of His promises
(verse 5): "Thou, O Lord, didst choose David (to be) king over Israel,
and swaredst to him touching his seed that never should his kingdom fail before Thee."

But Israel's sins kept these promises in abeyance and the author
draws a gloomy picture of the deeds of the Hasmonaean and Sadducean priests (verses 13-23). But now (verse 23 seq.): "Behold, O
Lord, and raise up unto them their king, the son of David, at the
time, in which Thou seest, O God, that he may reign over Israel
Thy servant. And gird him with strength, that he may shatter un-
righteous rulers, and that he may purge Jerusalem from nations
that trample [her] down to destruction."

The poet visualizes with delight the Messianic king destroying the
sinner as a potter's vessel and the nations fleeing before Him, and
then (verse 28): "He shall gather together a holy people, whom he
shall lead in righteousness, and he shall judge the tribes of the

398

people that has been sanctified by the Lord his God." There will be no alien living amongst them, and the heathen will serve him under his yoke (verses 32 seq.):

. . . .
And he shall purge Jerusalem, making it holy as of old:
So that nations shall come from the ends of the earth to see
his glory.

. . . .
And he (shall be) a righteous king, taught of God, over them,
And there shall be no unrighteousness in his days in their
midst,
For all shall be holy and their king be anointed of the Lord.
For he shall not put his trust in horse and rider and bow,
Nor shall he multiply for himself gold and silver for war,
Nor shall he gather confidence from a multitude for the day
of battle.
The Lord himself is his king. . . .

. . . .
And he himself (will be) pure from sin, so that he may rule a
great people.

. . . .
(He will be) shepherding the flock of the Lord faithfully
and righteously. . . .

Such is the realistic picture which the poet draws of the Davidic Messiah, and it conjures up a Messianic king who is not God, but a man chosen by God, anointed by Him, full of righteousness, science, and wisdom, holy, pious, just, and merciful, a good shepherd to his flock. His power being irresistible, he stands in no need of an army; he commands all nations. He will be king and priest in one and bless his people, in fulfilment of the law concerning Israelite kings laid down in Deuteronomy 17:14–18. The portrayal contains all the elements of the ideal king as adumbrated by the ancient East and perfected by the Jewish mind.

This Messianic kingdom is made to center around Jerusalem, with the Jews gathered from all over the world only forming its nucleus, since all nations will be at the service of the Messiah. It will be a kingdom of peace and justice, with no room for sin, where everybody will be happy and the fear of God will reign supreme. The Davidic king's reign will last forever, in realization of the ideal of the Jewish nation.

As this Messianic hymn reflects the ideals of every pious Jew at the close of Jewish history in Palestine, it will help us in our investigations, for it shows how a short period of national independence affected the Jewish spirit and made itself felt even in the Jewish concept of the Messiah. This concept gained in precision and focus. The national feeling roused by the victories of the Maccabees, and the national expansion that followed under their successors, proved, in spite of Pharisaic opposition, to be very soul-stirring factors which affected messianic expectations. The vague anticipations of a kingdom built on the faithful observance of the law, as found in the works of the early post-exilic period, now ceased. There was also less of the eschatological expectancy such as was inspired by the visions of Daniel and the Similitudes of the Book of Enoch. These pages had been written in the anxious days of persecution in an atmosphere of suffering and death, when the eyes of the pious were focussed on spiritual things. This time, the average Israelite was no longer content with the vague abstraction of a moral theocracy which had fascinated the pious of previous ages, but insisted on a visible and tangible state. So, in declaring "The Lord Himself is our King for ever and ever" (Psalms of Solomon, 17), the author meant it. He wanted Jahweh, supreme King of Israel, whose kingship had been his stand-by under the impious rule of the Hasmonaeans, to exercise His sovereignty in a tangible way by sending His anointed, a living descendant of David, to implement at last the promises made to David's seed: to set the Jewish monarchy on its feet again and make it a great, independent state and fatherland, where all Jews could foregather from the ends of the earth. It was to be a universal monarchy, including all nations by either conversion or subjugation and amalgamating the two Jewish ideals of a real theocracy and a national state. Such, and no other, was the Day of Jahweh to which the Israelites had been looking forward from the dawn of their history.

This was the last stage in the evolution of Jewish political and Messianic ideology. After this, the stage was set for the violent outburst of patriotism which inflamed the Zealots, the uncompromising defenders of the law and the sworn enemies of the Romans and the Idumaeans. Forcing the theocratic ideal to its most reckless conclusion, they were determined to overthrow by violent means every rule other than that of Jahweh, and their daggers threatened Herodians, Romans, and Jews alike, should any of them show signs of compromise with foreign rule. Their fanaticism, bitter hatred, and misplaced patriotism at last gained the upper hand over the Pharisees' pacifism and, as is well known, hastened the tragic end of the Temple, the city, and the nation. But it must be remembered that the inspiration of their religious and political fanaticism came from the picture of the messianic kingdom so eloquently outlined by the writer of Psalm 17 of Solomon.[182]

But the nation as such had not thrown in its lot with the Zealots in the years preceding the advent of the Messiah. The old spirit of the Hasidim was still alive and found a curious outlet in the sect at Qumran and among the Essenes,[183] the "over-righteous ones," who, by refusing to take oaths and other eccentricities, took the law more literally than the Sadducees and the Pharisees ever had. Bent on practicing purity and sanctity to the greatest possible degree of perfection, they preferred to emigrate from a corrupt society, and live in a community where everything was owned in common—becoming in many ways the forerunners of Christian ascetics and monks. But their influence on the Jews' political and messianic thought was very slight. Yet, their attitudes and manner of living predisposed them to accept the kind of kingdom of God preached by Jesus Christ. The bulk of the people, disillusioned by their leaders' tiresome politics, relied on the law and the great prophets

[182] Cf. K. Kohler, "Zealots," *The Jewish Encyclopedia*, 12, p. 639 seq.; H. Graetz, *Geschichte der Juden*, 3, pt. 1 (Leipzig, 1905), p. 250 seq. For more details on the Zealots, see Chapter Seven, pp. 433—440.

[183] Cf. K. Kohler, "Essenes," *The Jewish Encyclopedia*, 5, p. 224 seq.; E. Schürer, *Geschichte des jüdischen Volkes im Zeitalter Jesu Christi*, 2, 4th ed. (Leipzig, 1907), pp. 651–668; especially E. Meyer, *Ursprung und Anfänge des Christentums*, 2, pp. 393–402, and W. Bauer, "Essener," Pauly-Wissowa, Suppl. 4 (1924), cols. 386–430; also see C. D. Ginsburg, *The Essenes, Their History and Doctrines* (London, 1955), pp. 5–58. On the Essenes and early Christians, see Chapter Seven.

for their spiritual comfort and looked to the kind of Messiah they had learned to know from the "Similitudes" of Enoch. This was the flock which the Good Shepherd wanted to lead to greener spiritual pastures.

One thing is certain: at every stage of the history of political and messianic thought among the Jews, the Messiah stood out as the ideal king even when portrayed as suffering for his people; on his idealization, the best minds of the Egyptian, Sumerian, Babylonian, and Assyrian civilizations had worked for thousands of years. It was the common heritage of the East which was finally adapted to the Messiah by Israelite genius. This proves that the history of ideas is an organic growth and that the transmission of ideas is a succession whose strength, as in a chain, is equal only to the strength of each link. The knowledge of its beginning is as essential as that of its end.

This historical pattern of ideas is even more significant for the Christian who sees there the working of Providence. The whole East was invited to elaborate the idea of the Messiah, to prepare His way and thus foreshadow the universality of His teaching and of His Mission. What was best in Oriental political thought was preserved, developed, and deepened by Jewish genius to express the longing of the human heart for the ideal king, the ideal man, and the final reconciliation between God and man.

CHAPTER SEVEN

THE KINGDOM OF GOD

Spiritualization of the messianic kingdom in late Judaism — St. John the Baptist and Qumran — John's disciples — Jesus, Son of Man and Servant of God — The Kingdom of God and the Sermon on the Mount — The Kingdom of God in the parables — The Sermon on the Mount and the Dead Sea Scrolls — Temporal and eschatological elements in the Kingdom of God — Announcement of the foundation of the Kingdom of God — Christ and Hellenistic political thought — Payment of the tribute; Christ and the Zealots — The Apostles, the Church, and the Kingdom of God — State, Church, and Hellenistic polity in Paul's and Peter's Epistles — Conclusion.

As we have seen in the preceding chapter, the coming Messiah was, in the Jewish conception, a king, the founder of a new kingdom, and an ideal man, commissioned by God to represent and free Israel, to convert other nations, and to place their association with God on a new basis. Though a purely Jewish conception, this idea coincided to some extent with Eastern thought, the origin of which is traceable to the earliest civilization of the Nile valley and Mesopotamia, the cradle of Oriental culture. There all that was thought best in man had been emcompassed in the definition of the king, who was placed second only to the divinity; he was an intermediary between the nation and God, a superman. These postulates permeated not only Eastern thought but also that of the Greeks, who boasted a distinctive political philosophy, elaborated by their greatest thinkers. When the warlike Macedonians under Alexander conquered Persia, Egypt, and Babylonia, and reached the confines of India, the Greek genius enriched the civilization of these conquered territories with its own political structure, which then became the property of the known world and later was taken over by Rome. Since this combination of Hellenistic and Jewish ideas also formed the milieu in which the

Founder of Christianity lived and worked, it was only to be expected that His words would echo the language that had been current in the East for thousands of years, and that this same tradition would provide the foundations for the structure of Christian polity.

It must be assumed that Christ's contemporaries in Palestine expected the Messiah would be a king,[1] whose task it was to found a kingdom. Therefore they invested their image of Him with the royal prerogatives appropriate to such a mission. Any other assumption would sever the whole history of Israel and the pre-Christian era from its sequel and make it unintelligible. Even the successors to the Hasidim, the pious sectarians of Qumran, who were perhaps themselves Essenes,[2] were expecting a princely Messiah to lead them into war against the sons of Belial. He would reconquer Jerusalem and make it the center of the messianic kingdom. It remains to be seen now how far these expectations were realized.

On the other hand, a spiritualization of the messianic idea was achieved by the sectaries of Qumran through their influence upon the readers of their writings and of the similar revelations in Daniel and Enoch. The founder of Qumran, the Teacher of Righteousness, who acted as a prophet for the group, announced the impending arrival of the Messiah and gave precise directions for his followers to prepare themselves for the advent of His Kingdom. The Manual of Discipline starts with the following prescription for the members

[1] The best illustration of this general conviction is found in Matt. 2:19–23, where the apostle describes Herod the Great's reaction on learning that wise men from the East "were inquiring" about the birthplace of the king of the Jews whose star they had seen in the East. When Herod heard that, according to Micah's prophecy (Mic. 5:2), the expected "governor" and "shepherd"—both Oriental kingly titles—was to be born in Bethlehem, the murderer of the last Hasmonaeans decided to take no risks. To elude the Idumaean police who had orders to kill all the new-born boys of that city, Joseph took refuge in Egypt. He was later ordered to settle with his family, not in Bethlehem, where the presence of friends might have induced him to find a home, but in Nazareth, well out of reach of Herod's successor, Archelaus.

[2] On the Essenes, see H. Kosmala, *Hebräer, Essener, Christen* (Leiden, 1959), especially pp. 1–43, *re* the affinities between the teaching of the Essenes and the Letter to the Hebrews. Bibliographical indications are given by S. Wagner, *Die Essener in der wissenschaftlichen Diskussion*, Beihefte, *ZAW*, 79 (Berlin, 1960). Cf. also J. A. Fitzmyer, "The Qumran Scrolls, the Ebionites and Their Literature," in *The Scrolls and the New Testament*, ed. by K. Stendahl (New York, 1957), pp. 208–231. Cf. also, for general information, M. Black, *The Scrolls and Christian Origins* (New York, 1961).

of the sect (i, 1–15) :[3] "Everyone who wishes to join the community must pledge himself to respect God and man... to do what is good and upright in His sight, in accordance with what He has commanded through Moses and through His servants the prophets,... to act truthfully and righteously and justly on earth and to walk no more in the stubborness of a guilty heart and of lustful eyes...."

The war in which the Messiah was expected to lead his faithful to victory is also spiritualized in some respects, reflecting the sect's belief that God had appointed two spirits—the spirits of truth and of perversity—to reign over mankind. Truth originates in the Fountain of Light, perversity in the Wellspring of Darkness (Manual iii, 13 seq.). The two spirits try to dominate man, and an eternal enmity exists between them. In the end, God will destroy the spirit of perversity forever. Those who had followed the spirit of truth will be chosen partners of God's new, eternal covenant.

As it is presented in the Manual, this doctrine recalls the Persian dualistic belief, expressed especially in the Avesta in Yasna XLV, 2, and XXX, 3, 4, 5, 8, 10, 11.[4] However, the belief in two conflicting inclinations in men—to follow the road to good or to evil—has always existed in the Jewish religion. It is possible, however, that Persian influences—noticeable also in Daniel, whose book was favored by the sectaries of Qumran—influenced this Teacher of Righteousness and his disciples and helped them to express this doctrine in such telling terms.

The description of the war between the sons of righteousness, led by the Messiah, and the sons of Belial has an apocalyptic character. The whole tone of the imaginary final battle is eschatological and differs from the expectations, voiced by official circles, of an earthly Messiah and an earthly kingdom founded by him.

[3] Th. H. Gaster, *The Dead Sea Scriptures* (New York, 1956), p. 39.

[4] Quoted by A. Dupont-Sommer, *The Jewish Sect of Qumran and the Essenes* (London, 1954), pp. 118–130. An echo of this doctrine is also found in the Jubilees, Enoch, and the Testaments of the Twelve Patriarchs. The Evil Spirit is there also called Belial. Cf. B. Otzen, "Die neugefundenen hebräischen Sektenschriften und die Testamente der zwölf Patriarchen," *Studia Theologica*, 7 (Lund, 1954), p. 135 seq., on the dualistic tendencies in the Manual and the Testaments and on demonology and angelology in these works.

The spiritualization of the messianic idea in the Qumran community is also foreshadowed in their hostility toward the ritualization of the Sadducees, by their rejection of animal sacrifices, and by their stress on private prayers and community meetings. The beautiful psalms and songs recited on such occasions, composed by members of the community, testify to their profound and sincere faith and piety.

Although the traditional image of the Messiah is still reflected in their expectations, his arrival is regarded as near at hand,[5] and the idea of preparing themselves for that event by practicing and preaching penance is prominent in their writings.[6] The spirit of penance is also reflected in the common life of the Qumran sect under its strong discipline, with ceremonial repasts, lustrations, ablutions, and baths which stressed not only bodily but also spiritual cleanliness.

It is in such a milieu that the new doctrine of the true character of the coming Kingdom of God would be expected to find a sympathetic understanding. There seems, however, to have been more than mere coincidental agreement. There is evidence that Christ's predecessor, John the Baptist, was closely connected with the pious circle which had its center at Qumran. For example, the recluses of Qumran called their monastic establishment "the desert." It was also in the desert or "wilderness" that "the voice of God came to John the son of Zechariah" (Luke 3:2). It is thus quite possible that John was living at Qumran when the word of God came to him. He was a scion of a sacerdotal family. His father was certainly not a partisan of the Sadducees, but sympathized instead with the Sons of Zadok, as the Qumran priests called themselves. The father composed a hymn of thanksgiving after the birth of his son, and in this hymn he used words which were common among the Qumran community (Luke 1:67 seq.). He spoke about the service to God in holiness and righteousness, prophesied that his son would "prepare the ways" for the Messiah, "give knowledge of salvation to his people" and guide their feet "into the way of peace."

[5] Commentary to Habakkuk, ii, 3; Th. H. Gaster, *op. cit.*, p. 252.
[6] See especially the "confession" of the initiated (Manual i, 25 seq.).

Zechariah seems to have entrusted his son to the Qumran community for his education,[7] because Luke (1:80) says that the child was in the wilderness till the day of his manifestation to Israel. The life which John lived there was similar to that of the Essenes. He was an ascetic, whose food was locusts and wild honey (Matt. 3:4). The sectaries of Qumran must also have had similar fare, because the Zadokite Document (xii, 14) also speaks of locusts as a favorite dish, stipulating that they should be grilled or cooked while still alive. Although the sectaries were allowed to drink wine, many of them abstained from alcoholic beverages and practiced celibacy, as John did.

There are also similarities between John's preaching and the doctrines of the recluses of Qumran. The sectaries are convinced that "this is the time when 'the way is being prepared in the wilderness'" (Manual ix, 19). The words are a clear allusion to Isa. 40:3. The author of the Manual is even more outspoken in another passage (viii, 14) where he gives instructions on the attitude of the 'presbyters': "they may indeed 'go into the wilderness to prepare the way,' i.e., do what Scripture enjoins when it says, 'Prepare in the wilderness the way...make straight in the desert a highway for our God'" (Isa. 40:3). The same quotation is used in the same sense by John as recorded by Matt. 3:3 and John 1:23. This can hardly be simply a coincidence. It indicates that John was familiar with the spirit of Qumran and knew the literature of the sect.

It should also be noted that, in his preaching, John is very severe on the Pharisees and Sadducees, calling them "a brood of vipers" (Matt. 3:7), but he never mentions the Essenes, whose ideas were similar if not identical with those of the sectaries of Qumran. This seems to indicate that he sympathized with their moral and messianic conceptions and shared their dislike of the other groups.

When John speaks of the coming Messiah whose sandals he was not worthy to carry and who will baptize with the Holy Spirit

[7] Cf. W. H. Brownlee, "John the Baptist in the New Light of Ancient Scrolls," *Interpretation*, 9 (1955), pp. 71–90. Reprinted with additions in *The Scrolls and the New Testament*, pp. 33–53. On p. 73 (35), Brownlee quotes Josephus' statement that the Essenes adopted other men's children. John's parents may have died of old age and John may have been taken in by the Qumran sect for his education. Cf. also J. M. Allegro, *The Dead Sea Scrolls* (London, 1956), pp. 163–165.

and with fire (Matt. 3:11, 12), he gives the impression of having in mind the Messiah as represented in Enoch—the Son of Man, sublime, almost divine. The baptism with the Holy Spirit reminds us of a passage in the Zadokite Document (ii, 9–10) where it is said that God will "reveal the Holy Spirit at the hands of his Anointed" to the faithful.[8]

The baptism with fire is connected here with the judgment, because John's threat to the wicked, "the chaff," is that the Messiah will burn them "with unquenchable fire." C. H. Kraeling[9] has connected this baptism and judgment with fire to the Zoroastrian religion: In Persian eschatology the mountains are made of metal and at the end of the world will dissolve into a river of molten metal which all peoples will have to pass through; the good will be purified and saved, the bad will perish in fire. It appears that Daniel's river of fire (Dan. 7:10) is a variant of this idea. This is not surprising, as Daniel's book is full of Persian reminiscences. The idea must also have appealed to the sectaries of Qumran, because one of their hymns contains a vivid description of the river of fire:[10]

When the final doom of His [the Lord's] rage
    falls on all worthless things;
when the torrents of Death do swirl,
and there is none escape;
when the rivers of Belial
burst their high banks
— rivers that are like fire
devouring all that draw their waters...

---

[8] A. Dupont-Sommer, Les écrits esséniens découverts près de la Mer Morte (Paris, 1959), p. 139, translates wrongly "Les Oints" and thinks that the prophets are meant in this passage. Th. H. Gaster, op. cit., p. 63, translates "His anointed," but (p. 100) thinks that the anointed priests are meant. See, however, W. H. Brownlee, op. cit., p. 82 (44): "and through his Messiah he shall make them know His holy spirit."

[9] C. H. Kraeling, John the Baptist (London, 1951), pp. 117, 205.

[10] Hymns, III, 28 seq. Th. H. Gaster, op. cit., p. 139; Dupont-Sommer, op. cit., p. 225. Cf. W. H. Brownlee, op. cit., p. 80.; also A. Feuillet, "Le Baptême de Jésus." Revue biblique, 71 (1964), pp. 321–352. On Qumran practice, ibid., p. 337 seq.

The Manual of Discipline uses similar language. In iv, 12, 13 the author speaks of the final annihilation of the wicked in the fire. The people who had chosen the way of truth will be cleansed "by the Holy Spirit from all effects of wickedness" (iv, 20).

As for baptism, such a practice was common in Judaism for proselytes, and ritual baths were a special feature in the Qumran sect. John thus had plenty of opportunity to find a precedent for his practice. It is possible, however, as the threat of destruction of the "chaff" with fiery fire suggests, that John's practice had a deeper significance and had eschatological associations. It has been suggested "that the water of baptism represents and symbolizes the fiery torrent of judgment, and that the individual by voluntarily immersing himself in the water enacts in advance before God his willing submission to the divine judgment which the river of fire will perform." If this is so, John's baptism, practiced in running water, "dramatized an eschatological event."[11]

There is one final similarity to be mentioned between John and the Qumran community. The Teacher of Righteousness taught them that the time for the appearance of the Messiah had come. He himself, however, did not claim a messianic mission.[12] John also preached the immediate advent of the Messiah, but denied categorically that he himself was the expected Messiah (John 1:21).

It is therefore legitimate to see the movement which had its center at Qumran as the opening of the last stage in the Jewish expectation of the Messiah, and their Teacher of Righteousness as a perhaps prophetic predecessor to John the Baptist. With the latter, the period of waiting came to a close.

In spite of the many affinities between John's attitude and doctrine and that of Qumran, there are also some differences which distinguish John sharply from the sectaries. The Manual of Discipline and the Zadokite Document are concerned only with the conduct of the "Remnant," the members of the community opposed to any contact with the rest of the people and intent on keeping

---

[11] C. H. Kraeling, op. cit., pp. 117, 118.
[12] Cf. K. Elliger, Studien zum Habakuk-Kommentar vom Toten Meer (Tübingen, 1953), pp. 265 seq., 281–283.

the secret of their doctrine exclusively for the members of the community. They regard themselves as the remnant of the Hasidim to whom alone the Messianic message will be delivered, and through whom the rest will be converted or condemned.

No traces of such a spirit of exclusiveness are to be found in John. He does not keep his revelation to his disciples, but communicates it freely to any Israelite who will listen. When he had heard the voice of the Lord and received his special personal vocation, John left the community and became the "voice" in the desert preaching to pilgrims going to Jerusalem and to others whose business had brought them into the neighborhood of Qumran.[13] Later, when his preaching had become known and popular, crowds of curious and pious people visited the places near the Jordan where he preached.

John excluded no one from his teaching. It is true that he uttered a special rebuke to the Pharisees and Sadducees when they asked for baptism. He exhorted them to do penance, but promised them a place in the Kingdom of God if they repented (Matt. 3:7 seq; Luke 3:7 seq.) Not even the tax collectors and soldiers were excluded by him; if they did penance, abstained from sin, and performed the duties requisite to their vocations, they would all be saved. This idea of universality differs fundamentally from the exclusiveness practiced by the devotees of Qumran.

On the other hand, John outdistanced the Qumran sectaries in his rejection of the racial doctrine that descent from Abraham was a sufficient claim to participate in the Kingdom to be founded by the coming Messiah. "I tell you, God is able from these stones to raise up children to Abraham" (Matt. 3:9). Only sincere penance would cleanse them of sin through the baptismal waters, would reconcile them with God, and would make them worthy of entering the messianic kingdom.

John's converts were the first believers in Jesus Christ as the true Messiah. To his disciples John revealed the identity of Jesus Christ when he pointed to Him: "Behold, the Lamb of God, who

---

[13] W. H. Brownlee, *op. cit.*, p. 74, thinks that the first meeting places where he began his work were Bethany beyond the Jordan (John 1:28) and Aenon near Salim (John 3:23), trading places and important highways at the Jordan River. Cf. also C. H. Kraeling, *op. cit.*, p. 9 seq.

takes away the sin of the world! This is he of whom I said, 'After me comes a man who ranks before me, for he was before me'" (John 1:29 seq.). And he revealed to them how he had recognized Christ's identity when performing the baptism and seeing the Spirit descending upon Jesus.

His affirmation that the expected Messiah was before him, discloses perhaps that the true nature of Jesus was revealed to John by God. It should also be noted that John had in mind the Son of Man as described in Enoch, pre-existent, created by the Lord before all other creatures, sublime, almost divine. It is at least highly probable that John's disciples interpreted his description of Jesus in this way down to the time when the true nature of the Son of Man was revealed to them. John the Evangelist uses this designation; he even seems to give to it more prominence than to his teaching on the Logos—Word,—although the latter would seem better to explain the eternal pre-existence of the expected Messiah.[14]

It was among John's disciples that Jesus chose his first apostles. However, not all the disciples of John joined Jesus. Some of them remained faithful to John even after his death, and it can be gathered from Holy Writ that a group of Baptists continued to exist independently of the group which had joined Jesus.[15] Even after Jesus' death this group regarded John the Baptist as the true Messiah, because he came before Jesus.

This Baptist circle was rather dangerous to the first small group of Christians, as can be learned from the Pseudo-Clementine Recognitions.[16] It appears that the Baptist group was particularly numerous in the area where the Evangelist John lived, because his Gospel seems to minimize, in some ways, the importance of John the Baptist, stressing as it does in its first chapter the sublime pre-existence of Jesus and the more humble role of John whose vocation was only to give testimony "to the light," not more.[17]

[14] Cf. O. Cullmann, *Die Christologie des Neuen Testaments* (Tübingen, 1957), p. 186 seq., esp. p. 192.
[15] See especially Acts 18:25; 19:3.
[16] *Recognitiones*, I, 54, 60, PG, 1, cols. 1238, 1240.
[17] See for details O. Cullmann, *Le problème littéraire et historique du Roman Pseudo-Clementin* (Paris, 1930), p. 239 seq.; *idem*, "The Significance of the

It is quite probable that John the Evangelist was one of John the Baptist's disciples and was sympathetic to the Qumran group. Actually, his Gospel contains some phrases and expressions which remind us astonishingly of the doctrines pronounced in the Manual of Discipline. John's description of Christ's preaching in chapter 8:12:[18] "I am the light of the world; he who follows me will not walk in darkness, but will have the light of life" recalls the words of the Manual (iii, 20, 21): "All who practice righteousness are under the domination of the Prince of Light, and walk in the ways of light; whereas all who practice perversity are under the domination of the Angel of Darkness and walk in the ways of darkness." The light of life is also mentioned in Manual iii, 7.

The phrase "works of God" (John 6:28) is used also in Manual iv, 4. The instruction on methods of discerning the inspirations of the good or bad spirit, given by John in his first Epistle (4:1–3), is anticipated in Manual v, 23.

John was also captivated by the combat between the Spirit of Light and the Spirit of Darkness as were the sectaries of Qumran. To the Spirit of Darkness he opposes Jesus the Messiah.[19] He also seems to share the ideas of the Essenes and the Qumran community concerning the unimportance of worship in the Temple, rather than the views of the Christian Jews who still clung to institutionalized worship. His Gospel stresses the idea that Temple worship should be replaced by worship in spirit and in truth.[20]

It is thus possible that John the Evangelist sympathized with the group of Jewish Christians called Hellenists who were expelled

---

Qumran Texts for Research into the Beginnings of Christianity," *JBL*, 74 (1955), pp. 213–226, esp. pp. 218–219; reprinted in *The Scrolls and the New Testament*, pp. 18–32.

[18] Cf. also Luke 12:3, and I Thess. 5:4.

[19] See J. Daniélou, *Les manuscrits de la Mer Morte et les origines du Christianisme* (Paris, 1957), pp. 99–106 and especially R. E. Brown, "The Qumran Scrolls and the Johannine Gospel and Epistles" in *The Scrolls and the New Testament*, pp. 183–207. The author points out that if John was the disciple of the Baptist, these affinities can be easily explained. Cf. also F. M. Cross, *The Ancient Library of Qumrân and Modern Biblical Studies* (New York, 1958), pp. 146–180: "The Essenes and the Primitive Church."

[20] See for details O. Cullmann, *Early Christian Worship*, trans. by A. Steward Todd and J. B. Torrance (London, 1953), p. 72 seq. The Evangelist interprets the clearing of the Temple by Jesus as a replacement of Temple worship by the person of Christ.

from Jerusalem during the persecution reported in Acts 8:1. The Hellenists "scattered through the region of Judaea and Samaria." The mention of Samaria is the more interesting as its inhabitants also were adversaries of Temple worship.[21]

The idea that John was familiar with the doctrines and usages of the Qumran group and that he was also very close to the Hellenist group seems reasonably certain.[22] It is not excessive to suggest that John had even attempted in his Gospel a kind of rehabilitation of the Hellenists, discredited in the eyes of the other Jewish Christians by their opposition to Temple worship.

Thus, the spirit which animated the community of Qumran, the authors and readers of Daniel and Enoch, and the Essenes, served to prepare an atmosphere favorable to the new and true conception of the messianic idea which was to be defined by Jesus. He began his activity in the same regions near the Dead Sea in which the more spiritualized messianism was current. This was also near Qumran, where John the Baptist was preaching. In some way Jesus joined the group of new converts when He accepted John's baptism, and He followed the example of the recluses of Qumran when He retired into the "desert" for prayer and severe fasting during the forty days and nights. He did this perhaps as a kind of homage to the ascetics who had separated themselves from the sons of Belial. Jesus even allowed Himself to be tempted by Belial (Satan) and after His victory over temptation was served by the Angels. This scene reported by Matthew (4:1–12) and Mark (1:12, 13) recalls the doctrine of Qumran that every man is influenced by two spirits, the evil and the good (Manual iii, 13 seq.)—the Angel of Darkness and the Angel of God's Truth.

Jesus manifested his sympathy for the spiritualized messianic conception of these better spirits in Judaism. Like them He reject-

---

[21] See O. Cullmann, "The Significance of the Qumran Texts," p. 220 seq., for details. The affinity of John's Gospel with the writing of Qumran ends, of course, all discussions as to the late origin of this Gospel. Cf. W. F. Albright, "Recent Discoveries in Palestine and the Gospel of St. John," in *The Background of the New Testament and Its Eschatology*, ed. by W. D. Davies and D. Daube (Cambridge, 1956), pp. 153–171, esp. pp. 170–171.

[22] Stephen, the first Martyr, was also a Hellenist. In Acts 7:56 he applies to Christ the title Son of Man. See M. Simon, *St. Stephen and the Hellenists in the Primitive Church* (London, 1958).

ed outright, at every opportunity, the messianic ideas—which were national, political, and worldly—of the ruling circles and of the greater part of the nation. These ideas were so deeply rooted in Jewish minds that even His intimate companions, the apostles, often clung to them, not understanding the interpretations Jesus was giving to the role of the Messiah.

Perhaps to stress His rejection of such messianism, Jesus never used the word "Messiah" to designate himself, because it had for so many centuries symbolized the national and political aspirations of the Jews. Instead, He chose the title "Son of Man,"[23] which was familiar to the more esoteric literary and theological circles. It is important to bear in mind the origin of this title and its connection with Persian, Babylonian, and Hellenistic eschatological ideas, related to the legendary conception of Primordial Man, which had also influenced the Jewish evolution of the messianic idea. Is one not entitled to see in it a divine sanction for pagan contributions to the development of the messianic idea as God wished it to be realized from the beginning?[24]

Many of Jesus' followers must have understood the title Son of Man in the same sense as it was interpreted in the Ethiopian Enoch—designating a pre-existing creature of God who was supposed to live in Paradise before coming on earth. John the Apostle interpreted this title in such a way (John 3:13; 6:62), as did St. Paul also (II Cor. 8:9; Phil. 2:6 seq.). But Christ himself—so it appears from the Synoptic Gospels—preferred to stress the human side of the "Son of Man," because He combined with this title Isaiah's designation of the Saviour as the Servant of God—*Ebed Jahweh*.

[23] In this sense also the logion in Mark 12:35 seq. should be explained. "How can the scribes say that the Christ is the son of David? David himself, inspired by the Holy Spirit said to my Lord, Sit at my right hand... David himself calls him Lord; so how is he his son?" The descent of the Messiah from David was intimately connected with the earlier conception of a political Messiah. Jesus rejects this idea. The sonship from David is not sufficient for the Messiah. He originates from someone who is higher than David. The Davidic origin of the Messiah is denied by Christ. See O. Cullmann, *Die Christologie*, p. 133 seq.

[24] Cf. S. Mowinckel, *He that Cometh* (Oxford, 1956), p. 446 seq. One may not agree with many ideas of the author, but this last chapter of his work bears testimony to the sincere, humble, and profound faith of this great Protestant theologian.

Isaiah's description in chapter 53 revealed to the human nature of Jesus the role which the true Messiah had to play in God's plan. He should redeem men through suffering and death; only after that would the Son of Man triumph. At the most crucial moment, however, in the presence of the high priest and the whole council, Jesus referred clearly to the final glorification of the "Son of Man." "Hereafter you will see the Son of Man sitting at the right hand of Power, and coming in the clouds of heaven" (Matt. 26:64; Mark 14:62; Luke 22:69). There is, in this confession, a clear allusion to Enoch's prophecy and also to Psalm 110. At this crucial moment, also, the true character of the Son of Man—the Messiah—was revealed: He is the Son of God.

The idea of the Servant of God who, through his suffering and death, was to redeem his people is also connected with the idea of supreme priesthood. The author of the Letter to Hebrews recognized this connection well when he described the character of Jesus' supreme priesthood (chap. 7) and found the symbolic type of this priesthood in Melchizedek of whom it is said: "Thou art a priest for ever" (Ps. 110).[25]

Christ never spoke openly about his priestly character, but the two allusions to Psalm 110 in Mark 12:35 seq. and 14:62 indicate that He was conscious of its connection with the priesthood "after the order of Melchizedek." It is evident that this psalm was regarded generally in Jesus' time as messianic. The idea that the coming Messiah should also have a priestly character must have been familiar to many believers in the late Judaic period. It was foreshadowed by the stressing of the role of a high priest in connection with the Messiah as has been seen in the Testaments of the Twelve Patriarchs (Levi, 18) and in the Manual of Qumran.[26] It is therefore understandable that some started to ascribe the high-priestly role to the coming Messiah, although in the quoted texts the high priest is still differentiated from the kingly Messiah.

Although avoiding the title of Messiah, Jesus Christ did not renounce the royal dignity which this title implied in the minds of

[25] For details, see the well documented chapter on Jesus the High Priest in O. Cullmann, *Die Christologie*, pp. 82–107.

[26] Cf. *supra*, p. 392.

the Jews. He came to found a kingdom, different from that which the majority of the Jews had in mind. It was a Kingdom of God. John the Baptist's rebuke addressed to the Sadducees and Pharisees and his exhortations to penance had already revealed a concept of the Kingdom of God that did not coincide with that of the Jewish intellectual leaders, but resembled rather the messianic kingdom foreshadowed by Daniel and by the "Similitudes" of Enoch.

Such, then, was the first specification of the kingdom expected from the Messiah. On the foundation laid by John the Baptist, Jesus Christ proceeded to build and to preach His own concept of the Kingdom of God, which Matthew called the Kingdom of heaven, presumably in order to avoid using the divine name. Christ introduced the theme (Matt. 4:17) with John's words (Matt. 3:2) and maintained it throughout His active career. Many of His parables are prefixed with the words: "The kingdom of God [or of heaven] is likened unto..." and His listeners were so convinced that this was the object of His mission that the Synoptic Gospels make it the core of Jesus' preaching and of that of His disciples.[27]

The fact that Christ came forward as the founder of a new kingdom needs no further elaboration. What one should like to establish is the kind of kingdom which He had in mind; the extent to which it answered the expectations of the Jews; and which of its elements corresponded to the Oriental and Hellenistic ideology current at the time in the countries that lay open to His teaching.

If John lacked clarity on the nature of that kingdom, Jesus of Nazareth was explicit from the outset (Mark 1:14 seq.). Once He had aroused public attention by His preaching and His miracles and had selected twelve disciples as witnesses to His words and deeds, He considered the moment had arrived for making clear what sort of kingdom He had come to found.

His "inaugural speech" is fully reported, though certainly not in its original order and phraseology, by St. Matthew (chaps. 5–7) in

[27] Especially Matt. 2:23; 9:35; Luke 4:43; 8:1 seq.; 9:2; 10:11; 11:2; 16:16; Mark 1:14, 15. A critical comparison of all the references to the kingdom of God in the Synoptic Gospels was made by T. W. Manson, *The Teaching of Jesus* (Cambridge, 1935), p. 116 seq. The reader is referred to this excellent critical study for more complete information. On the parables in general, cf. J. Jeremias, *The Parables of Jesus*, trans. by S. H. Hooke (London, 1954).

the so-called Sermon on the Mount.[28] The opening words, "Blessed are the poor of spirit, for theirs is the kingdom of heaven," left no doubt in the listeners' minds that the kingdom thus launched was to differ from that expected by their leaders. The words reminded them of what they had read in the Book of Enoch. The beatitudes that followed made it clearer still that, unlike the earthly kingdoms, this one was intended to dominate not the world, but the hearts of men; and that, as confirmed on a different occasion (Matt. 22: 36 seq.), the first law of that kingdom was to love God and one's neighbor.

To be poor in spirit, to submit to the will of God in mourning, to be meek, to hunger and thirst for righteousness, to be merciful and pure in heart, to be a peacemaker, to suffer persecution for God; all these enactments only enlarged upon the law of love and formulated the first condition of God's royal dominion over the hearts of men with its attendant blessings. Those ready to accept this condition would be the salt of the earth and the lamp on the stand,[29] two similes intended to illustrate the kingdom's method of expansion, namely by the example of those of Christ's disciples who knew the blessing of God's dominion and of His law of love. As the people wondered how to achieve this, they were told to seek the necessary directives in the written Law, the greatest treasure of the Jews.

The Law was, therefore, far from being abrogated. He that shall observe and teach its commandments shall be called great in the kingdom of heaven. The Pharisees and Scribes were to be condemned for alienating people from the Law by their externalism and

[28] On the literary tradition concerning the evangelical reports of the Sermon, see especially Dom J. Chapman, *Matthew, Mark and Luke* (London, 1937), pp. 215–235. Cf. also W. Manson, *Jesus the Messiah* (London, 1943), pp. 78–93. Cf. also the exegetical study by H. Huber, *Die Bergpredigt* (Göttingen, 1932), and J. Dupont, *Les Béatitudes* (Bruges-Louvain, 1958), 2 vols.

[29] Matt. 5:15. Cf. also Mark 4:21 and Luke 8:16; 11:33. The simile of the lamp is used in three places in the Old Testament to describe the kingdom promised to the Anointed of the Lord: in Ps. 132:17, "I have ordained a lamp for mine anointed," and in II Kings 8:19 and II Chron. 21:7, "The Lord promised him [David] to give unto him a lamp for his children always." Cf. also II Sam. 22:29; Ps. 119:105; I Kings 11:36; 15:4. See E. Hoskyns and N. Davey, *The Riddle of the New Testament* (London, 1936), p. 162 seq. The coincidence would be significant, if it were certain that Christ had this symbolism in mind. It is not impossible, but there may also be another explanation of this phrase, see *infra*, p. 421.

their misinterpretations. The Law was to be observed in spirit as well as in deed, that is, hurtful words to one's brother and lustful glances at his wife were as wrong as murder and adultery.

As to swearing in God's name, those who accept God as the king of their hearts and belong to His kingdom have no need to confirm their words and their promises by an oath. The law of love toward one's neighbor is reiterated: we must love our enemies and do good to trespassers instead of claiming retribution. The candidates to this kingdom must strive to be as perfect as their heavenly Father and King.

God must be foremost in their minds. It is for His sake, not for earthly glory, that they fast, pray and do good. In praying, they must address God as Father and ask Him for the advent of His kingdom into all hearts, all in the spirit of the beatitudes. This is the only treasure worth coveting; bodily needs are as nothing in comparison and should be disregarded. "Seek ye first the kingdom of God and his justice and all these things shall be added unto you." Be more solicitous about the love of your neighbor. "Judge not that you be not judged." Remember that God provides for anyone who does his best to set up God's kingdom in his heart. Whoever believes his prayers are not heard prays without confidence, for the Heavenly Father hears all who trust Him.

But the treasure of the Kingdom of God is not obtainable without a struggle. It "suffers violence," (Matt. 11:12), is reached only by strife, and even at the cost of eye or hand and, if necessary, of all things that stand in its way. The gate to it is narrow, but there is no other. Do not listen to false prophets who show you comfortable alternatives. Their fruit is bad. Only on these conditions will you enter the kingdom and find mercy at the hands of the Lord when He will come to judge the world at its consummation. Only on this rock will you erect the building that will withstand rains and winds. Such must have been the true meaning of the Sermon on the Mount, whose short but epigrammatic sentences gripped the attention of all those who heard it.

In order to grasp the full meaning of the Kingdom of God which Jesus Christ came to found, every reference to it must be examined as it is recorded by the Synoptic Gospels. This will help us to see that the above interpretation is correct and to find in every one of Christ's sayings an expansion of the principles laid down in the Sermon.

The parables on the kingdom of heaven[30] contain many notions which clarify Christ's conception of His kingdom. In the parables on the kingdom recorded by Matthew (chap. 13)[31] the Lord first shows in the allegory of the Sower that, though every one receives the seed of His word, not all succeed in husbanding it into the kingdom; and those who do, must expect a period of long and slow growth before it ripens for the harvest. The seed of the kingdom is tiny, but like the mustard seed it spreads far and wide. It is likened to leavening that leavens the whole loaf, to a hidden treasure worth all possessions, to a pearl of great price.

The divine king is a shepherd who will go to any lengths to recover the one lost sheep;[32] He is forgiving if the sinner confesses his wrong and pleads for mercy; but merciless to him who refuses mercy to his fellow-men (Matt. 18:12 seq., 23 seq.). He is patient and will engage anyone at any time for work in his vineyard, i.e., He will set up the kingdom in a man's heart, even at the final moment of a wasted life. The same reward, the eternal kingdom in heaven, goes to all (Matt. 20:1 seq.). But once His rule is adopted, there remains the duty to persevere, not to look back (Luke 9:62), and to watch like the five wise virgins who provided themselves with oil as well as with a lamp.

Such are the parables introduced by the words, "the kingdom of heaven is likened to...." Other parables are commentaries on the principles laid down in the Sermon on the Mount. The Parable of the Talents (Matt. 25:14 seq.) tells us to use our faculties to the full to gain the eternal kingdom. The Good Samaritan (Luke 10:30 seq.) and the Friend at Midnight (Luke 11:5-8) illustrate love for our neighbor and explain the technique of repeated prayer.

---

[30] J. Pirot, *Paraboles et allégories évangéliques* (Paris, 1949). Cf. also G. Denzer, *The Parables of the Kingdom* (Washington, D. C., 1945); C. H. Dodd, *The Parables of the Kingdom*, 3rd. ed. (London, 1948).

[31] Cf. also Mark 4:27-39; Luke 13:18-21.

[32] Cf. Ezek. 34:11 seq.: "For thus says the Lord God: Behold, I myself will search for my sheep, and will seek them out."

The Rich Fool (Luke 12:16 seq.) shows the danger of concentrating on earthly things and neglecting the things of God the King. The Barren Fig Tree (Luke 13:6 seq.), the Lost Coin (Luke 15:8 seq.), and the Prodigal Son (Luke 15:11–32) exemplify God's mercy and patience. The Unjust Steward (Luke 16:1–9) is held up as a warning that earthly things should be used for the promotion of the Kingdom of God, while the Rich Man and Lazarus (Luke 16:19–31) should caution those who have wasted their lives, never giving a thought to the Kingdom of God.

There is in St. Luke's Gospel one particular passage which suggests that the term kingdom should be taken in a subjective and straightforward sense (Luke 17:20, 21): "And being asked by the Pharisees when the kingdom of God cometh, He answered them, and said: The kingdom of God cometh not with observation; neither shall they say: Lo here! or, there. For lo, the kingdom of God is within you." The words must not be taken in an eschatological sense, as though the Lord meant the sudden and unexpected end of things followed by the eternal Kingdom of God, for the Greek text does not admit of such an interpretation. The words *entos hymôn* imply that the Lord was thinking of a kingdom which already existed potentially within everybody. True enough, the Pharisees had in mind the eschatological messianic kingdom such as was generally expected at the time, and they wanted to know which signs would usher in its coming. The answer they got was that the Kingdom of God they were referring to was already potentially in everyone's possession, since participation in its blessings was made dependent on its acceptance here and now.[33]

Such a description of the Kingdom of God must have appeared strange to the men who were familiar only with the traditional and national conception of the messianic kingdom. It seems, however, that there were many among Christ's audience who were able to understand and to appreciate His words. Many of His sentences

---

[33] This eschatological interpretation was upheld by J. Weiss, *Die Predigt Jesu vom Reiche Gottes* (Göttingen, 1892), p. 41. His reading is ably refuted by W. Manson, *Christ's View of the Kingdom of God* (London, 1918), p. 82. Cf. also T. W. Manson, *The Teaching of Jesus*, p. 25.

were common knowledge among the Qumran people, the readers of Daniel and Enoch, and in Essenian circles.

The poor in spirit (Matt. 5:3; Luke 6:20) to whom full beatitude is promised are apparently not the destitute, but people who have given up worldly goods, who are voluntarily poor. This concept was familiar to the members of the Qumran sect who had to renounce private property when entering the community (Manual i, 11 seq.; vi, 19 seq.). The disciples of the Teacher of Righteousness called themselves "the poor," as is confirmed by their commentary on Habakkuk (xii, 3, 6, 10).[34] The Essenes too practiced voluntary poverty; Josephus[35] testifies that they held all their property in common. It is thus not improbable that many of those who heard Jesus' inaugural address on the character of His kingdom were familiar with the practices of the Qumran circle and other Essenian groups. Christ approved of the Essene spirit of poverty, without, however, recommending the renunciation of all worldly goods.

The promises given in the Kingdom of God to the persecuted and to those suffering unjustly (Matt. 5:12) for righteousness were also well understood by the "poor" of Qumran and the Essenes. Their Teacher of Righteousness and his disciples had been persecuted by the high priest and exiled to Damascus.[36]

There can also be found in the Manual (iii, 20) a parallel to Jesus' saying that His disciples should be the light of the world (Matt. 5:14–16). The Qumran document reads: "All the sons of justice tread in the way of light." Evidently, Christ chose comparisons which were easily comprehensible to his listeners.

The words of the Lord (Matt. 5:20), "Unless your righteousness exceeds that of the Scribes and Pharisees[36a] you will never enter the kingdom of heaven," must have found particularly ready

[34] See K. Elliger, op. cit., p. 221 seq.
[35] Jewish War, II, 122, ed. by H. St. J. Thackeray (Loeb, 1927), 2, p. 368.
[36] Cf. C. Schubert, "The Sermon on the Mount and the Qumran Texts," in The Scrolls and the New Testament, p. 123 seq. The author thinks that the Qumran people or the Essenes had a tradition that Isaiah was killed by Manasseh. This would explain why Christ mentioned the killing of prophets.
[36a] Cf. W. Beilner, Christus und die Pharisäer (Vienna, 1959), p. 89 seq. Cf. also A. Finkel, The Pharisees and the Teacher of Nazareth (Leiden, 1964), p. 128: The message of Jesus in the light of Pharisaic teaching.

listeners. Righteousness was the main condition for admittance to the sectarian communities, which were all hostile to the hypocritical piety of the Scribes and Pharisees. It must again be recalled that Christ never took the Essenes as a special target of reproach, an indication that he sympathized with many of their principles.

Christ's recommendation of love for one's neighbor (Matt. 18:15 seq.) also could be appreciated by those of his audience who were familiar with the rule of the Manual (v, 24–vi, 1): "When anyone has a charge against his neighbor, he is to prosecute it truthfully, humbly, and humanely. He is not to speak to him angrily or querulously or arrogantly or in any wicked mood. He is not to bear hatred toward him in the inner recess of his heart.... No man is to bring a charge publicly against his neighbor except he prove it by witnesses." Josephus[37] praises the Essenes because "they are just dispensers of their anger, curbers of their passions... ministers of peace."

Christ's precept of chastity also found sympathetic acceptance among these and similar circles. The Manual (i, 6) warns the candidates not to walk "in the stubbornness of a guilty heart and of lustful eyes." Similar exhortation can be read in the Zadokite Document (iii, 3): "...walking blamelessly in all his ways and not straying after thoughts of guilty lust or after whoring eyes." The same document also condemned divorce (iv, 21 seq.) as a "whorish practice of taking two wives at the same time," quoting Genesis (1:27; 7:9) and Deuteronomy (17:17) to give more weight to this condemnation.

With regard to taking oaths, Josephus states that the Essenes refused to swear an oath. They thought "that a man who is not believed unless he call upon the divinity is already condemned in advance."[38] The Zadokite Document also has a whole chapter on oaths which starts with the words (xv, 1): "No one is to take the oath by El or by Adonai."

This should suffice to show that the Essenian circles and the sectaries of Qumran were best prepared to understand Jesus'

---

[37] *Jewish War*, II, 135, *loc. cit.*, p. 374.
[38] *Ibid.* Cf. *Jewish Antiquities*, XV, 370 seg., ed. by R. Marcus (Loeb, 1963), 8, p. 178,

teaching on the kingdom of God which the Messiah had to found. It is legitimate to suppose that the teaching and practices of the Qumran and other sects and of the Essenes were known to a wider public. It was to this public that Jesus addressed himself at first.

But Jesus did not sanction all practices of the recluses of Qumran. He condemned their exclusivism[39] by implication, with His own actions: conversing freely with sinners, accepting invitations to meals with them and the Pharisees, even entering the house of a pagan centurion. He did not expect from His disciples ritual ablutions before meals and on other such occasions.

The Qumran recluses and the Essenes were even more severe than the Pharisees in their regulations concerning the observance of the Sabbath. The Zadokite Document (x, 14–xi, 18) contains strict ordinances. Not only is work on the Sabbath forbidden, but also "ribald or empty talk." "No one is to walk more than a thousand cubits outside his city." No food should be prepared on the Sabbath, nothing should be brought into or taken out of the house. If a beast drops its young into a cistern on the Sabbath, no one has the right to take it out. All these regulations are rejected by Jesus: "The Son of Man is Lord of the Sabbath" (Matt. 12:8).

In another important matter Jesus' teaching exceeded by far that of the Qumran circle. Their Manual contains many admonitions to love one's neighbors or brothers, but each time only the members of the sect—the remnant of Israel—are meant (for example, Manual i, 4; Zadokite Document ii, 20). On the other hand, the sons of darkness are to be hated (Manual i, 10). Against this doctrine of hate, Christ established his rule (Matt. 5:43 seq.): "You have heard that it has been said, 'You shall love your neighbor, and hate your enemy.' But I say unto you 'Love your enemies....'." Only the sin, not the sinner, is to be hated.[40]

[39] Manual v, 1–7, on social relations; Zadokite Document xii, 6–11, on the relations with pagans.

[40] P. Fiebig, *Jesu Bergpredigt* (Göttingen, 1924), collected many rabbinical texts, comparing them to Jesus' sermon. The comparison shows the originality and peculiarity of Jesus' presentation of the truth, some parts of which were familiar to his listeners. Cf. also H. L. Strack and P. Billerbeck, *Kommentar zum Neuen Testament aus Talmud und Midrasch*, 1 (Munich, 1922), pp. 189–474.

Christ did not overlook the eschatological aspect of the coming kingdom, for it is to be found at the very center of His teaching. It was not even excluded from the passage just quoted, since, after the dismissal of the Pharisees, Christ spoke to His disciples about the coming of the Son of Man and the end of the world. He was certainly referring to this aspect of His messianic message in the Parable of the Tares scattered among the Wheat. The farmer allowed them to grow together until the harvest: only then were the tares gathered and tied up in bundles to be burned and the wheat stored in the barn. The explanation showed that Christ was alive to both aspects of His kingdom (Matt. 13:36 seq.): "The good seed... are the sons of the kingdom." Here again, the meaning is that the sons of the Kingdom have it already in their hearts, but the blessing they enjoy is only a foretaste and a pledge of what is to come after the harvest, the end of the world, when the coming of the Son of Man is described in the traditional apocalyptic style. The same applies to the eschatological return of the Son of Man as the judge of all nations (Matt. 24; 25:31 seq.)[41] In this connection a third kingdom is mentioned over which the Son of Man shall have full power (Matt. 13:41), and this kingdom comprises all nations of the world. Here also Jesus conformed to general expectation, since all the great prophets had pictured the Messiah as the King of all nations, not only of the Jews.

The Jews' privileged position in Jahweh's plan as the chosen people is likewise respected in the Parable of the Wicked Husbandmen (Matt. 21:33–44; Mark 12:1–12; Luke 20:9–18). The unanimity of the three Synoptic Gospels in recalling this story proves that it was fully understood and that it left an impression on the listeners. The same privilege of first vocation and its refusal is implied in the parables of the Marriage of the King's Son (Matt. 22:1–14) and of the Great Supper (Luke 14:15–29), where the Jews are called "the sons of the kingdom" (Matt. 8:12), but are nevertheless cast aside.

Two component elements are thus present in Christ's teaching on the Kingdom of God. The one represents it as being already present on earth and in process of growing, the other as achieving maturity

[41] Cf. also the parable of the net with its fishes good and bad, Matt. 13:47 seq.

and glory in its eschatological aspect. Even the Sermon on the Mount, which certainly deals with a very tangible kingdom, has so pronounced an eschatological bent that many prominent scholars have discovered in Christ's message nothing but the announcement of an eschatological kingdom.[42] But such exclusiveness does no justice to Jesus' words. There were two elements in His announcement: the temporary messianic and the eschatological kingdoms, and in stressing both the Lord made use of the current notions of the kingdom of God.

His meaning, however, went far beyond that of the prophets and His contemporaries, when He sponsored the apocalyptic writers' concept of a spiritualized rule of Jahweh over Israel as against the narrow and nationalist interpretation of the Pharisees and the Scribes. The rabbinical kingdom of God had already lost most of

---

[42] The discovery and publication in the nineteenth century of some new Jewish eschatological writings, such as the Book of Enoch, the Testaments of the Twelve Patriarchs, the Apocalypses of Moses and of Ezra, contributed to the tendency, prevalent among the first modern scholars attracted by the problem of the Kingdom of God, to overstress the eschatological meaning of some of Christ's statements. The vogue was started by J. Weiss, *Die Predigt Jesu vom Reiche Gottes*, supported by P. Wernle, *Die Reichgotteshoffnung in den ältesten christlichen Dokumenten und bei Jesus* (Tübingen, 1903), and reached a climax with A. Schweitzer's work, *Das Abendmahl* (Strasbourg, 1901). The portion of the latter work which deals with our subject was translated into English by W. Lowrie under the title *The Mystery of the Kingdom of God* (London, 1914). This eschatological theory did much to shake public faith in the liberal theological school and its eccentric glosses on Jesus' teaching, but it also created a reaction, for it was argued that eschatological utterances were introduced into the Gospel by the early Christians, and were alien to the mind of Jesus Christ himself: J. Wellhausen, *Israelitische und jüdische Geschichte*, 7th ed. (Berlin, 1914); idem, *Einleitung in die drei ersten Evangelien* (Berlin, 1914); W. Bousset, *Jesus* (London, 1906); idem, "Das Reich Gottes in der Predigt Jesu," *Theolog. Rundschau*, 5 (1902), pp. 397–407, 437–449. The problem of the Kingdom of God provoked immediate interest among English students of the New Testament; the soundest views are, I think, to be found in A. Robertson, *Regnum Dei* (London-New York, 1901), W. Manson, *Christ's View of the Kingdom of God*, and in T. W. Manson, *The Teaching of Jesus*. A full bibliography on the subject will be found in J. Héring, *Le Royaume de Dieu et sa venue*, Etudes d'Hist. et de Phil. Rel., Fac. de Théol. Prot., Strasbourg, fasc. 35 (Paris, 1937), pp. 255–274; revised edition (Neuchâtel, 1959), pp. 267–290, with the most recent bibliography. See also C. J. Cadoux, *The Historic Mission of Jesus*, Lutterworth Library, 12 (London, 1941), another important contribution to the solution of the problem. Cf. also R. Otto, *The Kingdom of God and the Son of Man*, trans. by F. v. Filson and B. Lee-Woolf (London, 1943); 3rd German ed. (Munich, 1953); S. H. Hooke, *The Kingdom of God in the Experience of Jesus* (London, 1949). Cf. also H. Roberts, *Jesus and the Kingdom of God* (London, 1955).

its earthly content, the Apocalyptics had made a further step in spiritual directions, and Christ improved upon these by purging them of their last materialistic elements.

But most significant was the progress made in the notion of Jahweh's relations toward His subjects. Until then, almost all individualism had been submerged in the national triumph. God's transcendence and rigid legalism, so heavily stressed by the prophets and scribes of post-exilic days, had made Him almost inaccessible to the individual soul. Rabbinical literature, it is true, contains suggestions of a possible personal relationship between Jahweh and His subjects, but they are hesitant and vague.

Daniel's assertion of the resurrection of the body and the emphasis of the Apocalyptics on the eschatological aspect of God's kingdom were the first to break with this concentration on the collective relations of Israel with Jahweh to the neglect of the individual. But only Christ succeeded in bringing God nearer to the average worshipper. He revealed the King of Israel as a loving Father, who urged everyone to join His kingdom, was ready to pardon every sin, and would wait even until the last moment for the sinner to surrender to His invitation. Not only the chosen people, but every Israelite was made eligible; not the fear of God's immensity and severity, but the love of God as father and shepherd was made the law of this new kingdom. At once, God and the soul were placed on a footing of personal and intimate relationship. There lay the reality of God's rulership over Israel, though its final fulfillment was postponed until the Day of Jahweh.

In order to link His own view of the Kingdom of God with that of the Apocalyptics, Christ, as has already been shown, adopted the title Son of Man, which they had used. Descent from David had been the earliest feature of messianism, but Christ never used the title Son of David, and on one occasion actually disavowed it.[43]

---

[43] Mark 12:35 seq. In this passage Christ is said to have quoted Ps. 110:1. It will be remembered that this psalm was most probably a royal psalm, believed to have been written in the early period of Jewish royalty; for details, see *supra*, p. 297 seq. In quoting it, Jesus was merely conforming to usage which attributed the psalm to David and gave it a messianic meaning, without any intention of pronouncing on its authorship and origin. For an explanation of the passage, see C. H. Turner, "The Gospel According to

It had been too closely associated with primitive messianism and rather implied a restoration of the Davidic kingdom, an improvement no doubt on the older concept, but, as advocated by Pharisees and Scribes, too earthly. It connoted Jewish emancipation from foreign rule, the subjection of the Gentiles, and the Jews' sovereignty as the chosen people; elements that did not fit into Christ's spiritualized kingdom.

Furthermore, to eliminate the danger of setting the Kingdom of God in opposition to any worldly polity, He accentuated the mutual hostility between His kingdom and that of Satan, taking care to raise them both to a spiritual level. His parables, which threw the kingdom open to all the righteous, excluded every suspicion of racial or national preference which still lingered in Qumran writings and among the Essenes. This explains the apocalyptic turn of the Lord's teaching and the individualistic references to the immediate advent of His kingdom. It also reveals the logical connection between His teaching and the current Jewish tradition.

On listening to His teaching, with its profound and intimate knowledge of God as King and Father, and its emphasis on man's close relationship to God, the average pious listener must have felt intense relief. Here was a kingdom different from that which his leaders had awaited; here was a message holding rewards for every one. The average man knew earthly kingdoms and governments from personal experience, for he was the one who had to pay with his blood, his money, and his labor for the victories and the successes of his leaders. He feared instinctively that in the kingdom promulgated by the Pharisees and Sadducees his part might again be limited to what had been his onerous and humble share, while his leaders would reap the benefit of the Messiah's successes. But in Christ he found a prophet who offered him something that lay within everyone's reach and who assured to everyone his share in Jahweh's blessing. There was, besides, satisfaction given to the basic human yearning for a deeper intimacy with God and to the conviction that God cared for the humble as much as for the great.

St. Mark," *A New Commentary on Holy Scripture Including the Apocrypha,* ed. by Ch. Gore, H. L. Goudge, and A. Guillaume (London, 1936), pt. 3, p. 99 seq.

Christ did not just tell the Israelites what the Kingdom of God was and how it was to be founded, He also made it a reality in His own heart. Hence, He was able to declare that the kingdom was already on earth and in the very midst of the chosen people, and that He had placed it there. This His own disciples acknowledged, as witness Peter's solemn confession on being asked by the Master what he thought of Him: "Thou art the Christ" (Matt. 16:16). The words meant recognition of the fact that the historic event for which Israel had been waiting had actually happened; that the Messiah, the ideal king, the sole representative of Israel before Jahweh, stood in their presence; that His kingdom was all around them. To this admission may be attributed the change in Christ's treatment of the kingdom, for it was after that that the Lord spoke of it, not as coming, but as already existent in their midst. The use of the title "Son of Man" also belongs exclusively to this period.[44] Thenceforward, there was nothing left for Him to hide from His disciples. Their admission voiced by Peter was free, based on what they had seen and heard and on what their unsophisticated minds could safely infer. It was a turning point in Christ's mission when the presence of the Kingdom of God was made obvious to minds at once sincere and simple.

Peter's public confession and the disciples' recognition of Jesus' messianic mission were all the more significant in that Christ did not present Himself in regal attire, as the people generally imagined the founder of a mighty kingdom would do. There were in His demeanor, words, and deeds all the signs considered by the average Jew, who was familiar with the national tradition, as features distinguishing the promised Messiah. No one was expected to identify the prophet's true character at once; merely by exercising common sense one would recognize it of one's own free will.

More time and a better opportunity were given to the official representatives of the nation, the high priest and the members of the Sanhedrin, to read the signs and draw their own inference; for to them the Lord revealed His character and His mission at the supreme moment when His messianic activity had reached its

[44] For particulars, see T. W. Manson, *The Teaching of Jesus*, pp. 128 seq., 201 seq.

climax. After His capture and His cross-examination by the Sanhedrin court, Caiphas, the high priest, addressed Him in solemn
terms (Matt. 26:63 seq.): "I abjure thee by the living God, that
thou tell us whether thou be the Christ, the Son of God. Jesus
saith to him, Thou has said: nevertheless I say unto you, henceforth
ye shall see the Son of Man sitting at the right hand of Power, and
coming on the clouds of heaven." In that moment, the Messiah
announced the foundation of His kingdom to the official representatives of the nation, who expected the Kingdom of God as emphati-
cally as the humblest of the people. It was at the same time made
clear that God's foundation would last forever and that its second
final phase would begin when the Son of Man would appear again
at the right hand of God to judge the nations. All this was couched
in the language of Daniel and the apocalyptic writers with which
officials were supposed to be familiar.

The tragedy was that such a solemn declaration should have
provoked the formal rejection of the Messiah and his Kingdom by
the representatives of a nation that had been waiting for centuries
for its arrival. This same rejection cleared the way for the Lord to
assume his role of suffering and atoning Servant of God, as foretold by Isaiah, but this the high priest and the members of the
Sanhedrin did not know.

If we remember what has been said about the Oriental and
Hellenistic notions of kingship, it becomes easy to draw a parallel
between Christ's kingdom and the idea of kingship embodied in
the aspirations of the ancient East. For there lay in the background
of Eastern political thought the eternal longing of men for justice
and for a more intimate contact with the divinity. This desire, so
variously expressed, subconsciously led the Egyptians, the Babylonians, the Persians, and other nations to focus all their attention
on the person of the king representing divinity and its justice, the
ideal man, pattern of righteousness, an inspiration by word and
deed to all men. The same longing affected the Greeks and led
them to develop a political system of rule by the wisest and best
among them. It is enough to recall what Ecphantus wrote,[45] reflect-

---

[45] See *supra*, Chapter Six, p. 255.

ing thoughts typical of the Hellenistic age, of the king as an ideal man, so transformed by his approach to the divinity that the sight of him was enough to purify men and inspire them with finer feelings.

This ideal king, the pattern of righteousness for every life, was found at last in the person of Christ, the difference being that whereas the Greek philosophers were obliged to overlook human failings in their kings, the followers of Jesus found in Him the perfect and ideal man, whose very words and deeds effected an approach to God, a cleansing, and an acceptance of His rule. This aspect of Christ was, of course, not so evident to His contemporaries, but since His doctrine was followed in countries that were under the influence of Hellenistic philosophy, it is quite likely that Ecphantus' view, apparently popular at least among intellectuals, prepared the way for Christianity in the hearts of many.

Again, man's thirst for justice and righteousness found its gratification in the eschatological aspect of God's kingdom. God, as the source of justice, would in the end punish every sin and misdeed, rectify injustice, and reward virtue. The active agent of this last and supreme act of justice would be the Son of Man, who sits "on the right hand of the Power and is coming on the clouds of heaven."

It was clear, then, that the kingdom founded by the Lord would have nothing in common with an earthly realm. Even Christ's own disciples found this difficult to understand, though Jesus left them in no doubt on the point. When, after the multiplication of loaves and fishes, the crowd insisted on making Jesus king, He immediately withdrew into the wilderness. That was not the sort of royalty which concerned Him. The incident is reported only by John (6:15), but two Synoptic Gospels give some indication of what must have happened.[46] When the mother of the sons of Zebedee asked Christ to seat her sons next to Him in His kingdom, He answered by explaining to his listeners the difference between His kingdom and the one they envisaged; Matthew (20:25 seq.) characteristically quotes His words: "Ye know that the rulers of the Gentiles lord over them and their great ones exercise authority over them. Not so shall it be among you, but whosoever would become great

[46] Matt. 14:22; Mark 6:45.

430

among you shall be your minister: and whoseover would be first among you shall be your servant: even as the son of man came not to be ministered unto, but to minister, and to give his life a ransom for many." The same question must have troubled His disciples on another occasion, for Christ made use of the most emphatic terms to stress the spiritual character of His kingdom: "Verily I say unto you, except ye turn, and become as little children, ye shall in no wise enter into the kingdom of heaven. Whosoever therefore shall humble himself as this little child, the same is the greatest in the kingdom of heaven..." (Matt. 18:2 seq.; Mark 9:33–37; Luke 9:46–48).

The reference to the rulers of the Gentiles should be linked with the words quoted in Luke's Gospel as being uttered at the Last Supper (22:24 seq.): "And there arose also a contention among them, which of them is accounted to be greatest. And he said unto them, The kings of the Gentiles have lordship over them; and they that have authority over them are called benefactors. But ye shall not be so: but he that is the greater among you, let him become as the younger; and he that is chief, as he that doth serve."

This incident can be reconstructed with the help of St. John's Gospel which alone records the washing of the feet (John 13:3 seq.). As reported by St. Luke, Christ started the supper with the words: "With desire I have desired to eat this passover with you before I suffer: for I say unto you, I will not eat it, until it be fulfilled in the kingdom of God" (Luke 22:14 seq.). These words should logically be followed by the account of the disciples' dispute, and not, as is in fact the case, by that of the institution of the new covenant. It was probably the reference to the kingdom that recalled the presumption of the sons of Zebedee and raised the old quarrel again. Christ thereupon reminded them once more of the differences between the spiritual and the earthly kingdoms. To show them how little He, the king, made of earthly honors and to set an example of humility, He left the table, "poureth water into the basin, and began to wash the disciples' feet, and to wipe them with the towel wherewith he was girded" (John 13:5). This gentle rebuke may have been intended to remind them that it had occurred to none to render this service to their Master and their friends after the long journey from Bethany to Jerusalem.

In differentiating the two kingdoms, Christ showed His familiarity with Hellenistic political thought. The name "benefactors," which has puzzled so many exegetes, is simply a translation of the Greek *euergetes*, the official title affected by Hellenistic kings and conferred on them by Hellenistic philosophers. Their benefaction consisted in being the law animate and therefore indispensable to the state, in that without them justice could not be administered. That Christ should mention a Hellenistic royal title in contrast to His own task of love and humble service exposed in high relief the specific difference between the Kingdom of God and the political organization known at the time.

Palestine knew no other rule, having lived so long under the Ptolemies and the Seleucids. Even during the short span of the Hasmonaean dynasty, Hellenistic ideas on kingship persisted and somehow found favor with Hasmonaeans and Herodians alike. Rome, as we shall see presently, accepted this Eastern ideology. It is true that Luke alone mentions the title benefactor; but, as already stated, Matthew (20:25 seq.) and Mark (10:42 seq.) record almost the same words as Luke in connection with James's and John's ambition to sit on the right and the left of the Lord's throne. This is not just coincidence, nor is it necessary to assume interpolation by the Evangelist.

The Lord's declaration may also be read as an oblique attack on the excesses of Hellenistic political philosophy, especially its deification of kings. Far from boasting of His indispensability to the existence of society, such as was assumed by the doctrine of the king-law animate and his super-human origin or character, this ideal King rather meant to set an example of love for God and one's neighbor by humble service.

But the difference between the Kingdom of God and earthly governments, only hinted at by Christ in the incident of the sons of Zebedee, is made specific by the Lord's declaration, so vital for delimiting the two spheres, on payment of the emperor's tribute. The Lord's decision, which is reported by all the Synoptics,[47] "Render unto Caesar the things that are Caesar's, and unto God the things

[47] Matt. 22:17 seq.; Mark 12:14 seq.; Luke 20:22 seq.

that are God's," has at all times been acknowledged by every historian and political philosopher as the keystone of all political development down to the present day. It has also served as the basis for every theory concerning the relations between Church and state.

While it is understood that not all these theories were correct and that most of them were mutually contradictory, this was mainly because Christ's decision was separated by the theorists from the background of Jewish political and religious thought of His time. What has misled so many political theorists has been their excessive concentration on the Jews' spiritual leaders—Pharisees, Sadducees, and Herodians—as though these occupied the whole stage and as though Jesus and His questioners could think of nothing but the foreign pagan regime that oppressed the nation. But the problem is far more complex. When we come to think that the Lord's first concern was the foundation of the Kingdom of God, we presume that on the occasion also of the payment of tribute the nature and character of that Kingdom were uppermost in His mind.

There existed among the Jews of that time another concept of the kingdom of God, also derived from Daniel's visions and the apocalyptic writings, and also rooted in the Jewish creed and the Jewish national character: it was the logical inference drawn from post-exilic teaching that Jahweh alone was the king of His nation. From this, a group of extremists known as Zealots concluded that the chosen people should tolerate no other ruler but Jahweh and that His rule should be administered by the priests, His sole representatives. The Jewish historian Josephus Flavius,[48] who was well versed in Greek and Hellenistic letters and political philosophy, called the Zealot conception theocracy, or government by God. Thus, the concept of theocracy was introduced into the history of political philosophy.

This radicalism, which had helped the Romans in getting rid of the Hasmonaeans,[49] eventually turned against them as the Zealots

[48] *Against Apion*, II, 164 seq., ed. by H. St. J. Thackeray (Loeb, 1926), I, p. 358. Cf. A. Finkel, *op. cit.*, p. 118 seq.
[49] Josephus Flavius, *Jewish Antiquities*, XIV, 41, ed. by R. Marcus (Loeb, 1943), 7, p. 468, records that Pompey received envoys from the Jewish people in Damascus asking him to rid them of their national dynasty on the ground that the Jews had only one king, God, who should reveal His orders through His priests.

gained more power. Fanatically opposed to any payment of tribute to the Roman emperor, they professed contempt for every Jew who had any dealings with representatives of foreign rule, such as tax collectors and publicans, which explains their general unpopularity, and they stopped at nothing to undermine the emperor's authority in Palestine. What kindled their zeal was Daniel's explanation of Nebuchadnezzar's dream (Dan. 2:44): "And in the days of those kings shall the God of heaven set up a kingdom, which shall never be destroyed, nor shall the sovereignty thereof be left to another people; but it shall break in pieces and consume all these kingdoms, and it shall stand for ever." Many of them must have been expecting the Messiah to come to destroy the Roman Empire, and later, about the year of the sacking of Jerusalem by the Romans, they expressed their desire in an apocalyptic eagle vision which was included in the apocryphal fourth book of Ezra.[50]

Christ must have been well aware of the growing importance of this movement and of its danger, which was serious enough, since both He and the Zealots began their teachings with the same premises. Incidentally, this explains why His message found such favor with them. At least one of His disciples, Simon the Zealot (Luke 6:15; Acts 1:13), came from their ranks and possibly the sons of Zebedee were associated with the movement before they joined Christ, for their idea of the kingdom of God approximated that of the Zealots (Matt. 20:20–23). Their request, as expressed by their mother, to sit next to the Lord when He would come to judge Israel rang true to Zealot impetuosity, and their readiness to drink the bitter chalice with Jesus was consistent with the Zealots' eagerness to suffer martyrdom for their opinions. They brooked no compromise, for, as reported by Luke (9:54), they urged the Lord to send fire from heaven for the destruction of the Samaritans who refused to receive Him. This explains why Christ surnamed them Boanerges, that is, Sons of Thunder (Mark 3:17.).

There are indications that even John, although rather nearer to the Qumran sect, was under the influence of the Zealot move-

---

[50] Chapters 11, 12, trans. by G. H. Box, *The Ezra-Apocalypse* (London, 1912), p. 249 seq.

ment, for he also betrayed something of their fanatical temper when he forbade the young man to cast out evil spirits in the name of Jesus, since he was not one of His disciples (Mark 9:38); and the Lord reproved him, saying: "For he that is not against us is for us." John also displayed more daring and readiness to suffer with His Master than any other disciple. He followed Him after His arrest (John 18:15), he did not deny Him as did Peter, and he stood alone at the foot of the cross, regardless of the danger of being recognized, to share his Master's fate (John 19:26). He felt almost jealous of Peter who had the honor of dying the same death as his Lord, a grace that was denied to himself (John 21:19 seq.). We shall have occasion to study his subsequent attitude to Rome, as disclosed in Revelation, in connection with his prophecies on the tragic end of Babylon. His passionate description of the burning of that city would have delighted the Zealots, any of whom would gladly have given his life for the pleasure of seeing it go up in flames.[51]

The suggestion that Judas Ischariot also belonged to the Zealots would be quite plausible if we could substantiate the derivation of his name from the Latin *sicarius*,[52] to which the Greek word *lestes*, or bandit, corresponds. Josephus Flavius constantly uses this label for the Zealots.[53] The Romans held the Zealot movement in con-

---

[51] Rev. 14:8; 18:9–18; 19:17–18; 20. Cf. the judicious remarks by D. A. Schlatter, *Die Geschichte der ersten Christenheit*, 2nd. ed. (Gütersloh, 1926), p. 65 seq.

[52] On the etymology of Ischariot, see F. Schulthess, *Das Problem der Sprache Jesu* (Zurich, 1917), pp. 41, 55, and *idem*, "Zur Sprache der Evangelien," *ZNW*, 22 (1922), pp. 250–258. See also footnote 53.

[53] For particulars, see the short but well documented study on the Zealots by A. Stumpff in G. Kittel's *Theolog. Wörterbuch zum Neuen Testament*, 2 (Stuttgart, 1935), p. 886 seq., and K. H. Rengstorf's study on "ληστής," *ibid.*, 4 (Stuttgart, 1938), pp. 262–267. The bibliography on the movement of the Zealots is not abundant and the problem deserves better treatment by specialists. The two studies mentioned are therefore indispensable and record the results obtained up to recent years. Cf. also E. Meyer, *Ursprung und Anfänge des Christentums*, 2 (Stuttgart-Berlin, 1921), p. 402 seq., and especially O. Cullmann, *Der Staat im Neuen Testament* (Tübingen, 1956), p. 5 seq. It is M. Hengel's merit to have devoted a well documented book to this movement: *Die Zeloten. Untersuchungen zur jüdischen Freiheitsbewegung in der Zeit von Herodes I. bis 17 N. Chr.* (Leiden-Cologne, 1961), the first volume of the Arbeiten zur Geschichte des Spätjudentums und Urchristentum, published by the Institutum Iudaicum, Tübingen, ed. by O. Michel. After a critical review of all the sources on this movement (pp. 6–25), Hengel studies the history of the robber bands in the Roman Empire, especially in Syria and

tempt, and called its adherents bandits—*lestai, sicarii*—though whenever they captured one, they treated him not only as a bandit, but, by hanging on the cross, punished him also as a revolutionary.

Thus, when the Gospels mention bandits or *lestai*, the question arises whether they mean the revolutionary Zealots. This seems almost certain in some cases. That Christ's enemies affected to associate the unwanted prophet with the Zealots can be inferred from the words which He addressed to the hirelings of the chief priests who had come to arrest Him (Matt. 26:55): "Are ye come out as against a robber with swords and staves to seize me?" The word "robber," *lestes*, in this connection very probably meant the chief of a band of Zealots and Christ's rebuke could be amplified as follows: You are hunting me as though I were a leader of Zealots, yet "I sat daily in the temple, and ye took me not."[54] My words and my deeds might have shown you that I have nothing in common with the violent teaching and methods of the Zealots.

Another indication of a deliberate effort on the part of Christ's enemies to misrepresent Him as a Zealot before Pilate appears in

Palestine, showing in what circumstances the Zealots were identified with the *lestai* and the *sicarii* (pp. 25–53). The death sentence against the *lestai* was crucifixion or condemnation *ad bestias* (p. 33 seq.). See p. 45 on Josephus' identification of the Zealots with the *lestai*. On pp. 72–78, when describing what was said about the Zealots in the Christian sources, the author discusses the different factions of this movement and admits that the advocates of the Jewish struggle for freedom were called Zealots in the time of Christ. He is very cautious in examing the testimonies on the Zealot movement in Jesus' time (pp. 344–348) and among his Apostles, but admits that Barabbas was *lestes*— Zealot, and agrees that the Jews accused Christ as a leader of a Zealot band and that the two *lestai* crucified with him were Zealots (also p. 385). As to Judas (p. 49), Hengel is not inclined to accept Schulthess' interpretation. He ends his examination with the following statement: "Trotz gewisser Berührungspunkte stellte die Verkündigung Jesu und der ersten Christenheit die eigentliche Überwindung des zelotischen Versuches dar, die Herrschaft Gottes auf Erden mit Gewalt herbeizuführen." See this work also for more complete bibliographical references. Interesting ideas on the connection of Jewish nationalism with apocalyptic elements in the struggle of the Maccabees and in the movement of the Zealots will be found in W. R. Farmer's book, *Maccabees, Zealots, and Josephus. An Inquiry into Jewish Nationalism in the Greco-Roman Period* (New York, 1956). See the chapter on Jewish Nationalism and Jesus, pp. 175–204, which deserves special attention.

[54] In John's Gospel (18:3, 12), besides "officers from the chief priests," soldiers with the captain (*chiliarch*) are mentioned. O. Cullmann, *Der Staat*, p. 31, thinks that the Jews had already accused Jesus of Zealotism before his capture and that the Roman authorities had sent a cohort of soldiers to arrest him as a Zealot. Cf. also M. Hengel, *op. cit.*, p. 346.

the way the Roman procurator handled the case. He was holding imprisoned a notorious Zealot, Barabbas—some manuscripts of John's Gospel (18:40) call him *archilestes*,[55] or the leader of a gang of Zealots. When Pilate had seen for himself that Jesus was not a man of that persuasion, he placed Him side by side with Barabbas and asked the Jews to choose between the two in the hope that the Pharisees and the Sadducees would not claim the release of Barabbas. He must have known what they thought of the Zealots' violent methods.[56] But there he was mistaken. The Jewish leaders hated Jesus even more than they hated the Zealots. Their persistent attempts to identify Him with those revolutionaries would explain why they incited the mob to insist on the penalty of crucifixion for Christ, for it was generally applied to people convicted of sacrilege or insurrection, and frequently to the Zealots for their resistance to Roman rule.[57] Significant also is the fact that Christ was condemned to the cross and crucified between two *lestai*—bandits or Zealots. One of these through his suffering saw the true character of the kingdom of God which Christ had been preaching and accepted it, thus confessing that the Zealotic concept of the kingdom of God for which he had been fighting was erroneous. But the other persisted in his conviction and protested that Christ could be no Messiah if He failed to exterminate the enemy who had done them such wrong: no Zealot Messiah would spare the hated Roman and allow Israel to remain under his rule.

All this reveals a new aspect of Zealotism and the part it played in Christ's history. One comes to the conclusion that Christ dealt more often than is apparent with the Zealots' extremist doctrines and practices, in order to make it clear which of them He discarded and which He accepted. For instance, it is possible[58] that the robbers,

---

[55] C. von Tischendorf, *Novum Testamentum Graece*, Editio octava critica major, 1 (Leipzig, 1872), p. 935. Cf. K. H. Rengstorf, "ληστής," p. 257.

[56] This juxtaposition of Jesus and Barabbas would have been even more forceful were we justified in thinking with D. A. Deissmann ("The Name 'Jesus,'" *Mysterium Christi*, ed. by G. K. A. Bell and D. A. Deissmann [London, 1930], p. 22 seq.) that the first name of Barabbas was also Jesus but was omitted by the copyists of the Gospel out of respect for the Lord.

[57] Cf. H. F. Hitzig, "Crux," in Pauly-Wissowa, 4 (Stuttgart, 1901), col. 1730.

[58] See K. Bornhäuser, *Studien zum Sondergut des Lukas* (Gütersloh, 1934), p. 69. Cf. also Rengstorf, *op. cit.*, p. 266.

or *lestai*, mentioned (Luke 10:30,36) in the Parable of the Good Samaritan, were not ordinary malefactors, but Zealots, who, as was their custom, took from the Jew what they needed in their flight from the Roman authorities, and hurt him only because he offered resistance. They expected every Jew to support their "resistance" activities as a sacred and patriotic duty and to assist them in their task. If this explanation is valid, it is conceivable that Jesus chose to refer to the Zealots only to make it clear that He did not sanction their methods in the realization of the Kingdom of God in Israel.

It is also possible that in the parable of the shepherd who enters the sheepfold by the door while the thief and the robber "climb in some other way" (John 10:1 seq.), the word *lestes* or bandit was used deliberately. It was intended to brand the Zealots as interlopers who tried to force an entry into the Kingdom of God and to disregard the words of the true shepherd, the king, whose exclusive right it was to found and open His kingdom.[59] The place the Zealots occupied in Christ's time lends significance to His injunction to love one's enemies. It was all the more unjust to identify Christ with the Zealots, since he was preaching a law absolutely contrary to Zealot doctrine.

Another of Christ's sayings reported by Matthew (11:12) might also be taken as referring to the Zealots: "And from the days of John the Baptist until now the kingdom of heaven suffers violence and men of violence take it by force."[60] It would be plausible to read this as a rebuke addressed to the Zealots, who, for all their distorted notions, also believed in the Kingdom of God, but expected to hasten its advent by fighting the Romans. As the preaching of John the Baptist intensified the expectations of the pious, it is possible also that his words stimulated the revolutionary propaganda of the Zealots who interpreted them in their own favor. If this is correct, Christ's words may well connote a reaction to Zealotic methods.

If we bear this in mind, Christ's decision on the payment of tribute will appear in an entirely new light. The question was asked

[59] Cf. Rengstorf, *op. cit.*, p. 266.
[60] On this passage, consult C. J. Cadoux, *op. cit.*, pp. 130, 171, 173, 206, 232, and T. W. Manson, *The Teaching of Jesus*, p. 124.

during Jesus' last stay in Jerusalem, i.e., at a time when He was generally known to have assumed the title Son of Man, popularized by the apocalyptic writers, and when many people took Him to be the Messiah. The kingdom He announced closely resembled the one designated as the kingdom of Jahweh, which the Son of Man was prophesied as founding. Since the Zealots also upheld Jahweh as the sole king of Israel and drew from this theological principle political deductions which appealed neither to the Pharisees and the Sadducees nor to the Herodians, and since Christ's teaching showed similarities with Zealot political thought, it was only natural that the Pharisees and the Sadducees should call for a definite statement as to how Christ's preaching of the Kingdom of God could be reconciled with the emperor's political authority over Israel. It is understandable that they would have welcomed a declaration identifiable with Zealot doctrine, for this would have alienated all the upper classes, usually in favor of peaceful methods, and cast Roman suspicion on the new prophet, which was their main purpose. It appears that they tried hard to find an excuse for urging the authorities to put a stop to Jesus' activities, if we may judge from the charge they made against Him in the presence of Pilate (Luke 23:2): "We found this man perverting our nation and forbidding to give tribute to Caesar and saying that he himself is Christ a King."

The incident of the tribute, which occurred in the closing stage of Jesus' active career, must then be taken as the first deliberate attempt on the part of His enemies to brand Him a Zealot and a dangerous idealist who incited the people against Roman rule, and to provoke an admission that could be turned against Him. Had this attempt been successful, the rest would have followed as a matter of course: the Roman authorities would have taken the necessary steps and the danger of a popular rising against the Jewish authorities would have been averted. That Christ's enemies should persist in accusing Him as a Zealot in the presence of Pilate (Luke 23:2) rather confirms our conjecture.

It follows then that the dilemma which the Pharisees and the Sadducees forced on Jesus by their question concerning tribute was: Is the kingdom you are preaching compatible with the political system under which we must live? Given the premises on the

439

teaching about the Kingdom of God that were common to both Christ and the Zealots, the point of the whole maneuver was to inveigle Christ into giving an answer which would seem to support Zealot notions on the subject.

It is from this viewpoint that we can appreciate the importance of the Lord's answer, the clarity and straightforwardness of which must have baffled his questioners. By distinguishing between the emperor's sphere of influence in Israel's political life and Jahweh's sphere in Israel's spiritual life, the Lord condemned the theocratic regime upheld by the Zealots in a manner which his contemporaries must have understood better than we can today. There was in the Kingdom of God as Jesus understood it not the slightest pretension to any kind of political leadership; indeed, the nation could exist and thrive even under the rule of a pagan autocracy such as the Roman regime. In other words, Christ's answer implies the recognition of the rights of the civil state, for these rights rest on, and derive from, the natural law, which too is derived from God. Christ's answer defines at the same time the rights of the preachers and the members of the Kingdom of God, which the state must respect as scrupulously as they, in turn, must respect the rights of the existing political organization which ministers to their material interests.

Yet, though the Zealots' theocratic and hierocratic theory, as applied to the political field, stands condemned, their uncompromising condemnation of any kind of divinization, such as had been advocated by Hellenistic political thought and adopted by the Romans, is implicitly ratified by the words "render to God what is God's."

It should be noted here that nowhere does Christ identify his kingdom with the community of men who believe that they have set the Kingdom of God in their hearts or that they have been admitted into it as members—that is to say, with the "Church". On the other hand, He did select twelve disciples whom He invested with special powers to carry on His mission and preach the Kingdom of God. Those powers were carefully defined in the promises given first to St. Peter and then to all twelve. To Peter (Matt. 16:19): "I will give unto thee the keys of the kingdom of heaven: and whatsoever thou shalt bind on earth shall be bound in heaven: and

whatsoever thou shalt loose on earth shall be loosed in heaven."
To all the twelve (Matt. 18:18): "Verily I say unto you, what
things soever ye shall bind on earth shall be bound in heaven: and
what things soever ye shall loose on earth shall be loosed in heaven."
These words clearly imply that the twelve Apostles, and of course
their successors, would have full authority to teach what He had
taught and to decide all doubtful matters that might either promote
or hamper the expansion of the Kingdom of God. The authority
thus conferred on them was considerable and is defined in the
following chapter of the same Gospel (Matt. 19: 28): "Verily I say
unto you, that ye which have followed me, in the regeneration when
the Son of Man shall sit on the throne of His glory ye shall sit
upon the twelve thrones judging the twelve tribes of Israel." This
seems to imply that the disciples were given supreme jurisdiction
over all questions connected with the Kingdom of God and would
share the Founder's kingly powers. These powers are then amplified
with the addition of the authority to forgive sin (John 20:23).

That Jesus contemplated a special institution for the purpose of
preaching the Kingdom of God must be inferred from His declaration to Peter after the latter had witnessed to His being the
promised Messiah: "And I say unto thee that thou art Peter, and
upon this rock I will build my Church; and the gates of Hades
shall not prevail against it." These words, which are in some respects
the foundation charter of the Church, are also, however, open to
controversy in regard to their exact meaning as well as to their
authenticity. Since this controversy has some bearing on the foundation of the Kingdom of God, a short summary of it will be apposite.

With regard to the meaning of the logion, it is well-known
that Eastern theologians generally differ in their opinion with those
of Rome and the West. Easterners think that it is not the person
of Peter who is the rock on which the Church is to be built, but
his confession that Jesus was the promised Messiah; whereas
Westerners use the logion about Peter and the rock as their main
argument in favor of the primacy of Peter's successors in the
government of the Church.

The Eastern view, though universally accepted by present-day
Orthodox theologians, was not favored by the first Fathers of the

Church.[61] It was put forward for the first time by St. Cyril of Alexandria[62] and was adopted by some Western Fathers.[63] In spite of views to the contrary, the interpretation, which modern theologians in the East have now made their own, is not as unreasonable as it seems. We must remember what was said about the significance of Peter's confession for the foundation of the Kingdom of God. If our reading is correct, one can understand why the Lord could attribute such weight to it. The passage would read like a clever rhetorical device, since the author of the confession was called Peter or Rock and since he was the first openly and spontaneously to witness that Jesus was the expected Messiah.

Even if the Eastern explanation is accepted, the Western view loses nothing of its force, since the Lord addressed the rest of the sentence to Peter alone: "I will give unto thee the keys of the kingdom of heaven...." Keys, especially the keys of the Kingdom of God, the Lord's most valued creation, are entrusted to a single caretaker only and to one distinctly appointed. It is therefore plain that the Eastern Fathers were guided in their reading by the import of Peter's confession to Jesus' teaching mission, for it was the first recognition of Jesus' messianic claim and of the foundation of His messianic kingdom to come from a leader of the chosen people. Western Fathers, on the other hand, emphasized the part which Peter played in the incident. But once it is

[61] The following Fathers of the earlier period identify Peter with the rock on which the Church was to be built: Tertullian, *De monogamia*, 8, PL, 2, col. 989; *De praescriptionibus*, 22, loc. cit., col. 39; *De pudicitia*, 21, loc. cit., col. 1077. Cyprian, *Epistolae*, 71, PL, 4, col. 423, CSEL, 3, p. 773; *De habitu virginum*, 10, PL, 4, col. 461, CSEL, 3, p. 194; Origen, *In Exodum homilia* V, PG, 12, col. 329; *Comm. in Epistolam ad Romanos*, V, 10, loc. cit., 14, col. 1053.

[62] *De SS. Trinitate dialogus IV*, PG, 75, col. 865. Cf. also Photius, *Ad Amphilochium*, Questio 194, PG, 101, col. 933.

[63] Ambrose, *Expositio in Evangelium secundum Lucam*, VI, 97, PL, 15, col. 1781; *De incarnatione*, 5, 34, loc. cit., 16, col. 862. For other quotations from Western and Eastern Fathers, cf. Robertus Card. Bellarminus, *De Romano Pontifice* (*Opera omnia*, 1 [Rome, 1872]), p. 330 seq. A similar idea is expressed in the prayer of the Roman Mass on the Vigil of Sts. Peter and Paul: *Praesta quaesumus omnipotens Deus ut nullis nos permittas perturbationibus concuti, quos in* apostolicae confessionis petra *solidasti*. Cf. F. Dvornik, *The Photian Schism. History and Legend* (Cambridge, 1948), pp. 125 seq. For more details, see J. Ludwig, *Die Primatworte Mt 16, 18, 19 in der altkirchlichen Exegese*, Neutestam. Abhandlungen, 19, Heft 4 (Münster i. W., 1952).

admitted that his declaration had a direct bearing on the
setting up of the messianic kingdom, there is no fundamental
difference between the Eastern and the Western views on Matthew
16:18.[64]

Christ's estimation of Peter's confession provides an argument in
favor of the authenticity of His sayings in Matthew 16:18, which
has been questioned, chiefly by A. Harnack.[65] Apart from the
arguments in their favor based on textual criticism,[66] the mere fact
that the Lord attached such importance for His mission to Peter's
spontaneous confession makes the authenticity of this logion in
Matthew's version more than probable. Peter and his confession are
made the foundation of a Church that will be attacked by hell,
but never defeated. As a reward for being the first publicly to
acknowledge the Lord as the Messiah, Peter is entrusted with the
keys of the Kingdom of God, which had been made an earthly
reality through his faith.

Again, the Qumran Scrolls seem to provide some information on
the primitive organization of this society which was to promote the
Kingdom of God. Jesus Christ chose twelve Apostles from among
his disciples, three of whom, Peter, James, and John, had a kind of
precedence. The twelve tribes of Israel are thought to have been
the inspiration for this choice. It should be noted, however, that
the Qumran sect also had a hierarchic order composed of twelve
elders (presbyters) and three priests. The head of the community
was the high priest. Chapter eight of the Manual stresses with

---

[64] Such seems also to have been the opinion of that staunch defender of
the Roman primacy, Pope Nicholas I, the fierce antagonist of Photius, who
writes to him, in his letter of 18 March 862 (ep. 86, *Epistolae Karolini Aevi*, 4,
MGH, *Epistolae*, 6 [Berlin, 1925], p. 447): "When Our Lord and Redeemer
had given to Blessed Peter, Prince of the Apostles, the power to bind and to
loose in heaven and on earth and to close the gates of the heavenly kingdom,
He deigned to erect His holy Church on the solidity of the faith [*supra
soliditatem fidei suam sanctam dignatus est stabilire Ecclesiam*], according to
His authentic words, as He said: Verily, I say unto thee, thou art Peter..."
(Matt. 16:18, 19).

[65] "Der Spruch über Petrus als den Felsen der Kirche (Matth. 16, 17f.)," in
SB der Preuss, Akad. der Wiss., Phil.-hist. Kl., no. 32 (Berlin, 1918), pp.
637–654. On the controversy, cf. K. Guggisberg, "Matthaeus 16, 18 u. 19
in der Kirchengeschichte," *Zeitschr. für Kirchengeschichte*, 54 (1935), p. 276 seq.

[66] For particulars, see G. Glez, "Primauté du Pape," *Dict. de Théol. Cath.*,
13 (Paris, 1936), col. 250 seq.

eloquent words the importance of this hierarchic order to the existence of the sect.[67]

Similar organizations may have been established by other sects. It is thus quite natural to suppose that Jesus Christ followed a pattern already known to his disciples and understandable to all Jews because of its connection with the twelve tribes of Israel, and that He established a hierarchical order to help propagate the Kingdom of God and unite all the faithful who belonged to it. If we look at Christ's choice in this way, the privileged position of Peter among the three favored Apostles seems quite logical.

Once having been placed in the charge of Peter and the other disciples, however, the Church is not identified with the Kingdom of God, but is, rather, the organ for promoting that kingdom. Nor are its relations with the state expressly defined, though from the logion on the payment of tribute it can be inferred that it should exist independently of the state and concern itself only with the interests of the Kingdom of God.

Having established the true significance of Christ's logion on the relations between the two kingdoms, let us now examine the official attitude of the Roman Empire to the rising spiritual kingdom. This can be deduced from the manner in which Rome's representative in Jerusalem, Pontius Pilate, treated Jesus as He stood accused by the Jewish authorities of perverting the population and of disseminating subversive Zealotic doctrines. The three Synoptics agree that Pilate first examined the nature of the kingship that was the subject of the charge (Matt. 27:11 seq.; Mark 15:2; Luke 23:2 seq.). St. John's Gospel is more detailed, inasmuch as it gives the interrogation which the Judge put to the defendant (John 18:36 seq.): "Jesus answered, My kingdom is not of this world: if my kingdom were of this world, then would my servants fight, that I should not be delivered to the Jews: but now is my kingdom not from hence. Pilate therefore said unto him, Art thou a king then? Jesus answered, Thou sayest that I am king. To this end

---

[67] See, for details, S. E. Johnson, "The Dead Sea Manual and the Jerusalem Church of Acts," in *The Scrolls and the New Testament*, pp. 129–142, and B. Reicke, "The Constitution of the Primitive Church in the Light of Jewish Documents," *ibid.*, pp. 143–156.

have I been born and to this end am I come into the world, that I should bear witness unto the truth."[68]

It follows from this account that, though Christ explicitly claimed to be king of the Jews, yet Pilate detected the non-political nature of the claim, since he declared to the accusers "I find no fault in this man." This was the verdict of the Roman Empire, the highest political authority, on the Kingdom of Christ. It was also an admission that the two authorities could exist side by side; that the state would not be harmed by acknowledging the rights of the Kingdom of God. Pilate showed his deep conviction and his resentment of his defeat by insisting on his own wording of the inscription: "This is Jesus the king of the Jews" (Mark 15:26; Matt. 27:37; Luke 23:38). And when the chief priests protested: "Write not, the king of the Jews: but that he said, I am king of the Jews" (John, 19:21), Pilate retorted with characteristic brevity: "What I have written, I have written."[69] It may

[68] This is one of the three references to the Kingdom of God in John's Gospel. The other two are in 3:3 and 5. Generally, the Apostle uses the word "Life" instead of "Kingdom of God." Those who set it up in their hearts and are in union with the King, will have life everlasting (e.g., 3:36). Cf. A. Robertson, *Regnum Dei*, p. 94 seq., and R. H. Charles, *A Critical History of the Doctrine of a Future Life* (London, 1913), p. 425 seq.

[69] See J. Merkel, "Die Begnadigung am Passahfeste," *ZNW*, 6 (1905), pp. 293–316. Since this study was published two cases have been discovered which seem to point to a custom of releasing, on Roman authority, a prisoner under sentence of death, in order to placate the people. See A. Deissmann, *Light from the Ancient East*, trans. by L. R. M. Strachan from the 4th German ed. (London, 1927), p. 269 seq. The Governor of Egypt, G. Septimius Vegetus, according to a Florentine papyrus of the year A.D. 85, released a certain Thibion on public demand. Cf. also a similar case known from a Greek inscription of Phlegetius, Proconsul of Asia (*ca.* A.D. 441), who also released some criminals "owing to the outcry of this illustrious metropolis of the Ephesians and because their prayers could not be set aside." Cf. H. Grégoire, *Recueil des inscriptions grecques chrétiennes d'Asie Mineure* (Paris, 1922), p. 32; *idem*, "Miettes d'histoire byzantine," *Anatolian Studies, Pres.* worthy of closer study by exegetes of the New Testament. Apparently in to *Sir William M. Ramsay* (Manchester, 1923), p. 154 seq. The detail is Christ's case an old custom, perhaps borrowed by the Jews from the Babylonians (see *supra*, pp. 40, 342), was combined with a juridical procedure adopted by the Roman precursor of the popular courts. This places the legality of Pilate's action in a different light. O. Cullmann, *Der Staat*, p. 29, thinks that Pilate's inscription on the top of the cross was the *titulus* indicating that Jesus was condemned to crucifixion as a Zealot who was plotting against the Roman authority. It seems evident that this was taken by Pilate as a pretext for Jesus' condemnation on the accusation of the Sadducees and the Pharisees, whose testimony had to be respected. This,

have been his own personal retaliation, but it established the victim's innocence and made the Jews responsible for the murder of their own king.[70]

We find, then, that Jesus' logion on the payment of tribute and Pilate's verdict constitute two important decisions by the most competent authorities of both kingdoms to the effect that their coexistence was possible and that they were not in principle mutually exclusive. This meant that the Founder of the spiritual kingdom looked upon the state, not as a satanic institution, an evil which

---

however, does not imply that Pilate was convinced of Jesus' guilt. His attitude during the trial does not warrant that conclusion. On the historicity of the preliminary interrogation of Jesus by the Sanhedrin, see *ibid.*, p. 28. The author gives an account of the controversy, initiated by H. Lietzmann, "Der Prozess Jesu," *SB der Preuss. Akad. der Wiss.*, Phil.-hist. Kl., 1931 (Berlin, 1931), p. 313 seq.; continued by Lietzmann, "Bemerkungen zum Prozess Jesu," *ZNW*, 31 (1931), pp. 211–215; 32 (1932), pp. 78–84; and finally by J. Jeremias, "Zur Geschichtlichkeit des Verhörs vor dem Hohen Rat," *ZNW*, 43 (1950–51), p. 145 seq. O. Cullmann (*Der Staat*, p. 7) rightly refutes R. Eisler's claim that Jesus was a Zealot ('Ιησοῦς βασιλεὺς οὐ βασιλεύσας [Heidelberg, 1929–30], 2, p. 459 seq; *idem, The Messiah Jesus and John the Baptist* [London, 1931], pp. 469, 510 seq.). Cf. also M. Hengel, *op. cit.*, pp. 347, 385.

[70] It is impossible to discuss here in detail the problems relative to the trial of Jesus. A short outline of the considerable and controversial bibliography on this question is given by W. Beilner in his book *Christus und die Pharisäer*, pp. 235–237. He is more interested in the interrogation by the Sanhedrin. F. Doerr, *Der Prozess Jesu in rechtsgeschichtlicher Beleuchtung* (Berlin-Stuttgart-Leipzig, 1920), examined the problem from the angle of Jewish and Roman provincial criminal laws. J. Blinzler, *Der Prozess Jesu*, 3rd ed. (Regensburg, 1960), p. 232 seq., devoted an excursus to the custom of releasing a political prisoner before the Passover. The most recent work is that by P. Winter, *On the Trial of Jesus* (Berlin, 1961). On pp. 91–99 he discusses the Paschal Privilege and the release of Barabbas. He is too critical when discussing the reports of the Gospels. His conjecture that Pilate presented Jesus Barabbas with Jesus of Nazareth to the Jews only in order to determine which Jesus the Jews were accusing remains a conjecture which cannot be substantiated. Cf. also pp. 100–110 on the mockery and the inscription on the Cross. The whole question becomes clearer and the recital of the Gospels less puzzling if we accept the new thesis, namely that Jesus with his disciples followed the calendar of the Jubilees and of Qumran (see *supra*, p. 387 seq.), according to which the pre-Paschal meal was held on Tuesday, not on Thursday as was done by official circles using the reformed calendar. If this should be definitely established, then there was enough time for the investigation by Ananias, the Sanhedrin, Herod, and Pilate. On this problem, see A. Jaubert, "La date de la dernière Cène," *Revue de l'histoire des religions*, 146 (1954), pp. 140–173; *idem*, "Le calendrier des Jubilés et de la secte de Qumrân. Ses origines bibliques," *VT*, 3 (1953), pp. 250–264; *idem, La date de la Cène*, Etudes bibliques (Paris, 1957). See also E. Vogt, "Antiquum kalendarium sacerdotale," and "Dies ultimae coenae Domini," *Biblica*, 36 (1955), pp. 403–413.

one had to put up with, but as an organization which owed its existence to natural law, or the will of God. This is confirmed by the Lord's answer, according to John 19:10 seq., when Pilate tried to impress Jesus by reminding him of his power to release or to crucify Him. "Jesus answered him, Thou wouldst have no power against me, except it were given thee from above."

Christ's evaluation of the state has had far-reaching effects on the subsequent growth of the relations of the state with the Kingdom of God and its ancillary institution, the Church. Knowing on good authority that the state was not the Devil's invention, St. Paul, himself a Roman citizen familiar with Pharisaic opinion and Jewish hatred of the foreign and tyrannical power of the Roman Empire, felt free to write to the Romans (13:1–7) and to define the Christian attitude toward the state, in this case the Roman Empire: "Let every soul be in subjection to the higher powers; for there is no power but of God; and the powers that be are ordained of God. Therefore he that resisteth the power, withstandeth the ordinance of God: and they that withstand shall receive to themselves judgement." Here St. Paul only enlarges on Jesus' view of the state, adding precision to what Christ had only touched upon when He placed the state in some respects on a level with His own kingdom.[71]

But St. Paul goes further when he defines the role of the state and of the political authorities: "For rulers are not a terror to the good work, but to the evil. And wouldest thou have no fear of the power? do that which is good, and thou shalt have praise from the same: for he is a minister of God to thee for good. But if thou do that which is evil, be afraid; for he beareth not the sword in vain: for he is a minister of God, an avenger for wrath to

---

[71] G. Kittel, *Christus und Imperator* (Stuttgart, 1939), pp. 48–59, deals with the recent attempts made by K. Barth, G. Dehn, and others to explain the word "power" (ἐξουσία) used by St. Paul in this passage in a "demoniac" sense and he shows that such a hypothesis is groundless and untenable. See *ibid.*, the many bibliographical indications. See especially the convincing study by H. v. Campenhausen, "Zur Auslegung von Röm. 13: die dämonistische Deutung des Ἐξουσία -Begriffs," *Festschrift für A. Bertholet* (Tübingen, 1950), pp. 97–123, and G. Stählin's article "ὀργή" in *Theologisches Wörterbuch zum Neuen Testament*, 5 (1954), pp. 441–448.

him that doeth evil. Wherefore ye must needs be in subjection, not only because of the wrath, but also for conscience sake."[72]

The conclusion of Paul's definition shows that he only intended to comment with greater precision on Christ's logion about the tribute, and he must have had it in mind when he wrote: "For this cause ye pay tribute also; for they are ministers of God's service, attending continually upon this very thing. Render to all their dues: tribute to whom tribute is due; custom to whom custom; fear to whom fear; honor to whom honor." St. Paul was in a position to value the institutions of the state and to lay down his principles with such clarity and directness, for on his travels he benefited from the Roman administration far more than did those who stayed in Palestine. The growing menace of Zealot tendencies made St. Paul's firm attitude all the more timely, and one has the impression that he intended to prevent their penetration among Christians through the narrow zeal of Zealot converts.

The keynote of Hellenistic political philosophy, the divinization of kings, so distasteful to the Christian temperament, is directly attacked in Paul's Epistles to Timothy and to Titus. In his First Epistle to Timothy (2:1-6) he writes: "I desire therefore, first of all, that supplications, prayers, intercessions, and thanksgivings be made for all men; For kings, and for all that are in high place; that we may lead a tranquil and quiet life in all godliness and gravity. This is good and acceptable in the sight of God our Saviour, who willeth that all men should be saved, and come to the knowledge of the truth. For there is one God, one mediator also between

---

[72] A similar notion is believed to be found in St. Paul's Second Epistle to the Thessalonians, 2:3-8, where his words on the coming of Anti-Christ were understood by the ancient Fathers to mean that his advent would not be possible until there was a revolt against Rome and the Roman Empire was destroyed. This was interpreted as confirming the view that far from being evil, the state, as long as it remained true to its purpose, stemmed the coming of evil and helped the expansion of the Kingdom of God. However, this interpretation was questioned by O. Cullmann, *Christus und die Zeit* (Zurich, 1948), p. 145. The author thinks that the advent of Satan at the end of time is held back or retarded (κατέχων) by missionary preaching. See also *idem, Der Staat,* p. 43 on the explanation of I Cor. 6:1 seq., and pp. 67–80 on the author's defense of his interpretation of the double meaning of ἐξουσίαι (Staat und Engelmächte) against H. v. Campenhausen, *op. cit.* Cf. Chapter Nine, note 134.

God and men, himself the man Christ Jesus; Who gave himself a ransom for all; the testimony to be borne in its own time."

The juxtaposition of king and God is striking. Kings and state officials need the prayers and intercessions of the faithful, because they are human and fallible, with all the weaknesses of the average man. They therefore depend on the help God will give them, so that their rule be conducive to "a tranquil and quiet life." Hence, they are not divine; they can claim prayers, not divine honors.

Another Hellenistic notion on kings lends point to St. Paul's concluding words: "For there is one God, one mediator also between God and man, himself the man Christ Jesus; Who gave himself a ransom for all." Here the oblique thrust at the pretentious title *soter*, savior, arrogated by the Hellenistic kings is patent: there is but one *soter*, and He will save (*sothenai*) all, kings included; there is but one mediator between God and men, and that is Jesus. Readers of that period understood the reference and had no difficulty in detecting Paul's denial of the kings' divine privileges.

Paul is still more outspoken, though no less subtle and discreet, in his Epistle to Titus (3:1 seq.): "Put them [the faithful] in mind to be in subjection to rulers, to authorities, to be obedient, to be ready unto every good work...." Here the writer also admits the legitimacy of political authority and its recognition as a Christian duty. Christ's redeeming work has given the Christians an awareness of good works and a consciousness of the evil ways they have abandoned, which should make them all the more loyal to lawful authority: "For we also were aforetime foolish, disobedient, deceived, serving divers lusts and pleasures, living in malice and envy, hateful, hating one another. But when the kindness of God our Saviour, and His love towards man, appeared...according to His mercy He saved us...through Jesus Christ our Saviour; that being justified by His grace, we might be made heirs according to the hope of eternal life."

Note again St. Paul's insistence on Christ's title of Saviour and his obviously intended exclusion of the Hellenistic saviors. But there is further significance to his words: By his deliberate use of the word ἐπεφάνη in expressing the manifestation of God's kindness and love, Paul implicitly refers to the title Epiphanes, claimed by

449

Hellenistic kings to connote their divine majesty and kindness. However, he reserves to God alone the *philanthropia* (love of men) and *chrestotes* (kindness), which appeared on earth only when He sent down to man a visible Saviour in the person of Jesus Christ. Though Paul enjoins Christians to submit to civil rule, he is the first to recognize that their submission must be limited by certain reservations.

The "appearance" of the Lord is mentioned again in the Second Epistle to Timothy (1:10): "His own purpose and grace...hath now been manifested by the appearing of our Saviour Christ Jesus, Who abolished death...."[73] The word *epiphaneia* in this connection, too, must have sounded familiar to contemporary ears.[74] It was the association of the Hellenistic royal title Epiphanes with the *epiphaneia* of the true and only *Soter*, Jesus Christ, that later gave rise to the liturgical feast of the Epiphany, first in importance among the feasts of the Lord in the Eastern Church.

The principles of a Christian's attitude toward the state were not exclusively St. Paul's, for St. Peter writes in his First Epistle (2:13–17): "Be subject to every ordinance of man for the Lord's sake: whether it be to the king, as supreme; or unto governors, as sent by him for vengeance on evildoers and for praise to them that do well. For so is the will of God, that by well doing ye should put to silence the ignorance of foolish men: as free, and not using your freedom as a cloak of wickedness, but as bondservants of God. Honor all men. Love the brotherhood. Fear God. Honor the king."

The ideas are the same as St. Paul's: all earthly authority is human, but it is the Lord's wish that his followers be subject to it; the state's function is to punish and to praise; salvation is an additional reason for obedience; if people suspect the loyalty of the Christians, they are "foolish men"; good works and honoring the king will silence them. It seems that at the time of writing

[73] Φανερωθεῖσαν δὲ νῦν διὰ τῆς ἐπιφανείας τοῦ Σωτῆρος ἡμῶν Χριστοῦ Ἰησοῦ. In II Cor. 4:4 and Col. 1:15, St. Paul calls the Lord εἰκὼν τοῦ Θεοῦ—image of God. More often, he speaks about the second appearance of the Lord (I Tim. 6:14; II Tim. 4:1, 8; Titus 2:13; I Thess. 4:15 seq.; παρουσία, II Thess. 2:8).
[74] Cf. the interesting instances of epiphany or *adventus* (visits by Roman emperors) in Greece, quoted by A. Deissmann, *Light from the Ancient East*, pp. 271–273.

Christians were grievously calumniated, an indication that the Epistle may have been written at the beginning of Nero's persecution. Yet, in spite of provocation, Peter, as a faithful interpreter of Christ's commandment, enjoined in the logion on the tribute, insists on loyalty to the authorities.

This spirit is reflected in the oldest prayer of the Roman Christian community, which must have been written in the second half of the first century, since it is included in the first letter of St. Clement, bishop of Rome, written in A.D. 96. The following extract shows that the Christians of those days took the Apostle's admonitions very seriously and publicly prayed for the Roman authorities (paras. 60, 61):[75] "Guide our steps to walk in holiness and righteousness and singleness of heart, and to do such things as are good and well pleasing in Thy sight and in the sight of our rulers.... Give concord and peace to us...and to our rulers and governors upon the earth. Thou, O Lord and Master, hast given them the power of sovereignty through Thine excellent and unspeakable might, that we, knowing Thy glory and honour which Thou hast given them, may submit ourselves unto them, in nothing resisting Thy will. Grant unto them therefore, O Lord, health, peace, concord, stability, that they may administer the government which Thou hast given them without failure. For Thou, O heavenly Master, King of the ages, givest to the sons of men glory and honour and power over all things that are upon the earth. Do Thou, Lord, direct their council according to that which is good and wellpleasing in Thy sight, that, administering in peace and gentleness, with godliness, the power which Thou hast given them, they may obtain Thy favor."

The prayer needs no special comment beyond noting that it was said by the Christian community in the face of the persecution hinted at in the sixth chapter of St. Clement's letter.

It is clear that the Kingdom of God which Christ founded had not only an eschatological, but also an earthly character: It would

---

[75] *The Letter of the Romans to the Corinthians*, English translation in J. B. Lightfoot, *The Apostolic Fathers*, pt. 1: *Clement of Rome*, 1 (London, 1890), p. 383 seq.

be fully realized when the Son of Man appeared on the clouds to judge men, but it had also an earthly existence in the hearts of the faithful who accept the divine kingship. It could also be identified, in some respects, with the community of the faithful and with the Church which was the best organ for the diffusion of the Kingdom of God on earth.

The Kingdom of God could coexist within any state which was established by the natural law in order to care for the material welfare of men. Christians could not refuse to the state—even a pagan state—the necessary services and contributions which the state needed for the realization of its goal. They had also, however, to fulfill their duties to the Kingdom of God and render to God what is His. Because the full realization of the Kingdom of God, unknown to them yet actual, would come only in the future, they should not look upon the state as the only necessary and important establishment on earth.

On this basis the relationship of the state with the Church was to be established. The Church must not forget that her only role is to propagate the Kingdom of God in the hearts of men. It must not identify itself with the state and be merely an instrument of terrestrial goals; but neither must the state interfere with the Church and hamper her in the fulfillment of her sacred duties. Only where these two basic principles, set forth by Christ, are respected, can any state—even a pagan one—coexist with the Church which preaches the Kingdom of God on earth.